S0-DRS-284

POPULAR MUSIC, 1900-1919

The Popular Music Series

Popular Music, 1920-1979 is a revised cumulation of and supersedes Volumes 1 through 8 of the *Popular Music* series, all of which are still available:

Volume 1, 2nd ed., 1950-59	Volume 5, 1920-29
Volume 2, 1940-49	Volume 6, 1965-69
Volume 3, 1960-64	Volume 7, 1970-74
Volume 4, 1930-39	Volume 8, 1975-79

This series continues with:

Volume 9, 1980-84	Volume 11, 1986
Volume 10, 1985	Volume 12, 1987

Popular Music, 1900-1919 is a new, companion volume to the revised cumulation.

POPULAR MUSIC, 1900-1919

An Annotated Guide to American Popular Songs, Including Introductory Essay, Lyricists and Composers Index, Important Performances Index, Chronological Index, and List of Publishers

Barbara Cohen-Stratyner
Editor

Book Tower • Detroit, Michigan 48226

Barbara Cohen-Stratyner, *Editor*
Thomas M. Bachmann, *Contributing Editor*

Mary Beth Trimper, *Production Manager*
Darlene K. Maxey, *Production Associate*
Arthur Chartow, *Art Director*

Dennis LaBeau, *Editorial Data Systems Director*
Diane H. Belickas, *Supervisor of Systems and Programming*
Theresa Rocklin, *Program Design*

Doris D. Goulart, *Editorial Data Entry Supervisor*
Jean Hinman Portfolio, *Editorial Data Entry Associate*
Carolyn S. Lynch, Joyce M. Stone, *Senior Data Entry Assistants*

Linda S. Hubbard, *Senior Editor, Popular Music Series*

Library of Congress Cataloging in Publication Data

Cohen-Stratyner, Barbara Naomi.

Popular music, 1900-1919: an annotated guide to American popular songs, including introductory essay, lyricists and composers index, important performances index, chronological index, and list of publishers/Barbara Cohen-Stratyner, editor.

p. cm.

Companion volume to Popular music, 1920-1979.
Includes index.
ISBN 0-8103-2595-0
1. Popular music—United States—Bibliography. I. Title.
ML120.U5C6 1988
784.5'00973—dc19 88-21191
CIP
MN

Computerized photocomposition by
DataServe
Bethesda, Maryland

Printed in the United States

Contents

Acknowledgments. vii
About the Book and How to Use It ix
Popular Music, 1900-1919 xv
Song Listings, A-Z 1
Lyricists & Composers Index 419
Important Performances Index. 499
Chronological Index 615
List of Publishers 651

Acknowledgments

From its inception, the *Popular Music* series has depended upon the cooperation and assistance of the Index Department of the American Society of Composers, Authors, and Publishers (ASCAP) and of Broadcast Music, Inc. (BMI), and this remains true of this book as well. As so much of this volume concerns songs that are no longer in print or under copyright, the assistance of collectors, archives, and libraries has been invaluable, and the editor is deeply grateful to the staffs of all of the collections that she has visited or contacted; to the member institutions of the Music Library Association, the Theatre Library Association, and the Performing Arts Archivists' Round Table that made their files and expertise available to her; and to the unidentified cataloguers who have made RLIN (Research Library Information Network) into the resource that it is today.

The following institutions and their staffs deserve a special thank you: Suzanne Flandreau Steel and the Blues Archive of the University of Mississippi; the John Hay Library, Brown University; J. J. Wayne and the Office of Copyright; the E. Azalia Hackley Collection, Detroit Public Library; Gillian Anderson, Wayne D. Shirley, and the entire staff of the Music Division, Library of Congress; the Theatre Collection, Museum of the City of New York; the Popular Music Archives, Long Island University (formerly the Songwriters' Hall of Fame); William Howland Kenney, III, of Kent State University; and the archivists, staff, and fellows of the Shubert Archive.

The bulk of this research was done at two institutions—the Archive of Popular American Music (APAM) and the New York Public Library. Victor Cardell of APAM was a source of information, help, and friendship during my three stays at his collection, a division of the Music Library, University of California at Los Angeles. The volume could not have been completed without the assistance, support, and enthusiasm of the division chiefs, librarians, staff, conservators, reprographic services, microfilmers, and pages of the Research Centers of the New York Public Library. To list each individual's name might equal the 2600+ songs in the volume, but special thanks are due to Diana Lachatanare and Mary Yearwood of the Schomburg Center for Research in Black Culture and to the patient and helpful desk staffs of the Music Division, the Billy Rose Theatre Collection, and the Rodgers and Hammerstein Archive of Recorded Sound at the Performing Arts Research Center. I am especially grateful to Richard Jackson and John Shepard of Music and to Bob Kenselaar, then of R & H for their time-saving suggestions.

My thanks also to researchers Anya Bernstein and Jennifer Williams; to Shelley Berg, Carmen Cook, Julie Malnig, and May Wu, who assisted with the manuscript compilation; to the many colleagues who suggested songs; to collectors Bill Appleton and Bill Sommer; and to Robert Kimball and Brooks McNamara, who advised my earliest research on popular song.

About the Book and How to Use It

Popular Music, 1900-1919 sets down in permanent and practical form a selective, annotated list of more than 2600 significant popular songs of the first two decades of the twentieth century. Designed to provide access to the songs, their creators, publishers, and performers, this volume continues the uniquely detailed type of entries established in other volumes of the *Popular Music* series edited by Nat Shapiro and Bruce Pollock. The series was created to provide an objective, general overview of the music of a given era. *Popular Music, 1900-1919* offers a wealth of detail on an important period inadequately covered in resources available up to now.

Indexes Provide Additional Access

Three indexes make the valuable information in the song listings even more accessible to users. The Lyricists & Composers Index shows all the songs represented in *Popular Music, 1900-1919* that are credited to a given individual. The Important Performances Index tells at a glance what albums, musicals, films, vaudeville acts, or other media featured songs that are represented in the volume. The index is arranged by broad media category, then alphabetically by the show or album title, etc., with the songs listed under each title. Only currently available albums (whether recent releases or re-masterings) are listed in the index, although early recording information can be found in the entries themselves. Another index category, "Performer," allows the user to see with what songs an artist was associated and resurrects in vivid detail this era of Bert Williams, Edwin Foy, and Sophie Tucker, along with many less familiar names. Groups and ensembles, such as Sousa's Band or the Peerless Quartet, are also cited as "Performer," while theme songs for big bands can be found under "Orchestra." Finally, the Chronological Index lists songs according to their original copyright year, allowing the researcher to see what tunes filled the air at a given date.

List of Publishers

The List of Publishers is an alphabetically arranged directory providing performing rights affiliation (ASCAP, BMI, or SESAC) and addresses for the publishers of the songs represented in *Popular Music, 1900-1919.* Publishers known to be out of business are indicated as defunct.

Tracking Down Information on Songs

Previous indexes of popular music have concentrated on special genres such as jazz or theater and film music or have been concerned chiefly with "hit" songs as measured by the variably reliable music business trade indicators. Moreover, even the basic records kept by active participants in the music business are often casual, inaccurate, and transitory.

The editor of *Popular Music, 1900-1919,* Barbara Cohen-Stratyner, compiled information on songs from various sources, as did Nat Shapiro, the originator of the *Popular Music* series, and Bruce Pollock, the editor of volumes covering 1970 on. Before the publication of this book, there was no single source of comprehensive information of this type for the period nor did existing sources offer the scope of detail now available here.

The major performing rights societies—the American Society of Composers, Authors, and Publishers (ASCAP) and Broadcast Music, Inc. (BMI)—are two of the primary proprietors of basic information about popular music. The songwriters whose works are included in this volume were the charter and early members of ASCAP; these pioneers of Tin Pan Alley are still protected through its Index. Though founded decades later, BMI now represents the catalogues of some of the publishers of the period. Each of these organizations has considerable information about the songs of its own writer and publisher members and has also issued indexes of its own songs, but their files and published indexes are designed primarily for clearance identification by the commercial users of music. Their publications of annual or periodic lists of their "hits" necessarily include only a small fraction of their songs and provide limited information about even these. Much of the data and special knowledge of ASCAP and BMI is not readily accessible to the researcher. Both societies, however, remain invaluable and indispensable sources of data about popular music.

Another basic source of information about musical compositions and their creators and publishers is the Copyright Office of the Library of Congress. Through the massive volumes it published for many years and its more recent computer file, the Copyright Office lists each published, unpublished, republished, and renewed copyright of songs registered with the Office. The volumes covering this period are helpful in determining the precise date of the declaration of the original ownership of musical works, but contain no other information, are unwieldy, and, lacking a unified index, difficult to use. To complicate matters further, some authors, composers, and publishers have been known to employ rather makeshift methods of protecting their works legally, and there are several songs listed in Popular Music that are not to be found in the Library of Congress files. Moreover, approximately half the songs in this volume are now in the public domain in their original forms.

How the Series Was Compiled

When he originated *Popular Music,* Nat Shapiro faced a number of separate questions. The first and most important was that of selection. The stated aim of the project—to offer the user as comprehensive and accurate a listing of significant popular songs as possible—has been the guiding criterion. The purpose has never been to offer a judgment on the quality of any songs or to indulge a prejudice for or against any type of popular music. The series documents those musical works that (1) achieved a substantial degree of popular acceptance, (2) were exposed to the public in especially notable circumstances, (3) were accepted, promoted, and given important performances by musical and dramatic artists influential in their day or in ours, or (4) reflect or document an important historical or topical activity, movement, or common belief.

Another question was whether or not to classify the songs as to type. The editors have not done so because most works of music are subject to any number of interpretations. Although it is possible to describe a particular performance, it is more difficult to give a musical composition a label applicable not only to its origin but to its subsequent musical history. In fact, the most significant versions of some songs are often quite at variance with their origins. It could, therefore, seem arbitrary and misleading to label a given song as "rhythm and blues," "country and western," "folk," or "jazz." Instead, *Popular Music's* annotations provide the important facts about both the origins of songs and about their subsequent lives in best-selling records and other significant performances.

The principal sources of information for the titles, authors, composers, publishers, and dates of copyrights of the songs in these volumes were the Copyright Office of the Library of Congress, ASCAP, BMI, and individual writers and publishers. An effort was made to confirm or update all publisher information since the dates of original copyright. The song list and performer/recording information were compiled through the following sources: (1) a survey of the holdings of published songs and instrumentals in the New York Public Library, the Archive of Popular American Music, and the E. Azalia Hackley Collection; (2) a survey of recorded songs through published and computerized discographies of the Research Library Information Network (RLIN) and the New York Public Library; (3) a survey of advertising and promotional materials placed by publishers and recording companies in contemporary periodicals; and (4) a survey of the repertories of vaudeville performers and theatrical events as reviewed in trade and urban newspapers.

Contents of a Typical Entry

The primary listing for a song includes

- Title and alternate title(s)
- Country of origin (for non-U.S. songs)
- Author(s) and composer(s)
- Current publisher, copyright date
- Annotation on the song's origins or performance history

Title: The full title and alternate title or titles are given exactly as they appear on the Library of Congress copyright card or, in some cases, the sheet music. Since even a casual perusal of the book reveals considerable variation in spelling and punctuation, it should be noted that these are neither editorial nor typographical errors but the colloquialisms of the music trade. The title of a given song as it appears in this series is, in almost all instances, the one under which it is legally registered.

Foreign Origin: If the song is of foreign origin, the primary listing indicates the country of origin after the title. Additional information may be noted, such as the original title, copyright date, writer, publisher in country of origin, or other facts about the adaptation.

Authorship: In all cases, the primary listing reports the author or authors and the composer or composers. The reader may find variations in the spelling of a songwriter's name. This results from the fact that some writers used different forms of their names at different times or in connection with different songs. These variants appear in the Lyricists & Composers Index as well. In addition to this kind of variation in the spelling of writers' names, the reader will also notice that in some cases, where the writer is also the performer, the name as a writer may differ from the form of the name used as a performer.

Publisher: Since *Popular Music* is designed as a practical reference work rather than an academic study, and since copyrights more than occasionally change hands, the current publisher is given instead of the original holder of the copyright. If a publisher has, for some reason, copyrighted a song more than once, the years of the significant copyrights subsequent to the year of the original copyright are listed after the publisher's name. If the original publisher has ceased to function and many ASCAP and BMI editions are currently available, the arrangement that includes the largest amount of original lyrics has been selected for listing.

Annotation: The primary listing for a song includes a brief descriptive classification and a performance history, including: the introducer or most important performer in each medium or venue; early recordings and major revivals, with record label; significant uses in films or stage productions in later periods; and other relevant data. When a song was important as a historical document, background information on the electoral candidate, political movement, or event is noted. The name of a performer may be listed differently in connection with different songs, especially over a period of years. The name listed is the form of the name given in connection with a particular performance or record. It should be noted that the designation "best-selling record" does not mean that the record was a "hit." It means simply that the record or records noted as "best-selling" were the best-selling record or records of that particular song, in comparison with the sales of other records of the same song. Dates are provided for important recordings and performances. References under one song to another title covered in the volume are designated with (q.v.).

Cross-References

Any alternate titles appearing in bold type after the main title in a primary listing are also cross-referenced in the song listings.

Popular Music, 1900-1919

> "The word 'popular,' as used in this treatise in reference to songs, has been employed to expressly designate the various classes of songs which are written, published and sung, whistled and hummed by the great American 'unmusical' public, as distinguished from the more highly cultivated musical class which often decries and scoffs at the tantalizing and ear-haunting melodies that are heard from ocean to ocean in every shape and form. Argument in favor of their merit is undoubtedly proven beyond question by their enormous sale; and many a sad and weary heart has been made glad by the strains of these 'popular' songs."
>
> Charles K. Harris, *How to Write a Popular Song,* 1906

As we near the final decade of the twentieth century, there is a profound nostalgia for its early years. Then so many of the media that are now so commonplace had only been imagined and the role of radio, film, and television in determining "popularity" did not yet exist. Live performance—in parlors, vaudeville theatres, or revival meetings—was the medium of importance for popular music. The "great American 'unmusical' public" was purchasing pianos and pianolas, mandolins and ukuleles, cylinder and disc players, and, above all, printed songs. At the time of the above quote, Charles K. Harris was secure in his position as America's principal author of ballads and as one of its most successful publishers; he could, with knowledge and perception, attempt to define the merits of popular songs. By 1919, of course, his music was old-fashioned, his rhythms dated, but his criteria were still valid. Popular songs had even more enormous sales in 1919 because they still haunted the ears of America.

The continuing popularity of the songs of the early twentieth century is related to those "new" media. Radio, introduced in 1920, was controlled for decades by the vocal stars of vaudeville and the musical ensembles of the ragtime era. Film, itself developing into a popular form in the period, relied on creative talent honed by theatre experience; silent pictures' background music was supplied by the conductors, arrangers, and house musicians of vaudeville theatres. Talking pictures employed those same vocal stars and revived their most popular songs. As the novelty of soundtracks wore off, Hollywood turned to the lives of the great and lesser songwriters for plot inspiration, causing revived interest in their works. Now, of course, those films, and the whole range of musical pictures, are available on television and video, while cabaret artists, revue producers, and record companies are vying to rediscover popular songs of the past. It is ironic that the great performances of the last non-technological era of American music have been rediscovered through re-mastered compact discs and re-issued video tapes.

Popular Genres

The basic units of music in these first two decades were limited to the voice, the piano, the phonograph, and the piece of published sheet music. But the range of music available from 1900 to 1919 was tremendous. Styles, rhythms, vocal ranges, and themes went in and out of fashion as American life changed. A survey of the most important genres is necessary to compliment the 2600 songs listed in this volume.

Ballads: Harris's specialty, the sentimental ballad, had become the most popular song form by the 1890's. These songs were plotted, often encapsulating the story of a popular stage melodrama or novel. Early in the 1900's, the most prevalent forms, Paul Dresser's military sagas and Harris's tales of domestic pathos, were built around a time lapse, occurring between the first and second verses. For example, "The Waltz Must Change to a March" told of a soldier leaving a dance to go to war and returning to march up the aisle with his bride. In other ballads, characters died between verses, and the refrains served as both love songs and dirges. Many ballads were written for minstrel vocalists, such as R. J. Jose and J. Aldrich Libbey, who could enact different characters through their wide vocal ranges. One genre of ballads, including "Does This Railroad Go to Heaven" and the many "Hello Central" songs, were created for juveniles in vaudeville and in amateur performances. Most of Harris's output, and many works by his rivals, was devised specifically for performance with illustrated song slides or stereoptikons.

Unplotted ballads were most often love songs. A specialty of author Harry von Tilzer, they featured long titles proclaiming undying love and the promise to return at a specific time in the horticultural year, e.g., "When Flowers Bloom in Springtime, Mollie Dear." Nostalgic ballads, especially those set in the South, remained popular throughout the era and developed into the Western ballads of the 1910's and 1920's and into the Dixieland songs beloved by early radio listeners. Both forms of ballads enjoyed a rebirth of popularity during the years of World War I, when even the characters created for military farewell ballads were rejuvenated, among them, Will D. Cobb's "Good-bye, Dolly Gray." The new songs written from 1916 to 1918 in imitation of Dresser, Harris, and von Tilzer were themselves revived for World War II performance.

Romances: Two forms of romantic songs were prevalent in this period. Serious ones could be heard as parlor songs (for domestic performances), as "cross-over" art songs for opera stars on recordings and in concert, and in musical theatre. The love duet was especially popular on Broadway, as it has remained, and in operetta. The other form of romance in the era was devoted not to life-long devotion, but to an evening's flirtation. Many of the most popular songs were invitations, descriptions, or even instruction manuals on "spooning," among them, "By the Light of the Silvery Moon," "Shine On, Harvest Moon," and "Row, Row, Row." "Spoon/moon/June" tunes were varied to fit fads and new forms of transportation, including bicycles, balloons, ferris wheels, and "My Merry Oldsmobile."

Comic/Novelty Songs: In scripted musical theatre and in vaudeville, vocalists shared the stage with character comics. These men and women wrote or commissioned songwriters to create a seemingly unending stream of variations on their basic character in different situations. Lew Dockstader, Clarice Vance, and Bert Williams appeared as Jonahs oppressed by fate, spouses, and in-laws. Fanny Brice related stories about Jewish archetypes "Becky" or "Sadie" and her struggles with assimilation. Eddie Cantor specialized in suggestive songs that implied descriptions of seductions—always in the third person. As these stars and their scores of rivals and imitators toured on the vaudeville circuits, similar genres of songs were published for general distribution. Suggestive songs were written for men and women; Brice's ethnic portraits expanded to include the Irish, Swedish, and Italian—all trying to master both American culture and the latest fads of exotic and Hawaiian dance. Performance parodies became popular early in the decade, and the many satires by William Jerome, Jean Schwartz, and Maude Nugent for Lew Dockstader remain incisive descriptions of life and performance styles in minstrelsy, vaudeville, Wild West shows, and stock companies.

Thousands of topical novelties were published with references to politics (especially in Tammany-controlled New York), fashion, inventions, and fads. Many songwriters, such as William Jerome and Jean Schwartz, Gus Edwards, and Albert von Tilzer, specialized in novelties designed to last a single season only and filled their lyrics with allusions to sports figures, clothing, scandals, and ephemeral events. Occasionally, a song would outlast its seasonal novelty, as did von Tilzer's "Take Me Out to the Ball Game," which has a rebirth every April. This volume is peppered with novelty songs about expositions, including both promotional anthems, such as "When We Meet at the Golden Gate" (for San Francisco's 1915 Fair), and romances, among them the 1904 "Strolling the Pike" and "Meet Me in St. Louis, Louis."

American social history can be read in comic songs, their lyrics, their explicit illustrations, and their in-jokes. American attitudes towards in-laws, especially, can be seen, most noticeably in the "Everybody Works But Father" series. Attitudes towards women's rights can be traced through the period during which the Nineteenth Amendment was passed—from the political anthem "Votes for Women" to the dialect-novelty "Since My Margarette Become-a a Suffragette" to the ballad "She's Good Enough to Be Your Baby's Mother and She's Good Enough to Vote with You." Similarly, attitudes towards the Eighteenth Amendment can be traced through drinking songs, such as "Budweiser's a Pal of Mine," to anti- and evading-Prohibition novelties, like "You Cannot Make Your Shimmy Shake on Tea."

The wars, of course, were treated in serious and sentimental ballads, but they also engendered many comic novelties. The best-remembered of these are Irving Berlin's songs from World War I, but other examples could include the rationing complaint "When It Comes to a Lovingless Day" or "When I'm Thru with the Arms of the Army, I'll Come Back to the Arms of You."

A different study of American attitudes can be made through another category of comic novelties—the dialect song. They were written, performed, and popularized throughout the period with different ethnic groups as targets. Almost one fourth of the songs in this volume use Hebrew, Italian, Irish, Oriental, Swedish, or Black dialects, some to humorous ends, others to insult the group.

Songs purporting to reproduce a Black dialect cover the complete range of song genres from ballads to production songs. The comic novelties, derived as they are from minstrelsy, tend to be the most jarring. The "dialects" are so ill-conceived with so many inconsistencies that they disrupt the lyrics. When, as frequently happened, songs were reprinted without the dialect grammar and misspellings, they gained popularity as vocal standards; the performance history of "Bill Bailey, Won't You Come Home" exemplifies this. Some character comic songs, written for and by Black performers, use a different style of dialect, one which reproduces the individual speech patterns of the singer. The scores of songs associated with Bert Williams, George Walker, S. H. Dudley, Ernest Hogan, and members of their troupes bear out this distinction. Some art songs, spirituals, and settings of poetry were also written to duplicate a speech pattern.

To ignore or eliminate the dialect songs from this volume, because they may fairly be deemed offensive to the reader, would distort the presentation of the music of the era, since they were so popular between 1900 and 1919. Therefore, all dialect songs are identified as such with annotations noting the targeted ethnic group and/or the stereotype character. Many of these songs are grouped under D since they begin with "Dat," "Dat's," or "Dem." While many of them are now available in alternative versions, the dialect songs as written must stand as documents of an American cultural norm, acceptable and popular in the early twentieth century.

Production songs: The three genres—ballads, romances, and novelties—could be combined at will in musical theatre. A production song (observing the contemporary usage) was written specifically for each scene to introduce its theme and to frame solo specialty numbers or songs. Many production songs gained popularity on their own, among them Irving Berlin's "A Pretty Girl Is Like a Melody," but others are relevant only within the context of their musical comedy or revue.

Dance Songs: Exhibition ballroom dancing grew so in popularity that by 1913 it was a required feature of vaudeville, revues, cabarets, and musical shows. Most dances were performed to a purely instrumental score, but often a song version was published as well. They are now of interest principally as guides to dance steps, since they can be surprisingly explicit and informative. Dance songs that survived in popularity, primarily those by Chris Smith and Irving Berlin, are frequently categorized as ragtime.

Ragtime Songs: Three types of popular music were described as "ragtime" in the years from 1900 to 1919. Piano rags by such masters of the genre as Scott Joplin, Eubie Blake, and Thomas Allen were still being composed and recorded, although many of the classic rags were written just before the turn of the century. Tin Pan Alley ragtime, based on the cake-walk sections of the Joplin-style rags, was by far more prevalent. These piano pieces and songs were composed by the recent European immigrant, such as Max Hoffmann, Jean Schwartz, and Irving Berlin, who adapted the form as typically American. Their original melodies and their forays into "ragging the classics" of opera were syncopated, but lacked the chromaticism and complexity of Joplin's "rags" and "slow drags." There are literally hundreds of examples of Tin Pan Alley ragtime in this volume, much of it beginning with "O" (or "Oh") or with "That." The third type of popular music that can be described as "ragtime" was romances and production songs written for the Black musical comedies and vaudeville feature acts of the period. The publishing firms that printed music by Chris Smith, Cecil Mack, Alex Rogers, and their colleagues often advertised all of their songs as "ragtime," even when the individual works were purely ballads. Joseph W. Stern & Co. and Jerome Remick were especially prone to this misleading advertising. In current parlance, without the distinctions that the 1910 song and dance music purchasers used, it is common to categorize Smith's best-loved work, "Ballin' the Jack," as a "ragtime classic," although he specified that it was a "snake-hip dance" to be performed at a fox-trot rhythm.

Military Songs: The full range of soldiers' marches—many, like "Anchors Aweigh," still used—were written and promoted in this era, as well as lesser known ones by John Philip Sousa and his rivals Arthur Pryor and E. T. Paull. The three major wars between 1900 and 1919 are also documented in pro- and anti-militarist ballads, novelties, and anthems by almost every songwriter. The best documentation of America's decision-making process before entering World War I may well be in its songs, as lyricists took sides between the anti-interventionist "I Didn't Raise My Boy to Be a Soldier" and the preparedness forces' "America, Here's My Boy."

Political Anthems: An attempt has been made to give equal space to all sides of the major electoral campaigns and political battles between 1900 and 1919. Democratic, Republican, and Bull-Moose campaign songs are included, as well as unofficial songs decrying all of the candidates. Among them are memorial hymns for William McKinley, "Hooray for a Bryan to Lead Us," "Step into Line with Taft," "Our Hats Are Off to You, Mr. Wilson," and dozens of songs for and against Theodore Roosevelt. Songs about Tammany Hall (a New York political power) and references within songs about local campaigns are also noted. Suffragist, Temperance, and labor songs are listed, along with satires of those movements. Workers' songs range from the overtly political anthems published by Charles Kerr and Charles Ingersoll to the Yiddish-language "Mamenu," a lament for the victims of the Triangle Shirtwaist Company fire, and other songs that inspired the formation of unions, as well as songs written for the International Workers of the World ("Wobblies") by Joe Hill and the uncredited but world famous "Bread and Roses."

Religious Songs: Many of the gospel and country-western classics of today were introduced at revival meetings, often those associated with evangelist Billy Sunday as was "Love Lifted Me" and "Will the Circle Be Unbroken?" Others were originally Temperance anthems adapted from nineteenth-century hymnals, which are included since they were frequently copyrighted for the first time in the 1900's.

Promotional Songs: The final genre associated with the period was the advertisement set to music. This volume includes promotional songs for cosmetics, medical products, comic strips, amusement parks, and all of the major expositions in the period.

Songwriters

It is a tribute to the professionalism and flexibility of the Tin Pan Alley songwriters that all of those genres were in the repertories of each of the composers and lyricists. They had specialties, of course, and preferred styles, but they could and did write any kind of popular song. The songwriters can best be categorized by their favorite venue. Those who often wrote songs for unaffiliated performance (outside of the strictures of theatre) include balladists Paul Dresser, Charles K. Harris, the prolific Theodore F. Morse, Fred Fisher, and Albert and Harry von Tilzer; ragtime specialists Ted Snyder, Chris Smith, Shelton Brooks, Maceo Pinkard, and Cecil Mack; Irish specialists Ernest Ball and George Graff, Jr., and three whose careers blossomed in the 1920's and 1930's—Richard Whiting, B. G. De Sylva, and Gus Kahn. Songwriters who starred in, wrote, and produced their own shows included minstrels George Christy, George H. Primrose, Lew Dockstader, and Eddie Leonard; George M. Cohan, Irving Berlin, and Gus Edwards; the Chicago team of Adams, Hough, and Joseph E. Howard; comedians Richard Carle and Elsie Janis; Black theatre pioneers J. Leubrie Hill, Will Marion Cook, Bert Williams (with George Walker), his rivals S. H. Dudley and Ernest Hogan, and the team of Bob Cole, James Weldon Johnson, and J. Rosamond Johnson. In addition, many directors also were popular songwriters, among them, Gertrude Hoffmann, Ned Wayburn, Fanchon, and Earl Carroll.

Performers and Others as Writers

Many vaudeville vocalists wrote songs for their own vocal ranges that became generally popular, among them Nora Bayes, Anna Chandler, Hattie Burks, Dolly Connolly, Dolly Jardon, Maude Nugent, and Blossom Seeley. Members of juvenile dance teams frequently found adult success as songwriters, as did Martin Brown, Harry Puck, Joseph Santley, Marion Sunshine (of Tempest and Sunshine), and both of the Duncan Sisters.

Bandleaders and conductors who found success with their own songs included John Philip Sousa, Max Hoffmann, Rosario Bourdon, Ziegfeld's cabaret conductors Ford T. Dabney and Art Hickman, Sam Ash, and James Reese Europe, with his instrumentalists, Noble Sissle and Eubie Blake.

In an era when producers controlled both musical theatre and vaudeville, many songwriters became collaborators on long series of musical comedies and revues for the same individual or firm. They included Weber and Fields's regulars Edgar Smith and John Stromberg; the Shuberts' Harold Atteridge, Sigmund Romberg, Harry Carroll, William Jerome, and Jean Schwartz, Victor Herbert, and Rida Johnson Young; Jerome Kern with either Anne Caldwell (for C. B. Dillingham) or Guy Bolton (for Elizabeth Marbury); Raymond Hubbell and R. H. Burnside at the Hippodrome; British imports Adrian Ross and Andre Messager; Oscar Hammerstein I and II; and Blanche Merrill, who wrote on commission for Fanny Brice, and Florenz Ziegfeld, Jr.'s duo of Gene Buck and Dave Stamper. Even working critics formed long associations as songwriters, among them Channing Pollock and Rennold Wolf, who wrote for Ziegfeld, and "Zit" (C. Florian Zittel), a vaudeville critic associated with Eva Tanguay.

Composer/lyricists whose vocal works were popular on stage, in concerts, in domestic use, and on "crossover" recordings included Elsa Maxwell, Mary Earl, Anita Owen, Clare Kummer, Carrie Jacobs-Bond, Reginald De Koven, and H. W. Petrie, who was known for his sea ballads.

Finally, five fledgling talents contributed a handful of songs to the 1918-1919 seasons before taking over Broadway—Cole Porter, George and Ira Gershwin, and Richard Rodgers and Lorenz Hart.

The profession of songwriter was, in many ways, associated in the public's mind with inventors and industrialists. All were required to create novelties quickly every year, all worked for a minuscule royalty that could add up to wealth, and all were glorified in variants of the Horatio Alger story. Newspaper and magazine articles on "rags to riches" songwriters abounded.

Although it is obvious from even the brief list above that the roster of successful, influential composers and lyricists included many well-known women and Blacks, the commonly held image of a songwriter was that of a white male whose parents had recently immigrated from Europe. Those who did not fit the image were still credited with their songs and their talent, but, in general, they were denied the extra reward of personal publicity. This neglect persists to this day, although revisionist music and performance historians are re-publicizing the identities, as well as the songs, of such major contemporary figures as Chris Smith, Maceo Pinkard, Cecil Mack, Alex Rogers, Tom Lemonier, Bert Williams, Bob Cole, H. T. Burleigh, the Johnson brothers, and many other Black songwriters. Women composers, too frequently ignored or mis-categorized as "parlor song" writers, are being rediscovered as well.

It is important to remember that in this period songwriters were public figures, known through journalists and their firms' publicity offices. Many performed their own songs in vaudeville, whether they were trained vocalists, such as Cole and Johnson, or barely tonal, as critics said of Harry von Tilzer in 1909. Their social lives were as frequently covered by columnists as vaudeville stars, and they were often quoted on public events. Songwriters were not only stars, they were also entrepreneurs. Most at least attempted to control their product through self-publishing and, in 1913, formed the American Society of Composers, Authors, and Publishers (ASCAP) as a protective cooperative entity.

Publishing and Recording Industries

The industries of popular music—publishing and recording—established strong foundations in the 1900's and 1910's. Most songs were published as individual pieces of sheet music with illustrated covers and a back cover bearing advertisements. Many dance songs were also printed in seasonal folios, often by publishers Remick or Stern, and in arrangements for piano, mandolin or ukulele, or small band. Art songs and crossover ballads were available in albums of three to five related songs, by Riccordi, Schirmer, and other houses that also published classical music.

The Tin Pan Alley houses did have individual specialties; for example, Joseph W. Stern & Co. published more than 70% dance songs, and most maintained a similarly balanced catalogue. Many houses were established by successful songwriters in order to reap more of their own earnings, among them Charles K. Harris, Harry von Tilzer, Gus Edwards, and Irving Berlin. The less known companies grew, split, and recombined like amoeba over the two decades, as can be traced through the song listings. The major houses—Harms, Marks, Mills, Remick, and Witmark—maintained their catalogues by controlling show song publishing. They invested in productions in order to purchase exclusive rights to all of the unpublished songs from each musical comedy or revue. Some producers tried to print songs themselves, most notably the Rogers Brothers, Klaw and Erlanger, and Sam, Lee, and J. J. Shubert (Trebuhs Music Co.), as well as J. Leubrie Hill, whose Lafayette Theatre had its own press. They only other Black-controlled publishing house was formed by the merging of the Gotham and Attucks companies (1905-1911), which handled many of the Black vaudeville scores; due to its historical importance, Gotham-Attucks is listed as original publisher for its songs.

Recording came in with the century and, by 1919, had developed into a major international industry. Columbia, Edison, HMV Gramophone, Pathé, and Victor pioneered in the recording of popular music by vocalists from opera and vaudeville, instrumentalists, and bands. The number of families owning cylinder or disc players grew rapidly and, from the mid-1910's, those founding companies had to fight to preserve their shares of the market from new labels like Brunswick, Emerson, Gennett, Grey Gull, Little Wonder, Okeh, Rex, and Rainbow (which specialized in gospel).

Victor was the most efficient at reflecting and affecting music tastes. It was the first to promote authentic recorded Hawaiian music, the first to push "crossovers" for opera's Caruso, Gluck, and Schumann-Heink, and the first to make stars out of band leaders. It held exclusive contracts with both Sousa and Pryor and, most importantly for popular music, it sponsored military and dance bands of its own, led by Broadway conductors Rosario Bourdon, Max Hoffmann, and anonymous others. Columbia, in its effort to control the increasing ballroom market, hired a dance teacher, G. Hepburn Wilson, as "recording supervisor" for its Charles A. Prince Orchestra and Band. The Emerson Military Band and Pathé's American Republic Band soon followed. By 1917, the so-called "Band War" spilled out of the studio as each label attempted to sign famous cabaret and dance bands to exclusive contracts.

The major studios also maintained choruses, light opera ensembles, and close-harmony groups, such as Columbia's Stellar and Peerless Quartets. The Victor Light Opera Company of uncredited voices frequently recorded medleys or individuals songs from musical comedies, operettas, and revues.

A few vaudeville stars recorded their own hits, most notably Cantor, Brice, Jolson, and Tucker, while they made the transition to radio. Most popular songs, however, were recorded by studio vocalists whose names have long been forgotten. As those names can be found as recording artist on more than 2500 songs in this volume, it is impossible to ignore the tremendous impact that their vocal skills and ranges must have had on the public's perception of popular music. As soloists or in ever-shifting close-harmony duets, it can be truthfully said that almost every "tantalizing and ear-haunting melody" was first recorded by Henry Burr, Arthur Collins, Vernon Dalhart, Billy Murray, Elida Morris, Elise Stevenson, Walter J. Van Brunt, or Reinald Werrenrath.

The third arm of the music industry in this period comprised the companies that published music for automatic pianos or other mechanical instruments. QRS, Duo-Art, Ampico, and their rivals were more important in the 1920's, but they often kept older songs or dance instrumentals in their catalogues. Re-recordings of old piano rolls and live performances on extant pianolas are frequently issued now, among them rolls prepared by Eubie Blake and George Gershwin.

It is likely that more music from 1900 to 1919 is available today than at any time since 1920, thanks to the modern record companies that have re-mastered and re-issued original matrixes from Victor, Columbia, and other early labels. New World, Biograph, QRS, and other firms, as well as the Smithsonian Institution, are making the sound of 1900-1919 popular again today.

The Major Venues, Amateur and Professional

The two decades that began this century saw overwhelming changes in the venues of performance. Vaudeville, the medium of choice for popular music, was in its heyday, but minstrelsy, which had contributed the most popular song genres, was undergoing a steady decline. Cabaret was founded only to be sent underground by Prohibition, while modern musical theatre and revue forms were being established. It is important to understand the performance venues of the period before the popular music can be considered in its correct context.

The major venues for amateur performance were domestic (the "parlor" song), the revival meeting, and the political event.

Parlor songs: Sales of moderate-price pianos, mandolins, banjos, and guitars brought music to every household in middle-class America. Families purchased individual songs and albums of solos so that they could provide musical, inspirational, and morally correct entertainment for themselves and their guests. The most popular parlor songs were therefore semi-religious, like "Because," "The Rosary," and "I Love You Truly." Plotted ballads that preached conventional morality were also popular, among them "A Bird in a Gilded Cage," with its sequels and imitations about the dangers of marrying for money. Settings of spirituals by H. T. Burleigh joined art songs and reprintings of nineteenth-century songs on American pianos. The close-harmony songs now called "barbershop quartets" were originally aimed at domestic purchasers. Two- and four-part harmony arrangements of the chorus were printed in most sheet music between 1905 and 1915.

Revival Meetings: As a venue for amateur performance, the revival meeting combined elements of concerts and church attendance. Many of the activist meetings for such causes as Temperance adapted music from hymns that were known to the audience. Organizers distributed new texts on programs, fans, or other souvenirs so that the audience could sing along with the Blue Button Army, White Ribbon Army, or Women's Christian Temperance Union. The revivalists who engendered popular songs followed a similar pattern, although some, like Billy Sunday, employed professional choir leaders and composers.

Political Events: Whether Presidential campaign rallies or International Workers of the World protest meetings, political events depended on song to unify and educate the audience. Their songs were more likely to be adapted from folk melodies or non-denominational music (most often "The Battle Hymn of the Republic"), but lyrics were still distributed or taught by limning. Unlike revival songs, which could be used until the groups goals had been accomplished, political event songs tended to be discarded after a campaign. For this reason, they are easily dated and those listed in this volume are annotated with the name of the candidate, issue, or activity.

Also included in the book are songs written for quasi-political events such as inaugurations, investitures, openings of expositions or fairs, and World War I bond rallies. Although these were amateur venues, they usually involved a professional band or orchestra; lyrics were often printed by a local newspaper, as was the case with Sousa's occasional march-songs.

Professional performance venues included forms of theatre, film, and cabaret.

Theatre: Three theatrical forms from the nineteenth century maintained their popularity in the first decade of the period. Burlesques, a combination of topical parodies and individual specialties, were the province of Weber and Fields. Their company, which included Lillian

Russell, Fay Templeton, and DeWolf Hopper, introduced romantic ballads, such as Stromberg's "Come Down, Ma Evening Star," between satires of contemporary epics, politics, and plays. Pantomimes, an English form of Christmas operetta dedicated to lavish spectacle, were produced by Klaw and Erlanger. A plethora of interpolated songs by Cole and Johnson were included in their musical *The Sleeping Beauty and the Beast* (1901). The only example of pantomimes in the American theatre repertory now is Victor Herbert's *Babes in Toyland.*

The most controversial of the nineteenth-century forms is minstrelsy. The form had popularized two genres of song that have had a major impact on popular music—character novelty songs and nostalgic ballads. However, the minstrel characterizations of Blacks, as realized through caricaturish makeup ("corking up"), grotesque movement styles, and dialect humor, have made the minstrel show an anathema today. It must be remembered, albeit with regret, that minstrel shows were beloved in their day and recalled with nostalgia and affection by most of the creative talent of the period. Minstrel revivals were inserted into musicals and revues throughout the teens and twenties.

Both musical comedy and revues employed similar ranges of songs—character novelties, romances, flirtations, and production songs. One can generalize that, while the forms put limits on songwriters, they were considered the ideal venue for introducing, popularizing, and selling songs.

Vaudeville: Vaudeville gave the greatest freedom to songwriter and performer in the choice of music. A solo vocalist or comic/vocalist could sing anything that he or she desired, within the morality code of the theatre manager. Since most vaudeville acts were booked on a circuit of theatres for ten to one hundred weeks, a songwriter could be satisfied that his/her work would be heard by thousands of avid fans. However, due to the length of vaudeville tours, many soloists changed their acts by selecting (or allowing the audience to select) songs at each performance, requiring more and more new works. Al Jolson and Sophie Tucker were said to "devour" songs as they learned, sang, and discarded new ones every week.

Duets, close-harmony acts, juvenile acts, song and dance acts, and the stage appearances of such sports figures as Rube Marquand and Babe Ruth all required at least three songs per performance, generally including a romantic ballad or flirtation song, a comic novelty, and a rousing finale. Many songwriters also performed their own songs in vaudeville, both on the white Keith/Orpheum and Hammerstein circuits, and on the TOBA (Theatre Owners Booking Association) or

Black, circuit. Feature acts, miniature revues of twenty to thirty minutes, required more music, including at least one production song. Producer/songwriters Ned Wayburn, Gertrude Hoffmann, Gus Edwards, and Fanchon often wrote their own material for their annual touring features. An identification of the type of performer and act associated with the songs is, whenever possible, included in the entry annotations.

Plays: Popular songs were often associated with straight plays and comedies both on Broadway and in stock company tours. The songs were sometimes purely promotional tie-ins, as with the still popular "Peg o' My Heart." At other times, however, important songs were introduced within the context of a play, among them, "O Sole Mio" in *Over Night* and the title song of *Smilin' Though.* Occasionally a dramatic play had a tremendous influence on musical tastes; most notable of these was *The Bird of Paradise,* a melodrama credited with sparking the public's taste in South Sea music. That play introduced Broadway to "Aloha Oe" and engendered promotional theme songs by Fred Farrell and Irving Berlin.

Films: Most of the songs associated with films were promotional tie-ins. Their sheet music folders were often illustrated with stills from the film, even if they were not integrally related to its themes or plots. The film's star was occasionally co-credited with the lyrics, as Francis X. Bushman was for "My Ship of Dreams." Songs were frequently dedicated to stars, particularly Mary Pickford, or to directors; others were novelties about a film star, such as "That Charlie Chaplin Walk." Silent films had scores constructed from popular music as early as 1909, when the Edison company began issuing *Suggestions for Music* and cue sheets with its motion pictures. Popular songs were often given an irrelevant association by their frequent use in background music. Entry annotations distinguish between film scores and promotional tie-ins whenever possible.

Cabarets: Two forms of music were popularized in cabarets. Exhibition ballroom dance instrumentals, generally with their performers mentioned in the title (e.g., "The Castle Walk" for Vernon and Irene Castle), and their dance songs were performed by house bands, led by such masters as Ford T. Dabney, Art Hickman and James Reese Europe. The audience, who tried to pick up the steps after the trained dance teams' demonstration, purchased the song as sheet music, piano roll, or recording for home use. In this way, cabaret performance engendered domestic use.

Cabarets also featured their bands as filler, however, and those mentioned and their colleagues introduced the captive audience to jazz over dinner and drinks. Cabaret dance bands brought their audiences into the 1920's.

Concerts: The final form of professional performance venue was the vocal concert. Recitals presented by the greats of opera, such as Enrico Caruso, Alma Gluck, and Lucrezia Bori, by such non-operatic vocalists as John McCormack, and by instrumentalists like Fritz Kreisler, frequently included popular songs. Credit for this is often given to Charles K. Harris who wrote a ballad for Adelina Patti's farewell tour encores. Pressure from recording companies and the vocalists' genuine desire to leave their audiences with a recognizable tune also made the recital song popular. Composers like H. T. Burleigh, whose songs were featured by Bori and McCormack, gained respect, while many Tin Pan Alley regulars, such as Irving Berlin, experimented with art song forms.

The concert song, like ballroom dance songs, quickly became a domestic favorite as amateur singers tried to imitate their operatic favorites. For this reason, many of these art songs are included here as examples of popular music.

Topicality Characterizes the Period

Despite the ever-popular love songs, romantic ballads, and "June moon" tunes that one can still hear today, the overwhelming focus of these two decades was the songwriters' dedication to topicality. Songs were equivalent to newspapers and were often published in Sunday supplements on newsprint. Every event, from a marathon race to a subway tunnel opening, was celebrated or parodied in songs created for wide distribution. Even when the song itself was devoted to love, verses were created that discussed political figures, financiers, scandals, or popular sites for assignations. Whenever possible, entry annotations list such topics for satire (these are not, however, indexed).

Songwriters were intellectually, if not physically, situated between Tin Pan Alley and Broadway, even when their pianos were kept in Milwaukee, Chicago, Detroit, San Francisco, or Los Angeles. They all seemed to know each other and each others' works. Songs of these two decades are reflexive and filled with allusions to characters, situations, and musical motifs from other works. The writers, who had in many ways a monopoly over song production, could feel secure that each allusion would be picked up by the public. Songs about songs fill this volume, from "Just Because He Couldn't Sing 'Love Me and the World

Is Mine'" to the continuing adventures of Bill Bailey, Becky, Mariuccia, and Sadie Salome. Irving Berlin's "Alexander" had a most prolific life for over a decade with his rag-time, bag-pipe, and jazz bands, as well as a war career suspiciously similar to that of James Reese Europe. The first bars of the original Alexander song ("Come on and Hear") were integrated into scores of songs as a musical cue so that their listeners could expect to hear ragtime. Berlin wrote only the first two songs—his character and musical motif had a reflexive life of their own through other songwriters.

Popular music was pervasive in the twenty years covered in this volume. Songwriters fulfilled their roles as arbiters and documenters of social values. Their work's integral place in live theatre and film, its importance to new media and industries, and a veritable monopoly on production all made popular music into a potent force in America's early twentieth century.

POPULAR MUSIC, 1900-1919

A

The "A la Mode" Girl
Words by Joseph Herbert, music by Gustav Luders.
M. Witmark & Sons, 1903.
Production song created to introduce Anna Held, star of the musical *Mam'selle Napoleon* (1903), as the arbiter of stage fashion.

The Aba Daba Honeymoon
Words and music by Arthur Fields and Walter Donovan.
Leo Feist Inc., 1914.
Rag-time novelty duet popularized by Elizabeth Brice and Charles King and Ruby Raymond and Fred Heidler. Its performance by Debbie Reynolds and Carleton Carpenter in *Two Weeks with Love* (MGM, 1950) sparked renewed popularity as a novelty song; that excerpt was featured in MGM's *That's Entertainment I.*

ABCD (American-English)
Words by Wilkie Bard, Nora Bayes, and Jack Norworth, music by Wilkie Bard.
Francis, Day & Hunter, Ltd., London, England, 1905/Harms, Inc., 1909.
British music hall specialty for Bard; Bayes and Norworth Americanized the lyrics for their own vaudeville act.

Abie, the Sporty Kid
Words by Harry W. Fields, music by Alma L. Russell.
Original copyright, 1909.
Hebrew dialect novelty song performed by Fields in his vaudeville act, "The Napanese Vacation" (1909-1911). "Abie" was the standard male juvenile character in comedy dialect songs of the period, such as James Brockman's "Abie, Take an Example from Your Fader."

Absence Makes the Heart Grow Fonder, also known as **Longing to Be by Your Side**
Words by Arthur Gillespie, music by Herbert Dillea.
M. Witmark & Sons, 1900/Edward B. Marks Music Corp., 1940.
Sentimental waltz that became the first best-seller of the century as popularized by Blanche Ring and by Fred Gladdish of Primrose and Dockstader's Minstrels. The song was interpolated often into Broadway musicals, for example, by John Early into *The Floor Walkers* and Frederick Whitfield into *The Head Waiter* (both 1900). Recorded by Harry MacDonough and Walter B. Rogers for Victor and revived in the 1950's by the Ames Brothers (Coral).

Across the Sea
Words and music by Ernest K. Kaai, Ray Kinney, and Johnny Noble.
Miller Music Corp., 1919, 1947.
Hawaiian nostalgia standard that served as Kinney's theme song, with recordings on Decca and Brunswick; also recorded by June Ululani Leite (Hawaiian) and the Paradise Island Trio (Decca).

Acting
Words by Grant Stewart, music by Manuel Klein.
M. Witmark & Sons, 1902.
Introduced by DeWolf Hopper in *Mr. Pickwick* (1902), this comic song describes Victorian theatre.

Advertising
Words by Henry Blossom, music by John Golden.
Remick Music Corp., 1907.
Introduced by Elsie Janis as *The Hoyden* (1907); novelty song with topical references to advertising slogans for cigars, Pepsin Gum, and H.O. Oats.

The Aero Naughty Girls
Words by Harry B. Smith, music by Maurice Levi.
Remick Music Corp., 1909.
Production song from Ziegfeld's *Follies of 1909* created to introduce Lillian Lorraine, who then sang "Up, Up, Up in My Aeroplane" (q.v.).

The Aeroplane Waltz
Music by Charles Konedski-Davis.
Original copyright, 1914.
Novelty exhibition ballroom dance choreographed and popularized by Joan Sawyer at her New York cabaret, the Persian Gardens; published with instructions.

After All
Words by G. H. Kerr, music by Howard Webster.
Original copyright, 1900.
Waltz ballad popularized by Louisa Bates, identified on sheet music as "the sentimental ballad hit of 1900." Original copyright by Vandersloot.

After All That I've Been to You
Words by Jack Drislane, music by Chris Smith.
F. B. Haviland, 1912, 1929.
Romantic waltz ballad popularized by Rudy Vallee in the late 1920's.

After the Battle
Words and music by Paul Dresser (pseudonym for Paul Dreiser).
Paul Dresser Music Publishing Co., 1905/G. Schirmer Inc., 1905.
Anthem with a militarist first verse and a verse two filled with fear and death; performed and recorded by Paul Robeson (Gramophone) as a pacifist hymn.

After You, My Dear Alphonse
Words by Harlow Hyde, music by H. W. Petrie.
Original copyright, 1902.
Novelty song based on the characters and situations in F. B. Opper's comic strip, *Gaston and Alphonse;* featured by Clarence Wilbur.

After You've Gone
Words and music by Henry Creamer and Turner Layton.
Broadway Music Corp., 1918/Mayfair Music Corp., 1945.
Jazz standard first popularized concurrently as dance music (by the house orchestras of Columbia and Victor) and as a bluesy lament, by the team of Albert Campbell and Henry Burr (Pathe), Al Jolson (Decca), and Sophie Tucker who, throughout her carer, recorded it for Mercury, Odeon and Okeh. Memorable recordings also by jazz greats Bessie Smith (Columbia), Fats Waller (Gramophone), Art Tatum (Brunswick), Louis Armstrong (Parlophone), Bing Crosby (Columbia) and the ensembles of Sidney Bechet (V Disc), James P. Johnson (Blue Note), Paul Whiteman (Columbia), Tommy Dorsey (Columbia), and Benny Goodman (Columbia and Victor).

Ah, Sweet Mystery of Life, also known as **Dream Melody**
Words by Rida Johnson Young, music by Victor Herbert.
M. Witmark & Sons, 1910/Warner Brothers, Inc., 1984.
Introduced by Emma Trentini as the title character and answered by Orville Harrold as her hero in the operetta *Naughty Marietta* (1910). This rapturous ballad was recorded and performed often by Jeanette MacDonald and Nelson Eddy, stars of the 1935

MGM film version, as solos and duets for Columbia and RCA. Now considered a classic aria of American operetta, it has been performed in concert worldwide with major recordings by Anna Moffo, Beverly Sills, and Mario Lanza.

Ain't Dat a Shame?
Words by John Queen, music by Walter Wilson.
Howley, Haviland & Dresser, 1901/Jerry Vogel Music Co., Inc., 1939.
Comic song based on the reversal of the "Bill Bailey" situation (q.v.) popularized by Tascott.

Ain't Dat an Awful Feeling
Words and music by Chris Smith and Eustace Bowman.
Charles K. Harris Music Publishing Co., 1903.
Character complaint song written for Harry Brown.

Ain't It Funny Just What Money Does for You
Words by Jean Lenox, music by Harry O. Sutton.
M. Witmark & Sons, 1907.
Comic complaint song popularized by Grace Leonard.

Ain't It Funny What a Difference Just a Few Hours Make?
Words by Henry M. Blossom, Jr., music by Alfred G. Robyn.
Original copyright, 1903.
Character monologue and song introduced by Raymond Hitchcock, star of *The Yankee Consul* (1903, Chicago; 1904, Broadway). The lanky comic used this hangover lament frequently in vaudeville acts and as an interpolation in other musicals throughout his career; recorded by Hitchcock on Columbia and by Billy Murray for Victor.

Ain't It Tough to Be So Absent-Minded?
Words by Matthew C. Woodward, music by Ben M. Jerome.
Howley, Haviland & Dresser, 1902.
Character comedy song introduced by William Gould in the musical *The Rogers Brothers at Harvard* (1902).

Ain't You Coming Back, Mary Ann, to Maryland
Words by Noble Sissle, music by Eubie Blake.
M. Witmark & Sons, 1919.
Dixieland nostalgia popularized by its composers in their vaudeville act and their revue *Shuffle Along* (1921); recorded by Sissle for Pathe.

Ain't You Coming Back to Dixieland?
Words by Raymond Egan, music by Richard A. Whiting.
Remick Music Corp., 1917.

Up-beat nostalgia interpolated by Al Jolson into the musical *Robinson Crusoe, Jr.* (1917). Recorded in close harmony by the Orpheus Quartet (Victor) and as a fox trot by Jaudas' Society Orchestra on Edison.

Ain't You Coming Back to Old New Hampshire, Molly?
Words by Robert F. Roden, music by J. Fred Helf.
Helf & Hager, 1906.
Best-selling romantic ballad performed by most of the popular male and female solo vocalists of the first decade of the century, among them, Sadie Helf, James Emerson, Eleanor Henry, J. Aldrich Libbey, Gilda Rice, and James B. Brady.

Ain't You Got Nothing to Say?
Words by William Jerome, music by Jean Schwartz.
Francis, Day & Hunter, Inc., 1906.
Bluesy lament introduced by Emma Carus.

Alabama Lullaby
Words and music by Cal De Voll.
Leo Feist Inc., 1919, 1930.
Popular instrumental recorded for Pathe by Sherbo's Novelty Orchestra and for Victor by Campbell and Burr, Charles Hart, and Gere Austin.

Alamo
Words by Edward Madden, music by Dorothy Jardon.
Sol Bloom Publishing Co/Sol Bloom Music, 1906.
Novelty cowboy love song popularized by Jardon.

The Alcoholic Blues
Words by Edw. Laska, music by Albert von Tilzer.
Broadway Music Corp., 1919.
Soldiers' lament against the war-time Prohibition laws, recorded by Vernon Dalhart (Edison), Billy Murray (Victor), and DeFord Bailey (Vocalion) in the months between those laws and the enforcement of the 19th Amendment.

Alexander and His Clarinet
Words by Irving Berlin, music by Ted Snyder.
Snyder & Berlin Co., 1910.
Clarinet specialty by Snyder with Berlin patter rag lyrics; recorded as duet by Arthur Collins and Byron G. Harlan on Columbia.

Alexander, Don't You Love Your Baby No More?
Words by Andrew B. Sterling, music by Harry von Tilzer.
Harry Von Tilzer Music Publishing Co., 1904.

Raggy complaint popularized by May Ward, Charles McAvoy, and Pauline War and Her Plantation Quartet.

Alexander Jones
Words and music by Benjamin Hapgood Burt.
Remick Music Corp., 1909.
Song about minstrel show performer who breaks up marriages on tour; popularized by Nat M. Wills and Clarice Vance.

Alexander's Bag-Pipe Band
Words and music by E. Ray Goetz, Irving Berlin, and A. Baldwin Sloane.
Waterson, Berlin & Snyder, 1912.
One of a short-lived sub-genre of Scottish rag-time novelties, this answer song to "Alexander's Rag-Time Band" quotes its chorus and alludes to Harry Lauder's catch phrase "Hoot man!" It was recorded by Billy Murray (Zon-o-phone).

Alexander's Band Is Back in Dixieland
Words by Jack Yellin, music by Albert Gumble.
Remick Music Corp., 1919.
"Alexander's Rag-Time Band" (q.v.) served as a basis for other Tin Pan Alley song writers to chronicle America's taste in popular music. This one, introduced by the Farber Sisters in the musical *Sinbad* (1918) and also popularized by Elizabeth Murray, told of the return of American rag-time from France and the prevalence of Dixie nostalgia songs during the war. Recorded by Harry Fox for Columbia as a solo and by the Premier Quartet for Edison.

Alexander's Got a Jazz Band Now
Words by Bud De Sylva, music by Chris Schonberg.
Original copyright, 1917.
Answer song to Irving Berlin's "Alexander's Ragtime Band," reflecting the new popularity of jazz. A vaudeville success for Sophie Tucker, it quotes Berlin's opening phrase, "come on and hear." Other 1917 songs about "Alexander's Band" included Brice and Donaldson's "Alexander's Jazz Band" and Cobwell and Wendling's "Alexander's Back from Dixie with His Rag Time Band."

Alexander's Rag-Time Band
Words and music by Irving Berlin.
Ted Snyder Music Publishing Co., 1911/Irving Berlin Music Corp., 1938, 1966.
Considered by many the prototypical American song of the early Twentieth century, it was introduced by Berlin at the 1911 annual Friars' Club *Frolic* and first sung in vaudeville by Emma Carus. From its first recordings by Arthur Collins and Byron G. Harlan (Victor, Columbia), it was adopted by vocalists from theatre,

radio, jazz, and films, among them, Al Jolson (Decca, Brunswick; with Bing Crosby on Decca), Noel Coward (HMV), the Andrews Sisters (Decca), and Bessie Smith, whose Columbia cut is included on the Smithsonian Institution's album *American Popular Song.* Alice Faye sang it as the title song of Fox' 1938 film; Ethel Merman, Dan Dailey, Donald O'Connor, and Mitzi Gaynor sang it in *There's No Business Like Show Business* (20th Century-Fox, 1954). Its influence on other popular songwriters of the era can be suggested by the other "Alexander" songs (above) that trace the mythical band leader's evolution through the musical tastes of the period. Dozens of other songs quote from its music--adding to its status in American popular music.

Alias Jimmy Valentine, also known as **Look Out for Jimmy Valentine**
Words by Edw. Madden, music by Gus Edwards.
Gus Edwards Music Publishing Co., 1910/Remick Music Corp., 1920.
Production song about characters based on an O. Henry story; featured in Edwards' song revues of 1910 and 1913 and in the Metro Picture *Alias Jimmy Valentine* (1920). Sung by Bing Crosby and children to open the biographical film about Edwards, *The Star Maker* (Paramount, 1939).

Alice Blue Gown
Words by Joseph McCarthy, music by Harry Tierney.
Leo Feist Inc., 1919, 1940, 1947.
Introduced by Edith Day in the musical *Irene* (1919); as the title character's first song it was the hit of the show and an ASCAP all time top seller. The waltz ballad, which refers to a dress color popularized by Alice Roosevelt, was sung by Anna Nagle in the later R.K.O. film and by Debbie Reynolds in the 1973 stage revival. As an instrumental, it has been a best-selling recording for most of the major bands of the Swing and Jazz eras, among them, Harry James (Philharmonic), Louis Prima (Brunswick), Glen Miller (Victor), Eddy Duchin (Columbia), Red Nichols (Brunswick), and Guy Lombardo and His Royal Canadians. Day's performance was preserved on *They Stopped the Show!* (Audio Rarities).

Alice in Wonderland
Words and music by Irving Berlin.
Irving Berlin Music Corp., 1916.
Introduced by Hazel Dawn and Irving Fisher to lead into a production number in *The Century Girl* (1916), the song is based on the playing card sequences in Lewis Carroll's children's book. Popu-

larized as a romantic duet by Harry MacDonough and Anna Howard (Victor).

All Aboard for Dixie, also known as **All Aboard for Dixieland**
Words by Jack Yellin, music by George Cobb.
Original copyright, 1913.
Best-selling sheet music and Victor recording after interpolation by Elizabeth Murray into Rudolf Friml's score for *High Jinks* (1913-14). The vocal and jazz standard, now better known as "All Aboard for Dixieland," was also recorded by Ada Jones for Victor.

All Aboard for Dixieland, see **All Aboard for Dixie,**.

All Aboard for Dreamland
Words by Andrew B. Sterling, music by Harry von Tilzer.
Harry Von Tilzer Music Publishing Co., 1904.
Romantic ballad popularized by Harry and Eva Puck, Baby Zena Keefe, and Libbey Blondell.

All He Does Is Follow Them Around
Words by Grant Clarke, music by Maurice Abrahams.
Original copyright, 1914.
Comic novelty song about an errant husband popularized by Grace DeMar, Neil McKinley, and Jack Norworth; recorded by William Halley on Columbia and by the Victor Military Band.

All I Want in the Wide Wide World Is You
Words by Edgar Smith, music by Gus Edwards.
Gus Edwards Music Publishing Co., 1907.
Introduced by Amelia Stone and Harry Tighe as a proposal duet in *Hip! Hip! Hooray!* (1907).

All In Down and Out, also known as **Sorry, I Ain't Got It, You Could Have It If I Had It Blues**
Words by Cecil Mack, music by Chris Smith, Elmer Boman, and Billy B. Johnson.
Gotham-Attucks Music Publishing Co., 1906.
Character complaint song popularized and recorded by Bert Williams and by Clarice Vance, who often shared this genre.

All Is Fair in Love and War
Words by Will A. Heelan, music by James Brachman.
M. Witmark & Sons, 1902.
Plotted melodramatic ballad of the Spanish-American War sung by Fred Gladdish of the Primrose and Dockstader Minstrels.

All Night Long
Words and music by Shelton Brooks.
Will Rossiter, 1912.
Bluesy lament introduced by Belle Baker and recorded by Ada Jones and Billy Murray on Victor.

All of No Man's Land Is Ours
Words and music by James Reese Europe, Noble Sissle, and Eubie Blake.
M. Witmark & Sons, 1919.
Post-World War I romance popularized by Sissle as tenor with James Reese Europe's 369th U.S. Infantry "Hell Fighters" Band (Pathe).

All on Account of a Dear Little Girl
Words by Julia Marion Manley, music by William H. Penn.
Sol Bloom Publishing Co/Sol Bloom Music, 1900.
Sentimental ballad introduced by Josephine Harvey and Kitty Bingham in vaudeville; popular as a parlor song in the first decade of the century.

All Right!
Words by Jefferson de Angelis, music by Alfred R. Dalby.
M. Witmark & Sons, 1903.
Vernacular love song introduced by de Angelis in the musical *The Toreador* (1904).

All She Gets from the Iceman Is Ice
Words by Arthur J. Lamb, music by Alfred Solman.
Joseph W. Stern & Co., 1907.
Novel re-telling of an old joke; popularized by Vesta Victoria and interpolated into *The Girl Behind the Counter* (1907) by Connie Ediss.

All That Glitters Is Not Gold
Words by George A. Norton, music by James W. Casey.
M. Witmark & Sons, 1901.
Plotted melodramatic ballad popularized by Blanche Ring; later recorded by the Jimmy Dorsey Orchestra (Decca) and by vocalists Mildred Bailey (Majestic) and Dinah Shore (Columbia).

All That I Ask of You Is Love
Words by Edgar Selden, music by Herbert Ingraham.
Shapiro, Bernstein & Co., Inc., 1910.
Best-selling ballad, equally popular with male and female vocalists, including Mae Clark, Marie Laurent, Bessie Wynn, Harry Fields, Frank Morrell, Frank Mullane, and the Empire City Quartet.

Revived in the 1950's by Hugo Winterhalter's top-selling recording for RCA Victor.

All That I Had Is Gone
Words and music by Shelon Brooks and W. R. Williams.
Will Rossiter, 1914.
Ballad sung by Elizabeth D'Orsay as a solo but recorded in barbershop style by the Perfect Harmony Quartet (Okeh) and as dance music by the Original Jazz Hounds (Columbia).

All the Girls Love Me
Words and music by Richard Carle.
M. Witmark & Sons, 1906.
Comic song introduced by Carle in his musical *The Spring Chicken* (1906).

All the Little Lovin' That I Had for You Is Gone, Gone, Gone
Words by Jim Burris, music by Chris Smith.
Joseph W. Stern & Co., 1913.
Syncopated ballad popularized by Beatrice, the Rag-Time Violinist, in vaudeville.

All the Nice Girls Love a Sailor, see **Ship Ahoy,**.

All the Quakers Are Shoulder Shakers Down in Quaker Town
Words by Bert Kalmar and Edgar Leslie, music by Pete Wendling.
Waterson, Berlin & Snyder, 1919.
Novelty song promoting the popularity of the shimmy (dance); recorded by the All Star Trio on Victor and Bert Harvey on Okeh.

All the World Loves a Lover
Words by Robert B. Smith, music by Jean Gilbert.
Joseph W. Stern & Co., 1911.
Romantic waltz sung by Sallie Fisher in *Modest Suzanne* (1912) and by female impersonator Julian Eltinge in *The Fascinating Widow* (1911). George Graff, Jr. and Ernest R. Ball wrote a ballad of the same title in 1907.

All Those in Favor Say Aye
Words and music by Sam Downing and Tom Kennedy.
Joseph W. Stern & Co., 1919.
This novelty hit for Sophie Tucker uses phrases from *Robert's Rules of Order* in a topical parody of a lodge meeting.

Allessandro's Love Song, see **Ramona,**.

Allus' the Same in Dixie
Words by Richard Grant, music by Will Marion Cook.

Remick Music Corp., 1904.
Nostalgic, close-harmony dialect ballad introduced in the musical *The Southerners* (1904); recorded by Billy Murray and the Haydn Quartet on Victor.

Alma, Where Do You Live?
Words by George V. Hobart, music by Jean Briquet.
Remick Music Corp., 1910/Shapiro, Bernstein & Co., Inc., 1938.
Romantic title song from Hobart's version of Briquet's French musical comedy. Introduced by Kitty Gordon; recorded by Truly Shattuck who replaced Gordon in the cast. Title song also of the Monopol Photoplay film.

Aloha Oe, also known as **Farewell to Thee**
Hawaiian words and music by Queen Liliokalani.
Sherman, Clay & Co., 1908.
The first widely popularized version of the Hawaiian classic rose to prominence with the increased importance of the Hawaiian territories in trade, tourism, and foreign policy. The song was included in the mixed Hawaiian and composed score for the play *The Bird of Paradise* (1912) and was alluded to, quoted, or plagiarized for many of Tin Pan Alley and Broadway's exotic songs thereafter. Among the scores of recordings of this unofficial Hawaiian theme song are the currently available ones of Don Ho, whose signature tune it is (Reprise), Lawrence Welk (Ranwood), Andy Williams (Columbia), and Elvis Presley (*Blue Hawaii* sound track, RCA).

Aloma
Words by Sidney Mitchell, music by Archibald Joyce.
Leo Feist Inc., 1919.
Oriental fox-trot arranged by Theodore F. Morse from themes of Joyce's "Passing of Salome"; popularized and recorded as a Hawaiian novelty by Ray Kinney and His Hawaiians (Decca) and by the Hilo and Waikiki Hawaiian Orchestras on Grammophone and Edison.

Alone with You
Words and music by Melville Gideon and Cole Porter.
Original copyright, 1918.
Interpolated by Nelson Keyes into the London production of Kern's musical *Very Good Eddie* (1918).

Along Came Ruth
Words and music by Irving Berlin.
Irving Berlin Music Corp., 1914.
Promotional song for the H. W. Savage play *Along Came Ruth,*

starring Irene Fenwick; also popularized by Claire Rochester and recorded by Arthur Fields (Victor).

Although I Am a Soldier, I Prefer a Private Life
Words and music by Melville Ellis.
Original copyright, 1903.
Pun-filled comedy song introduced by Cyril Scott in *The Silver Slipper* as an interpolation late in its five-month Broadway run in 1902.

Altogether Too Fond of You
Words and music by Melville Gideon, James Heard, and Cole Porter.
Leo Feist Inc., 1918.
Introduced by Gerald Kirby and Birdie Courtney in the London revue *Telling the Tale* (1918); possibly used in the war comedy *Buddies* (1918), which had "special music" by Gideon. Original copyright shared by H. Darewski.

Always in the Way
Words and music by Charles K. Harris.
Charles K. Harris Music Publishing Co., 1903.
Plotted melodramatic ballad about an unwanted stepchild performed by Jere Sanford, Alta Yolo, and song illustrator Charles Falke.

Always Take a Girl Named Daisy ('cause Daisies Won't Tell)
Words by Alfred Bryan and Sam Lewis, music by George W. Meyer.
Original copyright, 1913/Shawnee Press, Inc.
Comedy song about a man who solves his breach-of-promise suits by only dating "Daisies," referring to a series of songs by Anita Owen ("Daisies Won't Tell," q.v.) based on the traditional language of the flowers. Sung in vaudeville by men, women, and teams, among them, Charlotte Taylor, Marmion Stone, the Awker Sisters, the Hodges Brothers, and the Melnotte Twins.

America First
Music by John Philip Sousa.
T. B. Harms, 1916/Warner Brothers, Inc., 1968.
This march was given a double premiere on Washington's Birthday, 1916. Sousa conducted his band's performance at the New York Hippodrome Theater while the United States Marine Band played it at a Daughters of the American Revolution convention in Washington, D.C. A new recording by the United States Marine Band appears on Volume 6 of *The Heritage of John Philip Sousa.*

America, Here's My Boy
Words by Andrew B. Sterling, music by Arthur Lange.
Edwin H. Morris Co., 1917.
Billed as "the sentiment of every American mother," this answer song to "I Didn't Raise My Boy to Be a Soldier" (q.v.) achieved greater popularity as pressure to enter World War I grew.

America Needs You Like a Mother, Would You Turn Your Mother Down?
Words by Grant Clarke, music by Jean Schwartz.
Kalmar, Puck & Abrahams Consolidated Mus, 1917.
Patriotic ballad popularized by Rae Samuels, Jimmy Hussey, and Thomas Potter Dunne.

America Never Took Water and America Never Will
Words and music by J. Keirn Brennan, Gus Edwards, and Paul Cunningham.
M. Witmark & Sons, 1919.
Anti-Prohibition song popularized by Belle Baker.

American Beauty
Words and music by Max Hoffmann.
Ballad by conductor Max Hoffmann for the musical *The Rogers Brothers in London* (1903).

The American Billionaire
Words by Edgar Smith, music by John Stromberg.
M. Witmark & Sons, 1901.
Topical humor sung by DeWolf Hopper in *Hoity-Toity* (1901).

The American Maid
Words and music by John Philip Sousa.
John Church Co., 1913.
Title song from the musical comedy, also performed as *The Glass Blowers* (1913); Sousa's rare Broadway production song's lyrics catalogue women of all nationalities, concluding that the American maid is the best.

The American Rag Time
Words and music by George M. Cohan.
George M. Cohan Music Publishing Co., 1908.
Every Broadway and Tin Pan Alley composer of the period wrote at least one song praising rag-time as an authentic and even patriotic musical form. Cohan wrote this for his *Cohan and Harris' Minstrel Show* (1908).

America's Popular Song
Words by Harold Atteridge, music by Sigmund Romberg and Jean

Schwartz.
Remick Music Corp., 1919.
Production song for "The Melting Pot of America's Popular Tunes," scene 5 of the *Passing Show of 1919*. Introduced by Eddie Miller and the Winter Garden High Steppers (a female chorus).

Amo
Words and music by Herbert Ingraham.
Shapiro, Bernstein & Co., Inc., 1909.
Cuban romance sung by Viola Dale and Suzanne Rocamora.

Anchors Aweigh
Words and music by Charles A. Zimmermann.
Robbins Music Corp., 1906, 1930.
Military anthem and band favorite composed by the then-musical director of the United States Naval Academy. Widely performed and recorded by military and marching bands, as well as by such vocalists as Pat Boone (WOR) and choruses, among them, the Mormon Tabernacle Choir (Columbia).

And a Little Bit More
Words by Alfred Bryan, music by Fred Fisher (pseudonym for Albert von Breitenbach).
Harms, Inc., 1907.
Suggestive romance popularized by the principal trio of rag-time specialists of the first decade--Ethel Levey, Maud Lambert, and Truly Shattuck.

And He Blames My Dreamy Eyes
Words by Arthur Lamb, music by Albert Gumble.
Remick Music Corp., 1907.
Vesta Victoria's comic success was an answer to "The Maiden with the Dreamy Eyes" (q.v.), which had been inspired by an illustration featuring Evelyn Nesbit.

And He'd Say Oo-la-la! Wee-Wee!
Words and music by Harry Ruby and George Jessel.
Waterson, Berlin & Snyder, 1919/Mills Music Inc.
Jessel's version of the adventures of a G.I. in liberated Paris was a great success for Billy Murray, who recorded it for Victor, Pathe, Paramount, and Columbia; also recorded as a novelty fox-trot by Yerkes' Jazarimba Orchestra.

And Other Things
Words by George Totten Smith, music by Melville J. Gideon.
Shapiro, Bernstein & Co., Inc., 1908.
Novelty song introduced by Lulu Glaser in *Mlle. Mischief* (1908). Topical verses refer to a performance of *Salome*.

And That Ain't All
Words by Bud Green, music by Sammy Stept.
Al Piantadosi Music, 1919.
This provocative novelty song uses slang but leaves room for the imagination. Popularized and recorded by Jack Norworth and Sophie Tucker; used in the vaudeville act of Babe Ruth and Wellington Cross with an additional verse about baseball; recorded by Billy Murray (Columbia) and Arthur Fields (Victor).

And the Green Grass Grew All Around
Words by William Jerome, music by Harry von Tilzer.
Harry Von Tilzer Music Publishing Co., 1912/T. B. Harms.
Edwin Foy's signature tune was a parody of spooning-amidst-nature songs.

And the World Goes on Just the Same
Words by Jean Lenox, music by Harry O. Sutton.
Joseph W. Stern & Co., 1905.
Raymond Hitchcock's comic character song about bankruptcy was interpolated into the musicals *A Yankee Tourist* (1906) and *Easy Dawson* (1905).

And Then
Words by Alfred Bryan, music by Herman Paley.
Original copyright, 1913.
Novelty song that initiated Mae West's reputation for risque material. Belle Baker and Bessie Wynn also sang this blow-by-blow description of a seduction.

Angel Eyes
Words by Alfred Bryan, music by James Kendis and Herman Paley.
Shapiro, Bernstein & Co., Inc., 1909.
Southern romantic ballad popularized by Anna Driver and Leon Errol; recorded by Elida Morris and Billy Murray for Victor. Jazz performances and recordings by Nat King Cole (Capitol) and Ella Fitzgerald (Decca) brought the song back into popularity in the 1950's.

Angelique
Words by Harold Atteridge, music by Louis A. Hirsch and Melville J. Gideon.
M. Witmark & Sons, 1911.
Production song for Gaby Deslys' entrance in *Vera Violette* (1911), with topical references to Isadora Duncan, Paris Green, and the Opera Comique.

The Animals' Convention
Words by James Weldon Johnson, music by J. Rosamond Johnson.

Joseph W. Stern & Co., 1902.
Raggy novelty song introduced by Charles K. French in the play *Huckleberry Finn* (1902).

Another Star
Words and music by Charlotte Perkins Gilman.
Original copyright, 1911.
A Suffragist anthem originally published in Gilman's magazine, *The Forerunner.* In the title's image, each star represented another state that had voted for women's suffrage in state-wide elections.

An Ante-bellum Sermon, see **Joshua Fit de Battl' ob Jericho,**.

Anti-Rag Time Girl
Words and music by Elsie Janis.
Remick Music Corp., 1913.
Spirited rag with lyrics about contentional love songs; introduced by Janis and also popularized by Sallie Fisher.

Any Little Girl That's a Nice Little Girl Is the Right Little Girl for Me
Words by Thomas J. Gray, music by Fred Fisher.
Shapiro, Bernstein & Co., Inc., 1910.
Generic romance popularized by Della Fox, May Ward, and the team of Burkes and Lorraine; recorded by Billy Murray and the American Quartet for Victor.

Any Old Place the Gang Goes I'll Be There
Words and music by William J. McKenna.
Broadway Music Corp., 1917.
Insouciant military song from World War I recorded by the Peerless Quartet (Columbia) and by William J. "Sailor" Reilley on Victor.

Any Old Place with You
Words by Lorenz Hart, music by Richard Rodgers.
Remick Music Corp., 1919.
Broadway's first Rodgers and Hart hit was a novelty romance introduced by Alan Hale and Eve Lynn in *A Lonely Romeo* (1919).

Any Old Port in a Storm
Words by Arthur J. Lamb, music by Kerry Mills.
Mills Music Inc., 1908/M. Witmark & Sons.
Marine anthem introduced in *Cohan and Harris' Minstrel Show* (1908).

Any Old Time at All
Words and music by William Jerome, music by Jean Schwartz.

Francis, Day & Hunter, Inc., 1906.
Although introduced as a duet between Georgia Caine and Edwin Nicander in *The Rich Mr. Hoggenheimer* (1906), this romance was most popular as a close harmony song; recorded as such by the Shannon Four (Columbia) and the Peerless Quartet (Columbia).

Any Rags?
Words and music by Thomas S. Allen.
Original copyright, 1902/Calumnet, 1940/Jerry Vogel Music Co., Inc., 1978.
Novelty song about a rag-picker was popularized by Tascott, Dan Coleman, and Stella Wiley; recorded as a song by Arthur Collins (Victor) and as an instrumental by the Columbia Band.

The Apple, Apple, Apple of My Eye, see **Love in an Orchard,**.

Araby
Words and music by Irving Berlin.
Waterson, Berlin & Snyder, 1915/Irving Berlin Music Corp.
Exotic song with a satirical alternate verse popularized by Eddie Cantor in vaudeville and recorded by Harry MacDonough on Victor.

Are You a Buffalo?, also known as **The Mysterious Melody**
Words by Edward P. Moran, music by Harry von Tilzer.
Shapiro, Bernstein & Co., Inc., 1901.
Lew Dockstader character song about the fraternal order of the Buffaloes. Revived as "The Mysterious Melody" in 1949 by Harry Salter and His "Stop the Music" Orchestra on radio.

Are You Coming Out Tonight, Mary Ann?
Words by Andrew B. Sterling, music by Harry von Tilzer.
Harry Von Tilzer Music Publishing Co., 1906.
Invitation to "spoon" extended by Nora Bayes and May Ellinore.

Are You from Heaven?
Words and music by L. Wolfe Gilbert and Anatol Friedland.
Original copyright, 1917.
Sentimental ballad in the repertories of most of vaudeville's principal vocalists in the war years; performed and recorded by Belle Baker, Bernard Granville, Elsie Janis, Dorothy Jardon, Charles King, Nonette, and others.

The Argentine
Words and music by Paul A. Rubens, words by Arthur Wimperis.
Chappell & Co., Inc., 1911.

Tango performed by Vernon Castle and Julia Sanderson in the musical *The Sunshine Girl* (1913).

Arise Ye Prisoners of Starvation, see **Workers of the World Awaken!,.**

The Army of Peace
Words by Raymond A. Browne, music by Theodore F. Morse.
American Music, Inc., 1902.
Interpolated by Mabelle Gilman into *The Hall of Fame* (1902). The march, which claims that "the army of industry is the army of peace for the future" remained popular as a statement of America's economic power. It was re-printed in 1904 and 1908 in Hearst newspaper supplements.

Arrah-Arabia
Words by Edward Madden, music by Dorothy Jardon.
Joseph W. Stern & Co., 1908.
Satiric portrait of exotic dancer "Maggie Brophy," who "never saw the Nile, she came from Erin's Isle"; Irish dialect version of "Becky" and "Sadie" songs (q.v.).

Arrah Go On, I'm Gonna Go Back to Oregon
Words by Sam M. Lewis and Joe Young, music by Bert Grant.
Waterson, Berlin & Snyder, 1916/Mills Music Inc., 1932.
Introduced by Maggie Cline, this ASCAP top seller was the Irish rube version of the return to the farm song.

Arrah-Wanna
Words by Jack Drislane, music by Theodore F. Morse.
F. B. Haviland, 1906/Jerry Vogel Music Co., Inc., 1943.
Billed as "An Irish Indian Matrimonial Venture," the novelty was popularized by Pauline Moran and Effie Brooklin and recorded by Billy Murray (Victor) and Arthur Collins (Columbia).

As Long as the World Goes Around
Words and music by J. Rosamond Johnson.
Remick Music Corp., 1909.
Romantic ballad introduced by Abbie Mitchell in *The Red Moon* (1908).

As on Moonlit Waves We Ride
Words by Edgar Smith, music by John Stromberg.
M. Witmark & Sons, 1901.
Romantic ballad introduced by Lillian Russell in *Hoity-Toity* (1901).

As the Sunflower Turns to the Sun
Words by Richard Grant, music by Will Marion Cook.
York Music Corp., 1904.
Ballad lyrics set to syncopation; introduced in the musical *The Southerners* (1904).

Ashes of Roses
Words by Mrs. F. G. de Fontaine, music by Maximilian Lichenstein Koevessy.
Original copyright, 1901.
Art song dedicated to, and popularized by Mme. Ernestine Schumann-Heink.

Ask Her in Tulip Time
Words by Joseph Santley, music by Henry I. Marshall.
Remick Music Corp., 1917.
Exhibition ballroom dance and song for lyricist Santley and Ivy Sawyer.

At Mammy's Fireside
Words by Ballard MacDonald, music by Harry Carroll.
Shapiro, Bernstein & Co., Inc., 1913.
Dixie nostalgia song interpolated by Al Jolson in *The Honeymoon Express* (1913); also popularized by Paul Russell Stone and the team of Doyle and Dixon.

At That Bully Wooly Wild West Show
Words by Edgar Leslie and Grant Clarke, music by Maurice Abrahams.
Fred Fisher Music Co., 1913.
Novelty song with syncopated patter sections. Introduced by William Montgomery and Florence Moore in *The Pleasure Seekers* (musical, 1913).

At the Ball, That's All
Words and music by J. Leubrie Hill.
Remick Music Corp., 1913/Jerry Vogel Music Co., Inc.
Chorus finale from Hill's musical *My Friend from Kentucky* (1913) with lyrics relating "mooche" dancing with seductions; interpolated into the author's *Darktown Follies* (1914) and into the *Ziegfeld Follies of 1913.* Recorded by the Victor Military Band as a tango one-step.

At the Devil's Ball
Words and music by Irving Berlin.
Irving Berlin Music Corp., 1912.
Novelty dance song popularized by close-harmony groups, among them, the Peerless Quartet (Victor).

At the Fall of Babylon, see **The Mountain Maid,.**

At the Levee on Revival Day
Words by Charles R. McCarron and Ferd E. Mierisch, music by Chris Smith.
Joseph W. Stern & Co., 1912.
Dialect rag with descriptions of a revival meeting; recorded by Arthur Collins and Byron G. Harlan on Victor.

At the Music Hall
Words by Edgar Smith, music by Jean Schwartz.
Shapiro, Bernstein & Co., Inc., 1904.
Schwartz wrote a series of novelty songs describing performances in contemporary venues for Weber and Fields' burlesques. This duet for Charles E. Bigelow and Christie McDonald, introduced in *The English Daisy* (1904), includes a cat duet, snatches from British music hall catch phrases, and an imitation bucolic ballad, "Down Where the Dandilions Grow."

At the Pan-I-Marry Can
Words by Harry Dillon, music by John Dillon.
M. Witmark & Sons, 1901.
Comic song about the midway of the Pan-American Exposition serving as a socially acceptable place for singles to meet.

At the Steeplechase
Words and music by Warren Ray Walker.
Original copyright, 1902.
Advertising song distributed by the Great Steeplechase Park, Coney Island, New York.

At the Yiddish Wedding Jubilee
Words by Joe McCarthy, music by Al Piantadosi and Jack Glogau.
Leo Feist Inc., 1914.
Yiddish-dialect novelty song popularized by both Sophie Tucker and Fanny Brice.

Auf Wiedersehn
Words by Herbert Reynolds (pseudonym for M. E. Rourke), music by Sigmund Romberg.
G. Schirmer Inc., 1915.
Romantic ballad integrated into the plot of the sentimental operetta *The Blue Paradise* (1915), where it was sung by and to Vivienne Segal. Recorded by many Victor artists, including Alice Green with Harry MacDonough, Julia Culp, Jesse Crawford and the Dance Orchestra, as well as Edison's Gladys Rice. Revived by Andre Kostelanetz and His Orchestra for Columbia.

The Awakening
Words and music by James Weldon Johnson and J. Rosamond Johnson.
G. Ricordi & C., SpA, Milan, Italy, 1913.
Art song associated with Frank Hamlin.

B

B-I-Double L Bill
Words by Monroe Rosenfeld, music by Rosie Lloyd.
Joseph W. Stern & Co., 1908.
Campaign song for William Howard Taft, the Republican presidential candidate in 1908.

Baby Lamb
Words by Felix F. Feist, music by Joel P. Corin.
Leo Feist Inc., 1909.
Full title, "Just Because I Let You Call Me Baby Lamb, Don't Pull the Wool Down Over My Eyes," proclaims it a Sophie Tucker lament.

Baby Love
Words by George Whiting and Paul Cunningham, music by Harry von Tilzer.
Harry Von Tilzer Music Publishing Co., 1914.
Introduced by Whiting's partner, Sadie Burt, in the *Ziegfeld Follies of 1914*. Recording by Billy Watkins for Columbia was a top-seller 78 rpm for that year.

Baby Mine
Words by Raymond A. Browne, music by Leo Friedman.
Sol Bloom Publishing Co/Sol Bloom Music, 1901.
Introduced by Marie George in *The Strollers* (musical, 1901).

Baby Rose
Words by Louis Weslyn, music by George Christie.
M. Witmark & Sons, 1911.
Introduced by Maud Lambert but most popular in close-harmony arrangements as performed by Wheeler Earl and Vera Curtis and recorded by Arthur Collins and Byron G. Harlan (Columbia) and by the American Quartet (Victor).

Baby Seals Blues
Words and music by W. C. Handy.
Handy Brothers Music Co., Inc., 1912.
Named for, and performed by, B. F. Seals, the vocalist of the team of Seals and Fisher on the TOBA vaudeville circuit.

Baby Shoes
Words by Joe Goodwin and Ed Rose, music by Al Piantadosi.
Shapiro, Bernstein & Co., Inc., 1916.
An ASCAP top seller of 1916, this sentimental ballad was recorded by the in-house vocalists for the major recording studios, among them, Elizabeth Spencer (Edison), Edna Brown (Victor), and Henry Burr (Columbia).

Baby, Won't You Please Come Home
Words and music by Charles Warfield and Clarence Williams.
Pickwick Music Corp., 1919, 1946/Clarence Williams Music, 1919, 1945.
Blues and jazz standard that has been recorded by most of the legendary performers in those genres, among them, Louis Armstrong (Decca), Ella Fitzgerald (Decca), Cab Calloway (Brunswick), Sidney Bechet (Victor), the Mills Brothers (Brunswick), Lionel Hampton (Victor), and Williams himself, with Eva Taylor on Okeh and with Bessie Smith on Columbia. Sung by Jo Stafford and Nat King Cole in the film *That's the Spirit* (Universal, 1945); recorded by (Capitol).

Baby's Prayers Will Soon Be Answered
Words and music by Billy Baskette, Gus Van, and Joe Schenck.
Shapiro, Bernstein & Co., Inc., 1918.
Post-war answer to the "Just a Baby's Prayer ..." (q.v.) songs popularized by Van and Schenck; recorded by Henry Burr (Columbia).

The Bacchanal Rag
Words and music by Louis A. Hirsch.
Shapiro, Bernstein & Co., Inc., 1912.
This classic example of "ragging the classics" was performed twice in the *Passing Show of 1912*-- sung by Louise Brunell and Willie Howard (playing David Belasco) and danced by Anna Wheaton and George Moon in imitation of Anna Pavlova and Mikhail Mordkin doing "L'Automne Bacchanale."

Back among the Clover and the Bees
Words by C. H. Scoggins, music by Charles Avril.
Original copyright, 1902.
Nostalgic ballad popularized by Frank Pearse of W. H. West's Minstrels. Frequently used in background scores for Westerns.

Back, Back, Back to Baltimore
Words by Harry Williams, music by Frank van Alstyne.
Shapiro, Bernstein & Co., Inc., 1904.
Novelty song describing life on tour with the McIntyre and Heath shows; popularized by Bonita, Marie Laurent, and Clarice Vance; recorded by Bob Roberts (Victor).

Back to My Old Home Town
Words and music by Nora Bayes and Jack Norworth.
Norworth Music Co., 1910/Jerry Vogel Music Co., Inc.
Nostalgic ballad popularized by Bayes and Norworth in their vaudeville acts and on Victor records.

Back to the Bleachers for Mine
Words by Harry Breen, music by Albert von Tilzer.
York Music Corp., 1910.
Baseball novelty answer song to von Tilzer's "Take Me Out to the Ball Game" (q.v.), popularized by Charlotte Greenwood.

Back to the Carolina You Love
Words by Grant Clarke, music by Jean Schwartz.
Waterson, Berlin & Snyder, 1914/Fred Fisher Music Co.
Nostalgia ballad made popular by vaudeville performances by Rae Samuels, the accordionist Peppino, and Jack Boyle; recorded by Owen J. McCormack (Edison, Rex), the Peerless Quartet (Victor), and Prince's Band (Columbia).

Back to the Woods
Words by William Jerome, music by Jean Schwartz.
Shapiro, Bernstein & Co., Inc., 1902.
This hit song for Lew Dockstader decries the audience's reaction to a bad performance. Also recorded by Joseph Natus and Arthur Collins (both Victor).

The Bal Tabarin, see **Meet Me at the Masquerade**,.

Ballin' the Jack
Words by Jim Burris, music by Chris Smith.
Joseph W. Stern & Co., 1913/Jerry Vogel Music Co., Inc.
One of the most widely known tunes of the period, its first popularity came as a promotional song for the fox trot of that name, performed by Donald Brian in *The Girl from Utah* (1914) and by Ziegfeld stars Fanny Brice and Lillian Lorraine. First recorded as dance music by the house bands of Columbia, Victor, Edison, and Little Wonder and, in England, by Elsie Janis and the Palace Theatre Orchestra. It has since become a jazz standard, with top-selling cuts by Jelly Roll Morton (Bluebird), Jonah Jones (Capitol), and Kid Orey's Creole Band (Exner). Sung by Dean Martin

and Jerry Lewis in *That's My Boy* (Paramount, 1951) and by Danny Kaye in *On the Riviera* (20th Century-Fox, 1951).

Ballooning
Words by Paul West, music by Jerome Kern.
T. B. Harms, 1907.
Flirtation song based on a newly popular fad. Introduced by Adele Ritchie in the 1907 musical *Fascinating Flora;* recorded by Harry Tally on Zon-o-phone.

The Baltimore Bombashay
Words by Stanley Murphy, music by Percy Wenrich.
Remick Music Corp., 1909.
Slow drag introduced by Mindell Kingston in Ziegfeld's *Follies of 1909.* A "bombashay" was an exhibition ballroom dance with exaggerated rhythms (slow drags or fast cakewalks) and poses derived from exotic dancing.

Baltimore Rag
Words and music by Tom Kelly and Dick Rogers.
Shapiro, Bernstein & Co., Inc., 1910, 1941.
Recorded by the orchestras of Jack Fina (MGM) and Ralph Flanagan (Victor). The Baltimore style involves dense chromaticism and slow tempi, now associated with Eubie Blake's compositions (heard in 1910 but not then copyrighted or published).

The Band of Reubenville
Words by Harry Williams, music by Jean Schwartz.
Remick Music Corp., 1905.
Novelty song about an Indiana small town band. Introduced by Elfie Fay in *The Belle of Avenue A* (1905).

The Band Played "Nearer My God to Thee" as the Ship Went Down
Words by Mark Beam, music by Harold Jones.
Original copyright, 1912.
Ballad dedicated to "the heroes of the ill-fated 'Titanic'."

Bandy Legs
Words and music by John B. Lowitz.
Novelty song about fashionable silhouettes revealing or concealing misshapen legs; popularized by Alice Lloyd and Ina Claire. The first two verses were written for a juvenile character, the final two for an adult male.

The Banquet in Misery Hall
Words by Arthur J. Lamb, music by Harry von Tilzer.
Harry Von Tilzer Music Publishing Co., 1902.
Plotted melodramatic ballad of a man who regrets having married

for wealth; sung by Tom Kelley, Hardie Langdon, and song illustrator Charles Falke.

Barnyard Blues
Music by D. J. La Rocca.
Leo Feist Inc., 1917, 1945.
Novelty instrumental with animal sound effects recorded by La Rocca's Original Dixieland Five (Gramophone) and Original Dixieland Jazz Band (Commodore) and by Ted Lewis and His Band (Columbia).

Barnyard Rag
Words and music by Chris Smith and Billy Johnson.
Original copyright, 1911/M. M. Cole, 1938.
Novelty rag with descriptions of barn dancing. Introduced by Florence Hobson.

The Baseball Glide
Words by Andrew B. Sterling, music by Harry von Tilzer.
Harry Von Tilzer Music Publishing Co., 1911.
Novelty song using baseball terminology to describe dance movements, e.g. "glide to first, dash for second, slide for third ..."

Bashful Betsey Brown
Words by Ed Gardinier, music by Winthrop Wiley.
Original copyright, 1901.
Comic song popularized by Anna Held in the musical *The Little Duchess* (1901).

The Bathing Lesson
Words and music by Joseph Hart.
Howley, Haviland & Dresser, 1902.
Hart starred in the title role of *Foxy Grandpa* (1902) and introduced this flirtatious duet with Carrie De Mar.

The Battle of Gettysburg
Music by E. T. Paull.
Paull-Pioneer Music Co., 1917, 1944.
Narrative march recorded by Conway's Band on Victor.

The Battle of the Nations
Music by E. T. Paull.
Paull-Pioneer Music Co., 1915, 1942.
Descriptive march with musical references to the European allies of World War I; recorded by Conway's Band (Victor).

Be Good! If You Can't Be Good Be Careful (English)
Words by John P. Harrington, music by James W. Tate.

Francis, Day & Hunter, Ltd., London, England, 1907.
British music hall favorite introduced to Americans by Lucy Weston in Ziegfeld's *Follies of 1907.*

Be Kind to Poor Pierrot
Words by Harry B. Smith, music by Victor Herbert.
M. Witmark & Sons, 1903.
Ballad introduced by Fritzi Scheff in *Babette* (1903).

Be My Little Baby Bumble Bee
Words by Stanley Murphy, music by Henry I. Marshall.
Remick Music Corp., 1912.
Novelty romance associated with Elizabeth Brice and Charles King, who interpolated it into *A Winsome Widow* (1912) and the *Ziegfeld Follies of 1913;* recorded by Ada Jones and Billy Murray (Victor) and revived by Bob Crosby and Marion Morgan (Columbia) and Doris Day (Columbia). Featured in the animated classic *Mr. Bug Goes to Town* (Fleischer and Fleischer for Paramount, 1941).

Be My Teddy Bear
Words by Vincent Bryan, music by Max Hoffmann.
Remick Music Corp., 1907.
Flirtation song introduced by Anna Held and a chorus of teddy bears in *A Pariaian Model* (1906) before its publication.

Be Satisfied with What You Have, Let Well Enough Alone
Words and music by Will Heelan and J. Fred Helf.
Sol Bloom Publishing Co/Sol Bloom Music, 1904.
Ballad comparing the lives of a poor laborer and a rich, but unloved, miser sung with great success by close-harmony groups, such as the Avon Comedy Four and the Reliance Quartette, and by minstrel show vocalists, among them, George Diamond, Charles Falke, and Billy Walsh.

Be Sweet to Me, Kid
Words by Will M. Hough and Frank R. Adams, music by Joseph E. Howard.
Charles K. Harris Music Publishing Co., 1907/Jerry Vogel Music Co., Inc.
Introduced by Junie McCree in *The Girl Question* (Chicago, 1907, New York, 1908); popularized by Joseph E. Howard and Ida Emerson in vaudeville; revived in the film *I Wonder Who's Kissing Her Now* (Fox, 1947) and recorded by Ray Bloch and His Orchestra (Signature).

Beale Street Blues
Words and music by W. C. Handy.

Handy Brothers Music Co., Inc., 1916, 1917, 1945.
Handy's best-selling blues of the period was recorded shortly after its composition by Ernest Hare (Vocalion), Marion Harris (Columbia), and Prince's Band (Columbia). Later recordings by major jazz figures include Alberta Hunter with Thomas "Fats" Waller (Victor) and the ensembles of Benny Goodman (Columbia), Duke Ellington (Victor), and Jelly Roll Morton (Hot Jazz Club of America).

Beans
Words by Elmer Bowman, music by Chris Smith.
F. B. Haviland, 1912.
Character complaint song set at a divorce hearing. Introduced by Charles Hart (of Avery & Hart) and recorded by Gus Van and orchestra on Columbia.

Beatrice Barefacts
Words by Glen MacDonough, music by Victor Herbert.
M. Witmark & Sons, 1904.
Satire of the advice columnist Beatrice Fairfax from the musical *It Happened in Norland* (1904).

Beatrice Fairfax, Tell Me What to Do
Words by Grant Clarke and Joe McCarthy, music by Jimmie V. Monaco.
Leo Feist Inc., 1915.
Bluesy lament featured by Emma Carus and Sophie Tucker, referring to the advice columnist for the King Features Syndicate; recorded by Ada Jones (Victor). Fairfax, herself a lyricist, was the topic of satirical songs from the 1904 *It Happened in Norland* to the 1937 *Pins and Needles.*

Beautiful Arizona
Words by Edgar Smith, music by John Stromberg.
M. Witmark & Sons, 1900.
Imitation Western ballad from the burlesque of the melodrama *Arizona.* Introduced by DeWolf Hopper in Weber and Fields's *Quo Vass-Iss?* (1901).

Beautiful Beautiful Girl
Words by John E. Hazzard, music by Raymond Hubbell.
Charles K. Harris Music Publishing Co., 1912.
Hommage to Ziegfeld *Follies* beauties of the past; introduced by Bernard Granville, Lillian Lorraine, and Ida Adams in the 1912 edition.

Beautiful Bird of Paradise
Words by Phil DeAngelis, music by Fred C. Farrell.

F. B. Haviland, 1912.
Theme song for Richard Walton Tully's exotic melodrama, *The Bird of Paradise,* which starred Lenore Ulrich. Also see Berlin's "My Bird of Paradise."

Beautiful Dreams of You
Words and music by Harold Freeman.
Charles K. Harris Music Publishing Co., 1912.
Romantic waltz popular as a piano solo and as a ballad by Bessie Wynn.

Beautiful Dreamy Eyes
Words by W. H. Wallis, music by Fred Terry.
M. Witmark & Sons, 1903.
Mock ballad satirizing "Mother" songs, about the beauty of a woman's eyes in the middle of the night after changing a baby, a fight, and a hangover. Introduced by Jefferson de Angelis in *The Toreador* (1902); recorded by Will F. Denny (Columbia).

Beautiful Eyes
Words by Carter De Haven and George Whiting, music by Ted Snyder.
Ted Snyder Music Publishing Co., 1909/Mills Music Inc.
Introduced by Laura Guerite in *Mr. Hamlet of Broadway* (1908), this song about a male hypnotist was popularized in vaudeville by Ila Grannon, Mabel Hite, and Willie and Eugene Howard; recorded by Ada Jones (Columbia, Victor). A different "Beautiful Eyes," a Yiddish-language ballad by Rumshinsky, recorded by Lucy Finkel for Emerson, was also popular in the 1910's.

Beautiful Eyes, also known as **Les Beaux Yeux**
English words by Louis W. Gilbert, French words and music by A. Nilson Fysher.
Joseph W. Stern & Co., 1915.
Waltz ballad for exhibition ballroom dancer Bonnie Glass, then partnered by Clifton Webb.

Beautiful Isle of Somewhere
Words by Jessie Brown Pounds, music by J. S. Fearis.
Original copyright, 1901.
This funeral hymn was performed by the Euterpean Quartet at the funeral of President William McKinley and was thereafter popular with close-harmony groups.

Beautiful Ohio
Words by Ballard MacDonald, music by Mary Earl.
Shapiro, Bernstein & Co., Inc., 1918.
This ASCAP top seller for 1918 was a nostalgic waltz ballad first

popularized through recordings by the major dance bands attached to record labels, among them, Pathe's American Republic Band, Edison's Jaudas' Society Orchestra, Prince's Orchestra (Columbia, Nation's Forum) and Victor's Waldorf-Astoria Dance Orchestra. Revival recordings have remained popular with such artists as Glenn Miller (Victor, Gramaphone, Bluebird), Tony Martin (Coral), and Fritz Kreisler (Victor).

Beautiful Roses
Words by Earl Carroll, music by Anatol Friedland.
Leo Feist Inc., 1914.
Waltz ballad popularized as a song by Marion Weeks and by female impersonator Bert Errol and as dance music by Prince's Band (Columbia).

Because (American-French)
English words by Edward Teschemacher, music by Guy d'Hardelot.
Chappell & Co., Inc., 1902.
Concert aria popularized through over fifty recordings and currently published in more than two dozen solo and choral arrangements. From the rival recordings of John McCormack and Enrico Caruso on both Victor and Victrola to the present, it has been a favorite "crossover" for opera stars, such as Lauritz Melchior and Jan Peerce (both RCA), Jussi Bjorling and Maggie Teyte (both Gramophone), and Rise Stevens (Columbia), as well as popular vocalists, among them, Perry Como (RCA), Deanna Durbin (Decca), and Mario Lanza (RCA).

Because I'm Married Now
Words and music by Herbert Ingraham.
Shapiro, Bernstein & Co., Inc., 1907.
Comic song introduced by Mabel Hite and interpolated into *The White Hen* by Maud Raymond; recorded by Billy Murray (Victor, Silverton) in an alternative male version.

Beckie, Stay in Your Own Backyard
Words and music by Young and Norman.
Mills Music Inc., 1910.
Hebrew-dialect novelty song of father warning against intermarriage; "Beckie" (or Becky) was a stock Lower East Side female archetype associated with Fanny Brice.

Becky Do the Bombashay
Words by Bobby Heath, music by Gus A. Benkhardt.
Remick Music Corp., 1910.
Hebrew dialect novelty song about two Lower East Side characters fighting over their dancing abilities. Introduced by Fanny Brice.

Becky's Got a Job in a Musical Show
Words and music by Irving Berlin.
Waterson, Berlin & Snyder, 1912.
The chorus-girl chapter in the continuing story of "Becky," a dancer from the Lower East Side developed over the decade in songs written by Berlin and others for Fanny Brice.

Bedelia
Words by William Jerome, music by Jean Schwartz.
Shapiro, Bernstein & Co., Inc., 1903/Photo Play Music Co., Inc.
"Bedelia" was the decade's first 3,000,000 seller, thanks to Blanche Ring's interpolation into *The Jersey Lily* (1903) and vaudeville performances by popular vocalists Elizabeth Murray, Emma Carus, and Clarice Vance. The Irish romance was recorded by Ed M. Favor (Columbia) and Dick Kuhn and His Orchestra (Decca).

The Bee That Gets the Honey Doesn't Hang Around the Hive
Words by Ed Rose, music by J. Fred Helf.
Helf & Hager Music Co/Helf Music Pub. Co, 1906/Larry Spier, Inc.
This comic song was a success for Lew Dockstader.

The Beer That Made Milwaukee Famous
Words and music by Dan McAvoy.
Sol Bloom Publishing Co/Sol Bloom Music, 1903.
Based on a still-popular advertising slogan, the novelty comic song was performed by McAvoy in *Mr. Bluebeard* (1903).

Believe Me!
Words by Alex Rogers, music by Bert A. Williams.
Will Rossiter, 1909.
Character complaint song popularized by Williams in vaudeville and in the 1909 *Follies;* also sung by black-face comic Ned "Cork" Norton.

The Belle of Brittany, see **I Can't Reach That Top Note,**.

Belle of the Ball
Words and music by Charles K. Harris.
Charles K. Harris Music Publishing Co., 1911.
Plotted ballad popularized and recorded by Frank C. Stanley (Victor).

The Belle of Washington, D.C., see **In the Swim,**.

The Bells of St. Mary's (American-English)
Words by Douglas Furber, music by A. Emmett Adams.
Chappell & Co., Inc., 1917.
Originally a ballad celebrating a wedding at St. Mary's church, it

became associated with the Bing Crosby film of 1945; his recordings for Decca are top sellers, but other popular performances by Frances Alda (Victor), Kenny Baker (Victor), Jesse Crawford (Decca), and Fred Waring and His Pennsylvanians (Decca) also maintained the song's importance.

Beneath the Moon
Words by William Jerome, music by Jean Schwartz.
Francis, Day & Hunter, Inc., 1907.
Spooning song introduced by Lulu Glaser in the musical *Lola from Berlin* (1907).

Beneath the Palms of Paradise
Words by Arthur J. Lamb, music by Harry von Tilzer.
Harry Von Tilzer Music Publishing Co., 1903.
Romantic ballad introduced by Edna Bronson in *The Fisher Maiden* (1902).

Berceuse Tendre, see **Love's Lullaby**,.

The Best of Everything
Words by B. G. De Sylva and Arthur Jackson, music by George Gershwin.
Harms, Inc., 1919, 1929/Francis, Day & Hunter, Inc., 1919, 1929.
Novelty romance that lists fashionable New York stores. Introduced by John E. Hazzard and chorus in the musical *La La Lucille* (1919).

Betty, You're the One Best Bet
Words by Paul West, music by Gus Edwards.
Gus Edwards Music Publishing Co., 1908.
Novelty romance using racing terminology to describe women was a major element in Edwards's plotted vaudeville feature playlet *30 Minutes at Sheepshead* and in his *Merry-Go-Round* revue.

Bible Stories
Words by John Lee Clarke, music by Al Johns.
M. Witmark & Sons, 1904/Jerry Vogel Music Co., Inc., 1938.
Comic novelty introduced by May Irwin in *Mrs. Black Is Back* (1904).

Big Indian Chief
Words by Bob Cole, music by J. Rosamond Johnson.
Joseph W. Stern & Co., 1904.
Novelty rag with Native American theme interpolated by Charles Bigelow into *The English Daisy* (1904); recorded by J. W. Myers on Columbia.

The Big Red Shawl
Words by Bob Cole, music by J. Rosamond Johnson.
Joseph W. Stern & Co., 1908.
Flirtation song introduced by composer Johnson in *The Red Moon* (1908).

Bill Bailey, Won't You Please Come Home
Words and music by Hughie Cannon.
Howley, Haviland & Co., 1902/Jerry Vogel Music Co., Inc., 1938.
A jazz and pop standard, it was first popularized in vaudeville by Harry Brown and by Tascott. It is associated with Pearl Bailey (Roulette), but has been recorded by most of the vocalists and major ensembles of jazz, among them, Sarah Vaughan (Mercury), Louis Armstrong (Van), Bobby Darin (Atlantic), Earl Fatha Hines (Crescendo), and the Preservation Hall Jazz Band (Columbia). The character of "Bill Bailey' was killed off in "He Done Me Wrong" (q.v.) and resurrected for "When Old Bill Bailey Plays the Ukelele" (q.v.).

Bill Taft for 1908
Words by Ada Shafer, music by H. Kirkus Dugdale.
Original copyright, 1908.
Campaign song for William Howard Taft, Republican candidate for President. Taft defeated William Jennings Bryan and became the twenty-seventh President.

Bill Was There
Words and music by Ren Shields.
Mills Music Inc., 1903.
Comic military character song similar to "Kilroy Was Here"; popularized by Nat M. Wills.

Bill? Bill Taft
Words and music by Cecil Marson.
Original copyright, 1908.
Republican William Howard Taft was elected President in 1908. His Democratic opponent, William Jennings Bryan, is referred to in the song as "Silver Bill" because of his monetary policies.

Billet Doux
Words by George V. Hobart and Walter H. Ford, music by John W. Bratton.
M. Witmark & Sons, 1900.
Punning romance introduced by Augusta Glose in *The Liberty Belles* (1900).

Billy
Words by Edgar Malone, music by Ted S. Barron.

Leo Feist Inc., 1904.
Romance introduced by Florence Bindley in *The Street Singer* (1905); recorded by Billy Murray for Columbia.

Billy, also known as **I Always Dream of Bill**
Words by Joe Goodwin, music by James Kendis and James Paley.
Mills Music Inc., 1911, 1938.
Romantic ballad recorded by Ada Jones and Billy Murray (each on Columbia); revived by Bonnie Baker and Orin Tucker (Vocalion) and by Peggy Nolan with Lang Thompson and His Orchestra (Regent).

Billy Billy, Bounce Your Baby Doll
Words by Joe McCarthy, music by Fred Fisher and Al Bryan.
Leo Feist Inc., 1912.
Comic novelty song interpolated by Al Jolson into *The Whirl of Society* (1912).

Bing! Bang! Bing 'Em on the Rhine
Words and music by Jack Mahoney and Allan Flynn.
Remick Music Corp., 1918.
World War I militarist song also known as "Bite 'Em on the Rhine," popularized by Blanche Ring who added couplets and catch phrases, including "This sounds ever so much sweeter on a 40 centimeter." Also recorded by the Premier Quartet (Edison).

A Bird in a Gilded Cage
Words by Arthur J. Lamb, music by Harry von Tilzer.
Shapiro, Bernstein & Co., Inc., 1900/Harry Von Tilzer Music Publishing Co., 1927.
A plotted ballad based on the characters and situations of melodrama and the stock theater company repertory, Lamb and von Tilzer's "moral lesson" was the first of scores that warned girls that marrying for wealth led to ruin. Although one of the most popular and best remembered songs of the decade, it was seldom recorded or performed by the stars of vaudeville. It was instead the favorite of song illustrators and amateur vocalists. Joan Morris included the entire ballad in her *After the Ball* album for Nonesuch.

Bird of the Wilderness
Words by Edward Horsman, music by Rabindranath Tagore.
G. Schirmer Inc., 1914.
Art song recorded and popularized by Alma Gluck on Victor and by Yvonne Gall on Pathe.

The Bird on Nellie's Hat
Words by Arthur J. Lamb, music by Arthur Solman.

Joseph W. Stern & Co., 1906/Edward B. Marks Music Corp., 1932/ Jerry Vogel Music Co., Inc.
Popular novelty song referring to a stuffed bird decorating a woman's hat who gossips about her wearer; associated with May Ward and Thomas Q. Seabrooke; recorded by Helen Trix on Victor and revived by Joan Morris on her *Vaudeville* album (Nonesuch).

The Bird That Never Sings
Words by Arthur J. Lamb, music by Monroe H. Rosenfeld.
Howley, Haviland & Dresser, 1902.
A sequel to Lamb's "A Bird in a Gilded Cage" (q.v.), this sentimental plotted ballad was sung and recorded by R. J. Jose.

A Bit o' Blarney
Words and music by Will Heelan and J. Fred Helf.
Sol Bloom Publishing Co/Sol Bloom Music, 1904/M. Witmark & Sons.
Irish romantic advice popularized by Josephine Sabel.

Blackberrying Today
Words and music by Bert Williams.
Remick Music Corp., 1912.
One of a series of Williams's specialties performed in the character of a Deacon. In this one, he presides at a funeral. It was interpolated into Ziegfeld's *Follies of 1912.*

Blarney
Words and music by Nora Bayes and Jack Norworth.
Remick Music Corp., 1909/Jerry Vogel Music Co., Inc., 1937.
Irish comedy popularized by Bayes and Norworth in the *Follies of 1909* and their own acts.

Bless Your Ever Loving Little Heart
Words by Stanley Murphy, music by Henry I. Marshall.
Charles K. Harris Music Publishing Co., 1911.
Romance associated with Elsie Janis who first sang it in *The Slim Princess* (1911); also performed by Nat Fields in *In and Out of Society* (1912) and recorded by Walter J. Van Brunt for Victor.

Blooming Lize
Words by Matt C. Woodward, music by Ben Jerome.
Howley, Haviland & Dresser, 1902.
A popular comic song about "Lize" who told lies, it was interpolated by the producers into Isadore Witmark's score for *The Chaperons* (1902 and subsequent national tours). Recorded by Dan W. Quinn (Victor).

Blow the Smoke Away
Words by Will M. Hough and Frank R. Adams, music by Joseph E. Howard.
Charles K. Harris Music Publishing Co., 1906/Edward B. Marks Music Corp., 1941.
Introduced by James Norval in *The Time, the Place and the Girl* (1905, Chicago; 1907, New York); recorded by composer Howard (Brunswick) and revived by Glen Gray and the Casa Loma Orchestra (Decca) and by Les Paul and Mary Ford on Capitol.

The Blue and the Gray: A Mother's Gift to Her Country
Words and music by Paul Dresser.
Howley, Haviland & Co., 1900/Shawnee Press, Inc.
Ballad of the Civil War dead associated with R. J. Jose; often interpolated by vocalists into minstrel shows and musical comedies, among them, the Rays in *A Hot Old Time* (1900) and Gilby Howe in *Miss Cuba, Jr.* (1902).

Blue Bell
Words and music by Edward Madden, Dolly Morse, and Theodore F. Morse.
Howley, Haviland & Co., 1904/Leo Feist Inc., 1933.
Military ballad with a romantic first verse and an alternative tragic second verse popularized by Anna Driver, Effie Brooklin, and Helen Trix; also performed and recorded by barber shop style ensembles, such as the Metropolitan Quartet, the Avon Comedy Four, the Messenger Boys Trio, and the Haydn Quartet (Victor).

The Blue Button Army
Words and music by Charles H. Stanley.
Original copyright, 1902.
Temperance anthem by Stanley, who billed himself as "The Converted Comedian"; other songs associated with the title's Temperance organization included Henry H. Hadley's "The Blue Button Men Are Coming."

The Blue Devils of France
Words and music by Irving Berlin.
Waterson, Berlin & Snyder, 1918.
Tribute to French soldiers introduced by Lillian Lorraine in the "Salute to the Allies" tableaux in the *Ziegfeld Follies of 1918.*

Blue Eyed Blond Haired Heart Breaking Baby Doll
Words and music by Cliff Hess and Sidney Mitchell.
Leo Feist Inc., 1919.
Signature tune for the Courtney Sisters.

Blue Eyed Sue
Words and music by James Reese Europe.
Sol Bloom Publishing Co/Sol Bloom Music, 1904.
Europe's first major success was a romantic ballad interpolated by Neva Aymar into *Mother Goose* (1903) and by Susie Fisher into *A Little Bit of Everything* (1904).

Blue Ridge, I'm Coming Back to You, also known as **The Boys in Navy Blue**
Words and music by John Philip Sousa.
T. B. Harms, 1917.
War-time nostalgia song given its premiere by Sousa's Band at a benefit concert for the Women's Auxiliary Naval Recruiting Station at the New York Hippodrome in 1917. A march version was re-named "Great Lakes" in tribute to the Naval Training Station just north of Chicago.

The Blues, also known as **I've Got the Blues But I'm Too Blamed Mean to Cry**
Words by Chris Smith, music by James Tim Brymn.
Shapiro, Bernstein & Co., Inc., 1912.
Generic blues popularized by Artie Hall.

Blues My Naughty Sweetie Gives to Me
Words and music by Arthur Swanstone, Charles K. McCarron, and Carey Morgan.
Edward B. Marks Music Corp., 1920, 1932.
Comic song with solo and duet patter choruses, associated with Ted Lewis (Columbia); also performed and recorded by novelty jazz stars such as Ted Doner, Billy Murray (Aeolian), and Irving Kaufman (Medallion). Became a BMI top seller after revivals by the jazz ensembles of Gene Krupa (Victor), Jimmie Noone (Brunswick), and Kay Kyser (Brunswick).

Bluin' the Blues
Words by Sidney D. Mitchell, music by H. W. Ragas.
Leo Feist Inc., 1919.
Popular success associated with the Original Dixieland Jazz Band (of which composer Ragas was a member) with multiple recordings for Victor; also recorded by other Dixieland ensembles, such as the New Orleans Rhythm Kings (Brunswick), Wilbur Sweatman's Original Jazz Band (Columbia), and Muggsy Spaniels' Ragtimers (Bluebird and the British Rhythm Society). Also available in arrangements published by the ODJB members La Rocco, Sbarbaro, and Shields.

Bo - la - Bo
Words and music by George Fairman.

M. Witmark & Sons, 1919.
An "Egyptian fox trot" associated with Ted Lewis and His Jazz Band. Introduced in the *Greenwich Village Follies of 1919* and recorded on Columbia; also recorded as dance music by the Emerson Xylo-Pheinds, Joseph Samuel's Orchestra (Pathe), and Lopez and Hamilton's Kings of Harmony (Edison).

Bohemian Rag
Words and music by Gus Edwards and Louis Silvers.
Remick Music Corp., 1914.
Raggy version of the male duet from Act IV of Puccini's *La Boheme.* Introduced by dancers Adelaide and Hughes in the *Passing Show of 1914.*

Bolsheveki Glide
Words by Carl Randall, music by Harry Tierney.
Remick Music Corp., 1918.
Exhibition ballroom dance for Randall in the *Century Grove Revue* (1918).

Bon Bon Buddy, also known as **The Chocolate Drop**
Words by Alex Rogers, music by Will Marion Cook.
Gotham-Attucks Music Publishing Co., 1907/Robbins Music Corp.
Introduced by George Walker in the Williams and Walker musical *Bandana Land* (1907) and recorded by Billy Murray on Victor; the song was the first wide-spread popular succss for the Gotham-Attucks publishing company.

Bonnie My Highland Lassie (English)
Words and music by William A. Dillon.
M. Witmark & Sons, 1908.
This imitative ballad was introduced by Blanche Ring in Weber's burlesque *The Merry Widow and the Devil* (1907); recorded by John E. Meyer on Columbia.

Bonnie Sue Sunshine
Words by Elmer Bowman and Ted Snyder, music by Eustace Bowman.
Mills Music Inc., 1907.
Introduced by May Irwin in *Mrs. Wilson-Andrews* (1908).

Boom-Tum-Ta-Ra-Ra-Zing-Boom
Words by Ferd E. Mierisch, music by Chris Smith.
Joseph W. Stern & Co., 1913.
Patter rag based on the "shave and a hair cut, two bits" rhythm. Introduced by Eli Dawson and by Smith in his vaudeville act.

Borrow from Me
Words by Jean C. Havez, music by Bert Williams.
Remick Music Corp., 1912.
Character monologue and song for Williams that sets impossible conditions for a loan; recorded on Columbia and interpolated into his acts at the Ziegfeld Moulin Rouge (cabaret) and the *Follies of 1912.*

Boy Scouts of America
Words by Booth Tarkington, music by John Philip Sousa.
T. B. Harms, 1943.
The official march of the Boy Scouts of America; a new recording by the United States Marine Band appears on Volume 9 of *The Heritage of John Philip Sousa.*

The Boy Who Stuttered and the Girl Who Lisped
Words and music by Louis Weslyn.
M. Witmark & Sons, 1907/Mills Music Inc., 1935.
Novelty duet stuttered and lisped respectively by William Rock and Maude Fulton.

The Boys in Blue Parade Today
Words by Thomas C. McDonald, music by Lylian M. Chapman.
Howley, Haviland & Dresser, 1903.
Military march popularized by Lottie Gilson.

The Boys in Navy Blue, see **Blue Ridge, I'm Coming Back to You,**.

The Boys in the Gallery for Mine
Words and music by Will A. Heelan and J. Fred Helf.
Sol Bloom Publishing Co/Sol Bloom Music, 1903.
Tribute to the audience sung in vaudeville by Johnnie Carroll and by the team of Evan and St. John.

Boys, the Old Flag Never Touched the Ground
Words by George E. Lothrop, music by Henry Mather.
Original copyright, 1909.
Patriotic anthem about the hero of the Black regiment in the Spanish-American War; sung by Sgt. William H. Carney. Also see "The Old Flag Never Touched the Ground."

BPOE, also known as **The Elks Song**
Words and music by Nat M. Wills.
Remick Music Corp., 1907.
Topical satire of lodge songs popularized and recorded by Wills (Emerson); reproduced on *They Stopped the Show!* (Audio Rarities).

Bread and Roses

Words by James Oppenheim, music by Caroline Kohlsaat.

This anthem for the textile workers' strike led by the International Workers of the World (I.W.W.) in Lawrence, Massachusetts (1912) has become symbolic of all women workers. Never copyrighted by its composer or the "Wobblies" (I.W.W.), it has been republished often in labor and feminist anthologies, including the International Ladies' Garment Workers' Union's *Let's Sing!,* the Rand School's *Rebel Song Book,* and Tom Glazer's *Songs of Peace, Freedom, and Protest* (1970). Among the many projects that have adopted the song's title are the play about the I.W.W. by Donald Hall (1975) and the National Union of Hospital and Health Care Employees' cultural program (1979-), documented on PBS in 1981.

Breeze, Blow My Baby Back to Me

Words and music by Ballard MacDonald, Joe Goodwin, and James F. Hanley.

Shapiro, Bernstein & Co., Inc., 1919.

The melody and rhythm of this song have made it popular with jazz and barbershop-style ensembles alike, with notable recordings by Clarence Williams' Jazz Band (Columbia, Vocalion), Jess Stacy (Varsity), and Andy Kirk and His Clouds of Joy (Decca). The earliest records were by the quartets of the major recording labels, such as Victor's American Quartet and Pathe's Premier Quartet.

Bridal Dawn

Words by Helen Taylor, music by Easthope Martin.

Original copyright, 1918.

Art song associated with John McCormack who recorded it for Victor.

Bright Eyes Good-Bye

Words by Harry H. Williams, music by Egbert van Alstyne.

Remick Music Corp., 1905.

Soldier's farewell popularized as a solo by Louise Dresser and in close harmony by the Empire City Quartette, Kelly and Violette, and the Four Musical Colbys.

Brighten the Corner Where You Are

Words by Ina Duley Ogden, music by Charles H. Gabriel.

Homer A. Rodeheaver, 1913/Robbins Music Corp., 1978.

The hymn most associated with the Billy Sunday evangelical campaigns was performed daily by Homer A. Rodeheaver's massive choir and reprinted by him as a *Victory Song* (1918) and a *Gospel Song* (1922). Now considered a gospel standard, it is still performed by church choirs and has been recorded by Rodeheaver (Rainbow), Frederick Wheeler (Victor), and Burl Ives (Decca).

Contemporary Ogden/Gabriel hymns also associated with Rodeheaver's choirs included "Carry Your Cross with a Smile" (1916) and "Lighten the Burden for Someone" (1919).

Bring Back My Daddy to Me
Words by William Tracey and Howard Johnson, music by George W. Meyer.
Leo Feist Inc., 1917.
Sentimental ballad of child's letter to Santa Claus, similar to the "Baby's Letter Over There" genre (q.v.); recorded by Robert Lewis (Columbia).

Bring Back My Lena to Me
Words and music by Irving Berlin and Ted Snyder.
Ted Snyder Music Publishing Co., 1910/Irving Berlin Music Corp.
Comic character song introduced by Sam Bernard in his vehicle *He Came from Milwaukee* (1910); recorded by Maurice Burkhardt (Victor).

Bring Back Those Wonderful Days
Words by Darl MacBoyle, music by Nat Vincent.
Original copyright, 1919.
Topical complaint song with specific referencs to rationing, Prohibition, taxes, and high rents, performed by Bert Williams in the *Ziegfeld Follies of 1919*; recorded by Arthur Fields (Edison) and Williams, whose Columbia version is reproduced on the Smithsonian Institution's album *Ziegfeld Follies of 1919.*

Bring Her Again to Me
Words by W. E. Henley, music by H. T. Burleigh.
G. Ricordi & C., SpA, Milan, Italy, 1914.
Art song published in Burleigh's *Two Poems.*

Bring Me a Rose
Words and music by Charles Shisler.
Kalmar, Puck & Abrahams Consolidated Mus, 1918.
This ballad was the first major success for vocalist and band leader Sam Ash (Brunswick and Columbia); also popularized and recorded by Harry Ellis (Okeh) and by Prince's Orchestra (Columbia).

Bring Me Back My Lovin' Honey Boy
Words by Jack Yellin, music by George L. Cobb.
Will Rossiter, 1913.
Bluesy romance popularized by Elizabeth Murray and by the Dolce Sisters.

The Brinkley Bathing Girl
Words by Harry B. Smith, music by Maurice Levi.
Remick Music Corp., 1909.
The first three editions of Ziegfeld's *Follies* had bathing suit choruses dedicated to the major illustrators of the era--Charles Dana Gibson, George Christy, and Nell Brinkley. The woman's chorus sang it in the *Follies of 1908.*

Brother Bill
Words by George Totten Smith, music by Alfred E. Aarons.
Sol Bloom Publishing Co/Sol Bloom Music, 1903.
Comedy song introduced by Josephine Hall in *The Knickerbocker Girl* (1903). Extra lyrics provide topical satires of Theodore Roosevelt, *Uncle Tom's Cabin,* and the most recent America's Cup.

Brother Masons
Words by Vincent Bryan, music by Gertrude Hoffmann.
M. Witmark & Sons, 1905.
Billed as a "Low comedy song of high degree" and introduced by Harry Bulger in *Woodland* (1904); recorded by Dan W. Quinn (Victor) and Frank Williams (Columbia).

Brother Noah Gave Out Checks for Rain
Words and music by Arthur Longbrake.
Original copyright, 1907.
Novelty comic song for the "Deacon Jones" character associated with Bert Williams. It combines references to Bible stories and baseball, such as "Eve stole first and Adam second ... Rebecca went to the well with a pitcher ... Ruth in the field won fame ..." Sung by Ed Morton and Tom Lancaster.

The Brotherhood of Man
Words by Raymond A. Browne, music by Theodore F. Morse.
Howley, Haviland & Co., 1901.
Pacifist anthem for the Spanish-American War.

Budweiser's a Friend of Mine
Words by Vincent Bryan, music by Seymour Furth.
Original copyright, 1907.
Advertising song distributed by the Anheuser-Busch Brewing Association. Performed by Grace LaRue in the Ziegfeld *Follies of 1907* and, in vaudeville, by LaRue, Ila Gannon, Charles J. Ross, and Dave Lewis.

Build Your Nest Away Down in My Heart
Words by Edward Madden, music by Dolly Jardon.

Shapiro, Bernstein & Co., Inc., 1907.
Ballad interpolated by Adele Ritchie into *Fascinating Flora* (1907).

Bumble Bee
Words by Jean C. Havez and Andrew Donnelly, music by James Blyler.
Remick Music Corp., 1911.
Novelty romance introduced by the Dolly Sisters in Ziegfeld's *Follies of 1911* and reprised by Lillian Lorraine in the *Follies of 1912.*

Bunker Hill
Words by Sam Ehrlich, music by Albert von Tilzer.
York Music Corp., 1904.
Patriotic march with anachronistic references to anthems, popularized by Raymond Teal; recorded by J. W. Myers for Columbia and Zon-o-phone.

The Burning of Frisco Town
Words by Bob Adams, music by Theron C. Bennett.
Original copyright, 1906.
Profits from the sale of this song's sheet music benefited charities following the San Francisco earthquake and fire of 1906.

The Burning of Rome
Music by E. T. Paull.
E. T. Paull, 1903, 1930.
Descriptive march narrating a chariot race and the destruction of Rome as related in the novel *Quo Vadis.*

But - After the Ball Was Over Then He Made Up for Lost Time
Words and music by Bud De Sylva and Arthur J. Jackson.
Remick Music Corp., 1918.
Eddie Cantor performed this comic song in the *Ziegfeld Follies of 1918,* satirizing Charles K. Harris's ballad "After the Ball" (q.v.).

By an' By
Words and music by H. T. Burleigh.
G. Ricordi & C., SpA, Milan, Italy, 1917.
Spiritual included in Burleigh's choruses and solos between 1917 and 1922; made famous in recordings by Roland Hayes and Paul Robeson.

By the Beautiful Sea
Words by Harold Atteridge, music by Harry Carroll.
Shapiro, Bernstein & Co., Inc., 1914, 1942.
This ASCAP top-seller and perennial standard was associated with Bessie Wynn but was equally popular in British music halls and

American vaudeville theatres. Early recordings by Ada Jones (Columbia) and the Heidelberg Quintette (Victor), revivals by Spike Jones and His City Slickers (RCA Victor), and frequent uses of the song as background in films have kept it popular as a romantic summertime tongue twister.

By the Honeysuckle Vine
Words and music by Bud De Sylva and Al Jolson.
T. B. Harms, 1919.
Dixie nostalgia interpolated by Jolson into the musical *Sinbad* in 1919; recorded by Ernest Hare on Pathe.

By the Light of the Honeymoon
Words by James O'Dea, music by Anne Caldwell.
Joseph W. Stern & Co., 1906.
Spooning song introduced by Maud Lambert in the musical *The Babes and the Baron* (1905); recorded by Frank C. Stanley for Victor.

By the Light of the Silvery Moon
Words and music by Edward Madden and Gus Edwards.
Remick Music Corp., 1909.
One of the most popular songs of the Tin Pan Alley era, it narrates a romance from a park flirtation to marriage. Performances by Nora Bayes and the principals of the *Follies of 1909* (in a "sing-along" review of the season's tunes) brought it into the repertories of the contemporary vaudeville stars until, by 1912, it had already sold 1.5 million copies of sheet music. Early recordings by Billy Murray (Victor), Al Jolson (Decca), and the Columbia Quartet foreshadowed its continuing popularity with pop and jazz artists, among them, Dennis Day (Victor), Doris Day (Columbia), Fats Waller (Victor), and the Bartlesville Barflies (Decca). Featured in a number of later films, including performances by Doris Day (title song, Warner Bros., 1953), Jane Powell (*Two Weeks with Love,* MGM, 1950), and Guy Lombardo and the Royal Canadians (*Birth of the Blues,* Paramount, 1941).

By the Old Oak Tree
Words by George V. Hobart, music by Max Hoffmann.
Popular ballad introduced by Dorothy Hunting and George Austin Moore in *The Rogers Brothers in Paris* (1904).

By the Pool at the Third Rosses
Words by Arthur Symons, music by H. T. Burleigh.
G. Ricordi & C., SpA, Milan, Italy, 1916.
Concert and parlor song.

By the Saskatchewan
Words by C. M. S. McLellan, music by Ivan Caryll.
Chappell & Co., Inc., 1910.
Comparison of French women by the Seine and Canadians by the Saskatchewan. Introduced by Ida Adams and John E. Young in the musical *The Pink Lady* (1910); recorded by Andrea Sarto (Columbia) and Reinald Werrenrath (Victor).

By the Silvery Rio Grande, see **My Heart's Tonight in Texas by the Silvery Rio Grande,**.

By the Sycamore Tree
Words by George V. Hobart, music by Max Hoffmann.
Introduced in *The Rogers Brothers in London* (1903), the spooning ballad was so popular that "Tree" songs became mandatory for romantic leads in Rogers Brothers shows.

Bye and Bye
Words by Blanche Merrill, music by Leo Edwards.
Charles K. Harris Music Publishing Co., 1912.
Romance popularized by the Courtney Sisters in Winter Garden revues.

Bye and Bye You'll See the Sun A-Shining
Words by Ed Moran and Vincent Bryan, music by Harry von Tilzer.
Harry Von Tilzer Music Publishing Co., 1918.
Romantic ballad popularized by Blanche Ring during World War I performances.

Bye Bye Dear Old Broadway
Words by Will D. Cobb, music by Gus Edwards.
Gus Edwards Music Publishing Co., 1907.
Finale performed by the entire company at the first Ziegfeld revue, his *Follies of 1907.*

Bye Bye Dearie
Words by Andrew B. Sterling, music by Harry von Tilzer.
Harry Von Tilzer Music Publishing Co., 1907.
Popular rag sung by the close-harmony duets Kelly and Violette and Eugene and Willie Howard; recorded by Harry Tally (Victor) as well as by Frank C. Stanley and Henry Burr (Columbia).

Bye-Bye, My Eva, Bye-Bye
Words and music by Chris Smith and Harry Brown.
Helf & Hager, 1905.
Comic song introduced by Brown; also sung by Carroll Johnson in the Dockstader Minstrel Troupe and recorded by Arthur Collins and Byron G. Harlan for Zon-o-phone.

Bye-O Baby Bunting
Words and music by Hen Wise and James Vaughan.
Will Rossiter, 1909.
Lullaby introduced by Henry Troy in the Williams and Walker company tour of *Bandana Land* (1908-1909).

Bygone Days in Dixie
Words and music by Charles Shackford.
Original copyright, 1902.
Nostalgic ballad popularized by Shackford; a standard for baritones in minstrel troupes.

C

California and You
Words by Edgar Leslie, music by Harry Puck.
Kalmar, Puck & Abrahams Consolidated Mus, 1914/Fred Fisher Music Co.
This Pacific nostalgia tune was popular as a song for Puck and Lottie Collins and as a fox-trot; recorded by Conway's Band (Victor) and the team of Albert Campbell and Henry Burr (Columbia).

Call 00-00-00-00-0, see **I Want a Real Nice Man,**.

Call Again
Words and music by Irving Berlin.
Waterson, Berlin & Snyder, 1912/Irving Berlin Music Corp.
Comic song about a flirt popularized by Lillian Bradley.

Call Me in the Morning
Words by A. Seymour Brown, music by Albert Gumble.
Remick Music Corp., 1912.
Traveling salesman situation comedy for Bessie Wynn.

Call Me Up Some Rainy Afternoon
Words and music by Irving Berlin.
Ted Snyder Music Publishing Co., 1910/Irving Berlin Music Corp.
Comic song about a woman setting up serial dates using the still-novel telephone; popularized by William Cahill and Joe Mack; recorded by Ada Jones with the American Quartet (Columbia).

Calligan - Call Again! (American-English)
Words and music by Herbert Rutter and Harry Lauder.
Francis, Day & Hunter, Ltd., London, England, 1900/T. B. Harms, 1900.
Lauder's character monologue and song about a Scottish tailor.

Calling to Her Boy Just Once Again
Words and music by Paul Dresser.

Howley, Haviland & Co., 1900.
Melodramatic plotted ballad associated with tenors R. J. Jose and Joseph Natus (Victor).

Can You Forget
Words by James Weldon Johnson, music by J. Rosamond Johnson.
Francis, Day & Hunter, Inc., 1910/T. B. Harms, 1910.
Romantic ballad interpolated by Grace von Studdiford into *The Bridal Trip* (1910); popularized as a fox-trot in recordings by many dance bands, including Clyde Doerr's Club Royal Orchestra and Theis' Detroit Ritz Orchestra.

Can You Tame Wild Wimmen?
Words by Andrew B. Sterling, music by Harry von Tilzer.
Harry Von Tilzer Music Publishing Co., 1918/T. B. Harms.
Comic complaint to a lion tamer popularized in vaudeville by Billy Glason and Jack Norworth and on records by Billy Murray (Victor) and Arthur Fields (Edison).

Can't Yo' Hear Me Callin', Caroline
Words by William H. Gardner, music by Caro Roma.
M. Witmark & Sons, 1914.
ASCAP top seller through recordings by Noble Sissle (Pathe) and Vernon Dalhart (Vocalion) and stage performances by George MacFarlane; revived by Red Nichols and His Five Pennies for Brunswick and by Jerry Colonna for Capitol.

Can't You See That I'm Lonely?
Words by Felix Feist, music by Harry Armstrong.
Leo Feist Inc., 1905, 1930.
After early recordings by Harry Ellis and Harry Tally (Victor), it was revised by Gus Kahn and Carmen Lombardo for Guy Lombardo and His Royal Canadians in 1930.

Can't You Take My Word?
Words by Harry Boden and James T. Powers, music by Bert Brandtford.
Original copyright, 1901.
Novelty character song introduced by Powers in *The Messenger Boy* (1901). His title character changed costume and identity constantly throughout the musical comedy and reprised the song with each appearance.

Captain Baby Bunting of the Rocking Horse Brigade
Words by Ed Gardinier and Will D. Cobb, music by J. Fred Helf.
Helf & Hager, 1906/Jerry Vogel Music Co., Inc., 1938.
Lullaby for child with toy soldiers becomes lament for a soldier kil-

led in action; recorded by Byron G. Harlan on Victor and Columbia.

The Captain of the Golf Club
Words and music by Salis Reya (pseudonym for S. H. Ayer).
Original copyright, 1902.
Novelty comic song describing typical golfers and dedicated to the United States Golfing Association.

Carissima
Words and music by Arthur A. Penn.
M. Witmark & Sons, 1912, 1928/Sol Bloom Publishing Co/Sol Bloom Music, 1905.
Ballad introduced by Cheridah Simpson in the musical *The Red Feather* (1903) and featured by Louise Brehany, Maud Williams, and Frances Alda, who recorded it for Victor.

Carmena
Words by Ellis Walton, music by H. Lane Wilson.
M. Witmark & Sons, 1902/G. Schirmer Inc.
This concert aria favorite of opera singer Alma Gluck (Victor) was also interpolated widely on Broadway by Maude Lillian Berri; currently published as an American art song.

Carnations, see **Clavelitos,**.

Carry Me Back to Old Virginny
Words and music by James Bland.
Oliver Ditson Co., 1906.
Although generally believed to be either a folk song or a Stephen C. Foster original, this nostalgic ballad was composed and copyrighted in 1906. In its first decades of popularity, it was performed as a parlor song and in barber-shop harmony; its first recordings fit these categories, with early discs by the quartets of the major labels--Columbia Stellar, Criteron (Zon-o-phone), and Orpheus (Victor). Associated with Alma Gluck, it was recorded by fellow opera singer Anna Case (Edison) with later popular performances by Rosa Ponselle (Gramophone), Helen Traubel and Bido Sayao (both Columbia), and Gluck (Victor and Victrola). Other notable recordings include those by Frances Langford (Decca), Jo Stafford and Paul Weston's Orchestra (V.Disc), and Louis Armstrong with the Mills Brothers (Decca).

Casey Jones
Words by T. Lawrence Seibert, music by Eddie Newton.
Original copyright, 1909/Shapiro, Bernstein & Co., Inc., 1936.
This comic West Coast version of the nineteenth-century railroad ballad was recorded by Gene Greene (Pathe) and Billy Murray

(Victor) and revived by Rudy Vallee and Ozzie Nelson. An anonymous political version, which accuses "Casey Jones" of scabbing for the railroad owners, can be heard on recordings by Pete Seeger and Tom Paxton (Folkways).

The Castle Combination
Music by James Reese Europe and Ford T. Dabney.
Joseph W. Stern & Co., 1914.
Waltz and fox-trot performed by Vernon and Irene Castle, the most widely known and imitated exhibition ballroom team in the United States, between 1912-1917; Europe and Dabney's orchestras played at the Castle House, Ziegfeld's Follies de Danse, and many other cabarets.

Castle Half and Half
Music by James Reese Europe and Ford T. Dabney.
Joseph W. Stern & Co., 1914.
Vernon and Irene Castle performed this exhibition ballroom dance to Europe and Dabney's orchestras; it was recorded by Prince's Band for Columbia and by the Victor Military Band as well. Another "Half and Half" (a one-step in 5/4 time), by F. Henri Klickmann, was also popular in 1914.

Castle of Dreams
Words by Joseph McCarthy, music by Harry Tierney.
Leo Feist Inc., 1919.
Fox-trot introduced in the musical *Irene* (1919) and popularized by contemporary and 1920's dance bands, including Art Hickman's Orchestra and Glen Gray and the Casa Loma Orchestra, who recorded it for Decca.

Castle Valse Classique
Music by Ford T. Dabney.
Joseph W. Stern & Co., 1914.
One of the Castles' most popular dances was this hesitation waltz based on Dvorak's *Humoresque;* its recordings by Earl Fuller's Rector restaurant Novelty Orchestra, Jaudas' Society Orchestra, Dabney's Orchestra, and George Hamilton Green sold more than a million copies combined.

The Castle Walk
Music by James Reese Europe and Ford T. Dabney.
Joseph W. Stern & Co., 1914.
Vernon and Irene Castle's signature dance (a trot and one-step) was a best-seller in sheet music, dance score, piano roll, and recording by Europe's Society Orchestra on Victor. Among the other 1914 Castle dances that Joseph W. Stern published were the "Innovation Tango," "Lame Duck," "Maxixe," and "Perfect Trot" (all by

Europe and Dabney), "Castles in Europe," and de Mesquita's "Innovation Waltz Esmeralda," all recorded by Europe's Society Orchestra.

Castles in the Air
Words by Joseph Herbert, music by Paul Lincke.
Apollo Verlag-Paul Lincke, Berlin, Federal Republic of Germany, 1900/Joseph W. Stern & Co., 1907.
Originally German, this parlor song was popularized in the United States through performances by Julius Steger in his touring productions of the melodrama *The Fifth Commandment* and in recordings by Richard Crooks (Gramophone).

Cecelia and Amelia
Words and music by Oscar Hammerstein, I.
Sol Bloom Publishing Co/Sol Bloom Music, 1901.
Producer Oscar Hammerstein wrote this popular romantic song for his musical *Sweet Maria* (1901), in which it was introduced by Eleanor Falk.

Central, Give Me Back My Dime
Words and music by Joseph E. Howard.
Charles K. Harris Music Publishing Co., 1905.
Howard made a hit out of his own variation of the classic telephone song, which usually started "Hello Central," (q.v.). This one was recorded by Arthur Collins and Byron G. Harlan for Victor.

The Chanticleer Rag
Words by Edward Madden, music by Albert Gumble.
Remick Music Corp., 1910.
Revues of the period often featured a "chicken" song, a slang reference to chorus women. Edmund Rostand's play *Chanticleer*--"The Rooster"-- with its impressive barnyard costumes inspired variations such as this one in 1909 and 1910. Arthur Collins and Byron G. Harlan recorded it for Columbia. Also see "White Folks Call It Chanticleer..."

Cheer Up Father, Cheer Up Mother
Words by Alfred Bryan, music by Herman Paley.
Remick Music Corp., 1918.
Post-World War I promise featured by Louise Dresser and recorded by the Peerless Quartet and by Prince's Orchestra for Columbia. Mary Earl's "Cheer Up Mother," published by Shapiro, Bernstein & Co., was also popular in 1918.

A Cheery Smile Is as Good as a Mile on the Road to Victory
Words and music by Anita Stewart.
Original copyright, 1918.

Patriotic song written and performed by silent film star Anita Stewart for Liberty Bond rallies.

Chere, a toi mon coeur, see **Love, Here Is My Heart!**,.

Cheyenne
Words by Harry Williams, music by Egbert van Alstyne.
Remick Music Corp., 1904.
Western romance of "Shy Ann" recorded by Billy Murray on Victor 78's.

Chic-Chic-Chic-Chic-Chicken
Words by Gene Buck, music by Dave Stamper.
Joseph W. Stern & Co., 1913.
Buck and Stamper used both meanings of the word "chicken" in this novelty song for Bessie Wynn; in verse 1, a farmer calls to hens, in verse 2, a young man approaches Broadway chorus dancers.

The Chicken Walk
Words and music by Irving Berlin.
Irving Berlin Music Corp., 1916.
Novelty song introduced by Elsie Janis and the Fairbanks Twins (Madeleine and Marion) as the Chickens in the "Hunting for a New Dance" sequence in *The Century Girl* (1916).

Chinatown, My Chinatown
Words by William Jerome, music by Jean Schwartz.
Remick Music Corp., 1910.
Originally a romantic serenade introduced by Edwin Foy in *Up and Down Broadway* (1910), it sped up and became one of the preeminent fox-trots of the decade with early recordings by Prince's Orchestra (Columbia), the Victor Military Band and major jazz revivals by Louis Armstrong (Vocalion), the Mills Brothers (Brunswick, Melotone, and Banner), and Glen Gray and the Casa Loma Orchestra (Decca). Featured recently as the "Mystery Song" in Woody Allen's *Radio Days.*

Chinese Lullaby
Words and music by Robert Hood Bowers.
G. Schirmer Inc., 1919/Fred Fisher Music Co., 1930/Venus Music Corp.
Theme song for *East Is West,* a 1919 play by Hymer and Shipman, it retells the plot in pidgin English (verse 1) and in poetry (verse 2). Revived in 1930 as theme song of Laemmle-Universal sound version of *East Is West* starring Lew Ayres and Lupe Velez. An ASCAP top seller in sheet music, as a fox-trot piano roll, and in

recordings by the Victor Salon Orchestra, the Waldorf-Astoria Dance Orchestra (Columbia), and Paul Whiteman (Columbia).

Chloe, I'm Waiting
Words by Edgar Smith, music by Reginald De Koven.
Edward Schuberth & Co., Inc., 1901.
Southern nostalgia ballad with banjo effects. Introduced by Anna Held in *The Little Duchess* (1901).

The Chocolate Drop, see **Bon Bon Buddy,**.

Chong, He Come from Hong Kong
Words and music by Harold Weeks.
Leo Feist Inc., 1919.
Chinese-dialect lyrics attached to dance music; recorded by the Premiere Quartet (Edison) and the Van Eps Banjo Quartet (Okeh). It was a short-lived ASCAP top seller.

The Christy Girl
Words by Harry B. Smith, music by Maurice Levi.
Remick Music Corp., 1909.
This tribute to the ideal woman of illustrator George Christy was introduced by Annabelle Whitford in the *Follies of 1909;* also see previous seasons' "Gibson" and "Brinkley Bathing Girls" songs.

Ciribiribin (Italian)
English words by Tell Taylor, Italian words by Rudolf Thaler, music by A. Pestalozzo.
Arnett Delonais, 1909/Mills Music Inc.
Italian novelty popularized as an instrumental by Sodero's Band on Edison. Scores of recordings range from those by opera singers Lucrezia Bori (Victrola) and Grace Moore (Brunswick, Victor) to the jazz ensembles of Carmen Cavallaro (Decca), Harry James (Victor), and Benny Goodman (Columbia). Over thirty arrangements of the song are currently registered with ASCAP alone.

Clavelitos, also known as **Carnations**
Words by Mrs. M. T. E. Sandwith, music by J. Valverde.
G. Schirmer Inc., 1909, 1941.
Concert aria popularized on Victor 78's and on Victrolas by opera divas Amelita Galli-Curci and Lucrezia Bori; revived by Deanna Durbin in the film *It Started with Eve* (Universal, 1941) and recorded most recently by Victoria de los Angeles with Gerard Moore on RCA.

Cleopatra
Words by Alfred Bryan, music by Harry Tierney.
Remick Music Corp., 1917.

Multiple ethnic jokes interpolated by Al Jolson into *Sinbad* (1918) through this song; recorded by Arthur Collins on Emerson.

Cleopatra Had a Jazz Band
Words by Jack Coogan, music by Jimmy Morgan.
Leo Feist Inc., 1917.
Novelty song featured by Emma Carus and Sophie Tucker; recorded as a fox-trot by Prince's Band (Columbia) and by Sam Ash (Columbia).

Clidee-Oh
Words by Carroll Flemming, music by Sidney Parker.
Southern ballad sung by Maud Raymond in William A. Brady's production of *Uncle Tom's Cabin* (1901).

Colleen Bawn
Words by Edward Madden, music by J. Fred Helf.
Helf & Hager, 1906/Larry Spier, Inc.
Irish ballad popularized by Bonita, Amy Butler, Eleanor Henry, Charles Perry, and the team of Mitchell and Marron.

Come After Breakfast, Bring 'long You' Lunch and Leave 'fore Supper Time
Words and music by James Tim Brymn, James Burris, and Chris Smith.
Joseph W. Stern & Co., 1909.
Character song and slow drag introduced by S. H. Dudley, producer and star of the Smart Set musical comedy touring company, for his vehicle *His Honor the Barber* (1909-1911); recorded by Arthur Collins for Columbia.

Come Along My Mandy (English)
Words and music by Tom Mellor and Harry Gifford, words by Nora Bayes and Jack Norworth.
Francis, Day & Hunter, Ltd., London, England/Francis, Day & Hunter, Inc., 1907, 1910/Jerry Vogel Music Co., Inc., 1938.
Bayes and Norworth "Americanized" the lyrics and interpolated this raggy song into *The Jolly Bachelors* (1907); Bayes recorded it for Victor as a solo and as a duet with Norworth. Francis, Day & Hunter also published "Come Along with Me, My Mandy Lee" (1907, credited to William Jerome and Jean Schwartz) which was introduced by Harry Bulger in *Noah's Ark.*

Come Along to Toy Town
Words and music by Irving Berlin.
Waterson, Berlin & Snyder, 1919.
Promotional song for the miniature village installed in the lower lobby of the New York Hippodrome; performed in the Hippo-

drome production *Everything* (1919) and recorded by Henry Burr (Pathe).

Come Along Up in the Flip Flap (English)
Words by Ballard MacDonald, music by James W. Tate.
Francis, Day & Hunter, Ltd., London, England, 1908/Francis, Day & Hunter, Inc., 1908.
Popularized by Vesta Victoria in British music halls and on American vaudeville tours, 1908-1911. A Flip Flap was an amusement park ride.

Come and Dance with Me
Words by Harold Atteridge, music by Louis Hirsch and Melville Gideon.
M. Witmark & Sons, 1911.
Romance introduced by Gaby Deslys and the male chorus dancing on a line of chairs in the musical *Vera Violette* (1911).

Come and Take a Stroll with Me
Words by George V. Hobart, music by Ludwig Englander.
Joseph W. Stern & Co., 1902.
Satire on social graces. Introduced by Marie Cahill and Joseph Herbert in *Sally in Our Alley* (1902).

Come Around on Our Veranda
Words by Paul West, words and music by Jerome Kern.
T. B. Harms, 1907.
Title continues "For We've Got a Phonograph." This song, performed by Irene Franklyn in *The Orchid* (1907) and by Melville Ellis in his Pianologue act, details popular records, rhyming Sousa with Caruso and plugging Blanche Ring's "Waltz Me Around Again, Willie" (q.v.).

Come Around to Mamie's
Words by John H. Flynn, music by J. N. Lowitz.
Original copyright, 1905.
Comedy song praising a local matchmaker popularized by Irene Bentley.

Come Back to Me (American-French)
English words by Worton David, music by Henri Christine.
Editions Salabert S.A., Paris, France, 1910/Leo Feist Inc., 1910/Leeds Music Corp., 1952.
This ballad associated with Gaby Deslys was revised in 1952 with new lyrics by Sylvia Dee and Sid Lippman; the later version was recorded by Tony Martin (Victor) and by Guy Lombardo and His Royal Canadians (Decca).

Come Back to Me
Words by Harold Atteridge, music by Sigmund Romberg and Jean Schwartz.
Remick Music Corp., 1919.
Waltz ballad interpolated by Al Jolson into *Monte Christo, Jr.* (1919).

Come Back to Me My Melody
Words and music by Irving Berlin and Ted Snyder.
Waterson, Berlin & Snyder, 1912.
Novelty song about a composer complaining about raggy arrangements; popularized by the ventriloquist Tilford.

Come Back to Playland with Me
Words and music by Maud Lambert.
M. Witmark & Sons, 1912.
Nostalgic ballad featured by Lambert.

Come Dance with Me
Words and music by George White and Billy Gaston.
Will Rossiter, 1913.
Exhibition ballroom dance number. Introduced by White and Minerva Coverdale in *The Red Widow* (1911) and maintained in White's acts.

Come Down from the Big Fig Tree
Words by Edward Madden, music by Theodore F. Morse.
F. B. Haviland, 1904.
In the parlance of Tin Pan Alley, "tree" songs referred to spooning and songwriters created strings of popular romances differentiated principally by the variety of the tree; this one was popularized by Anna Driver, Malcolm Shackleford, and George MacFarlane and recorded by Arthur Collins on Victor.

Come Down, Ma Evening Star
Words by Robert B. Smith, music by John Stromberg.
M. Witmark & Sons, 1902.
Stromberg's final song was introduced by Lillian Russell in Weber and Fields' *Twirly-Whirly* (1902) and recorded by her (released currently on CRS). Legend, perpetuated by the film biography of Russell, persists that the manuscript for the song was in Stromberg's pocket when he committed suicide. Recorded by Joan Morris on her *After the Ball* album (Nonesuch). Performed by Alice Faye in the film *Lillian Russell.*

Come Josephine in My Flying Machine
Words by Alfred Bryan, music by Fred Fisher.
Shapiro, Bernstein & Co., Inc., 1910, 1937.

The search for a place to spoon fascinated songwriters and performers alike in 1910 and gave them a reason to celebrate new inventions. Blanche Ring featured this song in vaudeville and on Victor 78's. It was revived for the Fred Fisher biographical film *Oh, You Beautiful Doll* (20th Century Fox, 1949) and, in a novelty version, by Spike Jones and His City Slickers (Bluebird).

Come On, Let's Razoo on Our Little Kazoo
Words and music by George Sping.
Shapiro, Bernstein & Co., Inc., 1913.
Novelty song alluding to the "composer, Herman von Bellow," from "Yip-I-Addy-I-Ay," (q.v.), featured by Reine Davies.

Come On Papa
Words and music by Edgar Leslie and Harry Ruby.
Waterson, Berlin & Snyder, 1918/Mills Music Inc.
World War I comedy song depicts French women beckoning to Yankee Doodle Boys; featured by Eddie Cantor in the *Ziegfeld Follies of 1918.* A fox-trot version remained popular through performances by Wellington Cross and Joseph C. Smith's Orchestra (Victor).

Come On, Play Ball with Me
Words by Edward Madden, music by Gus Edwards.
Gus Edwards Music Publishing Co., 1909/Remick Music Corp.
This audience participation number in the *Follies of 1909* saw theatre-goers pitching baseballs at Lillian Lorraine and the women's chorus. Eva Tanguay sang it on tour.

Come Out, Dinah, on the Green
Words by Bob Cole and James Weldon Johnson, music by J. Rosamond Johnson.
Howley, Haviland & Dresser, 1901.
Romantic ballad introduced in the pantomime *The Sleeping Beauty and the Beast* (1901).

Come Over on My Veranda
Words by John Kemble, music by Lester W. Keith.
Original copyright, 1905.
Summertime flirtation song popularized by female impersonator Julian Eltinge and, as a close-harmony number, by the Kimball Brothers.

Come Right In, Sit Right Down and Make Yourself at Home
Words by Bob White and Alfred Anderson, music by Will H. Dixon.
A. R. White, 1909/Jerry Vogel Music Co., Inc., 1939.

Bert Williams's response to "Come After Breakfast..." (q.v.) by rival S. H. Dudley.

Come, Take a Skate with Me
Words and music by Raymond Brown and Gus Edwards.
Gus Edwards Music Publishing Co., 1906.
Roller skating novelty flirtation song introduced by Blanche Ring in the musical *His Honor, the Mayor* (1906); recorded by Arthur Collins and Byron G. Harlan for Victor.

Come, Take a Trip in My Air-Ship
Words by Ren Shields, music by George Evans.
Charles K. Harris Music Publishing Co., 1904.
Romantic song performed by Edna Wallace Hopper and Ethel Robinson; recorded by Frank C. Stanley on Concert 78's.

Come to the Land of Bohemia
Words by Ren Shields, music by George Evans.
Mills Music Inc., 1907.
Drinking song popularized as a solo by John P. Curran and as a close-harmony specialty by That Quartette.

Come to the Moon
Words by Ned Wayburn and Lou Paley, music by George Gershwin.
T. B. Harms, 1919.
Finale of Ned Wayburn's *Demi-Tasse Revue* for the opening of the Capitol Theatre (1919); recorded by Gene Roderich's Orchestra on Brunswick. Revived as a major production number in *Celebrating Gershwin* televised worldwide in 1987 via PBS, BBC, and RAI.

The Comet and the Moon
Words by Harry B. Smith, music by Gus Edwards.
Remick Music Corp., 1910.
Florenz Ziegfeld, Jr.'s early *Follies* often featured filmed sequences projected onto curtains or scrims with on-stage vocal accompaniment. In this astronomical romance in the *Follies of 1910,* Anna Held appeared as "The Comet" (on film) and was serenaded by Harry Watson as "The Moon."

Common Sense
Words and music by Chris Smith and John Larkins.
Original copyright, 1907.
Character monologue and song popularized by Clarice Vance and by John Larkins.

The Concert in the Sky
Words by Ferdinand E. Mierisch and Charles R. McCarron, music by Chris Smith.
Joseph W. Stern & Co., 1913.
Rag version of the dance of the planets popularized by composer Smith in vaudeville.

Congo Love Song, see **Marie Cahill's Congo Love Song,.**

The Conjure Man
Words and music by Bob Cole and James Weldon Johnson.
Joseph W. Stern & Co., 1905.
Novelty love song interpolated by Marie Cahill into *Moonshine Mary* (1905).

Constantly
Words by Chris Smith and Jim Burris, music by Bert Williams.
Remick Music Corp., 1910/Jerry Vogel Music Co., Inc., 1938.
Complaint song for Williams in the *Follies of 1910;* recorded by him (Columbia) and revived by Phil Harris in the 1940's (Victor).

Coo! (English)
Words and music by Paul A. Rubens.
Chappell & Co., Inc., 1902.
British nostalgia song using imitations of children's voices in the chorus. Introduced by Lillian Eldee in the musical *A Country Girl* (1902).

Coster Rag
Words by Jack O'Malley, music by J. R. Shannon.
Original copyright, 1910.
Comic novelty song popularized by Alice Lloyd.

The Coster's Glide
Words by J. Leubrie Hill, music by J. Rosamond Johnson.
Remick Music Corp., 1911.
Cockney rag introduced by Billy B. Van and the Beaumont Sisters in *A Lucky Hoodoo* (1911).

Could You Be True to Eyes of Blue If You Looked into Eyes of Brown?
Words and music by Will D. Cobb and Gus Edwards.
Mills Music Inc., 1902, 1929, 1941.
Introduced by Van Rensselar Wheeler in *A Chinese Honeymoon* (1902) and featured in vaudeville by Lottie Gilson; revived for Edwards's juvenile feature acts in the 1910's.

Could You Learn to Love Me?, also known as **Ood-kay Oo-yay Earn-lay Oo-tay Ove-Lay Ee-may?**
Words by Junie McCree, music by Albert von Tilzer.
York Music Corp., 1909.
Pig latin novelty love song featured by McCree.

The Countess of Alagazam
Words and music by Bob Cole.
Joseph W. Stern & Co., 1904/Edward B. Marks Music Corp., 1932.
Novelty nonsense song from Cole's own vaudeville act with J. Rosamond Johnson.

The Country Girl (English)
Words by Stanislaus Stange, music by Julian Edwards.
M. Witmark & Sons, 1901.
Lulu Glaser's signature tune after introducing it in the musical *Dolly Varden* (1902).

Courting
Words and music by Frederick Solomon.
Sol Bloom Publishing Co/Sol Bloom Music, 1902.
Introduced in Mark Twain's own dramatization of his *Huckleberry Finn* (Hartford, 1902), it was performed in vaudeville by Florence Parker, Arthur Dunn, and John H. Slavin.

'Cross the Great Divide, I'll Wait for You
Words by Sam M. Lewis, music by George W. Meyer.
Original copyright, 1913.
Western love ballad referring to the nineteenth-century melodrama, *The Great Divide;* popularized by singer-band leaders Sam Ash and Phil Dolan and by female vocalists Charlotte Meyers, Charlotte Taylor, and Rene Dietrich; recorded by Harry Macdonough for Victor and by Henry Burr and Andrea Sarto for Columbia.

Crusade Glory
Words by Antoinette A. Hawley, music by Charles H. Gabriel.
Original copyright, 1900, 1928.
Anthem for the Women's Christian Temperance Union adapted by Gabriel from his own hymn "Glory"; also used by the Billy Sunday evangelical campaigns for Temperance.

Crusader and Tommy (English)
Words by Clifford Grey, music by Herman Finck.
Ascherberg, Hopwood & Crew, Ltd., London, England, 1918.
Patriotic song about a meeting between Richard the Lionheart and "Tommy Atkins," the archetypal British soldier character. Sung by Elsie Janis and, as a duet, by Stanley Lupino and Will West in the revue *Hullo America* (1918, Palace Theatre, London).

The Cubanola Glide
Words by Vincent Bryan, music by Harry von Tilzer.
Harry Von Tilzer Music Publishing Co., 1909.
After the dance (a glide with tango overtones) was premiered by Daphne Pollard, the music was popularized by recordings from Billy Murray (Victor) and Arthur Collins and Byron G. Harlan (Columbia). Revived as a novelty by Arthur (Guitar Boogie) Smith and the Cracker-Jacks (MGM).

The Cuckoo Bird
Words and music by Fred Meyer.
Sol Bloom Publishing Co/Sol Bloom Music, 1901.
Francis Wilson's popular novelty song from *The Strollers* (1901).

Cuddle Up a Little Closer, Lovey Mine
Words by Otto Hauerbach, music by Karl Hoschna.
M. Witmark & Sons, 1908, 1932.
Still a dance standard, this fox-trot was introduced by Alice Yorke in *The Three Twins* (1908) and popularized by Daisy Leon in vaudeville; contemporary recordings by Ada Jones, Billy Murray, and the Victor Novelty Orchestra, and Marion Harris's Columbia disc from the 1920's kept it popular. Performances in film include those by Betty Grable (20th Century Fox's *Coney Island,* 1943), Guy Lombardo (Paramount's *Birth of the Blues,* 1941), and Doris Day and Gordon McRae (*On Moonlight Bay,* Warner Brothers, 1951); recordings by Lombardo, the Pied Pipers (Capitol), Ray Coniff (Columbia), Sammy Kaye (Victor) and Meredith Willson and His Orchestra (Decca).

Cuddle Up Honey, Let's Make Love
Words by Henry S. Creamer (pseudonym for US), music by Will H. Vodery.
Original copyright, 1911.
Introduced by S. H. Dudley in his New Smart Set Company production of *Dr. Beans from Boston* (musical, 1911).

Cupid's I.O.U.
Words by Jack Drislane and Alfred Bryan, music by George W. Meyer.
Original copyright, 1910.
Popular romantic novelty with kisses included in the chorus lyrics, sung by Dot Raymond, Billy McDermott, and Flora Chalue; recorded by Ada Jones and Billy Murray (Victor).

The Curse of a Pretty Face
Words and music by Will F. Burke.
Original copyright, 1901.
Plotted ballad performed by Vogel's Minstrels.

The Curse of an Aching Heart
Words by Henry Fink, music by Al Piantadosi.
Leo Feist Inc., 1913, 1941.
Emma Carus's vaudeville hit was recorded frequently by vocalists and jazz pianists, among them Manuel Romain (Cort) and Vernon Dalhart (Columbia) in early decades and Ella Logan (Columbia) and Fats Waller (Victor) in the 1940's.

Cutey, Tell Me Who Tied Your Tie?
Words by Arthur Longbrake, music by Ed Edwards.
Original copyright, 1910.
Proposal song popular as a solo, duet, and close-harmony number. Introduced by Agnes Finley and George B. Fox in *The Soul Kiss* (1910) and sung in vaudeville by James A. Fleming, Mamie Champion, McAvoy & Brooks, Rose Black and Nat Jerome, and That Quartette.

D

Daddy Has a Sweetheart and Mother Is Her Name
Words by Gene Buck, music by Dave Stamper.
Penn Music Co., 1912.
Dixie nostalgia number for Lillian Lorraine that brought Buck and Stamper to the attention of Florenz Ziegfeld, Jr. He put the song in the *Follies of 1912* and hired its songwriters as members of his permanent staff; also revived in the *Ziegfeld Follies* of 1923 and 1927. Recorded by Edna Brown (Victor, Rex) and pianist Manuel Romain (Columbia).

Daddy, I Love You More and More Each Day
Words by Sophie Tucker, music by Fred Strasser.
Remick Music Corp., 1914.
Blues written by Sophie Tucker for her own performance.

Daddy Long Legs
Words by Sam M. Lewis and Joe Young, music by Harry Ruby.
Waterson, Berlin & Snyder, 1919/Warock Music, Inc.
Promotional title song for the Mary Pickford film (First National, 1919); recorded by Henry Burr (Pathe) and by Sam Ash (Emerson). Also promoting the film, which was based on a popular novel and play by Jean Webster, was Neville Fleeson and Albert von Tilzer's "Dear Old Daddy Long Legs" (1919).

Daddy's Little Girl
Words by Edward Madden, music by Theodore F. Morse.
F. B. Haviland, 1905.
Plotted melodramatic ballad sung by James T. Doyle, Genevieve Homer, and the team of Thomas Guyer and Beth Stone; recorded by Byron G. Harlan on Victor and Vim.

Daisies Won't Tell
Words and music by Anita Owen.
Remick Music Corp., 1908/Jerry Vogel Music Co., Inc., 1938.

Owen's most popular ballad in her "Flower" series was recorded by Arthur Clough for Columbia and by Helen Clark and Joseph A. Phillips for Edison.

Daisy Deane
Words by Richard Wilkens, words and music by Will Marion Cook.
York Music Corp., 1904.
Romantic ballad from the musical *The Southerners* (1904).

Daisy Dear
Words by George Totten Smith, music by A. M. Langstaff.
Francis, Day & Hunter, Inc., 1906.
Ballad based on petal counting popularized by Dorothy Jardon in Ned Wayburn's feature vaudeville act *Daisy Dancers* (1906-1908).

Daisy Donahue
Words by James O'Dea, music by Robert J. Adams.
Original copyright, 1903.
Romantic ballad popularized by Clara Morton and Nellie Florede and recorded by Arthur Pryor's Band (Victor).

Dallas Blues
Words by Lloyd Garrett, music by Hart A. Wand.
Mayfair Music Corp., 1912, 1940.
Fox-trot cited by W. C. Handy for its use of blues motifs; recorded by the ensembles of Isham Jones (Decca), Louis Armstrong (Okeh, Parlophone), Woody Herman (Decca), and by Glen Gray and the Casa Loma Orchestra (Brunswick).

Dancing Shoes
Words by Harold Atteridge, music by Harry Carroll.
Waterson, Berlin & Snyder, 1919.
Exhilarating tribute to syncopation as an aid in seduction sung by Bernard Granville and Lillian Lorraine in *The Little Blue Devil* (1919).

Dancing the Blues Away
Words and music by Joe McCarthy, Howard Johnson, and Fred Fisher.
Leo Feist Inc., 1914.
Plotted rag-time song interpolated by Al Jolson into *Dancing Around* (1914).

The Dandiest Boy in Town
Words and music by Fred Solomon.
Original copyright, 1900.
Cakewalk specialty popularized by Mabel Russell.

Danny Boy (American-English)
Words and music by Fred E. Weatherly.
Boosey & Hawkes Inc., 1913.
Imitative folk ballad that retained its popularity through the 1960's when Ray Price revived it as a best-seller on Columbia. Its earlier recordings have been split among such major jazz ensembles as Count Basie's (Columbia) and Glenn Miller's Orchestras (Gramophone, Bluebird), Irish crooners, among them Bing Crosby (Decca) and Dennis Day (Capitol), and operatic sopranos, including Ernestine Schumann-Heink (Victor), Eleanor Steber (Victor), and Eileen Farrell (Columbia). It also serves as a personal signature tune for comedian Danny Thomas.

Dardanella
Words by Fred Fisher, music by Felix Bernard and Johnny S. Black.
Fred Fisher Music Co., 1919/Fisher Music Corp., 1919.
Fox-trot billed as "an echo from the East," it has remained popular as a male solo and as an instrumental after early success as a piano roll (QRS). Memorable recordings include those by Billy Murray (Victor) and the Plantation Jazz Orchestra (Emerson) on early 78's and by the ensembles of Guy Lombardo and Borrah Minevitch (Decca) in the swing era; featured in the Fred Fisher biographical film *Oh, You Beautiful Doll* (20th Century-Fox, 1949).

Dark Grows the Sky (American-English)
Words by Harry Graham, music by H. Fraser-Simson.
Ascherberg, Hopwood & Crew, Ltd., London, England, 1918.
Waltz associated with Jose Collins and interpolated by her into the musicals *The Maid of the Mountains* (London) and *A Southern Maid* (London); recorded by Gladys Moncrieff (Vocalion).

Darktown Barbeque
Words and music by Will Marion Cook.
York Music Corp., 1904.
Introduced by Abbie Mitchell and the black chorus in *The Southerners* (a 1904 melodrama with music that featured two separate choruses); reprinted as a Sunday Music Supplement on April 16, 1905, in the New York *American.*

The Darktown Poker Club
Words by Jean C. Havez, music by Bert Williams and Will H. Vodery.
Remick Music Corp., 1914.
Bert Williams introduced this song during his famous one-person poker game skit in the *Ziegfeld Follies of 1914*; recorded by him (Columbia) and revived by Phil Harris (RCA Victor).

The Darktown Strutters' Ball
Words and music by Shelton Brooks.
Will Rossiter, 1917/Leo Feist Inc., 1945.
This jazz standard began its popularity as dance music listing and promoting specific ballroom dances of the period through early performances by Sophie Tucker and Blossom Seeley and recordings by the James Reese Europe's "Hell Fighters" (on the Pathe label) and the house bands of Pathe and Edison. Most of the major jazz ensembles and dance bands have performed and recorded the song (without all of the specific lyric references), among them, Hoagy Carmichael (Decca), Paul Whiteman (Victor), Ella Fitzgerald (Decca), and Fats Waller and His Rhythm Boys (RCA Victor).

Darling
Words by Arthur Gillespie and Carter De Haven, music by Arthur H. Gutman.
Shapiro, Bernstein & Co., Inc., 1913.
Featured by De Haven and his partner Flora Parker in their flirtation act in vaudeville, *Exceeding the Speed Limit* (1913-1915).

Darling
Words by Cyrus Wood, music by Sigmund Romberg.
Shapiro, Bernstein & Co., Inc., 1918, 1945, 1953.
Romantic waltz introduced by Isabelle Lowe and Jack Cagwin in *The Melting of Molly* (musical, 1918); re-issued in 1953 with new lyrics credited to Wood and Dick Rogers.

Dat Draggy Rag
Words and music by Irving Berlin.
Ted Snyder Music Publishing Co., 1910.
Promotional song for the latest craze in exhibition ballroom dancing -- elongated movements to slow rhythms.

Dat Lovin' Rag
Words by Victor H. Smalley, music by Bernard Adler.
F. B. Haviland, 1907.
Featured by Jerry Mills and Lottie Grady in Smalley's burlesque *The Merry Widower* (1907); has references to Lehar's music for *The Merry Widow* in the chorus.

Dat Lovin' Touch
Words by Sam M. Lewis, music by Leo Bennett.
Shapiro, Bernstein & Co., Inc., 1911.
This Al Jolson novelty specialty refers to the popularity of rag-time played on string instruments.

Dat Possum Rag
Words by Harold Atteridge, music by Phil Schwartz.
Original copyright, 1910.
Dialect character song introduced by Will Philbrick in *Jumping Jupiter* (musical done in Chicago, 1910).

Dat's Harmony
Words by Grant Clarke, music by Bert Williams.
Remick Music Corp., 1911/Fred Burch Music, 1939.
Bert Williams's character romance from the *Follies of 1911;* recorded by Arthur Collins on Zon-o-phone.

The Daughter of Rosie O'Grady
Words by Monty C. Brice, music by Walter Donaldson.
M. Witmark & Sons, 1918, 1946.
Dedicated to Maude Nugent, author of "Sweet Rosie O'Grady" (1896), this waltz-clog became the signature tune of Pat Rooney and Marion Bent, and of their son, Pat Rooney, Jr., in vaudeville, radio, and film. A success as an instrumental for the Victor Novelty Orchestra, it was revived by Gene Kelly (MGM), Phil Regan (Decca), and other Hollywood Irish vocalists; used as title song for the 1950 Warner Brothers film comedy.

The Dawn of a Tomorrow, also known as **Glad**
Words by Eden E. Greville, music by Walter Pulitzer.
Joseph W. Stern & Co., 1909.
Anthem introduced by Eleanor Robson as "Glad" in Francis Hodgson Burnett's symbolic play *The Dawn of a Tomorrow* (1909); revived for the 1924 Paramount film of the same title.

Day Dreams
Words and music by Chauncey Olcott.
M. Witmark & Sons, 1906.
Introduced by Olcott in his Irish melodrama *Eileen Asthorne* (1906) and recorded by Harry MacDonough (Victor).

Day of Hope and Day of Glory, see **Woman's Right Is Woman's Duty,**.

The Day That You Grew Colder
Words and music by Paul Dresser.
Paul Dresser Music Publishing Co., 1905.
Sentimental ballad associated with tenor R. J. Jose, who recorded it for Victor.

De Cakewalk Queen
Words by Harry B. Smith, music by John Stromberg.
M. Witmark & Sons, 1900.

Song and dance introduced by Bessie Clayton, whose specialty was cakewalking on point at Weber and Fields' Music Hall.

De Goblin's Glide
Words by Frederick Day, music by Jerome Kern.
T. B. Harms, 1911.
Slow rag interpolated into the musical *La Belle Paree* (1911).

De Little Pickaninny's Gone to Sleep
Words and music by James Weldon Johnson and J. Rosamond Johnson.
Oliver Ditson Co., 1910.
Art song based on dialect poem featured and recorded by Paul Robeson (Gramophone).

De Trop
Words by Harry B. Smith, music by Clifton Crawford.
Edward Schuberth & Co., Inc., 1901.
Novelty song performed by the male comics in *The Liberty Belles* (1901).

Deacon Jones
Words by James Melville, Jr., music by Clarence M. Chapel.
Original copyright, 1905.
Introduced by Caroline Hull in *The Winning Girl* (1905), this comic song featured the archetypal small town "Deacon Jones" after his first visit to the city.

Dear I Love You So
Words by Harold Atteridge, music by Franz Lehar.
Original copyright, 1908.
Early Atteridge lyrics for a Chicago production of the operetta *The Merry Widow* (1908).

Dear Land of Home (English)
Words and music by Graham Valmore.
Art song that became popular as a patriotic anthem during World War I, sung by Charles Tree and Trevelyan David in London; recorded by Anna Case for Edison.

Dear Little Boy of Mine
Words by J. Keirn Brennan, music by Ernest R. Ball.
M. Witmark & Sons, 1918/Anne-Rachel Music Corp.
Promotional song for the First National film based on Booth Tarkington's novel *Boy o' Mine* (1918); became a standard Irish "mother" ballad with recordings by Bing Crosby (Decca) and was revived in the film *Irish Eyes Are Smiling* (20th Century Fox, 1944). Original recordings by Carroll Clark (Black Swan), Elsie

Baker (Victor), Prince's Dance Orchestra (Columbia), and Will Oakland and His Orchestra (Edison) were also very successful.

Dear Mamie, I Love You
Words by Irving Berlin, music by Ted Snyder.
Ted Snyder Music Publishing Co., 1911.
Novelty love song written as a letter introduced by Billy Oakes.

Dear Old Girl
Words by Richard Henry Buck, music by Theodore F. Morse.
Howley, Haviland & Dresser, 1903.
Plotted anniversary ballad was a top seller twice--through recordings and performances by Frank Mullane, Harry MacDonough, and R. J. Jose (all Victor) in the 1910's and through revivals by Bing Crosby (Decca, V Disc) and Arthur Godfrey (Columbia) in the 1940's.

Dear Old Pal of Mine
Words by Harold Robe, music by Gitz Rice.
G. Ricordi & C., SpA, Milan, Italy, 1918/Bergman, Vocco & Conn Inc.
The last song by Rice, who died of poison gas at Viny Ridge, was a popular ballad during and after World War I, following its introduction in Manners and Hay's play *Getting Together* (1918); recorded as a sentimental tribute to the fallen by John McCormack (Victor, Victrola), but also as a waltz by Joseph C. Smith's Orchestra (Victor) and a fox-trot by Shep Fields (Bluebird).

Dearie
Words and music by Clare Kummer.
Joseph W. Stern & Co., 1905/Edward B. Marks Music Corp.
Romance introduced by Sallie Fisher in *Sergeant Brue* (1905) and recorded by Anna Case (Edison), Elsie Baker (Victor), and Arthur Pryor's Band (Victor). A parody version, also by kummer, was popularized and recorded by Billy Murray for Victor.

Dearie, Won't You Call Me Dearie, see **Next Sunday at Nine,**.

A Debutante's Engagement Book
Words and music by Fanchon (pseudonym for Fanny Wolff) and Marco (pseudonym for Mike Wolff).
Original copyright, 1919.
Novelty song delineating appropriate dress for every occasion. Written for Fanchon & Marco's revue *Let's Go* (1919), probably for a production number featuring evening clothes.

The Deedle-Dum-Dee
Words by Benjamin Hapgood Burt, music by Silvio Hein.

T. B. Harms, 1911/Francis, Day & Hunter, Inc., 1911.
Promotional song for the dance named the *deedle-dum-dee.* Introduced by Blanche Ring in *The Wall Street Girl* (1912) and recorded by Ada Jones.

Deep River
Words and music by H. T. Burleigh.
G. Ricordi & C., SpA, Milan, Italy, 1913, 1941.
Burleigh's best-known spiritual arrangement, popular both as a choral work and as a solo that has been recorded by many of the opera world's most important figures, among them, Clara Butt, Helen Traubel, Rosa Ponselle, and Ezio Pinza. Available recordings include those by Marian Anderson (RCA), Paul Robeson (Gramophone), Leontyne Price (RCA), Barbara Henricks (Angel), guitarist Christopher Parkening (Angel), and the Boston Pops. Choral versions copyrighted in 1916, 1928, and 1965.

Der Faderland for Mine
Words and music by Annie Andros Hawley.
M. Witmark & Sons, 1907.
Blanche Ring introduced this German (or "Dutch") dialect song into Lew Fields' *About Town* (1906) in tribute to his earliest stage persona.

Devotion
Words by George Totten Smith, music by Alfred E. Aarons.
Sol Bloom Publishing Co/Sol Bloom Music, 1903.
Wedding song from the finale of *The Knickerbocker Girl* (musical, 1903).

Didn't Know Exactly What to Do
Words by Frank Pixley, music by Gustav Luders.
M. Witmark & Sons, 1902.
Comic song introduced by John W. Ransome in *The Prince of Pilsen* (1903). The suggestive lyrics, in which "Hans" is taught how to approach a woman, were a well-appreciated scandal for the audiences of the half-dozen road companies of Luders's most popular musicals.

Dill Pickles Rag
Words by Alfred Bryan, music by Charles E. Johnson.
Remick Music Corp., 1910.
Patter rag first popularized by Arthur Pryor's Band (Victor) and revived by Eddie Condon (Decca) and Pee Wee Hunt (Capitol).

Dinah
Words by Stanley Murphy, music by Henry I. Marshall.
Remick Music Corp., 1913.

Dixieland nostalgia popularized by Marion Sunshine in *When Claudia Smiles* (1914) and Anna Held in the *All-Star Varieties Jubilee* (1914).

Ding Dong
Words and music by Irving Berlin.
Irving Berlin Music Corp., 1918.
Romantic song from the revue *Yip Yip Yahank* (1918) popular with such barbershop groups as the Peerless Quartet (Columbia).

The Dixie Volunteers
Words and music by Edgar Leslie and Harry Ruby.
Waterson, Berlin & Snyder, 1917/Mills Music Inc.
Introduced by Eddie Cantor in the *Ziegfeld Follies of 1917,* this novelty song integrates musical quotations from Dixie nostalgia and patriotic songs, such as "Over There" (q.v.) and "Look Away Dixieland." Recorded by the Premier Quartet for Edison and the American Quartet for Victor.

Djer-Kiss
Words and music by Milton Ager.
Leo Feist Inc., 1918.
Waltz popularized by Jaudas' Society Orchestra (Edison); the sheet music cover featured the nymph that was the title perfume's trademark.

Do It the Right Way
Words by Will A. Heelan, music by Seymour Furth.
Joseph Morris Co., 1911.
Fanny Brice gave dancing lessons in this novelty song in the *Follies of 1911.*

Do Re Me Fa So La Si Do
Words by William Cahill, music by Benjamin Hapgood Burt.
Joseph W. Stern & Co., 1906.
Topical song about the need for money-- "Dough re: Me." Introduced by Marie Cahill.

Do Something
Words and music by Edward Laska.
Waterson, Berlin & Snyder, 1917.
Patriotic song promoting alternative service and World War I industry jobs; sung by Joseph Santley and recorded by Arthur Fields (Columbia).

Do You Take This Woman for Your Lawful Wife?
Words by Andrew B. Sterling, music by Harry von Tilzer.
Harry Von Tilzer Music Publishing Co., 1913.

Sardonic answer song to "The Wedding Glide" (q.v.). Introduced by George Whiting in the *Passing Show of 1913;* recorded by the American Quartet for Victor.

Do You Think You Could Learn to Love Me?
Words and music by Charles K. Harris.
Charles K. Harris Music Publishing Co., 1900.
Proposal song introduced by Mabel Hite.

Does This Railroad Lead to Heaven?
Words and music by Lucy Schleif.
Original copyright, 1902.
Sentimental ballad about a train crash featured in the repertories of almost every juvenile performer in vaudeville.

Doing That Grizzly Bear, see **The Grizzly Bear,.**

Dolly
Words by W. Williams, music by William H. Penn.
Sol Bloom Publishing Co/Sol Bloom Music, 1904.
Sentimental ballad sung to a doll by Leonie Darden in the title role of *The Little Princess* (1904).

The Dolly Varden Song (English)
Words by Stanislaus Stange, music by Julian Edwards.
M. Witmark & Sons, 1901.
Title song introduced by Lulu Glaser in the comic opera based on Charles Dickens's novel *Barnaby Rudge* (1902).

Don't Be What You Ain't
Words by George V. Hobart and Edwin Milton Royle, music by Silvio Hein.
Joseph W. Stern & Co., 1905/Edward B. Marks Music Corp., 1931.
Advice delivered by Marie Cahill in *Molly Moonshine* (1905); recorded by Billy Murray for Zon-o-phone.

Don't Butt In
Words by Bob Cole and James Weldon Johnson, music by J. Rosamond Johnson.
Joseph W. Stern & Co., 1901.
Introduced in the musical *The Supper Club* (1900), but best known as a Lew Dockstader character solo.

Don't Cry Dolly Gray
Words and music by Alfred Bryan and Herman Paley.
Remick Music Corp., 1916.
Plotted ballad in which the "Dolly Gray" of the Spanish-American

War farewell song ("Good-bye, Dolly Gray," q.v.) sends her son to fight World War I.

Don't Cry, Little Girl, Don't Cry
Words and music by Maceo Pinkard.
Shapiro, Bernstein & Co., Inc., 1918.
Farewell ballad of the genre popular during World War I; top-selling recording by Henry Burr on Columbia; revived by Bob Eberly and the Song Spinners (Decca).

Don't Go in the Lion's Cage Tonight, Mother
Words by C. M. Denison, music by J. Fred Helf.
Helf & Hager, 1906/Jerry Vogel Music Co., Inc., 1939.
Satirical mock ballad. Introduced by Templar Saxe in *The Blue Moon* (1906).

Don't Go in the Water, Daughter
Words by William Jerome, music by Jean Schwartz.
Cohan & Harris, 1908/Shapiro, Bernstein & Co., Inc., 1908.
Satirical advice on bathing suits that look better dry given by female impersonator Julian Eltinge in the title role of *The Fascinating Widow* (1908).

Don't Let Us Sing Anymore about War, Just Let Us Sing of Love (American-English)
Words and music by Harry Lauder.
T. B. Harms, 1918/Francis, Day & Hunter, Inc., 1918.
Post-World War I ballad sung and recorded by Harry Lauder (Victor).

Don't Put Me Off at Buffalo Any More
Words by William Jerome, music by Jean Schwartz.
Shapiro, Bernstein & Co., Inc., 1901.
Novelty answer song to "Put Me Off at Buffalo" (1895); satirizes the Pan-American Exposition. Popularized by Maude Nugent.

Don't Take a Girlie to Coney (You May Find a Nicer One There)
Words and music by Will D. Cobb and Gus Edwards.
Gus Edwards Music Publishing Co., 1910.
Introduced by Mindell Kingston and the chorus of bathing beauties in their scene in Ziegfeld's *Follies of 1910.*

Don't Take Advantage of My Good Nature
Words by Howard E. Rogers, music by Jimmy V. Monaco.
Shapiro, Bernstein & Co., Inc., 1919.
The song about flirting in an automobile and its punch line ("'cause I got out and walked before") were popularized by the most

important character song comics of the era, among them Eddie Cantor, George Jessel, Rae Samuels, and Sophie Tucker.

Don't Take Your Beau to the Seashore
Words and music by E. Ray Goetz and Irving Berlin.
Ted Snyder Music Publishing Co., 1911.
Satirical song about bathing suit fashion. Introduced by female impersonator Julian Eltinge in *The Fascinating Widow* (1911).

Don't Try to Steal the Sweetheart of a Soldier
Words by Alfred Bryan, music by Gus Van and Joe Schenck.
Remick Music Corp., 1917, 1945.
World War I etiquette number sung by Anna Chandler, the Sterling Trio, and the team of Van and Schenck (Columbia).

Don't Turn My Picture to the Wall
Words by Robert B. Smith, music by Jerome Kern.
T. B. Harms, 1912.
Comic duet referring to the sentimental ballads of the previous decade. Introduced by Richard Carle and Hattie Williams in the musical *The Girl from Montmartre* (1912) and recorded by Helen Clarke and Walter J. Van Brunt (Victor).

Don't Wake Me Up I Am Dreaming
Words by Beth Slater Whitson, music by Herbert Ingraham.
Shapiro, Bernstein & Co., Inc., 1910, 1937.
Romantic ballad popularized by Frank Morrell, Bessie Wynn, and Walter Van Brunt, who recorded it for Victor.

Don't Walk So Fast
Words and music by Zit (pseudonym for C. Florian Zittel).
Joseph W. Stern & Co., 1910.
Vocal rag introduced in S. H. Dudley's black vaudeville feature act, *Smart Set* (1910-1911), and later popularized by Sophie Tucker. "Zit" was a pen name for theatre and vaudeville critic C. Florian Zittel.

Don't Worry, also known as **It May Not All Be True**
Words and music by Ed Rose and Ted Snyder.
Original copyright, 1907.
March song popularized by Elizabeth Murray.

Don't You Think It's Time to Marry?
Words by Addison Burkhardt, music by Gus Edwards.
Gus Edwards Inc., 1906.
Proposal song introduced by Josie Cohan in *The Blue Moon* (1906); also sung and recorded by Grace LaRue, Billy Murray (Victor), and Ada Jones (Zon-o-phone).

Don't You Want a Paper, Dearie?
Words by Paul West, music by Jerome Kern.
T. B. Harms, 1906.
Romantic song recommending newspapers to shield spooning couples from the public (and the audience). Introduced by Georgia Caine in *The Rich Mr. Hoggenheimer* (1906) and recorded by Ada Jones (Victor).

Don't You Wish You Were Back Home Again?
Words and music by Charles K. Harris.
Charles K. Harris Music Publishing Co., 1913.
Harris reverted to his earliest genre, the plotted melodramatic ballad, for this moralistic song, which was popularized by Joseph Gillespie, lead tenor of the George Evans' Honey Boy Minstrels.

Dooley's Alibi
Words by R. H. Burnside, music by Henry Walker.
Original copyright, 1902.
Irish novelty song performed by Jefferson de Angelis in *The Emerald Isle* (musical, 1902) and in vaudeville. Dooley's alibi for horse-stealing is given by the horse that he stole.

Douce Fievre, also known as **Whisper That You Love Me** (French)
English words by Louis Weslyn, French words and music by Y'Ener.
A. Durand & Fils, Paris, France, 1914/Manus Music, 1914.
Used as the love theme in the film *The Big Parade* (MGM, 1925).

Down Among the Sheltering Palms
Words by James Brockman, music by Abe Olman.
La Salle Music Publishers, Inc., 1914/Leo Feist Inc.
Homage to California popularized in close harmony by the Lyric and Columbia Quartets and the Victor Military Band; revived in the 1940's by the Boswell Sisters with the Dorsey Orchestra (Columbia), Al Jolson, the Mills Brothers (Decca), and Johnny Mercer and the Pied Pipers (Capitol). Featured by "Sweet Sue and Her Society Syncopators" in *Some Like It Hot* (UA, 1959).

Down Among the Sugar-Cane
Words by Avery and Charles Hart, music by Chris Smith and Cecil Mack.
Gotham-Attucks Music Publishing Co., 1908/Mills Music Inc., 1936.
Romantic ballad. Introduced by Avery and Hart in close harmony and popularized by Clara Morton; Arthur Collins and Byron G. Harlan recorded the duet version for Victor in the 1910's; revived by Phil Harris in 1936.

Down at the Old Bull and Bush, see **Under the Anheuser Bush,.**

Down by the Old Mill Stream
Words and music by Tell Taylor.
The Star Music Publishing Co., 1910/Forster Music Publishers, Inc., 1932.
This classic of the barbershop quartet genre has been sung fervently by amateurs throughout its life but it was first popularized in vaudeville by Frank Morrell and on records by Harry MacDonough (Victor). Its frequent recordings include those by Kenny Baker (Victor), Bing Crosby (Brunswick, Decca), Gene Krupa (Okeh), and Arthur Godfrey and His Chordettes (Columbia).

Down De Lover's Lane
Words by Paul Lawrence Dunbar, music by Will Marion Cook.
Joseph W. Stern & Co., 1900.
Ballad introduced by Virginia Earl in *The Casino Girl* (1900); revived and recorded by Paul Robeson (Victor, Gramaphone) in tribute to Dunbar's poetry.

Down in Chattanooga
Words and music by Irving Berlin.
Waterson, Berlin & Snyder, 1913/Irving Berlin Music Corp.
Dixie nostalgia song with railroad rhythm effects. Introduced by Belle Baker and sung in close harmony by Arthur Collins and Byron G. Harlan (Victor).

Down in Dear Old Sunny Georgia Years Ago, see **Down in Sunny Georgia Years Ago,.**

Down in Honky-Tonk Town
Words and music by Charles McCarron and Chris Smith.
Broadway Music Corp., 1916, 1944.
This raggy song promoting rag-time dances was popularized by Sophie Tucker; recorded by Louis Armstrong on Decca.

Down in Mulberry Bend
Words by James Weldon Johnson, music by J. Rosamond Johnson.
Joseph W. Stern & Co., 1904.
Ballad about poor children playing on Mulberry Street in New York. Introduced by Nellie Daly in the musical *Humpty-Dumpty* (1904).

Down in Sunny Georgia Years Ago, also known as **Down in Dear Old Sunny Georgia Years Ago**
Words by C. H. Scoggins, music by Charles Avril.
Original copyright, 1902.

Nostalgic ballad introduced by Alma Adderly, the "Western Nightingale."

Down in the Subway
Words by William Jerome, music by Jean Schwartz.
Shapiro, Bernstein & Co., Inc., 1904.
This song offers urban recommendations for spooning; popularized by May Yohn and by Billy Murray (Victor).

Down on the Farm
Words by Raymond A. Browne, music by Harry von Tilzer.
Harry Von Tilzer Music Publishing Co., 1902/Jerry Vogel Music Co., Inc., 1938.
Pastoral ballad associated with minstrel vocalist and producer George H. Diamond; recorded by Ada Jones (Victor).

Down the Line with Molly
Words by George Totten Smith, music by George L. Spaulding.
Original copyright, 1902.
Romantic song about trolley lines as a location for dating.

Down Where the Cotton Blossoms Grow
Words by Andrew B. Sterling, music by Harry von Tilzer.
Remick Music Corp., 1901/Harry Von Tilzer Music Publishing Co., 1929.
Ballad included in the repertories of most minstrel troupes of the early 1900's and popularized by Harry A. Ellis, George H. Diamond, and Harry MacDonough (Victor).

Down Where the Swanee River Flows
Words by Andrew B. Sterling, music by Harry von Tilzer.
Harry Von Tilzer Music Publishing Co., 1903.
Nostalgic ballad popularized in minstrelsy by George H. Diamond.

Down Where the Swanee River Flows
Words by Charles McCarron and Charles S. Alberts, music by Albert von Tilzer.
Broadway Music Corp., 1916.
Al Jolson's Dixieland nostalgia hit interpolated into *Robinson Crusoe, Jr.* (1917) and recorded for Columbia; also recorded by Frank Howard (Zon-o-phone) and Arthur Collins (Emerson).

Down Where the Wurzburger Flows (American-English)
Words by Vincent P. Bryan, music by Harry von Tilzer.
Harry Von Tilzer Music Publishing Co., 1902.
Mock nostalgia ballad honoring "flowing rivers of beer" popularized by the Empir City Quartet, Nora Bayes (after 1907), and the family act of Joe, Nora, and Buster Keaton.

Dream Melody, see **Ah, Sweet Mystery of Life,.**

Dream One Dream of Me
Words by Edgar Smith, music by John Stromberg.
M. Witmark & Sons, 1902.
Romantic ballad. Introduced by Fay Templeton in Weber and Fields' musical *Twirly-Whirly* (1902).

Dreaming
Words by L. W. Heiser, music by J. Anton Dailey.
Remick Music Corp., 1906/Jerry Vogel Music Co., Inc., 1940.
Instrumental popular as dance music; revised in 1926 by Gus Kahn and Egbert van Alstyne as a fox-trot and as the theme song for Paramount's *Jennie Gerhardt,* starring Sylvia Sidney.

Dreaming
Words by Earl Carroll, music by Archibald Joyce.
Leo Feist Inc., 1913.
Waltz introduced by Kitty Gordon in *The Pretty Mrs. Smith* (1914); billed as "the sensation of two continents," it was popular as dance music with recordings by Marek Weber and His Orchestra (Odeon) and Prince's Band on Columbia.

Dreaming in the Trenches
Words by Ed Gardinier, music by Henry W. Armstrong.
Original copyright, 1901.
Military ballad sung by Charles Chapman.

Dreams of Long Ago
Words by Earl Carroll, music by Enrico Caruso.
Leo Feist Inc., 1912.
Nostalgic ballad recorded by Caruso for Victor, Victrola, Gramophone, and Polydor (and available on RCA Victor compilation albums of the present); featured in the play *The Million* (1911).

Dreamy Alabama
Words and music by Mary Earl.
Shapiro, Bernstein & Co., Inc., 1919.
Follow-up to Earl's "Beautiful Ohio" (q.v.) recorded by Conway's Band (Okeh), Lewis James (Edison), and Albert Campbell and Henry Burr (Columbia).

Dreamy Fandango Tune
Words by William Jerome, music by Jean Schwartz.
Remick Music Corp., 1910.
Patter rag based on the Act I finale of Gilbert and Sullivan's *The Gondoliers.* Introduced by Edwin Foy in *Up and Down Broadway* (1910).

Dress Up Your Dollars in Khaki and Help Win Democracy's Fight
Words by Lester R. Allwood, music by Richard A. Whiting.
Remick Music Corp., 1918.
Promotional anthem for the War Savings Stamps campaign.

Dry Your Tears
Words and music by Art Hickman and Ben Black.
Sherman, Clay & Co., 1918.
Dance music featured by Hickman's band at the New Amsterdam Roof and recorded by Joseph C. Smith's Orchestra (Victor).

Du Barry, the Doll of the World
Words by George Taggart, music by J. Fred Helf.
Sol Bloom Publishing Co/Sol Bloom Music, 1902.
Promotional song for Mrs. Leslie Carter's starring vehicle *Du Barry*.

The Duchess of Central Park
Words by J. Cheever Goodwin, music by Maurice Levi.
Original copyright, 1900.
Romantic song introduced by Jeannette Bageard in the Rogers Brothers' *In Central Park* (1900).

Duna
Words by Marjorie Pickthall, music by Josephine McGill.
Boosey & Hawkes Inc., 1915.
Ballad popularized and recorded by John McCormack and Cantor Joseph Rosenblatt.

The Dusky Salome
Words and music by Edward Madden and Benjamin M. Jerome.
Original copyright, 1908.
Novelty song for Edwin Foy in response to the craze for Salome dance performances in vaudeville; Ed Wynn performed and co-wrote (with Stanley Murphy) the similar "I'm Going to Get Myself a Black Salome."

E

Early in the Morning (English)
Words and music by Harry Lauder.
Francis, Day & Hunter, Ltd., London, England, 1900.
Although Lauder performed it for Victor as a Scottish dialect song, it has also been recorded as folk music, most notably by Burl Ives and Roy Clark.

Eastern Moon
Words by M. E. Rourke, music by Jerome D. Kern.
T. B. Harms, 1907.
Exotic ballad interpolated by Marie D'Oro into the play *The Morals of Marcus.*

Easy Money, also known as **Ma Poppy Belle**
Words by Edgar Smith, music by John Stromberg.
M. Witmark & Sons, 1901/Bell & Cee Music Co.
Comic romance introduced by Fay Templeton in *Hoity-Toity* (1901).

Easy Pickins'
Words and music by Maceo Pinkard.
Shapiro, Bernstein & Co., Inc., 1919.
Raggy dance promotion recorded as a fox-trot by Ford T. Dabney's Band and the Yerkes' Novelty Five (Columbia).

Easy Street
Words by Raymond A. Browne, music by William A. Penn.
Sol Bloom Publishing Co/Sol Bloom Music, 1905.
Novelty song popularized by Josephine Sabel.

The Edinboro Wiggle
Words by M. E. Rourke, music by Jerome Kern.
T. B. Harms, 1911.

Scottish-dialect novelty song about the popularity of rag-time from the musical *La Belle Paree* (1911).

Egypt, My Cleopatra
Words and music by Clare Kummel.
Joseph W. Stern & Co., 1903.
Exotic ballad interpolated into *The Girl from Kay's* (1903); also popular as a parlor song.

Eight Little Girls
Words by M. E. Rourke, music by Jerome Kern.
T. B. Harms, 1910.
Tribute to the eight-woman chorus interpolated into *Our Miss Gibbs* (1910).

Eight Little Letters Make Three Little Words
Words by Bert Kalmar, music by Ted Snyder.
Ted Snyder Music Publishing Co., 1911.
May Irwin's popular hit extolling the phrase "I Love You."

Eighth Avenue
Words by William Jerome, music by J. Sherrie Mathews and Harry Bulger.
Original copyright, 1901.
Novelty song about the Bowery denizens moving uptown; performed by James H. Cullen. Composers Mathews and Bulger, themselves a famed comedy team, also performed the song in their touring vehicle *The Ham Tree.*

El Choclo
Music by A. G. Villoldo.
Joseph W. Stern & Co., 1913/Robbins Music Corp.
A tango Argentine featured by Elsie Janis.

Eli Eli
Original copyright, 1919.
Whether performed in Yiddish, Hebrew, or English, "Eli Eli" was the staple of Yiddish vaudeville, concert, and stock company circuits. The most popular arrangements of the traditional, Eastern European song were by R. A. Zagler (S. Schenker, 1919), popularized by actress Sophia Karp; by J. J. Kammen (1919), sung by Belle Baker; and by Jacob Schindler, performed by Boris Thomashefsky and members of his theatre companies. Recorded for Victor by Cantor Joseph Rosenblatt, in an edition distributed free during World War I by Sunshine Biscuit's kosher foods division, and by the Victor Salon Orchestra.

The Elks Song, see **BPOE**,.

Emalyne, My Pretty Valentine
Words and music by Max Hoffmann.
Introduced by Eula Lee, this cakewalk was an early rag-time success for arranger-conductor Hoffmann.

Enid Waltz, also known as **Joyous Springtime Bring Me Love**
Words by Thomas Field, music by Mary Earl.
Shapiro, Bernstein & Co., Inc., 1919.
Novelty waltz popularized in recordings by the Columbia Orchestra, under G. Hepburn Willson, and the Aeolian Dance Orchestra for Vocalion.

Ephraham Played Upon the Piano
Words and music by Irving Berlin and Vincent Bryan.
Ted Snyder Music Publishing Co., 1911.
Character song for Bert Williams, who introduced it in his specialty slot in Ziegfeld's roof garden revue at the Jardin de Paris and in the *Follies of 1911.*

Ethiopia Saluting the Colors
Words by Walt Whitman, music by H. T. Burleigh.
G. Ricordi & C., SpA, Milan, Italy, 1915.
Concert aria based on the Whitman poem.

Every Day Will Be Sunday When the Town Goes Dry
Words and music by William Jerome and Jack Mahoney.
Leo Feist Inc., 1918.
Anti-Prohibition comedy song with references to evangelist Billy Sunday and to the New York "blue laws" that banned alcohol sales on Sundays. Among the many similarly themed songs is "What'll We Do on a Saturday Night When the Town Goes Dry?" by Harry Ruby (1919).

Every Girl Is Fishing
Words by Gene Buck, music by Dave Stamper.
T. B. Harms, 1916.
Audience participation dance for the female chorus in the *Ziegfeld Midnight Frolics of 1916* in which the women dangled fishing rods towards the front row of tables. The audience attempted to hook souvenir fish onto their lines.

Every Laddie Loves a Lassie (English)
Words and music by Harry Lauder.
Francis, Day & Hunter, Ltd., London, England, 1910.
Scottish-dialect romance performed by Lauder.

Every Little Movement
Words by Otto Hauerbach, music by Karl Hoschna.

M. Witmark & Sons, 1910.
Perhaps the best known song (or, first line of a song) of the era, it was created as a theme that is sung or danced by each couple in the Broadway farce *Madame Sherry* (1910). Frances Demarest actually introduced the song during a lesson at the Sherry School of Aesthetic Dancing. Despite its very specific parody of pre-modern dance, pioneering choreographer Ted Shawn chose it as the title of his 1945 text. It has been recorded as a concert aria by Ernestine Schumann-Heink (Victor), as a comic novelty by Harry MacDonough (Victor), and as an instrumental by ensembles from Edison's Hungarian Orchestra and Jerry Murad's Harmonicats (Mercury) to the Robert Shaw Chorale (RCA) and Lawrence Welk.

Every Saturday Afternoon
Words by James O'Dea, music by Anne Caldwell.
Joseph W. Stern & Co., 1906.
Invitation to spoon interpolated by Julia Frary into the musical *Sergeant Brue* (1905).

Everybody Has a Whistle Like Me
Words and music by Ed Rogers.
Joseph W. Stern & Co., 1901.
Whistling novelty song popularized by Gertie Gibson; it sold over 50,000 copies in 1901 alone.

Everybody Loves a Chicken
Words and music by Bobby Jones.
Original copyright, 1912.
Sung by the author to a chorus of female dancers (known in theatrical slang as "chickens") in *Broadway to Paris* (1912).

Everybody Loves a Jazz Band
Words and music by Coleman Goetz and Leon Flatow.
Leo Feist Inc., 1917.
Raggy song belted out by Emma Carus.

Everybody Rag with Me
Words by Gus Kahn, music by Grace LeBoy.
Remick Music Corp., 1914.
Introduced by Al Jolson in *Dancing Around* (1914) and recorded as a rag by the American Quartet (Victor) and Prince's Band (Columbia).

Everybody Shimmies Now
Words by Eugene West, music by Joe Gold and Edmund J. Perry.
Charles K. Harris Music Publishing Co., 1918.

Tribute to the dance in which you "move everything except your feet"; performed by Sophie Tucker and Mae West.

Everybody Sometime Must Love Some One
Words by Gene Buck, music by Dave Stamper.
Joseph W. Stern & Co., 1913.
Romantic ballad introduced by Blanche Ring in the musical *When Claudia Smiles* (1913).

Everybody Wants a Key to My Cellar
Words and music by Ed Rose, Billy Baskette, and Lew Pollack.
Mills Music Inc., 1919.
Comic complaint referring to the clause in the 19th Amendment which allowed the personal storage of prohibited alcohol. Associated with Bert Williams, who sang it in the *Ziegfeld Follies of 1919;* recorded by Al Bernard (Edison), Irving Kaufman (Emerson), Billy Murray (Vocalion), and Williams, whose performance on Columbia is included in the Smithsonian Institution's compilation album *Ziegfeld Follies of 1919.*

Everybody Works But Father
Words and music by Jean C. Havez.
Helf & Hager, 1905/Edward B. Marks Music Corp., 1933.
Comic character song introduced by Lew Dockstader and associated with him throughout his long career; as a result of its popularity, it was imitated widely, producing similar songs, such as McClintock and Lehrman's "We All Go to Work But Father" (1905) for Dockstader's rival, George Primrose. Havez and others also created a "family" of related songs, among them, his "Uncle's Quit Working Too" (q.v.) and Arthur Gillespie's "Mother Has Got the Habit Now" (q.v.). The original was recorded as a comic novelty by Dockstader (Columbia), Billy Murray (Victor), Arthur Collins (Vim), and Riley Puckett (Columbia).

Everybody's Doin' It Now
Words and music by Irving Berlin.
Ted Snyder Music Publishing Co., 1911.
Novelty song promoting and describing rag-time dances that became a standard; popularized by Lydia Barry in Winter Garden revues and by Ruby Raymond and Maud Tiffany in vaudeville; recorded in close harmony arrangements by the Columbia Quartet and Arthur Collins and Byron G. Harlan (Victor). Later performances include those by Julie Andrews (Columbia), Ann Sothern (Tops), and many others as solos; also featured in the film *Alexander's Rag-Time Band* (Fox, 1938).

Everybody's Ragtime Crazy
Words by William Jerome, music by Jean Schwartz.

Shapiro, Bernstein & Co., Inc., 1909.
Broadway songwriters, having adopted ragtime at the turn of the century, kept creating promotional songs for the new rhythms throughout the decades; this was written for the chorus in McIntyre and Heath's vehicle *In Hayti* (1909).

Everything Is Peaches Down in Georgia
Words by Grant Clarke, music by Milton Ager and George W. Meyer.
Leo Feist Inc., 1918/Fred Fisher Music Co.
ASCAP top seller first popularized by the Farber Sisters; recorded by them on Pathe, but even more successful as instrumental dance music, in recordings by Prince's Band (Columbia), and in barbershop arrangements, as that by the American Quartet on Victor.

Everything Is Rosy, Rosie
Words by Edward P. Moran, music by Seymour Furth.
M. Witmark & Sons, 1906.
Romance introduced by Trixie Friganza.

Everything Looks Rosy and Bright
Words and music by E. Ray Goetz, Jean Schwartz, and Willy White.
M. Witmark & Sons, 1917.
Wedding narrative performed as a chorus processional in the revue *Words and Music* (1917), which, according to its program, was written by William Shakespeare and Ludwig Beethoven.

Ev'ry Day
Words by W. R. Williams, music by Shelton Brooks.
Will Rossiter, 1918.
Bluesy lament popularized by Sophie Tucker and Olive Callaway.

Ev'ry Morning She Makes Me Late
Words and music by Bud De Sylva, Gus Kahn, and Al Jolson.
Remick Music Corp., 1918.
Suggestive romance introduced by Jolson.

Eyes of Blue
Music by Andrew Mack.
Howley, Haviland & Dresser, 1900/Warner Brothers, Inc.
Irish imitative ballad introduced by Mack in his play *The Rebel* (1900).

Eyes of Youth
Words and music by Irving Berlin.
Irving Berlin Music Corp., 1919.

Waltz with a mystic theme promoting the Equity Pictures release of the same name, starring Clara Kimball Young.

F

The Face in the Firelight
Words and music by Charles Shackford.
Original copyright, 1902.
Nostalgic sentimental ballad sung by Emma Carus but usually performed by minstrel show tenors, such as Edward J. Foye or William Phillips, or as a parlor song.

The Fairest of the Fair
Words and music by John Philip Sousa.
John Church Co., 1936.
Written for and premiered at the 1908 Boston Food Fair, it is considred one of Sousa's finest and most melodious marches. It has been recorded by the Goldman Band, the Decca Band, the Band of Her Majesty's Royal Marines, the United States Marine Band, and the marching bands of the universities of California and Michigan. Available on such albums as *The Heritage of John Philip Sousa* and *Stars and Stripes Forever.*

Fall in for Your Motherland
Words by Woodrow Wilson, music by Frank Black and John Golden.
T. B. Harms, 1916.
Producer/composer Golden adapted a speech by President Woodrow Wilson for a patriotic anthem that closed his all-soldier show *Army Play-by-Play* (2nd Service Command, 1916); it was performed frequently at Liberty Loan and Reserve rallies since it emphasized civilian war service.

Falling Star
Words and music by Nora Bayes and Jack Norworth.
Remick Music Corp., 1909.
Spooning song introduced by Bayes and Norworth in Ziegfeld's *Follies of 1909;* recorded by Frank C. Stanley for Remick Perfection Records, a short-lived enterprise by the publishing house.

Farewell Killarney
Words by Edward Madden, music by Gus Edwards.
Gus Edwards Inc., 1906/Mills Music Inc.
Irish soldier ballad featured by Julius (Groucho) Marx as an adolescent member of Edwards' Newsboys.

Farewell to Thee, see **Aloha Oe,**.

Farmyard Blues
Words and music by Chris Smith and Henry Troy.
Joseph W. Stern & Co., 1917.
Novelty blues with farmyard sound effects introduced by Smith and Troy in vaudeville.

The Farrar Waltz, see **Gay Butterfly,**.

Fas' Fas' World
Words by Alex Rogers, music by Bert Williams.
Gotham-Attucks Music Publishing Co., 1907.
Typically ironic character song for Williams in *Bandana Land* (musical, 1907).

The Fatal Ring
Words by Charles R. McCarron and Arthur J. Jackson, music by James F. Hanley.
Shapiro, Bernstein & Co., Inc., 1917.
Promotional title song for a Pathe serial starring Pearl White. The first verse describes the film's plot; verse 2 and the chorus warn of the dangers of marriage and a fatal wedding ring.

Father's Got a Job
Words by Bob Cole and James Weldon Johnson, music by Bob Cole.
Joseph W. Stern & Co., 1906.
Answer song to "Everbody Works But Father" (q.v.) with specific references to pickle advertising -- Father "quit the factory in 57 ways, got 57 jobs in 57 days"; popularized, like its source, by Lew Dockstader.

Faugh-a Ballagh
Words by Ed Rose, music by Abe Olman.
Forster Music Publishers, Inc., 1917.
Irish patriotic song performed by Blanche Ring in *What's Next* (musical, 1917).

Feed the Kitty
Words by Ed Moran, music by J. Fred Helf.
Helf & Hager, 1908.

Comic novelty song complaint popularized by Broadway and vaudeville's foremost character comics, among them, Lew Dockstader, Edwin Foy, Jack Norworth, George Evans, and Trixie Friganza.

The Fife and Drum
Words by Rida Johnson Young, music by Paul Rubens.
Original copyright, 1903.
Military song associated with Ermine Earle and also performed as a band number.

Fifteen Years on the Erie Canal, see **Low Bridge - Everybody Down,**.

Fifty-Fifty
Words by Jim Burris, music by Chris Smith.
Joseph W. Stern & Co., 1914.
One of Smith's most famous variations on the cake-walk rhythm was originally an ironic lament by a cheated-on wife introduced by Miss Patricola; Lynn Thigpen's performance of the song in the musical *Tintypes* (1980; also on cast album) has given it new life in a feminist repertory.

Fireflies
Words by Ballard MacDonald, music by Paul Lincke.
Joseph W. Stern & Co., 1908.
Follow-up to Lincke's "Glow Worm" (q.v.) introduced in *The Summer Widowers* (1900); popularized as dance music by Prince's Orchestra (Columbia) and the Reed Orchestra (Edison).

The First Rose of Summer
Words by Anne Caldwell, music by Jerome Kern.
T. B. Harms, 1919.
Fox-trot with musical references to Flatow. Introduced by exhibition ballroom dance team of Ivy Sawyer and Joseph Santley in *She's a Good Fellow* (1919); recorded by the Happy Six for Columbia.

Fishing
Words by James Weldon Johnson, music by J. Rosamond Johnson.
Joseph W. Stern & Co., 1904.
Novelty song about fishing for husbands. Introduced by Fay Templeton in the Summer 1904 Aerial Theatre revue; recorded by Harry Tate for Zon-o-Phone.

Fishing
Words and music by Chris Smith.
Original copyright, 1911.

Suspicious wife's revenge introduced by Rae Samuels, billed as "The Rag-Time Girl."

Flippity-Flop
Words and music by Junie McCree and Sophie Tucker.
York Music Corp., 1910.
Sophie Tucker popularized this euphemistic song about flirtation etiquette in different cities.

Flirtation Song
Words by Harry B. Smith, music by Reginald De Koven.
Edward Schuberth & Co., Inc., 1901.
Introduced by Anna Held in her starring vehicle, *The Little Duchess* (1901).

Floating Down the River
Words by Roger Lewis, music by James White.
Will Rossiter, 1913/Jerry Vogel Music Co., Inc.
Dixie nostalgia with steamboat sound effects. Introduced by Sophie Tucker and popularized by Elizabeth Murray and Winnie Lightner.

Flora, I Am Your Adorer
Words by Vincent P. Bryan, music by Charles Robinson.
Original copyright, 1901.
Comedy song about the husband of a *Florodora* Octette member; performed by Harry Bulger in the burlesque *The Sleeping Beauty and the Beast* (1901).

Floreine
Music by Ernest J. Schuster.
Original copyright, 1913.
Waltz recorded by the major studio bands of the era, including the Victor Military Band, Royale's Grand Military Orchestra, and Prince's Band (Columbia).

The Florida Blues
Words by Dave Huffman and Arthur Neale, music by William King Phillips.
Handy Brothers Music Co., Inc., 1914, 1917, 1926.
Blues by Phillips, saxophonist/clarinetist for Handy's Band; recorded by Prince's Orchestra (Columbia) and by Wilbur Sweatman and His Orchestra (Vocalion).

A Flower from the Garden of Life
Words and music by Thurland Chattaway.
Howley, Haviland & Dresser, 1900.
Wedding ballad popularized by May A. Bell and Joseph Natus.

The Flower Garden Ball
Words by William Jerome, music by Jean Schwartz.
Original copyright, 1913.
Novelty rag-time song integrating dance instructions with flower names. Introduced by Belle Story and interpolated by Blanche Ring into *When Claudia Smiles* (1914); recorded as a turkey trot by the Victor Military Band.

Flowers of Dixieland
Words by Edgar Smith, music by J. Rosamond Johnson.
Joseph W. Stern & Co., 1903.
Nostalgic Dixie ballad introduced by Lillian Russell in *Whoop-Dee-Doo* (1903).

Follow the Crowd
Words and music by Irving Berlin.
Waterson, Berlin & Snyder, 1914/Irving Berlin Music Corp.
Introduced by the chorus in the musical parody of moral reformers *Queen of the Movies* (1914).

Follow the Man That Leads the Band
Words by Harry B. Smith, music by Aime Lachaume.
M. Witmark & Sons, 1902.
March introduced by Harry Davenport in *The Liberty Belles* (musical, 1902).

Following in Father's Footsteps (English)
Words and music by E. W. Rogers.
Francis, Day & Hunter, Ltd., London, England, 1902.
Vesta Tilley's character monologue and song was performed in British music halls, in her United States vaudeville tours, and on Broadway in *Algy* (1901).

The Fond Dove and His Lady Love
Words and music by Anita Baldwin.
Original copyright, 1900.
Romantic ballad sung by Helen Merrell at the Tivoli Roof Theatre in New York.

A Fool There Was
Words by Alexander Dubin, music by Gustav Benkhart.
Original copyright, 1913.
Ballad based on Rudyard Kipling's poem performed by Robert Hilliard; a play of the poem was popular in stock companies.

Foolish Questions
Words by William Lee, music by A. Baldwin Sloane.
Charles K. Harris Music Publishing Co., 1909/Jerry Vogel Music

Co., Inc., 1937.
Six verses of topical humor introduced by Jefferson de Angelis in *The Beauty Spot* (musical, 1909). Recorded by Billy Murray (Victor).

Football
Words by Vincent Bryan, music by Charles Zimmerman.
Original copyright, 1905.
Novelty song about football injuries performed by Montgomery and Stone in the musical *The Wizard of Oz* (1905).

For Dixie and Uncle Sam
Words by J. Keirn Brennan, music by Ernest R. Ball.
M. Witmark & Sons, 1916.
Patriotic march featured by Nora Bayes (Victor) and recorded by the Consolidated Quartet (Standard) and the Peerless Quartet (Columbia).

For Freedom and Ireland
Words and music by Matthew Woodward and Andrew Mack.
Original copyright, 1900.
Anthem introduced by Mack in his play *The Rebel* (1900) and recorded by Harry MacDonough (Victor).

For God and Home and Native Land
Words and music by Anna A. Gordon.
Original copyright, 1904.
Setting of the "Battle Hymn of the Republic" that served as the theme song for the Cold Water Army, the children's brigade of the Women's Christian Temperance Union.

For Me and My Gal
Words by Edgar Leslie and E. Ray Goetz, music by George W. Meyer.
Waterson, Berlin & Snyder, 1917/Mills Music Inc., 1932.
Wedding narrative featured by the teams of Elizabeth Brice and Charles King and Gladys Clark and Henry Bergman. A perennial best-seller through recordings by Billy Murray (Edison), Van and Schenck (Victor), and Al Jolson, who recorded it for Cedda and sang it in *Jolson Sings Again* (Columbia, 1949). Title song of the retrospective MGM film whose stars, Gene Kelly and Judy Garland, recorded it for Decca.

For You
Words by William Jerome, music by Jean Schwartz.
Original copyright, 1904.
Novelty love song with topical references to shredded wheat, auto-

mobiles, and political figures, from Schwartz' first complete Broadway score -- *Piff! Paff!! Pouf!!!* (1904).

For You Alone
Words by P. J. O'Reilley, music by Henry E. Geehl.
Edward Schuberth & Co., Inc., 1909/Leonard Gould Bottler.
Ballad associated with Enrico Caruso (Gramophone); revived for recordings by opera singers Lauritz Melchior (MGM), Richard Tauber (Parlophone), and Ezio Pinza (RCA Victor).

For Your Boy and My Boy
Words by Gus Kahn, music by Egbert van Alstyne.
Remick Music Corp., 1918.
War Bond recruiting song for the National Liberty Loan Organization recorded by the Peerless Quartet (Victor).

For Your Country and My Country
Words and music by Irving Berlin.
Waterson, Berlin & Snyder, 1917/Irving Berlin Music Corp.
Patriotic anthem from World War I billed as the "Official Recruiting Song" for the armed forces, performed and recorded by almost every vocalist of the era, from opera singer Frances Alda to comic Willie Weston (both on Victor and Victrola); interpolated into Berlin's revue *Yip Yip Yahank* (1918) and editions of *This Is the Army* (World War II service show).

Forget
Words by Will D. Cobb, music by Gus Edwards.
Howley, Haviland & Dresser, 1901.
Ballad introduced by Helene Mora.

The Fortune Telling Man
Words and music by Bert Williams and George Walker.
Joseph W. Stern & Co., 1901/Edward B. Marks Music Corp., 1920.
Novelty song for Williams and Walker in their musical *Bandana Land* (1901-1903); revived by Leonard Feather's Hiptet (Savoy).

Forty-five Minutes from Broadway
Words and music by George M. Cohan.
Mills Music Inc., 1906/George M. Cohan Music Publishing Co.
Victor Moore first sang this complaint about suburban New Rochelle night life as the title song in Cohan's hit musical; featured by James Cagney and chorus in the biographical film *Yankee Doodle Dandy* (Warner Brothers, 1942) and by Joel Grey and Loni Ackerman in *George M!* (musical, 1968).

Fou the Noo (English)
Words and music by Harry Lauder, words by Gerald Grafton.

Francis, Day & Hunter, Ltd., London, England, 1905/T. B. Harms, 1905.
Drunken monologue, patter, and song for Scottish-dialect comic Harry Lauder.

France, Glorious France
Words by Sydney Rosenfeld, music by A. Baldwin Sloane.
Joseph W. Stern & Co., 1902.
Patriotic march introduced by Mabelle Gilman and the chorus for the Act I finale of *The Mocking Bird* (1902).

Freedom of the C's
Words by Alfred Bryan, music by Jean Schwartz.
Remick Music Corp., 1919.
Mock patriotic anthem introduced by Harry Fender and the female chorus in the revue *Gaieties of 1919;* the topical parody of World War I songs offers freedom for "Carrie to smoke...for Caroline to bet...for Cecile to shimmy...for Clara to powder her nose...for Claudie to wear hose..."

French Fandango, also known as **Philomene** (American-French)
English words by John L. Golden, music by Henri Christine.
T. B. Harms, 1910/Francis, Day & Hunter, Inc., 1910.
Exuberant dance number led by Bessie McCoy and the chorus in *The Echo* (musical, 1910).

The Friars
Words by Charles Emerson Cook, music by Victor Herbert.
M. Witmark & Sons, 1907.
Toasting song for the Friars, a theatrical club in New York City.

Frisco's Kitchen Stove Rag
Words by C. Francis Reisner, music by Jimmie Morgan.
Original copyright, 1918/M. Witmark & Sons, 1919.
Promotional song based on music to which Joe Frisco performed his eccentric dance act in the *Ziegfeld Follies of 1918.*

From Here to Shanghai
Words and music by Irving Berlin.
Waterson, Berlin & Snyder, 1917/Irving Berlin Music Corp.
Ballad popularized as a solo, as a romantic duet, and in close harmony by Al Jolson (Columbia), Gene Greene (Victor), the team of Gladys Clark and Harry Bergman, and the Peerless Quartet (Victor).

From Now On
Words by Arthur J. Jackson and B. G. De Sylva, music by George Gershwin.

T. B. Harms, 1919/Francis, Day & Hunter, Inc., 1919.
Marriage vows exchanged by Janet Velie and John E. Hazzard in *La La Lucille* (musical, 1919).

G

The Gaby Glide
Words by Harry Pilcer, music by Louis A. Hirsch.
Shapiro, Bernstein & Co., Inc., 1911.
The Shubert Brothers, producers of *Vera Violette* (1911), commissioned this two-step as a specialty dance for Gaby Deslys and her partner, Pilcer. Their next Shubert show featured "When Gaby Did the Gaby Glide" (q.v.); recorded by Billy Murray (Victor) and by the Zon-o-phone Concert Band.

The Gambling Man
Words by William Jerome, music by Jean Schwartz.
Francis, Day & Hunter, Inc., 1902.
"Philosophical ballad" featured by Emma Carus, Anna Driver, Maude Nugent, and Tascott in American vaudeville and by Carlotta Levey at the London Coliseum.

The Game of Love
Words by Edgar Smith, music by Maurice Levi.
Charles K. Harris Music Publishing Co., 1904.
Introduced by Anna Held and Trixie Friganza in Weber and Ziegfeld's extravagant revue/pantomime *Higgeldy-Piggeldy* (1904).

The Garden of Allah
Words and music by George A. Little, Billy Baskette, and Leon Flatow.
Leo Feist Inc., 1917.
Promotional title song for the controversial novel by Robert Hitchens and for the Rex Ingram film based on it.

The Garden of Dreams
Words by Charles Emerson Cook, music by Reginald De Koven.
Joseph W. Stern & Co., 1903.
Romantic ballad and concert aria introduced by Grace van Studdiford in *The Red Feather* (1903).

The Garden of Dreams
Words and music by Clare Kummer.
Remick Music Corp., 1908.
Ballad introduced by Sallie Fisher in *A Knight for a Day* (musical, 1907); recorded by Elise Stevenson and Harry MacDonough for Victor.

Garden of Roses
Words by J. E. Dempsey, music by Johann Schmid.
Remick Music Corp., 1909, 1922/Jerry Vogel Music Co., Inc., 1937.
Romantic ballad recorded by Harry MacDonough with the Haydn Quartet (Victor), Lewis James (Edison), and Harvey Hindermeyer (Columbia).

Gay Butterfly, also known as **The Farrar Waltz**
English words and music by Annie Andros Hawley, French words by Marie Madeleine Suck.
M. Witmark & Sons, 1908.
Concert aria for coloratura Geraldine Farrar.

Gee But Ain't America a Grand Old Place
Words and music by Chris Smith.
Joseph W. Stern & Co., 1909.
American history lesson in the form of a patter rag.

Gee! But There's Class to a Girl Like You
Words and music by W. R. Williams.
Will Rossiter, 1908.
Top-selling proposal song popularized by Dan Healey and Maud Lambert.

Gee! But This Is a Lonely Town
Words and music by Billy Gaston.
Original copyright, 1905/Shapiro, Bernstein & Co., Inc., 1930.
Song for character comic Edwin Foy to interpolate during the second season of *Piff! Paff!! Pouf!!!*. Later recorded by Billy Murray for Victor.

Gee! I Wish I Had Someone to Rock Me in the Cradle of Love
Words by Noble Sissle, music by Eubie Blake.
M. Witmark & Sons, 1919.
Bluesy ballad popularized by the composers in their vaudeville act; recorded by Sissle as vocalist (Pathe) and by Blake as a piano roll, re-released on the Biograph label in Volume I of their Blake series. Ethel Beatty's rendition of the song with its wide range and slow, sensuous tempo in *Eubie!* (1980, original cast recording on

A & R) brought it back to favor with cabaret artists and popular vocalists.

Gee! I'd Like to Be the Mayor
Words and music by Zit (pseudonym for C. Florian Zittel).
Shapiro, Bernstein & Co., Inc., 1909.
Eva Tanguay vaudeville song satirizing New York City municipal politics.

Gee! I'm Glad That I'm from Dixie
Words by Noble Sissle, music by Eubie Blake.
M. Witmark & Sons, 1919.
The opening number from Sissle and Blake's vaudeville act; recorded by Sissle for Victor.

Gee, Its a Wonderful Game
Words by R. N. Lardner, music by G. Harris (Doc) White.
Remick Music Corp., 1911.
Ring Lardner's comical tribute to baseball.

General Hardtack on Guard
Words and music by Dave Reed, Jr.
Howley, Haviland & Dresser, 1903.
Novelty song introduced by Nat M. Wills as the cowardly "General Fourflush" in the military comedy *A Son of Rest* (1903); recorded by Dan W. Quinn for Monarch and Victor.

The Gertrude Hoffmann Glide
Words and music by Max Hoffmann.
T. B. Harms, 1912/Francis, Day & Hunter, Inc., 1912.
Sung by Gertrude Hoffmann in *Broadway to Paris* (revue, 1912). The lyrics describe her vaudeville imitation act. Also used in her vaudeville acts, 1913-1916; recorded by the Victor Military Band.

Get a Girlie!
Words by Harold Atteridge, music by Harold Timberg.
G. Schirmer Inc., 1916.
Grace Fisher introduced this audience participation number in which patrons tossed balls at the Winter Garden Peaches (female chorus) in an on-stage mid-way in *The Show of Wonders* (1916).

Get Behind the Girls Behind the Boys
Words by Anita Day Downing, music by Nat Goldstein.
Original copyright, 1918.
Patriotic anthem adopted as the official song of the Young Women's Christian Association.

Get Busy Over Here or Over There, also known as **Work or Fight**
Words and music by Edward Laska.
Original copyright, 1918.
World War I anthem urging all Americans to enlist or to do non-military service.

Get Happy
Words and music by Melville Collins.
Original copyright, 1907.
Eva Tanguay's "cyclonic hit" in vaudeville.

Get in Line for Big Bill Taft
Words by D. M. Kinnear, music by Frederick W. Mills.
Original copyright, 1908.
Campaign song for William Howard Taft, successful 1908 candidate for President on the Republican ticket.

The Ghost That Never Walked
Words by William Jerome, music by Jean Schwartz.
Shapiro, Bernstein & Co., Inc., 1904.
Novelty song referring to the theatrical slang for a troupe stranded on the road. Introduced by Edwin Foy in *Piff! Paff!! Pouf!!!* (1904) and recorded by Billy Murray (Victor) and Arthur Collins (Zono-o-phone).

Gianina Mia
Words by Otto Hauerbach (pseudonym for Otto Harbach), music by Rudolf Friml.
G. Schirmer Inc., 1912, 1940, 1955.
Romantic ballad introduced by Emma Trentini in *The Firefly* (operetta, 1912), but sung by Allan Jones as the male lead in the 1937 MGM film version; memorable recordings by Jones, Mario Lanza (RCA), and the duet of Jeanette MacDonald and Nelson Eddy.

The Gibson Bathing Girl
Words by Paul West, music by Alfred Solman.
Joseph W. Stern & Co., 1907.
Introduced by Annabelle Whitford in Florenz Ziegfeld's first *Follies* (revue, 1907). Whitford and the chorus dressed in swim suits popularized in the illustrations of Charles Dana Gibson.

The Gibson Widow
Words by Paul West, music by Alfred Solman.
Joseph W. Stern & Co., 1908.
Double parody of the fad for Charles Dana Gibson-style dresses, hats, and manners and of the popularity of *The Merry Widow;* from vaudeville's *The Gibson Girl Review.* (1908).

Gimme de Leavins'
Words by James Weldon Johnson, music by Bob Cole.
Joseph W. Stern & Co., 1904.
Character complaint song introduced by John Rucker.

Gimme Hush Money or I'll Tell on You
Words and music by Chris Smith and Harry Brown.
Original copyright, 1905/Helf & Hager.
Character comedy song about a craps-playing deacon. Introduced by Brown; also popularized by Kitty Hart.

A Girl, A Man, A Night, A Dance
Words by William Le Baron, music by Fritz Kreisler.
Francis, Day & Hunter, Inc., 1919/Harms, Inc., 1919.
Romance defined by Florence Shirley in the revue *Apple Blossoms* (1919).

Girl of My Dreams
Words and music by Charles K. Harris.
Charles K. Harris Music Publishing Co., 1903.
Art song written for Mme. Eugenie Mantelli.

The Girl of the Great Divide
Words by Robert B. Smith, music by Raymond Hubbell.
Charles K. Harris Music Publishing Co., 1907.
Plotted ballad referring to the nineteenth-century melodrama *The Great Divide.* Introduced by John Slavin in *A Knight for a Day* (1907).

The Girl on the Magazine Cover
Words and music by Irving Berlin.
Waterson, Berlin & Snyder, 1915/Irving Berlin Music Corp.
The most famous "elimination picture," in which chorus women posed in frames designed to look like contemporary illustrations, was created for Berlin's *Stop! Look! Listen!* (1915) and sung by Harry Fox; revived as a production number for the film *Easter Parade* (MGM, 1948). The song was also popular as a fox-trot on Victor dance records by Harry MacDonough and the Military Band; Joan Morris' recent recording is the title song on her Berlin album.

The Girl Who Cares for Me
Words by Will D. Cobb, music by Gus Edwards.
Gus Edwards Inc., 1904.
Romantic early hit for the new combination of Cobb and Edwards; popularized by Emma Carus and Frank C. Stanley (Zon-o-phone, Marconi).

The Girl Who Loves the Races
Words by Matt C. Woodward, music by Ben M. Jerome.
Howley, Haviland & Dresser, 1902.
Novelty song using race track slang; the third verse integrates a race call spoken over a raggy vamp.

The Girl with the Baby Stare
Words by Ernest Hanegan, music by William H. Penn.
Sol Bloom Publishing Co/Sol Bloom Music, 1902.
Comedy song about naive-looking sophisticate, who "has read that book by what's-her-name" performed by Frank Daniels in *Miss Simplicity* (1902) and by Dan McAvoy in *Sally in Our Alley* (1902).

The Girl with the Big Toy Bear
Words by Earle C. Jones, music by Max S. Witt.
Joseph W. Stern & Co., 1907.
Theodore Roosevelt had popularized "Teddy" bears and Anna Held had taught the audience how to flirt through them when Adele Ritchie introduced this parody in *Fascinating Flora* (1907).

The Girl with the Eyes and the Golden Hair
Words and music by Anna Held.
Sol Bloom Publishing Co/Sol Bloom Music, 1904.
Sung by Anna Held about herself in vaudeville.

The Girl You Can't Forget
Words and music by W. R. Williams.
Will Rossiter, 1916.
Romantic description of an ideal woman popularized by Maud Lambert.

The Girl You Love (American-English)
Words and music by Paul A. Rubens.
Sol Bloom Publishing Co/Sol Bloom Music, 1901.
The romantic song hit of the turn-of-the-century, it was interpolated into many musical comedies by popular female vocalists, among them, Beatrice Golden and Edna Wallace Hopper in *The Silver Slipper* (1901) and Delia Mason in *Three Little Maids* (1903).

Give an Imitation of Me
Words and music by Blanche Merrill.
Original copyright, 1910.
When vaudeville star Eva Tanguay was plagued by her many imitators in the 1909-1910 season, she commissioned this comic song from Merrill for her own act.

Give Me a Syncopated Tune
Words by Eugene West, music by Joe Gold.
Charles K. Harris Music Publishing Co., 1919.
Introduced by shimmy dancer Bee Palmer.

Give Me One More Chance
Words and music by Shelton Brooks.
Will Rossiter, 1914.
Bluesy lament popularized by Lee White (of White and George Perry).

Give Me the Moonlight, Give Me the Girl and Leave the Rest to Me
Words by Lew Brown, music by Albert von Tilzer.
Broadway Music Corp., 1917.
Introduced by Elsie Janis in the London revue *Hullo America* (1917) and recorded by her with the Palace Theatre Orchestra (Victor), and by Henry Burr (Emerson) and Sam Ash (Columbia).

Give Me the Sultan's Harem
Words by Alex Gerber, music by Alex Silver.
M. Witmark & Sons, 1919.
Comic monologue and song popularized by Al Herman, who introduced it in the *Greenwich Village Follies* of 1919, Nellie V. Nichols, and Eddie Cantor, who recorded it for Emerson.

Give My Regards to Broadway
Words and music by George M. Cohan.
Sol Bloom Publishing Co/Sol Bloom Music, 1904/Robbins Music Corp.
One of Cohan's most popular songs was, in the context of *Little Johnny Jones* (1904), a plot-effecting production song, performed by Cohan before and after a transformation scene and a still-famous ship effect--both replicated in the biographical film *Yankee Doodle Dandy* (Warner Brothers, 1942) with James Cagney; revived by Joel Grey in the musical *George M!* (1968).

Glad, see **The Dawn of a Tomorrow,**.

The Glad Song, see **Pollyanna,**.

The Glory of the Yankee Navy
Words by Kenneth S. Clark, music by John Philip Sousa.
John Church Co., 1909.
The song was dedicated to Blanche Ring and interpolated by her into *The Yankee Girl* (1909). Without its lyrics, the march remained in the repertory of Sousa's bands throughout his career. It has been recorded by the United States Marine Band, the Band of Her Majesty's Royal Marines, the Goldman Band, and the

Eastman Wind Ensemble. Sousa's own 1909 recording can be heard on New World's *The Sousa and Pryor Bands.*

The Glow Worm (American-English)
Words by Lilla Cayley Robinson, music by Paul Lincke.
Apollo Verlag, Berlin, Federal Republic of Germany, 1902/Joseph W. Stern & Co., 1902/Edward B. Marks Music Corp., 1932, 1952.
Introduced by May Naudain during the long run of *The Girl behind the Counter* (1907), the song, already a European favorite, became an instant best-seller. Recordings by the Edison and Victor Concert Bands, Pryor's Band (Victor), and Prince's Orchestra (Columbia) soon followed, as did parodies, such as the *Follies'* "Nix on the Glow Worm" (q.v.). Revivals by the Mills Brothers (Decca) and by Spike Jones and His City Slickers (RCA). New lyrics were added by Johnny Mercer in 1952.

Go Down Moses, also known as **Let My People Go**
Words and music by H. T. Burleigh.
G. Ricordi & C., SpA, Milan, Italy, 1917, 1920, 1926/Belwin-Mills Publishing Corp.
One of Burleigh's most famous spiritual arrangements popularized internationally by recordings and performances by Roland Hayes and Paul Robeson.

Go Easy Mabel
Words by Ren Shields, Edward Moran, and Will D. Cobb, music by J. Fred Helf.
Helf & Hager, 1909/Edward B. Marks Music Corp., 1942.
Comic novelty narrative of a cheap date worrying about Mabel's dinner order; featured by Emma Carus and Lew Dockstader.

Go Slow Joe
Words by Gus Kahn, music by Grace LeBoy.
Original copyright, 1911.
An early collaboration by LeBoy and Kahn featured romantic advice from Louise Dresser.

Golden Shores of Miami, see **On Miami Shore,**.

The Golden Stairs of Love
Words by Harold Atteridge, music by Jean Schwartz.
Original copyright, 1913.
Introduced by Wellington Cross and Lois Josephine in the revue *Passing Show of 1913.* Ned Wayburn staged the scene (Act 1 finale) on a replica of the Capitol steps and the exhibition ballroom team danced up and down the risers to enact the lyrics' depiction of their rocky romance.

The Golden Star
Words and music by John Philip Sousa.
Chappell & Co., Inc., 1946.
Dedicated to Gold Star mother Mrs. Theodore Roosevelt after the death of her son Quentin in World War I. Once popular in organ and orchestral arrangements and still in the band repertory of the United States Marine Band, who recorded it for *The Heritage of John Philip Sousa.*

Goo-Goo Eyes
Words by Fred W. Leigh, music by C. W. Murphy.
T. B. Harms, 1908.
Introduced by Melville Ellis in *The Midnight Songs* (1908).

Good-By, Teddy! You Must March! March! March!
Words by Paul West, music by John W. Bratton.
Original copyright, 1904.
Campaign march against Theodore Roosevelt's re-election. The Democratic candidate, Alton B. Parker, is mentioned only twice in the lyrics that list Roosevelt's shortcomings in detail.

Good-bye Alexander, Good-bye Honey-Boy
Words and music by Henry S. Creamer and Turner Layton.
Broadway Music Corp., 1918.
Farewell ballad for the archetypal characters "Alexander" and "Dinah Lee;" recorded as a fox-trot by Arthur Collins and Byron G. Harlan (Vocalion, Pathe), Marion Harris (Victor), and Prince's Band (Columbia).

Good-bye Cabarabian Nights
Words by Richard Egan, music by Richard A. Whiting.
Remick Music Corp., 1918.
Early lament for Prohibition.

Good-Bye Christina Swanson
Words by Bob Adams, music by Terry Sherman.
Original copyright, 1909.
A Swedish-dialect song performed by Montgomery and Stone in *The Old Town* (1910). "Swanson" was the standard female in Swedish-dialect songs since she rhymed with Wisconsin.

Good-Bye, Dolly Gray
Words by Will D. Cobb, music by Paul Barnes.
Howley, Haviland & Dresser, 1900/Jerry Vogel Music Co., Inc., 1939.
The classic farewell ballad of wartime America was first popularized by Harry Ellis, then of Primrose and Dockstadter's Minstrels. Recordings by Harry MacDonough and by Conway's Band

(both Victor) kept it popular until World War I, when it was revived and re-popularized. Despite the original plot, in which the soldier dies on the battlefield, the character of "Dolly Gray" developed a song biography of her own, marrying the British archetype Tommy Atkins (q.v) and sending her own son to war in "Don't Cry, Dolly Gray" (q.v.).

Good-bye, Eliza Jane
Words by Andrew B. Sterling, music by Harry von Tilzer.
Harry Von Tilzer Music Publishing Co., 1903.
Popular romance featured by Harry Brown and Allie Spooner and recorded by Bob Roberts (Victor).

Good-bye France
Words and music by Irving Berlin.
Waterson, Berlin & Snyder, 1918.
Post-World War I farewell to colleagues and fellow soldiers; introduced by Nora Bayes, who recorded it for Columbia.

Good-Bye Girlie and Remember Me
Words by Irving Berlin, music by George W. Meyer.
Ted Snyder Music Publishing Co., 1909.
Raggy romance popularized by the juveniles Willie and Eugene Howard.

Good Bye Girls I'm Through
Words by John Golden, music by Ivan Caryll.
Chappell & Co., Inc., 1914.
ASCAP top seller was introduced by Douglas Stevenson in *Chin-Chin* (1914) and popularized as a one-step by Prince's Band (Columbia).

Good Bye, Good Luck, God Bless You
Words by J. Keirn Brennan, music by Ernest R. Ball.
M. Witmark & Sons, 1916.
An old-fashion ballad of renunciation, it became an ASCAP top seller through recordings by its composer (Columbia), Henry Burr (Victor), Herbert Payne (Zon-o-phone), and Gladys Rice and Walter J. Van Brunt (Edison).

Good-Bye, I'll See You Some More
Words and music by Chris Smith and Billy B. Johnson.
Original copyright, 1905.
Complex farewell song for the trio act of Smith with Estelle and Billy B. Johnson, followed in 1906 by their "Good-bye, Ma Honey, I'm Gone."

Good-Bye, Little Girl, Good-Bye
Words by Will D. Cobb, music by Gus Edwards.
Gus Edwards Inc., 1904.
Patriotic farewell song as a follow-up to Cobb's "Good-bye, Dolly Gray" featured by George Lydecker and May Bouton in *The Strollers,* by Emma Carus in vaudeville, and by Madge Lessing at the London Coliseum. Recorded by Byron G. Harlan (Columbia) and by the Old Homestead Double Quartet (Victor); featured in the film *The Strawberry Blonde* (Warner Brothers, 1941).

Good-Bye, Maggie May
Words by Vincent Bryan, music by Paul Barnes.
Original copyright, 1905.
Military farewell ballad sung by male impersonator Della Fox.

Good-Bye Mister Caruso
Words by Billy Dunham, music by Al Piantadosi.
Original copyright, 1909.
Italian-dialect novelty song about Caruso losing his voice and returning to Italy.

Good Bye Mister Ragtime
Words by William Jerome, music by Jean Schwartz.
Cohan & Harris Music Publishers, 1908.
Premature obituary for rag-time "since the Merry Widow has come to town." Introduced in the touring *Cohan & Harris' Minstrels* (1908--).

Good Bye My Home Sweet Home
Words by Paul Benedek, music by Alfred Solman.
Original copyright, 1913.
Ballad introduced by French singer Chapine, star and title character of *Little Dolly Dimples* (1913).

Good Bye, My Lady Love
Words and music by Joseph E. Howard.
Charles K. Harris Music Publishing Co., 1904/Mills Music Inc., 1931/T. B. Harms.
The first rag-time song to "cross-over" into national popularity through performances by Ida Emerson, Blanche Ring, and the Hengler Sisters, as well as recordings by Harry MacDonough (Victor) and Frank Howard (Vocalion). Now best known as the cakewalk from the 1900 scenes in the musical *Show Boat,* in which it has always been interpolated; notable performances there by, among many others, Sammy White and Eva Puck in the Broadway original cast and Marge and Gower Champion in the 1951 MGM film. Also featured in the film *I Wonder Who's Kissing Her Now* (20th Century Fox, 1947).

Good-Bye, Sweet Old Manhattan Isle
Words by William Jerome, music by Jean Schwartz.
Remick Music Corp., 1905.
In their vehicle *The Ham Tree* (1905), McIntyre and Heath sing that "when you leave Manhattan Isle, you're only camping out;" Harry Tally recorded the comic song for Columbia and Zon-o-phone.

Good Fellows
Words by F. A. Woods, music by H. W. Petrie.
Original copyright, 1903.
Drinking song that, according to front cover advertisements, earned its composer over $100,000. Like all of Petrie's successes, it was written for the basso voice, and popularized by William McDonald of the Bostonians (an opera company).

Good Luck and God Be with You, Laddie Boy, also known as **Laddie Boy**
Words by Will D. Cobb, music by Gus Edwards.
M. Witmark & Sons, 1917.
Patriotic farewell ballad in the tradition of Cobb's song for the Spanish-American War; featured and recorded by Nora Bayes (Victor) and Henry Burr and Albert Campbell (Columbia). After the conclusion of World War I, Cobb and Edwards wrote "Welcome Home, Laddie Boy, Welcome Home" for Bayes.

Good Luck Mary
Words by Alfred Bryan and Edgar Leslie, music by Al Piantadosi.
Original copyright, 1909.
Close-harmony standard popularized by the Empire City Quartette.

A Good Man Is Hard to Find
Words and music by Eddie Green.
Handy Brothers Music Co., Inc., 1918/Mayfair Music Corp., 1927/Edwin H. Morris Co.
Blues standard first popularized by Sophie Tucker and by Jack Norworth; recorded by Les Brown and His Band of Renown using lyrics revised in 1940 to mention radio and the rhumba.

Good Morning Carrie!
Words by R. C. McPherson (pseudonym for Cecil Mack), music by Chris Smith and Elmer Bowman.
Original copyright, 1901/Jerry Vogel Music Co., Inc., 1938.
Proposal song that was a standard part of the vaudeville acts of black couples and teams at the turn of the century, among them, Jones and Sutton, the Wilson Family, and Williams and Walker with Aida Overton Walker and Lottie Williams; recorded as dance music by the Columbia Band.

Good Night, Angeline
Words and music by Noble Sissle, Eubie Blake, and James Reese Europe.
M. Witmark & Sons, 1919.
Pre-wedding serenade popularized by the authors in their vaudeville act and in *Shuffle Along* (1921). Blake recorded it on piano roll, which has been reissued on Volume I of the Biograph record series, and on piano in Volume I of his own retrospective album series (EBM). Also recorded by the authors (Pathe), the Peerless Quartet (Columbia), and Yerkes' Jazarimba Orchestra (Columbia). Revived for *Eubie!* in performance by Ethel Beatty, Lonnie McNeill, Janet Powell, and Mel Johnson, Jr. (1980, original cast recording on A & R).

Good Night Dear
Words and music by Will R. Anderson.
M. Witmark & Sons, 1908.
Ballad featured by Billie Burke in the comedy *Love Watches* and revived by George MacFarlane for *The Midnight Girl* (musical, 1914); recorded by Elizabeth Wheeler (Victor) and Harvey Hindermeyer (Columbia).

Good Night Is But Your Last Good Bye
Words by Leo Friedman, music by Jeffrey T. Branen.
Sol Bloom Publishing Co/Sol Bloom Music, 1901.
Ballad of renunciation popularized by Jessie Bartlett Davis and later a parlor song standard.

Good Night Lucindy
Words by R. C. McPherson (pseudonym for Cecil Mack), music by James T. Brymn.
Shapiro, Bernstein & Co., Inc., 1902.
Ballad introduced by John E. Slavin in the play *Huckleberry Finn* (1902).

The Good Old U.S.A.
Words by Jack Drislane, music by Theodore F. Morse.
F. B. Haviland, 1906.
Patriotic anthem dedicated to William Randolph Hearst at a time when the newspaper magnate was considering a run for national office; sung in vaudeville by Lillian Burt and James Purvis; recorded by J. W. Myers (Victor) and Byron G. Harlan (Columbia).

The Good Ship Mary Ann
Words by Gus Kahn, music by Grace LeBoy.
Remick Music Corp., 1914.
Ballad to Mississippi steam boat popularized by Nora Bayes (Vic-

tor), Blossom Seeley, Rae Samuels, and the team of Hattie Burke and Ted Lorraine.

Goodbye Broadway, Hello France
Words by C. Francis Reisner and Benny Davis, music by Billy Baskette.
Leo Feist Inc., 1917.
Patriotic anthem sung at the conclusion of the war-time *Passing Show of 1917;* recorded by Bob Grant for Decca, Arthur Fields for Edison, and the Peerless Quartet for Columbia; also popular as a one-step by Conway's Band (Victor) and Jaudas' Society Orchestra (Edison).

Goodbye, Mother Machree
Words by J. Keirn Brennan, music by Ernest R. Ball.
M. Witmark & Sons, 1918.
Used as a promotional song for the film *Mother Machree* (Wm. Fox, 1928); recorded by Henry Burr for Columbia.

Goodbye, Sweetheart, Goodbye
Words by Arthur Lamb, music by Albert von Tilzer.
York Music Corp., 1905/Jerry Vogel Music Co., Inc., 1939.
Romantic ballad recorded by John McCormack (Victor, Victrola), Frank C. Stanley (Zon-o-phone), and Alan Turner (Victor).

Googy-Oo
Words and music by Edward E. Rice.
Original copyright, 1908.
Parody of the "Goo-Goo Eyes" songs popularized by Anna Held. Introduced by Frank Lalor in *The Candy Shop* (1909); recorded by Ada Jones and Billy Murray (Victor).

G.O.P.
Words by Vincent Bryan, music by Gertrude Hoffmann.
Original copyright, 1905.
Comedy song about graft interpolated into *Fantana* (1905) by Jefferson de Angelis and *The Duke of Duluth* (1905) by Nat M. Wills; also popularized by Lew Dockstader in his minstrel shows.

A Great Big Girl Like Me
Words by Edgar Smith, music by Maurice Levi.
Charles K. Harris Music Publishing Co., 1904.
Descriptive comic song introduced by Marie Dressler in the Weber and Ziegfeld extravaganza *Higgeldy-Piggeldy* (1904).

The Green above the Red
Words and music by Paul Dresser.
Howley, Haviland & Dresser, 1900.

Overtly political military anthem praising Irish soldiers for their fighting in the Boer War, but threatening England with their fight for Irish freedom; performed by R. J. Jose, then with West's Minstrel Jamboree.

Greenwich Village
Words by John Murray Anderson, music by A. Baldwin Sloane.
M. Witmark & Sons, 1917.
Rag-time ball description from the cabaret revue *Venus of Broadway,* staged by Anderson, who would develop the *Greenwich Village Follies* annual series.

The Grizzly Bear, also known as **Doing That Grizzly Bear**
Words by Irving Berlin, music by George Botsford.
Waterson, Berlin & Snyder, 1910/Irving Berlin Music Corp.
"Animal" dances, variations on the "turkey trot" or one-step were generally dispensible, but "The Grizzly Bear" survived in popularity throughout the decade. Fanny Brice introduced it as a novelty dance in the *Follies of 1910,* but it remains associated with Sophie Tucker, who did it in vaudeville and recorded it for Mercury; also recorded by Billy Murray and the American Quartet for Victor; frequently used in films for atmosphere and featured in *Wharf Angel* (Paramount, 1934).

The Gypsy's Warning
Words and music by Henry A. Coard.
Original copyright, 1907.
Plotted parlor song in imitation of a folk ballad.

The Gypsy's Wedding
Words by Harry B. Smith, music by Ludwig Englander.
Original copyright, 1902.
Showy soprano aria introduced by Irene Bentley in *The Wild Rose* (musical, 1902).

H

H-A-Double R-I-G-A-N, also known as **Harrigan**
Words and music by George M. Cohan.
Cohan & Harris, 1908/George M. Cohan Music Publishing Co.
Cohan's tribute to the Irish of the Boston area (and to nineteenth-century actor/manager Ned Harrigan) was a show stopper from its introduction by James C. Marlowe in *Fifty Miles from Boston* (1908). Recorded as a novelty by Billy Murray (Victor) and featured by James Cagney and the cast of *Yankee Doodle Dandy* (Warner Brothers, 1942); revived by Joel Grey in the title role of *George M!* (1968).

Had She Only Let Me Dream an Hour More
Words and music by Nat M. Wills.
Joseph W. Stern & Co., 1903.
Comic character monologue and song performed by Wills.

Hail the Waistmakers!
Words and music by anonymous composer/lyricist .
Original copyright, 1947.
Labor anthem by an uncredited International Ladies Garment Workers' Union (ILGWU) member for the 1909 strike by waist (blouse) makers in New York, subtitled "The Uprising of the 20, 000." Published by the union.

Hail to the Spirit of Liberty
Words and music by John Philip Sousa.
John Church Co., 1928.
Sousa's Band represented the United States at the Paris Exposition of 1900 and premiered this march at the July 4th unveiling of a statue of General Lafayette. A piano transcription appears in Dover Books' *Sousa's Great Marches.* The march has been recorded by the United States Marine Band on the album *The Heritage of John Philip Sousa* and by Her Majesty's Royal Marine Band.

Hamlet Was a Melancholy Dane
Words by William Jerome, music by Jean Schwartz.
Shapiro, Bernstein & Co., Inc., 1902.
Edwin Foy's famous parody of Shakespeare, featured in *Mr. Bluebeard* (musical, 1903; staged in Chicago).

The Hand That Rocked the Cradle Rules My Heart
Words and music by Irving Berlin.
Irving Berlin Music Corp., 1919.
Ballad dedicated to Berlin's mother and recorded by the era's foremost male vocalists, among them John Steel (Victor) and Henry Burr (Emerson); its title is derived from the maternal archetype, "The Hand That Rocks the Cradle," in D. W. Griffith's film *Intolerance* (1916).

Handle me with Care
Words by William Jerome, music by Jean Schwartz.
Francis, Day & Hunter, Inc., 1907.
Introduced by Nora Bayes and Harry Watson, Jr. in the first Ziegfeld *Follies* (1907); also popularized by Emma Carus.

Hannah Dooley, Pride of Ballyhooley
Words by George V. Hobart, music by Max Hoffmann.
Original copyright, 1905.
Irish rag-time jig performed by Bessie De Voie in *The Rogers Brothers in Ireland* (1905).

Hannah, Won't You Open the Door?
Words by Andrew B. Sterling, music by Harry von Tilzer.
Harry Von Tilzer Music Publishing Co., 1904.
Errant lover's plea featured in vaudeville by Bonita, Tascott, and Elizabeth Murray.

Happiness
Words and music by Fred Fisher and Joe Jordon.
Charles K. Harris Music Publishing Co., 1918.
Promotional title song for J. Hartley Manners's play starring Laurette Taylor.

Happy Hooligan
Music by Theodore F. Morse.
Original copyright, 1902.
Novelty piano cakewalk dedicated to the comic strip character. Other songs about F. B. Opper's strip, such as "Happy Hooligan" (by Stillman and Vogel) and "Happy Hooligan's Reception" (by Dunham and Wilson), were published in music supplements to the Hearst syndicate newspapers in which the cartoon ran.

Happy Little Country Girl
Words and music by Irving Berlin.
Waterson, Berlin & Snyder, 1913.
Comic romance popularized and recorded by Elida Morris (Victor).

The Harbor of Lost Dreams
Words by Alex Rogers, music by Bert A. Williams.
Will Rossiter, 1909.
Ballad (with "ensembles" credited to J. Rosamond Johnson) from Williams's star vehicle *Mr. Lode of Koal* (1909).

Hard Trials
Words by Deems Taylor, music by H. T. Burleigh.
G. Ricordi & C., SpA, Milan, Italy, 1919, 1921, 1956/Belwin-Mills Publishing Corp.
Taylor's lyrics, based on New Testament texts, were recorded and performed by Marian Anderson.

Harem Life, also known as **Outside of That Every Little Thing's All Right**
Words and music by Irving Berlin.
Irving Berlin Music Corp., 1919.
The male and female comics in the harem scene in the *Ziegfeld Follies of 1919* each had Berlin solos--this was sung by Rae Samuels, while Bert Williams responded as "I'm the Guy Who Guards the Harem ... and My Heart Is in My Work."

Harrigan, see **H-A-Double R-I-G-A-N,.**

Has Anybody Here Seen Kelly?
Words by C. W. Murphy and Will Letters, music by Wm. J McKenna.
Harms, Inc., 1909.
Already featured in vaudeville by Emma Carus, the Irish novelty song became a best-seller in sheet music and 78's (Victor) when Nora Bayes adopted it to interpolate into *The Jolly Bachelors* in 1910. Later recordings by Ada Jones (Columbia), Phil Regan and Jesse Crawford (Decca), the De Marco Sisters (Majestic), and Frank Novak and His Rootin' Tootin' Boys (Vocalion, Columbia, Okeh) maintained its popularity, especially on St. Patrick's Day when its plot is set.

Hat Song
Words by Harry B. Smith, music by Maurice Levi.
Cohan & Harris, 1908.
Parody of contemporary millinery fashions from Ziegfeld's *Follies of 1908,* where it introduced the "Nell Brinkley Girl" chorus (q. v.).

Havana
Words by E. Ray Goetz, music by James Kendis and Herman Paley.
Original copyright, 1910.
Nostalgic love song referring to Havana as a honeymoon site; popularized by Cheridah Simpson and Daisy Leon.

Have a Heart
Words by Gene Buck, music by Jerome Kern.
Harms, Inc., 1916.
Chorus dance specialty from the *Ziegfeld Follies of 1916* coupled with a romantic duet of the same name that followed; recorded as a duet by Anita Boyer and George Griffin (Victor) and Alice Green and Raymond Dixon (both Victor) and as dance music by the Victor Military Band, Conway's Band (Victor), and Jaudas' Society Orchestra (Edison). Kern wrote a different "Have a Heart" that year with P. G. Wodehouse as title song for their musical comedy with Guy Bolton.

Have You Seen My Baby?
Words by Will D. Cobb, music by Gus Edwards.
Gus Edwards Music Publishing Co., 1908.
Novelty romance with a whistled chorus performed in *Gus Edwards' School Days* (vaudeville feature act, 1907-1910) and in the Raymond Hitchock comedy *Merry-Go-Round* (1908).

Have You Seen My Sweetheart in His Uniform of Blue?
Words by Will D. Cobb, music by Gus Edwards.
Mills Music Inc., 1902.
Tragic ballad of the Spanish-American War. Introduced by Leila McIntyre in *The Sleeping Beauty and the Beast* (1901).

Hawaiian Butterfly
Words and music by George A. Little, Billy Baskette, and Joseph Santley.
Leo Feist Inc., 1917.
Oriental fox-trot associated with Elizabeth Brice and Charles King (Columbia) and also featured by Emma Carus, Larry Comer, Gene Greene, Blossom Seeley, Sophie Tucker, and other vaudeville greats. As dance music, it was the signature tune of Earl Fuller's Orchestra at Rector's and was recorded by Prince's Band (Columbia), the Victor Military Band, and Jaudas' Society Orchestra (Edison).

He Died on the Fighting Line, also known as **Just a Message from the Camp Fire**
Words by Robert H. Brennan, music by Pauline B. Story.
Original copyright, 1901.

Patriotic ballad about a casualty of the Spanish-American War introduced by Story.

He Done Me Wrong
Words and music by Hughie Cannon.
Howley, Haviland & Dresser, 1904.
Originally a plotted lament about the death of "Bill Bailey" (q.v.) of cholera. Introduced by Maud Lambert, it became popular as a generic blues and was a top seller for Marion Harris (Columbia) in the 1920's.

He Draws No Color Line, see **When the Good Lord Makes a Record of a Hero's Deed, He Draws No Color Line,.**

He Goes to Church on Sunday
Words by Vincent Bryan, music by E. Ray Goetz.
Shapiro, Bernstein & Co., Inc., 1907.
Portrait of a hypocrite interpolated by Edwin Foy in *The Orchid* (1907) where it stopped the show nightly.

He Handed Me a Lemon
Words and music by Bob Cole.
Joseph W. Stern & Co., 1906.
Character complaint song associated with Lew Dockstader; a topical second verse describes the Philippines Territory secession as a "lemon."

He Laid Away a Suit of Gray to Wear the Union Blue
Words by Edw. M. Wickes, music by Ben Jansen.
Leo Feist Inc., 1901.
Patriotic ballad popularized by J. Aldrich Libbey, Lydia Barry, and Lillian Mack, among many others. The theme of a Confederate veteran or Southern boy adopting the blue of the U.S. Army was frequently heard in Spanish-American War songs of the early 1900's.

He Likes Their Jukelele
Words and music by James Kendis.
Original copyright, 1917.
Hebrew-dialect imitation Hawaiian song performed in close-harmony by the team of Van and Schenck in *The Century Girl* (revue, 1917).

He May Get Over It But He'll Never Look the Same
Words and music by Ernest Hogan, W. C. Steele, and E. D. Cole.
Joseph W. Stern & Co., 1903.
Animal trainers and their mishaps were frequent targets for the rag

songs written for Ernest Hogan, the star of a series of musical comedies in vaudeville.

He Ought to Have a Tablet in the Hall of Fame
Words by Arthur L. Robb, music by John W. Bratton.
M. Witmark & Sons, 1901.
Topical comedy song about unsung heroes, husbands, politicians, and songwriters. Introduced by Francis Wilson in *The Troubador* (musical, 1901); recorded by Ed. M. Favor for Zon-o-phone.

He Played It on His Fid, Fid, Fiddle-dee-dee
Words and music by Ray Goetz and Irving Berlin.
Waterson, Berlin & Snyder, 1912.
Novelty rag associated with Lew Dockstader (Columbia, Audio) and Victor's vocalist Walter J. Van Brunt.

He Sleeps beneath the Soil of France
Words and music by Tell Taylor.
Original copyright, 1917.
Patriotic anthem extolling the death of an American on duty in World War I.

He Was a Sailor
Words by William Jerome, music by Jean Schwartz.
Shapiro, Bernstein & Co., Inc., 1903.
Comic monologue and novelty song introduced by Edwin Foy, includes puns on loan shark, floating a bond, and sail boats, with topical references to Sir Thomas Lipton, unsuccessful challenger for the America's Cup.

He Was Always Fooling Around
Words by William Jerome, music by Abner Greenberg.
Original copyright, 1914.
Popular comedy song introduced by Charles Evans at the Lambs Club's revue, *Lambs' Gambol of 1914,* makes topical references to American and Mexican political leaders. Also sung as a marital complaint duet by William Montgomery and Florence Moore and by Willie and Eugene Howard.

A Heart That's Free, also known as **Valse de Concert** (American-Italian)
English words by Thomas T. Railey, Italian words by Carmen Stanzione, music by Alfred G. Robyn.
Leo Feist Inc., 1908, 1910.
Concert aria revived by Jane Powell in *Two Weeks with Love* (MGM, 1950).

Hearts of the World
Words and music by Lee Johnson.
Original copyright, 1918.
Ballad promoting D. W. Griffith's World War I silent film of the same name. Other songs dedicated to the film and its theme of peace were written by Bartley Costello and James W. Casey and by George Graff, Jr. and Bert Grant (both 1918).

Hearts You Lose
Words and music by Andrew B. Sterling.
Leo Feist Inc., 1903.
Plotted sentimental ballad about rivals who draw cards for the woman they both love; popularized by Hardie Langdon and the team of Bohannon and Corey.

The Heaven Born Banner
Words by Vincent Bryan, music by Gertrude Hoffmann.
Original copyright, 1905.
Anthem dedicated to the school children of America written by Bryan and dance director Hoffmann for Harry A. Ellis of the Dockstader minstrel troupe. The song was published in the music supplement pages of the Hearst newspapers in spring, 1906.

Heaven Will Protect the Working Girl
Words by Edgar Smith, music by A. Baldwin Sloane.
Charles K. Harris Music Publishing Co., 1909/Jerry Vogel Music Co., Inc., 1937.
Burlesque of labor ballads. Introduced by Marie Dressler in *Tillie's Nightmare* (musical, 1910).

Heavenly Twins
Words by Stanley Murphy, music by Henry I. Marshall.
Remick Music Corp., 1916.
Romantic song for and about the twin tandem act of Roszika and Jansci Dolly in their vehicle *His Bridal Night* (1913).

He'd Have to Get Under, Get Out and Get Under to Fix Up His Automobile
Words by Grant Clarke and Edgar Leslie, music by Maurice Abrahams.
Mills Music Inc., 1913, 1931.
Comic novelty about car repairs, popularized by Al Jolson and Belle Baker and recorded by Billy Murray (Victor); also popular as dance music, it was recorded by Prince's Band (Columbia), the Victor Military Band, and the Hoosier Hot Shots (Vocalion). Revived by Debbie Reynolds and Carleton Carpenter in the film *Two Weeks with Love* (MGM, 1950, recorded on the MGM label).

Heidelberg, also known as **The Stein Song**
Words by Frank Pixley, music by Gustav Luders.
M. Witmark & Sons, 1902.
Drinking song from the musical *The Prince of Pilsen* (1903); recorded on Victor by Harry MacDonough, Frank Mazziolla, the Haydn Quartet, and the Heidelberg Concert Choir.

Hello Central, Give Me France
Words by James M. Reilley, music by Harry De Costa.
M. Witmark & Sons, 1917.
Pathetic baby ballad of World War I with a very detailed plot in which the switchboard operator, "Central," calls the White House which relays a message in code to the father in the trenches.

Hello Central, Give Me Heaven
Words and music by Charles K. Harris.
Charles K. Harris Music Publishing Co., 1901/Edward B. Marks Music Corp., 1941.
This melodramatic ballad enjoyed tremendous popularity in the early years of the twentieth century. "Hello Central" were the words used to reach a switchboard operator on the still-new telephone system. Harris's frequently copied and parodied ballad was introduced by J. Aldrich Libbey and popularized by Byron G. Harlan (Victor), Ed. M. Favor (Columbia), and generations of juveniles; revived in 1937 by Vic Abbs and the Four Californians.

Hello Central, Give Me No Man's Land
Words by Sam M. Lewis and Joe Young, music by Jean Schwartz.
Waterson, Berlin & Snyder, 1918/Mills Music Inc., 1946/Warock Music, Inc.
The most famous of the baby ballads of World War I was introduced by Frank Carter and interpolated by Al Jolson into *Sinbad*--both within a few weeks of its composition. An ASCAP top seller during the war, it was also recorded by Edna Brown (Victor) and Irving Gillette (Pathe).

Hello Cupid, Send Me a Fellow
Words by Melville Alexander, music by Anatol Friedland.
Remick Music Corp., 1912.
Raggy romance from Gertrude Hoffmann's vehicle *Broadway to Paris* (1912).

Hello Honey
Words by George V. Hobart, music by Raymond Hubbell.
Harms, Inc., 1913.
Telephone novelty romance introduced by Elizabeth Brice as an operator at an on-stage switchboard in the *Ziegfeld Follies of 1913.*

Hello Wisconsin, Won't You Find My Yonnie Yonson
Words by Bert Kalmar and Edgar Leslie, music by Harry Ruby.
Kalmar, Puck & Abrahams Consolidated Mus, 1917.
Swedish-dialect song using the popular gimmick of telephone conversation; featured in the vaudeville acts of Anna Chandler, Sophie Tucker, and Willie Weston.

Her Boy in the Rank and File
Words by Will A. Heelan, music by Silvio Hein.
Shapiro, Bernstein & Co., Inc., 1903.
Sentimental ballad introduced by George Diamond. In typical minstrel troupe ballad format, the mother sees her son off to war in verse 1 and learns of his death in verse 2; the title, repeated in the chorus, serves as a statement of her pride and as the son's epitaph.

Her Eyes of Irish Blue
Words by William Jerome, music by Jean Schwartz.
Shapiro, Bernstein & Co., Inc., 1903.
Irish ballad adapting themes from "Molly Malone" featured by the Ellinore Sisters in *Mrs. Delaney of Newport* (musical, 1904).

Herald of Peace
Music by E. T. Paull.
Original copyright, 1914.
Promotional march for the National Relief Board of the American Red Cross.

Here's to Our Absent Brothers
Words and music by J. Fred Helf.
Original copyright, 1903.
Sentimental ballad dedicated to the Benevolent Paternal Order of Elks' tradition of toasting "Absent Brothers."

Here's to You, My Sparkling Wine
Words by Blanche Merrill, music by Leo Edwards.
G. Schirmer Inc., 1915.
Drinking song introduced by Cecil Lean, Teddy Webb, Walter Armin, and chorus in *The Blue Paradise* (musical, 1915).

He's a Cousin of Mine
Words by Cecil Mack, music by Chris Smith and Silvio Hein.
Gotham-Attucks Music Publishing Co., 1906/Mills Music Inc., 1934.
One of the most popular novelty rag songs of the decade. Introduced by Marie Cahill in *Marrying Mary* (1906), and repeated five times as her character's excuse for being found in a romantic situation; contemporary recordings were by Bert Williams (Columbia), Arthur Fields (Zon-o-phone), and Clarice Vance

(Victor); revived in 1934 by Phil Harris in his repertory of Dixie novelty songs. Among the many popular answer songs were Smith's "She's a Patient of Mine" and "He's My Cousin..." (q.v.).

He's a Devil in His Own Home Town
Words by Grant Clarke, words and music by Irving Berlin.
Waterson, Berlin & Snyder, 1914/Fred Fisher Music Co., 1942.
This ASCAP top seller repopularized "rube" songs making fun of country bumpkins; performed by Fanny Brice and recorded by Ed Morton (Columbia) and Billy Murray (Victor); revived by Kay Kyser and His Orchestra (Brunswick).

He's a Fan, Fan, Fan
Words and music by Cecil Lean and Florence Holbrook.
M. Witmark & Sons, 1909.
Baseball slang duet from Lean and Holbrook's vaudeville act.

He's a Rag Picker
Words and music by Irving Berlin.
Waterson, Berlin & Snyder, 1914.
Novelty song describing and imitating a rag-time pianist; popularized by Sophie Tucker and Rae Samuels and recorded in close harmony by the Peerless Quartet on Victor and Columbia; also featured often as a piano roll.

He's Coming Home on the 8 O'Clock Train
Words by Marguerite Kendall, music by J. Russel Robinson.
Original copyright, 1912.
Blues lament written for Sophie Tucker.

He's Had No Lovin' for a Long, Long Time
Words by William Tracey, music by Maceo Pinkard.
Broadway Music Corp., 1919.
"Big mama" blues sung to welcome troupes home from World War I; popularized by Arthur Fields and Frantzen's Society Orchestra (Victor).

He's Me Pal
Words by Vincent Bryan, music by Gus Edwards.
M. Witmark & Sons, 1905.
This "East Side love song" in Edwards's series of New York dialect songs for adolescents has an additional verse for a mother character; featured by Eleanor Falk, Willa Holt Wakefield, and Edwards's School Boys and Girls juvenile acts.

He's My Cousin If She's Your Niece
Words by Alfred Bryan, music by Chris Smith.
Remick Music Corp., 1914.

Title continues "... What's Game for the Gander Is Game for the Geese." Feminist answer song to "He's a Cousin of Mine" (q.v.) popularized by its performer, Clarice Vance.

He's the Whole Show Now
Words by Edward Gardinier, music by William Gould and Max Dreyfus.
Harms, Inc., 1903.
Novelty song for Marie Dressler satirizes (without naming) Irish actor-directors turned managers and authors, such as George M. Cohan, Chauncey Olcott, and Andrew Mack.

The Hesitating Blues
Words and music by W. C. Handy.
Handy Brothers Music Co., Inc., 1915.
Recorded by Adele Rowland (Columbia), Esther Bigeon (Okeh), and by Art Hickman's Orchestra (Columbia).

Heure exquise qui nous grise (French)
French words by Gaston de Caillavet, music by Franz Lehar.
Editions Max Eschig, Paris, France, 1909, 1934.
This standard European version of the "Merry Widow Waltz" was distributed in the United States beginning in 1909, then re-issued for the 1934 film *The Merry Widow,* starring Maurice Chevalier and Jeanette MacDonald.

Hiawatha
Words by James O'Dea, music by Neil Morel.
Original copyright, 1903.
Indian novelty cakewalk introduced by David Lythgoe in the touring *Show Girl* company. An ASCAP all-time top seller, it was also sung in vaudeville by Grace LaRue, Clara Norton, and Louise Brehany and was interpolated in *The Runaways* (musical, 1903).

The High Cost of Loving
Words by Alfred Bryan, music by George W. Meyer.
Leo Feist Inc., 1914.
Lew Fields introduced this comic title song for his play; also popularized by Emma Carus and Elida Morris.

Hike!
Words by George Ade, music by Alfred G. Wathall.
M. Witmark & Sons, 1902.
Parody of soldiers' marching songs with topical verses about businessmen draftees who seek foreign trade while on maneuvers; from *The Sultan of Sulu* (musical, 1902).

Hindustan
Words and music by Oliver Wallace and Harold Weeks.
Forster Music Publishers, Inc., 1918, 1945/Fred Fisher Music Co., 1946/Venus Music Corp., 1953.
Oriental fox-trot first popularized by Albert Campbell and Henry Burr (Columbia), the Emerson Military Band, Joseph C. Smith's Orchestra (Victor), and a top-selling piano roll by Max Kortlander (QRS). Major revivals include those by Sammy Kaye (Columbia), Artie Shaw, (Victor) and Frankie Carle (Columbia).

Hiram Green, Good-Bye
Words by Henry A. Gillespie, music by Clarence M. Chapel.
Original copyright, 1905.
Comic number about a small town "rube" who travels to New York; it was introduced by Dave Lewis in *Kafoozelum* (musical, 1905 in Chicago) and later popularized by Lew Fields.

His Eye Is on the Sparrow
Words by Mrs. C. D. Martin, music by Charles H. Gabriel.
Original copyright, 1906.
Gospel standard and hymn first popularized by Homer A. Rodeheaver's massive choirs performing with Billy Sunday's evangelical campaigns. It became the signature tune of Ethel Waters, who sang it as gospel and as blues in concert and also in her role as "Berenice" in Carson McCullers' play, *The Member of the Wedding* (1951), in which it was also performed by Julie Harris and Brandon de Wilde; Waters used it as the title of her autobiography (1951, with Charles Samuels).

His Majesty, the American
Words by Lew Brown, music by Albert von Tilzer.
York Music Corp., 1919.
Promotional title song for Douglas Fairbanks's film (United Artists, 1919).

Hitchy's Garden of Roses, also known as **In Hitchy's Garden**
Words and music by Cole Porter.
Francis, Day & Hunter, Ltd., London, England, 1919/Harms, Inc., 1919.
Production song from the revue *Hitchy-Koo of 1919.* Introduced by Lillian Kemble Cooper and female chorus; the scene also included Porter's "Old Fashioned Garden," which became a British dance band success in the 1920's.

Holding Hands, also known as **You Don't Say Nothing at All**
Words by Jack Norworth, music by Albert von Tilzer.
York Music Corp., 1906.

Spooning instructions offered by Georgia Caine, Toby Claude, and female impersonator Julian Eltinge.

Homesickness Blues
Words and music by Cliff Hess.
Waterson, Berlin & Snyder, 1916/Mills Music Inc., 1944.
Blues recorded and popularized by Nora Bayes and Marion Harris (both on Columbia).

Homeward Bound
Words by Howard Johnson and Coleman Goetz, music by George W. Meyer.
Leo Feist Inc., 1917.
Optimistic ballad from the beginning of World War I; featured by Belle Baker, Emma Carus, Dorothy Jardon, Joseph Santley, and Willie Weston.

Honey Boy
Words and music by William H. Penn.
Original copyright, 1904.
Lilting ballad associated with Leila McIntyre, who introduced it in the burlesque *Mother Goose* (1903).

Honey Boy
Words by Jack Norworth, music by Albert von Tilzer.
York Music Corp., 1907/Broadway Music Corp./Jerry Vogel Music Co., Inc., 1935.
Farewell ballad popular as a solo and in a barbershop quartet arrangement featured by Louise Dresser, Harry Fox, and lyricist Norworth in vaudeville; recorded by Billy Murray (Victor), Frank C. Stanley (Victor), and the quartets of Columbia, Emerson, and Harmony. Revived by Ray Bloch and vocalist Beatrice Kay for Columbia.

Honey, I Will Long for You
Words by Arthur Longbrake, music by Edw. Edwards.
Original copyright, 1910.
Sentimental ballad introduced by the Metropolitan Quartette but also popularized by solo male vocalists, among them Frank Morrell and Vaughn Comfort.

Honey Love
Words by Jack Drislane, music by George W. Meyer.
F. B. Haviland, 1911/Shawnee Press, Inc.
Proposal song popularized by Lottie Gilson and by Gladys Clark, who also sang it in vaudeville as a duet with her partner Harry Bergman.

Honey Love Me All the Time
Words by William Jerome, music by Jean Schwartz.
Remick Music Corp., 1905.
Flirtatious ballad sung by the team of McIntyre & Heath to the female chorus in their comedy vehicle *The Ham Tree* (1905).

Honey Man, also known as **Little Lovin' Honey Man**
Words by Joe McCarthy, music by Al Piantadosi.
Leo Feist Inc., 1911.
Introduced by Bessie Wynn, but most popular in close-harmony arrangements by the teams of Carter De Haven and Flora Parker, Irene and Bobbie Smith, Mike Bernard and Willie Weston, and Gus Van and Joe Schenck.

Honey Will You Miss Me When I'm Gone?
Words and music by Joseph E. Howard and Billy Emerson.
Charles K. Harris Music Publishing Co., 1902.
Romantic song introduced by Sidney Dean and Maud Alice Kelly in *The Sweet Girl* (musical, 1902, at the New York Roof Garden) and quickly popularized in minstrelsy by its authors.

Honey, You Were Made for Me
Words by Earl Carroll, music by Jack Glogau.
Leo Feist Inc., 1913.
Romantic duet also called "You Were Meant for Me." Introduced by Carter De Haven and Flora Parker in *All Aboard* (1913).

Honeymoon
Words by Will M. Hough and Frank R. Adams, music by Joseph E. Howard.
Charles K. Harris Music Publishing Co., 1906, 1929/Edward B. Marks Music Corp., 1942.
Romantic ballad, also called "Waning Honeymoon," in *The Time, the Place, and the Girl* (1906) where it was introduced by Harriet Burt. Used as a theme for the Warner Brothers film *The Time, the Place, and the Girl* 1926), starring Betty Compson, and the Joseph E. Howard biographical film, *I Wonder Who's Kissing Her Now* (20th Century Fox, 1947); revived by Kay Starr for Capitol.

The Honeysuckle and the Bee
Words by Alb. H. Fitz, music by William H. Penn.
Original copyright, 1901.
Romantic ballad with buzzing voice effects that has become a favorite nostalgic song; originally introduced by Lulu Glaser in *The Prima Donna* (1901) and performed widely in vaudeville and minstrel troupes by, among others, Della Fox, J. Aldrich Libbey, and George H. Primrose.

The Honky-Tonky Monkey Rag
Words and music by Chris Smith.
Original copyright, 1911.
Top-seller for Sophie Tucker; see also Smith and McCarron's "Down in Honky-Tonk Town."

Honolulu, America Loves You
Words by Grant Clarke and Eddie Cox, music by Jimmie V. Monaco.
Leo Feist Inc., 1916.
Comic song featured by the Avon Comedy Four, Gene Greene, and the team of Elizabeth Brice and Charles King; recorded by Arthur Fields (Edison) and Victor's Military Band and American Quartet.

The Honolulu Blues
Words by Grant Clarke and Eddie Cox, music by Jimmie V. Monaco.
Leo Feist Inc., 1916.
Exotic nostlagia featured by Emma Carus, Joseph Santley, and the team of Bert and Betty Wheeler.

Hoop-la, I'm Having the Time of My Life
Words by Will D. Cobb, music by John H. Flynn.
Shapiro, Bernstein & Co., Inc., 1910.
Novelty song describing a day at a county fair; popularized in vaudeville by Anna Driver and Grace Leonard.

Hooray for a Bryan to Lead Us
Words by E. C. Hicks, music by John Martin.
Original copyright, 1908.
Campaign song for Democratic candidate William Jennings Bryan, who lost the presidential race to William Howard Taft.

The Hope of the Ages (English)
Words by Edith Nesbit.
Original copyright, 1901.
Edith Nesbit, leader of the British Fabian Socialist movement, set new words to "Columbia, the Gem of the Ocean" for this popular anthem, published by Charles Kerr. For Kerr's settings of music with posthumous poetry, see "The March of the Workers."

The Hornpipe Rag
Words by Edward Madden, music by Ben M. Jerome.
Rag-time sailor dance introduced by Edwin Foy in the musical *Mr. Hamlet of Broadway* (1908).

The Hour of Memory
Words by J. Will Callahan, music by Anton Dvorak.
Original copyright, 1916.
Sentimental setting of Dvorak's famous piano piece, "Humoresque."

How Can I Forget When There's So Much to Remember?
Words and music by Irving Berlin.
Waterson, Berlin & Snyder, 1917.
Sentimental ballad recorded by Alan Turner (Victor) and Robert Lewis (Columbia).

How Do You Do It Mabel on $20 a Week?
Words and music by Irving Berlin.
Ted Snyder Music Publishing Co., 1911/Irving Berlin Music Corp.
Risque comic song about a chorus dancer who lives suspiciously well on her salary; popularized by Neil McKinley as her "rube" home-town boyfriend.

How 'Ya Gonna Keep 'Em Down on the Farm After They've Seen Paris?
Words by Sam M. Lewis and Joe Young, music by Walter Donaldson.
Mills Music Inc., 1919, 1932.
Originally a "rube" song, it became a symbol for the real sociological problems facing the United States after World War I. In its time, it was popular both as a comic solo, most notably by Eddie Cantor (Decca, V Disc), and as dance music, with recordings by Noble Sissle and Europe's Hell Fighters (the 369th Infantry Band) on Pathe, Joseph C. Smith's Orchestra (Victor), and Earl Fuller's Orchestra (Pathe). Revived often in films to identify the period.

How'd You Like to Float Me
Words by Vincent Bryan, music by E. Ray Goetz.
Original copyright, 1907.
The "Gibson Bathing Girls" chorus (q.v.) specialty in Ziegfeld's *Follies of 1907* included this seaside flirtation song. Introduced by Grace Leigh.

How'd You Like to Spoon with Me?
Words by Edward Laska, music by Jerome Kern.
Harms, Inc., 1905, 1931.
Romantic duet introduced by Georgia Caine and Victor Morley in *The Earl and the Girl* (musical, 1905).

Huckleberry Finn
Words by Sam M. Lewis and Cliff Hess, music by Joe Young.

Waterson, Berlin & Snyder, 1917/Mills Music Inc., 1931/Warock Music, Inc.
Narrative of the Mark Twain novel recorded by Sam Ash (Columbia), Prince's Band (Columbia), the Little Wonder Band, and Gus Van and Joe Schenck (Victor); revived by Guy Lombardo and His Royal Canadians.

Huckleberry Pie
Words by Bert Hanlon, music by Con Conrad.
Harry Von Tilzer Music Publishing Co., 1918.
Novelty spelling song introduced by Willie Solar.

The Humpty-Dumpty Kid
Words by F. J. Hamill, music by Percy Wenrich.
Original copyright, 1908.
Advertising song for the stockings manufactured by A. B. Andrews Company. The song was distributed free with all sales of Miss Moffett, Cinderella, Mother Goose, Prince, and King Cole socks and stockings.

A Hundred Years from Now
Words by John Bennett, music by Carrie Jacobs-Bond.
Original copyright, 1914.
Art song popularized and recorded by Elsie Baker (Victor).

Hurrah for Baffin's Baby
Words by Vincent Bryan, music by Theodore F. Morse.
Howley, Haviland & Dresser, 1903.
Satirical sea chanty introduced by Dave Montgomery and Fred Stone as the "Tin Woodsman" and "Scarecrow," respectively, in the 1903 musical *The Wizard of Oz.*

The Hurricane
Music by S. L. Alpert.
E. T. Paull, 1906.
Descriptive march-two-step with storm effects recorded by Edison's Concert Band and often excerpted for silent film accompaniments.

Hymn to Liberty
Words and music by Edwards P. Ingersoll.
Original copyright, 1914.
Socialist anthem written and published by Ingersoll for his Church of the Social Responsibility, New York City.

Hypnotizing Lize
Words by Vincent P. Bryan, music by Theodore F. Morse.
Shapiro, Bernstein & Co., Inc., 1901.

Comedy song with tongue-twisting monologue. Introduced by Dan McAvoy.

I

I Ain't a-Goin' to Weep No More
Words by George Totten Smith, music by Harry von Tilzer.
Shapiro, Bernstein & Co., Inc., 1900.
Dialect lament featured by Emma Carus and Grace Leonard.

I Ain't Gonna Give Nobody None o' This Jelly Roll
Words and music by Spencer Williams and Clarence Williams.
Clarence Williams Music, 1919/Shapiro, Bernstein & Co., Inc., 1919.
Jazz classic associated with Sidney Bechet and His New Orleans Feet Warmers (Gramophone) and Phil Harris (Victor).

I Ain't Got Nobody Much and Nobody Cares for Me
Words by Roger Graham, music by Spencer Williams.
Original copyright, 1916/Jerry Vogel Music Co., Inc.
The archetypal torch song, "I Ain't Got Nobody" has been a top seller since its release and first performances by Sophie Tucker and Kitty Hart; recordings by jazz ensembles are numerous, among them, Art Tatum (Decca), Fats Waller (Victor, Bluebird), Louis Armstrong (Vocalion), and Coleman Hawkins (Decca), but it remains associated with female vocalists, such as Ruth Etting (Columbia), Bessie Smith (Columbia), Tucker (Victor, Odeon, Okeh), and Marion Harris, whose 1920 recording for Columbia is included in the Smithsonian Institution's *American Popular Song* (CBS). A variation on the song, which was derived from traditional blues, was copyrighted by David Young and Charles Warield in 1914 (Frank K. Root & Co.; now: Jerry Vogel Music Corp.).

I Ain't Got'en No Time to Have the Blues
Words by Andrew B. Sterling, music by Harry von Tilzer.
Harry Von Tilzer Music Publishing Co., 1919.
Close harmony song, also entitled "I Ain't-en Got'en...," in imitation of the dialect laments of the first decade, featured by the

Duncan Sisters, Gus Van and Joe Schenck, Irving and Jack Kaufman (Columbia), Billy Murray (Victor), and the Louisiana Five Jazz Orchestra (Columbia).

I Ain't Gwin ter Work No Mo'
Words by James Weldon Johnson and Bob Cole, music by J. Rosamond Johnson.
Joseph W. Stern & Co., 1919.
Dialect comedy song commissioned, copyrighted, and performed by May Irwin.

I Ain't Had No Lovin' in a Long Time
Words by Bob Cole, music by James Reese Europe.
Joseph W. Stern & Co., 1908.
Character complaint song recorded by Bob Roberts (Columbia); performed by Europe's Society Orchestra as dance music.

I Ain't Married No More
Words by Rennold Wolf, music by Les Copeland.
M. Witmark & Sons, 1917.
Bert Williams's comic complaint from the *Ziegfeld Follies of 1917.*

I Always Dream of Bill, see **Billy,.**

I Always Wish 'Twas You
Words and music by J. Louis MacEvoy.
Original copyright, 1902.
Art song introduced by Emma Nevada.

I Am Longing for Tomorrow When I Think of Yesterday
Words by Arthur Longbrake, music by Edward Edwards.
Original copyright, 1909.
Sentimental ballad of man left at the altar sung by Charles Bradley, Eleanor Cameron, and the team of Harvard and Cornell.

I Am So Particular
Words by Matt Woodward, music by Louis A. Hirsch.
Helf & Hager, 1908.
Character comedy song introduced by rag-time specialist Ethel Levey in the musical *Nearly a Hero* (1908).

I Called You My Sweetheart
Words by Howard Johnson and Grant Clarke, music by Jimmie V. Monaco.
Leo Feist Inc., 1917/Fred Fisher Music Co.
Waltz ballad popularized by Neil McKinley and Willie Weston and recorded by Henry Burr (Columbia) and James F. Harrison (Victor).

I Can Always Find a Little Sunshine in the Y.M.C.A.
Words and music by Irving Berlin.
Irving Berlin Music Corp., 1918.
World War I tribute from *Yip Yip Yahank* (1918); recorded by the Peerless Quartet (Victor).

I Can Dance with Everybody But My Wife
Words and music by Joseph Cawthorne and John Golden.
Harms, Inc., 1916.
This comic character song introduced by Cawthorne in *Sybil* (musical, 1916) tells of a couple who "tangle when they tango;" recorded by Cawthorne (Victor), Billy Murray (Edison), and the Victor Military Band.

I Can Live without You
Words by Gene Buck, music by Dave Stamper.
Joseph W. Stern & Co., 1913.
Top-selling romantic song popularized by Elizabeth Brice as a solo and as a duet with partner Charles King in the *Ziegfeld Follies of 1913;* recorded by Olive Kline for Victor.

I Can't Get Enough of Your Love
Words and music by George White and Billy Gaston.
Will Rossiter, 1913.
Popularized and recorded by Sophie Tucker.

I Can't Help Dreaming of You
Words and music by Neal Byrden.
Original copyright, 1917.
Waltz ballad sung in vaudeville by Truly Shattuck and Marta Golden.

I Can't Help It
Words and music by Blanche Merrill.
Original copyright, 1910.
Answer song to Eva Tanguay's greatest success, "I Don't Care" (q. v.).

I Can't Reach That Top Note, also known as **The Belle of Brittany**
Words and music by David Worton and George Arthurs.
Original copyright, 1909.
Novelty song about unsuccessful opera singers popularized in London music halls by Wilkie Bard and Frank Daniels. Daniels introduced it to New York in the brief Broadway run of his *The Belle of Brittany* (1909).

I Can't Take My Eyes off You
Words by Rida Johnson Young, music by Paul Rubens.

Original copyright, 1904.
Romantic song for Constance Windom in *Three Little Maids* (1903).

I Can't Tell Why I Love You But I Do
Words by Will D. Cobb, music by Gus Edwards.
Howley, Haviland & Co., 1900/Paull-Pioneer Music Co., 1939/ Mills Music Inc., 1944.
Composer Edwards's first major success was introduced by Emma Carus, to whom it was dedicated, and featured by Clarice Vance, Harry MacDonough (Victrola), and Pryor's Band (Victor); revived in the late 1930's and 1940's in films ranging from the Edwards biography *The Star Maker* (Paramount, 1939) with Bing Crosby to International's *Belle of the Yukon* (1944) in which it was sung by Dinah Shore (Victor, V Disc).

I Can't Think of Nothing in the Wide, Wide World But You
Words by Bob Cole, music by J. Rosamond Johnson.
Joseph W. Stern & Co., 1907.
Ballad introduced in *The Shoo-Fly Regiment* (1908) and featured in Cole and Johnson's vaudeville act.

I Could Learn to Love You If You Let Me Try
Words and music by Verne C. Armstrong.
Original copyright, 1905.
This song was a vaudeville success for Emma Carus and Virginia Earl.

I Could Love You in a Steam Heat Flat
Words by Vincent Bryan, music by J. B. Mullen.
Harry Von Tilzer Music Publishing Co., 1903.
Novelty vaudeville number for Emma Carus about a woman who rejects suitors by citing song titles.

I Didn't Go Home at All
Words and music by Edgar Leslie and Irving Berlin.
Shapiro, Bernstein & Co., Inc., 1909.
Comic song for British music-hall star Alice Lloyd.

I Didn't Raise My Boy to Be a Soldier
Words by Alfred Bryan, music by Al Piantadosi.
Leo Feist Inc., 1915.
The most popular ballad of 1915 was sung in vaudeville by Gene Greene, Nellie V. Nichols, Will J. Ward, and many others and was recorded by Morton Harvey (Victor), the Peerless Quartet (Columbia), and Jaudas' Society Orchestra (Edison). Described in the *Pittsburgh Gazetter-Times* as "the song that would end the war," it was a controversial anthem for the anti-interventionist

movement in America before World War I. Among the many songs specifically protesting Bryan's ballad as unpatriotic were Jack Crawford's "My Mother Raised Her Boy to Be a Soldier" (1915) and Dempsey and Burke's "If I Had a Son for Each Star in Old Glory..." (1917, q.v).

I Don't Care
Words by Jean Lenox, music by Harry O. Sutton.
Remick Music Corp., 1905/Jerry Vogel Music Co., Inc., 1938.
Eva Tanguay's signature tune was part of her vaudeville act from 1905 to her retirement; featured on *They Stopped the Show!* (Audio Rarities) from the late 1910's. When it was revived for film, it was still identified with her, by Judy Garland's character in *In the Good Old Summertime* (MGM, 1949) and by Mitzi Gaynor in Tanguay's biographical film *The "I Don't Care" Girl* (20th Century Fox, 1953). Even Joan Morris's recording on her *Vaudeville* album (Nonesuch) does not use the full song, which included eight verses of topical parodies of, at various times, Theodore Roosevelt and his Presidential opponent, Alton B. Parker, William Randolph Hearst, the Russo-Japanese War, and the "Great Vaudeville War," between Tanguay and Gertrude Hoffmann.

I Don't Feel No Way Tired
Words and music by H. T. Burleigh.
G. Ricordi & C., SpA, Milan, Italy, 1917, 1919.
Performed and recorded as a spiritual by Marian Anderson, James Cleveland (Savoy), and the Mighty Clouds of Joy (MYRR).

I Don't Like Them Minstrel Folks, see **When Mr. Shakespeare Comes to Town,**.

I Don't Want To
Words and music by A. Seymour Brown.
Original copyright, 1913.
Novelty song about a honeymoon popularized in vaudeville by Daisy Leon, Emma O'Neil, and Florence Timponi.

I Don't Want to Get Well
Words by Harry Pease and Howard Johnson, music by Harry Jentes.
Leo Feist Inc., 1917.
World War I novelty song of a wounded soldier in love with his nurse; recorded by Gus Van and Joe Schenck (Victor) and by Arthur Fields (Columbia, Edison); revived for World War II by Kay Kyser and His Orchestra (Brunswick).

I Gave Her That
Words and music by Bud De Sylva and Al Jolson.
T. B. Harms, 1919.
Jolson novelty song interpolated into the musical *Sinbad* and recorded by him on Columbia and by Ernest Hare on Pathe. One version is romantic with compliments to the sweetheart's "dress... look of happiness... eyes of black"; an alternate lyric includes a couplet about "the left is blacker than the right ... I gave her that."

I Get Dippy When I Do That Two-Step Dance
Words by Edgar Selden, music by Bert Fitzgibbon and Louis Fitzgibbon.
Shapiro, Bernstein & Co., Inc., 1907.
Descriptive dance song that includes references to individual steps ("dip," "glide," "slide") performed by Clara Thropp and recorded by Arthur Collins (Columbia).

I Got a Rock
Words and music by Blanche Merrill.
Charles K. Harris Music Publishing Co., 1911.
Italian-dialect comedy song about a wife anticipating the return of her errant husband; popularized by Lillian Shaw.

I Guess I'll Take the Train Back Home
Words by Jeffrey T. Branen, music by Billee Taylor.
Original copyright, 1906.
Interpolated by Taylor into *Comin' thro' the Rye* (1906).

I Hate to Lose You, also known as **I'm So Used to You Now**
Words by Grant Clarke, music by Archie Gottler.
Waterson, Berlin & Snyder, 1918/Blossom Music Corp., 1945/Fred Fisher Music Co., 1946.
Close-harmony specialty recorded by the Peerless Quartet (Victor) and revived in the 1940's by the Andrews Sisters, the Barry Sisters, and Benny Goodman (Capitol).

I Hates to Get Up Early in the Morning
Words by John Queen, music by Hugh Cannon.
Howley, Haviland & Dresser, 1901.
Comic song introduced by Peter F. Dailey in *Champagne Charlie* (musical, 1901).

I Have Just One Heart for Just One Boy
Words and music by Irving Berlin.
Irving Berlin Music Corp., 1918.
Romance explained by Julia Sanderson to the male chorus in *The Canary* (1918).

I Have Never Seen the Russian Ballet
Words and music by Elsa Maxwell.
Original copyright, 1916.
Comic song, also titled " I Will Never Dally with the Russian Ballet," written for Marie Dressler in her role as a over-cultured socialite in the operetta *Melinda and Her Sisters;* given a single performance in 1916 as a benefit for the New York Suffragist campaign. Dressler retained the song in her vaudeville act until the conclusion of the Diaghilev Ballet Russe tour of America in 1916-1917.

I Have Shed My Last Tears for You
Words by N. H. Jefferson, music by Chris Smith.
Joseph W. Stern & Co., 1914.
Sentimental ballad in close harmony sung by Willie and Eugene Howard.

I Hear You Calling Me
Words by Harold Harford, music by Charles Marshall.
Boosey & Hawkes Inc., 1908.
Art song associated with John McCormack (Victor, Victrola, Columbia) and also recorded by Henry Scott (Cameo), Charles Harrison (Victor), Elizabeth Spencer (Edison), and Lucrezia Bori (Victor, Victrola).

I Introduced
Words and music by Cole Porter.
T. B. Harms, 1919.
Typical Porter list novelty (also known as "I Presented") introduced by Raymond Hitchcock, star and producer of the revue *Hitchy-Koo of 1919.*

I Just Can't Help from Lovin' That Man
Words by Andrew B. Sterling and Vincent P. Bryan, music by Harry von Tilzer.
Harry Von Tilzer Music Publishing Co., 1902.
Bluesy song introduced by May Irwin and featured by Billy Single Clifford.

I Just Can't Keep My Eyes Off You
Words by Lester A. Walton, music by Will H. Vodery and Ernest Hogan.
M. Witmark & Sons, 1907.
Romantic ballad introduced by Hogan, billed as "the unbleached American," in his vehicle *The Oyster Man* (1907).

I Just Can't Make My Eyes Behave
Words and music by Will D. Cobb and Gus Edwards.

Gus Edwards Music Publishing Co., 1906/Shapiro, Bernstein & Co., Inc., 1936.
The prototypical Anna Held song introduced in *A Parisian Model* (1906) and featured in all of her vaudeville and cabaret performances thereafter; recorded by Ada Jones (Standard, Edison) and revived by Joan Morris on her *Vaudeville* album.

I Just Can't Make My Feet Behave
Words by Harold Atteridge, music by Sigmund Romberg and Jean Schwartz.
Remick Music Corp., 1918.
Introduced by Adele Astaire as "Miss Dansant" in the *Passing Show of 1918.*

I Just Couldn't Do without You
Words by Paul West, music by Jerome Kern.
T. B. Harms, 1907.
Ballad interpolated by Edna Wallace Hopper into the play *The White Chrysanthemum* (1907).

I Knew at First Sight That I Loved You
Words and music by Addison Burkhardt and Raymond Hubbell.
Charles K. Harris Music Publishing Co., 1903.
Ballad introduced by Pauline Hall.

I Know What It Means to Be Lonesome
Words and music by James Kendis, James Bockman, and Nat Vincent.
Leo Feist Inc., 1919.
A two-time ASCAP top seller in recordings by Henry Burr (Victor) and Margaret Freer (Edison) and in the revival by Connee Boswell (Decca).

I Know Why--Because I'm in Love with You
Words by Benny Davis, music by Ted Lewis and Jimmy Morgan.
Irving Berlin Music Corp., 1919/Shawnee Press, Inc.
Featured by vocalist and band leader Ted Lewis in the *Greenwich Village Follies of 1919* and on Columbia 78's; also recorded by Selvin's Novelty Orchestra (Victor).

I Live Up-Town
Words by Alfred Bryan, music by George W. Meyer.
F. B. Haviland, 1911.
Flirtation song set on a subway introduced by Tempest and Sunshine, a sister act in which Florenz Tempest played male roles; recorded by Ada Jones and Walter Van Brunt (Standard Disc).

I Lost My Heart in Dixieland
Words and music by Irving Berlin.
Irving Berlin Music Corp., 1919.
Introduced and recorded by Harry Fox (Columbia).

I Love a Lassie, also known as **Ma Scotch Bluebell** (English)
Words and music by Harry Lauder and Gerald Grafton.
Francis, Day & Hunter, Inc., 1905/T. B. Harms, 1905.
Lauder's most famous Scottish dialect romance, recorded for Victor.

I Love a Piano
Words and music by Irving Berlin.
Waterson, Berlin & Snyder, 1915/Irving Berlin Music Corp.
Novelty rag introduced by Harry Fox with six pianos in *Stop! Look! Listen!* (musical, 1915); recorded by Billy Murray (Victor), Arthur Collins and Byron G. Harlan (Little Wonder), and Blossom Seeley (Mercury); best known from Judy Garland and Fred Astaire's revival for *Easter Parade* (MGM, 1948).

I Love But One, I Love But You
Words by Julian Jordon, music by Henrietta Markstein.
Joseph W. Stern & Co., 1900.
Art song introduced by Zelie de Lussan and popular in the early 1900's as a wedding aria.

I Love But You
Words and music by Anna Chandler, Gus Chandler, and Dave Dreyer.
Shapiro, Bernstein & Co., Inc., 1917.
Romantic ballad introduced and recorded by Anna Chandler.

I Love Her Oh! Oh! Oh!
Words by Joe McCarthy and E. P. Moran, music by James V. Monaco.
Broadway Music Corp., 1913, 1940.
Introduced by Al Jolson in *The Honeymoon Express* (1913) but most associated with his arch-rival Eddie Cantor, who recorded it for Victor; also recorded as a turkey trot by Conway's Band (Victor) and by Enoch Light and His Clover Leaf Four (Lincoln).

I Love My Babe, My Baby Loves Me
Words by J. Leubrie Hill, music by J. Rosamond Johnson.
Remick Music Corp., 1911.
Duet with patter recorded by Jan Garber and His Orchestra (Capitol) as a one-step.

I Love My Billy Sunday But Oh, You Saturday Night
Words by Edgar Leslie and Grant Clarke, music by George W. Meyer.
Waterson, Berlin & Snyder, 1917.
The most topical of the "I Love My ____, But Oh, You ____" genre (see below), it was popular during the evangelist's ten-week revival in New York City (April-June, 1917) and included in the repertories of almost every comic/vocalist, among them, Eddie Cantor and Al Jolson. The song is based on the pun of Sunday's name and the New York Blue Laws that prohibited alcohol, theatre, and baseball on Sundays, mandating Saturday night as appropriate for social dating and drinking; additional topical material in the lyrics refer to Elinor Glyn's banned novel *Three Weeks.*

I Love My Husband But Oh You Henry
Words by Edgar Selden, music by Herbert Ingraham.
Shapiro, Bernstein & Co., Inc., 1909.
Answer song to "I Love My Wife But Oh, You Kid!" (q.v.) with a literary pun on popular novelist O. Henry; sung by Georgie Kelly and Kathryn Ryan.

I Love My Shirt Waist Best
Words and music by George V. Hobart.
Original copyright, 1900.
Celebration of separate blouses and skirts introduced by Peter F. Dailey in *Hodge, Podge & Co.* (1900), a musical comedy noted for its semi-dressed female chorus.

I Love My Steady, But I'm Crazy for My Once-in-a-While
Words by Irving Hinkley, music by Allan W. S. MacDuff.
Original copyright, 1910.
Novelty romance using contemporary slang terms, popularized by Al Jolson and Carrie Starr.

I Love My Wife But Oh, You Kid!
Words and music by Harry Armstrong and Billy Clark.
Original copyright, 1909/Jerry Vogel Music Co., Inc., 1937.
Popularized by Daphne Pollard in vaudeville and by Billy Murray on records (Victor), the comic song was the basis of a long series of punch lines and other songs, such as Branen and Lange's "I Love My Wife But Oh, Her Family! (1909), Harry von Tilzer's "I Love, I Love, I Love My Wife, But Oh, You Kid" (1909) and others above and below.

I Love the Heart of Dixie
Words by Alfred Bryan, music by Al Jolson and Jean Schwartz.
Remick Music Corp., 1918.

One of a score of Dixie nostalgia songs interpolated serially into *Sinbad* (1918) by Al Jolson.

I Love the Moon (English)
Words and music by Paul A. Rubens.
Chappell & Co., Ltd., London, England, 1902/T. B. Harms, 1902.
Romantic ballad from *Three Little Maids* (1901, London; 1902, New York); revived successfully by Rudy Vallee and Richard Tauber (Parlophone).

I Love the U.S.A.
Words and music by Will Hardy.
Original copyright, 1915.
Temperance anthem for the Flying Squadron for Constitutional Prohibition.

I Love to Quarrel with You
Words and music by Irving Berlin.
Waterson, Berlin & Snyder, 1914/Bourne Co.
Duet novelty associated with the juvenile vaudeville act of Fred and Adele Astaire.

I Love to Sit and Look at You
Words by Edward Madden, music by Pat Rooney.
Shapiro, Bernstein & Co., Inc., 1908.
Romantic ballad sung by Jack Gardner to the title character in *Fluffy Ruffles* (musical, 1908) and later used in Rooney's own flirtation act with his wife Marion Bent.

I Love You All the Time
Words and music by Will R. Anderson.
M. Witmark & Sons, 1904.
Romantic ballad introduced by Hattie Williams in *The Girl from Kay's* (1903) and recorded by Harry MacDonough (Victor).

I Love You Dolly
Words by George V. Hobart, music by Max Hirschfield.
Joseph W. Stern & Co., 1903.
Doll song interpolated by Blanche Ring into *The Jewel of Asia* (1903).

I Love You Just the Same, Sweet Adeline
Words and music by Harry Armstrong and Clarence Gaskill.
M. Witmark & Sons, 1919.
Answer song to "Sweet Adeline," (q.v.) on the occasion of the fictional characters' golden anniversary; recorded by the Premier Quartet (Edison).

I Love You, Ma Cherie (American-English)
Words and music by Paul Rubens.
Original copyright, 1900.
Ballad introduced by Edna May and recorded by Henri Leoni (Victor).

I Love You So (American-English)
Words by Adrian Ross, music by Franz Lehar.
Chappell & Co., Inc., 1907/T. B. Harms, 1907.
Soon after the London premiere of *The Merry Widow* in June, 1907, American producers planned Broadway and touring productions here. Henry W. Savage, who won the race to open his New York production first, arranged for the London show's lyrics to the Lehar score to be published in the United States in an attempt to establish that version as the "official" *Merry Widow.* Although Adrian Ross was not credited in Savage's first printing with T. B. Harms, the lyrics to this version of the waltz are definitly his creation. Ross's waltz was introduced by Joseph Coyne and Lily Elsie in London and by Donald Brian and Ethel Jackson in New York. It can be heard on the Dorothy Kirstein/Robert Rounseville 1952 recording of the operetta on Columbia and on Eleanor Steber's early recording for Victor.

I Love You Truly
Words and music by Carrie Jacobs-Bond.
Boston Music Co., 1901, 1906.
Originally published as one of seven art songs by Jacobs-Bond, it became an international standard, associated with wedding ceremonies; recorded by opera singers, such as Helen Traubel (Columbia), Frances Alda (Victor), and Lauritz Melchior (Victor), as well as popular film vocalists Allan Jones, Perry Como, and Jeanette MacDonald (each on Victor).

I May Be Crazy But I Ain't No Fool
Words and music by Alex Rogers.
Gotham-Attucks Music Publishing Co., 1904.
Ironic character song introduced by Bert Williams.

I May Be Gone for a Long, Long Time
Words by Lew Brown, music by Albert von Tilzer.
Broadway Music Corp., 1917.
Soldier's ballad introduced by Grace LaRue in the revue *Hitchy-Koo of 1917;* recorded by Edison's Shannon Quartet and by Columbia's Peerless Quartet.

I Might Be Your "Once in a While"
Words by Robert B. Smith, music by Victor Herbert.
T. B. Harms, 1919.

Romantic ballad that has become a standard, introduced in *Angel Face* (musical, 1919) and interpolated into *Sweethearts* in its 1947 revival; early recordings were made by Arthur Fields (Pathe), Olive Kline (Victor), and Joseph C. Smith's Orchestra (Victor).

I Miss You in a Thousand Different Ways
Words by Will D. Cobb, music by Gus Edwards.
Gus Edwards Music Publishing Co., 1906.
Romantic ballad popularized by Willie Solar and Nellie McCoy.

I Must Have Been a-Dreamin'
Words and music by Bob Cole.
Howley, Haviland & Co., 1900.
Ballad featured in vaudeville by Harcourt and May and recorded by the Four Clefs on Bluebird.

I Need the Money
Words and music by Raymond A. Browne.
Sol Bloom Publishing Co/Sol Bloom Music, 1900.
Comic song introduced by Attie Spencer at Koster & Bial's Music Hall, New York City.

I Never Knew
Words by Elsie Janis, music by Irving Berlin.
Irving Berlin Music Corp., 1919.
Ballad co-authored and introduced by Janis in her *Her Gang* revues; recorded by Arthur Fields (Emerson) and George Meader (Columbia).

I Never Knew How Much I Loved You Until There Was Somebody Else
Words by Frank Fay, music by Dave Dreyer.
Harry Von Tilzer Music Publishing Co., 1919.
Bluesy ballad introduced by Fay in his vehicle *Oh, Mamma* (1919).

I Remember You
Words by Vincent Bryan, music by Harry von Tilzer.
Harry Von Tilzer Music Publishing Co., 1908.
Comic song about a young woman rejecting a masher. Introduced by Louise Dresser in *The Girls from Gottenburg* (musical, 1908).

I Sent My Wife to the 1000 Isles
Words by Andrew Sterling and Ed Moran, music by Harry von Tilzer.
Harry Von Tilzer Music Publishing Co., 1916.
Husband celebrating wife's absence introduced by Jolson in *Robinson Crusoe, Jr.* (1916) and recorded by him on Columbia;

also recorded by Billy Murray (Victor) and by Prince's Orchestra (Columbia) as a one-step.

I Sing a Little Tenor
Words by Harry Linton, music by John Gilroy.
Howley, Haviland & Dresser, 1902/Jerry Vogel Music Co., Inc., 1939.
Comic novelty about vocal ranges (and bad singers). Introduced by Al Hart in *The Wild Rose* (1902).

I Think I Could Be Awfully Good to You
Words by Will D. Cobb, music by Kerry Mills.
Mills Music Inc., 1905.
Flirtatious song introduced by Emma Carus.

I Think It Must Be Love
Words by Raymond A. Browne, music by Leo Friedman.
Sol Bloom Publishing Co/Sol Bloom Music, 1901.
Novelty romance relating illness to love; introduced by Frank Lalor in *The Press Agent* (musical, 1901).

I Think of Thee
Words and music by T. C. Weston, Sr.
Original copyright, 1903.
Ballad popularized by Mabel Talliaferro.

I Think You're Absolutely Wonderful (What Do You Think of Me?)
Words by Joe McCarthy, music by Harry Carroll.
Original copyright, 1918.
Romance introduced by Harry Fox in *Oh, Look!* (musical, 1918).

I Thought I Wanted Opera
Words and music by Max Hoffmann.
Conductor and arranger Hoffmann Specialized in "ragging the classics." In this song, which Maud Raymond introduced in *The Young Turk* (1910), he adapted themes from Puccini and Wagner.

I Thought My Troubles Were Over, But They'd Scarce Begun
Words by Roger Gray, music by Stephen O. Jones.
F. B. Haviland, 1906.
Typical "situation tragedy" song and monologue interpolated by Bert Williams into his musical *Abyssinia* (1906).

I Told My Love to the Roses
Words by J. A. Middleton, music by J. Rosamond Johnson.
G. Schirmer Inc., 1916.

Art song, published with "Morning, Noon, and Night" (q.v.), popularized and recorded by Louis Graveure.

I Want a Gibson Man
Words and music by Edward Madden.
Remick Music Corp., 1907.
One of a continuing series of "Fluffy Ruffles" and "Gibson Girl" songs written for Gertrude Hoffmann's vaudeville acts.

I Want a Girl Just Like the Girl That Married Dear Old Dad
Words by Will Dillon, music by Harry von Tilzer.
Harry Von Tilzer Music Publishing Co., 1911, 1938/Jerry Vogel Music Co., Inc., 1938.
Ballad sung on the occasion of the character's parents' anniversary has become a classic example of the period's bathetic but powerful music; featured by Al Jolson in recordings (Decca, Columbia), on radio, and in *The Jolson Story* (Columbia, 1946). Also recorded by the American Quartet (Victor, 1911) and revived by Sammy Kaye (Victor) and by Frankie Carle (V Disc, Columbia).

I Want a Little Lovin' Sometimes
Words and music by Chris Smith.
T. B. Harms, 1911.
Associated with Marie Cahill who interpolated it into *Judy Forgot* (1910) and *The Opera Ball* (1912); recorded by Edna Brown on Victor.

I Want a Man Made to Order for Me
Words by Arthur Gillespie, words and music by Nat D. Mann.
M. Witmark & Sons, 1905.
Novelty song introduced by Zelma Rawlston in *The Earl and the Girl* (1905); succeeding verses describe the ideal man from Germany, Italy, and Ireland; the choruses are in the respective dialects.

I Want a Real Nice Man, also known as **Call 00-00-00-00-0**
Words and music by Belle Blanche.
Shapiro, Bernstein & Co., Inc., 1910.
Popularized and recorded by Blanche.

I Want Someone to Flirt with Me
Words by Barney Costello and Andrew Sterling, music by Albert von Tilzer.
York Music Corp., 1910.
Romance popularized by Vera Hoppe, Louise Meyers, and the juvenile Irish dialect singer Baby Athlone.

I Want Something New to Play With
Words by Will D. Cobb, music by Gus Edwards.
Original copyright, 1911.
Juvenile novelty song about a child requesting a baby brother; as performed by Anna Held, however, the song took on a suggestive tone.

I Want to Be a Drummer in the Band
Words by Matt C. Woodward, music by Silvio Hein.
Shapiro, Bernstein & Co., Inc., 1902.
Novelty song introduced by Arthur Dunn in the title role in the play *Huckleberry Finn* (1902).

I Want to Be a Lidy (American-English)
Words by George Dance, music by George Dee.
Ascherberg, Hopwood & Crew, Ltd., London, England, 1901.
Cockney novelty song introduced by Miss Louie Freear in *A Chinese Honeymoon* (London, 1901; New York, 1902), and recorded by Ed. M. Favor (Zon-o-phone).

I Want to Be a Merry Merry Widow
Words by Edward Madden, music by Theodore F. Morse.
F. B. Haviland, 1907.
Descriptive comedy song about fashionable styles in women's hats and corsets associated with the opera; popularized by Jeannette DuPre and Kathryn Pearl and recorded by Ada Jones (Victor).

I Want to Be a Prima Donna
Words by Edgar Malone, music by Tom Sherman.
M. Witmark & Sons, 1909.
Opera burlesque with comic references to Emma Eames, Caruso, Tetrazini, and critic Alan Dale; popularized by Florence Bindley and Maggie Cline.

I Want to Be a Soldier
Words and music by William Cahill.
Joseph W. Stern & Co., 1904.
Patriotic ballad introduced by Harry Ellis as part of a tableaux finale for the 1904 edition of Lew Dockstader's Minstrels.

I Want to Be an Actor Lady
Words by Vincent Bryan, music by Harry von Tilzer.
Harry Von Tilzer Music Publishing Co., 1902.
Topical parody of legitimate and popular theatre performed in vaudeville by juvenile Baby Zena Keefe.

I Want to Be in Dixie, see **I'm Going Back to Dixie,**.

I Want to Be Loved Like a Leading Lady
Words by Paul West, music by Herman Avery Wade.
Joseph W. Stern & Co., 1908.
Topical satire introduced by Louise Dresser in *The Girl behind the Counter* (1907) and later sung in that show by Kathryn Miley. The lyrics allude to the romantic power of matinee idols Henry Miller, William Favesham, E. Southern, and more recent stars: "I want a kiss that has steam to back it, like Andrew Mack or James K. Hackett." Revived in the 1980 tribute to turn-of-the century music *Tintypes* and included on the show's cast album.

I Want to Be Naughty Too
Words by Harry B. Smith, music by Ludwig Englander.
Joseph W. Stern & Co., 1908.
Flirtatious song introduced by Anna Held in *Miss Innocence* (1908).

I Want to Go Back to Michigan
Words and music by Irving Berlin.
Waterson, Berlin & Snyder, 1914/B. Feldman & Co., Ltd., 1914.
An ASCAP top seller in 1914 and thirty years later, it was originally popularized in vaudeville by Daisy James, Frank Mullane, and Bobbie Russell and recorded by Morton Harvey; Judy Garland revived it as her first song in *Easter Parade* (MGM, 1948) and kept it in her concert repertory.

I Want to Go Back to the Land of Cotton
Words and music by Eddie Leonard.
Joseph W. Stern & Co., 1908.
Dixie nostalgia production number for Leonard's minstrel show.

I Want to Go to Paree, Papa
Words and music by George M. Cohan.
Original copyright, 1903.
Comic romance introduced by Josephine Cohan in *Running for Office* (1903).

I Want to Learn to Jazz Dance
Words by Gene Buck, music by Dave Stamper.
Concord Music, Ltd., London, England, 1918/T. B. Harms.
Reflexive song from the *Ziegfeld Follies of 1918* that refers to the revue's s pecialty dancers by name.

I Want to Linger
Words by Stanley Murphy, music by Henry I. Marshall.
Remick Music Corp., 1914.
This romance popularized by Baby Zena Keefe refers to the "Linger Longer" series (q.v.).

I Want to Look Like Lillian Russell
Words by Channing Pollock and Rennold Wolf, music by Charles J. Gebest.
Remick Music Corp., 1913.
Topical novelty song about contemporary actresses and their most admired physical attributes, from Raymond Hitchcock's musical *The Beauty Shop* (1914).

I Want to See My Ida Hoe in Idaho
Words by Alex Sullivan, music by Bert Rule.
M. Witmark & Sons, 1918.
Jazzed-up rural nostalgia song performed by the Duncan Sisters in vaudeville and in *Tip-Top* (musical, 1920).

I Want to Shimmie
Words and music by Shelton Brooks and Grant Clarke.
Leo Feist Inc., 1919.
Bee Palmer's "shimmie" specialty song lists passe popular dances.

I Want to Spoon to the Tune of the Silvery Moon
Words and music by Gus Edwards.
Gus Edwards Music Publishing Co., 1911.
Generic flirtation number included in Edwards's *Song Revue of 1911.*

I Want to Spread a Little Sunshine
Words and music by Clifton Crawford.
Francis, Day & Hunter, Ltd., London, England, 1919/T. B. Harms, 1919.
Romantic ballad introduced by Crawford in his musical *My Lady Friends* (tour company, 1919); popularized and recorded by Jack Norworth (Pathe).

I Want What I Want When I Want It
Words by Henry Blossom, music by Victor Herbert.
M. Witmark & Sons, 1905.
Plutocratic claims made by William Pruette in *Mlle. Modiste* (1905); revised for the Broadway revue (and recording) *Tintypes* (1980). Recorded by Lauritz Melchior for the MGM film *Thrill of a Romance* (1945).

I Wants a Man Like Romeo
Words by James O'Dea, music by Robert Adams.
Original copyright, 1902.
Novelty song about a stage-struck woman popularized by Nellie Burt.

I Wants to Be the Leading Lady
Words by George Totten Smith, music by Harry von Tilzer.
Shapiro, Bernstein & Co., Inc., 1901.
Novelty song with topical backstage references popularized by Flossie Allen and Helene Mora.

I Wants to Be the Villain in the Show
Words and music by Stanley Crawford.
Shapiro, Bernstein & Co., Inc., 1902.
Comic song with descriptions of melodrama popularized by Claude Thardo.

I Was So Young, You Were So Beautiful
Words by Irving Caesar and Al Bryan, music by George Gershwin (pseudonym for Jacob Gershovitz).
T. B. Harms, 1919.
Romantic duet introduced by Charles and Mollie King in *Good Morning, Judge* (musical, 1919); recorded as dance music by Joseph C. Smith's Orchestra for Victor.

I Went to See Them March Away
Words by S. E. Keisser, music by R. J. Jose.
Howley, Haviland & Co., 1902.
Sentimental ballad introduced by Jose; concerns a veteran whose son died in the Spanish-American War and, in verse 3, is buried in Cuba.

I Wish I Could Shimmy Like My Sister Kate
Words and music by A. J. Piron.
Clarence Williams Music, 1919/Pickwick Music Corp., 1941, 1950, 1962.
Descriptive song promoting the "Shimmie" that, like the dance, speeds up to the finish. Always considered a novelty, it was recorded by Clarence Williams and Eva Taylor on Okeh, Leonia Williams and Her Dixie Band (Columbia), the California Ramblers (Vocalion), and Helen Forrest (MGM).

I Wish I Had a Girl
Words by Gus Kahn, music by Grace LeBoy.
Original copyright, 1907/Remick Music Corp., 1909/Robbins Music Corp., 1951.
Kahn and LeBoy's first major hit was popularized by Grace LaRue as an interpolation in *Nearly a Hero* (1908) and in her own vaudeville act. It was recorded by Billy Murray (Victor) and Al Jolson (Decca) in the 1910's; after Doris Day sang the ballad in the Kahn biographical film *I'll See You in My Dreams* (Warner Brothers, 1951), it was recorded and re-popularized by her with Paul Weston, Alvino Rey, and Arthur Godfrey (Columbia).

I Wish I Had My Old Girl Back Again
Words by Ballard MacDonald, music by Paul Wallace.
Joseph W. Stern & Co., 1909.
Performances of the nostalgic ballad by minstrel tenors, such as Glen Ellison and Thomas Davis, and recordings of the innovation waltz versions by Manuel Romain, Art Gillham ("The Whispering Pianist"), and Mike Speciale and His Bamboo Gardens Orchestra made this a top-seller of 1909.

I Wonder If They're True to Me
Words and music by Nora Bayes (pseudonym for Dora Goldberg).
Remick Music Corp., 1908.
Novelty romance popularized by Bayes with a parody of a different style of nostalgia song (relating to a different lover) in each verse.

I Wonder If You Love Me
Words by Mabel Hite, music by Tom Kelly.
Shapiro, Bernstein & Co., Inc., 1910.
Ballad popularized by Hite in vaudeville.

I Wonder If You're Lonely
Words by Ned Wayburn, music by George Byrd Dougherty.
Romantic ballad introduced by Flora Parker in *The Girl and the Wizard* (musical, 1909).

I Wonder What Will William Tell
Words by Thomas S. Allen.
Original copyright, 1914.
Originally credited "with apologies to Rossini," the comic song adapted the *Lone Ranger* theme to relate the story of little brother Will spying on his older sister and her beau. It was sung in vaudeville by juveniles such as the Charles Twins, the midget Little Jerry, and such adult women as Zella Russell; recorded by the Van Eps Trio for Victor.

I Wonder What's the Matter with My Eyes?
Words by Harry Williams, music by Egbert van Alstyne.
Remick Music Corp., 1908.
Sequel song to "I Just Can't Make My Eyes Behave" (q.v.). Introduced by Anna Held in *Miss Innocence* (musical, 1908).

I Wonder What's the Matter wiz My Oo-la-la
Words by Jack Frost, music by F. Henri Klickmann.
Original copyright, 1919.
Comic answer song to "How're You Gonna Keep 'Em Down on the Farm" (q.v.). Introduced by Eddie Cantor.

I Wonder Where My Easy Rider's Gone
Words and music by Shelton Brooks.
Will Rossiter, 1913/Edwin H. Morris Co.
Typical Brooks lament written for Sophie Tucker; uses the character of the errant jockey, "Easy" or "E. Z. Rider," from blues.

I Wonder Where My Lovin' Man Has Gone
Words by Earle C. Jones, music by Richard A. Whiting and Charles I. Cooke.
Remick Music Corp., 1914.
Dialect blues popularized by Gene Greene.

I Wonder Who's Kissing Her Now
Words by Will M. Hough and Frank R. Adams, music by Joseph E. Howard.
Charles K. Harris Music Publishing Co., 1909, 1929/Jerry Vogel Music Co., Inc., 1937.
Introduced by composer Howard in *The Prince of To-Night* (1909, Chicago), this most enduring of the Hough-Adams songs became the title of Howard's film biography. Major recordings by Henry Burr on early Columbia 78's, by Cliff Edwards for the Reliance B, *Red Salute*, and by Bobby Darin (Capitol) have maintained its popularity. Gerald Boardman, in his *Chronicles of the American Musical Theatre,* claims that the song was co-written by Harold Orlob.

I Wonder Why Bill Bailey Don't Come Home
Words and music by Frank Fogerty, Matt C. Woodward, and William Jerome.
Howley, Haviland & Dresser, 1902.
Answer song to "Bill Bailey, Won't You Please Come Home" (q.v.). Introduced by Fogerty. Lyrics refer to Bailey's wife writing for advice to Beatrice Fairfax (q.v.).

I Wonder Why She Kept On Saying Si Si Si Si Si Senor
Words by Joe Young and Sam Lewis, music by Ted Snyder.
Waterson, Berlin & Snyder, 1918.
Al Jolson introduced this novelty song about a Spanish seductress in *Sinbad* (1918) and recorded the song that year for Columbia.

I Won't Be an Actor Any More
Words and music by George M. Cohan.
Shapiro, Bernstein & Co., Inc., 1900.
Comic song describing the difficult conditions on a minstrel tour introduced by Frances Curren.

I Won't Come Back
Words by Harold Atteridge, music by Ted S. Barron.

M. Witmark & Sons, 1911.
Novelty dialogue song with patter interpolations written for Stella Mayhew and Billee Taylor in Winter Garden Midnight revues.

I Would If I Could But I Can't
Words and music by Manuel Romain.
Original copyright, 1903.
Ballad introduced and recorded by Romain.

I Would Like to Be Your Pal
Words and music by Junie McCree.
York Music Corp., 1905.
Proposal song introduced by McCree and Carrie Behr in *The Babes and the Baron* (musical, 1905).

I Would Like to Marry You
Words and music by Edward Laska.
Original copyright, 1905.
Proposal duet sung by Georgia Caine and Victor Morley in *The Earl and the Girl* (1905) and by Junie McCree and Carrie Behr on tour in *Babes in the Woods.*

I Wouldn't Give 'That' for the Man Who Couldn't Dance
Words and music by Irving Berlin.
Irving Berlin Music Corp., 1919.
Introduced by Julia Sanderson in *The Canary* (1918).

I-yay Ove-lay Oo-yay Earie-day, see **Pig Latin Love,**.

I'd Be Happy Anywhere with You
Words by Rida Johnson Young, music by Sigmund Romberg.
G. Schirmer Inc., 1916.
Romantic duet for Sidonie Spiro and Ward DeWolfe in *Her Soldier Boy* (1916); recorded by Bettina Bergere and George Wilton Ballard for Edison.

I'd Lay Down My Life for You
Words by Thomas J. Keating, music by Lyn Udall.
M. Witmark & Sons, 1901.
Plotted nuptial ballad introduced by Louise Dresser.

I'd Like to Be a Gunner in the Navy
Words by Harry B. Smith, music by Will Accooe.
Edward Schuberth & Co., Inc., 1901.
Comic song from *The Liberty Belles* (musical, 1901).

I'd Like to Be a Real Lady
Words by Alex Rogers, music by Tom Lemonier.

Shapiro, Bernstein & Co., Inc., 1902.
Introduced by Aida Overton Walker in *In Dahomey* (1903).

I'd Like to Be the Fellow That Girl Is Waiting For
Words by Ed Rose, music by Kerry Mills.
Mills Music Inc., 1909.
Novelty romance popularized by Frank Morrell, Jimmy Doherty, and Marie Fisher.

I'd Like to Live in Loveland with a Girl Like You
Words and music by W. R. Williams.
Original copyright, 1910.
Ballad introduced by Maud Lambert in *The Midnight Sons* (musical, 1910) and sung in vaudeville by her, Clara Nelson, and the violinist/vocalist Nonette. Bing Crosby revived the song with great success in the 1930's.

I'd Like to Meet Your Father
Words by M. E. Rourke, music by Jerome Kern.
T. B. Harms, 1907.
Julia Sanderson interpolated this early Kern romantic song into her vehicle *The Dairymaids* (1907) and popularized it in her vaudeville tours.

I'd Rather Love What I Cannot Have Than Have What I Cannot Love
Words and music by Elsie Janis.
Remick Music Corp., 1911.
Romantic ballad popularized by Janis and used in her wartime appearances to entertain the troupes and *Her Gang* tours throughout the decade.

I'd Rather See a Minstrel Show
Words and music by Irving Berlin.
Irving Berlin Music Corp., 1919.
Introduced by Eddie Cantor and Bert Williams as end-men of "The Follies Minstrels," in the Act I finale of the *Ziegfeld Follies of 1919.*

I'd Rather Two-Step Than Waltz, Bill
Words and music by Benjamin Hapgood Burt.
Remick Music Corp., 1907.
Introduced by Adele Ritchie as the title character in *Fascinating Flora* (1907), the topical song was adopted by rag-specialist Ethel Levey in vaudeville and London revue performances; recorded by Billy Murray and Clarice Vance on Victor.

Ida from Idaho
Words and music by John H. Flynn.
Mills Music Inc., 1901.
Top-selling song introduced by Grace Leonard.

Ida, Sweet as Apple Cider
Words by Eddie Leonard, music by Eddie Munson.
Joseph W. Stern & Co., 1903/Edward B. Marks Music Corp., 1920.
Eddie Leonard's hit from his minstrel tours became Eddie Cantor's theme song, adopted to honor his long-time wife, Ida. As well as Cantor's for Decca, vocalists and jazz instrumentalists who have made records of the song include Eddie Condon (Decca), Gene Kelly (MGM), Glenn Miller (Victor), and Red Nichols (Brunswick, Vocalion).

If a Boy Like You Loved a Girl Like Me
Words by Will D. Cobb, music by Gus Edwards.
Gus Edwards Music Publishing Co., 1905.
Romantic ballad introduced by Lillian Russell and recorded by Harry MacDonough on Victor. When Edwards's juvenile Newsboys included his song in their vaudeville act, it was warbled by Julius (soon to be Groucho) Marx.

If a Table at Rector's Could Talk
Words by Will D. Cobb, music by Raymond Hubbell.
T. B. Harms, 1913.
Introduced and recorded by Nat M. Wills in Ziegfeld's *Follies of 1913,* this topical comic song refers to the New York late night restaurant known as the site of assignations.

If Adam Hadn't Seen the Apple Tree
Words and music by Bob Cole.
Joseph W. Stern & Co., 1906.
Novelty introduced by Cole in *The Shoo-Fly Regiment* (1907).

If All My Dreams Were Made of Gold, I'd Buy the World for You
Words by J. F. Bradley and C. F. Quigley, music by George Christy.
M. Witmark & Sons, 1911.
Romantic ballad popularized by Christy's Minstrels, Reese Prosser of the Honey Boy Minstrels, Maud Lambert, Ernest Ball, and Emma Partridge; recorded and performed as well in barber-shop close harmony by the Orpheus Quartet.

If All the Stars Were Mine
Words by Harry B. Smith, music by John Stromberg.
Allan & Co., Melbourne, Australia, 1900.
Romantic ballad introduced by Carrie Moore as Maid Marian in the comic operetta *Robin Hood* (in a revival of the 1891 success)

and interpolated by Grace von Studdiford in the title role of its successor *Maid Marian* (1902).

If Anybody Wants to Meet a Jonah, Shake Hands with Me
Words and music by Harry Hoyt.
Shapiro, Bernstein & Co., Inc., 1906.
Signature tune for blues singer Clarice Vance in vaudeville. Songs about the bad luck character, also associated with Bert Williams, were frequently up-dated with topical references to new inventions (that didn't work), political scandals, and financial dealings in the news.

If He Can Fight Like He Can Love, Good Night Germany
Words by Grant Clarke and Howard E. Rogers, music by George W. Meyer.
Leo Feist Inc., 1918.
Patriotic version of a popular comic song style associated with Eddie Cantor and Rae Samuels. Sung and recorded by female teams, such as the Dream Girls and the Farber Sisters, and by solo men and women, among them, Maurice Burkhardt, Grace Wallace, Arthur Fields, and Eddie Nelson.

If He Comes In, I'm Going Out
Words by Cecil Mack, music by Chris Smith.
Original copyright, 1910/Mills Music Inc.
Novelty song about an unwanted guest at a seance. Introduced by Stella Mayhew in the roof garden show *A Barnyard Romeo* (1910); recorded by Ed Morton (Victor).

If I Could Only Sleep Like Rip Van Winkle
Words and music by Chris Smith.
Joseph W. Stern & Co., 1909.
Introduced by Eddie Leonard in his minstrel show.

If I Could Peep through the Window Tonight
Words and music by Joe McCarthy, Gus Van, and Joe Schenck.
Original copyright, 1918.
World War I nostalgic ballad for close-harmony team Van and Schenck.

If I Ever Get Back to Cincinnati
Words and music by Chris Smith and S. H. Dudley.
F. B. Haviland, 1906.
Introduced by Dudley with his Smart Set Company's production of *The Black Politician* (1906-1907).

If I Forget
Words by Alfred Anderson, music by DeKoven Thompson.
Art song introduced by Mme. Ernestine Schumann-Heink.

If I Had a Son for Each Star in Old Glory, Uncle Sam, I'd Give Them All to You
Words by J. E. Dempsey, music by Joseph A. Burke.
Leo Feist Inc., 1917.
Patriotic "Mother" song in answer to the pre-World War I "I Didn't Raise My Boy to Be a Soldier" (q.v.); popularized by Elizabeth Brice and Charles King, Larry Comer, and Monte Austin. The title refers to the "Service" flag with a star for each member of the family serving in the military forces.

If I Had My Way
Words by Lou Klein, music by James Kendis.
Original copyright, 1913/Paull-Pioneer Music Co., 1939.
After early popularity in performance and recordings by Ethel Green, Gene Austin, and the Peerless Quartet, the ballad became a major hit in 1940's radio and recordings by the top vocalists and teams, among them, Bing Crosby, Kate Smith, and the Mills Brothers. Bands that adopted the song included Guy Lombardo and His Royal Canadians, Meyer Davis' Hotel Astor Orchestra, Ray Noble and His Orchestra, and Glen Gray and the Casa Loma Orchestra.

If I Knock the 'L' Out of Kelly, It Still Would Be Kelly to Me
Words by Sam M. Lewis and Joe Young, music by Bert Grant.
Waterson, Berlin & Snyder, 1916.
Irish comic novelty song. Introduced by Marguerite Farrell in *Step This Way* (musical, 1916); recorded by Farrell, by the Victor Military Band, and by Frank Novak and His Rootin' Tootin' Boys.

If I Only Knew Just How I Stood with You
Words by Jean C. Havez, music by Gus Edwards.
Joseph W. Stern & Co., 1916.
Romantic song introduced by "Cuddles" Edwards (Lila Lee) in the feature act *Gus Edwards' Bandbox Revue* (1916-1917).

If I Should Die Before I Wake, How Will I Know I'm Dead?
Words by Thomas J. Gray, music by Bert A. Williams.
Joseph W. Stern & Co., 1910.
Williams's character monologue and song about a skeptic at a revival meeting.

If I Thought You Wouldn't Tell
Words by Irving Berlin, music by Ted Snyder.

Ted Snyder Music Publishing Co., 1909/Irving Berlin Music Corp.
Ballad popularized by Billy Oakes and Harry Leybourne.

If I Were a Bee and You Were a Red, Red Rose
Words and music by Shelton Brooks.
Kalmar, Puck & Abrahams Consolidated Mus, 1915.
Romantic duet introduced by Elizabeth Brice and Charles King.

If I Were on the Stage, see **Kiss Me Again,**.

If I Were Only Mister Morgan
Words and music by George M. Cohan.
George M. Cohan Music Publishing Co., 1903.
Topical comedy song introduced by Cohan in his *Running for Office* (1903); title refers to banker J. P. Morgan.

If She Means What I Think She Means
Words and music by Arthur J. Jackson and Bud De Sylva.
Remick Music Corp., 1918.
Comic song about American soldiers in Paris. Introduced by Frank Carter in the *Ziegfeld Follies of 1918.*

If That's Your Idea of a Wonderful Time, Take Me Home
Words and music by Irving Berlin.
Waterson, Berlin & Snyder, 1914/Irving Berlin Music Corp.
Novelty song complaining about a cheap date popularized and recorded by Ada Jones (Victor).

If the Wind Had Only Blown the Other Way
Words and music by Edna Williams and Bessie Wynn.
Joseph W. Stern & Co., 1909/Jerry Vogel Music Co., Inc., 1937.
Novelty comic song about the wind blowing open the drapery of a sheath gown; introduced by Wynn.

If They'd Only Fight the War with Wooden Soldiers
Words by Bert Fitzgibbon, music by Theodore F. Morse.
M. Witmark & Sons, 1915.
Pacifist song introduced by Fitzgibbon from the anti-Interventionist era preceeding World War I.

If We Can't Be the Same Old Sweethearts
Words by Joseph McCarthy, music by Jimmie V. Monaco.
Leo Feist Inc., 1915.
Romantic ballad first recorded by Rose Bryant and Henry Burr for Columbia; revived by Perry Como (RCA).

If Yankee Doodle Hadn't Come to Town
Words by Alfred Bryan, music by Silvio Hein.

Shapiro, Bernstein & Co., Inc., 1902.
Comic song introduced by Jerome Sykes in *The Billionaire* (musical, 1902) speculating on American society if the United States had lost the Revolutionary War and Edward VII was King of Washington.

If You Ain't Got It, Go and Get It
Words by Alfred Bryan, music by Chris Smith.
Remick Music Corp., 1909/Mills Music Inc.
Response to proposal, associated with Bert Williams.

If You Can't Be a Bell-Cow, Fall in Behind
Words by A. L. Robb, music by J. Fred Helf.
Sol Bloom Publishing Co/Sol Bloom Music, 1902.
Comic song about a nagging farmer's wife, popularized by Tascott the Great and Clarice Vance.

If You Can't Get a Girl in the Summertime, You'll Never Get a Girl at All
Words by Bert Kalmar, music by Harry Tierney.
Mills Music Inc., 1915.
Rollicking flirtatious advice popularized by Lou Lockett and Jack Waldron, Cissy Ramsden, Harry Tierney, and the violiste Lillian Mascot; Ada Jones's recording for Columbia was a top seller of 1916. Used in the 20th Century Fox period musical *Three Little Girls in Blue* (1946).

If You Can't Say Something Good, Don't Say Nothing at All
Words and music by Claude Thardo.
Helf & Hager, 1906.
Originally a dialect comedy for Thardo and rival minstrel vocalists, the chorus became a popular piano rag in the mid-1910's.

If You Don't Want Me
Words and music by Irving Berlin.
Waterson, Berlin & Snyder, 1913.
Bluesy lament introduced by Belle Baker and featured by Gladys Clark and Harry Bergman in Jesse Lasky's vaudeville feature act *The Trained Nurses* (1913-1914).

If You Don't Want Me, Send Me to My Ma
Words and music by Chris Smith and Cecil Mack.
Original copyright, 1916.
Classic blues introduced by Elida Morris and recorded by Arthur Collins (Rex), Morton Harvey (Emerson), and May Stafford and Her Jazz Band (Columbia).

If You Had All the World and Its Gold
Words by Harry Edelheit and Barney Costello, music by Al Piantadosi.
Al Piantadosi Music, 1916/Laurel Music Corp., 1944.
"The Greatest of All Mother Songs," as Eva Tanguay described this ballad, was re-popularized and recorded in the 1950's by the Ames Brothers and Perry Como.

If You Knew What I Know about Men
Words by Vincent Bryan, music by E. Ray Goetz.
Shapiro, Bernstein & Co., Inc., 1911.
Novelty song about a gossiping telephone switchboard operator. Introduced by Belle Blanche.

If You Love Your Baby Google Google All the Time
Words and music by Julia Rooney.
Shapiro, Bernstein & Co., Inc., 1908.
Flirtation song praising "goo-goo eyes" introduced by the Rooney Sisters---Julia and Josie.

If You Want a Little Doggie, Whistle and I'll Come to You
Words by Blanche Merrill, music by Leo Edwards.
Charles K. Harris Music Publishing Co., 1915.
Flirtatious song interpolated by Nora Bayes into *Maid in America* (1915).

If You Were the Only Girl in the World (English)
Words by Clifford Grey, music by Nat D. Ayer.
B. Feldman & Co., Ltd., London, England, 1916/Chappell & Co., Inc., 1916.
Introduced by George Robey and Violet Loraine in *The Bing Boys Are Here* (1916, London) and a popular favorite in British music halls as sung and recorded by Stanley Holloway on his *Join in the Chorus* album (Vanguard). Its American popularity came in later revivals by Rudy Vallee (in *The Vagabond Lover,* Radio Pictures, 1929, and on Victor), Dick Haymes (Decca) and Perry Como (RCA).

If You'll Walk with Me
Words by Edgar Selden, music by Paul Rubens.
Shapiro, Bernstein & Co., Inc., 1907.
Flirtatious duet introduced by William Rock and Topsy Siegrist in *The Girl behind the Counter* (1907).

I'll Be There, Mary Dear
Words by Andrew B. Sterling, music by Harry von Tilzer.
Harry Von Tilzer Music Publishing Co., 1902.
Plotted sentimental ballad of soldier returning from the Spanish-

American War. Introduced by Jenny Eddy; this was one of the few post-war ballads to deal with disabilities. Its chorus promises that "one arm will do to fold her to you."

I'll Be True to the Whole Regiment, see **Madelon,**.

I'll Be Waiting in the Gloaming, Sweet Genevieve
Words and music by J. Fred Helf.
Helf & Hager, 1905.
Dixie nostalgia ballad introduced by Harry A. Ellis and popular with minstrel troupes throughout the early twentieth century.

I'll Be with You Honey in the Springtime
Words and music by Harry Freeman.
M. Witmark & Sons, 1902.
Romance interpolated by Anna Laughlin as "Dorothy" in *The Wizard of Oz* (musical, 1902).

I'll Be With You Honey When It's Honeysuckle Time
Words and music by Olive Fields Newman.
Will Rossiter, 1910.
Romantic ballad performed by many of vaudeville's best-known vocalists, among them Frank Morrell, Kathryn Miley, and Suzanne Rocamora; also popular in a barber-shop quartet version arranged for the Imperial Comedy Quartette.

I'll Be with You When the Roses Bloom Again
Words by Will D. Cobb, music by Gus Edwards.
Mills Music Inc., 1901/Paull-Pioneer Music Co., 1928.
Plotted sentimental ballad that remained popular throughout the first third of the twentieth century; sung by Edward Flowers, Dorothy Morton, and Joseph Natus in vaudeville and recorded on Victor, Victrola, and Edison cylinders by Vernon Dalhart, Harry MacDonough, and Walter Scanlon.

I'll Be Your Rain-Beau
Words by Ed Gardinier, music by J. Fred Helf.
Sol Bloom Publishing Co/Sol Bloom Music, 1902.
Romance introduced by Emma Carus in *The Defender* (musical, 1902).

I'll Break the Fighting Line Like You Broke This Heart of Mine
Words by Will D. Cobb, music by Kerry Mills.
Mills Music Inc., 1905.
Military blues popularized by Flo Adler, song illustrator Charles Falke, and male soldier impersonator Della Fox.

I'll Change the Shadows to Sunshine
Words by George Graff, Jr., music by Ernest R. Ball.
M. Witmark & Sons, 1913.
Romantic ballad introduced by Maud Lambert; recorded soon after its composition by Harry Burr (Columbia), Mary Carson (Edison), and Helen Clark (Victor).

I'll Come Back to You When It's All Over
Words by Lew Brown, music by Kerry Mills.
Leo Feist Inc., 1917.
World War I ballad performed in vaudeville by Frank Mullane, Ruth Roland, and Elsie White and recorded during the war by Prince's Band and Arthur Fields.

I'll Get You
Words by Will D. Cobb, music by Gus Edwards.
Remick Music Corp., 1913.
Romantic duet introduced by Gaby Deslys and Harry Pilcer in Winter Garden performances and also featured by George Jessel and Ethel Movey in their vaudeville act; recorded as a fox-trot by Polla's Clover Garden Orchestra and as a vocal solo by Helen Clarke (Victor).

I'll Keep a Warm Spot in My Heart for You
Words by James Weldon Johnson, music by J. Rosamond Johnson.
Joseph W. Stern & Co., 1906.
Ballad introduced by Aida Overton Walker in the musical *Abyssinia* (1906).

I'll Lend You Everything I've Got Except My Wife
Words by Jean C. Havez, music by Harry von Tilzer.
Harry Von Tilzer Music Publishing Co., 1910/Jerry Vogel Music Co., Inc., 1937.
Recorded and performed by Bert Williams in Ziegfeld's *Follies of 1910.*

I'll Never Love Another Like I Love You
Words by Will D. Cobb, music by Gus Edwards.
Shapiro, Bernstein & Co., Inc., 1904.
Ballad introduced by Bessie Wynn.

I'll Say She Does
Words and music by Bud De Sylva, Gus Kahn, and Al Jolson.
Remick Music Corp., 1918.
Jolson introduced this suggestive song into *Sinbad* (1918) and recorded it that year; also recorded as a comic song by Ernest Hare and Eddie Nelson and as a fox-trot by Yerkes' Jazarimba Band and Bob Wills and the Texas Playboys.

I'll Still Believe in You
Words and music by Al Piantadosi.
Leo Feist Inc., 1913.
Ballad of faith in an errant lover; popularized by Emma Carus.

I'll Take You Back to Italy
Words and music by Irving Berlin.
Irving Berlin Music Corp., 1917.
Berlin's Italian-dialect hit was introduced by Fred Stone in his *Jack O'Lantern* (1917); as the organ grinder hero, Stone offered to give his monkey to Irene Castle, known for her advocacy of animal shelters; recorded by Ada Jones and Billy Murray for Victor.

I'll Wed You in the Golden Summertime
Words by Alfred Bryan, music by Stanley Crawford.
Shapiro, Bernstein & Co., Inc., 1902.
Romantic ballad introduced by John P. Curran.

I'm a Bringing Up the Family
Words and music by Irene Franklyn and Burt Greene.
Leo Feist Inc., 1909.
Comic song introduced by Irene Franklyn, who specialized in juvenile characters in her vaudeville act.

I'm a Crazy Daffydil
Words by Bessie McCoy, music by Jerome Kern.
T. B. Harms, 1911.
Novelty comic song with riddles and puns; introduced by McCoy in Ziegfeld's *Follies of 1911*.

I'm a Jonah Man
Words and music by Alex Rogers.
M. Witmark & Sons, 1903.
The archetypal character song for Bert Williams; introduced in the musical *In Dahomey* (1903); also recorded by Arthur Collins (Victor).

I'm a Lady
Words by Ed Gardinier, music by Maurice Levi.
Comic character portrait introduced by Hattie Williams in the musical *The Rogers Brothers at Harvard* (1902).

I'm a Lonesome Melody
Words by Joe Young, music by George W. Meyer.
Kalmar, Puck & Abrahams Consolidated Mus, 1915.
Novelty song about a melody begging to be syncopated; popularized by Ed Morton, Claire Rochester, Bert and Betty Wheeler, and the

Manhattan Trio; recorded by Olive North for Victor and George Wilton Ballard for Edison cylinders.

I'm a Member of the Midnight Crew
Words by William Jerome, music by Jean Schwartz.
Shapiro, Bernstein & Co., Inc., 1909.
Comic character song associated with young male performers such as Carter De Haven and McKee Richmond. The "Midnight Crew" referred to young men-about-town who habituated Broadway cabarets and roof gardens after dark.

I'm a Poor Unhappy Maid
Words by William Jerome, music by Jean Schwartz.
Shapiro, Bernstein & Co., Inc., 1903.
Character monologue and song introduced by Edwin Foy in his spinster role in *Mr. Bluebeard* (musical, 1903).

I'm a Respectable Working Girl
Words by Edgar Smith, music by John Stromberg.
M. Witmark & Sons, 1901.
Cockney comic song introduced by Fay Templeton in *Quo Vass-Iss?* (musical, 1901).

I'm a Yankee Doodle Dandy, see **Yankee Doodle Boy,**.

I'm a Yiddish Cowboy, also known as **Tough-Guy Levi**
Words by Edgar Leslie, music by Al Piantadosi and Halsey K. Mohr.
Original copyright, 1908.
Hebrew-dialect comedy song revived for the interpolation repertories of Fanny Brice and Eddie Cantor in the late 1910's.

I'm Afraid to Come Home in the Dark
Words by Harry Williams, music by Egbert van Alstyne.
Remick Music Corp., 1907.
Top-selling comic song based on a husband's excuse for staying out all night. Introduced by May Vokes in *A Knight for a Day* (1906); adopted by most of the female character comics in vaudeville, among them, Della Fox, May Irwin, May A. Bell, Clara Morton, Elizabeth Murray, and Clarice Vance, who recorded it for Victor.

I'm After Madame Tettrazzini's Job
Words and music by Gus Edwards.
Gus Edwards Music Publishing Co., 1909.
Opera burlesque introduced by Bessie Wynn in Ziegfeld's *Follies of 1909;* topical song rhymes "Hammerstein" with "Puccini" and "Verdi" with "birdie" for a scene set in Oscar Hammerstein's Manhattan Opera House office.

I'm All Bound 'Round with the Mason-Dixon Line
Words by Sam M. Lewis and Joe Young, music by Jean Schwartz.
Waterson, Berlin & Snyder, 1917/Mills Music Inc., 1945.
ASCAP top-seller as sheet music, one of the most popular raggy Dixieland nostalgia songs of the decade was sung by Harry Fox, Grace Lindon, James Nazarro, and Vernon Dalhart, who recorded it for Edison cylinders. Al Jolson recorded it for Columbia and maintained it in his repertory throughout his career.

I'm All Dressed Up and No Where to Go
Words by Thomas S. Allen, music by Joseph M. Daly.
Original copyright, 1913.
Character comic song introduced by Joe Rath but also associated with Raymond Hitchcock and interpolated into his revues.

I'm All O.K. with K. and E.
Words and music by George M. Cohan.
Cohan & Harris, 1909.
Comic novelty song introduced by Raymond Hitchcock in his musical *The Man Who Owns Broadway* (1909); the topical lyrics refer to the Syndicate of Klaw and Erlanger (who controlled vaudeville and Broadway employment), the Shubert Brothers, and "that showman Frohman."

I'm Always Chasing Rainbows
Words by Harry Carroll, music by Joseph McCarthy.
Original copyright, 1918/Robbins Music Corp., 1918, 1946.
An ASCAP top seller, the ballad (based on Chopin) was introduced by Harry Fox and the Dolly Sisters in *Oh, Look!* (1918) and recorded by Sam Ash (Emerson), Charles Harrison (Victor), and Prince's Band (Columbia). It was revived for the 20th Century Fox film biography of Roszika and Jansci Dolly (1945) and MGM's *Ziegfeld Girl* (1946), and recorded by Benny Goodman (Columbia), Perry Como (RCA), and Guy Lombardo and His Royal Canadians (Decca).

I'm Awfully Glad I Met You
Words by Jack Drislane, music by George W. Meyer.
F. B. Haviland, 1909.
Romantic ballad popularized by Billy McDermott and May Ward.

I'm Awfully Glad I'm Irish
Words by Edgar Leslie, music by Al Piantadosi.
Leo Feist Inc., 1910.
Introduced by burlesque veteran Rose Sydell and also sung by the close-harmony team of Larkin and Larkin.

I'm Crazy about My Daddy in a Uniform
Words and music by Charles R. McCarron and Carey Morgan.
Joseph W. Stern & Co., 1918.
Patriotic tribute to a lover who "knows about manoeuvres." Introduced by Sophie Tucker and recorded by her and by the Farber Sisters.

I'm Crazy 'bout the Turkey Trot
Words by Joe Goodwin, music by George W. Meyer.
F. B. Haviland, 1911.
Novelty turkey-trot with barnyard sound effects. Introduced by Anna Chandler; recorded as dance music by Arthur Collins and Byron G. Harlan on Victor.

I'm Crazy to Go on the Stage
Words by Will D. Cobb, music by Gus Edwards.
Shapiro, Bernstein & Co., Inc., 1904.
Novelty comic song with allusions to legitimate drama and descriptions of melodrama. Introduced by Edwards in vaudeville.

I'm Cured
Words by Jean C. Havez, music by Bert Williams.
Remick Music Corp., 1914.
Williams's specialty from the *Ziegfeld Follies of 1914.*

I'm Down in Honolulu Looking Them Over
Words and music by Irving Berlin.
Waterson, Berlin & Snyder, 1916.
Berlin's response to "They're Wearing 'Em Higher in Hawaii" (q. v.), popularized by Al Jolson in his Winter Garden revues.

I'm Falling in Love with Some One
Words by Rida Johnson Young, music by Victor Herbert.
M. Witmark & Sons/Warner Brothers, Inc., 1984.
Waltz ballad introduced by Orville Harrold as the hero, "Captain Dick," in *Naughty Marietta* (operetta, 1910). Nelson Eddy sang it in the 1935 MGM film and recorded it often; it was also a favorite aria of Mario Lanza.

I'm Forever Blowing Bubbles
Words and music by Jean Kenbrovin and John William Kellette.
Remick Music Corp., 1919.
A success after its interpolation into the *Passing Show of 1919,* the ballad was recorded almost instantly by Charles Hart (Victor), Albert Campbell and Henry Burr (Columbia), Helen Clark and George Wilton Ballard (Edison), and Selvin's Novelty Orchestra (Victor). It has retained its popularity through recordings by Mildred Bailey (Vocalion), Ella Logan (Columbia), Les Paul (Capi-

tol), and many others; featured by Doris Day in Warner Brothers' film *On Moonlight Bay* (1951) and on Columbia records.

I'm Getting Kind of Lonesome for My Old Kentucky Pal
Words by Thomas J. Gray, music by Blossom Seeley.
Joseph W. Stern & Co., 1911.
Bluesy ballad introduced by Seeley.

I'm Getting Sleepy
Words by Wilbur U. Gumm, music by Joe Hollander.
Harry Von Tilzer Music Publishing Co., 1905.
Suggestive romance song popularized as a solo by Grace Cameron and as a duet by the Rooney Sisters.

I'm Glad I Can Make You Cry
Words and music by Charles R. McCarron and Carey Morgan.
Joseph W. Stern & Co., 1918.
Romantic song introduced by Gus Hill's Minstrels and sung by Harry Tenney and Bessie Hamilton; also popular as dance music and recorded as a shimmie fox-trot by Henry Burr and by Riley's Cabaret Orchestra.

I'm Glad I'm a Boy/I'm Glad I'm a Girl
Words and music by Nora Bayes (pseudonym for Dora Goldberg) and Jack Norworth.
Remick Music Corp., 1909.
Duet with alternating verses introduced by Bayes and Norworth in Ziegfeld's *Follies of 1909;* recorded as a duet by Ada Jones and Billy Murray on Victor.

I'm Glad I'm Married, also known as **Yes She Does**
Words by Jack Norworth, music by Albert von Tilzer.
York Music Corp., 1908.
The catch phrase of this comic song ("Yes She Does") caught on with the general public. Introduced by Norworth and popularized by Irene Jarman, Viola Gillette, George MacFarlane, and Billy Murray, who recorded it for Victor.

I'm Goin' to Live Anyhow 'Till I Die
Words and music by Shepard N. Edmonds.
Joseph W. Stern & Co., 1901.
One of the first "shouter" songs to gain a wide audience, it was popularized by male and female, black and white vocalists in vaudeville and minstrelsy, among them, Eddie Leonard, Clarice Vance, Carroll Johnson, and Ernest Hogan.

I'm Going Back to Carolina
Words and music by Billy Downs and Ernie Erdman.

Original copyright, 1913/Jerry Vogel Music Co., Inc., 1940.
Dixie nostalgia song introduced by Janet Adair in *Little Dolly Dimples* (1913); recorded and popularized by Sophie Tucker, Frank Morrell, and Arthur Collins.

I'm Going Back to Dixie, also known as **I Want to Be in Dixie**
Words and music by Irving Berlin and Ted Snyder.
Ted Snyder Music Publishing Co., 1911.
Nostalgia song with railroad rhythm effects. Introduced by May Irwin in *She Knows Better Now* (1912); popular in close-harmony arrangements and recorded by Gene Greene and the American Quartet (Pathe), the Courtney Sisters (Victor), and Arthur Collins and Byron G. Harlan on Victor and Silvertone.

I'm Going to Do What I Please
Words by Alfred Bryan, music by Ted Snyder.
Ted Snyder Music Publishing Co., 1909.
An early success for Sophie Tucker, the bluesy song was also associated with Ruby Raymond and Billy Oakes.

I'm Going to Spend My Vacation with a Dear Old Relation
Words by Al Wilson, music by Louis Silvers.
Al Piantadosi Music, 1918.
Patriotic parody introduced by Willie Howard in the *Passing Show of 1918;* the "vacation" referred to World War I spent with Uncle Sam.

I'm Gonna Make Hay While the Sun Shines in Virginia
Words by Joe Young and Sam Lewis, music by Archie Gottler.
Mills Music Inc., 1916, 1944.
Bluesy Dixie song popularized and recorded by Sophie Tucker and Marion Harris; revived in the 1940's through performances and recordings by Victor Lombardo and His Orchestra.

I'm Learning Something Every Day
Words and music by Nora Bayes (pseudonym for Dora Goldberg) and Jack Norworth.
Remick Music Corp., 1909.
Romance introduced by Anna Held in *Miss Innocence* (1909) and performed by Bayes and Norworth in their vaudeville acts.

I'm Longing for My Old Kentucky Home
Words by Vincent Bryan, music by J. B. Mullen.
Shapiro, Bernstein & Co., Inc., 1904.
Dixie nostalgia ballad popularized by George H. Diamond, Clarice Vance, Louise Brehany, and Zoa Mathews in vaudeville.

I'm Looking for a Dear Old Lady
Words by J. W. Hamer, music by Al Piantadosi.
Leo Feist Inc., 1910.
Romantic ballad about a man seeking an ideal mother so that he can marry her morally brought up daughter. Introduced by Stuart Barnes.

I'm Looking for a Dear Old Lady
Words by Edgar Selden, music by Tom Kelley.
Shapiro, Bernstein & Co., Inc., 1910.
Bessie Wynn's juvenile specialty song about a runaway child searching for her grandmother.

I'm Looking for the Man That Wrote "The Merry Widow Waltz"
Words by Edgar Selden, music by Seymour Furth.
Shapiro, Bernstein & Co., Inc., 1907.
Novelty song complaining about the popularity of "The Merry Widow Waltz" (q.v.); performed in vaudeville by Virginia Earl, May Ward, and Trixie Friganza.

I'm Not Jealous
Words by Harry Pease, music by Edward G. Nelson and Fred Mayo.
Original copyright, 1919.
Comic romance interpolated into many Shubert productions, including *Good Morning, Judge* (sung by Mollie King) and *Sinbad* (performed by the Farber Sisters).

I'm Off for Mexico
Words by J. Will Callahan, music by F. Henri Klickmann.
Original copyright, 1914.
Militarist anthem for the conflict with Mexico (1911-1916).

I'm on My Way to Dublin Bay
Words and music by Stanley Murphy.
Remick Music Corp., 1905, 1915.
Introduced by Julia Sanderson in *The Girl from Utah* (musical, 1914); became the hit of the season, with the song doubling as an Irish romance for female teams such as Irene and Bobbie Smith and the Home Town Girls, and as dance music, recorded by various labels' house orchestras, among them, the Columbia Band, the Victor Military Band, Prince's Orchestra, and Jaudas' Society Orchestra.

I'm on My Way to Manadalay
Words by Al Bryan (pseudonym for Albert Von Breitenbach), music by Fred Fisher.
Leo Feist Inc., 1913.

Exotic ballad of nostalgia popularized by Belle Rutland and Carrie Lilie; recorded as a fox-trot by Elizabeth Spencer and Henry Burr.

I'm on My Way to Reno
Words by William Jerome, music by Jean Schwartz.
Remick Music Corp., 1910.
Introduced by Mabel Hite in *A Certain Party* (musical, 1911), this song about divorce sets its chorus to "shouting the Battle Cry of Freedom."

I'm Proud to Be a Mother of a Soldier Like You
Words by Andrew B. Sterling, music by Harry von Tilzer.
Harry Von Tilzer Music Publishing Co., 1915.
Pro-interventionist ballad of pre-World War I period in opposition to "I Didn't Raise My Boy to Be a Soldier" (q.v.). Introduced by George MacFarlane but also popularized and recorded in a close-harmony version by the Peerless Quartet.

I'm Saving Up Coupons
Words by Joe Weston, music by Billy James and Abe Wilsky.
Original copyright, 1914/Jerry Vogel Music Co., Inc., 1914, 1942.
Comedy song about saving cigarette coupons--after he acquires a wife, a divorce, a child, and a car, the narrator dies from smoking.

I'm Simply Crazy over You
Words by William Jerome and E. Ray Goetz, music by Jean Schwartz.
Mills Music Inc., 1915.
Novelty flirtation song introduced by Artie Mehlinger as "Percy Bonehead" in *Hands Up* (musical, 1915); billed as "That Cutest Little Dimple Song," it was recorded as a one-step by the Victor Military Band, Harry MacDonough (Victor), and Sam Ash on Silvertone; revived by Guy Lombardo and His Royal Canadians.

I'm So Used to You Now, see **I Hate to Lose You,.**

I'm Sorry
Words by Jack Norworth, music by Albert von Tilzer.
York Music Corp., 1906.
Ballad interpolated by Louise Dresser into *About Town* (1906) and popularized in vaudeville by Norworth, Ula Gannon, and Ida O'Day; recorded by Ada Jones and Billy Murray as a duet.

I'm Sorry I Ain't Got It You Could Have It If I Had It Blues
Words by Sam M. Lewis and Joe Young, music by Ted Snyder.
Waterson, Berlin & Snyder, 1919.
Character monologue and song popularized by Bert Williams whose

1919 recording is included in the Smithsonian Institution's compilation album *Ziegfeld Follies of 1919.*

I'm Sorry I Made You Cry
Words and music by N. J. Clesi.
Leo Feist Inc., 1916, 1944, 1958.
ASCAP top seller of 1916 was popularized by Belle Baker and Jack King and recorded by Henry Burr, George Wilton Ballard, and Prince's Orchestra. It became a jazz standard from the mid-1920's with recordings as a fox-trot by Fats Waller and by Earl Fuller's Famous Jazz Band. Jazz recordings returned to the ballad mood in the 1940's and 1950's, with popular performances by Red Nichols, Jack Teagarden and the Capitol Jazzmen, Connie Francis, and Frank Sinatra.

I'm the Man Who Makes the Money in the Mint
Words and music by Will D. Cobb and Gus Edwards.
Mills Music Inc., 1902.
Character comedy song introduced by Dan McAvoy in *The Hall of Fame* (musical, 1902).

I'm the Money Burner
Words by Harry B. Smith, music by Gustave Kerker.
Sol Bloom Publishing Co/Sol Bloom Music, 1902.
Comic character portrait introduced by Jerome Sykes in *The Billionaire* (musical, 1902).

I'm the Only Mother That You Ever Knew
Words by Vincent Bryan, music by E. Ray Goetz.
Shapiro, Bernstein & Co., Inc., 1911.
Sentimental ballad sung by a child's nursemaid. Introduced by Belle Blanche.

I'm the Only Star That Twinkles on Broadway
Words by Andrew B. Sterling, music by Harry von Tilzer.
Harry Von Tilzer Music Publishing Co., 1905.
Novelty comedy song introduced by Emma Carus as a hopeful actress; includes topical references to performers and critics.

I'm Thinking 'bout You Honey All the While
Words by Rose Melville, music by Frank Minzey.
F. B. Haviland, 1904.
Top-selling romantic ballad introduced by Minzey on national tours of Melville's starring vehicle *Sis Hopkins* (1904-1908).

I'm Tired
Words by William Jerome, music by Jean Schwartz.
Shapiro, Bernstein & Co., Inc., 1901.

Character comedy song introduced by Edwin Foy in *The Strollers* (musical, 1901), with topical extra verses on Sir Thomas Lipton's attempts to win the America's Cup.

I'm Trying to Find a Sweetheart
Words by Jean Lenox, music by Henry O. Sutton.
Remick Music Corp., 1905.
Romantic ballad associated with Adele Ritchie.

I'm Trying to Teach My Sweet Papa Right from Wrong
Words by Will E. Skidmore, music by Marshall Walker.
Charles K. Harris Music Publishing Co., 1918.
Bluesy complaint popularized by Sophie Tucker.

I'm Tying the Leaves So They Won't Come Down
Words by E. S. S. Huntingdon, music by J. Fred Helf.
Helf & Hager, 1907.
Plotted sentimental ballad popularized by juveniles and adult vocalists, among them Baby Nellie McCoy, Sadie Helf, and Ruth Wright. The pathos of the tragic situation, in which a boy overhears a doctor saying that his playmate will die when Autumn comes and tries to stop the changing of the season, became symbolic of the early twentieth century. George Burns refers to this song in his current act as the worst ballad of his youthful career.

I'm Unlucky
Words by William Jerome, music by Jean Schwartz.
Shapiro, Bernstein & Co., Inc., 1902.
Character song introduced by Edwin Foy in *The Wild Rose* (1902); describes himself as "a disappointed double-jointed poor unlucky man."

I'm Wearing My Heart Away for You
Words and music by Charles K. Harris.
Charles K. Harris Music Publishing Co., 1902.
Romantic ballad associated with male vocalists in minstrelsy and vaudeville and popular as a parlor song. Introduced by Jere Sanford and recorded by Henry Burr and Harry MacDonough.

Imagination
Words by Vincent Bryan, music by J. B. Mullen.
Shapiro, Bernstein & Co., Inc., 1904.
Character monologue and song introduced by Jess Dandy in *The Prince of Pilsen* (musical, 1903); includes topical references to the Russo-Japanese War, Christian Science, and the Temperance movement.

In a Hammock Built for Two
Words by Andrew B. Sterling, music by Harry von Tilzer.
Harry Von Tilzer Music Publishing Co., 1905.
Flirting song popularized by Anna Laughlin, Toby Claude, and Sue Smith; recorded by von Tilzer.

In a Kingdom of Our Own
Words and music by George M. Cohan.
M. Witmark & Sons, 1919.
Ballad interpolated by the author into his own "Cohanized Opera Comique" *The Royal Vagabond* (1919). Recorded as dance music by the Aeolian Orchestra and Joseph C. Smith's Orchestra.

In a Little Cottage by the Railroad Track
Words and music by Blanche Merrill.
Waterson, Berlin & Snyder, 1913.
Domestic romance introduced then-juvenile balladeer Herman Timberg in his vaudeville musical comedy *Davey's Troubles.*

In Berry Pickin' Time
Words by Jack Yellin, music by Percy Wenrich.
Leo Feist Inc., 1917.
Romantic nostalgia popularized by Dolly Connolly; recorded by Henry Burr (Columbia) and Harry Williams (Lyric).

In de Evenin'
Words by Alex Rogers, music by Will Marion Cook.
Harry Von Tilzer Music Publishing Co., 1910.
Dixie song written for Bert Williams in the *Follies of 1910.*

In Dear Old Georgia
Words by Harry H. Williams, music by Egbert van Alstyne.
Remick Music Corp., 1905.
Dixie nostalgia popularized by soloists, such as Claude Thardo and Lydia Barry, by duets, like Kelly and Violette, and by close-harmony teams, among them the Mound City Four and the Quaker City Quartet; recorded by label vocalists Frank C. Stanley for Victor and Harry Tally for Zon-o-phone.

In Disguise
Words by Harry B. Smith, music by Arthur Weld.
Original copyright, 1901.
Description of flirting at masquerade parties introduced by Katie Seymour in *The Casino Girl* (musical, 1900).

In Dreamland, In Dreamland
Words by Edward S. Abeles, music by William T. Francis.
M. Witmark & Sons, 1904.

Romantic ballad introduced by Lillian Russell in *Whoop-Dee-Doo* (1903); recorded by Corinne Morgan on Victor.

In Flanders' Fields (American-English)
Words by John McCrae, music by Frank E. Tours.
M. Witmark & Sons, 1918.
Setting of Lieutenant Colonel John McCrae's pacifist poem performed and recorded by John McCormack. The poem was also set to music in 1918 by John Philip Sousa, by Charles Gilbert Spross, and by Arthur William Foote (1919).

In Florida
Words by Harry B. Smith, music by Louis F. Gottschalk.
Edward Schuberth & Co., Inc., 1901.
Descriptive song from *The Liberty Belles* (1901) that introduced the chorus of bathing beauties in the final act.

In Hitchy's Garden, see **Hitchy's Garden of Roses,**.

In My Dreams of You
Words and music by Claire Kummer.
Remick Music Corp., 1910.
Romantic ballad introduced by Sallie Fisher in *The Girl on the Trail* (musical, 1910) as an interpolation and maintained in her vaudeville repertory.

In My Harem
Words and music by Irving Berlin.
Waterson, Berlin & Snyder, 1913/Irving Berlin Music Corp.
Dialect comedy song (for an Irish and/or Hebrew clothing salesman character) popularized by Josie Flynn and recorded by Walter J. Van Brunt; revived for the film *Alexander's Rag-Time Band.*

In My Merry Oldsmobile
Words by Vincent Bryan, music by Gus Edwards.
M. Witmark & Sons, 1905, 1933/Clef Music Publishers, 1961.
Romantic song with a double life as a commercial and as a novelty about automobile dating; popularized by Anna Fitzhugh in vaudeville and recorded by Billy Murray (Victor). Also recorded by the jazz ensembles of Les Brown (Columbia) and Bix Beiderbecke (Biltmore).

In My Old Home
Words by "Mord" Allen, music by Tom Lemonier.
Gotham-Attucks Music Publishing Co., 1908.
Dixie nostalgia from the musical *Bandana Land* (1902).

In Naples Fair
Words by Charles Horwitz, music by Frederick V. Bowers.
Original copyright, 1900.
Ballad performed by Camille D'Arville in vaudeville; also popular as parlor song.

In Old Kentucky
Words and music by Anita Stewart.
Waterson, Berlin & Snyder, 1919.
Promotional title song for Stewart's silent film for 1st National/ Vitagraph, which was based on Charles Dazey's nineteenth-century melodrama.

In Old New York
Words by Henry M. Blossom, Jr., music by Alfred G. Robyn.
M. Witmark & Sons, 1903.
Satirical song about municipal politics from *The Yankee Consul* (musical, 1904); recorded as dance music by Al Goodman and His Orchestra (Victor) in the mid-1910's.

In Old New York, see **The Streets of New York,.**

In Silence
Words by Sydney Rosenfeld, music by A. Baldwin Sloane.
Joseph W. Stern & Co., 1902.
Ballad introduced by Mabelle Gilman in *The Mockingbird* (musical, 1902).

In Society
Words by Harry B. Smith, music by Reginald De Koven.
Edward Schuberth & Co., Inc., 1901.
Satirical song about imitation aristocrats from Anna Held's starring vehicle *The Little Duchess* (1901).

In the Candlelight
Words and music by Fleta Jan Brown.
M. Witmark & Sons, 1913.
Ballad introduced by Bessie Wynn; popular as a parlor song after recordings by Edna Brown and Nora Watson, and in its close-harmony version, as recorded by the Peerless Quartet.

In the City of Sighs and Tears
Words by Andrew B. Sterling, music by Kerry Mills.
Mills Music Inc., 1902.
Sentimental ballad performed by song illustrator Charles Falke and by vocalists John P. Curran, May Adams, and Josie Flynn.

In the Cold Grey Dawn
Words by Rita Di Milo, music by Irene Bentley.
Original copyright, 1905.
Plotted melodramatic ballad introduced by Bentley.

In the Days of Girls and Boys
Words by Blanche Merrill, music by Leo Edwards.
Leo Feist Inc., 1911.
Nostalgic ballad popularized by Lillian Russell and Helen Vincent.

In the Folds of the Starry Flag
Words by Paul West, music by Victor Herbert.
M. Witmark & Sons, 1904.
Patriotic anthem commissioned by the newspaper *New York World,* July 3, 1904.

In the Good Old-Fashioned Way
Words and music by Charles K. Harris.
Charles K. Harris Music Publishing Co., 1901.
Romantic ballad of a fiftieth wedding anniversary. Introduced by May Shirk Garnella.

In the Good Old Summertime
Words by Ren Shields, music by George Evans.
Howley, Haviland & Dresser, 1902/Edward B. Marks Music Corp., 1932, 1949.
"Summer" songs were a feature of Broadway and Tin Pan Alley in the first decade of the century; this one was introduced by Blanche Ring in her seasonal hit, *The Defender* (1902). It was recorded by Sousa's Band, Harry MacDonough, and the Haydn Quartet (all on Victor) and became a top seller in piano rolls as well. A nostalgia favorite in the 1940's and 1950's, it was revived by the Andrews Sisters (Decca) and Bing Crosby (V Disc, Ward) and used behind the credits in the MGM film named for it (1949).

In the Heart of the City That Has No Heart
Words by Thomas S. Allen, music by Joseph M. Daly.
Original copyright, 1913/Mills Music Inc., 1926.
Plotted melodramatic ballad of the style of 1900-1902; popularized by Phil Dolan and Emma O'Neill in 1913 and by the Bennett Twins in its 1926 revival. Recorded on Columbia by Henry Burr.

In the Heart of the Mighty Deep
Words by Arthur J. Lamb, music by Harry von Tilzer.
Shapiro, Bernstein & Co., Inc., 1901.
Ballad of sailor dreaming before his death in a shipwreck; popular as a parlor song for low male voices.

In the Hills of Old Carolina
Words and music by Charles K. Harris.
Charles K. Harris Music Publishing Co., 1902.
Sentimental ballad of the Spanish-American War sung by Will J. Cook and Allen May.

In the House of Too Much Trouble
Words and music by Will A. Heelan and J. Fred Helf.
Joseph W. Stern & Co., 1900.
Plotted sentimental ballad of a neglected baby boy; popularized by George H. Diamond, the Troubadour Four, and the vaudeville vocalist billed as "The Woman in White."

In the *Ladies' Home Journal*
Words and music by Clifton Crawford.
Original copyright, 1904.
Satire of the etiquette question-and-answer page in the venerable women's magazine; introduced by Joseph Cawthorne in *Mother Goose* (musical, 1903).

In the Land of Beginning Again
Words by Grant Clarke, music by George W. Meyer.
Leo Feist Inc., 1918/Fred Fisher Music Co., 1946, 1960.
Ballad associated with Bing Crosby (Decca) in *The Bells of St. Mary's* (RKO, 1945); recorded soon after its composition by Charles Harrison (Victor), George Wilton Ballard (Edison), and Prince's Band (Columbia).

In the Land of Harmony
Words by Bert Kalmar, music by Ted Snyder.
Kalmar, Puck & Abrahams Consolidated Mus, 1911.
One of Tin Pan Alley's most popular rag songs, it was introduced by Bonita and performed in vaudeville by her, Lew Hearn, Josie Flynn, Rose Felmar, Claire Maynard, and many others.

In the Land of Wedding Bells
Words by Howard Johnson, music by George W. Meyer.
Leo Feist Inc., 1917.
Romantic song introduced by female impersonator Julian Eltinge, but soon adopted as a standard by both male and female vocalists, among them, Belle Brooks, Frank Mullane, Willie Weston, Al Herman, and Elsie White.

In the Land Where Poppies Bloom
Words by Billy Baskette, music by Gus Van and Joe Schenck.
Remick Music Corp., 1918.
Romantic ballad sang and recorded by Van and Schenck in their close-harmony duet act.

In the Shade of the Old Apple Tree
Words by Harry H. Williams, music by Egbert van Alstyne.
Remick Music Corp., 1905.
Best-selling sheet music of the year and popular with all vocal categories of vaudeville singers--single women, men, juveniles, duets, and close-harmony groups. Among its most prominent performers were Louise Dresser, Anna Driver, male impersonator Della Fox, the Italian Trio, Baby Zena Keefe, Kelly and Violette, Marie Laurent, and Claude Thardo.

In the Shadows
Words by E. Ray Goetz, music by Herman Finck.
Joseph W. Stern & Co., 1911/Edward B. Marks Music Corp., 1932.
Popular piano and dance band piece from Europe given American lyrics by Goetz for interpolation in *The Hen Pecks* (musical, 1911).

In the Swim, also known as **The Belle of Washington, D.C.**
Words by Harry B. Smith, music by Maurice Levi.
Satirical song about Washington society introduced by Jeannette Bageard in *The Rogers Brothers in Washington* (1901).

In the Valley of Broken Hearts
Words by Fred C. Farrell, music by Theodore F. Morse.
Original copyright, 1903.
Sentimental advice from a mother to her son. Introduced by Fannie Trimbell.

In the Valley of Kentucky
Words and music by Tony Stanford.
Leo Feist Inc., 1901.
Sentimental plotted ballad introduced by Sallie Fisher; also performed for many years by Henry and Gallot, song illustrators, who used projected slides to relate the tragic story of Nellie, buried in Kentucky.

In the Valley of Mont Bijou
Words by M. E. Rourke, music by Jerome Kern.
T. B. Harms, 1911.
Imitative folk ballad written for Julia Sanderson in *The Siren* (musical, 1911).

In the Village by the Sea
Words by Andrew B. Sterling, music by Stanley Crawford.
Shapiro, Bernstein & Co., Inc., 1903.
Plotted melodramatic ballad sung by minstrel show vocalists, such as John P. Curran, George H. Diamond, and the Empire City

Quartette, and by women, among them, Louise Brehany and Emma Carus.

In the Wildwood Where the Bluebells Grew
Words and music by Herbert H. Taylor.
Original copyright, 1907.
Nostalgic ballad popularized by vaudeville's premier male vocalists R. J. Jose and J. Aldrich Libbey.

In Vacation Time
Words by Andrew B. Sterling, music by Harry von Tilzer.
Harry Von Tilzer Music Publishing Co., 1905.
Summertime romance popularized by Louise Grandy, Dorothy Russell, and Baby Zena Keefe.

In Washington
Words by Vincent Bryan, music by Gertrude Hoffmann.
Remick Music Corp., 1906.
Topical satire introduced by Anna Held and Charles Bigelow in *A Parisian Model* (musical, 1906).

In Zanzibar
Words by Will D. Cobb, music by Gus Edwards.
Shapiro, Bernstein & Co., Inc., 1904.
Comic song using Black dialect; interpolated by Emma Carus into *The Medal and the Maid* (1904); also interpolated by Agnes Fraser into the London production of *The Earl and the Girl* (1904).

Indiana
Words by Ballard MacDonald, music by James F. Hanley.
Shapiro, Bernstein & Co., Inc., 1917.
Popular instrumental that was first recorded as a barbershop ballad by the Knickerbocker Two (Columbia) and the Sterling Trio (Victor); major jazz recordings by Lester Young Trio (Philo), Art Tatum (V Disc), the Dave Brubeck Octet (Fantasy), and Red Nichols and His Five Pennies (Brunswick).

Indianola
French words by G. Helene Barker, English words by Frank Warren, music by S. R. Henry and D. Onivas.
Joseph W. Stern & Co., 1918.
A BMI top-seller that served as a patriotic World War I song about a Native American fighting the German army, as performed by Billy Murray; it also doubled as a novelty fox-trot recorded by the Emerson and Edison Military Bands, Prince's Band, Wilbur Sweatman's Original Jazz Band, and James Reese Europe's Hell Fighters.

The Indians Along Broadway
Words and music by Benjamin Hapgood Burt.
Joseph W. Stern & Co., 1905.
Satirical song complaining about the stores that cheat tourists in New York City. Introduced by Sam Bernard and Hattie Williams in *The Rollicking Girl* (musical, 1905).

Innocent Bessie Brown
Words and music by Irving Berlin.
Ted Snyder Music Publishing Co., 1910.
Novelty comic song about a small-town girl in New York City; popularized by Ethel Green and Mindell Kingston.

Instrumental Man
Words and music by John Gilroy and Harry Linton.
Sol Bloom Publishing Co/Sol Bloom Music, 1902.
Novelty song featuring instrument imitations performed by Gilroy and Linton in *The Liberty Belles* (1901).

Inverary (American-English)
Words by James Malackey, words and music by Harry Lauder.
Francis, Day & Hunter, Ltd., London, England, 1905/T. B. Harms, 1905.
Scottish-dialect flirtation song performed and recorded by Lauder.

The Invincible Eagle
Words and music by John Philip Sousa.
John Church Co., 1929.
Premiered by Sousa's Band at the Pan-American Exposition of 1901 in Buffalo, New York. A piano transcription appears in Dover Books' *Sousa's Great Marches.* It has been recorded by the bands of the United States Marines, Her Majesty's Royal Marines, the Royal Netherlands Marines, and Warner Brothers, as well as the Decca and Goldman Bands and the Eastman Wind Ensemble.

Iola
Words by James O'Dea, music by Charles L. Johnson.
Original copyright, 1901/Remick Music Corp., 1906/Jerry Vogel Music Co., Inc., 1938.
The most famous of the Indian rag songs was featured in vaudeville by Harry Ellis, Louise Brehany, and the team of Kelly and Violette, and recorded by Sousa's Band and the teams of Frank C. Stanley and Henry Burr and Stanley and Byron G. Harlan (all for Victor).

Ireland! A Gra Ma Chree
Words and music by Chauncey Olcott.

M. Witmark & Sons, 1900.
Patriotic Irish anthem performed by Olcott in his play *Garrett O'Magh.*

Ireland Must Be Heaven for My Mother Came from There
Words and music by Joseph McCarthy, Howard Johnson, and Fred Fisher.
Leo Feist Inc., 1916, 1944.
ASCAP top-seller in sheet music with special editions printed with cameos for Emma Carus, Dorothy Meuther, and the Avon Comedy Four in 1916 alone; recorded by John McCormack (Victor, RCA) and the studio balladeers Henry Burr (Rex), Charles Harrison (Victor), and Walter van Brunt (Edison); featured in the film *Oh, You Beautiful Doll* in a montage of ethnic types to show the popularity of Fisher's songs.

Ireland, My Land of Dreams
Words and music by George M. Cohan.
M. Witmark & Sons, 1918.
Patriotic song written for Chauncey Olcott in his play *The Voice of McConnell.*

Irish Fluffy Ruffles
Words by Will A. Heelan, music by Albert Gumble.
Remick Music Corp., 1907.
Irish version of the "Fluffy Ruffles" songs (q.v.). Introduced by Blanche Ring as an assimilated immigrant in *The Gay White Way* (musical, 1907).

The Irish Girl I Love
Words by George V. Hobart, music by Max Hoffmann.
Romantic duet introduced by Bessie DeVoie and Maurice Darcy in *The Rogers Brothers in Ireland* (1905).

An Irishman's Lilt
Words by Alice, music by Andrew Mack.
Original copyright, 1903.
Self-descriptive song interpolated by Mack into Dion Boucicault's play *Arrah-na-Pogue.*

Is Everybody Happy?
Words by Frank Williams, music by Ernest Hogan and Tom Lemonier.
Charles K. Harris Music Publishing Co., 1905.
Signature theme for Hogan, introduced in *Rufus Rastus* (musical, 1905).

The Island of By and By
Words by Alex Rogers, music by Bert Williams.
Gotham-Attucks Music Publishing Co., 1906.
Ballad introduced by Aida Overton Walker in *Abyssinia* (1906).

The Island of Roses and Love
Words by Earle C. Jones, music by Neil Moret.
Remick Music Corp., 1911.
Romantic standard introduced by Lillian Russell in Weber and Fields' reunion revue *Jubilee* (1911).

It Ain't All Honey and It Ain't All Jam
Words and music by Fred Murray and George Everard.
B. Feldman & Co., Ltd., 1906.
Character comic monologue and song about the perils of vacationing with a small child. Introduced by Vesta Victoria.

It Gets Them All
Words by Arthur Hammerstein, music by Herbert Stothart.
Shapiro, Bernstein & Co., Inc., 1918.
Tribute to the seductive qualities of gypsy violins from *Somebody's Sweetheart* (1918).

It May Not All Be True, see **Don't Worry,**.

It Must Have Been Svengali in Disguise
Words by Vincent P. Bryan, music by Harry von Tilzer.
Harry Von Tilzer Music Publishing Co., 1902.
Comic character song about the power of hypnotism. Introduced by Edwin Foy in *The Wild Rose* (1902).

It Never, Never Can Be Love
Words by Rida Johnson Young, music by Victor Herbert.
M. Witmark & Sons, 1910.
Romantic duet introduced by Emma Trentini and Orville Harrold as the lovers in *Naughty Marietta* (operetta, 1910). Recorded by Beverly Sills as a bel canto aria.

It Rained a Mist
Words by Clyde Fitch, music by William Furst.
Howley, Haviland & Dresser, 1902.
Gothic plotted ballad of a child disappearing into a misty castle; written by the popular author of melodramas, Clyde Fitch; sung by Annie Russell in the play *The Girl and the Judge.*

It Takes a Long Tall Brown-Skin Gal to Make a Preacher Lay His Bible Down
Words by Marshall Walker, music by Will E. Skidmore.

Joseph W. Stern & Co., 1917/Edward B. Marks Music Corp.
A BMI top-seller, this satirical song was introduced by Rae Samuels.

It Was Just a Song at Twilight That Made Me Come Back to You
Words by Bernard Granville and Arthur J. Jackson, music by Rubey Cowan.
Original copyright, 1915.
Granville and Alice Moss found success with this nostalgic ballad that quotes and alludes to Molloy and Bingham's 1884 song, "Love's Old Sweet Song," known also as "Just a Song at Twilight" (the first line of the chorus). Similarly, J. Will Callahan and Paul Pratt wrote "An Old Time Song 'Just a Song at Twilight'" for vaudeville in 1912.

It Was Me
Words by George W. Day, music by Seymour Furth.
Joseph Morris Co., 1911.
Comic complaint from the victimized. Introduced by Bert Williams in the Ziegfeld *Follies of 1911.*

It Was the Dutch
Words by Vincent Bryan, music by J. B. Mullen.
Original copyright, 1903.
Dutch-dialect novelty song performed by Jess Dandy in *The Prince of Pilsen* (1903); also sung in minstrel troupes by Lew Dockstader and John W. Ransome.

Italian Street Song
Words by Rida Johnson Young, music by Victor Herbert.
M. Witmark & Sons, 1910/Warner Brothers, Inc., 1984.
Introduced by Emma Trentini as the title character in the 1910 operetta *Naughty Marietta.* Jeanette MacDonald performed the showy aria in the 1935 MGM film and on three recordings. Popular with opera singers, it has also been recorded by Beverly Sills and Anna Moffo.

It's a Long Way to Berlin But We'll Get There
Words by Arthur Fields, music by Leon Flatow.
Leo Feist Inc., 1917.
Patriotic marching song introduced by Henry Bergman in the *Passing Show of 1917* and performed by most of the male vocalists in the United States and England during the war; recorded by Prince's Band for Columbia.

It's a Long Way to Dear Old Broadway
Words and music by Ernest Breuer.
Leo Feist Inc., 1918.

Signature song for Elsie Janis in her World War I performances with the American Expeditionary Forces.

It's a Waste of Time to Worry
Words and music by Raymond A. Browne.
Sol Bloom Publishing Co/Sol Bloom Music, 1905.
Typical novelty song for comedian-monologuist Raymond Hitchcock in his touring vehicle, *Easy Dawson* (1905).

It's All Right in the Summertime (American-English)
Words and music by Fred Murray and George Everard.
Francis, Day & Hunter, Ltd., London, England, 1904.
Vesta Victoria's signature tune in British music halls and American vaudeville. The song, about an artists' model who catches cold easily, was considered highly risque in the United States.

It's All Your Fault
Words by Noble Sissle and Eddie Nelson, music by Eubie Blake.
Original copyright, 1915.
The first published Sissle and Blake collaboration was popularized by Sophie Tucker; recorded by Blake on Record 2 of the 1968 retrospective of his works, *The Eighty-Six Years of Eubie Blake* (Columbia).

It's Delightful to Be Married
Words by Anna Held, music by Vincent Scotto.
Edward B. Marks Music Corp., 1906, 1907, 1935.
Anna Held's signature tune introduced in *A Parisian Model* (1906); recorded by Giselle MacKenzie (Vik) and featured in *Tintypes* (1980) and on its album. An identical song, "How Delightful to Be Married," by *A Parisian Model*'s composers, Harry B. Smith and Max Hoffmann, was published by Witmark in 1906. Parodies of it (them) abounded, most notably Jack Lowitz's "Oh, It's Lovely to Be Single," featured by Edwin Foy (1906).

It's Good Enough for Me
Words by Neal Harper, music by Clarence West.
T. B. Harms, 1905.
Satirical song introduced by Edwin Foy in *The Earl and the Girl* (1905); includes topical references to John D. Rockefeller and other millionaires and to New York City restaurants and night spots.

It's Got to Be a Minstrel Show Tonight
Words by Ren Shields, music by George Evans.
Original copyright, 1902.
"Honey Boy" Evans's novelty song, promoting his own minstrel

show, describes the audience's reaction to a performance of *Othello* in Eagle's Nest, out West.

It's Hard to Love Somebody Who's Loving Somebody Else
Words by Cecil Mack, music by Chris Smith.
Gotham-Attucks Music Publishing Co., 1907.
Introduced by Aida Overton Walker in *Bandana Land* (1908).

It's Lonesome Here
Words and music by Bliss Milford.
F. B. Haviland, 1916.
Sophie Tucker popularized this song responding to rural nostalgia--her character has returned to the farm but wants to move back to Broadway.

It's Moonlight All the Time on Broadway
Words by Ren Shields, music by Percy Wenrich.
F. B. Haviland, 1908.
Romantic song about neon lights providing the suitable atmosphere for spooning; popularized by Flossie Allen and the Avon Comedy Four.

It's Nobody's Business But My Own
Words and music by Will E. Skidmore and Marshall Walker.
Joseph W. Stern & Co., 1919/Edward B. Marks Music Corp., 1932.
One of the "Deacon" series of character songs for Bert Williams, performed in the *Ziegfeld Follies of 1919* and recorded for Columbia in 1920.

It's the Man in the Sailor Suit
Words by Fred C. Farrell, music by Theodore F. Morse.
Howley, Haviland & Dresser, 1902.
Patriotic romance of the Spanish-American War sung by F. W. Hollis and Eva Mudge.

It's the Pretty Things You Say
Words by Alfred Bryan, music by Ted Snyder.
Ted Snyder Music Publishing Co., 1908.
Romantic song popularized in vaudeville by Lulu Beeson, Amy Butler, Ray Cox, Grace Delmore, and Mirsky Gynt, "The Boy Caruso."

It's Time for Every Boy to Be a Soldier
Words by Alfred Bryan, music by Harry Tierney.
Remick Music Corp., 1917.
Patriotic recruitment anthem that ends with a quotation from the Gettysburg Address; recorded by the Gennett Military Band, Prince's Band (Columbia), and Charles H. Hart on Victor.

I've a Longing in My Heart for You, Louise
Words and music by Charles K. Harris.
Charles K. Harris Music Publishing Co., 1900.
Proposal song popular as a parlor song but also sung in vaudeville by Lydia Barry, Louise Beaton, and Margaret Kingore.

I've a Million Reasons Why I Love You
Words by M. E. Rourke, music by Jerome Kern.
T. B. Harms, 1907.
Romantic song introduced by Julia Sanderson in *The Dairymaids* (musical, 1907).

I've Been Floating Down the Old Green River
Words by Bert Kalmar, music by Joe Cooper.
Waterson, Berlin & Snyder, 1915/Mills Music Inc., 1943.
Comic song filled with coded references to alcoholic beverages (including Green River). Introduced by Florence Moore in *Maid in America* (1915). Prohibition (1919-1932) made the song more popular as a political statement, but by the 1940's, it was treated as a folk song. Recorded as a comic novelty by Billy Murray (Victor), by Phil Harris and His Dixieland Syncopators, who lived up to the band's mythic reputation for drinking in their performances in *Wabash Avenue* (20th Century Fox, 1950), and by Guy Lombardo and His Royal Canadians, who often played it New Year's Eve.

I've Been Looking for a Girl Like You
Words by Carter De Haven, music by Morris Silver and Thomas R. Confare.
Original copyright, 1907.
Flirtation duet for De Haven and Flora Parker, performed with alternating male and female verses. It became their signature tune for twenty years of vaudeville and film comedy.

I've Got My Captain Working for Me Now
Words and music by Irving Berlin.
Irving Berlin Music Corp., 1919.
Post-World War I novelty song written for Eddie Cantor's solo specialty act in the *Ziegfeld Follies of 1919*; his recording for Pathe is included in the Smithsonian Institution's album of the same name, but releases by Billy Murray (Victor, Emerson) and Al Jolson (Columbia) were equally popular. Revived and featured in *Blue Skies* (Paramount, 1946) by Bing Crosby and Billy DeWolfe (V Disc).

I've Got Rings on My Fingers
Words by Weston and Barnes, music by Maurice Scott.
T. B. Harms, 1909.

Blanche Ring's signature tune was interpolated into at least four of her musicals--*The Midnight Sons* (1909), *The Yankee Girl* (1910), *When Claudia Smiles* (1914), and, in a cameo role, *Right This Way* (1938)--and was one of her very few contemporary recordings (Victor). Originally a plotted novelty song about an Irish sailor who becomes the king of a South Sea isle, it has been made less specific over the past decades with revised lyrics that seem to refer to fashion and jewelry. Also recorded by Billy Murray (Victor), Ada Jones (Columbia), and Frank Novak and His Rootin' Tootin' Boys (Columbia). Ring's recording is included in *They Stopped the Show!* (Audio Rarities).

I've Got the Blues But I'm Too Blamed Mean to Cry, see **The Blues,**.

I've Got the Blues for Home Sweet Home
Words by William Jerome and E. Ray Goetz, music by George W. Meyer.
Kalmar, Puck & Abrahams Consolidated Mus, 1916.
Nostalgic ballad popularized by Willie Weston, Myrtle Young, and Harry Du-For.

I've Got the Time, I've Got the Place, But It's Hard to Find the Girl
Words by Ballard MacDonald, music by S. R. Henry.
Joseph W. Stern & Co., 1910/Edward B. Marks Music Corp., 1938.
Frustrated romance sung and recorded by Hetty King; revived by Guy Lombardo and His Royal Canadians.

I've Got to Dance Till the Band Gets Through
Words and music by G. A. Spink.
M. Witmark & Sons, 1906.
Early Broadway rag duet sung by Mabel Barrison and John P. Slavin in *The Three Graces* and by Melville Ellis and Maud Raymond in *The Social Whirl* within the same week -- April 2-7, 1906.

I've Got Troubles of My Own
Words by Bob Cole and James Weldon Johnson, music by J. Rosamond Johnson.
Joseph W. Stern & Co., 1900.
Novelty song interpolated by Marie Cahill into *The Belle of Bridgeport* (musical, 1900).

I've Grown So Used to You
Words and music by Thurland Chattaway.
Original copyright, 1901.
Sentimental ballad for a fiftieth wedding anniversary sung by R. J. Jose, E. J. Baldwin, Walter Talbot, Hazel Burt, and many others.

I've Lost My Teddy Bear
Words and music by Bob Cole, music by J. Rosamond Johnson.
Joseph W. Stern & Co., 1908.
Coy song featured by Abbie Mitchell in *The Red Moon* (1909) and interpolated by Anna Held into *Miss Innocence* (1908); recorded by Alice Stevenson for Zon-o-phone.

I've Lost You So Why Should I Care?
Words and music by Richard Howard.
Original copyright, 1916/Shapiro, Bernstein & Co., Inc., 1945.
Romantic ballad popular at first as a hesitation (and played by the house bands of cabarets and night clubs) and associated with Theda Bara (whose photograph was displayed on the 1916 cover); revived as a ballad in the 1940's by Joan Brooks.

I've Loved Her Ever Since She Was a Baby (English)
Words and music by Harry Lauder and Bob Beaton.
Francis, Day & Hunter, Ltd., London, England, 1909/T. B. Harms.
Scottish-dialect song performed and recorded by Lauder.

I've Made My Plans for the Summer
Words and music by John Philip Sousa.
John Church Co., 1907.
Promotional song commissioned by Luna Park, the amusement arcade at Coney Island.

I've Made Up My Mind to Mind a Maid Made Up Like You
Words by Alfred Bryan, music by Jean Schwartz.
Remick Music Corp., 1919.
Romantic duet introduced by Stewart Baird and Marjorie Gateson in the revue *Gaieties of 1919;* recorded by Helen Clarke and Joseph A. Phillips on Edison.

I've Only One Idea about the Girls and That's to Love 'Em
Words by Earl Carroll and Joe McCarthy, music by Al Piantadosi.
Leo Feist Inc., 1914.
Raggy romance popularized by Elizabeth Brice, Helen Vincent, and Al Abbott.

I've Told His Missus All about Him
Words and music by John P. Harrington and James W. Tate.
Francis, Day & Hunter, Inc., 1907.
Vesta Victoria's specialty number was the revengeful answer song to her "Waiting at the Church."

J

Ja-Da
Music by Bob Carleton.
Leo Feist Inc., 1918, 1939, 1946.
Novelty instrumental originally published as a fund-raiser for the Navy Relief Society during World War I; an ASCAP best-seller as sheet music, piano roll, and recording, it has retained its popularity and can now be heard in a computer commercial. Major recordings include those by popular and jazz ensembles ranging from Lieutenant Jim Europe's "Hell Fighters" Band (Pathe) to the Jefferson Airplane (Grunt/RCA), as well as Bunny Berigan (Decca sessions on Jazz Heritage), Count Basie (Pablo), Erroll Garner (Columbia), Art Tatum (Pathe), and Eddie Condon and the Windy City Seven (Commodore).

Jack O'Lantern
Words by Harry B. Smith, music by Mae Auwerda Sloane.
Original copyright, 1901.
Chorus production number from *The Liberty Belles* (muscial, 1901).

Jack O'Lantern Girl
Words by Glen MacDonough, music by Victor Herbert.
M. Witmark & Sons, 1904.
Specialty song and production number for toe dancer Bessie Clayton in *It Happened in Nordland* (musical, 1904).

A Japanese Love Song
Words and music by Thomas Clayton.
Boosey & Hawkes Inc., 1900.
Novelty ballad introduced by Mme. Alberto Randegger about the love between figures painted on a fan and on a package of tea.

Jazz Babies' Ball
Words by Charles Bayha, music by Maceo Pinkard.

Shapiro, Bernstein & Co., Inc., 1919.
Novelty rag that delineates preferable "new" dances of 1919. Introduced by Sophie Tucker in the Shuberts' *Gaieties of 1919;* recorded by the Peerless Quartet (Vocalion).

Jazz Baby
Words by Blanche Merrill and William Jerome, music by William Jerome.
Mills Music Inc., 1919.
Preview of the Flapper era recorded by Marion Harris (Victor), by Arthur Fields (Lyrophone), and by James Reese Europe's 369th Infantry Band (Pathe, under C. Creighton Thompson).

The Jazz Band
Words and music by Elsie Janis, music by Dan Kildare.
Ascherberg, Hopwood & Crew, Ltd., London, England, 1918.
Rag song introduced by Janis in the London revue *Hullo America* (1918).

Jennie
Words and music by Harry von Tilzer.
Harry Von Tilzer Music Publishing Co., 1902/Tempo Music.
Romantic ballad introduced by Flo Adler.

Jennie Lee
Words by Arthur Lamb, music by Harry von Tilzer.
Shapiro, Bernstein & Co., Inc., 1902.
Romantic ballad sung in minstrel shows and vaudeville by John P. Curran, Jos. F. Horitz, and Helene Mora.

Jerry, You Warra a Warrior in the War
Words by Dannie O'Neill, music by Billy Baskette.
Leo Feist Inc., 1919.
Irish romantic ballad popularized in vaudeville by Gladys Clark and Henry Bergman, Jerry Vogel, Bert Fitzgibbons, and Margaret Young.

Joan of Arc, They Are Calling You
Words by Arthur Bryan, Willie Weston, and Liane Held Carrera, music by Jack Wells.
Waterson, Berlin & Snyder, 1917/Venus Music Corp./Mills Music Inc.
This ASCAP top seller was popular as an instrumental for dance bands and as a pro-interventionist ballad.

Joan Sawyer Tango
Music by Leonard Stagliano.
Joseph W. Stern & Co., 1914.

Sawyer, an exhibition ballroom dancer and cabaret impresario, commissioned music for fashionable dance forms and for her own inventions, such as her "Mexi-Tango" and "Aeroplane Glide" (q.v).

Joe Turner Blues
Words and music by W. C. Handy.
Handy Brothers Music Co., Inc., 1915, 1943.
Classic chain-gang blues that was first popularized as a fox-trot by Prince's Band (Columbia) and the Victor Military Band; more appropriate performances were given by Handy's own band and by Johnny Dodds and the Black Bottom Stompers (Brunswick).

John Would Never Do That
Words by John Gilroy, music by Harry Linton.
Sol Bloom Publishing Co/Sol Bloom Music, 1902.
Comic duet of sibling rivalry sung by the authors in *The Liberty Belles* (musical, 1901).

Johnny, Get a Girl
Words by Stanley Murphy, music by Harry Puck.
Original copyright, 1916.
Summertime romantic advice introduced by Harry and Eva Puck; also popularized by Mabel Burke.

Johnny's in Town
Words by Jack Yellin, music by George W. Meyer and Abe Olman.
Leo Feist Inc., 1919.
Eddie Cantor interpolation comedy song from the *Ziegfeld Follies of 1919* about an American soldier who learned a lot in Paris. One in a continuing series of suggestive songs for Cantor and his rival Al Jolson, answering "How You Gonna Keep Them Down on the Farm ..." (q.v).

Johnson Rag
Words by Jack Lawrence, music by Gus Hall and Henry Kleinkauf.
Robbins Music Corp., 1917, 1940.
Jazz standard with many memorable recordings by vocalists and ensembles including Pearl Bailey (Columbia), Liberace (Columbia), Glenn Miller (RCA), and Jimmy Dorsey and His Band (Columbia). It was used as a theme song for Art Fallon on radio station WWSW and Doug Arthur on WIBG.

Josephine, My Jo
Words by R. C. McPherson, music by James T. Brymn.
Shapiro, Bernstein & Co., Inc., 1901.
Romance popularized by Flossie Allen and the Blondells.

Joshua Fit de Battl' ob Jericho, also known as **An Ante-bellum Sermon**
Words by Paul Lawrence Dunbar, music by H. T. Burleigh.
G. Schirmer Inc., 1901.
Dunbar's rendition of a Black sermon set as one of Burleigh's *Plantation Melodies Old and New.*

Joyous Springtime Bring Me Love, see **Enid Waltz,**.

Jubilo
Words by Anne Caldwell, music by Jerome Kern.
T. B. Harms, 1919.
Imitative Southern hymn introduced in *She's a Good Fellow* (musical, 1918); revived as the title song of the Samuel Goldwyn film (1919).

The Judgement Is at Hand
Words and music by Paul Dresser (pseudonym for Paul Dreiser).
Joseph W. Stern & Co., 1906.
Hymn first performed at Dresser's funeral; composed three days before his death and described at the time as "his requiem."

Julie
Words by William Jerome, music by Jean Schwartz.
Shapiro, Bernstein & Co., Inc., 1903.
Novelty comic song about a slang popularization of *Romeo and Juliet.* Introduced by Herbert Cawthorne in *Mr. Bluebeard* (musical, 1903).

June
Words and music by Clare Kummer.
Joseph W. Stern & Co., 1903.
Ballad introduced by Marie Cahill.

The Junk Man Rag
Words by Chris Smith and Ferd E. Mierisch, music by C. Luckeyth Roberts.
Joseph W. Stern & Co., 1913/Shawnee Press, Inc.
Novelty dance music introduced by Maurice Mouvet and his exhibition ballroom dance partner Florence Walton. It features plotted lyrics about junk man Peter, a rag-time violinist; recorded by composer "Lucky" Roberts on Circle records.

Just a Baby's Prayer at Twilight to Her Daddy Over There
Words by Sam M. Lewis, music by M. K. Jerome.
Waterson, Berlin & Snyder, 1918/Mills Music Inc., 1948.
Tremendously popular World War I sentimental plotted ballad in the style of 1900-1902; performed by most vaudeville stars and

recorded by each label's resident vocalists, such as Victor's Henry Burr, as well as by Prince's Orchestra of Columbia records. Revived in World War II as a novelty song by Guy Lombardo and His Royal Canadians. Similar retrospective ballads include Grossman and Lawrence's 1918 "Just a Baby's Letter Found in No-Man's Land."

Just a Dream of You, Dear
Words by C. F. McNamara, music by F. Henri Klickmann.
Original copyright, 1910/Paull-Pioneer Music Co., 1939.
Ballad popularized by Gene Greene and George Austin Moore, but recorded in barbershop arrangements by the Peerless and Haydn Quartets (Victor), the Capitol City Four (Victor), the Maple City Four (Mercury) and, more recently, the Mills Brothers (Decca).

Just a Kiss, also known as **The Raffles Dance**
Words and music by Bobby Clark.
Original copyright, 1913.
Romance based on the Raffles, or "kiss burglar," theme sung by Clark in the revue *Broadway to Paris* (1913); later used in Maurice Mouvet and Florence Walton's exhibition ballroom act.

Just a Little Rocking Chair and You
Words by Bert Fitzgibbon and Jack Drislane, music by Theodore F. Morse.
F. B. Haviland, 1905.
Flirtation song introduced by the duet team of Thomas Guyer and Beth Stone; also popularized by solo women, such as Flossie Allen and Mabel Russell.

Just a Little Word Unspoken, also known as **Let Us Be Sweethearts Again**
Words and music by Augustus Barratt.
Leo Feist Inc., 1912.
This romantic ballad as performed by Percival Knight became the most popular song in the musical *The Quaker Girl* (1911).

Just a Message from the Camp Fire, see **He Died on the Fighting Line,.**

Just a Tender Spot for Father Dear
Words by William Jerome, music by Jean Schwartz.
Shapiro, Bernstein & Co., Inc., 1902.
Ballad introduced by Arthur Dunn as the title character in the play *Huckleberry Finn* (1902, Hartford); parodied within the show with an additional verse complaining that too many songs were written about mothers.

Just a-Wearying for You
Words by Frank L. Stanton, music by Carrie Jacobs-Bond.
Boston Music Co., 1901.
Art song based on a poem by Atlanta writer Stanton recorded by Anna Case (Columbia), Frances Alda (Victor), and Arthur Tracy (Decca); revived by Paul Robeson in his program of American folk-derived songs (Victor).

Just Another Poor Man Gone Wrong
Words by Andrew B. Sterling, music by Harry von Tilzer.
Harry Von Tilzer Music Publishing Co., 1919.
Satirical song about marriage sung and recorded by Billy Glason.

Just Around the Corner
Words by Raymond B. Egan, music by Richard A. Whiting.
Remick Music Corp., 1919.
Optimistic romance introduced by Elizabeth Brice in the revue *Tout Suite Elizabet* (1919; also called *The Overseas Revue,* Paris); recorded by her in France and the United States.

Just as Washington Crossed the Delaware, So Will Pershing Cross the Rhine
Words by Howard Johnson, music by George W. Meyer.
Leo Feist Inc., 1917.
Patriotic anthem of World War I. Introduced by Elinore and Williams and sung frequently at bond rallies.

Just Because He Couldn't Sing "Love Me and the World Is Mine"
Words and music by Bert Fitzgibbon.
M. Witmark & Sons.
Introduced by Louise Dresser in *The Girl behind the Counter* (1907), this comic novelty told of the rejection of the suitor who could not sing Reed and Ball's popular romantic ballad (q.v.).

Just Because It's You
Words by C. M. S. McLellan, music by Ivan Caryll.
Chappell & Co., Inc., 1913.
Romantic song introduced by Hazel Dawn and John E. Young in *The Little Cafe* (1913), one of the season's most popular musicals; recorded by the principal studio vocalists of the era, among them, Elise Baker (Victor), Elizabeth Spencer (Edison), and Helen Clarke (Rishell).

Just Because She Made Dem Goo-Goo Eyes
Words by John Queen, music by Hughey Cannon.
Howley, Haviland & Dresser, 1900/Jerry Vogel Music Co., Inc., 1937.
An early example of the "Goo-Goo Eye" flirtation song, popular-

ized by Querita Vincent and recorded by Arthur Collins and Dan W. Quinn (both on Victor); revived by Bonnie Blue Eyes and Bob Atcher in the early 1940's era of nonsense songs.

Just for the Sake of Society
Words by Alfred Bryan, music by Kerry Mills.
Mills Music Inc., 1904.
Plotted melodramatic ballad of a mother who dresses for the ball while her baby is burning to death in his nursery. Introduced by Joseph Natus.

Just for Tonight
Words and music by Frank O. French.
M. Witmark & Sons, 1902.
Spanish-American War era farewell ballad. Introduced by countertenor R. J. Jose.

Just for Tonight
Words and music by George L. Cobb.
Will Rossiter, 1913.
Introduced by Franklyn Batie, this best-selling song uses the standard Broadway blues pattern of sustained notes over heavily syncopated vamps. It was billed as "a bigger hit than 'Some of These Days'" (q.v.), which it resembles, and was sung and recorded by many of that song's promoters, among them, Winnie Baldwin, Montgomery & Moore, and Sophie Tucker.

Just Like a Gypsy
Words and music by Seymour B. Simons and Nora Bayes.
Remick Music Corp., 1919.
Romantic ballad introduced by Bayes in her suffragist musical *Ladies First* (1918).

Just Next Door
Words and music by Charles K. Harris.
Charles K. Harris Music Publishing Co., 1902.
Plotted melodramatic ballad of poor child dying while rich children are giving a party; sung by juveniles, such as Baby Lund and Baby Zena Keefe, and by adults, among them George Diamond and Ida Emerson.

Just One Day
Words by Bobby Heath, music by Arthur Lange.
Original copyright, 1916.
Romantic song popularized by Kathryn Miley in vaudeville; also performed by male barbershop quartets, such as the Carnival Four.

Just 'Round the Corner from Broadway
Words by Blanche Merrill, music by Gus Edwards.
Shapiro, Bernstein & Co., Inc., 1914.
Romantic tune introduced by Sallie Seeley and juvenile chorus in *Gus Edwards' 1914 Song Revue.*

Just Try to Picture Me Back Home in Tennessee
Words by William Jerome, music by Walter Donaldson.
Waterson, Berlin & Snyder, 1915.
Dixie nostalgia interpolated by Al Jolson in *Robinson Crusoe, Jr.* (musical, 1916); an ASCAP top seller of 1915 after recordings by George Wilton Ballard on Edison and by the Pathe Dance Orchestra.

Just What the Good Book Taught
Words and music by Will A. Heelan and J. Fred Helf.
Joseph W. Stern & Co., 1900.
This plotted sentimental ballad introduced by Charles Falke tells of a father who forgives his son and second wife.

Just You
Words by Madge Marie Miller, music by H. T. Burleigh.
G. Ricordi & C., SpA, Milan, Italy, 1915.
Art song popularized by Lucrezia Bori, to whom it is dedicated, and Maggie Teyte, who recorded it for Columbia.

K

K-K-K-Katy
Words and music by Geoffrey O'Hara.
Leo Feist Inc., 1918.
ASCAP top seller through popular support for the sheet music by amateurs and soldiers, rather than vaudeville performers. The stuttering novelty by Army Song Leader O'Hara was widely distributed through the *A.E.F. Songbook* and the Y.M.C.A. Frequently used in films as period-setting background music, as in *The Cockeyed World* (Fox Films, 1929) and *Tin Pan Alley* (20th century Fox, 1940). See also "Thtop your Thrtuttering."

Kansas City
Words and music by Willard Robinson and Euday L. Bowman.
Original copyright, 1914/Shapiro, Bernstein & Co., Inc., 1949.
Blues popularized on automatic pianos; also recorded by the Victor Military Band and by Lonnie Johnson (Okeh).

Kashmiri Song
Words by Lawrence Hope, music by Amy Woodforde Finden.
Boosey & Co., Ltd., London, England, 1903, 1930.
Art song recorded by studio vocalists, such as Reinald Werrenrath (Victor) and Walter Scanlan (Edison), and by opera stars, among them, Maggie Teyte (Edison) and John McCormack (Victor). Also a popular instrumental with a range of recordings from Xavier Cugat (Columbia) to Yehudi Menuhin (Victor). Rudolph Valentino's recording has been re-issued by CRS.

Kate Kearney
Words and music by Fay and Oliver.
M. Witmark & Sons, 1904.
A traditional Irish ballad introduced in this arrangement by Chauncey Olcott in his play *A Romance of Athlone;* also performed by Blanche Ring and recorded by Harry MacDonough (Victor) and Jesse Crawford (Decca).

Katrina
Words and music by Edward W. Corliss.
Original copyright, 1902.
Sung by Adele Archer in *The Show Girl* (musical, 1902).

Katy Did
Words by Edgar Selden, music by Ben M. Jerome.
Joseph W. Stern & Co., 1902.
Romantic close-harmony song introduced by the Orpheus Comedy Four.

The Katy-Did, the Cricket and the Frog
Words by James Weldon Johnson, music by Bob Cole.
Joseph W. Stern & Co., 1903.
Introduced by Marie Cahill in *Nancy Brown* (1903) and interpolated into her musicals thereafter.

Keep a Little Cozy Corner in Your Heart for Me
Words by Jack Drislane, music by Theodore F. Morse.
F. B. Haviland, 1905, 1916/Jerry Vogel Music Co., Inc., 1943.
Flirtation song popularized by Flo Allen.

Keep Away from the Fellow Who Owns an Automobile
Words and music by Irving Berlin.
Ted Snyder Music Publishing Co., 1912/Irving Berlin Music Corp.
Novelty song about the dangers of dating in a car; popularized by the ventriloquist Tilford.

Keep on the Sunny Side
Words by Jack Drislane, music by Theodore F. Morse.
F. B. Haviland, 1906/Jerry Vogel Music Co., Inc.
Popular romantic tune performed in vaudeville by Charles Falke, Grace Leonard, Kathryn Miley, and Eddie and Cecilia Weston.

Keep on Walking
Words and music by Irving Berlin.
Waterson, Berlin & Snyder, 1913.
Novelty song relating a mother's advice to her daughter; popularized by Sophie Tucker.

Keep the Home Fires Burning (English)
Words by Lena Guilbert Ford, music by Ivor Novello.
Chappell & Co., Inc., 1915.
The song that symbolized the British experience in World War I was popularized in the United States through recordings by John McCormack (Victor) and Rosa Ponselle (Columbia, with the Stellar Quartet); it also serves as the title song of the Biograph album devoted to World War I music.

Keep Your Eye on the Girlie You Love
Words by Howard Johnson and Alex Gerber, music by Ira Schuster.
Leo Feist Inc., 1916.
Romantic song introduced by Elizabeth Brice and Charles King in their flirtation act, but also popularized as a suggestive warning from Sophie Tucker.

Keep Your Golden Gate Wide Open
Words by J. B. Silverwood, music by Gus Edwards.
Remick Music Corp., 1913.
Promotional song for the San Francisco Exposition of 1915 celebrating the completion of the Panama Canal trade route.

Keep Your Head Down, 'Fritzie Boy'
Words and music by Gitz Rice and Carey Morgan.
Leo Feist Inc., 1918.
This song of comic military advice during World War I became an ASCAP top seller.

The Kellerman Girlie
Words by William Jerome, music by Jean Schwartz.
Remick Music Corp., 1910.
Descriptive comedy song about beach fashion and etiquette. Introduced by Edwin Foy in *Up and Down Broadway* (1910), it derives its title from diver and vaudeville star Annette Kellermann, who popularized form-fitting one-piece bathing suits.

Kelly Has Gone to Kingdom Come
Words by Sax Rohmer, music by T. W. Thurban.
Will Rossiter, 1910.
This answer song to "Has Anyone Here Seen Kelly" (q.v) describes Kelly as a flyer who drowned while trying to cross the Atlantic. Introduced by Maud Lambert in *The Midnight Sons* (musical, 1910).

Kentucky Rose
Words and music by Shelton Rose.
Original copyright, 1915.
Nostalgic ballad introduced by vocalist and violinist Nonette.

Kerry Mills' Barn Dance
Words by Thurland Chattaway, music by Kerry Mills.
Mills Music Inc., 1908/Jerry Vogel Music Co., Inc.
Popular piano piece and instrumental based on country fiddling.

Kewpie Doll
Words by Edward Madden, music by Melville Morris and Albert Gumble.

Remick Music Corp., 1914.
Typical song for Anna Held, who overlaid its juvenile lyrices with suggestive performances.

Khaki Sammy
Words and music by John Alden Carpenter.
G. Schirmer Inc., 1917.
Patriotic ballad by art song composer Carpenter was dedicated to Nora Bayes; also recorded by Mabel Garrison and Percy Hemus.

Kidland
Words by Will D. Cobb, music by Gus Edwards.
Gus Edwards Music Publishing Co., 1910.
Comic song and production number for Lillian Lorraine in Ziegfeld's *Follies of 1910.*

Killarney, My Home o'er the Sea
Words and music by Frederick Knight Logan.
Leo Feist Inc., 1911/Jerry Vogel Music Co., Inc., 1942.
Nostalgic ballad featured and recorded by America's foremost Irish vocalists, ranging from Broadway's Chauncey Olcott and Blanche Ring to John McCormack. The ballad gave its name to a melodrama for the stage and silent film; in the 1950's, it was revived and recorded by Morton Downey and Lawrence Tibbett.

Killiecrankie (American-English)
Words and music by Harry Lauder.
Francis, Day & Hunter, Ltd., London, England, 1900.
Performed and recorded by Scottish dialect comic Harry Lauder.

Kinky
Words by "Mord" Allen and J. Ed. Green, music by Will Marion Cook.
Gotham-Attucks Music Publishing Co., 1908/Jerry Vogel Music Co., Inc.
Aida Overton Walker's song introducing her character in *Bandana Land* (musical, 1907).

Kiss All the Girls for Me
Words by J. J. Walker, music by John Heinzman.
Joseph W. Stern & Co., 1906.
This top-selling romantic march with lyrics by the future New York mayor was performed by the popular vaudeville feature act *Max Witt's Six Sophomores and a Freshman.*

The Kiss Burglar
Words by Harold Atteridge, music by Sigmund Romberg and Jean Schwartz.

Remick Music Corp., 1919.
Waltz introduced in the *Passing Show of 1919,* parodies the musical comedy *The Kiss Burglar* (1918); performed by the Mellette Sisters and recorded as dance music by Sam Ash.

A Kiss for Each Day of the Week
Words and music by Raymond Hubbell and Addison Burkhardt.
Charles K. Harris Music Publishing Co., 1903.
Romantic novelty song introduced by Arthur Dunn in *The Runaways* (musical, 1903).

A Kiss in the Dark
Words by Sydney Rosenfeld, music by C. M. Zierhrer.
The Shubert brothers, under the name Trebuhs, commissioned this "Americanized" ballad for Lulu Glaser to sing in their production of the Viennese operetta *Mlle. Mischief* (1908).

Kiss, Kiss, Kiss, If You Want to Learn to Kiss
Words by Harry B. Smith, music by Gertrude Hoffmann.
M. Witmark & Sons, 1906.
Romantic song introduced by Anna Held and Henri Leoni in *A Parisian Model* (1906) and recorded as a duet by Ada Jones and Billy Murray.

Kiss Me Again, also known as **If I Were on the Stage**
Words by Henry Blossom, music by Victor Herbert.
M. Witmark & Sons, 1905, 1933, 1961.
The 1905 musical *Mlle. Modiste* featured a complex song for its star, Fritzi Scheff, in which she gave short examples of the different characters that she could portray in the theatre (a genre derived from Viennese operettas such as *Die Fledermaus*) -- "Kiss Me Again" is the example of a romantic ballad. It became a standard and lost the framing device. As a ballad, it was soon recorded by Mabel Garrison (Victor) and Charles A. Prince's Columbia Orchestra. Many opera and film sopranos have recorded the song, among them, Amelita Galli-Curci (Victor, Victrola), Rosa Ponselle and Lily Pons (Columbia), Dorothy Kirsten (Victor), and Deanna Durbin (Decca); its male vocalists have included Richard Tauber (Parlophone) and Frank Sinatra (V Disc). In addition, the orchestras of Andre Kostelanetz (Columbia), Mantovani (London), and Victor Herbert himself (Victor) have recorded it as a waltz.

Kiss Me Good Night, Dear Love
Words and music by Malcolm Williams and Israel Zangwill.
Original copyright, 1904.
Introduced by Eleanor Robson as the title character in Zangwill's play *Merely Mary Ann* (1904).

Kiss Me, My Honey, Kiss Me
Words by Irving Berlin, music by Ted Snyder.
Ted Snyder Music Publishing Co., 1910/Irving Berlin Music Corp.
Popularized by "Little" Amy Butler and Elida Morris, who recorded it for Victor and Columbia; featured in the film biography of Eva Tanguay, *The "I Don't Care" Girl* (20th Century-Fox, 1953).

Kiss This Rose and Say "He Loves Me", see **While the Old Mill Wheel Is Turning,**.

The Kiss Waltz
Words by Rida Johnson Young, music by Sigmund Romberg.
G. Schirmer Inc., 1916.
Romantic duet with intervals left for on-stage kissing, introduced by Beth Lydy and Tom Richards in *Her Soldier Boy* (musical, 1916); popularized as dance music in a recording by Jaudas' Society Orchestra on Edison.

Kitty
Words by J. Cheever Goodwin, music by Frederick Solomon.
M. Witmark & Sons, 1901.
Romantic ballad introduced by the Hengler Sisters in *The Sleeping Beauty and the Beast* (musical, 1901).

The Kodak Girl
Words by George V. Hobart, music by Ludwig Englander.
Original copyright, 1901.
Novelty comic solo sung by Dan Daly in *The New Yorkers* (musical, 1901); lyrics use the language of photography to describe girls with "snap" or those who use "frozen negatives."

L

The Ladder of Roses
Words by R. H. Burnside, music by Raymond Hubbell.
T. B. Harms, 1915.
Romantic ballad written for the climax of a floral production number involving over two hundred dancers, each dressed as a flower, in Burnside's *Hip Hip Hooray* (1915) at the New York Hippodrome; popularized as a recorded one-step by Prince's Band.

Laddie Boy, see **Good Luck and God Be with You, Laddie Boy,**.

The Laddies Who Fought and Won (American-English)
Words and music by Harry Lauder.
T. B. Harms, 1916.
Patriotic anthem popularized and recorded by Scottish balladeer and dialect comic Lauder.

Lady Angeline
Words by Dave Reed, music by George Christie.
M. Witmark & Sons, 1912.
Dixie romance sung as a ballad, as a patter song, or in close harmony; popularized by Franklyn Batie, Willie and Eugene Howard, and Weston, Fields, and Carroll.

Lady Bountiful
Words by Robert Hobart Davis, music by Louis F. Gottschalk.
Original copyright, 1902.
Mamie Gilroy introduced this title song of the musical (1902), based on the comic strip by Gene Carr.

Lafayette
Words and music by Wellington Cross and Ted Shapiro.
Waterson, Berlin & Snyder, 1919.
Wellington Cross performed this patriotic ballad in vaudeville following his return from World War I military service.

The Lambs' March
Words and music by John Philip Sousa.
John Church Co., 1942.
Written for the 1914 *Lambs' Gambol,* a benefit revue by the Lambs, a New York theatrical club. Still a popular band march, it can currently be heard on recordings by Her Majesty's Royal Marine Band and the United States Marine Band.

The Land of "Let's Pretend"
Words by Harry B. Smith, music by Jerome Kern.
T. B. Harms, 1914.
Ballad introduced by Julia Sanderson, Donald Brian, and Joseph Cawthorne in *The Girl from Utah* (musical, 1914).

The Land of Nicotine, also known as **My Cigarette Maid**
Words by Jean C. Havez, music by Louis Hirsch.
Helf & Hager, 1907.
Production number and Cuban ballad featured in vaudeville by Lew Dockstader's Minstrels.

The Land Where the Good Songs Go
Words by P. G. Wodehouse, music by Jerome Kern.
T. B. Harms, 1917.
Originally a production song from the revue *Miss 1917* to introduce Bessie McCoy Davis's rendition of old favorites, revived from the mythical land of the title; ironically, the ballad was itself retrieved as a lost masterpiece for the biographical film about composer Kern, *'Till the Clouds Roll By* (MGM, 1946); recorded as a ballad by Alice Green and Charles Harrison on Victor.

The Language of Flowers
Words and music by Jessie H. Campbell.
Original copyright, 1903.
Introduced by Dorothy Jardon in *A Chinese Honeymoon* (musical, 1903); popular as a parlor song after publication in Sunday supplements of 1904 newspapers.

The Language of Love
Words by Bud De Sylva, music by Jerome Kern.
T. B. Harms, 1919.
Romantic duet introduced by Marie Carroll and Harry Fox in *Zip Goes a Million* (musical, 1920).

The Language of Lover's Smiles
Words by Channing Pollock and Rennold Wolf, music by Augustus Barratt.
M. Witmark & Sons, 1912.
Complex song with ballad and rag sections reflecting the lover's

changing expressions. Introduced by Clifton Crawford as an interpolation into his own musical *My Best Girl* (1912).

The Language of the Flowers (English)
Words by Percy Greenbank, music by Lionel Mockton.
Chappell & Co., Inc., 1901.
Satirical comic song introduced by Joseph Coyne in the musical *The Toreador* (1900, London; 1902, New York) about interpreting the nineteenth-century symbolic language of flowers as evidence in a breech of promise suit.

The Last Farewell
Words and music by Charles K. Harris.
Charles K. Harris Music Publishing Co., 1903.
Ballad written for operatic soprano Adelina Patti to sing as an encore to concerts on her farewell tour of 1903.

Last Night Was the End of the World
Words by Andrew Sterling, music by Harry von Tilzer.
Harry Von Tilzer Music Publishing Co., 1912.
Sentimental ballad introduced by Clare Rochester, recorded for Victor by Henry Burr and by the Victor Military Band.

The Last Rose of Summer Is the Sweetest Song of All
Words by Arthur Gillespie, music by Harry Sidney.
Joseph W. Stern & Co., 1907.
Nostalgic ballad referring to Flatow's aria from *Martha;* sung by Dorothy Jardon, Grace Wilson, and the vaudeville feature act *Max Witt's Singing Colleens;* recorded by Harry MacDonough and the Haydn Quartet (Victor).

The Last Shot Got Him
Words and music by Cecil Mack and Cecil Smith.
Harry Von Tilzer Music Publishing Co., 1912.
Billed as "The Great Bloo-ie Song," this patter rag described two Western shoot-outs with syncopated sound effects; recorded as a novelty by Ed Morton (Victor) and the Chenoweth Cornfield Symphony Orchestra on Okeh.

Late Hours
Words by David Kempner, music by Bert Williams.
Gotham-Attucks Music Publishing Co., 1907.
Bert Williams's character song about hangovers from *Bandana Land* (musical, 1907).

Laugh and the World Will Laugh with You, Weep and You'll Weep All Alone
Words and music by Chauncey Olcott and Manuel Klein.

M. Witmark & Sons, 1908.
Advice offered by Chauncey Olcott appearing in his plays *Ragged Robin* (1908) and *Barry of Barrymore* (1911).

Lazy Moon
Words by Bob Cole, music by J. Rosamond Johnson.
Joseph W. Stern & Co., 1903.
Close-harmony standard first popularized by George Primrose and his minstrel troupes; recorded by Billy Murray and the Haydn Quartet for Victor.

Lead Me to That Beautiful Band
Words and music by E. Ray Goetz and Irving Berlin.
Waterson, Berlin & Snyder, 1912.
Introduced by "Happy" Jack Lambert in *Cohan & Harris' Minstrels* (1911).

The Leader of the Frocks and Frills
Words by Robert H. Smith, music by Melville Ellis.
M. Witmark & Sons, 1902.
Ellis, a costume designer and composer, co-authored this description of contemporary fashion. Introduced by Adele Ritchie in *A Chinese Honeymoon* (1902).

The Leader of Vanity Fair
Words by Robert B. Smith, music by William T. Francis.
M. Witmark & Sons, 1903.
Parody of fashionable behavior; introduced by Lillian Russell in *Twirly-Whirly* (musical, 1902).

The Legend of the Maguire
Words and music by Andrew Mack.
Original copyright, 1904.
Ballad introduced by author Mack in his Irish melodrama *The Way to Kenmare.*

A Lemon in the Garden of Love
Words by M. E. Rourke, music by Richard Carle.
M. Witmark & Sons, 1906/Jerry Vogel Music Co., Inc., 1935.
Comic complaint introduced by composer Carle in his *The Spring Chicken* (1906) and, with its tremendous popularity there, in his subsequent revues. The song was interpolated into Kaufman and Hart's play *The American Way* (1939), with Frederick March.

Les Beaux Yeux, see **Beautiful Eyes**,.

A Lesson in Flirtation
Words by Harry B. Smith, music by Ludwig Englander.

Original copyright, 1901.
Performed by Irene Bentley and the male officers' chorus in *The Strollers* (musical, 1901).

Let Bygones Be Bygones and Let Us Be Sweethearts Again
Words by Harry Williams and Joe Young, music by Bert Grant.
Original copyright, 1914/Mills Music Inc., 1931.
Romantic ballad that became a signature tune for (Hattie) Burke and (Ted) Lorraine; also performed and recorded by Helen Clark on Victor.

Let It Alone
Words by Alex Rogers, music by Bert Williams.
Gotham-Attucks Music Publishing Co., 1906.
Ironic character song for Bert Williams; introduced in the musical *Abyssinia* (1906) and recorded on Columbia.

Let Mary Go Round on the Merry-Go-Round
Words and music by Dave Reed, Jr.
Howley, Haviland & Dresser, 1901.
Novelty romance introduced by Josephine Sabel.

Let Me Call You Sweetheart
Words and music by Beth Slater Whitson and Leo Friedman.
Original copyright, 1910/Shawnee Press, Inc., 1937.
One of America's favorite ballads; its many recordings include those by Vernon Dalhart (Brunswick), Ruth Etting (Banner), George Olsen (Majestic), and Xavier Cugat's Waldorf Astoria Orchestra. It is now performed most often as a barbershop nostalgic novelty. In 1925 Whitson and Friedman wrote their own answer song, "Since You Called me Sweetheart."

Let Me Live and Stay in Dixieland
Words and music by Elizabeth Brice and Charles King.
Ted Snyder Music Publishing Co., 1910.
One of the first Dixie nostalgia songs to become a best seller as sheet music and recording, it was introduced on Broadway by Elsie Janis as the title character in *The Slim Princess* (January 2, 1911). A month later, the songwriters brought it back to New York from their successful vaudeville tour and interpolated their own song into *The Hen Pecks* (February 4, 1911). In addition to Janis, Elizabeth Brice and Charles King recorded the song for Victor.

Let Me See You Smile
Words and music by Fred Fisher.
Mills Music Inc., 1905.
Romance sung in vaudeville by Thomas J. Quigley, Maud Packwell,

and Cordelia ("The Creole Belle") Mitchell and the Three Mitchells.

Let My People Go, see **Go Down Moses,**.

Let the Flag Fly!
Words and music by L. Wolfe Gilbert.
Original copyright, 1917.
Patriotic anthem suggested by the slogan of *The New York World.*

Let the Rest of the World Go By
Words by J. Keirn Brennan, music by Ernest R. Ball.
M. Witmark & Sons, 1919.
ASCAP top-selling ballad of 1919 was widely recorded by studio vocalists, among them, Albert Campbell and Henry Burr (Columbia), Charles Hart (Emerson), Harvey Hindermeyer (Edison), and Elizabeth Spencer and Charles Hart (Victor). Revived in the 20th Century-Fox film *Irish Eyes Are Smiling* (1944). Recorded by Joan Morris on her *Vaudeville* album (Nonesuch).

Let Us Be Sweethearts Again, see **Just a Little Word Unspoken,**.

Let Us Build a Little Nest
Words and music by Jerome Kern, words by Edgar Allan Woolf.
T. B. Harms, 1912.
Lullaby doubling as romantic ballad. Introduced by Mitzi in the musical *Head Over Heels* (1918).

Let Us Have Peace
Words by George Graff, Jr., music by Ernest R. Ball.
M. Witmark & Sons, 1911.
Anthem of the "Let Us Have Peace" political movement cosponsored by Julius Witmark. Dedicated to then-President William Howard Taft, it was introduced at the July 7, 1911 Christian Endeavor Convention. Recorded by Reinald Werrenrath for Victor and Edison.

Let's All Be Americans Now
Words and music by Irving Berlin, Edgar Leslie, and George W. Meyer.
Waterson, Berlin & Snyder, 1917.
Patriotic anthem of World War I popularized and recorded by barbershop-style ensembles, such as the American Quartet (Victor) and the Knickerbocker Quartet (Columbia).

Let's All Go Up to Maud's
Words by Joseph C. Farrell, music by Kerry Mills.
Mills Music Inc., 1904.

Invitation to spoon with Maud and her sisters. Introduced by Lottie Gilson.

Let's Be Ready, That's the Spirit of '76
Words and music by Charles Bayha and Rubey Cowan.
Original copyright, 1916.
Interventionist march sung in vaudeville by Wellington Cross. Similar songs of 1916 included Heath and James's "Let's Be Prepared" and Bunce and Donaldson's "Prepare the Eagle to Protect the Dove."

Let's Get the Umpire's Goat
Words and music by Nora Bayes and Jack Norworth.
Remick Music Corp., 1909.
This novelty song introduced by Bayes and Norworth has a chorus that lists insults to umpires at a baseball game.

Let's Go to a Picture Show
Words by Junie McCree, music by Albert von Tilzer.
York Music Corp., 1909.
Descriptions of movie dating in the early twentieth century sung by Irene Jermon, Maud Gray, and lyricist McCree.

Let's Help the Irish Now
Words by Bernie Grossman, music by Billy Frisch.
Original copyright, 1919.
Introduced by Frank Mullane, this patriotic ballad was distinctly in favor of the Irish Free State.

Let's Help the Red Cross Now
Words and music by Ted S. Barron.
Original copyright, 1917.
Recruitment song for the American Red Cross during World War I.

Let's Make Love among the Roses
Words by William Jerome, music by Jean Schwartz.
Remick Music Corp., 1910.
Romantic ballad introduced by Blanche Ring in *The Yankee Girl* (musical, 1910).

The Letter That Never Reached Home
Words by Edgar Leslie and Bernie Grossman, music by Archie Gottler.
Kalmar, Puck & Abrahams Consolidated Mus, 1916/Leeds Music Corp., 1944.
Plotted ballad of World War I introduced by Anna Chandler. The image of the dead soldier's letter lying on the battlefield was

adopted on posters and promotional campaigns for service organizations in the United States. Recorded by Harry MacDonough and the Orpheus Quartet (Victor).

Liberty Bell, It's Time to Ring Again
Words by Joe Goodwin, music by Halsey K. Mohr.
Shapiro, Bernstein & Co., Inc., 1917, 1940.
Patriotic anthem recorded by the Peerless Quartet (Emerson) and distributed in the *A.E.F. Songbook;* re-issued in 1940 for World War II.

Liberty Forever, also known as **Per Sempre Liberta!**
Italian words and music by Enrico Caruso and Vincenzo Bellezza, English words by Frederick H. Martens.
G. Schirmer Inc., 1918/Carl Fischer, Inc.
Patriotic march song popularized by Caruso in both Italian and English versions; recorded by the Victor Military Band.

The Liberty Loan March
Words and music by John Philip Sousa.
Original copyright, 1917.
Sousa wrote songs and marches for his band's performances to benefit the World War I Liberty Loan campaigns. Most, like "Victory Chest" and "Pushing On," written for the fourth campaign in 1918, were published by newspapers. This title was recorded by the United States Marine Band on Volume 7 of *The Heritage of John Philip Sousa.*

Life, Let Me Live My Life for You
Words by "Rube" Goldberg, music by Ethel Broaker.
Leo Feist Inc., 1919.
Ballad based on situations in lyricist Goldberg's cartoon strip, *Life's Little Jokes.*

Lift Every Voice and Sing
Words and music by James Weldon Johnson and J. Rosamond Johnson.
Joseph W. Stern & Co., 1900, 1921, 1940, 1959.
As the anthem of the National Association for the Advancement of Colored People (NAACP), this song's status as the "Negro National Anthem" has been dramatically depicted in many works of documentary prose, fiction, and theatre. Two books, in which the amateur performance of the anthem had enormous impact, were translated into highly acclaimed made-for-television movies -- Maya Angelou's *I Know Why the Caged Bird Sings* (20 Century-Fox-TV, 1979) and Alex Haley's *Roots: The Next Generation* (WB-TV, 1979, episode 3). Recorded as a hymn by the Juanita Hall Choir (Decca) and the Southern Sons (Bluebird). Published

as complete text in *Lift Every Voice! The Second People's Songbook* (1953, 1957).

The Light That Failed
Words and music by Charles E. Baer.
Original copyright, 1901.
Sentimental ballad that provides a happy ending for the situation suggested by Rudyard Kipling's 1890 novel of the same title; sung by Tom O'Brien.

Lights of Home
Words and music by Al Trahern.
Original copyright, 1905.
Promotional title song for Lottie Blair Parker's popular melodrama; also interpolated by Jessie Mae Hall into *The Street Singer* (musical, 1905 in Chicago).

Like a Star That Falls from Heaven
Words by Arthur Lamb, music by Kerry Mills.
Mills Music Inc., 1903.
Melodramatic ballad of a girl gone astray in the city. Introduced by Charles Foreman and performed by song illustrator Charles Falke.

Li'l Gal
Words by Paul Lawrence Dunbar, music by J. Rosamond Johnson.
Joseph W. Stern & Co., 1901, 1917/Edward B. Marks Music Corp., 1932.
Art song featured by Paul Robeson on recordings with an orchestra (Gramophone) and with pianist Lawrence Brown (Victor, Gramophone).

Lila
Words by Archie Gottler, music by Maceo Pinkard.
Original copyright, 1907.
Fox-trot that maintained its popularity through the 1940's with recordings by the Dixie Jazz Band (Okeh), the University Six (Harmony), and Fred Waring's Pennsylvanians (Victor).

Lillies Mean You to Me
Words by Lillian Gibson, music by Fred Bernhardt.
Original copyright, 1911.
Promotional song for the American vaudeville tours of Gaby Deslys, using her name as a rationale for a floral romance ballad of the type more popular in the early 1900's.

Lily of the Valley
Words and music by L. Wolfe Gilbert and Anatol Friedland.

Joseph W. Stern & Co., 1917.
This BMI top seller uses a plot frame for the verses about a songwriter's struggle to compose the romantic ballad chorus; sung and recorded by Sophie Tucker, Adele Rowland, and Kathryn Miley; revived by Jimmy Dorsey in the late 1930's.

The Lily or the Rose
Words by Monroe H. Rosenfeld, music by Alfred Solman.
Original copyright, 1902.
Sentimental ballad combining a soldier's farewell to his sweetheart, typical of the Spanish-American War era, with lyrics derived from the language of the flowers, popular in early-twentieth-century parlor songs; introduced by Lara Rogers.

The Limerick Girls
Words and music by Chauncey Olcott.
M. Witmark & Sons, 1902.
Irish imitative romance introduced by Olcott in his play *Old Limerick Town* (1902).

Linda, Look Out de' Windah
Words by Edward Gardinier, music by Maurice Levi.
Comic dialect song introduced by the Rogers Brothers in their vehicle *The Rogers Brothers at Harvard* (1902); later sung by cast member Pat Rooney in his vaudeville acts.

Lindy, also known as **Sound of the Times**
Words by James Weldon Johnson, music by Bob Cole and J. Rosamond Johnson.
Joseph W. Stern & Co., 1903.
Introduced by Fay Templeton in the "Evolution of Rag Time" sequence in her act at the Klaw and Erlanger Aerial Theatre, 1903; recorded by Marguerite Dunlap (Victor), by many close-harmony ensembles, including the Proximity Quartet (Columbia) and the Vocalion Harmonizers, and by the Original Dixieland Jazz Band (Victor). The scene also featured Peter F. Dailey singing the same writers' "Spirit of the Banjo."

Line Up for Bryan
Words and music by George W. Gale.
Original copyright, 1908.
Campaign song supporting William Jennings Bryan, Democratic candidate for President.

The Linger Longer Girl
Words by Arthur J. Lamb, music by Alfred Solman.
Joseph W. Stern & Co., 1906.
Maud Lambert introduced this invitation to spoon longer 'neath

the moon. The phrase entered contemporary slang, re-emerging in 1917 in the title and title song of Charlotte Greenwood's show *Linger Longer Letty,* which opened on Broadway in 1919.

Linger Longer Letty
Words by Bernie Grossman, music by Alfred Goodman.
Leo Feist Inc., 1919.
Title song for the musical comedy starring Charlotte Greenwood and Olin Howard that had toured for many seasons before opening on Broadway in 1919; also used as a theme song for Greenwood's silent and early sound film comedies about "Letty."

Linger Longer Lingerie
Words by Harry B. Smith, music by Maurice Levi.
Remick Music Corp., 1909.
Production number for Lillian Lorraine and the lingerie-clad chorus in Ziegfeld's *Follies of 1909;* this parody of fashion recalls Maud Lambert's "The Linger Longer Girl" (q.v.).

Listen to Me
Words and music by Clare Kummer.
T. B. Harms, 1912.
Marie Cahill's stentorian voice introduced this interpolation in *The Opera Ball* (musical, 1912).

A Little Bit o' Honey
Words and music by Carrie Jacobs-Bond.
Original copyright, 1917.
Popular art song recorded by Olive Kline and Evan Williams, each on Victor and Victrola.

A Little Bit of Heaven, Shure They Call It Ireland
Words by J. Keirn Brennan, music by Ernest R. Ball.
M. Witmark & Sons, 1914.
Ballad associated with two generations of Irish tenors, beginning with Chauncey Olcott, who introduced it in Rachel Crother's play *The Heart of Paddy Whack* (1914), and continuing to Bing Crosby, Dennis Day, and Phil Regan. Featured in the film *Irish Eyes Are Smiling.*

A Little Bit of Irish
Words by Gus Kahn, music by Grace LeBoy.
Shapiro, Bernstein & Co., Inc., 1911.
Tribute to "Lena Herman" by an Irish boyfriend who describes her by using lines from other Irish songs; popularized by Ila Grannon, Maggie Cline, and Frank Mullane.

A Little Boy Named 'Taps'
Words by Edward Madden, music by Theodore F. Morse.
F. B. Haviland, 1904.
This top-selling sentimental ballad about a young bugler killed in battle was performed by Kathryn Miley, Madeleine Clark, and Amy Butler. It became a popular parlor song during the World War I era.

The Little Church around the Corner
Words by Thomas J. Gray, music by Harry Carroll.
Shapiro, Bernstein & Co., Inc., 1913.
Popular romance introduced by Alice Lloyd in the vaudeville number *A Night in the Jardin de Danse* (1913) and featured by Frank Mullane and Harry Carroll. Other songs with this title were by M. E. Rourke and Jerome Kern (1907, for *Fascinating Flora*) and by Alex Gerber and Sigmund Romberg (1919, for *Magic Melody*).

A Little Empty Nest
Words by Will A. Heelan, music by J. Fred Helf.
Joseph W. Stern & Co., 1901.
Pathetic ballad of a mother crying over her dead infant. Introduced by Edna May Spooner and popular as a parlor song.

A Little Girl Like Me
Words by Charles J. Campbell and Ralph M. Skinner, music by Alfred E. Aarons.
M. Witmark & Sons, 1905.
Flirtatious song interpolated by Blanche Ring into *His Honor the Mayor* (1905) and used frequently in her vaudeville acts.

Little Girl, You'll Do
Words by Benjamin Hapgood Burt, music by Alfred Solman.
Joseph W. Stern & Co., 1905.
This proposal song was so popular in 1904-1905 that it was reprinted three times, with a new "introduced by" banner each time. During that season, it was interpolated with great success by Sophie Brandt into *The Madcap Princess* (September 5, 1904), by Harry Leighton into *The Rollicking Girl* (May 1, 1905), and by Talleur Andrews into *The Catch of the Season* (August 25, 1905).

Little Grey Home in the West
Words by D. Eardley-Wilmot, music by Hermann Lohr.
Chappell & Co., Inc., 1911.
Descriptive ballad that became a frequently heard concert aria for opera singers such as John McCormack (Victor), Alma Gluck (Victor), and Maggie Teyte (Columbia) and for popular vocalists,

including Jesse Crawford (Decca), Kenny Baker (Victor), Dorothy Jardon (Brunswick), and Sam Ash (Vocalion).

The Little Gypsy Maid
Words by Harry B. Smith and Cecil Mack, music by Will Marion Cook.
Harry Von Tilzer Music Publishing Co., 1902.
Ballad interpolated by Irene Bentley into *The Wild Rose* (musical, 1902), where it became the hit of the show.

The Little House upon the Hill, see **There's a Light That's Burning in the Window of the Little House upon the Hill,**.

Little Lost Sister
Words by Caspar Nathan, music by F. Henri Klickmann.
Original copyright, 1914.
The cover of this song proclaims it "The Moral-Uplife Song Founded on Virginia Brooks' Great White Slavery Play of the Same Name."

A Little Love But Not for Me
Words by Elsie Janis, music by Jerome Kern.
T. B. Harms, 1915.
Introduced by Janis in the musical *Miss Information* (1908).

Little Lovin' Honey Man, see **Honey Man,**.

Little Mary (English)
Words by Leslie Mayne, music by Lionel Monckton.
Chappell & Co., Inc., 1903.
Song about a gold-digger introduced by Gertie Millar in *The Orchid* (musical, 1904 in London; 1907 in New York).

Little Mary Gardeners
Words by Glen MacDonough, music by Raymond Hubbell.
Original copyright, 1909.
Introduced by Nan Brennan in the opera parody in the musical *The Midnight Sons* (1909), this song refers to the histrionic powers of actresses Ethel Barrymore, Mabel Barrison, and Alla Nazimova but concludes "... we prefer to these Mary Garden in *Thais.*"

Little Miss No-One from No-Where
Words by Robert B. Smith, music by Gus Edwards.
M. Witmark & Sons, 1904.
Comic song about a know-it-all. Introduced by Della Fox performing in military drag.

Little Mother of Mine
Words by Walter H. Brown, music by H. T. Burleigh.
G. Ricordi & C., SpA, Milan, Italy, 1917.
Nostalgic ballad associated with John McCormack (Victor) and also recorded by John Charles Thomas (Vocalion) and Theo Karle (Brunswick).

Little Nemo and His Bear
Words by Dave Clarke, music by Albert Gumble.
Remick Music Corp., 1907.
This song, based on the comic strip characters created by Winsor McCay, was interpolated into a touring production of Montgomery and Stone's great musical *The Wizard of Oz.*

Little One, Good Bye
Words by E. P. Moran, music by Silvio Hein.
Shapiro, Bernstein & Co., Inc., 1906.
Romantic ballad featured by vaudeville's most popular singers, including Irene Franklyn, Grace LaRue, and Claude Thardo.

Little Rag Baby Doll
Words by L. Wolfe Gilbert, music by Lewis F. Muir.
Mills Music Inc., 1913/Alfred Music Co., Inc., 1940.
Novelty rag-time version of "Rockabye Baby" performed and recorded by Sophie Tucker.

Little Tommy Murphy
Words by Matthew Woodward, music by Andrew Mack.
Howley, Haviland & Co., 1900.
Imitative Irish ballad from Mack's play *The Bold Soger Boy.*

Little Widow Brown
Words by Edgar Smith, music by W. T. Francis.
M. Witmark & Sons, 1903.
Portrait of a merry widow introduced by Lillian Russell in *Twirly-Whirly* (musical, 1902).

The Little Wooden Soldier (English)
Words by Basil Hood, music by Arthur Sullivan.
Chappell & Co., Inc., 1901.
Robert Evett introduced one of the famous composer Sullivan's final songs in *The Emerald Isle* in London (1901) and New York (1902).

Liz'
Words by Jean Lenox, music by Harry O. Sutton.
Joseph W. Stern & Co., 1905.
Minstrel show dialect romance introduced by George Primrose.

Liza
Words by Richard Carle, music by Gus Edwards.
Mills Music Inc., 1902.
Rhyming patter song claiming that "wiser guys are making eyes at Liza"; written and performed by Carle for interpolation into his musical *The Storks* (1902). Composer Edwards later used the song in his vaudeville feature acts for juveniles-- his *Song Revue* (1913) and *Blonde Typewriters* (1915).

The Load That Father Carried
Words by Frank Fogerty, music by J. B. Mullen.
Original copyright.
Novelty song in three verses; if only the first two verses are performed, it is a sentimental ballad about a father's responsibilities; the third verse turns it into a comedy song about an alcoholic father whose "load was loaded." Sung by Nick Conroy, the Imperial Four, and others.

Lola
Words by Louise Brehany, music by Anne Caldwell.
Shapiro, Bernstein & Co., Inc., 1904.
Romantic ballad introduced by Brehany; also featured in a close-harmony arrangement by the Castle Square Quartette.

Lonesome
Words by Joseph Rosey, music by Albert von Tilzer.
York Music Corp., 1904.
Ballad introduced by Edna May in *The School Girl* (revue, 1904).

Lonesome
Words by Edgar Leslie, music by George W. Meyer.
Mills Music Inc., 1909/Paull-Pioneer Music Co., 1936.
Romantic song introduced by Corinne in the musical *Mlle. Mischief* (1908) and performed in vaudeville by Julia Frary and Florence Turner.

Lonesome Honey for You
Words by Kenneth Bisbee, music by Harry H. Williams.
Original copyright, 1912.
Bluesy ballad popularized by Bonita.

The Longest Way 'Round Is the Sweetest Way Home
Words by Ren Shields, music by Kerry Mills.
Mills Music Inc., 1908/Jerry Vogel Music Co., Inc., 1936.
Comic song about spooning in an automobile popularized in vaudeville by Jack Devereaux, Irma LaPomme, and Frank Morrell.

Longing to Be by Your Side, see **Absence Makes the Heart Grow Fonder,**.

Look in Her Eyes
Words by M. E. Rourke, music by Jerome Kern.
Harms, Inc., 1913/Francis, Day & Hunter, Inc., 1913.
Ballad introduced by George MacFarlane in *Miss Caprice* (musical, 1913). Revised by Kern and Herbert Reynolds as "Look in His Eyes" for *Have a Heart* (1917). Recorded by MacFarlane for Victor and by Vernon Archibald for Edison.

Look into Mine Eyes Dear Heart (American-English)
Words and music by Arthur Trevelyan.
T. B. Harms, 1900.
Sentimental ballad introduced by Pauline Hall in vaudeville and popular as a parlor song and concert aria.

Look It Up in the Dream Book
Words by Robert Smith, music by Harry T. MacConnell.
Edward Schuberth & Co., Inc., 1901.
Parody of dream analysis introduced by Francis Wilson in *The Strollers* (1901).

Look Out for Jimmy Valentine, see **Alias Jimmy Valentine,**.

Look Who's Here
Words by Andrew B. Sterling, music by Harry von Tilzer.
Harry Von Tilzer Music Publishing Co., 1906.
Nora Bayes's rollicking song of a sailor on home leave.

Lord Have Mercy on a Married Man
Words by Edgar Leslie, music by J. Fred Helf.
Original copyright, 1911/Larry Spier, Inc.
Lew Dockstader's signature song in his minstrel troupe and in vaudeville; up to eight extra choruses allowed Dockstader to insert topical references that updated the song through the 1910's and 1920's.

Lotus San: A Japanese Romance
Words by Edward Madden, music by Dorothy Jardon.
Original copyright, 1908.
Song and instrumental background for dance solo by Madden's sometime composer colleague, Gertrude Hoffmann; also performed as a ballad by Jardon.

Louie, Take Me to the Frisco Fair
Words by Jack M. Lipton, music by D'Amasus G. Gallur.
Original copyright, 1912.

This promotional song for the San Francisco Pan-American Exposition uses the characters introduced in "Meet Me in St. Louis, Louis" (q.v.).

Louisiana
Words and music by Harry Tierney.
G. Schirmer Inc., 1916.
Dixie nostalgia rag performed by Sam White and Lew Clayton and danced by Marie Lavarre in the pullman car scene in the revue *The Show of Wonders* (1916).

Louisiana Louise
Words by Andrew B. Sterling, music by Gus Edwards.
Mills Music Inc., 1902.
Syncopated romance introduced by Billy Clifford in vaudeville.

Love
Words by R. H. Burnside, music by A. Baldwin Sloane.
Original copyright, 1903.
Popular song introduced by Virginia Earl as the title character in *Sergeant Kitty* (musical, 1904).

Love a la Mode
Words by Edgar Smith, music by John Stromberg.
M. Witmark & Sons, 1902.
Opera burlesque for Lillian Russell and DeWolf Hopper from Weber and Fields's annual comic revue *Hoity-Toity* (1901).

Love at the Door (English)
Words by Adrian Ross, music by Ivan Caryll.
Chappell & Co., Inc., 1903.
Romantic waltz introduced by Kitty Gordon in *The Girl from Kay's* (1903).

Love Days
Words by William Jerome, music by Jean Schwartz.
George M. Cohan Music Publishing Co., 1908.
Romantic ballad introduced by Frank Morrell in the vaudeville act *Cohan & Harris' Minstrels.*

Love Has Claimed Its Own
Words by S. R. Cassin, music by Will Accooe.
Shapiro, Bernstein & Co., Inc., 1901.
Ballad introduced by Harry Farleigh in *The Casino Girl* (1900).

Love, Here Is My Heart!, also known as **Chere, a toi mon coeur** (American-French)
French words by Louis Delamarre, English words by Adrian Ross,

music by Lao Silesu.
Leo Feist Inc., 1915, 1943, 1952.
Romantic concert aria recorded by John McCormack (Victor), Richard Tauber (Parlophone), the Paradise Island Trio (Decca), and, most memorably, by Mantovani (London).

Love in an Orchard, also known as **The Apple, Apple, Apple of My Eye**
Words by Matt C. Woodward, music by Ben M. Jerome.
Sol Bloom Publishing Co/Sol Bloom Music, 1903.
Love song using fruit imagery performed by Albert Hart in *The Girl from Dixie* (musical, 1903).

Love Is Elusive
Words by Richard Carle, music by H. L. Heartz.
M. Witmark & Sons, 1903.
Ballad associated with Richard Carle throughout his career and interpolated into his musicals *The Tenderfoot* (1904) and *Mary's Lamb* (1908).

Love Is Like a Firefly
Words by Otto Hauerbach (pseudonym for Otto Harbach), music by Rudolf Friml.
G. Schirmer Inc., 1912, 1940, 1955.
Romantic ballad introduced by Emma Trentini in the operetta *The Firefly* (1912) and revived by Jeanette MacDonald in the 1937 MGM film of the same title; recorded by MacDonald and by Allan Jones, her film co-star.

Love Is Mine
Words by Edward Teschemacher, music by Clarence G. Gartner.
M. Witmark & Sons, 1911.
Concert aria associated with Enrico Caruso (Victor); also recorded by Lloyd Chandos (Odeon) and Mario Laurenti (Edison).

Love Laughs at Locksmiths
Words by R. H. Burnside, music by A. Baldwin Sloane.
Original copyright, 1903.
Romantic song that sums up the plot of the musical *Sergeant Kitty* (1904); sung by Virginia Earl as the title character.

Love Lifted Me
Words by James Rowe, music by Howard E. Smith.
Homer A. Rodeheaver, 1912, 1922.
This gospel standard associated now with Roy Rogers and Dale Evans was first popularized by Homer A. Rodeheaver's 2000-voice choir for the Billy Sunday evangelical movement (1912-

1918) and by Anna Case, who made it one of Edison's earliest top-selling sacred recordings.

A Love-Lorn Lily
Words by Louis Harrison and George V. Hobart, music by A. B. Sloane.
M. Witmark & Sons, 1900.
Parody of the "language of the flowers" type of romantic ballad. Introduced by Fay Templeton in *Broadway to Tokio* (musical, 1900); a piano waltz version of the song became popular as dance music.

Love Me All the Time
Words and music by Joseph E. Howard.
Original copyright, 1909.
Popular bluesy love song performed by Mabel Barrison in Clyde Fitch's play *The Blue Mouse* and by her and Anna Laughlin in vaudeville.

Love Me and the World Is Mine
Words by Dave Reed, Jr., music by Ernest R. Ball.
M. Witmark & Sons, 1906.
Irish ballad featured by Dave Carter and Sue Smith in vaudeville and recorded by studio vocalists Albert Campbell, Harry MacDonough, and Blanche Thebon (all Victor), Henry Burr (Columbia), and organist John Hassel (Harmony, Velvet Tone).

Love Me at Twilight
Words by William Jerome and Joe Young, music by Bert Grant.
Waterson, Berlin & Snyder, 1916.
Popular romantic ballad introduced and recorded by Grace LaRue; interpolated by her in *Step This Way* (musical, 1916).

Love Me Like I Want to Be Loved
Words by Earle C. Jones and Alfred Bryan, music by George W. Meyer.
Original copyright, 1908.
Bluesy ballad performed by the black vocalist Ella Jones and further popularized by Emma Carus.

Love Me Like the Ivy Loves the Old Oak Tree
Words by George J. Moriarty, music by Richard A. Whiting.
Remick Music Corp., 1914.
Romance performed in vaudeville by Moriarty and by Jack Driscoll.

Love Me, Make Me Love You Like I Never Loved Before
Words by Alfred Bryan, music by Fred Fisher.

Shapiro, Bernstein & Co., Inc., 1911/Fred Fisher Music Co., 1939, 1951.
Romantic song with a complex syncopated chorus. Introduced by James T. Powers, it became a staple of male/female flirtation acts in vaudeville throughout the 1920's and 1930's. Revived in 1951 by Bill Darnel on Carol Records.

Love Me While the Loving Is Good
Words by Stanley Murphy, music by Harry von Tilzer.
Harry Von Tilzer Music Publishing Co., 1913.
Spooning instructions introduced by Whiting and Burt in the *Passing Show of 1913.*

Love Me with a Tiger Love
Words by Addison Burkhardt, music by Will Marion Cook.
Harry Von Tilzer Music Publishing Co., 1910.
Introduced by Clara Palmer in *The Deacon and the Lady* (musical, 1910).

Love Sends a Little Gift of Roses
Words by Leslie Cooke, music by John Openshaw.
T. B. Harms, 1919, 1947.
ASCAP top seller of 1919 through recordings by John McCormack and Fritz Kreisler for Victrola and by Reinald Werrenrath, Rosario Bourdon, and the Victor Novelty Orchestra (Victor); revived by Tommy Dorsey and the Pied Pipers (RCA Victor) and by the Andrews Sisters (Okeh).

Love Will Find a Way
Words and music by Charles Shackford.
Joseph W. Stern & Co., 1900.
Sentimental ballad introduced by May Mooney.

Loveland Days
Words and music by W. R. Williams.
Will Rossiter, 1915.
This juvenile romantic ballad in the "Loveland" series was a top-seller in 1915-1916 as sung by the Dolce Sisters, Dixie Harris, and Ethel Mae Butler.

Lovely Daughter of Allah
Words by James Weldon Johnson, music by J. Rosamond Johnson.
Joseph W. Stern & Co., 1912.
"Arabian episode" featured by Charles Hart, J. Rosamond Johnson's vaudeville partner after Bob Cole's death.

The Lover's A.B.C.
Words by M. E. Rourke, music by Max S. Witt.

Joseph W. Stern & Co., 1903.
Romantic advice song introduced by Irene Bentley in *The Girl from Dixie* (musical, 1903).

Love's Lullaby, also known as **Berceuse Tendre** (American-French)
English words by Ballard MacDonald, music by Leo Danideroff.
Joseph W. Stern & Co., 1912.
French ballad and waltz glide given English lyrics for its U.S. publication; one of the season's most popular dance scores after its introduction by Arthur Monday and Sylvia Sunday, the resident exhibition ballroom team at New York's famous Follies Marigny cabaret.

Love's Lullaby of Dreams, see **Sing Me Love's Lullaby,**.

Love's Own Sweet Song (American-Austrian)
English words by C. C. S. Cushing and E. P. Heath, music by Emmerich Kalman.
Josef Weinberger, Frankfurt, Federal Republic of Germany, 1912/ Joseph W. Stern & Co., 1914/Edward B. Marks Music Corp., 1938.
Romantic ballad introduced by Mitzi in the operetta *Sari* (Vienna, 1912; New York, 1914) with English-language lyrics; recorded by the Victor Light Opera company in its 1914 medley from *Sari.*

Lovesick
Words by Louis Weslyn, music by Herbert Spencer.
M. Witmark & Sons, 1908.
Novelty song for Weslyn's vaudeville act that could also be performed as a duet with alternating "conversations" in the lyrics.

Lovie Dear
Words by Fred Bonny, music by Tom Lemonier.
Bluesy song popularized by Aida Overton Walker.

Lovie Joe
Words by Will Marion Cook, music by Joe Jordon.
Harry Von Tilzer Music Publishing Co., 1910/Jerry Vogel Music Co., Inc., 1937.
One of the first blues to become a mainstream success through popular performances by Fanny Brice in Ziegfeld's *Follies of 1910* and by Elizabeth Brice in Shubert revues and vaudeville; also recorded by Arthur Collins (Columbia) and as an instrumental by Louis Jourdan and His Tympany Five (Decca).

Loving Eyes
Words and music by Harry Puck and George W. Meyer.
Original copyright, 1907.

Romantic song about flirtation and the language of the eyes; featured by Harry and Eva Puck in their vaudeville song-and-dance act and by Julian Eltinge in his female impersonation routines.

Loving Moon
Words by J. Leubrie Hill, music by J. Rosamond Johnson.
Remick Music Corp., 1911.
Romantic ballad featured in *Ned Wayburn's Hello, Paris* (1911), a vaudeville "Revuette" at the Folies Bergere, New York.

Loving Time
Words by A. Seymour Brown, music by Nat D. Ayer.
M. Witmark & Sons, 1908.
Romantic ballad from the musical comedy *The Newlyweds and Their Baby* (1909), based on the cartoons by George McManus in the New York *World*.

Low Bridge - Everybody Down, also known as **Fifteen Years on the Erie Canal**
Words and music by Thomas S. Allen.
F. B. Haviland, 1913/Jerry Vogel Music Co., Inc.
Currently accepted as a folk song.

Lucky in Love
Words and music by Louis Weslyn and Felix Arndt.
M. Witmark & Sons, 1913.
Two-step introduced by Weslyn and Rhoda Nichells in the exhibition ballroom dance and vaudeville act *Cupid's Ladder*.

Lucy Anna Lou
Words by Edward Madden, music by Gus Edwards.
Gus Edwards Music Publishing Co., 1910.
Dixie nostalgia introduced by Lillian Boardman in the finale of *Gus Edwards' Song Revue of 1910* and recorded by Arthur Collins and Byron G. Harlan for Victor and Edison.

M

M-i-s-s-i-s-s-i-p-p-i
Words by Bert Hanlon and Benny Ryan, music by Harry Tierney.
Leo Feist Inc., 1916.
An ASCAP top seller of 1916, this novelty spelling song was introduced by Frances White (Victor) in her juvenile character in the *Ziegfeld Midnight Frolics of 1915.* Revived in the 1930's by Paul Whiteman and in the 1940's by Paul Mahoney.

M-O-N-E-Y Spells Money
Words by J. Sherrie Matthews, music by Max Hoffmann.
Original copyright, 1901.
A Bulger & Matthews specialty, the comic song was interpolated by Harry Bulger into *The Night of the Fourth* (musical, 1901).

M-O-T-H-E-R
Words by Howard Johnson, music by Theodore F. Morse.
Leo Feist Inc., 1915, 1943.
Classic "Mother" song introduced by Eva Tanguay and popularized by balladeers Monte Austin, Gene Greene, George MacFarlane, Henry Burr (Columbia), and George Wilton Ballard (Edison). Often revived and more often parodied, the spelling out of words was a frequent motif in vaudeville songs of the decade.

Ma Blushin' Rosie, My Posie Sweet
Words by Edgar Smith, music by John Stromberg.
M. Witmark & Sons, 1900, 1940.
An ASCAP top seller, this romantic ballad was introduced by Fay Templeton in *Fiddle-dee-dee,* the Weber and Fields show for 1900. It became associated with Templeton and Al Jolson (Decca, Columbia), and received new popularity in the 1950's after film biographies of Jolson and Lillian Russell were released.

Ma, He's Making Eyes at Me
Words by Sidney Clare, music by Con Conrad.

Fred Fisher Music Co., 1918/Mills Music Inc., 1928.
Comic blow-by-blow description of spooning always associated with Eddie Cantor who recorded it for Decca, Ward, and United States; also recorded by Pearl Bailey (Columbia) and the Merry Macs (Decca). Title song for the Constance Moore comedy (Universal, 1940).

Ma Mamselle Honee
Words by Edgar Smith, music by Gus Edwards.
Shapiro, Bernstein & Co., Inc., 1903.
Novelty duet that combines dialect with fractured French. John C. Rice told Fred Lennox that his girl was "charmant like ze possum" in *The English Daisy* (musical, 1904).

Ma Poppy Belle, see **Easy Money,**.

Ma Scotch Bluebell, see **I Love a Lassie,**.

Mack and Teddy
Words by J. B. Robinson, music by T. C. O'Kane.
Original copyright, 1900.
This campaign song favored the re-election bid of President William McKinley and vice-presidential candidate Theodore Roosevelt.

Mack Sennett Girls
Words and music by Fanchon and Marco.
Original copyright, 1919.
Performed by the Sunkist Beauties, a precision troupe, in a tribute to the silent film *Bathing Beauties* in Fanchon and Marco's *Let's Go* (revue, 1919).

MacNamara's Band (American-Irish)
Words by John J. Stamford, music by Shaumus O'Connor.
Original copyright, 1914/Jerry Vogel Music Co., Inc., 1940.
Novelty song known in its 1940 "Americanized" version by the Three Jesters (Red Latham, Wemp Carlson, and Guy Bonham) was recorded by them with Bing Crosby (Decca) and by Spike Jones and His City Slickers (Victor).

Madame Venus, see **Take a Tip from Venus,**.

Madelon, also known as **I'll Be True to the Whole Regiment** (French)
French words by Louis Bousquet, English words by Alfred Bryan, music by Camille Robert.
Remick Music Corp., 1918.
This ASCAP top seller of 1918 was popularized by the Emerson and

Victor military bands as a one-step march; also recorded by Arthur Fields (Pathe, Edison) and revived by Ray Benson and His Orchestra (Decca).

Magdaline, My Southern Queen
Words by Bob Cole and James Weldon Johnson, music by J. Rosamond Johnson.
Joseph W. Stern & Co., 1900.
Introduced by May Irwin in *The Belle of Bridgeport* (musical, 1900).

Maggie McDonahue
Words and music by Oscar Hammerstein.
M. Witmark & Sons, 1903.
Hammerstein wrote this Irish romantic ballad for *Punch, Judy and Co.* (1903), the extravaganza with which he opened his Paradise Roof Garden.

Mah Moonlight Lou
Words by C. J. Campbell and Ralph M. Skinner, music by Herbert Dillea.
M. Witmark & Sons, 1901.
A dialect romance introduced by Lucy Daly in *The Head Waiters* (musical, 1902).

The Maid in the Moon
Words by Sydney Cowell, music by Ellen Wright.
Boosey & Hawkes Inc., 1901.
A "spiritual love song" based on a poem by Sydney Cowell that had been published in the *New York Dramatic Mirror;* sung by Winifred Hare.

The Maid of Old Madrid
Words by Ruth Deppman, music by Alphonse Zelaya.
Original copyright, 1911.
A Spanish romance popularized in an instrumental version by its composer, "the Paderewski of South America, the sensation of the music world."

The Maid of Timbucktoo
Words by James Weldon Johnson, music by Bob Cole.
Joseph W. Stern & Co., 1903.
An exotic ballad introduced by Lillian Russell in *Whoop-Dee-Doo* (musical, 1903).

The Maiden with the Dreamy Eyes
Words by Bob Cole and James Weldon Johnson, music by J. Rosamond Johnson.
Joseph W. Stern & Co., 1901.

Romantic ballad inspired by an illustration of showgirl Evelyn Nesbit that was often interpolated into Broadway musical comedies--by Mabelle Gilman into *The Hall of Fame* (1902), by Thomas Q. Seabrooke into *The Supper Club* (1902) and, most memorably, by Anna Held into *The Little Duchess* (1901).

Make a Noise Like a Hoop and Roll Away
Words by Ren Shields, music by J. Fred Helf.
Helf & Hager, 1908/Larry Spier, Inc.
A slang rejection song introduced by Emma Carus. Lew Dockstader also featured the lyrics "kidoo, skidoo" in his act.

Make Believe
Words by Jack Brislane, music by Theodore F. Morse.
Original copyright, 1907.
Popular flirtation and proposal waltz sung by male and female vaudeville teams, including Cartnell and Harris and Fleman and Miller; revived in the mid-1910s by such exhibition ballroom dance teams as (Wellington) Cross and (Lois) Josephine.

Make Yourself at Home
Words and music by Pat Rooney.
Original copyright, 1904.
A novelty song by comedian Pat Rooney for his vaudeville act with his sisters; also sung as a woman's solo by Marie Walsh.

Mamenu
Yiddish words by A. Scherr, music by J. M. Rumshisky.
Original copyright, 1909.
Yiddish-language protest song written as a dirge by the parents and unborn children of the victims of the 1909 fire at the Triangle Shirt-waist Factory in New York; recorded by Simon Paskal and His Orchestra (Columbia) at the time and performed today as a labor and feminist ballad.

Mamie, Don't You Feel Ashamie
Words by Will D. Cobb, music by Gus Edwards.
Howley, Haviland & Dresser, 1901.
Comic song popularized as a solo by Elizabeth Murray and Belle Brooklin and as a close harmony ballad by the Mozart Comedy Four and the Orpheus Quartet.

Mamma's Little Alabama Love
Words by Andrew B. Sterling, music by Harry von Tilzer.
Harry Von Tilzer Music Publishing Co., 1903.
The first major success associated with the vaudeville act of the Two Pucks, brother and sister--Eva and Harry.

Mammy o' Mine
Words by William Tracey, music by Maceo Pinkard.
Shapiro, Bernstein & Co., Inc., 1919.
Pinkard's contribution to the year's most popular genre was popularized by female vocalist Adele Rowland (Victor), the barbershop Acme Male Quartet (Pathe), and, as a one-step by the Emerson Military Band, Joseph C. Smith's Orchestra (Victor), and Yerkes' Jazarimba Orchestra (Columbia).

Mammy's Chocolate Soldier
Words by Sidney Mitchell, music by Archie Cottler.
Waterson, Berlin & Snyder, 1918.
Bluesy dialect song crooned by Sophie Tucker and Marion Harris (Victor).

Mammy's Little Choc'late Cullud Chile
Words by Noble Sissle, music by Eubie Blake.
M. Witmark & Sons, 1917.
Popularized and recorded by the authors (Pathe); revived by Amanda Randolph in *The Chocolate Dandies* (revue, 1924).

Mammy's Little Coal Black Rose
Words by Raymond Egan, music by Richard A. Whiting.
Remick Music Corp., 1916.
A dialect lullaby popularized by Al Jolson, Blossom Seeley, and Adele Rowland; recorded as an instrumental by Manuel Romain (Edison) and as barbershop specialties by the Broadway Quartet on Columbia and the Orpheus Quartet on Victor.

Mammy's Shufflin' Dance
Words by L. Wolfe Gilbert, music by Melville J. Gideon.
Will Rossiter, 1911.
Dialect song performed as a solo by Grace Wilson, Nonette, and the Sousa Band's Alma Yolo, in female close harmony arrangements by the Dolce and Farber Sisters, and in male versions by Arthur Collins and Byron G. Harlan (Columbia) and the American Quartet (Victor).

Mamselle (American-English)
Words by Harry B. Smith, music by Arthur Nevin.
Edward Schuberth & Co., Inc., 1900.
The song portrays fractured French compliments paid to an American girl; introduced by Mabel Gilman in *The Casino Girl* (1900).

The Man Behind
Words by Vincent Bryan, music by J. B. Mullen.
Original copyright, 1904.

Monologue and comic song performed by character comics Lew Dockstader, Nat M. Wills, James T. Power, and S. H. Dudley.

The Man of the Hour
Words and music by Robert Mortimer.
Original copyright, 1916.
Official campaign song of the National Democratic Committee and its 1916 presidential candidate, Woodrow Wilson.

The Man Who Fights the Fire
Words by Felix F. Feist, music by Joseph S. Nathan.
Leo Feist Inc., 1908.
Descriptive march performed by Bohannon and Corey with moving picture projection effects to dramatize the plot.

The Man Who Plays the Tambourine
Words by William Jerome, music by Jean Schwartz.
Shapiro, Bernstein & Co., Inc., 1901.
Novelty song describing minstrel show jokes and parades. Introduced by Joseph Herbert in *The Little Duchess* (musical, 1901).

The Man with the Ladder and the Hose
Words and music by T. Mayo Geary.
Original copyright, 1904.
Tribute to volunteer firemen.

Mandy
Words and music by Irving Berlin.
Irving Berlin Music Corp., 1919, 1946.
Berlin's tribute to the heroine and cliches of minstrel romances was introduced by Private John Murphy to Private Dan Healy in the soldier show *Yip Yip Yahank* (1918) and featured by Eddie Cantor in the *Ziegfeld Follies of 1919,* recordings for Melotone and Conqueror, and in his film vehicle *Kid Millions* (Goldwyn Productions, 1934); revived by Danny Kaye and Bing Crosby as a duet (Decca). The close harmony team of Van and Schenck's recording of the song for Columbia is included in the Smithsonian Institution's *Follies* album.

Mandy Lane
Words and music by William J. McKenna.
Remick Music Corp., 1908/Famous Music Corp.
Dixie nostalgia sung in vaudeville by Ray Bailey, Eveleen Dunmore, and the team of De Haven and Sidney; recorded by Harry MacDonough (Victor) and Ada Jones (Zon-o-phone).

The Mansion of Aching Hearts
Words by Arthur Lamb, music by Harry von Tilzer.

Harry Von Tilzer Music Publishing Co., 1902/Jerry Vogel Music Co., Inc.
This plotted melodramatic ballad continues the theme of a woman unhappily married to wealth that was associated with Lamb's songs since "A Bird in a Gilded Cage" (q.v.); it was featured by Kathryn Miley and Raymond Teal and sung by most vaudeville and parlor song vocalists in the early years of the twentieth century. Recorded by Harry MacDonough for Victor and Victrola.

March of the Toys
Words by Glen MacDonough, music by Victor Herbert.
M. Witmark & Sons, 1903.
This instrumental work introduced the "Toyland" sequence in the operetta *Babes in Toyland* (1903), and also was sung in the original production by William Norris and Mabel Barrison. Composer Herbert's own recording of 1911 is included on the Smithsonian Institution's *Music of Victor Herbert* album; other popular recordings include those by Eugene Ormandy and the Philadelphia Orchestra and Arthur Fiedler and the Boston "Pops." Revived as an instrumental in both film versions of *Babes in Toyland* -- MGM's 1934 production with Laurel and Hardy and the Disney/Buena Vista picture, 1961.

The March of the Workers (English)
Words by William Morris and Charles Kerr, music by Charles Kerr.
Original copyright, 1901.
Charles Kerr's volumes of *Socialist Song with Music* featured settings of traditional melodies by late nineteenth-century poets. William Morris, founder of the British Socialist League, was the source for Kerr's anthem based on the "Battle Hymn of the Republic." See also Kerr's "Onward Brothers" and "True Freedom."

Marie Cahill's Congo Love Song, also known as **Congo Love Song**
Words by James Weldon Johnson, music by J. Rosamond Johnson.
Joseph W. Stern & Co., 1903.
Interpolated by Marie Cahill into *Nancy Brown* (musical, 1903) and her shows thereafter.

Marie from Sunny Italy
Words by Irving Berlin, music by Nick Nicholson.
Joseph W. Stern & Co., 1907/Irving Berlin Music Corp.
Generally considered Berlin's Opus 1, this was an answer song to Al Piantadosi's "My Mariuccia Take a Steamboat" (q.v.) with musical quotes from "O Maria, Mari" (q.v.). Introduced by Berlin (then a waiter) and also performed by Leah Rubell; recorded by Joe Brenner (Coronet).

Mariutch Down at Coney Island, also known as **Mariutch Make a the Hootch a Ma Kootch**
Words by Andrew B. Sterling, music by Harry von Tilzer.
Harry Von Tilzer Music Publishing Co., 1907.
"Mariutch" (or "Mariuccia") was the most popular female Italian archteype in comic songs of the first decade of the century. Like her Jewish equivalents "Becky" and "Sadie," she used dance to achieve upward mobility -- here, as a hootchy-cootchy dancer in New York's amusement park boardwalk; see "The Police Won't Let Mariuccia Dance..." Among those who sang this dialect song in vaudeville were Baby Eleanor, Ed Norton, Sadie Fields, and the Empire City Quartette.

Mariutch Make a the Hootch a Ma Kootch, see **Mariutch Down at Coney Island,.**

Mariutch, She Come Back to Me
Words by Harry L. Newton, music by Mike Bernard.
Original copyright, 1907.
Answer song to "My Mariuccia Take a Steamboat" (q.v.); popularly performed by Madge Maitland and Grace Wilson.

The Marquand Glide
Words by Rube Marquand and Thomas J. Gray, music by Blossom Seeley and W. Ray Walker.
Remick Music Corp., 1912.
Seeley introduced this song in her vaudeville act with then-husband Marquand, which was called *Breaking the Record, or The 19th Straight* (1912-1913). Marquand, a baseball idol, included sports teminology in the descriptive dance lyrics with puns on "sliding home" and references to contemporary players.

Mary, also known as **Mary Is a Grand Old Name**
Words and music by George M. Cohan.
Mills Music Inc., 1906/Dajon.
Introduced by Fay Templeton as "Mary" in *Forty-five Minutes from Broadway;* featured by Irene Manning in *Yankee Doodle Dandy* (Warner Brothers, 1942) and on Broadway by Jacqueline Alloway in *George M!* (1968).

Mary Be Wary
Words by Ed. Gardinier, music by Maurice Levi.
Comic song introduced by Clara Palmer in *The Rogers Brothers at Harvard* (1902).

Mary Had a Little Lamb
Words by Will D. Cobb, music by Leo Edwards.
Shapiro, Bernstein & Co., Inc., 1903.

Leah Russell introduced this suggestive song about a "Merry Merry" (or chorus girl) and her "lamb" (or show backer).

Mary Is a Grand Old Name, see **Mary,.**

Mary Pickford, the Darling of Them All
Words and music by Dave Radford, Daisy Sullivan, and Richard A. Whiting.
Remick Music Corp., 1914.
Promotional song dedicated to the film star. Among the many other Pickford songs of the era were "Sweet Little Mary Pickford" (by Earle and Williams, 1914), "Sweetheart of Mine" (by Daniels and Friedman, 1914), and "The Mary Pickford Waltz" by Leo Bennett (1917).

Mary Regan
Words and music by Anita Stewart.
Waterson, Berlin & Snyder, 1919.
Promotional song for Anita Stewart's own film of the same name (Stewart-Weber Productions De Luxe, 1919).

Maud, Maud, Maud (American-English)
Words by Harry B. Smith and Adrian Ross, music by John Stromberg.
M. Witmark & Sons, 1901.
Early example of the novelty song genre that complains about a woman's bad voice. Introduced by Claire Romaine in the London version of *The Toreador* (1900) with the Ross lyrics. Maud Lambert introduced the Smith version in New York (1902).

Maudie
Words and music by George M. Cohan.
George M. Cohan Music Publishing Co., 1901.
Romantic ballad introduced by Josephine Cohan in *The Governor's Son* (musical, 1901).

The Maurice Glide
Music by Gustav Haenschen.
T. B. Harms, 1912/Francis, Day & Hunter, Inc., 1912.
Glide (slow ballroom dance in which the female stands closest to the audience) performed by Maurice Mouvet and Madeleine d'Harville; recorded by the Edison Band and the American Republic Band (Pathe).

The Maurice Tango
Words and music by Silvio Hein.
T. B. Harms, 1912/Francis, Day & Hunter, Inc., 1912.
Tango for Maurice Mouvet and his exhibition ballroom dance part-

ner Madeleine d'Harville; recorded by the Edison Band, by Fred Van Eps, and by the Victor Military Band.

Maurice's Rag
Words and music by William H. Penn.
Original copyright, 1912.
Exhibition ballroom dance number for Maurice Mouvet in his performances at Louis Martin's cabaret and in the musical comedy *Over the River* (1912).

May, May, May (American-English)
Words by George Arthurs, music by Orlando Powell.
Francis, Day & Hunter, Inc., 1907.
Novelty song about a flirtatious girl named May who may be in love. Introduced by Alice Lloyd on a Victor-label recording.

May Sweet May
Words by R. J. Jose, music by Robert S. Roberts.
Howley, Haviland & Dresser, 1902.
Lyricist Jose introduced this sentimental ballad.

Maybe
Words by Frank Tannehill, Jr., music by George Rosey.
Joseph W. Stern & Co., 1901.
Proposal song introduced by Fred Gladdish of the Primrose and Dockstader minstrel troupe; it was very popular as a parlor and wedding song in the early years of the Twentieth century.

McGinnis
Words by William Jerome, music by Jean Schwartz.
Cohan & Harris, 1908.
Topical satire of New York City's Tammany Hall and corrupt politicians from *Cohan & Harris' Minstrels* vaudeville routine.

McKinley, Our Hero, Now at Rest
Words and music by Joseph L. Hain.
Original copyright, 1901.
Memorial anthem for President William McKinley, assassinated in September, 1901, early in his second term of office.

The Meaning of U.S.A.
Words and music by Raymond A. Browne.
Original copyright, 1902.
Patriotic march sung by Blanche Ring, John Nestor, and others. In various verses the initials "U.S. and A" are said to represent "Uncle Sam, Ships and Almighty," "Union Eternal, Stripes and Stars and Army," and "Unlucky to Uncage the Eagle,Success and Admiral;" recorded by Harry MacDonough (Victor).

Meet Me at the Masquerade, also known as **The Bal Tabarin**
Words by Harry B. Smith, music by Paul Lincke.
Joseph W. Stern & Co., 1904.
Song and production number for the finale of the musical *The Soul Kiss* (1908) set in the Bal Tabarin cabaret. Introduced by Ralph Herz and sung by the entire cast.

Meet Me at the Station
Words by Sam M. Lewis and Joe Young, music by Ted Snyder.
Waterson, Berlin & Snyder, 1917.
Romantic song introduced by Gladys Clark and Henry Bergman in the *Passing Show of 1917.* One of the most popular vaudeville songs of the year, it was performed by dozens of male/female flirtation acts, among them Fanchon and Marco and George Burns and Gracie Allen; also, as a solo, by Harry Fox.

Meet Me at Twilight
Words by F. Clifford Harris, music by Jerome Kern.
Harms, Inc., 1906.
Invitation to spoon offered by Winnona Winter in *The Little Cherub* (1906).

Meet Me Dear, on Saturday, a Little after Two
Words and music by D. K. Stevens.
Original copyright, 1903.
Interpolated by Blanche Ring into *Sergeant Brue* (1905) and performed by her in vaudeville throughout her long career. A typical situation comedy song, the first verse describes a date; the second, the same couple after marriage and children, spending the Saturday pay-check.

Meet Me Down at the Corner
Words by Will D. Cobb, music by Harry Hoyt.
Shapiro, Bernstein & Co., Inc., 1906.
Irish-dialect proposal and elopement song. Introduced by Clara Palmer in *The Blue Moon* (musical, 1906); recorded by Ada Jones (Columbia).

Meet Me in Frisco and We'll Go Out to the Fair
Words and music by Will A. Fentress.
Original copyright, 1915.
Promotional song for the San Francisco Exposition of 1915.

Meet Me in Rose Time Rosie
Words by William Jerome, music by Jean Schwartz.
Cohan & Harris, 1908/Shapiro, Bernstein & Co., Inc.
Best-selling romantic song introduced by Earl Benham in Cohan & Harris' Minstrels (1908) and interpolated by Fannie Ward into

Jerome K. Jerome's play *The New Lady Bantock.* Recorded by Billy Murray and the Haydn Quartet (Victor) and by Frank C. Stanley and Byron G. Harlan (Columbia).

Meet Me in St. Louis, Louis
Words by Andrew B. Sterling, music by Kerry Mills.
Mills Music Inc., 1904/Harms, Inc.
Promotional song for the 1904 St. Louis Exposition that became a best seller and remained popular for over fifty years. In 1904 alone, it went through a dozen editions, popularized through performances by Ethel Levey, Lottie Gilson, Lew Dockstader, Nora Bayes, and many others. Recorded by Billy Murray (Columbia, Victor) and by Pryor's Band (Victor), but it earned most success through performances by Judy Garland in the MGM film *Meet me in St. Louis* (1944) and on recordings for Decca.

Meet Me Tonight in Dreamland
Words by Beth Slater Whitson, music by Leo Friedman.
Will Rossiter, 1909/Shapiro, Bernstein & Co., Inc., 1936.
Whitson received $7000, publicized as the largest advance ever paid for a song, for her poem which was immediately featured by Maud Lambert, Reine Davies, Henry Burr (Columbia, Oxford) and Vernon Dalhart (Supertone). New editions were printed in the 1920's for popular performances by Jessie Royce Landis and saxophiste Kathryne Thompson, in the 1930's for Wayne King, and in the 1940's for the Mills Brothers (Decca). The song is remembered as the ballad that Judy Garland's character demonstrated in the music store in *In the Good Old Summertime* (MGM, 1949).

Meet Me When the Sun Goes Down
Words by Vincent P. Bryan, music by Harry von Tilzer.
Harry Von Tilzer Music Publishing Co., 1902.
Suggestive rag-time song introduced by Emma Carus in *The Hall of Fame* (musical, 1902).

Meet Me with Spangles and Bells On
Words and music by Martin G. Brown.
M. Witmark & Sons, 1907.
Syncopated invitation to the audience from Nora Bayes in Ziegfeld's first *Follies* (1907).

Melody Chimes
Words by Dave Manley, music by Rennie Cormack.
Original copyright, 1912.
Romantic description of a wedding sung with great popularity in vaudeville by men, such as Edwin Morgan and Joe Weston, women, like Fritzie Lyton, and female close-harmony acts, among

them the Shepperly Sisters, the Duncan Sisters, and Sunshine and Tempest.

Melody of Love
Music by H. Engelmann.
Theodore Presser Co., 1903/Shapiro, Bernstein & Co., Inc., 1954.
Romance recorded by George Hamilton Green (Edison) and the Victor Orchestra. See Popular Music, 1920-1979 for recordings using the Tom Glazer lyrics (1954).

Memories
Words by Gus Kahn, music by Egbert van Alstyne.
Remick Music Corp., 1915.
This ASCAP best seller of 1915 had at least ten editions within that year and recordings by John Barnes Wells (Victor) and Prince's Orchestra (Columbia); revived by Lee Wiley (Majestic).

Merrily We'll Roll Along
Words by Andrew B. Sterling, music by Abner Silver.
Original copyright, 1918.
World War I novelty song popularized by Al Herman in vaudeville; makes references to specific military goals on the European front.

Merry Widow Waltz
Music by Franz Lehar.
Tin Pan Alley versions of the "Merry Widow Waltz" included "Dear, I Love You So" (q.v.), "I Love You So" (q.v.), and "When Your Lips Pressed Mine" (q.v.). For songs about the impact of this waltz on music and dance, see "I'm Looking for the Man That Wrote the 'Merry Widow Waltz'" and "Since My Mariuccia Learned the 'Merry Widow Waltz'."

The Merry Widow Waltz Song
Words by Beatrice Fairfax, music by Franz Lehar.
Original copyright, 1908.
This version of the "Merry Widow Waltz," with lyrics by the syndicated advice columnist Beatrice Fairfax and music arranged by Theo. F. Morse, was printed in the Chicago *Evening American,* February 17, 1908.

The Message of the Rose
Words by Will A. Heelan, music by Leo Edwards.
Shapiro, Bernstein & Co., Inc., 1902.
Plotted melodramatic ballad introduced by Helene Mora. In this clear statement of the nineteenth-century language of sentiment associated with flowers, the heroine was to answer with a white rose if she was pure and with a red one if she "bore a nameless stain."

The Message of the Violet
Words by Frank Pixley, music by Gustav Luders.
M. Witmark & Sons, 1902.
This classic of the "language of the flowers" genre was the hit tune of the popular musical *The Prince of Pilsen* (1903), in which it was introduced by Albert Parr and Anna Lichter. Recorded by J. W. Myers and by Olive Kline for Victor and by Irene Williams for Brunswick.

The Messiah of Nations
Words by James Whitcomb Riley, music by John Philip Sousa.
John Church Co., 1942, 1946, 1947.
Sousa set Riley's poem as a hymn for public performance at the dedication of Indianapolis' Soldiers and Sailors Monument in 1902. It was distributed free to the audience then, but was published in 1914 when it regained popularity as a patriotic anthem.

Mexi-Tango
Music by W. L. Beardsley and D. S. Lindeman.
Original copyright, 1914.
Tango composed for Joan Sawyer and John Jarrott, the era's most innovative exhibition ballroom team.

Mexico
Words and music by Bob Cole, words by James Weldon Johnson.
Joseph W. Stern & Co., 1904.
Ballad introduced by Maude Lillian Berri in *Humpty-Dumpty* (musical, 1904) and recorded by J. W. Myers (Victor).

Mickey
Words by Harry Williams, music by Neil Moret.
Waterson, Berlin & Snyder, 1919/Jerry Vogel Music Co., Inc., 1945.
Promotional title song for the Mack Sennett film series in which Mabel Normand played "Mickey". Recorded by Vernon Dalhard (Edison), Arthur Fields (Emerson), and Joseph C. Smith's Orchestra and Trio (Victor).

Microbes on the Brain, see **Poor Barney Mulligan,**.

The Midnight Fire Alarm
Music by Harry J. Lincoln.
E. T. Paull, 1900, 1928.
This march gallop (a lively dance with side-to-side sliding steps) arranged by E. T. Paull featured sound effects of horses, bells, etc. It was recorded by the Emerson Military Band and often excerpted for silent film scores.

Midnight in Dreamy Spain
Words and music by Joe McCarthy, Gus Van, and Joe Schenck.
Original copyright, 1918.
Van and Schenck introduced this romantic ballad in their close-harmony specialty act in the revue *Miss 1917* and also performed it at the Century Grove roof garden and in vaudeville.

Midnight Maid
Words and music by Joe Meyer and Ben Black.
Sherman, Clay & Co., 1919.
Flirtation song from Fanchon and Marco's revue *That's It* (in San Francisco, 1919).

A Midnight Romance
Words and music by Anita Stewart.
Waterson, Berlin & Snyder, 1919.
Promotional title song for Stewart's silent film for the First National/Vitagraph Studio.

Mighty Lak' a Rose
Words by Frank L. Stanton, music by Ethelbert Nevin.
John Church Co., 1901.
This art song based on Stanton's poem about a small boy was recorded by the major opera singers of the era, among them, Anna Case (Edison), Lillian Nordica (Columbia), Frances Alda (Victor), John McCormack (Gramophone), and Geraldine Farrar with Fritz Kreisler (Victor, Victrola); major revivals were by Bing Crosby (Decca) and Paul Robeson (Victor, Gramophone). Reissued in 1923 as title song for the First National Films silent picture.

Mind the Paint (English)
Words by Arthur Pinero, music by Jerome Kern.
T. B. Harms, 1912.
Title song for Pinero's play *The Mind the Paint Girl* (1912), starring Billie Burke.

Mirandy, also known as **That Girl o' Mine**
Words and music by James Reese Europe, Noble Sissle, and Eubie Blake.
M. Witmark & Sons, 1919.
Europe's final published song was popularized as a fox-trot by his 369th U.S. Infantry ("Hell Fighters") Band with vocals by Sissle (Pathe); recorded as a piano roll by Blake.

Miss Bob White
Words and music by Willard Spenser.
Original copyright, 1901.

Title song introduced by Ethel Jackson (and performed by her replacement Marguerite Sylva) in the musical *Miss Bob White* (1901, in Philadelphia), featuring bird call cadenzas.

Miss Hannah from Savannah
Words by R. C. McPherson, music by Thomas Lemonier.
Joseph W. Stern & Co., 1901.
Comic song introduced by Aida Overton Walker.

Mister Dooley
Words by William Jerome, music by Jean Schwartz.
Shapiro, Bernstein & Co., Inc., 1902.
Tribute to the columnist Peter Finley Dunne and his persona "Mr. Dooley." Introduced by Thos. Q. Seabroke as an interpolated specialty in *A Chinese Honeymoon* (musical, 1902); also performed as a character monologue and sung by Alexander Clark, John E. Slavin and Elizabeth Murray, and Dan W. Quinn (Victor).

Mister E. Z. Mark
Words and music by Earle Remington.
Original copyright, 1903.
Comedy song based on the characters created in F. M. Howarth's comic strip for the Hearst syndicate.

Mister Jazz Himself
Words and music by Irving Berlin.
Waterson, Berlin & Snyder, 1917.
The Watson Sisters introduced this syncopated song, which used Berlin's own nickname as its title.

Mister Monkey
Words by Will D. Cobb, music by Gus Edwards.
Gus Edwards Inc., 1906.
Novelty rag written for interpolation by Anna Held into *A Parisian Model* (musical, 1906).

Mister Pagliatch
Words by Edward Madden, music by Gus Edwards.
Remick Music Corp., 1912.
An answer song to Madden and Edwards's Italian-dialect series based on opera themes. Introduced by Lillian Boardman in *Gus Edwards' Song Revue of 1912.*

Mister Wilson, That's All
Words by Henry Williams, music by Egbert van Alstyne.
Shapiro, Bernstein & Co., Inc., 1904.
Comic monologue and song about a hen-pecked husband. Introduced by Lew Dockstader.

Mister Yodeling Man
Words and music by Chris Smith.
Ted Snyder Music Publishing Co., 1911.
Comic novelty portrait of black minstrel end-man (whose role traditionaly involved repartee with the group's spokesman); with yodeling effects.

The Modern Maiden's Prayer
Words by Ballard MacDonald, music by James F. Hanley.
Shapiro, Bernstein & Co., Inc., 1917.
Eddie Cantor introduced this topical comedy song in the *Ziegfeld Follies of 1917* and recorded for Victor.

The Modern Sandow Girl
Words by Will D. Cobb, music by Gus Edwards.
Gus Edwards Music Publishing Co., 1907.
This chorus song from Ziegfeld's *Follies of 1907* refers to Eugen Sandow, the weight-lifter whom Ziegfeld managed in the 1880's. The song connected the seaside scene featuring "The Gibson Bathing Girls" (q.v.) with Nora Bayes' specialty, "Handle Me with Care" (q.v.) and "The Ju-Jitsu Waltz" (q.v.).

Molly
Words by Rida Johnson Young, music by Victor Herbert.
M. Witmark & Sons, 1919.
Irish ballad associated with John McCormack (Victor).

Molly Dear, It's You I'm After (American-English)
Words by Frank Wood, music by Henry E. Pether.
Remick Music Corp., 1915/Francis, Day & Hunter, Inc., 1915.
Irish romance popularized by Blanche Ring, Hattie Burke, Elizabeth Murray, and Lillian Ross; interpolated into the 1915 revival of the musical *The Girl from Urah.* Recorded by Walter J. Van Brunt (Edison), the Orpheus Quartet (Victor), and the Victor Military Band.

Molly Malone, My Own
Words by Roscoe Arbuckle, music by Hale N. Byers and Chris Schonberg.
Remick Music Corp., 1919.
Irish romantic ballad introduced by Olga Cook in the *Passing Show of 1919.*

Molly-O Oh Molly
Words and music by Irving Berlin.
Ted Snyder Music Publishing Co., 1911.
Irish proposal song introduced by Emma Carus.

Mon Amour, also known as **My Sweetheart**
Words by Edgar Allen Woolf, music by Armand Kalisz.
Leo Feist Inc., 1911.
Waltz ballad introduced by Amelia Stone and Armand Kalisz in their feature vaudeville act.

The Monk of Malabar
Words by J. Cheever Godwin, music by Ludwig Englander.
Original copyright, 1900.
Drinking song introduced by Francis Wilson in the comic opera of the same name (1900).

Montezuma
Words by Earl Carroll, music by Charles Eggert.
Leo Feist Inc., 1912.
Atmospheric Mexican ballad introduced by Jeanette Methuin in *Over the River* (1912). The sheet music bills the song as including "the highest note ever reached by the Human Voice."

Moon Dear
Words and music by Manuel Klein.
M. Witmark & Sons, 1905.
Popular romantic ballad written by the New York Hippodrome's resident composer for its extravaganza *A Society Circus* (1905).

The Moon Has His Eyes on You
Words by Billy Johnson, music by Albert von Tilzer.
York Music Corp., 1905/Jerry Vogel Music Co., Inc., 1933.
Romantic ballad about spooning popularized by Adele Ritchie, Netta Vesta, and Toby Claude; recorded by Corinne Morgan and Frank C. Stanley for Columbia and Victor.

The Moon Shines on the Moonshine
Words by Francis De Witt, music by Robert Hood Bowers.
Shapiro, Bernstein & Co., Inc., 1920.
This Prohibition satire was sung by Bert Williams in *Ziegfeld Follies of 1919* and *Ziegfeld Midnight Frolics* (1919). The recording by Bert Williams (Columbia, 1919) is included in the Smithsonian Institution's album *Ziegfeld Follies of 1919.*

Moonlight
Words by James O'Dea, music by Neil Moret.
Remick Music Corp., 1905.
Ballad popularized by Louise Brehany, Marie Lambert, and the team of Kelly and Violette; recorded by Sousa's Band (Victor) and Selvin's Dance Orchestra (Vocalion).

Moonlight Bay, also known as **On Moonlight Bay**
Words by Edward Madden, music by Percy Wenrich.
Remick Music Corp., 1912.
Barbershop quartet classic in amateur performance and on recordings from the Premier Quartet (Edison) to the Mills Brothers (Decca). It regained popularity in the 1940's through recordings by Bing Crosby (V Disc and on Decca, with son Gary), Gene Kelly (MGM), Glenn Miller (Decca), and Doris Day, who sang it in the Warner Brothers film named for the song (1951).

Moonlight Waltz
Words by Virginia Knight Logan, music by Frederic Knight Logan.
Forster Music Publishers, Inc., 1916.
Romantic waltz that served as a signature tune for Charles A. Prince's Orchestra, the dance band associated with early Columbia recordings.

The More I See of Hawaii, the Better I Like New York
Words by Bert Kalmar, music by Archie Gottler.
Kalmar, Puck & Abrahams Consolidated Mus, 1917.
Comic complaint that Hawaii doesn't have enough jazz to suit urban tastes. Introduced by Florence Moore.

Moriarty
Words by Charles Horwitz, music by Fred. V. Bowers.
Original copyright, 1903.
Character monologue and song introduced by composer Bowers in Lew Dockstader's Minstrels and recorded by Arthur Collins and Byron G. Harlan for Columbia.

Morning, Noon, and Night
Words by James Weldon Johnson, music by J. Rosamond Johnson.
G. Schirmer Inc., 1916.
Art song featured and recorded by Roland Hayes.

Mother Has Got the Habit Now
Words and music by Arthur Gillespie.
Charles K. Harris Music Publishing Co., 1906.
Answer song to "Everybody Works But Father" (q.v.) in which Mother has joined "the Knights of Rest;" popularized by Elizabeth Murray.

Mother Hasn't Spoken to Father Since
Words by William Jerome, music by Jean Schwartz.
Shapiro, Bernstein & Co., Inc., 1908.
This specialty song and monologue for Vesta Victoria related the events leading up to a divorce in seven verses. The final verse and chorus string together song titles for comic effect; also recorded

by Billy Murray (Victor) and by Arthur Collins and Byron G. Harlan (Zon-o-phone).

Mother o' Mine (American-English)
Words by Rudyard Kipling, music by Frank E. Tours.
Chappell & Co., Inc., 1903.
Art song associated with John McCormack, who performed it in recital and recorded it for Victor. Based on a poem from *The Light That Failed,* it was introduced by Herbert Witherspoon and also recorded by tenors John Charles Thomas (Vocalion) and Emilio de Gogorza (Victor). It is frequently called the most popular male vocal solo of the twentieth century.

Mother's Hymn to Me
Words and music by James R. Homer.
Original copyright, 1901.
Sentimental ballad performed by the author, by Dan Coleman, and by Tascott.

Mothers of America, You Have Done Your Share
Words by Harry A. Ellis, music by Lew Porter.
Original copyright, 1919.
This post-World War I ballad thanking American mothers for their sacrifices was made popular in vaudeville by Eva Tanguay and in minstrelsy by Charles Kent and by lyricist Ellis.

Mother's Sitting Knitting Little Mittens for the Navy
Words by R. P. Weston, words and music by H. E. Dareweski.
T. B. Harms, 1915.
Al Jolson and Nora Bayes both found success with this tongue-twister answer song to "Sister Suzie's Sewing Shirts for Soldiers" (q.v.).

The Mountain Maid, also known as **At the Fall of Babylon**
Words and music by Fred Fisher.
Fred Fisher Music Co., 1919.
Promotional song for D. W. Griffith's silent film masterpiece *Intolerance* (1916). The lyrics relate the plot of the Babylon sequence, which involved the attempt of "The Mountain Maid" (played by Constance Talmadge) to rescue the King.

Movin' Man Don't Take My Baby Grand
Words by Bert Kalmar, music by Ted Snyder.
Ted Snyder Music Publishing Co., 1911/Mills Music Inc.
Popularized and recorded by Al Jolson, this bluesy complaint was also sung in vaudeville by Jack Manion, Marie Fenton, and the King Trio.

Mozart Lincoln
Words by John Gilroy, music by Ben M. Jerome.
Sol Bloom Publishing Co/Sol Bloom Music, 1903.
A very early example of "ragging the classics," this dialect song adapts themes from the Pilgrims' Chorus from Richard Wagner's *Tannhauser*; it was interpolated into *The Darling of the Gallery Gods* (1903), a roof garden revue by Ned Wayburn, then Broadway's foremost promoter of rag-time.

Mrs. Carter, You're a Tartar
Words and music by Edward Rogers.
Shapiro, Bernstein & Co., Inc., 1901.
Comic portrait of a seductive widow. Introduced by Emma Carus.

"Mumms" the Word
Words by Will D. Cobb, music by Gus Edwards.
M. Witmark & Sons, 1904.
Drinking song introduced by May Irwin in *Mrs. Black Is Back* (musical, 1904).

Musical Moon
Words and music by George M. Cohan.
George M. Cohan Music Publishing Co., 1911.
This parody of moon/June songs was introduced by author Cohan in *The Little Millionaire* (musical, 1911); it features satirical references to his fellow songwriters, who extolled the "funny moon, Honeymoon, always get's the money moon."

Must We Say Good Bye Forever, Nellie Dear?
Words and music by Charles K. Harris.
Charles K. Harris Music Publishing Co., 1901.
Plotted sentimental ballad that reverses the situation of Harris's "After the Ball" and allows the couple to reunite following the revelations at the party; popularized by Margaret Kingore.

Must You?
Words by Harry Boden and Dave Montgomery, music by Bert Branford.
M. Witmark & Sons, 1903.
Montgomery's specialty number was interpolated into *The Wizard of Oz* (musical, 1903), in which he played the Tin Woodsman.

My Angemima Green
Words by James Weldon Johnson, music by Bob Cole.
Joseph W. Stern & Co., 1902.
Introduced by Dan McAvoy and Louis Harrison in *The Hall of Fame* (musical, 1902).

My Baby Talking Girl
Words by Gus Kahn, music by Egbert van Alstyne.
Remick Music Corp., 1918.
Novelty song performed by Frank Fay and Charles Ruggles with the Baby Talking Girls in the *Passing Show of 1918* and by Nancy Fair in *Oh, What a Girl* (musical, 1918); recorded by Arthur Fields for Victor and Gennett.

My Baby's Arms
Words and music by Harry Tierney and Joseph McCarthy.
Leo Feist Inc., 1919.
Close harmony duet for Gus Van and Joe Schenck in the *Ziegfeld Follies of 1919* and their subsequent vaudeville acts; recordings by them and by John Steel (on Victor) are included in the Smithsonian Institution's compilation album *Ziegfeld Follies of 1919* (Columbia).

My Belgian Rose
Words and music by George Benoit, Robert Levenson, and Ted Garton.
Leo Feist Inc., 1918/Jerry Vogel Music Co., Inc.
Ballad for war brides sung by Louise Glamm and Yvette, and recorded by Charles Hart (Victor) and Henry Burr (Emerson, Okeh).

My Billy Boy
Words by Felix Feist, music by Joel P. Corin.
Leo Feist Inc., 1906.
Popular romantic ballad introduced by Florence Bindley in *The Street Singer* (musical, 1905, in Chicago).

My Bird of Paradise
Words by Edward Madden, music by Max Hoffmann.
Remick Music Corp., 1912.
Imitative Hawiian love song interpolated by Gertrude Hoffmann into *Broadway to Paris* (1912) in response to the Richard Walton Rully play *The Bird of Paradise.* See also "Beautiful Bird of Paradise," its theme. Recorded by Jaudas' Society Orchestra (Edison).

My Bird of Paradise
Words and music by Irving Berlin.
Waterson, Berlin & Snyder, 1915/Irving Berlin Music Corp.
Introduced by Blossom Seeley in Winter Garden revues, the title refers to the Lenore Ulrich 1912 vehicle of the same name; recorded by the Peerless Quartet (Victor) and by the Hilo Orchestra (Victor).

My Brudda Sylvest'
Words by Jesse Lasky, music by Fred Fisher.
Fred Fisher Music Co., 1908, 1936, 1964.
Italian-dialect comedy song about "Sylvester," a superman at work, circus, battle, boxing, and baseball. Introduced by Sam Dody in Lasky's feature act *Seven Hoboes* and performed in vaudeville by Mabel Hite and Mike Donlin. The title character re-appears in Italian dialect songs throughout the decade, among them, "Teddy da Roose" (q.v.).

My Castle on the Nile
Words by Bob Cole and James Weldon Johnson, music by J. Rosamond Johnson.
Joseph W. Stern & Co., 1901.
Featured by Bert Williams in the Williams and Walker vaudeville act; recorded by such close-harmony ensembles as the Camp Hill Male Quartet (V Disc), the Eton Boys (Victor), and the Wonder State Harmonists (Vocalion), and by Joan Morris, on her *Vaudeville* album (Nonesuch).

My Charcoal Charmer
Words by Will D. Cobb, music by Gus Edwards.
Howley, Haviland & Dresser, 1900.
Introduced by Peter F. Dailey in *Hodge, Podge & Co.* (musical, 1900). This novelty proposal song has a sentimental first verse and chorus, but the second verse describes a shotgun wedding from which the hero runs away.

My Chilly Baby
Words and music by Hattie Starr.
Leo Feist Inc., 1900.
Comic complaint that a girl is "so frappe'd," introduced by author Starr, was popular enough to be reprinted in the Hearst syndicate's Sunday supplement of October 7, 1906.

My Cigarette Maid, see **The Land of Nicotine,**.

My Cleopatra Girl
Words by Harold Atteridge, music by Sigmund Romberg.
Joseph W. Stern & Co., 1914.
Syncopated exotica introduced by Lillian Lorraine in the finale of the Winter Garden revue *The Whirl of the World* (1914).

My Cosy Corner Girl
Words by Charles Noel Douglas, music by John W. Bratton.
M. Witmark & Sons, 1903.
Rag-time romance based on the traditional song, "In a Cosy Corner". Introduced by Edna May and George Grossmith, Jr. as

an interpolation in *The School Girl* (musical, 1904). Recorded by Billy Murray (Columbia) and by Harry MacDonough (Victor).

My Country Right or Wrong
Words and music by Cecil Mack and Chris Smith.
Joseph W. Stern & Co., 1915.
Patriotic march song introduced by Bernard Granville in the *Ziegfeld Follies of 1915.*

My Cousin Caruso
Words by Edward Madden, music by Gus Edwards.
Gus Edwards Inc., 1909/Remick Music Corp.
The first of Madden and Edwards' Italian dialect opera parodies, this topical novelty song described the negotiations among Oscar Hammerstein's Manhattan Opera, Otto Kahn's Metropolitan Opera, and the famous tenor. Enrico Caruso was so taken with the song that he provided a self-portrait as Pagliacci for the sheet music cover. Edwards and his singer/songwriter brother, Leo, performed it in their *Song Revues* of 1909 and 1910. Victor, which had Caruso under exclusive recording contract, made 78 r.p.m. recording with Byron G. Harlan and Billy Murray.

My Croony Melody, also known as **Tia Da Da Tia Da Da**
Words and music by Joe Goodwin and E. Ray Goetz.
Waterson, Berlin & Snyder, 1914/Mills Music Inc.
Maxixe (a Brazilian two-step) performed by Fred and Adele Astaire as a dance number; also done by Ethel Mae Barker, Violet Carleton, and Ethel Kirk as a syncopated song and recorded by Arthur Collins and Byron G. Harlan (Victor).

My Daddy Long-Legs
Words by Ray Goetz, music by Bert Grant.
Waterson, Berlin & Snyder, 1914.
Promotional title song for the popular play by Jean Webster (1914); recorded by the Peerless Quartet (Columbia).

My Desert Rose, see **Sand Dunes,**.

My Dixie Land Daisy
Words and music by Max Hoffmann.
Shapiro, Bernstein & Co., Inc., 1903.
Southern nostalgia rag featured by the chorus in Ned Wayburn's *Minstrel Misses,* a vaudeville feature act at the New York Theatre Roof Garden. Wayburn and Hoffmann were New York's foremost promoters of rag in the early years of the twentieth century.

My Drowsy Babe
Words by George Totten Smith, music by George A. Nichols.

Shapiro, Bernstein & Co., Inc., 1900.
Introduced by George H. Diamond as a minstrel dialect novelty song, it was also performed as a lullaby by Elinore Falk, Louise Montrose, and the black male/female team of Larkins and Patterson.

My Dusky Rose
Words and music by Thomas S. Allen.
Original copyright, 1905.
Originally a dialect number for minstrel shows, the ballad was also popularized by black vocalists in vaudeville and on the T.O.B.A (Theater Owners Bookings Association) circuits, among them, the teams of Al Anderson and T. H. Goines and Gordon and Chacon. Recorded by Harry Tally (Victor) and Arthur Collins (Vim).

My Eulah Eulah, My Indian Maid
Words and music by Max Hoffmann.
Shapiro, Bernstein & Co., Inc., 1902.
The connecting of early Broadway rags with Indian characters was prevalent in the roof garden songs of the first seasons of the century. Gertrude Hoffmann introduced this rag at the Hammersteins' Victoria Roof Garden, where she doubled as dance director.

My Evalyne
Words and music by Mae Auwerda Sloane.
Original copyright, 1901.
Dialect romance sung by Marie Cahill in *The King's Carnival* (musical, 1901).

My Filopena Pet
Words by Harry B. Smith, music by Aime Lachaume.
M. Witmark & Sons, 1901.
As the Spanish-American War progressed, Broadway songwriters became aware of a new focus for standard exotica songs. In *The Liberty Belles* (1901), this ballad was set in the Philippines, where U.S. troops were stationed.

My Firefly
Words by Raymond A. Browne, music by Harry von Tilzer.
Harry Von Tilzer Music Publishing Co., 1902.
Romantic ballad introduced by Grace LaRue.

My Fisher Maid, see **Tess of the Storm Country,**.

My Fluff-a de Ruff
Words by Ed. Gardinier, music by James Brockman.
Original copyright, 1908.

Italian-dialect song popularized by Lalla Selbini. A "Fluffy Ruffle," a phrase popularized by the *New York Herald,* was a Gibson Girl, who sported long white skirts and shirt waists trimmed with pleats or ruffles.

My Fox Trot Girl
Words by Jack Frost, music by Paul Biose and F. Henri Klickmann.
Original copyright, 1907.
Dance music with very descriptive lyrics that include names of cabarets and titles of songs good for fox-trotting.

My Gal Sal, also known as **They Call Her Frivolous Sal**
Words and music by Paul Dresser.
Joseph W. Stern & Co., 1905/Shawnee Press, Inc.
Dresser's best remembered song was introduced by Louise Dresser as an homage to a dead woman. Memorable recordings were made by the Critereon Quartet (Victor), the Mills Brothers (Decca), Fletcher Henderson (Columbia), and Jerry Murad's Harmonicats (Universal). It was heard on screen in *The Jazz Singer* (Warner Brothers, 1927) as sung by Bobbie Gordon as Jakie at age thirteen, and in *My Gal Sal* (20th Century-Fox, 1942), a fictionalized biography of the songwriter, where it was performed by Rita Hayworth and chorus.

My Gal's Another Gal Like Galli-Curci
Words by Louis Weslyn, music by Felix Arndt.
Joseph W. Stern & Co., 1919.
Novelty song built on references to Italian soprano Amelita Galli-Curci and American Geraldine Farrar, both then popular in opera performances and recordings. Featured in vaudeville by Lillian Lane, Leonora McDonough, and Sally Taylor.

My Gypsy Queen
Words by William Jerome, music by Jean Schwartz.
Shapiro, Bernstein & Co., Inc., 1902.
Written for the Original English Pony Ballet, an eight-woman precision dance troupe that toured with its own vaudeville feature act and also appeared in Broadway revues.

My Hawaiian Sunrise
Words and music by L. Wolfe Gilbert and Carey Morgan.
Joseph W. Stern & Co., 1916/La Salle Music Publishers, Inc.
Exotic love ballad sung by Harry Jolson, Marie Russell, and the close-harmony team of Van and Schenck. Recorded by Albert Campbell and Henry Burr (Victor) and by Sam Ash (Columbia).

My Heart's Tonight in Texas by the Silvery Rio Grande, also known as **By the Silvery Rio Grande**

Words by Robert F. Roden, music by Max S. Witt.
Joseph W. Stern & Co., 1900/Edward B. Marks Music Corp., 1933.
Correspondence ballad from a Texan in England to her lover at home. Introduced by Jane Whitbeck.

My Hindoo Man
Words by Harry H. Williams, music by Egbert van Alstyne.
Remick Music Corp., 1905.
Syncopated hit song introduced by Marie Cahill in *It Happened in Nordland* (musical, 1904); also performed by Libbie Blondell, Josephine Gassman, and the team of Kelly and Violette.

My Honey's Back
Words by George Getsey, music by Moe Thompson.
Leo Feist Inc., 1918.
Popularized and recorded by Sophie Tucker.

My Honolulu Lu
Words by George Totten Smith, music by Emil Bierman.
Leo Feist Inc., 1901.
Exotic love song introduced by Dan Daly in *The New Yorkers* (1901).

My Hula Lula Girl
Words by William Jerome, music by Jean Schwartz.
Shapiro, Bernstein & Co., Inc., 1903.
Comic novelty song declaring love for a Midway (or side show) dancer; it may have been the first of many songs about an Irish exotic dancer. Introduced by Alice A. Leslie.

My Irish Daisy
Words by William Jerome, music by Jean Schwartz and Maude Nugent.
Remick Music Corp., 1905.
Romantic ballad introduced by Joseph Cawthorne in the title role of *Fritz in Tammany Hall* (1905), a musical satire of New York municipal politics.

My Irish Gibson Girl
Words by William Jerome, music by Jean Schwartz.
T. B. Harms, 1907.
The Gay White Way (musical, 1907) featured this in-joke answer song to Jerome and Schwartz's multi-million copy seller, "Bedelia" (q.v.). Here Blanche Ring sang of the assimilated immigrant who "makes Bedelia look like a failure."

My Irish Girl
Words by Harry Williams, music by Egbert van Alstyne.

Remick Music Corp., 1906.
Romantic waltz introduced by Maud Raymond and the chorus in *Girlies'* a vaudeville act.

My Irish Indian
Words by William Jerome, music by Jean Schwartz and Maude Nugent.
Remick Music Corp., 1905.
Syncopated tribute to Mary Ann McCue, a character that experimented with exotic cultures in Jerome/Schwartz songs; performed in vaudeville by Nugent and by Lottie West Symonds.

My Irish Maid
Words by George V. Hobart and Max Hoffmann, music by Max Hoffmann.
Romantic ballad introduced by Bessie DeVoie (and thereafter sung by her replacement Marion Stanley) in *The Rogers Brothers in Ireland* (1905); recorded by Billy Murray (Victor).

My Irish Molly O
Words by William Jerome, music by Jean Schwartz.
Remick Music Corp., 1905.
Irish romantic ballad that became a signature tune (and frequent interpolation) for Blanche Ring; it was used in *Sergeant Brue* (1905) and *His Honor the Mayor* (1906). Recorded by Billy Murray (Zon-o-phone) and by Harry Tally (Victor).

My Irish Rose
Words by William Jerome, music by Jean Schwartz.
Francis, Day & Hunter, Inc., 1906.
Romantic "moon/spoon" song introduced by Hattie Williams in *The Little Cherub* (musical, 1906). Also sung and recorded by Bonita, John P. Curran, and Lee Tong Foo.

My Isle of Golden Dreams
Words by Gus Kahn, music by Walter Blaufuss.
Remick Music Corp., 1919.
This ASCAP top seller was introduced by Jansci and Roszika Dolly in *Oh, Look!* (musical, 1919); it was frequently performed and recorded as dance music as by Selvin's Novelty Orchestra (Victor), the Tuxedo Dance Orchestra (Edison), and Joe Thomas's Sax-o-tette (Okeh). Revived by the Andrews Sisters (Decca), Bing Crosby (Decca), and Dinah Shore (Victor).

My Japanese Cherry Blossom
Words by Edgar Smith, music by John Stromberg.
M. Witmark & Sons, 1901.
This ballad retells the opera *Mme. Butterfly* from Cho-Cho San's

viewpoint. Introduced by Fay Templeton in *Hoity-Toity* (musical, 1901).

My Jersey Lily
Words by Arthur Trevelyan, music by Harry von Tilzer.
Shapiro, Bernstein & Co., Inc., 1900.
Romantic song performed by the Rays in the vaudeville feature act *A Hot Old Time* and by Rita Redmond and Nellie Sylvester. Recorded by Joseph Natus (Zon-o-phone).

My Lady Hottentot
Words by William Jerome, music by Harry von Tilzer.
Shapiro, Bernstein & Co., Inc., 1901.
This syncopated exotic romance (with an alternative dialect version) was performed with great success in vaudeville by "shouters" Bonita, May A. Bell, Maude Nugent, and Libbie Blondell.

My Landlady
Words by Ferd E. Mierisch and James T. Brymn, music by Bert Williams.
Leo Feist Inc., 1912/Jerry Vogel Music Co., Inc., 1944.
Character complaint written for Williams in the *Follies of 1911;* recorded by him on Columbia.

My Little Chick
Words by George Totten Smith, music by Ned Wayburn.
Sol Bloom Publishing Co/Sol Bloom Music, 1904.
Rag-time chorus number from Wayburn's vaudeville act, *Ned Wayburn's Girls* (1904-1906).

My Little Coney Island
Words by Andrew B. Sterling, music by Harry von Tilzer.
Harry Von Tilzer Music Publishing Co., 1903.
Comic romance about the New York amusement park. Introduced by Harry and Eva Puck.

My Little Creole Babe
Words and music by Maude Nugent.
Shapiro, Bernstein & Co., Inc., 1903.
Lullaby introduced by Nugent; recorded by Harry Tally (Victor).

My Little Hindoo Belle
Words and music by Addison Burkhardt and Raymond Hubbell.
Original copyright, 1903.
Rag-time song interpolated by Fay Templeton into *The Runaways* (musical, 1903, in Chicago and New York).

My Little Japaneesee
Words and music by Max Hoffmann.
Shapiro, Bernstein & Co., Inc., 1903.
Comic version of the opera *Mme. Butterfly,* sung in vaudeville by Mary Marble and used in Ned Wayburn's feature act *Daisy Dancers* (1906-1908).

My Little Lady Bug
Words by Walter H. Ford, music by John W. Bratton.
M. Witmark & Sons, 1900.
Comic romance introduced by Otis Harlan in the musical farce *Star and Garter* (1900).

My Little Rambling Rose
Words and music by Harold Freeman.
Joseph W. Stern & Co., 1906.
A top-selling song and piano roll popularized and recorded by the close-harmony duet of Van and Schenck.

My Little Rang Outang
Words by Edward Madden, music by Theodore F. Morse.
Howley, Haviland & Dresser, 1903.
Syncopated romance interpolated into the Chicago musical *A Son of Rest* (1903) by Mona Wynne.

My Little Service Flag Has Seven Stars
Words by Stanley Murphy, music by Harry Tierney.
Remick Music Corp., 1918.
World War I comic song about a Ziegfeld chorus girl with seven admirers--each in a different branch of the service.

My Little Star, I'm Looking Up to You
Words by John Hyams, music by Theodore Northrup.
M. Witmark & Sons, 1903.
Ballad introduced by Leila McIntyre in *The Sleeping Beauty and the Beast* (musical, 1901).

My Lonesome Little Louisiana Lady
Words by Will D. Cobb, music by Gus Edwards.
Mills Music Inc., 1901.
Pastoral nostalgic ballad introduced by Anna Nagore.

My Madagascar Maid
Words and music by Richard Carle.
M. Witmark & Sons, 1902.
Syncopated romance performed by Carle in his successful Chicago musical farces, among them, *The Explorers* (1902) and *Mary's Lamb* (1908, Chicago and New York).

My Marguerite
Words and music by Billy Gaston and Edgar Selden.
Original copyright, 1912.
Romantic ballad performed and recorded by Billy Gaston and by George S. Reed and the Lads of Melodie.

My Mariuccia Take a Steamboat
Words by George Ronklyn, music by Al Piantadosi.
Original copyright, 1906.
Italian-dialect lament about the archetypal Italian immigrant woman returning to Italy; sung by Madge Maitland, Idalene Cotton, Kathryn Miley, Ben Welch, and the Broadway Quartet.

My Melancholy Baby
Words by George A. Norton and Maybelle E. Watson, music by Ernie Burnett.
Shapiro, Bernstein & Co., Inc., 1939/Jerry Vogel Music Co., Inc.
Originally a two-step published by a rag-time house, this song has maintained its popularity as a vocal standard for blues, jazz, and pop singers from Walter Scanlan (Edison) to Barbra Streisand (Columbia). Among its most memorable singers were Bing Crosby (Brunswick, Decca), Ella Fitzgerald (Columbia), Kate Smith (RCA), and early crooner Gene Austin, whose 1927 Victor cut is included on the Smithsonian Institution's *American Popular Song* album (CBS). Major jazz ensemble recordings by Paul Whiteman (Columbia), Earl Hines (Victor), Glenn Miller (Bluebird), and Benny Goodman (RCA).

My Mississippi Missus Misses Me
Words by Earle C. Jones, music by Max S. Witt.
Joseph W. Stern & Co., 1906.
Nostalgic ballad interpolated into many musicals and vaudeville feature acts, among them, *The Shoo-Fly Regiment* (musical, 1907), *Buster Brown's Holiday,* and *Gorman's Minstrels.*

My Mother's Rosary
Words by Sam M. Lewis, music by George W. Meyer.
Waterson, Berlin & Snyder, 1915/Mills Music Inc.
Sentimental ballad which, like "The Rosary" (q.v.), found more popularity with amateur singers than on stage.

My Onliest Little Dolly, also known as **The Pawn Shop Man**
Words by George O. Poole, music by Hattie Starr.
Original copyright, 1901.
A genre of parlor songs that condensed plots from melodrama was popular at the turn of the century. This pathetic ballad, in which a child pawns her doll to buy bread for her ailing mother, is typical.

My Otaheite Lady
Words by Charles H. Taylor, music by Jerome D. Kern.
Francis, Day & Hunter, Inc., 1902.
A very early Jerome Kern exotic nostalgia song about a sailor mourning his lost cannibal love. Introduced by Billie Burke in the comedy *The Amazones.*

My Own Dear Irish Queen
Words and music by Chauncey Olcott.
M. Witmark & Sons, 1903.
Introduced by Olcott in his own play *Terrance.*

My Own United States
Words by Stanislaus Stange, music by Julian Edwards.
M. Witmark & Sons, 1902, 1916.
The patriotic hit song of the Civil War melodrama *When Johnny Comes Marching Home* (1902), where it was sung by William G. Stewart. Re-issued with new even more patriotic (un-credited) lyrics in 1917, it found new popularity during World War I.

My Pajama Beauty
Words by George V. Hobart, music by Mae A. Sloane.
Original copyright, 1902.
This hit tune describes the female chorus in *The Hall of Fame* (musical, 1902).

My Palm Leaf Maid
Words by Aaron S. Hoffman, music by Byrd Dougherty.
Original copyright, 1903.
Like many early rag-time songs, it celebrated the beauty of a tropical or oriental woman; sung by Josephine Sabel, Charlotte Wehle, and Johnnie Carroll.

My Particular Friend
Words by Wilton Lackaye, music by W. T. Francis.
M. Witmark & Sons, 1902.
Comic song about an actress whose "particular friend is an intimate friend of an intimate friend" of a producer. Introduced by Fay Templeton in Weber and Fields's *Twirly-Whirly* (musical, 1902).

My Pocahontas
Words by Edgar Selden, music by Seymour Furth.
Shapiro, Bernstein & Co., Inc., 1907.
Ziegfeld's first *Follies* (of 1907) had a plot in which Pocohontas and John Smith come to life in New York of that year. Grace LaRue introduced the characters in this *Follies* song.

My Pony Boy
Words by Bobbie Heath, music by Charlie O'Donnell.
Remick Music Corp., 1909/Jerry Vogel Music Co., Inc., 1937.
Comic novelty interpolated by Lillian Lorraine into *Miss Innocence* (musical, 1908). Recorded by Ada Jones (Victor) and the Columbia Quartet.

My Pretty Little Kick-a-poo
Words by Andrew B. Sterling, music by Harry von Tilzer.
Harry Von Tilzer Music Publishing Co., 1904.
The title and lyrics to this romantic ballad include clue words that connect "Kick-a-poo" to its identity as a patent medicine brand name--not a Native American tribe; performed in vaudeville by Harry and Eva Puck.

My Pretty Zulu Lu
Words and music by Max Hoffmann.
Original copyright, 1902.
Juvenile novelty song introduced by Marie Marble and Little Chip in *The Man of Mexico* (touring musical, 1902).

My Princess Zulu Lulu
Words and music by Dave Reed, Jr.
Howley, Haviland & Dresser, 1902.
Novelty dialect song introduced by Harry Bulger in *The Sleeping Beauty and the Beast* (musical, 1901).

My Samoan Beauty
Words by Arthur Trevelyan, music by Will Accooe.
Shapiro, Bernstein & Co., Inc., 1901.
An exotic song introduced by Emma Carus.

My Ship of Dreams
Words by Francis X. Bushman, music by Frank M. Suttle.
Will Rossiter, 1915.
Waltz ballad and promotional title song for the Essanay film *My Ship o' Dreams.*

My Sist' Tetrazzin'
Words by Edward Madden, music by Anatol Friedland.
Original copyright, 1909.
Originally published as written by Friedland "with due credit to Mascagni," this Italian-dialect opera satire rags themes from the composer's *Cavalleria Rusticana.* Maud Lambert introduced it in the Lew Fields farce *The Midnight Sons* (1909).

My Star
Words and music by Elsa Maxwell.

Leo Feist Inc., 1918.
This World War I hymn referring to service star flags was sung and recorded by Anna Fitzin and the Princeton, Harvard, and Yale Glee Clubs in benefits.

My Starlight Queen
Words by Ed Gardinier, music by Maurice Levi.
Original copyright, 1902.
Romantic ballad sung by Hattie Williams and parodied by the Rogers Brothers in their musical *The Rogers Brothers at Harvard* (1902).

My Sulu Lulu Loo
Words by George Ade, music by Nat D. Mann.
M. Witmark & Sons, 1902.
Exotic nostalgic song performed by Frank Moulan and the chorus in *The Sultan of Sulu* (musical, 1902).

My Sumurun Girl
Words by Al Jolson, music by Louis A. Hirsch.
Shapiro, Bernstein & Co., Inc., 1912.
Novelty comic song about a rube quoting romantic verse from *Sumurun* (q.v.) to his lover to no avail. Introduced by Jolson and Stella Mayhew in *The Whirl of Society* (musical, 1912), just after Max Reinhardt's *Sumurun* opened in New York; recorded as a novelty by Arthur Collins (Columbia) and Walter J. Van Brunt (Victor).

My Sunflower Sue
Words by Walter H. Ford, music by John W. Bratton.
M. Witmark & Sons, 1900.
Promoted as a "Darktown Botanical Fascination." Introduced by Peter F. Dailey in *Hodge, Podge & Co.* (musical, 1900).

My Swee' Kimona
Words and music by Maude Nugent.
Shapiro, Bernstein & Co., Inc., 1901.
Nugent's romance, which she also performed, was considered risque since it referred to an item of lingerie.

My Sweet
Words by William Jerome, music by Jean Schwartz.
Remick Music Corp., 1905.
Urban romance with lyrics about "the cosy little corner in the subway of my heart." Introduced by Joseph Cawthorne in *Fritz in Tammany Hall* (musical, 1905).

My Sweet Suzanna
Words and music by Blossom Seeley.
Shapiro, Bernstein & Co., Inc., 1911.
This western romance about "Susanna from Butte, Montana" was featured by Seeley in her own vaudeville act.

My Sweetheart, see **Mon Amour,**.

My Sweetheart Is Somewhere in France
Words and music by Mary Earl.
Shapiro, Bernstein & Co., Inc., 1917.
World War I patriotic ballad performed by Earl; recorded by Elizabeth Spencer (Victor).

My Sweetie
Words and music by Irving Berlin.
Waterson, Berlin & Snyder, 1917/Irving Berlin Music Corp.
Ballroom dance music popularized as a one-step and trot in a recording by Joseph C. Smith's Orchestra on Victor.

My Syncopated Gypsy Maid
Words by Edgar Smith, music by Maurice Levi.
Original copyright, 1905.
This hit song from Joe Weber's *Twiddle Twaddle* (revue, 1906) ragged the classics of rag-time by listing the heroines and title characters of popular songs in its lyrics.

My Syncopated Melody Man
Words and music by Blanche Merrill and Eddie Cox.
Original copyright, 1918.
A rag-time recording success for Marion Harris.

My Teddy Girl
Words by William Jerome, music by Jean Schwartz.
Francis, Day & Hunter, Inc., 1907.
A tribute to athletic young women who emulate Theodore Roosevelt. Introduced by Helen Hale in *A Yankee Tourist* (musical, 1907).

My Toreador
Words and music by Paul A. Rubens.
Boosey & Hawkes Inc., 1901.
Maidie Hope performed this title song from a British musical comedy, which featured a vivid description of a bull fight.

My Turkey Trotting Boy
Words by Harold Atteridge, music by Harry Carroll.
Shapiro, Bernstein & Co., Inc., 1914.

In *The Belle of Bond Street* (musical, 1914), this syncopated tune was sung by Lottie Collins and reprised as a exhibition ballroom dance for Gaby Deslys and Harry Pilcer.

My Twilight Queen
Words by Jean C. Havez, music by Louis A. Hirsch.
Helf & Hager, 1907.
Ballad featured by Will Oakland in appearances with Lew Dockstader and His Big Minstrels.

My Virginian
Words and music by Charles K. Harris.
Charles K. Harris Music Publishing Co., 1914.
This promotional song for the Jesse Lasky Feature Play Company silent film *The Virginian* also served as the official anthem of the Motion Picture Exhibitors' Convention of 1914.

My Waikiki Mermaid
Words and music by A. R. Cunha.
Miller Music Corp., 1903.
This exotic novelty was dedicated to "The Surf-Rider of Hawaii."

My Wife's Gone to the Country
Words by George Whiting and Irving Berlin, music by Ted Snyder.
Ted Snyder Music Publishing Co., 1909.
Mabel Hite and the Chantal Twins popularized the more topical version of this comic song with additional verses by Berlin. Recorded in close-harmony arrangements by Arthur Collins and Byron G. Harlan (Columbia) and the Victor mixed-voice chorus.

My Yiddische Butterfly
Words by Al Dubin, music by Joseph Burke.
M. Witmark & Sons, 1917.
Hebrew dialect novelty answer song to the raft of butterfly songs written during the decade. With this one, Willie Howard invited his butterfly to "flutter, flutter, flutter, 'round your Abie Perlmutter" in *The Show of Wonders* (revue, 1917).

My Yiddische Colleen
Words by Edward Madden, music by Gus Edwards.
Gus Edwards Inc., 1911.
Ziegfeld's *Follies of 1911* included this parody of *Abie's Irish Rose* and similar intermarriage plays; it was performed by Bobby North to Shirley Kellogg.

The Mysterious Melody, see **Are You a Buffalo?,**.

N

'N' Everything
Words and music by Bud De Sylva, Gus Kahn, and Al Jolson.
Remick Music Corp., 1918.
Jolson achieved success with this song as a recording for Columbia and interpolation into the musical *Sinbad* (1918); it was a slang appreciation of a woman's beauty.

Nancy Brown
Words and music by Clifton Crawford.
Howley, Haviland & Dresser, 1901/Jerry Vogel Music Co., Inc., 1938.
Novelty song about a "rube" taken in by the title character who claims that her father owns Fifth Avenue. When Marie Cahill interpolated it into *The Wild Rose* (1901), the musical's composers, Harry B. Smith and Ludwig Englander, protested and attempted to fire her. Cahill won what is considered a test case for the performer's right to interpolate songs at will. Recorded by Harry MacDonough (Victor).

Nancy Clancy
Words by Edgar Smith, music by Maurice Levi.
Original copyright, 1904.
Introduced by Anna Held in *Higgeldy-Piggeldy* (revue, 1904); also a popular success for Trixie Friganza.

Nancy, Oh Miss Nancy
Words and music by Mae Auwerda Sloane.
Original copyright, 1902.
Comic romance introduced by Emma Carus in *The Hall of Fame* (musical, 1902).

Naughty Eyes
Words by Harry Sylvester, music by Percy Wenrich.
Remick Music Corp., 1908.

Flirtatious song performed by Dolly Connolly, Grace Drew, and Mary Lawrence.

Naughty! Naughty! Naughty!
Words by Joe Goodwin and William Tracey, music by Nat Vincent.
Shapiro, Bernstein & Co., Inc., 1916.
This ASCAP top seller was introduced as a song by Grace Fisher in *The Show of Wonders* (1916); also popular as an instrumental two-step for dancing in records by Prince's Band (Columbia) and the Victor Military Band. Recorded as a song by Marguerite Farrell (Victor) and Gladys Rice (Edison).

Nava Jo
Words by Harry Williams, music by Egbert van Alstyne.
Shapiro, Bernstein & Co., Inc., 1903/Remick Music Corp., 1916.
Novelty Indian rag interpolated by Marie Cahill into *Nancy Brown* (1903) and recorded by her; also interpolated by Ellaline Terriss into *The Cherry Girl.* Recorded by J. W. Myers (Columbia).

The Navy Took Them Over and the Navy Will Bring Them Back
Words by Howard Johnson, music by Ira Schuster.
Leo Feist Inc., 1918.
Military rally song introduced by Frank Carter in the *Ziegfeld Follies of 1918;* recorded by the Peerless Quartet (Victor, Columbia).

'Neath the Old Acorn Tree, Sweet Estelle
Words by C. M. Denison, music by J. Fred Helf.
Original copyright, 1907.
Nostalgic ballad performed in vaudeville and revived as a popular parlor song after 1917; sung by Thomas Hackett, Emma O'Neil, Eleanor Wisdom, etc.; recorded by Albert Campbell (Columbia) and Harry MacDonough (Victor).

'Neath the Old Cherry Tree, Sweet Marie
Words and music by Harry Williams and Egbert van Alstyne.
Remick Music Corp., 1907.
Nostalgic ballad first popularized by Harry Ellis but recorded most successfully by close harmony teams, among them, the American Quartet, the Empire City Quartette, and the White City Quartette.

The Nell Brinkley Girl
Words by Harry B. Smith, music by Maurice Levi.
Cohan & Harris, 1908.
Ziegfeld's *Follies of 1908* featured this chorus production number. Nell Brinkley was a popular illustrator of the era, who later became famous as a theatrical caricaturist. The song was a

response to the previous seasons' "Gibson Bathing Girl" (q.v.) and "Christy Girl" (q.v.) and introduced "The Brinkley Bathing Girl" (q.v.) onto the scene.

Nellie Dean, also known as **You're My Heart's Desire**
Words and music by Harry Armstrong.
M. Witmark & Sons, 1905.
This ballad by the master of barbershop harmony, was popularized and recorded by the quartets attached to Columbia records--Columbia, Shannon, and Stellar. It is still a standard close-harmony song.

Never Let the Same Bee Sting You Twice
Words and music by Cecil Mack and Chris Smith.
Broadway Music Corp., 1916.
Popularized and recorded by Anna Chandler on Columbia.

The New Moon
Words and music by Irving Berlin.
Irving Berlin Music Corp., 1919.
Promotional song for the Norma Talmadge silent film drama of the same name.

The New York Hippodrome March
Words and music by John Philip Sousa.
T. B. Harms, 1915/Warner Brothers, Inc., 1968.
The composer dedicated this march to Charles B. Dillingham at the end of his band's ten-month engagement at Dillingham's Hippodrome Theater in New York City. Current recordings include those by the United States Marine Band and the Band of Her Majesty's Royal Marines on the album *The Heritage of John Philip Sousa.*

The Next Horse I Ride On (English)
Words and music by Fred Murray and George Everard.
Francis, Day & Hunter, Ltd., London, England, 1906.
Vesta Victoria performed this specialty number for British music halls and American vaudeville; it was a comic monologue and song about a novice fox hunter. Recorded by Victoria and by Helen Trix (both on Victor).

Next Sunday at Nine, also known as **Dearie, Won't You Call Me Dearie**
Words and music by Evans Lloyd.
Will Rossiter, 1912.
Romantic duet with wedding chime effects featured in vaudeville by male/female teams, among them Alexander and Scott and

Dale and Boyle. Recorded by the team of Helen Clark and Walter J. Van Brunt (Victor).

Next to Your Mother Who Do You Love?
Words by Irving Berlin, music by Ted Snyder.
Ted Snyder Music Publishing Co., 1909/Irving Berlin Music Corp.
Proposal song popularized by Kathryn Miley, Slater Brockman, and Kate Elinore; sung by Eddie Cantor at his first engagement--at Coney Island.

Nijinski
Words by Gene Buck, music by Dave Stamper.
T. B. Harms, 1916/Francis, Day & Hunter, Inc.
Comic monologue and song introduced by Fanny Brice in "The Ballet Loose," the satire of Diaghilev's Ballet Russe in the *Ziegfeld Follies of 1916.* Brice kept the song in her repertory throughout the 1920's.

No Bird Ever Flew So High He Didn't Have to Light
Words by Will D. Cobb, music by Harry Bulger.
M. Witmark & Sons, 1904.
Comic advice interpolated by Bulger into the musical *Woodland* (1904).

No, No, Positively No
Words and music by Chris Smith and Harry Brown.
Original copyright, 1907.
Character monologue and song for Brown; recorded by Al Bernard on Grey Gull, Radiex, and Okeh.

No One Can Take Your Place
Words by Ed Gardinier, music by J. Fred Helf.
Original copyright, 1904.
Ballad popularized by Lew Dockstader.

No One Knows
Words and music by Francis Mack.
M. Witmark & Sons, 1907.
Sentimental ballad popular with such minstrel show tenors as Walter Sherwood of Al Field's Greater Minstrels.

No One Knows Where the Old Man Goes
Words by Thomas J. Gray, music by E. Raymond Walker.
Original copyright, 1912.
Here Elizabeth Murray and Reine Davis told the vaudeville audiences that "the Old Man" went out to turkey trot in the cabarets.

No One Seems to Love Me Now
Words and music by Joseph Maxwell.
Shapiro, Bernstein & Co., Inc., 1904.
Melodramatic ballad of an orphanage performed by Maxwell in his song illustration vaudeville act, Maxwell and Simpson.

No Wedding Bells for Me
Words by E. P. Moran and Will A. Heelan, music by Seymour Furth.
Shapiro, Bernstein & Co., Inc., 1906.
The male version of this comic song as introduced by Lew Dockstader in his minstrel show; May Irwin and Trixie Friganza both performed the woman's version in vaudeville. Recorded by Billy Murray (Victor) and Bob Roberts (Columbia).

Nobody
Words by Alex Rogers, music by Bert A. Williams.
Gotham-Attucks Music Publishing Co., 1905/Jerry Vogel Music Co., Inc., 1937.
Bert Williams's best remembered character song originally included a variety of extra verses with political, topical, and theatrical references. He performed it often as an interpolation in his shows with George Walker and as one of his specialty numbers in the *Follies*, as well as recording it for Columbia. Others who attempted to perform "Nobody" include Arthur Collins (Victor), Lew Dockstader, Perry Como (Victor), Bing Crosby (Decca), and Avon Long, who revived it as a tribute to Williams in the revue *Bubbling Brown Sugar* (1976).

Nobody Knows and Nobody Seems to Care
Words and music by Irving Berlin.
Irving Berlin Music Corp., 1919.
Lament recorded by Irving and Jack Kaufman on the Columbia and Emerson labels.

Nobody's Lookin' But de Owl and de Moon
Words by Bob Cole and James Weldon Johnson, music by J. Rosamond Johnson.
Joseph W. Stern & Co., 1901.
Introduced in *The Sleeping Beauty and the Beast* (musical, 1901) and featured in Cole and Johnson's vaudeville act; recorded by Corinne Morgan and Frank C. Stanley for Columbia, Oxford, and Manhattan.

Nola
Words by James F. Burns, music by Felix Arndt.
Original copyright, 1915/Sam Fox Publishing Co., Inc., 1926.
An ASCAP top seller of 1916, this Vincent Lopez theme song has

been a popular instrumental since its first publication. Lopez's recordings with his various ensembles on Victor, International, Edison, Bluebird, and Okeh, as well as a recording by Arndt (Victor) brought the syncopated piano base into preeminence; other major recordings include those by Isham Jones' Juniors (Decca), Tommy Dorsey and His Orchestra (Victor), and Lionel Hampton (Decca). Paul Whiteman's Orchestra, featuring the banjo, can be seen and heard in the 1929 musical film *The King of Jazz.*

None of Them's Got Anything on Me
Words by William Jerome, music by Jean Schwartz.
Cohan & Harris, 1908.
Novelty bragging song about actors from *Cohan and Harris' Minstrels* (1908); the second verse consists entirely of compliments to Cohan's acting style.

Nora Malone, Call Me by Phone
Words by Junie McCree, music by Albert von Tilzer.
York Music Corp., 1909/Broadway Music Corp.
This combined Irish romance with telephone novelty song was interpolated by Blanche Ring in *The Yankee Girl* (musical, 1910); recorded by Ring (Victor) and by Ada Jones (Victor) and Byron G. Harlan (Columbia).

Nosie Rosie Posie
Words by Blanche Merrill, music by Leo Edwards.
Charles K. Harris Music Publishing Co., 1912.
Trixie Friganza's novelty song about the belle of New York, Paris, and London, performed in New York, French, and British accents.

Not Because Your Hair Is Curly
Words and music by Bob Adams.
Original copyright, 1906/Jerry Vogel Music Co., Inc., 1935.
Romance song interpolated with great success by Mable Barrison into *The Three Graces* (Chicago, 1906) and by Johnny Fogarty into *His Highness the Bey* (Chicago, 1904); recorded by Billy Murray (Victor and Columbia).

Not for Me
Words and music by Bessie Wynn.
Leo Feist Inc., 1907.
Juvenile novelty song for author Wynn.

Nothing Bothers Me
Words and music by Zit (pseudonym for C. Florian Zittel).
Shapiro, Bernstein & Co., Inc., 1907.

Zit's sequel song to "I Don't Care" (q.v.) for Eva Tanguay's vaudeville act.

Nothing Doing
Words by Edgar Smith, music by John Stromberg.
Original copyright, 1900.
Character comedy song introduced by DeWolf Hopper in Weber and Fields' *Quo Vass-Iss?* (musical, 1900).

Nothing's Good Enough for a Good Little Girl If She's Good Enough for You
Words by Alfred Bryan, music by Harry Tierney.
Remick Music Corp., 1917.
One-Step and patter song introduced by Clark and Bergman in *The Passing Show of 1916;* also performed as dance music.

Nulife
Words and music by J. S. Nathan.
Original copyright, 1908.
Advertising song for Professor Charles Munter's Nulife, a back brace described as "the belt of health."

Nursery Rhymes
Words by William Jerome, music by Jean Schwartz.
Shapiro, Bernstein & Co., Inc., 1902.
Comedy song introduced by Joseph Cawthorne in *The Sleeping Beauty and the Beast* (musical, 1901), with topical references to cornering the wheat market and Carrie Nation.

O

O
Words and music by Byron Gay and Arnold Johnson.
Leo Feist Inc., 1919.
Instrumental popular for dance music in recordings by Sauter-Finegan Orchestra (Victor), Pee Wee Hunt (Capitol), and Lawrence Welk and His Champagne Music Orchestra (Coral).

O Dry Those Tears (American-English)
Words and music by Teresa Del Riego.
Chappell & Co., Inc., 1901.
Art song popularized by Leland Langley.

O Mona San
Words by George V. Hobart, music by Alfred E. Aarons.
M. Witmark & Sons, 1900.
Ballad based on *Mme. Butterfly* (although here narrated by Pinkerton) and dedicated to producer David Belasco. Introduced by Josephine Hall in *The Military Maid* (musical, 1900).

O Promise Me You'll Write to Him Today
Words by Harry Clarke, music by Jerome Kern.
T. B. Harms, 1918.
This patriotic ballad urging the audience to write to soldiers overseas was interpolated into *The Canary* (musical, 1918) by Julia Sanderson.

O, Southland
Words by James Weldon Johnson, music by J. Rosamond Johnson.
G. Schirmer Inc., 1919.
James Weldon Johnson's poem was set to music for Anna Cook Pankey, J. Rosamond Johnson, and the male chorus in their 1908 musical *Shoo-Fly Regiment,* but was not published until 1919, in a choral arrangement for mixed voices and soprano solo.

O'Brien Is Tryin' to Learn to Talk Hawaiian
Words by Al Dubin, music by Rennie Cormack.
M. Witmark & Sons, 1916.
Irish dialect songs set in the South Seas were typical of 1916; this one was performed and recorded by Ada Jones on Edison and Horace Wright and His Ukelele Orchestra on Victor.

Oh by Jingo! Oh by Gee! You're the Only Girl for Me
Words by Lew Brown, music by Albert von Tilzer.
Broadway Music Corp., 1919, 1946.
Comic romance introduced by Charlotte Greenwood in *Linger Longer Letty* (1919); it was recorded extensively as a romance, but most successfully as a novelty song by Danny Kaye (Decca) and by Spike Jones and His City Slickers. Sung by Vivian Blaine in the film *Skirts Ahoy* (MGM, 1952).

Oh! Didn't He Ramble
Words and music by Will C. Handy.
Joseph W. Stern & Co., 1902/Edward B. Marks Music Corp., 1920.
Comic novelty with seven additional verses of topical humor by Bob Cole in the version introduced by George Primrose in his minstrel troupe; recorded by Arthur Collins (Zon-o-phone) and Dan W. Quinn (Victor). Also popularized as if traditional with recordings by Kid Ory's Creole Jazz Band (Crescent, Jazz Man, Good Time Jazz) and by Jelly Roll Morton's New Orleans Jazzmen (Gramophone, Bluebird).

Oh! Frenchy
Words by Sam Ehrlich, music by Con Conrad.
Broadway Music Corp., 1918.
ASCAP top seller about a Red Cross nurse who stays in Paris after World War I; sung and recorded by Arthur Fields and Ray Benson. A fox-trot version was recorded in 1918 by Joseph C. Smith's Orchestra for Victor and revived in the 1940's by Fats Waller.

Oh Fudge!
Words by George Sidney, music by Paul Schindler.
Shapiro, Bernstein & Co., Inc., 1901.
This plotted comedy song uses "Oh Fudge!" as an expletive. Introduced by Dan Daly in the musical *The New Yorkers* (1901).

Oh God! Let My Dream Come True!
Words by Blanche Merrill, music by Al Piantadosi.
Shapiro, Bernstein & Co., Inc., 1916.
Pacifist anthem given wide distribution by its Tin Pan Alley authors.

Oh! Harry! Harry!
Words and music by Nat Vincent and Lew Pollack.
Shapiro, Bernstein & Co., Inc., 1918.
Blues belted by Sophie Tucker.

Oh Helen!
Words and music by Charles R. McCarron and Carey Morgan.
Joseph W. Stern & Co., 1918.
This stuttering novelty song flirted with expletives ("Oh Hell...en, Oh Dam...sel") and was dedicated to Roscoe ("Fatty") Arbuckle; popularized by Wellington Cross, Henry Lewis, and Sophie Tucker.

Oh! How I Hate to Get Up in the Morning
Words and music by Irving Berlin.
Irving Berlin Music Corp., 1918.
Berlin performed his best remembered World War I song himself in the revue *Yip Yip Yahank* (1918) and repeated the performance in the film *This Is the Army* (1942; WB 1943). The song was also performed by Eddie Cantor in the *Ziegfeld Follies of 1918,* and by Rae Samuels and Florence Timponi.

Oh, How I Laugh When I Think How I Cried about You
Words by Roy Turk and George Jessel, music by Willy White.
Waterson, Berlin & Snyder, 1919/Mills Music Inc.
This bluesy lament equally popular with male and female vocalists was recorded throughout the 1920's by Arthur Fields (Emerson), Billy Murray (Pathe), and Nora Bayes (Columbia).

Oh, How I Love My Teacher
Words and music by Harry H. Williams and Egbert van Alstyne.
Remick Music Corp., 1906.
Novelty comic song introduced by Will West in *The Little Cherub* (musical, 1906); also popularized by Edwin Foy, who added topical lyrics about politics.

Oh, How I Wish I Could Sleep Until My Daddy Comes Home
Words by Sam M. Lewis and Joe Young, music by Pete Wendling.
Waterson, Berlin & Snyder, 1918.
Al Jolson popularized this old-fashioned sentimental ballad during World War I.

Oh! How She Can Dance
Words by Emma Carus, music by Walter Leopold.
Charles K. Harris Music Publishing Co., 1919.
Novelty song popularized by lyricist Carus.

Oh! How She Can Sing
Words by Jack Yellin, music by Gus Van and Joe Schenck.
Harry Von Tilzer Music Publishing Co., 1919.
Novelty duet for the close harmony team Van and Schenck as a specialty for the *Ziegfeld Follies of 1919,* with allusions and quotations from other popular songs, including "Sweet Adeline" and "'N' Everything" (q.v.). Van and Schenck's recording for Columbia is reproduced on the Smithsonian Institution's compilation album *Ziegfeld Follies of 1919.*

Oh, How She Could Yacki Hacki Wicki Wacki Woo, also known as **That's Love in Honolulu**
Words by Stanley Murphy and Charles R. McCarron, music by Albert von Tilzer.
Broadway Music Corp., 1917.
A Hawaiian novelty song that served as Eddie Cantor's audition and opening act for the *Ziegfeld Midnight Frolics of 1915;* recorded by Arthur Collins and Byron G. Harlan for Victor.

Oh, I Want to Be Good But My Eyes Won't Let Me
Words by Anna Held and Alfred Bryan, music by Harry Tierney.
Remick Music Corp., 1916.
This retrospective flirtation song for Anna Held in *Follow Me* (musical, 1916) reminded the audience of her theme song, "I Just Can't Make My Eyes Behave" (q.v.).

Oh Johnny, Oh Johnny, Oh!
Words by Ed Rose, music by Abe Olman.
Forster Music Publishers, Inc., 1917, 1944, 1956.
An ASCAP top seller in 1917 and in the 1940's thanks to revivals by the Andrew Sisters (Decca) and Glenn Miller (Bluebird). One of a series of songs about unattractive young men with secret skills as a lover, it was introduced by Henry Lewis as a novelty in *Follow Me* (1917) and quickly adopted by Nora Bayes and Sophie Tucker. Their vaudeville performances and recordings by Elizabeth Brice (Rex) and Ada Jones (Rex) helped the song sell out five editions in 1917 alone; also recorded as a fox-trot by Joseph C. Smith's Orchestra (Edison) and Jaudas' Society Orchestra (Victor) and as a barbershop number by the Premier Quartet (Edison) and the American Quartet (Victor).

Oh! London, Where Are Your Girls Tonight?
Words and music by R. P. Weston and Bert Lee.
Francis, Day & Hunter, Inc., 1918.
This World War I song popularized by Vesta Tilley refers to trenches named for London streets.

Oh, Miss Malinda, also known as **When Evening Time Comes 'Round**
Words and music by Bonita and Max Armstrong.
Original copyright, 1908.
Romantic ballad sung with great success by its author Bonita and her rival contralto Maud Lambert.

Oh, Mr. Dream Man
Words and music by Jimmie V. Monaco.
Harry Von Tilzer Music Publishing Co., 1911.
Romantic ballad originally written for the vaudeville act of baseball players Cy Morgan and Coombs Bender.

Oh, Mr. Webster
Words and music by Raymond A. Browne.
Howley, Haviland & Dresser, 1902.
Novelty song of man searching for better words to express his love introduced by Raymond Teal.

Oh! Oh! Miss Phoebe
Words by Andrew B. Sterling, music by Harry von Tilzer.
Shapiro, Bernstein & Co., Inc., 1900.
Raggy love song popularized by Mamie Grant.

Oh! Papa, Oh! Papa, Won't You Be a Pretty Papa to Me?
Words and music by Nat Vincent and James F. Hanley.
Shapiro, Bernstein & Co., Inc., 1917.
Originally introduced by the midget Hoy Sisters in the musical *Jack O'Lantern* (1917), this song was popularized and recorded by Sophie Tucker.

Oh, So Gently (American-English)
Words by George Grossmith, Jr., music by Ivan Caryll.
Chappell & Co., Inc., 1905.
Flirtation song that could be performed as a parody introduced by Olive Morrell in *The Spring Chicken* (1905) and interpolated in 1911 into Caryll's own musical *The Pink Lady.*

Oh! Take Me to My Mamma Dear
Words by W. W. Hall, music by Edmund Braham.
Original copyright, 1903.
Introduced by Jenny Hawley, this narrative ballad about a kidnapped child was sung by all of vaudeville's juvenile stars.

Oh! The Last Rose of Summer Was the Sweetest Rose of All
Words and music by Harry Ruby, Eddie Cantor, and Phil Ponce.
Waterson, Berlin & Snyder, 1919.
Novelty comic song parody of Flatow's aria from *Martha* and the

"language of the flowers" genre ballads. Introduced by Eddie Cantor in the *Ziegfeld Midnight Frolics* and *Ziegfeld Follies of 1919.* Cantor's recording for Emerson is included in the Smithsonian Institution's album *Ziegfeld Follies of 1919.*

Oh! What a Beautiful Dream You Seem
Words by Dave Oppenheim, music by Joe Cooper.
Shapiro, Bernstein & Co., Inc., 1912.
Romantic ballad popularized by Frank Mullane, Reine Davis, and Florenz Tempest.

Oh, What a Night
Words and music by L. Wolfe Gilbert, Lewis F. Muir, and Maurice Abrahams.
Mills Music Inc., 1912/Alfred Music Co., Inc., 1940.
Euphemistic novelty romance popularized by Emma Carus and Al Jolson; revived by Charles Bartholomew in the 1940's.

Oh! What a Pal Was Mary
Words by Edgar Leslie and Bert Kalmar, music by Pete Wendling.
Waterson, Berlin & Snyder, 1919/Mills Music Inc.
This ASCAP top seller was popular both as a ballad, sung and recorded by Henry Burr, Charles Hart, and Edward Allen, and as a fox-trot, recorded by Emerson's Dance Orchestra, Victor's house band, and Joseph C. Smith's Orchestra. Frank Sinatra revived its sentimental ballad form.

Oh! Wouldn't That Jar You?
Words and music by Will D. Cobb.
Howley, Haviland & Dresser, 1900.
Situation comedy song introduced by Lew Dockstader.

Oh, You Beautiful Doll
Words by Seymour Brown, music by Nat D. Ayer.
Remick Music Corp., 1911.
Perennial favorite through early recordings by Gene Greene (Pathe), Billy Murray (Victor), and Arthur Pryor's Band (Victor) and with revivals by vocalists like Mel Torme (Capitol); also a favorite with country ensembles such as the Hoosier Hot Shots (Vocalion), Homer and Jethro and the Rootin' Tootin' Boys (King), and Stan Fritts and His Korn Kobblers. Featured as title song in the 1949 film biography of Fred Fischer.

Oh, You Candy Kid
Words and music by Bob Adams and John Golden.
Charles K. Harris Music Publishing Co., 1909/Jerry Vogel Music Co., Inc., 1937.
Romantic song using candy brand names. Introduced by Maude

Fulton in *The Candy Shop* (musical, 1909) and popularized by Louise Dresser. A brief craze for similar novelty songs that year also gave Dresser "Oh, You Spearmint Kiddo with Wrigley Eyes" by Jerome and Schwartz.

Oh! You Circus Day
Words and music by Edith Maida Lessing and Jimmie V. Monaco.
Will Rossiter, 1912/Jerry Vogel Music Co., Inc., 1941.
An ASCAP top seller of 1912 and Monaco's first major success, this novelty song was popularized by Maud Lambert, the Dolce Sisters, and the team of Billy Montgomery and Florence Moore. Re-issued as the promotional theme song of the Jackie Coogan film *Circus Days* (First National, 1923).

Oh, You Devil Rag
Words and music by Ford T. Dabney.
Shapiro, Bernstein & Co., Inc., 1909.
Cake-walk featured by Aida Overton Walker.

Oh! You Georgia Rose
Words by Shelton Brooks and W. R. Williams, music by Bob Cole and Johnnie Waters.
Will Rossiter, 1912.
Proposal duet popularized by Lee White and George Perry.

Oh! You Gray Haired Kid
Words by Alfred Bryan, music by Harry Tierney.
Remick Music Corp., 1916.
Novelty song tailored to the specialties of character dancer William Rock and juvenile-imitator Frances White for their appearances in the *Ziegfeld Midnight Frolics of 1916.*

Oh, You Wonderful Girl
Words and music by George M. Cohan.
Cohan & Harris, 1911.
Introduced by Cohan in his musical *The Little Millionaire* (1911); revived on Broadway by Bernadette Peters as "Oh, You Wonderful Boy" in *George M!* (1968).

The Old Flag Never Touched the Ground
Words by James Weldon Johnson and Bob Cole, music by J. Rosamond Johnson.
Joseph W. Stern & Co., 1901, 1916/Edward B. Marks Music Corp., 1928, 1932.
Military anthem sung by the entire company for the finale of *The Shoo-Fly Regiment* (1907); a BMI top seller in revivals during and after World War I.

The Old Maids' Ball
Words and music by Irving Berlin.
Waterson, Berlin & Snyder, 1908/Irving Berlin Music Corp.
Novelty comic song recorded by Arthur Collins and Byron G. Harlan on Columbia.

The Old, Old Story
Words and music by Lew Dockstader.
Original copyright, 1904.
Dockstader sang his own comic song about lying to one's wife.

The Old Postmaster
Words and music by Edward B. Marks and Joseph W. Stern.
Joseph W. Stern & Co., 1900.
Plotted sentimental ballad of a New England postmaster waiting for a letter from his prodigal son.

Old Reliable Jokes
Words by Benjamin Hapgood Burt, music by Silvio Hein.
Joseph W. Stern & Co., 1906.
Introduced by Marie Cahill in *Marrying Mary* (1906), this comic novelty song re-tells bad jokes.

Ole Miss
Words and music by W. C. Handy.
Handy Brothers Music Co., Inc., 1916, 1944.
Railroad blues in song-and-trio form recorded by Handy's Orchestra (Columbia), Wadsworth's Novelty Orchestra (Pathe), and the Bechet Quintet (King Jazz).

On a Beautiful Night with a Beautiful Girl
Words by Will D. Cobb, music by Gus Edwards.
Remick Music Corp., 1912.
Spooning ballad with an echo effect in the chorus; introduced by Edwards's juvenile chorus in his *Song Revue of 1912* and also popularized as a solo by Arthur Deacon and Elphye Barnard.

On a Little Farm in Normandie
Words by Ballard MacDonald, music by Nat Osbourne.
Shapiro, Bernstein & Co., Inc., 1919.
Introduced by Frank Tinney in the service show *Atta Boy* and later popularized by Marie Cahill, this nostalgic ballad was later adapted to post-World War I use.

On a Spoony Moony Night
Words by Ed Gardinier, music by Leo Edwards.
Original copyright, 1903.

Bonnie Maginn told the chorus that "I croon when I spoon 'neath the moon in June" in *Mr. Bluebeard* (musical, 1903).

On a Starry Night
Words and music by Felix F. Feist.
Leo Feist Inc., 1903.
Ballad popularized by the Doherty Sisters and by Gertrude Stanley in vaudeville; also often performed as a parlor song.

On a Sunday Afternoon
Words by Andrew B. Sterling, music by Harry von Tilzer.
Harry Von Tilzer Music Publishing Co., 1902.
Romance popularized by juveniles in vaudeville, among them, Baby Lund and the Two Pucks; revived in the 1910's as dance music and in the 1940's as atmosphere for films, such as Republic Picture's *Atlantic City* (1944).

On an Automobile Honeymoon
Words by William Jerome, music by Jean Schwartz.
Remick Music Corp., 1905.
Novelty romance from the musical *The Ham Tree* (1905).

On Furlough
Words by Sam Richards, music by Walter Tilbury.
Francis, Day & Hunter, Inc., 1900.
Military novelty song for British male impersonator Vesta Tilley.

On Lalawana's Shore
Words by James Weldon Johnson, music by J. Rosamond Johnson.
Joseph W. Stern & Co., 1904.
South Sea Island love song introduced by Maude Lillian Berri in *Humpty-Dumpty* (musical, 1904) and recorded by Frank Howard on Zon-o-phone.

On Miami Shore, also known as **Golden Shores of Miami**
Words by William Le Baron, music by Victor Jacobi.
Chappell & Co., Inc., 1919.
An ASCAP top seller as a vocal and instrumental, it was recorded by the house bands of Vocalion, Columbia, Victor, and the Waldorf-Astoria, with a Victrola edition by Fritz Kreisler; used in the film *Las Vegas Nights* (Paramount, 1941).

On Moonlight Bay, see **Moonlight Bay,**.

On Patrol in No Man's Land
Words and music by James Reese Europe, Noble Sissle, and Eubie Blake.
M. Witmark & Sons, 1919.

This World War I song based on snatches on conversations and military orders was performed by the authors with their 369th Infantry ("Hell Fighters") Band (Pathe); Sissle and Blake popularized it in vocal duet and piano form in vaudeville and in their revue *Shuffle Along* (1921).

On San Francisco Bay
Words by Vincent Bryan, music by Gertrude Hoffmann (pseudonym for Kitty Hayes).
M. Witmark & Sons, 1906.
Romantic ballad interpolated by the Hedges Brothers and Jacobson into *A Parisian Model* (musical, 1906); recorded as dance music by the Victor Military Band.

On the Banks of the Bronx
Words by William Le Baron, music by Victor Jacobi.
T. B. Harms, 1919/Francis, Day & Hunter, Inc., 1919.
A New York City romance introduced by Percivål Knight in the operetta *Apple Blossoms* (1919).

On the Banks of the Rhine with a Stein
Words by Andrew B. Sterling, music by Harry von Tilzer.
Harry Von Tilzer Music Publishing Co., 1905.
One of von Tilzer's many drinking songs for vaudeville, popularized by Josie Sadler, Sadie Fields, and the Doherty Sisters.

On the Exposition Zone
Words and music by Don J. Gono.
Original copyright, 1915.
Promotional song for the Panama Pacific International Exposition in San Francisco, 1915, with descriptive references to its popular "Zone" (or Boardwalk).

On the 5:15
Words by Stanley Murphy, music by Henry I. Marshall.
Remick Music Corp., 1914.
An ASCAP top seller of 1914-1915, this novelty romance about commuters to the suburbs was introduced by Elizabeth Murray; recorded by Arthur Collins and Byron G. Harlan (Columbia), the American Quartet (Victor), and the Jesters (Decca).

On the Grand Old Sand
Words by Will D. Cobb, music by Gus Edwards.
Gus Edwards Music Publishing Co., 1907.
Billed as "Edwards' annual summer success," it was introduced by Florenz Tempest in the "Bathing Beauties" scene of Ziegfeld's *Follies of 1907*.

On the Level, You're a Devil
Words by Joe Young, music by Jean Schwartz.
Waterson, Berlin & Snyder, 1918/Mills Music Inc., 1946.
Title continues "But I'll Soon Make an Angel Out of You." Introduced by Frank Fay and Isabel Lowe in the *Passing Show of 1918.*

On the Mississippi
Words by Ballard MacDonald, music by Harry Carroll and Fields.
Shapiro, Bernstein & Co., Inc., 1912.
Dixie nostalgia introduced by Carroll and Fields in their close-harmony act; recorded by Gene Greene (Pathe), Sousa's Band (Victor), Prince's Band (Columbia), the Victor Military Band, and both the American and Peerless quartets on Victor. Phil Harris revived the song in his Dixie repertoire of the 1940's.

On the Old See-Saw
Words by Edward Gardinier, music by Gus Edwards.
Gus Edwards Music Publishing Co., 1907.
Answer song to the past season's "School Days" (q.v.) popularized by Daisy Leon, Maude Earle, and Suzanne Rocamora; used in Edwards's *Rube Kids* and *School Days* juvenile vaudeville feature acts.

On the Road That Leads to Home
Words and music by Gitz Rice.
G. Ricordi & C., SpA, Milan, Italy, 1918.
Military ballad interpolated into J. Hartley Manners and Percival Knight's play *Getting Together* (1918).

On the Road to Calais
Words by Alfred Bryan, music by Al Jolson.
Remick Music Corp., 1919.
Romantic ballad introduced by Al Jolson in *Sinbad* (1918) and recorded for Columbia.

On the Road to Home Sweet Home
Words by Gus Kahn, music by Egbert van Alstyne.
Remick Music Corp., 1917.
Nostalgic ballad that gained popularity during World War I; recorded by John Young and George Reardon on Edison cylinders and by Percy Hemus for Victor.

On the Road to Mandalay
Words by Rudyard Kipling, music by Oley Speaks.
G. Schirmer Inc., 1907.
Speaks's art song based on Kipling's *Barrack Room Ballads* became a favorite for male vocalists as a concert aria and parlor song. One of the first best-selling non-operatic vocal recordings on all avail-

able formats, it has been recorded by early studio regulars Henri Scott (Edison) and John Charles Thomas (Vocalion), opera singers Leonard Warren and Lawrence Tibbett (both Victor), and a host of popular vocalists from Frankie Laine (Columbia) to Frederick Wheeler (Victor). Sung by Tibbett in the film *Metropolitan* (20th Century-Fox 1935).

On the Shores of Italy
Words and music by Al Piantadosi, Dave Oppenheim, and Jack Glogau.
Leo Feist Inc., 1914, 1950.
Imitative Italian folk song featured in vaudeville by Emma Carus, Marie Russell, and Elizabeth Brice and Charles King; recorded by Albert Campbell and Henry Burr (Victor).

One Called "Mother" and the Other "Home Sweet Home"
Words by William Cahill, music by Theodore F. Morse.
F. B. Haviland, 1905/Jerry Vogel Music Co., Inc., 1933.
Blanche Washburn introduced this pathetic ballad about sentimental songs.

One Day in June
Words by Joe Goodwin, music by James F. Hanley.
Shapiro, Bernstein & Co., Inc., 1917.
Sentimental ballad most popular in close harmony duets; recorded by Albert Campbell and Henry Burr (Pathe and Victor) and by authors Goodwin and Hanley for Victor.

One - Two - Three - Four
Words and music by S. Kalama and Jack Alan.
F. B. Haviland, 1917/Jerry Vogel Music Co., Inc., 1917.
A Hawaiian instrumental introduced on Broadway in the Lenore Ulrich melodrama *The Bird of Paradise* in a ukelele arrangment by May Singhi Breen; a version of the same song by F. Henri Klickmann was published by the John Franklyn Music Corp. also in 1917.

Only a Dream of a Golden Past
Words by Alfred Bryan, music by Stanley Crawford.
Shapiro, Bernstein & Co., Inc., 1903.
Plotted sentimental ballad based on the "Bird in a Gilded Cage" genre (q.v.); popularized by Flo Allen and Anna Driver.

Onward Brothers (English)
Words by Havelock Ellis and Charles Kerr, music by Charles Kerr and Ludwig von Beethoven.
Original copyright, 1901.
Charles Kerr published this Socialist anthem created from

Havelock Ellis's setting of the *Ode to Joy* from Beethoven's Ninth Symphony. It remained a popular political version of the chorale at least through the 1930's when it was republished at the Brookwood Labor College, Katonah, New York.

Ood-kay Oo-yay Earn-lay Oo-tay Ove-Lay Ee-may?, see **Could You Learn to Love Me?**,.

O'O'O'Brien
Words by M. B. Kirby, music by Jean Schwartz.
Shapiro, Bernstein & Co., Inc., 1902.
Irish-dialect romance introduced by Maggie Cline.

Open Up the Golden Gates to Dixieland and Let Me into Paradise
Words by Jack Yellin, music by Gus Van and Joe Schenck.
Harry Von Tilzer Music Publishing Co., 1919.
Raggy specialty song for close harmony duet Van and Schenck.

The Opera
Words by Edgar Smith, music by John Stromberg.
M. Witmark & Sons, 1900.
An elaborate opera burlesque written for Lillian Russell and DeWolf Hopper in *Quo Vass-Iss?* (musical, 1900). Published at twelve pages, this is the only full text available of the annual parodies of opera performance in Weber and Fields's shows.

Other Eyes
Words and music by Clare Kummer.
Remick Music Corp., 1916.
Ballad introduced by Lola Fisher in Kummer's play *Good Gracious Annabelle* (1916).

Our Ancestors
Words by Harold Atteridge, music by Sigmund Romberg.
G. Schirmer Inc., 1918.
Production song comparing rag-time dancers to chimpanzees. Introduced by Kitty Donner and Mabel Withee and the Cave Men and Girls in *Sinbad* (1918).

Our Boys in Overalls
Words and music by Henry V. Neal and Julia Smith.
Original copyright, 1901.
Patriotic anthem praising the home front support of the Spanish-American War.

Out of His Heart He Builds a Home
Words by Edward Childs Carpenter, music by Victor Herbert.
M. Witmark & Sons, 1916.

Ballad in praise of the ordinary man introduced in Carpenter's play *The Cinderella Man.*

Out Where the Breakers Roar
Words by Harlow Hyde, music by H. W. Petrie.
Joseph W. Stern & Co., 1903.
Introduced by bass Carl A. Koenig; like Hyde and Petrie's other sea songs, it was most popular as a concert aria or parlor song.

Outside of That Every Little Thing's All Right, see **Harem Life,**.

Over the Moonlit Sea
Words by Vincent Bryan, music by Max Hoffmann.
M. Witmark & Sons, 1904.
Ballad from *Me, Him, and I,* a musical about the Alaska Gold Rush (1905, in Chicago); like most of Hoffmann's songs, it had a second life as dance music in a recording by the Victor Military Band.

Over the Pilsner Foam
Words by Vincent Bryan, music by J. B. Mullen.
Original copyright, 1903.
Comic song about romance and drinking featured by female performers, among them, Winnifred Greenwood and the Sisters Howard.

Over There
Words and music by George M. Cohan.
Original copyright, 1917/Leo Feist Inc., 1917/Jerry Vogel Music Co., Inc.
Introduced by Nora Bayes, Cohan's patriotic anthem of World War I became a top seller in sheet music and recordings that retains its popularity today. Early recordings by Bayes (Victor) and the studios' regulars, such as Billy Murray (Edison), Arthur Fields (Columbia), and the Pathe, Victor, Continental, and Prince's Bands, were joined by Enrico Caruso's still famous cuts for Gramophone, Victor, and Victrola. The same range of vocalists, from Dick Powell and Fred Waring (Decca) to Placido Domingo (DGG), have kept it in stock through the years; Cohan himself recorded it for Victor. Featured in the Cohan biographical entertainments *Yankee Doodle Dandy* (Warner Brothers, 1942) and by Frances Langford in *George M!* (on Broadway, 1968) by Joel Grey and company. Cohan also wrote a tribute to the Red Cross for the benefit of War Relief the next year -- "Their Hearts Are Over Here" (Waterson, Berlin & Snyder, 1918).

P

Pack Up Your Troubles in Your Old Kit Bag and Smile, Smile, Smile, also known as **Smile, Smile, Smile** (American-English)
Words by George Asaf, music by Felix Powell.
Chappell & Co., Inc., 1915.
World War I soldiers' song equally popular with British and Americans. Originally introduced by Adele Rowland in the musical comedy *Her Soldier Boy* (1915; London, 1916). Recorded by the Victor Military Band, Prince's Band (Columbia), and the Peerless Quartet (Lyrophone) and revived for World War I by Bob Crosby and His Bob Cats with Martha Tilton (V Disc, Decca) and by the Andrews Sisters (Decca); there was also a popular novelty version by Spike Jones and His City Slickers (Bluebird).

Pack Your Duds for San Francisco
Words and music by Joe Meyer.
Original copyright, 1915.
This march promotes the 1915 San Francisco Exposition, describing "fair weather, streets of gold ... and buildings all brand new."

Paint Me a Picture of Mama
Words by Addison Burkhardt, music by Raymond Hubbell.
Original copyright, 1902.
Sentimental ballad of an orphaned child sobbed by Ola Hayden and other juvenile singers in vaudeville.

Pajama Polly
Words and music by Max Hoffmann.
Shapiro, Bernstein & Co., Inc., 1902.
Novelty rag-time song introduced by Elinore Falk.

The Palm Beach Dip
Words by Stanley Murphy, music by Harry Tierney.
Original copyright, 1917.

Exhibition ballroom dance number from the revue *Miss 1917* where it was sung by Brice and King and dipped by the chorus dancers.

Pan-Am Rag
Words and music by Thomas M. J. Turpin.
Original copyright, 1914.
Rag written for the Pan-American Exposition of 1915 in San Francisco; recorded by rag revival pianist John Arpin on his album *They All Play Ragtime.* A third edition was registered for copyright in 1966.

Pan, Pan, Pan
Words by Will D. Cobb, music by Gus Edwards.
Howley, Haviland & Dresser, 1901.
Promotional song for the Buffalo, New York, Pan American Exposition in imitation of the popular "Lam' Lam' Lam'."

Pansies Mean Thoughts and Thoughts Mean You
Words by Fleta Jan Brown, music by Herbert Spencer.
M. Witmark & Sons, 1908.
Romantic ballad based on the "language of the flowers"; popularized by Frances Gerard and Nell Capron.

Pansy
Words and music by Pat Rooney.
Howley, Haviland & Dresser, 1901.
Romantic ballad introduced by Georgia Caine and Hattie Waters in *The Messenger Boy* (musical, 1901).

Pansy Faces
Words and music by William H. Penn.
Sol Bloom Publishing Co/Sol Bloom Music, 1903.
Romantic flower ballad introduced in Klaw and Erlanger's *Mother Goose* (1903) by Leila McIntyre and interpolated within the month by Irene Bentley into *The Girl from Dixie.*

Pansy of the Dell
Words by John Gilroy, music by Harry Linton.
Sol Bloom Publishing Co/Sol Bloom Music, 1902.
Producers Klaw and Erlanger featured a flower ballad for Leila McIntyre in each of their annual pantomime extravaganzas -- in 1902, she sang this in *The Sleeping Beauty and the Beast.*

Paree, also known as **The Wiggle-Woggle Dance**
Words by Matt C. Woodward, music by Gus Edwards.
Gus Edwards Music Publishing Co., 1907.
Promotional dance song for Mlle. Di Dio, a rival to Gaby Deslys.

Paree's a Branch of Broadway
Words and music by Max Hoffmann.
T. B. Harms, 1912/Francis, Day & Hunter, Inc.
Novelty song in "Tampo Catchouchka" about the popularity of American rag-time in France. Introduced by George Austin Moore in *Broadway to Paris* (musical, 1912).

A Parisian Model
Words by Harry B. Smith, music by Max Hoffmann.
M. Witmark & Sons, 1906.
Title song for the famous Anna Held vehicle, produced for her by Florenz Ziegfeld, Jr. in 1906.

Parisienne
Words by Lew Brown, music by Albert von Tilzer.
York Music Corp., 1912.
Novelty song describing new exhibition ballroom dances; popularized by Valeska Surratt, Olive Morgan, and Frankie Heath.

Patria
Words by George Graff, Jr., music by Mrs. Vernon Castle (pseudonym for Irene Foote Castle).
Waterson, Berlin & Snyder, 1917.
Introduced by popular ballroom dancer Irene Castle in her vaudeville appearances; this song promoted her starring role in the silent film serial *Patria* (1917).

The Pawn Shop Man, see **My Onliest Little Dolly,**.

Pawnee
Words by James O'Day, music by Silvio Hein.
Shapiro, Bernstein & Co., Inc., 1906.
In the middle of the first decade of the century, rag-time novelty songs often had Native American heroines; Nora Bayes and Anna Driver each found success with this tribute to a "little love so tawny."

Peace Song
Words by Victor L. Schertzinger, music by Thomas H. Ince.
Leo Feist Inc., 1916.
Promotional theme for composer Ince's film spectacle *Civilization* (1916).

The Peach That Tastes the Sweetest Hangs the Highest on the Tree
Words by Will D. Cobb, music by Gus Edwards.
Gus Edwards Music Publishing Co., 1907.
Novelty flirtation song introduced by May Irwin.

Peaches
Words by P. G. Wodehouse, music by Jerome Kern.
T. B. Harms, 1917.
Production song that introduced the female chorus in the revue *Miss 1917.*

Peggy
Words by Harry Williams, music by Neil Moret.
Leo Feist Inc., 1919/Jerry Vogel Music Co., Inc., 1946.
Romantic fox-trot introduced by Dorothy Dickson in the *Century Midnight Whirl* (revue, 1919).

People Who Live in Glass Houses Never Should Throw Any Stones
Words by Carroll Fleming, music by Theodore F. Morse.
Leo Feist Inc., 1903.
Plotted melodramatic ballad that tells sentimental stories of childhood and of a faithless marriage; popular as a parlor song and in vaudeville performance by song illustrators Charles Falke and Gillot and Henry.

Per Sempre Liberta!, see **Liberty Forever,.**

Percy
Words by Vincent Bryan, music by Gertrude Hoffmann.
Original copyright, 1906.
Rag-time ballad sung by Etta Pearce in *The Duke of Duluth* (musical, 1905).

Percy
Words by William Jerome, music by Jean Schwartz.
Francis, Day & Hunter, Inc., 1906.
Rag-time portrait of a shy mama's boy, sung by Toby Claude.

The Perfect Song
Words by Clarence Lucas, music by Joseph Carl Briel.
Chappell & Co., Inc., 1915, 1929.
Originally published as a promotional song for D. W. Griffith's *Birth of a Nation,* it became popular thirty years later as the theme for *The Pepsodent Hour Featuring Amos and Andy.* Recorded by Jesse Crawford (Decca) and the Victor Salon Orchestra and revivied by Guy Lombardo and His Royal Canadians (Bluebird).

Personality
Words and music by George Spink.
M. Witmark & Sons, 1909.
Self-descriptive novelty song for Eva Tanguay's vaudeville act.

Philomene, see **French Fandango,.**

The Phonograph March
Music by Charles William Harrison.
Original copyright, 1902.
Promotional piece for Harrison's method of teaching the piano quickly. He advertised a series of concerts of piano accompanying recordings of vocal, cornet, violin, and xylophone solos "given by pupils after receiving only one month's instruction" on the back of this march, which was dedicated to Thomas Alva Edison.

The Phrenologist Coon
Words by Ernest Hogan, music by Will Accooe.
Joseph W. Stern & Co., 1901.
Lyricist Hogan and Bert Williams both found success with this satirical monologue and song using the spiel of the pseudoscience of phrenology, reading the bumps on a person's head.

Pick, Pick, Pick, Pick on the Mandolin, Antonio
Words and music by Irving Berlin.
Waterson, Berlin & Snyder, 1912.
Italian-dialect song with imitations of the then-popular instrument in the chorus, popularized by Belle Blanche and Al and Ruby Raymond.

A Picnic for Two
Words by Arthur J. Lamb, music by Albert von Tilzer.
York Music Corp., 1905.
This romance was performed by most of the popular female vocalists in vaudeville, among them, Grace Cameron, Adele Ritchie, Josie Sadler, and La Belle Estellita.

The Picture I Want to See
Words by P. G. Wodehouse, music by Jerome Kern.
Original copyright, 1917/T. B. Harms, 1917/Francis, Day & Hunter, Inc., 1917.
Invitation to a movie date sung by Elsie Janis and Owen Nares in the revue *Hullo America* (in London, 1918).

A Picture without a Frame
Words and music by Al Wilbur and Harry Jonnes.
Joseph W. Stern & Co., 1900.
Song illustrator Charles Falke introduced this plotted melodramatic ballad of quarreling lovers reunited in death.

Pierrot and Pierrette (American-English)
Words and music by Ivan Caryll.
Chappell & Co., Inc., 1906.
Plotted ballad introduced by Hattie Williams in *The Little Cherub* (musical, 1906).

Pierrot and Pierrette, also known as **Valse Exquisite**
Words and music by Leo Edwards and Jean Lenox.
Joseph W. Stern & Co., 1916.
This waltz written for the exhibition ballroom dance team of Adelaide and Hughes was their most famous ballet specialty.

Pig Latin Love, also known as **I-yay Ove-lay Oo-yay Earie-day**
Words and music by L. Wolfe Gilbert and Anatol Friedland.
Original copyright, 1919.
Novelty love song recorded by Arthur Fields on Columbia.

Piking the Pike, also known as **Take a Pike at the Pike with Me**
Words by Mark L. Stone and George Totten Smith, music by William H. Penn.
Sol Bloom Publishing Co/Sol Bloom Music, 1904.
This was the official and authorized promotional song for the St. Louis Fair Midway, then called "the Pike."

The Ping Pong Song (American-English)
Words by Percy Greenbank, music by Ivan Caryll.
Francis, Day & Hunter, Ltd., London, England/T. B. Harms, 1901.
Novelty song using the by-play of ping pong as a metaphor for romance. Introduced by Edna Wallace Hopper and Cyril Scott in *The Silver Slipper* (musical, 1902).

The Pink Lady Waltz
Music by Ivan Caryll.
Chappell & Co., Inc., 1911.
Waltz popularized in the musical comedy *The Pink Lady* (1911) and recorded by the Victor Dance Orchestra and by the Melachrino Strings (Gramophone).

Pinkerton Detective Man
Words and music by Nora Bayes and Jack Norworth.
T. B. Harms, 1912.
Novelty romance comparing the Pinkerton logo ("the eye that never closes") to the moon that spies on spooners. Introduced by Bayes and Norworth in *The Sun Dodgers* (musical, 1912).

Pinky Panky Poo
Words by Aaron S. Hoffman, music by Andy Lewis.
Sol Bloom Publishing Co/Sol Bloom Music, 1902.
This comic Oriental romance was the hit song of the summer of 1902 and was interpolated by Marguerite Clark into *The Wild Rose* in May and by Blanche Ring into *The Defender* in July.

Pirate Song
Words by Robert Louis Stevenson, music by Henry F. Gilbert.

Original copyright, 1902.
Gilbert's setting of "Fifteen men on a dead man's chest" from the novel *Treasure Island* was one of the most popular art and parlor songs of the period; recordings by bassos David Bispham (Columbia), Herbert Witherspoon (Victor), and especially Reinald Werrenrath on Victrola were among the best selling early discs.

Plain Mamie O'Hooley
Words by Harry B. Smith, music by Ludwig Englander.
Joseph W. Stern & Co., 1903.
Comic description of romance introduced by Frank Daniels in *The Office Boy* (musical, 1903).

Play a Simple Melody
Words and music by Irving Berlin.
Irving Berlin Music Corp., 1914, 1942.
Patter rag with vocal obligato now performed as a duet or re-recorded solo. Introduced by Sallie Fisher and Charles King in *Watch Your Step* (1914) and recorded shortly thereafter by Billy Murray and Edna Brown (Victor); the revival by Ethel Merman and Dan Dailey in the Zanuck film *There's No Business Like Show Business* (1954) led to top-selling recordings by Phil Harris (RCA), Jo Stafford (Capitol), Dinah Shore (Columbia), and Bing and Gary Crosby (Decca).

Play That Fandango Rag
Words by E. Ray Goetz, music by Lewis F. Muir.
Shapiro, Bernstein & Co., Inc., 1909.
Spanish novelty rag introduced by Lillian Lorraine in Ziegfeld's *Follies of 1910.*

Please Don't Take Away the Girls
Words by Alfred Bryan, music by Jean Schwartz.
Remick Music Corp., 1919.
William Kent and a chorus of Cocktail Girls in the *Gaieties of 1919* introduced this preview of Prohibition.

Please Don't Take My Lovin' Man Away
Words by Lew Brown, music by Albert von Tilzer.
York Music Corp., 1912.
Blues-style song popularized by Valeska Surratt, Frankie Heath, and Perqueta Courtney.

Please Go Away and Let Me Sleep
Words by Cecil Mack (pseudonym for R. C. McPherson), music by James T. Brymn.
Harry Von Tilzer Music Publishing Co., 1902.

Comic song popularized by Raymond Teal and Billy Single Clifford; recorded by Arthur Fields on Grey Gull.

Please Keep Out of My Dreams
Words and music by Elsa Maxwell.
Original copyright, 1915.
Romantic ballad performed and recorded by Frances Alda and Nora Bayes, both on Victor.

Please Leave the Door Ajar
Words by Robert F. Roden, music by J. Fred Helf.
Edward B. Marks Music Corp., 1902.
Plotted pathetic ballad about a dying child. Song illustrators Charles Falke and Dietrich and Sheridan used projected slides to present the melodramatic story during their vaudeville performances.

Please Mother, Buy Me a Baby
Words and music by Will D. Cobb and Gus Edwards.
Mills Music Inc., 1903, 1910.
Plotted melodramatic ballad performed by song illustrator Charles Falke.

The Police Won't Let Mariutch-a Dance, Unless She Move-a-da-Feet
Words and music by Edgar Leslie and Halsey K. Mohr.
Original copyright, 1907.
Answer song to "Mariutch Down at Coney Island" (q.v.), an Italian-dialect number about a "hootch-a ma kootch" dancer who shimmied but never moved her feet. In the summer of 1907 police did raid midway booths at Coney Island's amusement parks, claiming that the hootchy-kootchy dancers violated obscenity laws.

Pollyanna, also known as **The Glad Song**
Words by Will J. Hart, music by Gilbert Dodge.
Original copyright, 1917.
Promotional song for Chatherine Chisolm Cushing's play starring Patricia Collinge (1916), which was based on the popular children's novel by Eleanor H. Porter.

The Pony Ballet Girl
Words and music by Irene Franklyn and Bert Green.
Leo Feist Inc., 1909.
Satirical song about the Original English Pony Ballet, an eight-woman precision team. Introduced by Franklyn in her vaudeville act; references to the history of the team and descriptions of its specialties are valuable sources.

Poor Barney Mulligan, also known as **Microbes on the Brain**
Words by W. W. Hall, music by Edmund Braham.
Original copyright, 1902.
Comic novelty song for Trixie Friganza based on F. Opper's comic strip character.

Poor Butterfly
Words by John Golden, music by Raymond Hubbell.
Harms, Inc., 1916, 1944.
This romantic ballad based on the plot of *Mme. Butterfly* was introduced in the Hippodrome Theater spectacle *The Big Show* (revue, 1916) and popularized in vaudeville by Grace LaRue. Recorded as a concert aria by Frances Alda (Victor), Deanna Durbin (Decca), and violinist Fritz Kreisler (Victor), but more recently popular with jazz ensembles led by Paul Whiteman (Victor), Russ Morgan (Decca), Erroll Garner (Columbia), Art Tatum (V Disc), Elizabeth Welch (Vocalion), and Benny Goodman (Columbia), among many others.

Poor John
Words by Fred W. Leigh, music by Henry E. Pether.
Francis, Day & Hunter, Inc., 1906.
Signature tune for Vesta Victoria in British music halls and American vaudeville; Rita Hayworth sang the song about a conflict with a mother-in-law in the film *Cover Girl* (Columbia, 1944). Recorded by Victoria (Victor), Ada Jones (Victor), and Gertrude Lawrence (Decca); revived by Joan Morris for her *Vaudeville* album (Nonesuch).

Poor Little Butterfly Is a Fly Girl Now
Words by Sam M. Lewis and Joe Young, music by M. K. Jerome.
Waterson, Berlin & Snyder, 1919/Mills Music Inc./Warock Music, Inc.
Comic answer song to "Poor Butterfly" (q.v.), itself a response to *Mme. Butterfly*. Billy Murray recorded and popularized this very-Americanized Butterfly who "knows that Ballin the Jack will bring Pinkerton back." As a fox-trot, it was recorded by Ford T. Dabney's Orchestra on Vocalion and by the All-Star Trio on Victor.

Poor Little Rich Girl's Dog
Words and music by Irving Berlin.
Irving Berlin Music Corp., 1917.
Topical comic song introduced by Joseph Cawthorne in *The Rambler Rose* (musical, 1917); the title is derived from Eleanor Gate's popular novel and play (1913) and the recently released Mary Pickford film *Poor Little Rich Girl.*

The Poor Old Man
Words and music by Vincent Bryan.
Original copyright, 1906.
Comic monologue and song about fatherhood popularized by Edwin Foy and Nat C. Wills; recorded by Bob Roberts (Victor).

Poor Pauline
Words by Charles McCarron, music by Raymond Walker.
Broadway Music Corp., 1914.
Promotional song for the Pearl White film serial, *The Perils of Pauline.*

Poor Robinson Crusoe
Words by Edward P. Moran, music by Seymour Furth.
Mills Music Inc., 1904.
Comic song introduced by Billy Van in *The Messenger Boy* (musical, 1903).

Popular Songs
Words and music by Clare Kummer.
Joseph W. Stern & Co., 1906.
Complex parody on each of five popular song genres--dialect/minstrel, Indian rags, Spanish, Irish ("Molly O'Mary"), and rural nostalgia, sung "when the jay-birds were warbling in the wild wood." Introduced by Hattie Williams in *The Little Cherub* (1906).

The Portobello Lassie (English)
Words by Gilbert Wells and Harry Lauder, music by Harry Lauder.
Francis, Day & Hunter, Ltd., London, England, 1914/T. B. Harms, 1914.
Cockney novelty romance popularized and recorded by Lauder, who usually performed as a Scottish dialect singer.

Pots and Pans
Words by Charley Grapewin, music by Jean Schwartz.
Original copyright, 1911.
Character song about a failed actress. Introduced by Fanny Brice in Ziegfeld's *Follies of 1911.*

The Preacher and the Bear
Words and music by Joe Arizona.
Original copyright, 1904/Lewis Music Publishing Co., Inc., 1947.
Comic "Deacon" novelty song popularized by Sousa's Band (Victor) and by Arthur Collins (Operaphone, Victor, Columbia); revived by Phil Harris (RCA) as a Southern novelty in the 1940's.

Pretty Baby
Words and music by Gus Kahn, Tony Jackson, and Egbert van Alstyne.
Remick Music Corp., 1916.
Introduced by the chorus in the Shuberts' *A World of Pleasure* (musical, 1915) and, within a few months, interpolated by Dolly Hackett into their *Passing Show of 1916,* soon becoming an ASCAP best seller. Early recordings as a fox-trot by Prince's Band (Columbia) and the Orpheus Quartet (Victor) were followed by discs by such major vocalists as Al Jolson (Decca), Bing Crosby (Decca), Sammy Davis, Jr. (Circle, with Jelly Roll Morton), and Doris Day, who revived it for Columbia and the Kahn film biography.

Pretty Desdemona
Words and music by F. Collis Wildman.
Gotham-Attucks Music Publishing Co., 1905.
Bert Williams and George Walker's performance of this romantic ballad was the hit of their appearances at the Hammersteins' Victoria Theater, New York City.

A Pretty Girl Is Like a Melody
Words and music by Irving Berlin.
Irving Berlin Music Corp., 1919.
The song that symbolizes the spectacle and glory of the *Ziegfeld Follies* was introduced by John Steel, the tenor, in the 1919 edition. In the number he presented five show girls, each costumed to illustrate a semi-classical piano work (with unpublished lyrics, probably by Gene Buck), such as the Humoresque, Spring Song, and Traumerei. Steel's recording for Victor (without the interludes) is included in the Smithsonian Institution's *Ziegfeld Follies of 1919* album. The song was revived for Berlin's *Blue Skies* (Paramount, 1946) and *Alexander's Ragtime Band* (Fox, 1938), but is now best remembered for the extravaganza that ended *The Great Ziegfeld* (MGM, 1936) which was excerpted in *That's Entertainment I* (1974). That production, sung by Dennis Morgan, had additional lyrics by Harold Adamson and a new "vocal development," bridge and introduction by Arthur Lange.

Pretty Kitty-San
Words by Addison Burkhardt and Aaron S. Hoffman, music by Leo Edwards.
Original copyright, 1904.
Marie Dressler introduced this love song of the Russo-Japanese War.

Pretty Little Dinah Jones
Words and music by J. B. Mullen.

Harry Von Tilzer Music Publishing Co., 1902.
Romance sung by minstrel vocalists, such as Dan Coleman, and black vaudeville performers, among them the team of Avery and Hart.

Pretty Maid Adelaide
Words by Addison Burkhardt, music by Raymond Hubbell.
Charles K. Harris Music Publishing Co., 1902.
Comic romance introduced by the Hengler Sisters in *The Runaways* a 1902 musical about naive country maidens visiting the city.

Pretty Polly!
Words by George V. Hobart, music by Max Hoffmann.
Novelty song relating the romance of two parrots from *The Rogers Brothers in Paris* (1904).

The Pride of Newspaper Row
Words and music by A. B. Sloane.
M. Witmark & Sons, 1900.
Nellie O'Neil introduced this tribute to the newsboy character, "Jimmy."

Pride of the Prairie
Words by Harry Breen, music by George Botsford.
Remick Music Corp., 1907, 1930/Jerry Vogel Music Co., Inc., 1943.
Cowboy love song popularized by Cheridah Simpson, Violet Carleton, and Carter De Haven.

Prohibition Blues
Words by Ring Lardner, music by Nora Bayes.
Remick Music Corp., 1919.
Dirge for alcohol prior to the enactment of the Nineteenth Amendment. Introduced by composer Bayes in the suffragist musical *Ladies First* (1919).

Prohibition, You Have Lost Your Sting
Words and music by J. Russel Robinson, Al Siegel, and Billy Curtis.
Original copyright, 1919.
Sophie Tucker and the Five Kings of Syncopation found success recommending kisses as substitutes for intoxicants.

The Proper Way to Kiss
Words by Raymond A. Browne, music by Theodore F. Morse.
Original copyright, 1902.
Demonstrated by Louise Grunning and Frank Daniels in *The Office Boy* (musical, 1903).

Prunella
Words by Harold Atteridge, music by Harry Carroll.
Shapiro, Bernstein & Co., Inc., 1914.
Romance introduced by Harry Pilcer in *The Belle of Bond Street* (musical, 1914).

Prunella Mine
Words by Gene Buck, music by Dave Stamper.
T. B. Harms, 1914.
Love song from the *Ziegfeld Follies of 1914,* possibly in response to "Prunella."

Psyche
Words and music by Edward W. Corliss.
Original copyright, 1902.
The most popular song from the musical *The Show Girl* (1902), it was introduced by Kathryn Hutchinson as "Amor."

Pull the Cork Out of Erin and Let the River Shannon Flow
Words by Addison Burkhardt, music by Fred Fisher (pseudonym for Albert von Breitenbach).
Fred Fisher Music Co., 1917.
Anthem of the Irish Free State as represented on Broadway by Nora Bayes and Andrew Mack.

The Pussy and the Bow-Wow
Words by James Weldon Johnson, music by J. Rosamond Johnson.
Joseph W. Stern & Co., 1904/Edward B. Marks Music Corp., 1920.
Romantic ballad introduced by Nellie Daly and John McVeigh in *Humpty-Dumpty* (musical, 1904); re-issued as a children's song by Marks.

Put Me Among the Girls
Words by C. W. Murphy, music by Dan Lipton.
Francis, Day & Hunter, Inc., 1907.
Introduced by Joseph Cawthorne in *The Hoyden* (musical, 1907) and popular in British music halls; the suggestive song was interpolated into John Osbourne's portrait of an aging music hall performer *The Entertainer* on stage and film (1960), starring Laurence Olivier.

Put Me Upon an Island
Words and music by Will Letters.
Shapiro, Bernstein & Co., Inc., 1908.
Anti-suffragist novelty song popularized by character comics John T. Powers, Ed Wynn, and London musical hall's Wilkie Bard.

Put on Your Old Grey Bonnet
Words by Stanley Murphy, music by Percy Wenrich.
Remick Music Corp., 1909.
This golden anniversary song was often performed and recorded as a genuine folk or country-western tune, as by the Sweet Violet Boys (Vocalion), Ray Burke's Speakeasy Boys (Paradox), and the Merry Macs (Decca); also recorded by jazz artists, among them, Jimmie Launceford (Decca), the Mills Brothers (Decca), and the Casa Loma Orchestra (Okeh).

Q

A Quaint Old Bird
Words by Edward Madden and Charles H. Taylor, music by Theodore F. Morse.
F. B. Haviland, 1904.
Advice song introduced by Arthur Collins in *The Catch of the Season* (musical, 1905).

Quand les Francaise apprennent a "Do You Speak English?", see **When Yankee Doodle Learns to "Parlez-Vous Francaise?"**,.

The Queen of Society
Words by Edgar Smith, music by John Stromberg.
M. Witmark & Sons, 1901.
Lillian Russell introduced this satirical song in *Hoity-Toity* (musical, 1901); the lyrics are filled with French and English malapropisms.

Queen of the Bungalow
Words by Ed Gardinier, music by Gus Rogers and Max Rogers.
The Rogers Brothers wrote this raggy song for Neva Aylmer to introduce in their musical *The Rogers Brothers in London* (1903); recorded by Harry MacDonough (Victor).

The Queen of the Night
Words by Ballard MacDonald, music by Paul Lincke.
Apollo Verlag, Berlin, Federal Republic of Germany, 1907/Joseph W. Stern & Co., 1909.
This ballad, probably English-language lyrics set to a piano work by Lincke, was introduced by Maud Lambert in *The Midnight Sons* (musical, 1909).

The Queen of the Track
Words by Addison Burkhardt, music by Raymond Hubbell.
Original copyright, 1902.

This novelty romance uses horse and betting slang to describe a beautiful woman; from the musical *The Runaways* (1903).

R

R-E-M-O-R-S-E
Words by George Ade, music by Alfred G. Wathall.
Original copyright, 1902.
Frank Moulan as "Ki-Ram" introduced this hangover dirge in *The Sultan of Sulu* (musical, 1902).

The Radiance in Your Eyes (English)
Words and music by Ivor Novello.
Ascherberg, Hopwood & Crew, Ltd., London, England, 1915.
Popularized and recorded by the foremost balladeers of the era, among them, Orville Harrold, Percy Remus (Pathe), and Reinald Werrenrath (Victor).

The Raffles Dance, see **Just a Kiss,**.

Rag Babe
Words and music by George M. Cohan.
George M. Cohan Music Publishing Co., 1908.
Exhibition ballroom dance introduced by George M. and Josephine Cohan in his musical *The Yankee Prince* (1908); recorded by Arthur Collins (Victor).

Rag-Time Cowboy Joe
Words by Grant Clarke, music by Lewis F. Muir and Maurice Abrahams.
Mills Music Inc., 1912/Fred Fisher Music Co., 1940/Robbins Music Corp.
Novelty hit about an Arizona cowpoke whose horse is "syncopated gaited"; sung and recorded by Gene Greene on Pathe. Paul Whiteman and Jo Stafford kept the song popular through the 1920's and 1940's. It was performed in films by Alice Faye in *Hello, Frisco, Hello* (Fox, 1942) and by Betty Hutton in *Incendiary Blonde* (Paramount, 1945).

Rag-Time Violin
Words and music by Irving Berlin.
Waterson, Berlin & Snyder, 1911/B. Feldman & Co., Ltd., 1911/Irving Berlin Music Corp.
At the turn of the decade, rag-time music for string instruments was at its most popular; Berlin's song has a plotted verse and a chorus that imitates the sound of a fiddle. It was popularized in London by Fred Barnes and in American vaudeville by Gene Greene, Eddie Cantor, and many close-harmony ensembles, such as the Melody Monarchs, the R.A.G. Trio and the American Quartet (Victor); revived by Judy Garland and Fred Astaire in the montage sequence in the film *Easter Parade* (MGM, 1948).

Ragging the Baby to Sleep
Words by L. Wolfe Gilbert, music by Lewis F. Muir.
Mills Music Inc., 1912.
Novelty song popularized by Bonita.

Ragging the Chopsticks
Words and music by Archie Gottler, music by Abe Frankel.
Leo Feist Inc., 1919.
Novelty song and fox-trot popularized by Arthur Fields, who recorded versions for Edison, Emerson, and Pathe.

Ragging the Old Vienna Roll
Words by Vincent Bryan, music by Jean Schwartz.
Remick Music Corp., 1911/Mills Music Inc.
Patter rag introduced by Al Jolson as an interpolation into the musical *The Honeymoon Express.* One of the cleverest of the Broadway rags, it explains that flour from Savannah made New York's Viennese bakers get syncopation.

The Ragtime College Girl
Words by E. Ray Goetz, music by Kerry Mills.
Mills Music Inc., 1911.
Female impersonator Julian Eltinge introduced this satirical song in *The Fascinating Widow* (musical, 1911).

Ragtime Eyes
Words by Grant Clarke and Edgar Leslie, music by Jean Schwartz.
Original copyright, 1912.
Clever chromatic rag popularized by Emma Carus.

Ragtime Jockey Man
Words and music by Irving Berlin.
Waterson, Berlin & Snyder, 1912.
Novelty song narrated by a race tout betting on the jockey. Introduced by Willie Howard in the *Passing Show of 1912.*

Ragtime Mockingbird
Words and music by Irving Berlin.
Waterson, Berlin & Snyder, 1912.
Novelty song popularized and recorded by Dolly Connolly (Columbia).

Ragtime Soldier Man
Words and music by Irving Berlin.
Waterson, Berlin & Snyder, 1912.
Ragged response to the popular "Dolly Gray" songs (q.v.); recorded by Arthur Collins and Byron G. Harlan on Victor.

The Ragtime Volunteers Are Off to War
Words by Ballard MacDonald, music by James F. Hanley.
Shapiro, Bernstein & Co., Inc., 1917.
The ragged up patriotic anthem was World War I's contribution to American music; this popular example was introduced by Emma Carus.

Rainbow
Words by Alfred Bryan, music by Percy Wenrich.
Remick Music Corp., 1908/Jerry Vogel Music Co., Inc., 1938.
Indian serenade popularized through recordings by the house quartets, vocalists, and dance orchestras of the major 1910's record labels, among them, Victor's Orchestra, the Shannon and Haydn Quartets, and Billy Murray and Columbia's Band, and singers Henry Burr, Frank Stanley, and Andrea Sarto; revived by Chet Atkins for RCA.

Rainbows Follow After Rain
Words by J. Cheever Goodwin, music by Maurice Levi.
Romantic ballad introduced in *The Rogers Brothers at Harvard* (musical, 1902).

Ramona, also known as **Allessandro's Love Song**
Words and music by Lee Johnson.
Original copyright, 1903.
Ballad based on characters from Helen Jackson's novel *Ramona;* re-issued in 1910 concurrent to the Biograph Company film of that name.

Ramona
Words and music by L. Wolfe Gilbert and Mabel Wayne.
Leo Feist Inc., 1917.
This promotional title song for the second silent version of Helen Jackson's novel (Clune, 1916) became a major success for vocalists and ensembles; its over sixty recordings include those by Ruth Etting (Columbia), Paul Whiteman and His Orchestra (Vic-

tor and Gramophone), and Louis Armstrong and Sy Oliver together on Decca.

Razzberries
Words and music by Sidney D. Mitchell and Frank E. Banta.
Original copyright, 1919.
Novelty one-step with sound effects; popularized by the Van Eps Trio (Victor).

Red Domino
Words by James O'Dea, music by S. R. Henry.
Joseph W. Stern & Co., 1906.
Promotional song for "La Domino Rouge," a so-called Parisian dancer appearing at Hammerstein's roof garden theater. In a typical Hammerstein twist, the song, performed at the same theater, identified the French dancer as "Birdie Maloney from faraway Coney." In fact, she was Daisy Peterkin from St. Louis.

Red Pepper Rag
Words by Harold Atteridge, music by Henry Lodge.
M. Witmark & Sons, 1911.
Introduced by George Austin Moore in the *Passing Show of 1912,* it was a popular dance recording by Prince's Band (Columbia).

Red Red Rose
Words by Alex Rogers, music by Will Marion Cook.
Gotham-Attucks Music Publishing Co., 1908/Carl Fischer, Inc.
Ballad introduced by Abbie Mitchell in *Bandana Land* (musical, 1907); recorded by Arthur Clough and the Haydn Quartet in its popular barbershop version (Victor).

The Red Rose Rag
Words by Edward Madden, music by Percy Wenrich.
Remick Music Corp., 1911.
One of the most popular Broadway rags, it was associated with Dolly Connolly, who recorded it on Columbia. The fox-trot version was a dance standard for decades, with recordings on Victor (by Arthur Pryor's Band and Billy Murray) and Capitol. The patter version is associated with George Burns, who performed it in his concert monologues (1970's and 1980's).

Red Wing
Words by Thurland Chattaway, music by Kerry Mills.
Mills Music Inc., 1917/Shawnee Press, Inc., 1939.
Indian novelty popular as a romantic ballad in recordings by Harry MacDonough (Victor), Henry Burr (Columbia), and Prince's Military Band (Columbia); revived as a novelty by Spike Jones and His City Slickers (Bluebird, Decca).

Redhead
Words and music by Irene Franklyn and Bert Green.
Leo Feist Inc., 1908.
Franklyn's signature tune, a juvenile novelty song that lists slang terms for hair color. It is included in the album *They Stopped the Show!* (Audio Rarities).

Regretful Blues
Words by Grant Clarke, music by Cliff Hess.
Kalmar, Puck & Abrahams Consolidated Mus, 1917.
Bluesy lament with topical second verse threatening that Kaiser Wilhelm will be made to feel regret. Introduced by Nora Bayes in the *Cohan Revue of 1918.*

A Regular Girl
Words by Bert Kalmar and Harry Ruby, music by Elsie Janis.
Waterson, Berlin & Snyder, 1919.
A catch phrase associated with Elsie Janis became the title of her Paramount film (1919), for which this was a promotional song.

Remember Dear
Words and music by Vans Lloyd.
Original copyright, 1905.
The final ballad associated with contralto Jessie Bartlett Davis.

Remember Me to My Old Girl
Words by George Moriarty, music by Al H. Brown and J. Brandon Walsh.
Original copyright, 1912.
This rag-time romance had lyrics written by one baseball player (Moriarty was captain of the Detroit team) and popularized in vaudeville by three more, "those Heroes of the World Series"--Bender, Coombes, and Morgan.

Returned
Words by Paul Lawrence Dunbar, music by Will Marion Cook.
Harry Von Tilzer Music Publishing Co., 1902.
Ballad based on Dunbar's poem featured by Abbie Mitchell.

Right Is Might
Words by Fannie J. Barnes, music by T. Martin Towne.
Original copyright, 1904.
Recitation and song about a filthy slum child who keeps clean her white ribbon (symbol of the Women's Christian Temperance Union) and stops her parents from drinking; published in Anna Gordon's *Marching Songs for Young Crusaders* (1904).

Ring-Ting-a-Ling
Words by William Jerome and Grant Clarke, music by Jean Schwartz.
Original copyright, 1912.
Telephone novelty love song introduced by Edwin Foy and Lillian Lorraine in *Over the River* (musical, 1912).

Rip van Winkle Was a Lucky Man
Words by William Jerome, music by Jean Schwartz.
Shapiro, Bernstein & Co., Inc., 1901.
Comic song praising Mrs. Rip van Winkle for paying her own rent for twenty years. Introduced by Harry Bulger in *The Sleeping Beauty and the Beast* (musical, 1901); also popularized by Maude Nugent. For an alternative version, see "Who Paid the Rent for Mrs. Rip van Winkle...".

Rip Van Winkle Was a Lucky Man But Adam Had Him Beat a Mile
Words by James H. Burris, music by Chris Smith.
Shapiro, Bernstein & Co., Inc., 1909/Leeds Music Corp.
Comic character song introduced by Bert Williams and recorded by Dan W. Quinn (Victor).

The Road for You and Me
Words by James Donaldson, music by George Lyons and Bob Yosco.
M. Witmark & Sons, 1917.
Sentimental ballad performed and recorded by Lyons and Yosco, a harp and mandolin duet.

The Road to Romany
Words and music by Olga Petrova.
M. Witmark & Sons, 1919.
Gypsy ballad and promotional title song for the Vitagraph film starring Petrova.

The Road to Yesterday
Words and music by Clare Kummer.
Remick Music Corp., 1908.
Nostalgic ballad introduced by Louise Gunning in the title trouser role of the play *Tom Jones* (1907).

Roamin' in the Gloamin' (American-English)
Words and music by Harry Lauder.
T. B. Harms, 1911/Francis, Day & Hunter, Inc.
Lauder's most popular Scottish dialect romantic ballad; recorded by Lauder (Victor) and his rival Glen Ellison (Edison); revived by Pete Daily and His Chicagoans (Capitol) and Sam Lanin's Orchestra (Banner).

Roaming Romeo
Words by Billy Duval, music by Jimmie Morgan.
Original copyright, 1918.
This salacious tribute to Shakespeare's character was performed by Eddie Cantor in the *Ziegfeld Follies of 1918.*

The Roaring Volcano
Music by E. T. Paull.
Paull-Pioneer Music Co., 1923, 1940.
Descriptive music based on the destruction of Pompeii.

Rob Roy McIntosh (American-English)
Words and music by Harry Lauder and Frank Folloy.
Francis, Day & Hunter, Inc., 1907.
Scottish dialect comedy song popularized and recorded by Lauder, who like the title character was "enchanting wi ma lilt."

Robinson Crusoe's Isle
Words and music by Benjamin Hapgood Burt.
Joseph W. Stern & Co., 1905.
Comic song introduced by Marie Cahill in *Molly Moonshine* (musical, 1905); novelty songs about Defoe's hero remained popular throughout the two decades, from "Poor Robinson Crusoe" (q.v.) to "What Did Robinson Crusoe Do with Friday on Saturday Night?" (q.v.).

Rock-a-bye Your Baby with a Dixie Melody
Words by Joe Young and Sam M. Lewis, music by Jean Schwartz.
Waterson, Berlin & Snyder, 1918/Mills Music Inc., 1946.
Written for interpolation into the "Dixieland" slot in Al Jolson's *Sinbad* (1918--), it became an ASCAP top seller. Associated with Jolson through recordings for Decca, Columbia, and Harmony and performed in the film *Jolson Sings Again* (Columbia, 1949), it is a vocal standard, with major recordings by Arthur Fields (Pathe), Wilbur C. Sweatman's Original Jazz Band (Columbia), and Jerry Lewis (Decca).

Rock Me in the Cradle of Love
Words and music by J. Leubrie Hill.
T. B. Harms, 1914.
Bluesy ballad introduced by Alice Ramsey in *My Friend from Kentucky* (musical, 1913) and interpolated into the *Ziegfeld Follies of 1914.*

Rockaway
Words by Howard Johnson and Alex Rogers, music by C. Luckeyth Roberts.
Leo Feist Inc., 1917.

Song promoting the revived slow drag dance; popularized by Sophie Tucker and recorded by Irving Kaufman on Columbia.

Roll Dem Cotton Balls
Words by James Weldon Johnson, music by J. Rosamond Johnson.
Joseph W. Stern & Co., 1914.
Dixie nostalgia song introduced by Trixie McCoy and recorded by the Heidelberg Quartet (Victor).

Roll Them Roly Boly Eyes
Words and music by Eddie Leonard.
Harry Von Tilzer Music Publishing Co., 1912/Edward B. Marks Music Corp., 1939.
Leonard also performed this dialect song referring to his trademark, which was emphasized by the blackface that he used in his minstrel show throughout his career. Revived for the musical *Roly-Boly Eyes* (1919).

Rolling Stones All Come Rolling Home Again
Words by Edgar Leslie, music by Archie Gottler.
Kalmar, Puck & Abrahams Consolidated Mus, 1916.
Bluesy lament popularized by Anna Chandler and Sophie Tucker.

Romance
Words and music by Lee David.
Original copyright, 1919.
Popularized by vaudeville vocalists Amelia Stone and Armand Kaliz in their "artistic offering," *A Song Romance* (1918-1921).

A Romance of Happy Valley
Words by Miles Overbolt, music by L. F. Gottschalk.
Waterson, Berlin & Snyder, 1919.
Promotional title song for D. W. Griffith's 1919 film for Paramount-Artcraft.

Romany, also known as **When the Sun Goes Down in Romany, My Heart Goes Roaming Back to You**
Words by Sam M. Lewis and Joe Young, music by Bert Grant.
Waterson, Berlin & Snyder, 1916.
Gypsy romance introduced by Clark and Bergman in *Step This Way* (musical, 1916).

Romeo
Words by Edgar Smith, music by W. T. Frances.
M. Witmark & Sons, 1902.
This comic novelty song lists seduced women. Introduced by Charles Bigelow in *Twirly-Whirly* (musical, 1901).

Roosevelt

Words by C. H. Congdon.

Original copyright, 1912.

Campaign song set to the German Christmas carol "O Tannenbaum" promotes the Presidential candidacy of Theodore Roosevelt on the Progressive ticket in 1912; it was introduced at a Madison Square Garden rally on October 30, 1912.

The Rosary

English words by Robert Cameron Rogers, French words by Mme. C. Eschig, music by Ethelbert Nevin.

G. Schirmer Inc., 1900, 1911.

The period's most popular concert aria found almost instant success at publication and retained its place as a cross-over vocal solo all the way through the 1950's. It was one of the first songs recorded by opera stars on phonographs and victrolas; the singers included Ernestine Schumann-Heink, John McCormack, Alma Gluck, and more recently, Clara Butt, Nelson Eddy, Rosa Ponselle, Jan Peerce, Lauritz Melchior, and Richard Tauber. Instrumental versions by Fred Waring, Andre Kostelanetz, Liberace, Victor Herbert's Orchestra, Fritz Kreisler, and the Hilo Hawaiian Orchestra were also top sellers. Parodies of the song abounded in the 19910's, among them "When Ragtime Rosie Ragged the Rosary" (q.v.). Responsive songs, that reflected its gravity, were also very popular, among them, "A Mother's Rosary" (q.v.).

The Rose of No Man's Land

Words by Jack Caddigan, music by James A. Brennan.

Leo Feist Inc., 1918/Jerry Vogel Music Co., Inc., 1945.

World War I sentimental tribute to the Red Cross Nurse working on the European battlefront. It was recorded at least once by each of the major studios within a year of its composition by, among others, the Moonlight Trio (Edison), Charles Hart and Elliot Shaw (Columbia), the American Republic Band (Pathe), and the Emerson Military Band.

Rose of Washington Square

Words by Ballard MacDonald, music by James F. Hanley.

Shapiro, Bernstein & Co., Inc., 1919, 1939, 1946.

This song achieved double popularity with a comic version, associated with Fanny Brice from performances in the *Ziegfeld Midnight Frolics* and her own radio shows, and a romantic ballad version, associated with Alice Faye, as title song of her 20th Century-Fox film. Also recorded as a ballad by Henry Burr (Columbia), as British dance music by Ambrose' Orchestra (London), and as jazz by Bob Crosby (Decca) and Red Nichols and His Five Pennies (Brunswick).

Rose Room
Words by Harry Williams, music by Art Hickman.
Sherman, Clay & Co., 1917/Miller Music Corp., 1945, 1949.
Signature tune for Hickman's Band, in residence at the New Amsterdam Roof for *Ziegfeld's Midnight Frolics* and at popular New York hotels and cabarets (Columbia). Having out-lived its use as ballroom dance music, it became a jazz standard with major recordings by Sidney Bechet (Victor, Gramophone), Paul Whiteman (Decca), and Benny Goodman (V Disc, Columbia).

A Rose with a Broken Stem
Words by Carroll Fleming, music by Everett J. Evans.
Leo Feist Inc., 1901.
Melodramatic ballad condemning a strayed woman; popularized by Imogene Comer and the Morrisey Sisters.

Roses Bring Dreams of You
Words and music by Herbert Ingraham.
Shapiro, Bernstein & Co., Inc., 1908, 1936.
Ballad popularized by Thomas J. Quigley, Viola Dale, and Bessie Wynn.

Roses of Picardy
Words by Fred E. Weatherly, music by Haydn Wood.
Chappell & Co., Inc., 1916.
First popularized by Grace LaRue, this romantic ballad became an ASCAP top seller during the return to sentimental ballads in World War I. Early major recordings were made by Charles Harrison (Columbia, Gennett), Jesse Crawford (Victor), and John McCormack (Victor, Victrola); it was revived by Perry Como (RCA), the George Shearing Quintet (MGM), and opera singer Richard Tauber (Parlophone, Decca). A different song of the same title, by Alfred Bryan and Jean Schwartz, was introduced by Vivian Holt ("Aunt Jemima") in the 1919 musical *Hello Alexander.*

Rosie and Josie
Words and music by Maude Nugent.
Joseph W. Stern & Co., 1900.
Comic romance about twins introduced by Nugent.

Rosie Rosinsky
Words by William Jerome, music by Jean Schwartz.
Shapiro, Bernstein & Co., Inc., 1904.
Hebrew-dialect song about an erring husband's return. Introduced by John C. Rice.

Round Her Neck, She Wears a Yeller Ribbon
Words and music by George A. Norton.
Leo Feist Inc., 1917.
Title continues "...for Her Lover Who is Fer Fer Away." Imitative American folk ballad popularized through recordings by Byron G. Harlan as a solo (Pathe) and with Arthur Collins (Pathe). See *Popular Music, 1920-1979* for a 1949 version "'Round Her Neck She Wore a Yellow Ribbon," used in the similarly titled John Ford film.

Row Row Row
Words by William Jerome, music by Jimmie V. Monaco.
Harry Von Tilzer Music Publishing Co., 1912.
This spooning song, introduced by Elizabeth Brice in Ziegfeld's *Follies of 1912,* has been recorded frequently as a vocal standard, as by Arthur Collins (Columbia), Gene Greene (Pathe), Ada Jones (Victor), and the American Quartet (Victor); revived by Phil Harris (Victor), Pearl Bailey (Columbia), and Bing Crosby (Decca).

Royal Garden Blues
Words and music by Clarence Williams and Spencer Williams.
Shapiro, Bernstein & Co., Inc., 1919.
The ASCAP top seller, actually a rag using the standard language of the hypnotic power of that form, was first featured in the *Johnson and Dean Review.* Now a jazz standard, it has been recorded by the major ensembles from the Original Dixieland Jazz Band and Noble Sissle and His Sizzling Syncopators (both on Victor soon after its composition) to Duke Ellington (Victor), Count Basie (Columbia), Bix Beiderbecke (Hot Record Society), and Benny Goodman (Columbia).

The Royal Will
Words and music by Harry Heisler.
Original copyright, 1901.
This ballad based on the last words of President William McKinley includes a vivid description of his assassination.

Rufus Johnson's Harmony Band
Words and music by Shelton Brooks and Maurice Abrahams.
Kalmar, Puck & Abrahams Consolidated Mus, 1914/Jerry Vogel Music Co., Inc.
Joyous praise of jazz rhythms performed by Willie Weston and Emma O'Neil and recorded by Gene Greene (Victor) and the team of Arthur Collins and Byron G. Harlan (Columbia).

Rufus Rastus Johnson Brown, see **What You Goin' to Do When the Rent Comes 'Round?,.**

Rum-Tiddely-Um-Tum-Tay Out for the Day Today (English)
Words by Fred Leigh, music by Orlando Powell.
Joseph W. Stern & Co., 1907.
Comic novelty for British music hall favorite Marie Lloyd.

Run Home and Tell Your Mother
Words and music by Irving Berlin.
Ted Snyder Music Publishing Co., 1911.
Novelty song associated with such juvenile vaudeville stars as Baby Edna Nickerson and Rutan's Song Birds; recorded by Molly Ames with the Columbia Quartet.

S

Sabre and Spur
Words and music by John Philip Sousa.
Sam Fox Publishing Co., Inc., 1946.
Dedicated to the 311st Cavalry Regiment, this march remained popular throughout Sousa's career in live performance and on Victor cylindars. Current recordings include those by the Decca Band, the Goldman Band, the Eastman Wind Ensemble, and the Bands of the Royal Netherlands Marines, the United States Marines, and Her Majesty's Royal Marines. It is included on the album *The Heritage of John Philip Sousa.*

Sadie (American-English)
Words by J. P. Harrington, music by Leo LeBrun.
Edward Schuberth & Co., Inc., 1901.
This comedy song from the musical *The Little Duchess* describes the wardrobe of fashionable clothes worn by star Anna Held.

Sadie Salome Go Home
Words and music by Irving Berlin and Edgar Leslie.
Ted Snyder Music Publishing Co., 1909/Irving Berlin Music Corp.
Novelty song introducing the character of "Sadie," a Lower East Side woman who attempted to work as an exotic dancer; associated with Fanny Brice, who performed it for her Ziegfeld audition, Rhodo Berman, and Lizzie B. Raymond; recorded by Bob Roberts (Columbia).

Sadie, You'se Ma Lady-Bird
Words by Arthur Trevelyan, music by William H. Penn.
Sol Bloom Publishing Co/Sol Bloom Music, 1901.
Dialect romance popularized by Camille D'Arville.

The Saftest of the Family (English)
Words by Harry Lauder and Bobry Beaton, music by Harry Lauder.

Francis, Day & Hunter, Ltd., London, England, 1904.
Scottish-dialect monologue and song for Lauder.

Sail On!
Words and music by Charles H. Gabriel.
Homer A. Rodeheaver, 1909, 1918.
Hymn performed by the 2000-voice choir that Homer A. Rodeheaver directed for Billy Sunday's evangelical campaigns (1912-1918).

Sailin' Away on the Henry Clay
Words by Gus Kahn, music by Egbert van Alstyne.
Remick Music Corp., 1917.
Syncopated barbershop quartet song featured by Elizabeth Murray in *Oh So Happy* (1917) and by the Marx Brothers in their vaudeville act; recorded by the American Quartet (Victor), Arthur Collins (Emerson), and Prince's Band (Columbia); revived by Mel Torme (Capitol).

St. Louis Blues
Words and music by W. C. Handy.
Handy Brothers Music Co., Inc., 1914, 1942.
Recorded by Handy on Varsity and Philharmonic and by Cecil Mack and Ethel Waters for Brunswick; revived by Art Tatum on Brunswick.

Sallie, Mah Hot Tamale
Words by George V. Hobart, music by Mae Auwerda Sloane.
Original copyright, 1901.
Comic dialect romance interpolated by Dan McAvoy into *The Hall of Fame* (musical, 1902).

Sally in Our Alley
Words and music by Harry Carey.
Original copyright, 1902.
This title song for the Marie Cahill vehicle (1902) lacks references to the plot of Lower East Side Jewish immigrant milieu of the musical comedy. It was recorded by many of the 1910's major close-harmony ensemble groups, among them, the Knickerbocker (Edison), Whitney Brothers (Victor), Critereon (Regal), and Strand (Brunswick) quartets. Sally's vacation was chronicled in Heelan and Helf's 1903 "Since Sally Left Our Alley"; see also "When Sally in Our Alley Sang..."

Sally's Sunday Hat
Words by Will D. Cobb, music by Gus Edwards.
Howley, Haviland & Dresser, 1901.
Parody of women's millinery fashion featured by George Crawford.

Salome
Words by John P. Harrington, music by Orlando Powell.
Remick Music Corp., 1909.
Clarice Vance performed this parody of the "Salome" dance that had been popularized in concert by Maud Allan and in vaudeville by Gertrude Hoffmann, Amalia Caine, Eva Tanguay, and many others. See also "A Vision of Salome" and "Sadie Salome, Go Home."

Sambo and Dinah
Words by Bob Cole and James Weldon Johnson, music by J. Rosamond Johnson.
Joseph W. Stern & Co., 1904.
Syncopated duet introduced by Lillian Coleman and John McIveagh in *Humpty-Dumpty* (musical, 1904) and recorded by Frank C. Stanley and Miss Nelson for Victor.

The Same Old Crowd
Words by Fred C. Farrell, music by Theodore F. Morse.
Howley, Haviland & Dresser, 1903.
Blanche Ring featured this tribute to her adoring audience in *The Jewel of Asia* (musical, 1903) and used it in encores thereafter.

Same Sort of Girl
Words by Harry B. Smith, music by Jerome Kern.
T. B. Harms, 1911.
Conversational duet interpolated into the musical *The Girl from Utah* by its stars Julia Sanderson and Donald Brian and recorded in 1941 by Sanderson and Frank Crummit (Decca). Also popular as a fox-trot in recordings by the Victor Military Band.

Sammy
Words by James O'Dea, music by Edward Hutchinson.
Sol Bloom Publishing Co/Sol Bloom Music, 1902.
Tremendously popular novelty song interpolated into *The Wizard of Oz* (musical, 1903--) by Mabel Barrison and Lotta Faust during the spectacle's Broadway run and many years of touring.

San Diego, California, the Gem of the U.S.A.
Words by Scott A. Palmer and Bert H. Carlson, music by Bert H. Carlson.
Original copyright, 1916.
Promotional song for the San Diego Exposition of 1916 and for California as "the pride of the Golden West." Other locally written songs about the Panama-California Exposition include "Welcome to All Is San Diego's Call" (q.v.).

San Francisco
Words by Sam M. Lewis, music by George W. Meyer.
Original copyright, 1914.
Promotional song for what the lyrics call the "San Fran Pan American Fair" in 1915.

Sand Dunes, also known as **My Desert Rose**
Words and music by Byron Gay.
Leo Feist Inc., 1919.
One-step featured by Earl Fuller's Orchestra at Rector's cabaret (and recorded on Columbia), Lyric's Dance Band, and the Nicholas Orlando Orchestra (Victor); also popularized, like Gay's other works, on piano rolls for QRS.

Sasparilla, Women, and Song
Words by Alfred Bryan, music by Jean Schwartz.
Remick Music Corp., 1919.
Prohibition version of a comic opera toasting song. Introduced by Roy Atwell in the musical *Oh, My Dear!* (during its 1918-1919 run).

Save It for Me
Words by James Weldon Johnson, music by Bob Cole.
Joseph W. Stern & Co., 1903.
Insistent love song interpolated by Marie Cahill into *Nancy Brown* (musical, 1903) and recorded by Washboard Sam and His Band (Bluebird) as a fox-trot.

Say a Prayer for the Boys Out There
Words by Bernie Grossman, music by Alex Marr.
Billed as "The Greatest Patriotic Ballad of the Season," it was introduced by Neil Mack in the Irish play *Acushla Machree* (1917). This is not the same song that was popular during World War II.

Say! Fay!
Words and music by Marie Doro.
Joseph W. Stern & Co., 1906.
Comic rag introduced by Hattie Williams in *The Little Cherub* (musical, 1906).

Scaddle-de-Mooch
Words and music by Cecil Mack and Chris Smith.
Joseph W. Stern & Co., 1915.
Scatted mooch (slow drag) introduced by Nora Bayes with Ford T. Dabney's Ziegfeld roof garden orchestra in the *Ziegfeld Midnight Frolics of 1915.*

Scarecrow
Words by L. Frank Baum, music by Paul Tietjens.
M. Witmark & Sons, 1902.
Fred Stone introduced his character with this song in *The Wizard of Oz* (musical, 1903).

School Days, also known as **When We Were a Couple of Kids**
Words by Will D. Cobb, music by Gus Edwards.
Mills Music Inc., 1906/Shapiro, Bernstein & Co., Inc., 1935.
Composed as a nostalgic tribute to the nineteenth century, this title sold over 1,000,000 copies in its first five years and has been a popular favorite ever since. Introduced by Herman Timberg in *Gus Edwards' School Boys and Girls* feature vaudeville act (1907-1914), it was first recorded by Byron G. Harlan for Victor. Revived often (especially in September and June) with memorable recordings by Horace Heidt (Brunswick), Johnny Mercer and the Pied Pipers (Capitol), Louis Jordan and His Tympany Five (Decca), and Bing Crosby (Decca); Crosby also sang it as Edwards in the film *The Star Maker* (Paramount, 1939).

Scissors to Grind
Words and music by Thomas S. Allen.
Original copyright, 1904.
Companion song to "Any Rags?" (q.v.). Also featured by Gladys Fisher.

The Seaside Sultan (English)
Words and music by C. W. Murphy and William Hargreaves.
T. B. Harms, 1903.
British music hall favorite performed by Vesta Tilley, who interpolated it into *Algy* (musical, 1903).

Semiole
Words by Harry Williams, music by Egbert van Alstyne.
Shapiro, Bernstein & Co., Inc., 1904.
Indian novelty song featured by Bonita, Emma Carus, and Blanche Ring.

Send Me a Kiss by Wireless
Words and music by Earl Carroll.
Joseph W. Stern & Co., 1911.
Waltz novelty from Carroll's vaudeville feature act *The Wireless Belles* (1911-1912); it uses "C.Q.D." (Come Quick--Danger) not "S.O.S." in its chorus's pun.

Send Me Away with a Smile
Words and music by Louis Weslyn and Al Piantadosi.
Al Piantadosi Music, 1917/Robbins Music Corp.

World War I farewell ballad popularized by John McCormack (Victor), Arthur Fields (Edison), and Van and Schenck (Columbia); also popular as a two-step from Prince's Band (Columbia).

The Sentinel Asleep
Words by Arthur J. Lamb, music by Harry von Tilzer.
Shapiro, Bernstein & Co., Inc., 1900.
Military ballad popularized by minstrel troupe vocalists J. Aldrich Libbey and Tascott.

Shadowland
Words by Blanche Merrill, music by Gus Edwards.
Shapiro, Bernstein & Co., Inc., 1914.
This novelty introduced by Sally Seeley in *Gus Edwards' 1914 Revue* was performed by dancers in back of a scrim, to imitate a film.

Shadows
Words by Ray Sherwood, music by Howard Lutter.
Original copyright, 1919.
Geraldine Farrar popularized this promotional ballad for her own silent film *Shadows* (Goldwyn, 1919).

Shall They Plead in Vain?
Words by Joe Young and Sam M. Lewis, music by Ray Perkins.
Waterson, Berlin & Snyder, 1919.
This promotional post-war anthem for the American Jewish Relief Committee asked "Our boys freed them, shall we feed them?"

She Is Ma Daisy (English)
Words by J. D. Harper and Harry Lauder, music by Harry Lauder.
Francis, Day & Hunter, Ltd., London, England, 1905/T. B. Harms, 1905.
Scottish-dialect romance for Lauder, who recorded it for Victor; also recorded by Glen Ellison (Edison) and the Jesters (Decca).

She Was a Dear Little Girl
Words by Irving Berlin, music by Ted Snyder.
Ted Snyder Music Publishing Co., 1909.
Portrait of a golddigger. Introduced by Marie Cahill in *The Boys and Betty* (musical, 1908).

She's a Princess Just the Same
Words by Charles Horwitz, music by Frederick V. Bowers.
Original copyright, 1900.
Tribute to American peerage of beautiful women popularized by Attie Spencer.

She's Dancing Her Heart Away
Words by L. Wolfe Gilbert, music by Kerry Mills.
Mills Music Inc., 1914.
Sentimental ballad featured by Emma Carus and Grace LaRue and recorded by Manuel Romain and his orchestra for Columbia.

She's Getting More Like the White Folks Every Day
Words and music by Bert Williams and George Walker.
Shapiro, Bernstein & Co., Inc., 1901.
Williams and Walker included this satirical song in their Theater Owners Booking Association (TOBA) vaudeville act; published verses refer to fashion trends, but their performance version may have had more topical barbs.

She's Good Enough to Be Your Baby's Mother...
Words by Alfred Bryan, music by Herman Paley.
Remick Music Corp., 1916.
Title continues: "and She's Good Enough to Vote with You." Except for its suffragist overtones this is an otherwise conventional "Mother" ballad; it was sung by vaudeville's more political blues shouters, such as Marie Dressler, Louise Dresser, Clarice Vance, and Anna Chandler (Columbia).

She's the Daughter of Mother Machree
Words by Jeff Nebarb (pseudonym for Jeff Branen), music by Ernest R. Ball.
M. Witmark & Sons, 1915/Jerry Vogel Music Co., Inc., 1944.
Answer song to Ball's "Mother Machree" (q.v.) recorded by Manuel Romain (Columbia) and Charles Harrison (Victor). Nebarb was the pseudonym for Jeff Branen.

Shim-me-sha-wabble
Words and music by Spencer Williams.
Original copyright, 1916/Edward B. Marks Music Corp., 1932.
Combining the rhythms and names of the era's most important black-influenced dances (the shimmie, shim-sham, and wobble), this song was most popular as a band instrumental, from the early recordings by McKinley's Cotton Pickers (Victor) to jazz standards from Red Nichols and His Five Pennies (Brunswick), Ted Lewis (Columbia), and Benny Goodman (Columbia).

Shine On, Harvest Moon
Words and music by Nora Bayes and Jack Norworth.
Remick Music Corp., 1908, 1941/Jerry Vogel Music Co., Inc.
This most famous song by one of vaudeville's most famous teams was introduced by Bayes in the *Follies of 1908* and recorded by the duo in 1910 (Victor); revived in the 1909 *Follies* by Bayes and in the 1931 edition by Ruth Etting. Memorable recordings

include those by Connee Boswell (V Disc), Kate Smith (Velvet Tone), Count Basie (Victor), and the Boswell Sisters with Jimmy and Tommy Dorsey (Brunswick). Joan Morris recorded the original Bayes lyrics and the Etting second chorus on her *Vaudeville* album (Nonesuch). It also served as the title song for the 1944 Warner Brothers musical.

Ship Ahoy, also known as **All the Nice Girls Love a Sailor**
Words by A. J. Mills, music by Bennett Scott.
B. Feldman & Co., Ltd., London, England/The Star Music Publishing Co., 1909/Edward B. Marks Music Corp., 1920.
Signature tune for male impersonator Hetty King.

The Ship of Uncle Sam
Words and music by Daisy M. Pratt Erd.
Original copyright, 1917.
Patriotic anthem for the Naval Reserve Society by its Chief Yeoman; lyrics list ships on active duty in the U.S. Navy.

Shoot Me Back to California Land
Words and music by Byron Gay.
Original copyright, 1915.
Song advertising the San Francisco Exposition of 1915.

The Shorter They Wear 'Em the Longer They Look
Words by Will J. Harris, music by Nat Vincent.
Shapiro, Bernstein & Co., Inc., 1917.
Satire of women's fashions featured by Johnny Dooley.

Shovelin' Coal
Words and music by Jean C. Havez.
Original copyright, 1906.
Character song for Lew Dockstader; although it was performed in blackface with Dockstader's Minstrels, the song shows a sympathetic view of a black man who, despite a classical education, can find work only as a steevedore.

Sierra Sue
Words and music by Joseph B. Carey.
Original copyright, 1916/Shapiro, Bernstein & Co., Inc., 1940.
This nostalgic ballad became a vocal standard in the swing era with major recordings by Gene Autry (Okeh), Glen Gray and the Casa Loma Orchestra (Decca), Gene Krupa (Columbia), and Bing Crosby (Decca).

Silver Sleigh Bells
Music by E. T. Paull.
Paull-Pioneer Music Co., 1906.

"Novelette-descriptive" instrumental or piano work based on a story of racing sleighs; recorded by the Victor Military Band.

Simple Little Sister Mary Green
Words and music by Clifton Crawford.
Howley, Haviland & Dresser, 1901.
Satirical portrait of a golddigger. Introduced by Crawford in *My Lady* (1901) and interpolated into productions at the Cherry Blossom Grove and Paradise Garden roof theaters by William Gould.

Sinbad Was in Bad All the Time
Words by Stanley Murphy, music by Harry Carroll.
Remick Music Corp., 1917.
Comic song interpolated by Al Jolson into *Robinson Crusoe, Jr.* (1917); later that season, Jolson played "In Bad" in *Sinbad.*

Since Father Went to Work
Words and music by William Cahill.
Joseph W. Stern & Co., 1906.
Further adventures of "Everybody Works But Father" (q.v.) and family; featured by Cahill and the act of Charles D. Lawlor and Daughters.

Since Little Dolly Dimples Made a Hit
Words by William Jerome, music by Jean Schwartz.
Shapiro, Bernstein & Co., Inc., 1904.
Introduced by Grace Cameron in the musical *Piff! Paff!! Pouf!!!* (1904); a "dolly dimples" was a euphemism for a chorus girl/ golddigger.

Since My Mariutch Learned the Merry Widow Waltz
Words and music by Bert Fitzgibbon.
M. Witmark & Sons, 1908.
One of many Italian-dialect songs on the Americanization of "Mariutch" (or "Mariuccia") by various authors. Interpolated by Lillian Shaw into *The Soul Kiss,* it was also popularized by Fitzgibbon and Thomas Potter Dunne in vaudeville. The chorus begins with a musical quote from Lehar's "Merry Widow Waltz."

Since Nellie Went Away
Words and music by Herbert H. Taylor.
Original copyright, 1906.
Sentimental nostalgic ballad popularized by R. J. Jose, who recorded it for Victor in 1905. The song was the basis for a four-act melodrama by Owen Davis that toured extensively after its 1907 opening.

Since Reuben's Gone Away
Words by Vincent Bryan, music by Theodore F. Morse.
Leo Feist Inc., 1902.
This final chapter in the "Wedding of the Reuben and the Maid" (q.v.) is set after their divorce; popularized by the Blondells.

Since Sister Nell Heard Paderewski Play
Words by William Jerome, music by Jean Schwartz.
Shapiro, Bernstein & Co., Inc., 1902.
George Manion played and sang this rag on the classical repertory in *The Little Duchess* (musical, 1901).

Sing Me a Song of Other Days
Words and music by Sadie Koninsky.
Original copyright, 1900.
Descriptive nostalgic ballad sung by DeForest West.

Sing Me Love's Lullaby, also known as **Love's Lullaby of Dreams**
Words by Dorothy Terris, music by Theodore F. Morse.
Leo Feist Inc., 1917.
Art song associated with Frances Alda (Victor); also recorded by Marie Rappold (Edison), Henry Burr (Columbia), and by Prince's Orchestra (Columbia), as an instrumental.

The Singer
Words and music by Elsa Maxwell.
Boston Music Co., 1923.
Francis Alda popularized this art song about a soprano who compares herself to a small bird. She featured it in her earliest recordings for Victor.

A Singer Sang a Song
Words by Will Heelan, music by Seymour Furth.
Original copyright, 1908.
Parody of a musicale during which a vocalist mauls "The Merry Widow Waltz"; performed by Sam Bernard in *Nearly a Hero* (1908).

Sipping Cider thru' a Straw
Words and music by Lee David and Carey Morgan.
Joseph W. Stern & Co., 1919.
Lisping novelty popularized by Roscoe Arbuckle and recorded by Arthur Collins and Byron G. Harlan for Edison.

Sister Ann
Words by Matt C. Woodward, music by Ben M. Jerome.
Sol Bloom Publishing Co/Sol Bloom Music, 1903.
Edwin Foy dressed in comic drag to relate the woes of the disaster-

prone "Sister Ann" in *Mr. Bluebeard* (musical, 1903) and his own vaudeville act thereafter.

Sister Susie's Sewing Shirts for Soldiers
Words by R. P. Weston, music by Hermann E. Drewski.
T. B. Harms, 1914.
Pre-World War I tongue twisting hit for Al Jolson who interpolated it often into Winter Garden shows and recorded it for Columbia; Billy Murray also sang it for Victor, but the other popular recordings were by Victor's Military Band and Columbia's house dance orchestra, Prince's Band. Weston and Darewski's follow-up, "Mother's Sitting Knitting..." (q.v.) was also a hit for Jolson.

Sister Susie's Started Syncopation
Words by Harold Atteridge, music by Sigmund Romberg.
T. B. Harms, 1915/Francis, Day & Hunter, Inc., 1915.
Introduced by Bly Brown as "The Spirit of Ragtime" in *Maid in America* (musical, 1915); also featured by Blossom Seeley.

Six Times Six Is Thirty-Six
Words by Bert Hamlon, music by William White.
T. B. Harms, 1917.
Juvenile novelty song introduced by Frances White in the revue *Hitchy-Koo of 1917* and recorded by her for Victor.

Sleepy-Headed Little Mary Green
Words and music by George W. Gage.
Original copyright, 1900.
Novelty song for Fay Templeton featuring yawns written into the chorus.

Slowly Stealing Up and Down the River
Words and music by G. Romilli.
M. Witmark & Sons, 1917.
Art song performed and recorded by Geraldine Farrar (Victor, Victrola).

Sly Musette
Words by Sydney Rosenfeld, music by A. Baldwin Sloane.
Joseph W. Stern & Co., 1902.
Romantic song introduced by Mabel Gilman as the heroine of *The Mocking Bird* (musical, 1902).

Smarty
Words by Jack Norworth, music by Albert von Tilzer.
York Music Corp., 1908/Broadway Music Corp.
Juvenile novelty song popularized by Norworth, Lulu Beeson,

Trixie Friganza, and Baby Zena Keefe; recorded by Ada Jones and Billy Murray (Victor).

Smile and Show Your Dimple
Words and music by Irving Berlin.
Waterson, Berlin & Snyder, 1917/Irving Berlin Music Corp.
World War I-era brave farewell song recorded by Sam Ash (Columbia) as dance music; its chorus was adapted for "Easter Parade" (for which, see *Popular Music, 1920-1979*).

Smile, Smile, Smile, see **Pack Up Your Troubles in Your Old Kit Bag and Smile, Smile, Smile,**.

Smile the While You Kiss Me Sad Adieu, see **Till We Meet Again,**.

Smiles
Words by J. Will Callahan, music by Lee S. Roberts.
Remick Music Corp., 1917, 1941.
ASCAP top seller with continued popularity to this day. Introduced by Nell Carrington in the *Passing Show of 1918* and recorded by Albert Campbell and Henry Burr and by Prince's Band (all Columbia). Major revivals and recordings were done by Eddy Duchin (Columbia), Red Nichols and His Five Pennies (Brunswick), Jo Stafford (Capitol), Guy Lombardo and His Royal Canadians (Decca), and Joan Morris on her *Vaudeville* album.

Smilin' Through
Words and music by Arthur A. Penn.
M. Witmark & Sons, 1919, 1922.
Title song for a sentimental play by Allan Langdon Martin pseudonym for Jane Cowl and Jane Murfin; it was performed by Cowl on Broadway (1919). Penn's imitation Irish ballad links the past and present plot themes and was so closely associated with the script that it was used as a theme for the silent film (First National, 1922, starring Norma Talmadge) and was performed by Norma Shearer in the 1932 MGM version and by Jeanette MacDonald in the 1941 MGM motion picture. Popular recordings were made by MacDonald, Judy Garland, and the Mormon Tabernacle Choir. A British musical comedy based on the play featured Penn's ballad during curtain calls by Lauverne Gray as "Moonyeen"

Smother Me with Kisses and Kill Me with Love
Words by Alfred Bryan, music by Harry Carroll.
Shapiro, Bernstein & Co., Inc., 1914.
Popular favorite associated with Lillian Lorraine in *The Whirl of the World* (1914) and other Winter Garden revues.

Snap Your Fingers and Away You Go
Words by William Jerome, music by Harry von Tilzer.
Harry Von Tilzer Music Publishing Co., 1912.
Al Jolson specialty number from the musical *The Honeymoon Express* and recordings for Victor.

So Long Letty
Words and music by Earl Carroll.
M. Witmark & Sons, 1915.
Title song from the musical comedy of 1915 based on Charlotte Greenwood's continuing character, "Letitia Proudfoot," and from her Warner Brothers/Vitagraph film *So Long Letty;* recorded by Helen Clark and Joseph A. Phillips (Edison), Ada Jones (Rex), Grace Nash and M. J. O'Connell (Pathe), and Prince's Band (Columbia).

So Long, Mary
Words and music by George M. Cohan.
Mills Music Inc., 1906/George M. Cohan Music Publishing Co./Dajon.
Introduced by the cast and chorus of *Forty-five Minutes from Broadway* (1906); featured by Irene Manning in *Yankee Doodle Dandy* (Warner Brothers, 1942) and by Joel Grey, Angela Martin, Harvey Evans, and Loni Ackerman in the musical *George M!* (1968).

So Long Mother
Words by Raymond Egan and Gus Kahn, music by Egbert van Alstyne.
Remick Music Corp., 1917.
Military farewell ballad associated with Al Jolson and recorded by George Wilton Ballard (Edison), Charles Hart (Victor), and Prince's Band (Columbia).

A Soldier's Dream
Words and music by Byron Gay.
Original copyright, 1918.
World War I anthem performed and recorded by Ernestine Schumann-Heink.

Some Boy
Words by Gene Buck, music by Dave Stamper.
Joseph W. Stern & Co., 1912.
Lillian Lorraine's specialty song from the *Follies of 1912* was recorded by Ada Jones for Victor.

Some Girls Do and Some Girls Don't
Words and music by Howard Johnson, Alex Gerber, and Harry Jen-

tes.
Leo Feist Inc., 1916.
Title continues "... So You're Taking a Chance All the Time." Leering comedy song featured by William Gaxton, Joseph Santley (with Ed. Norton), Sophie Tucker, and Oscar Shaw, who recorded it for Columbia.

Some Sort of Somebody
Words by Elsie Janis, music by Jerome Kern.
T. B. Harms, 1915.
Romantic song written for Janis' vehicle *Miss Information* (1915) and re-used by Ann Orr in Kern's musical *Very Good Eddie* two months later. Recorded by Edna Brown and Billy Murray (Victor), Prince's Band (Columbia) and the Victor Military Band. Often revived for tributes to Kern because of *Very Good Eddie's* importance to the integrated musical.

Some Sunday Morning
Words by Gus Kahn and Raymond Egan, music by Richard Whiting.
Remick Music Corp., 1917.
Preview of wedding featured by the team of Elizabeth Brice and Charles King; recorded as a duet by Ada Jones with Billy Murray (Victor), Robert Grant (Emerson) and with M. J. O'Connell (Columbia); revived by Kate Smith (Columbia) and Louis Prima (Majestic).

Somebody Lied
Words and music by Jeff T. Branen and Evans Lloyd.
Will Rossiter, 1907.
Character complaint song adapted by Bert Williams for his own use in *Bandana Land* (musical, 1907); recorded by Ed Morton on Victor.

Somebody Stole My Gal
Words and music by Leo Wood.
Robbins Music Corp., 1918, 1940, 1946.
An ASCAP top seller; since its debut in a rare women's minstrel troupe, the Lady Bountifuls, it has become a jazz standard. Major recordings were done by the ensembles of Cab Calloway (Perfect), Ted Lewis (Columbia), and Fats Waller (Victor) and, in the big band era, Benny Goodman (Columbia), Count Basie, and Bix Beiderbecke (Special Editions).

Somebody's Coming to Town from Dixie
Words by Raymond A. Browne, music by Henry Clay Smith.
Original copyright, 1912.
Raggy Dixieland song performed in vaudeville by Kitty Flynn, Belle

Gold, and the team of McCormack and Margaret Irving; recorded by Billy Murray (Victor).

Somebody's Waiting for You
Words by Vincent Bryan, music by Al. Gumble.
Remick Music Corp., 1906.
Waltz ballad popularized by Bessie Wynn, Bonita, Harry A. Ellis, and Trixie Friganza.

Someday Sweetheart
Words and music by John C. Spikes and Benjamin Spikes.
Spike's Music, 1919/George Simon, Inc., 1939.
Originally featured by Sophie Tucker, the bluesy lament has been recorded by most of the jazz greats, among them, the Benny Goodman Trio (Victor), Eddie Condon (Decca), and Jimmy Dorsey and His Orchestra (Decca). Major vocal recordings include those by Bing Crosby (Decca, Brunswick), Helen Traubel (Decca), Kay Starr (Capitol), and Ethel Waters (Columbia).

Somehow It Seldom Comes True
Words by Arthur J. Jackson and B. G. De Sylva, music by George Gershwin.
T. B. Harms, 1919/Francis, Day & Hunter, Inc., 1919.
Romantic song introduced by Janet Velie in *La La Lucille* (musical, 1919).

Someone Else May Be There While I'm Gone
Words and music by Irving Berlin.
Waterson, Berlin & Snyder, 1917/Irving Berlin Music Corp.
Associated with Al Jolson who introduced it in his Winter Garden revues and recorded it in 1916 for Columbia and 1947 for Decca.

Something about Love
Words by Lou Paley, music by George Gershwin.
T. B. Harms, 1919/Francis, Day & Hunter, Inc., 1919.
Introduced by Adele Rowland and Donald MacDonald in *The Lady in Red* (musical, 1919).

Somewhere in France
Words by William Vaughan Dunham, music by Shelton Brooks.
Will Rossiter, 1917.
Patriotic ballad of the World War I era.

Somewhere in France Is the Lily
Words by Philander Johnson, music by Joseph E. Howard.
M. Witmark & Sons, 1917.
March of the World War I allies, each represented by a flower, e.g. English rose, Scots thistle, Irish shamrock, etc.; recorded by

Henry Burr (Columbia), Charles Hart (Victor), and Prince's Band (Columbia).

The Song That I Hear in My Dreams
Words and music by Walter Rolfe.
Original copyright, 1902.
Sentimental tribute to "a Mother's lullaby" sung in vaudeville by Julia Crosby, James Wood, and the team of Browne and Scott.

Sorry, I Ain't Got It, You Could Have It If I Had It Blues, see **All In Down and Out,**.

Sound of the Times, see **Lindy,**.

Southern Gals
Words by Jack Yellin, music by Albert Gumble.
Remick Music Corp., 1917.
Dixieland ballad featured by Florence Moore, Nellie V. Nichols, and Rae Samuels in vaudeville and recorded by Gus Van and Joe Schenck (Victor).

The Spaniard That Blighted My Life
Words and music by Billy Merson.
T. B. Harms, 1911.
Jolson's first unique success with this number stopped the show nightly in *The Honeymoon Express* (musical, 1911); he recorded the imitation Spanish lament about a toreador who stole his fiancee as a solo on Victor, and as a duet with Bing Crosby (Decca, 1947), and performed it in the films *The Singing Fool* (Warner Brothers, 1928) and *The Jolson Story* (Columbia, 1946).

Spanish Love
Words and music by Vincent Bryan, Irving Berlin, and Ted Snyder.
Ted Snyder Music Publishing Co., 1911.
Exotic ballad introduced by Ethel Levey and the hit of Jesse Lasky's New York Follies Bergere revues *Gaby* and *Temptations* (1911); recorded by Andrea Sarto for Columbia.

Spoon Time
Words by Addison Burkhardt, music by Albert von Tilzer.
York Music Corp., 1905.
"Moon time, morn, and noon time ..." are recommended in the lyrics; performed by John Parks and Amelia Stone in *Coming thro' the Rye* (1906) and by Columbia's Berkes and LaCalle Orchestra.

A Sprig of Rosemarie (English)
Words by Basil Hood, music by Edward German.

Chappell & Co., Inc., 1903.
Nostalgic romance introduced by Pauline Frederick in *A Princess of Kensington* (musical, 1903 in London).

Spring and Fall
Words and music by Irving Berlin.
Waterson, Berlin & Snyder, 1912.
Art song described by Berlin as a "Tone Poem."

Spring Fashions
Words by Harry B. Smith, music by Mae Auwerda Sloane.
Original copyright, 1901.
Comic descriptions of contemporary fashion sung by Edna Hunter and Margaret Walker in *The Liberty Belles* (musical, 1901).

Spring Song
Words by Arthur Lamb, music by Felix Mendelssohn-Bartholdi.
Joseph Morris Co., 1906.
A parlor song setting of the popular piano solo, "Spring Song." Another setting of the music, which was often used by concert dancers, was written by James O'Dea (Remick, 1904, 1906).

Sprinkle Me with Kisses If You Want My Love to Grow
Words by Earl Carroll, music by Ernest R. Ball.
M. Witmark & Sons, 1915/Anne-Rachel Music Corp.
Ballad featured by Evelyn Nesbit in her exhibition ballroom dance act and recorded by Ada Jones (Columbia), Edna Brown (Victor), and Prince's Band (Columbia).

The Star and the Flower
Words and music by Raymond Hubbell.
Original copyright, 1900.
Plotted ballad of wealthy girl leaving home for a poor but honest man performed in vaudeville by Ola Hayden and Ben Gittelman; also popular as a parlor song.

Star of Happiness
Words by Francis Trevelyan Miller, music by George Alfred Lewis.
Shapiro, Bernstein & Co., Inc., 1919.
Pacifist anthem dedicated to and "suggested by" the blind and deaf author-lecturer Helen Keller.

Stars of the National Game
Words by James O'Dea, music by Anne Caldwell.
Remick Music Corp., 1908.
Tribute to baseball featured by Mabel Hite and Mike Donlin in vaudeville.

Stay Down Here Where You Belong
Words and music by Irving Berlin.
Waterson, Berlin & Snyder, 1914/Irving Berlin Music Corp.
Anti-militarist song of Satan telling his son to avoid the uncivilized people above; recorded by Henry Burr (Victor) and Arthur Fields (Columbia).

The Stein Song, see **Heidelberg,**.

Step into Line for Taft
Words and music by J. M. Hagen.
Original copyright, 1908.
Campaign song for William Howard Taft, in his 1908 bid for the presidency on the Republican ticket. The lyrics state his platform, "a continuation of the Big Stick and Square Deal Policy" associated with his predecessor, Theodore Roosevelt.

The Stolen Melody
Words by Harold Atteridge, music by Paul Schwartz and Nora Bayes.
T. B. Harms, 1915/Francis, Day & Hunter, Inc., 1915.
Bayes's song success in *Maid in America* (musical, 1915) and vaudeville.

Stop That Rag
Words by Irving Berlin, music by Ted Snyder.
Ted Snyder Music Publishing Co., 1909.
Rag-time promotion introduced by Stella Mayhew in *The Jolly Bachelors* (revue, 1910).

Stop Your Tickling Jock! (English)
Words by Harry Lauder and Frank Folloy, music by Harry Lauder.
Francis, Day & Hunter, Ltd., London, England, 1904.
Scottish-dialect seduction featured and recorded by Lauder (Victor, Zon-o-phone).

The Story Book Ball
Words and music by Billie Montgomery and George Perry.
Original copyright, 1917.
Specialty dance song performed in vaudeville by its authors (a male vocal team) and by Jessie Royce Landis; recorded by Billy Murray (Victor), Albert Campbell, and Henry Burr (Columbia) and the Castle (label's) Jazz Band.

The Story of a Clothes Line (English)
Words by James Tate, music by Clifford Harris.
Original copyright, 1904.
Marriage and family as seen, according to the alternate title,

through "another pair of stockings on the line"; featured by Alice Lloyd in British music halls and American vaudeville; recorded by Helen Trix (Zon-o-phone).

The Streets of New York, also known as **In Old New York**
Words by Henry Blossom, music by Victor Herbert.
M. Witmark & Sons, 1906, 1916.
One of the city's most beloved unofficial anthems was introduced by Fred Stone and David Montgomery in the comic operetta *The Red Mill* (1906) and sung by Eddie Foy, Jr. and Michael O'Shea in their roles in the 1945 New York revival. *The Red Mill* was recorded by the Victor Light Opera companies in 1911 and 1930 and in studio recordings in the United States and England; individual recordings of the song were made by Billy Murray (Columbia), Victor Herbert and His Orchestra (Victor), and Andre Kostelanetz (Columbia).

Strike Up the Band
Words by Andrew B. Sterling, music by Charles B. Ward.
Original copyright, 1900/Harry Von Tilzer Music Publishing Co., 1900, 1927, 1942.
An ASCAP top seller of 1900, this naval novelty was revived during World War II by Fred Waring and His Pennsylvanians.

String a Ring of Roses 'Round Your Rosie
Words by William Jerome, music by Jean Schwartz.
Original copyright, 1912.
In this proposal song the female initiates the action. Introduced by Elizabeth Brice and Charles King in *A Winsome Widow* (musical, 1912).

Strolling Along the Beach
Words by James Weldon Johnson and Bob Cole, music by J. Rosamond Johnson.
Joseph W. Stern & Co., 1902.
Summertime flirtation song featured by Anna Held in *The Little Duchess* (musical, 1901).

Strolling on the Pike
Words and music by G. G. Zarn.
Original copyright, 1904.
Promotional song for the St. Louis Exposition including descriptions of Pike (or midway) attractions.

Sugar Blues
Words by Lucy Fletcher, music by Clarence Williams.
Pickwick Music Corp., 1919, 1949/MCA, Inc.
Jazz standard recorded by Fats Waller (Victor), Count Basie

(Columbia), Ella Fitzgerald (Decca), and Horace Heidt and His Brigadiers (Brunswick).

Sugar Mine
Words and music by Eddie Leonard and Eddie Cupero.
Original copyright, 1906.
Romance composed for Lew Dockstader's Minstrels, printed by its short-lived publishing house.

The Sum of Life
Words and music by Elsa Maxwell.
Leo Feist Inc., 1909.
Art song performed and recorded by Frances Alda in concert and Grace LaRue in vaudeville.

Sumurun (American-English)
Words by Arthur Gillespie, music by Victor Hollaender.
Joseph W. Stern & Co., 1912.
Ballad and instrumental work derived from Hollaender's score for the dance pantomime *Sumurun;* recorded by his Mayfair Orchestra on Gramophone. See also "My Sumurun Girl."

Sunbonnet Sue
Words by Will D. Cobb, music by Gus Edwards.
Gus Edwards Inc., 1908/Shapiro, Bernstein & Co., Inc., 1937.
Bucolic version of the authors' "School Days." Introduced by Betty Joss in the feature act *Gus Edwards' School Boys and Girls* (1908--); recorded by Harry MacDonough andthe Haydn Quartet (Victor) and revived by Frank Crummit (Decca) and the Lyn Duddy Swing Choir (MGM). Featured by Bing Crosby in the film biography of Edwards, *The Star Maker* (Paramount, 1939) and used as title song by Phil Regan and Gale Storm for the 1945 Monogram Studio B-musical.

The Sunflower and the Sun
Words by Carrie W. Colburn and C. N. Schneider, music by William H. Penn.
Sol Bloom Publishing Co/Sol Bloom Music, 1901.
Romantic duet introduced by Mabel Gilman and Frank Doane in *The Hall of Fame* (1902); sung in vaudeville by duets Kelly and Violette and Libbey and Trayer.

Sunrise at the Zoo
Words by Edward Madden, music by Max Hoffmann.
Rag-time duet sung by the Hengler Sisters in the Rogers Brothers' final show, *The Rogers Brothers in Panama* (1907).

The Sunshine of Your Smile
Words by Leonard Cooke, music by Lillian Ray.
Francis, Day & Hunter, Inc., 1915.
Ballad popularized by John McCormack (Victor) and Walter Scanlan (Emerson) and revived by Frank Sinatra (V Disk) and Meredith Willson and His Orchestra (Decca). It became the standard silent film cue for bathos and, in film and animation, for drunkeness.

Susan, Dear Sue
Words by James O'Dea and Arthur Gillespie, music by Herbert Dillea.
M. Witmark & Sons, 1901.
Comic narrative of a breach-of-promise suit, a typewriter and a phonograph, from the farce *The Head Waiter* (1900), starring Ward and Vokes.

Swanee
Words by Irving Caesar, music by George Gershwin.
T. B. Harms, 1919/Francis, Day & Hunter, Inc., 1919/New World Music Corp. (NY).
Al Jolson's signature tune, and Caesar and Gershwin's first major hit, was first sung by Muriel De Forrest and the chorus in *Ned Wayburn's Demi-Tasse Revue* (1919) for the opening of his Capitol Theater. It was first popularized by Arthur Pryor's Band at the Capitol. Jolson, whose appetite for Dixieland nostalgia songs almost singlehandedly kept that nineteenth-century form alive, first interpolated this one into the 1920 touring company of *Sinbad* and recorded it that year for Columbia. He revived it for Decca albums and for the film *The Jolson Story* (Columbia, 1946).

Sweet Adeline, see **You're the Flower of My Heart, Sweet Adeline,**.

Sweet and Low, see **That Lullaby of Long Ago,**.

Sweet Cider Time When You Were Mine
Words by Joe McCarthy, music by Percy Wenrich.
Leo Feist Inc., 1916.
War-time return to the nostalgic ballads of the earlier decade popularized by Emma Carus, Sophie Tucker, and the Avon Comedy Four; recorded by Dolly Connolly (Columbia), the Peerless Quartet (Victor), and Joseph A. Phillips (Edison); revived by Eddie Condon and His Orchestra for Decca.

Sweet Genevieve
Words by George Cooper, music by Henry Tucker.
Original copyright, 1916.

Although it was first popularized by John McCormack (Victor), it is best known in barbershop arrangements and has been recorded by early labels' Peerless Quartet (Victor) and the Mills Brothers (Decca) and Merle Tillotson (Columbia) in more recent years.

Sweet Hawaiian Moonlight, Tell Her of My Love
Words by Harold G. Frost, music by F. Henri Klickmann.
Original copyright, 1918/Morley Music Co., Inc.
An ASCAP top seller of 1918, this exotic ballad was recorded by both the conventional orchestras of the early labels, such as Joseph Samuel's (Pathe), Joseph C. Smith's (Victor), and Prince's (Columbia), and by Hawaiian ensembles, among them, the Kalawaottawaiian Orchestra (Lyrophone), the Kalaluki Hawaiian Orchestra (Columbia), and Ray Kinney and His Hawaiians (Decca).

Sweet Italian Love
Words by Irving Berlin, music by Ted Snyder.
Ted Snyder Music Publishing Co., 1909.
Italian dialect novelty introduced by the songwriters in *Up and Down Broadway* (musical, 1910).

Sweet Kisses That Came in the Night
Words by Lew Brown and Eddie Buzzell, music by Albert von Tilzer.
Broadway Music Corp., 1919.
Close-harmony ballad written for Van and Schenck in the *Ziegfeld Follies of 1919.* Their recording for Columbia is on the Smithsonian Institution's album *Ziegfeld Follies of 1919.*

Sweet Marie Make-a Rag-a Time-a-Dance with Me
Words and music by Irving Berlin and Ted Snyder.
Snyder & Berlin Co., 1909.
Italian-dialect answer song to "Marie from Sunny Italy" (q.v.) and the Coney Island adventures of "Mariuccia" (q.v.). Introduced by Emma Carus in *The Jolly Bachelors* (musical, 1910).

Sweet Thoughts of Home
Words by Stanislaus Stange, music by Julian Edwards.
M. Witmark & Sons, 1904.
Ballad associated with Ernestine Schumann-Heink, who premiered it in the musical *Love's Lottery* and recorded it for Victor.

Sweetest Gal in Town
Words and music by Bob Cole and J. Rosamond Johnson.
Joseph W. Stern & Co., 1908.
Close-harmony syncopated ballad featured by songwriters Cole and Johnson in vau deville and recorded by Arthur Collins and Byron

G. Harlan for Columbia and Victor; revived by Frank Messina and the Mavericks for MacGregor records.

The Sweetheart of Sigma Chi
Words by Byron D. Stokes, music by F. Dudleigh Vernon.
Original copyright, 1912/Melrose Music Corp., 1927/Edwin H. Morris Co.
Romantic ballad popularized twenty years after its composition through recordings by Gene Austin (Bluebird, Victor), Ted Lewis and His Orchestra (Decca), and Bing Crosby (Decca); revived periodically by, among many others, Ozzie Nelson (Victor), Robert Merrill (Victor), and Dean Martin (Diamond). Also served as the title song of the 1946 Monogram film.

Sweetheart, Sweetheart, I Wear the Blue
Words by Catherine Ziegler, music by Rachel Ziegler.
Original copyright, 1901.
Spanish-American War ballad arranged and popularized by Hattie Starr.

Sweetie Dear
Words by Will Marion Cook, music by Joe Jordan.
Original copyright, 1906.
Raggy song popularized by Ethel Levey; recorded as dance music by Conway's Band (Victor) and as jazz by Sidney Bechet and His New Orleans Feet Warmers (Brunswick, Gramophone).

Swing Me High, Swing Me Low
Words by Ballard MacDonald, music by Victor Hollander (pseudonym for Victor Hollaender).
Edward B. Marks Music Corp., 1905.
Lillian Lorraine's famous swing song from the *Follies of 1910,* which she performed on a rose-covered trapeze propelled out above the audience.

Sylvia
Words and music by Olin Speaks.
G. Schirmer Inc., 1914.
This ASCAP top seller as a romantic ballad is now considered an American art song. It has been recorded by Paul Robeson (Victor), Louis Graveure (Columbia), Nelson Eddy (Columbia, Victor), Jan Peerce (RCA), and by the Philadelphia Orchestra under Eugene Ormandy (RCA).

The Syncopated Walk
Words and music by Irving Berlin.
Waterson, Berlin & Snyder, 1914.
Walk (or one-step) dance introduced by Vernon and Irene Castle in

Watch Your Step (musical, 1914); popularized as dance music by the Peerless Quartet (Victor) and the Victor Military Band; see, however, "The Castle Walk" by Europe.

T

'Taint No Use in Lovin' That Way
Words and music by May Irwin.
M. Witmark & Sons, 1904.
Complaint performed by Irwin In *Mrs. Black Is Back* (musical, 1904).

Take a Little Tip from Father
Words and music by Irving Berlin and Ted Snyder.
Ted Snyder Music Publishing Co., 1912/Irving Berlin Music Corp.
Advice popularized by Maud Tiffany and Lillian Bradley and recorded by Billy Murray (Victor).

Take a Pike at the Pike with Me, see **Piking the Pike,.**

Take a Tip from Venus, also known as **Madame Venus**
Words by Harry B. Smith, music by Maurice Levi.
Remick Music Corp., 1909.
Introduced by Annabelle Whitford in Ziegfeld's *Follies of 1909.*

Take a Trip Down to Luna with Me
Words by William Cahill, music by S. R. Henry.
Joseph W. Stern & Co., 1908.
Official promotional song for Luna Park, the permanent exposition at Coney Island.

Take Me Around Again
Words by Ed Rose, music by Kerry Mills.
Mills Music Inc., 1907.
Mlle. Fougere had a summer roof garden success with this song that refers to the rides at Luna Park.

Take Me Back to Babyland
Words by Frank J. Tannehill, music by Pat Rooney.
M. Witmark & Sons, 1909/Jerry Vogel Music Co., Inc., 1937.

A nostaligic imitative lullaby featured by Louise Dresser in vaudeville.

Take Me Back to Herald Square
Words by George V. Hobart, music by Ludwig Englander.
Original copyright, 1901.
Urban nostalgia sung by Dan Daly in *The New Yorkers* (musical, 1901).

Take Me Back to New York Town
Words by Andrew B. Sterling, music by Harry von Tilzer.
Harry Von Tilzer Music Publishing Co., 1907/Harms, Inc.
Tribute to New York City featured by Nellie Florede and Cecilia Weston.

Take Me Back to the Garden of Love
Words by E. Ray Goetz, music by Nat Osbourne.
Ted Snyder Music Publishing Co., 1911/Mills Music Inc., 1932.
A romantic duet introduced by Bonita and Lew Hearn in *A Real Girl* (vaudeville act, 1911); it was featured as a vaudeville solo by Belle Story, Josephine Sabel, and Frank Mullane, among many others.

Take Me Back to the Old Virginia Shore
Words and music by Raymond A. Browne.
Original copyright, 1902.
Published both as advertising for the summer Atlantic Ocean resort and as a standard nostalgic ballad.

Take Me in Your Arms and Say You Love Me
Words and music by J. Rosamond Johnson.
Joseph W. Stern & Co., 1912.
Ballad featured by Dorothy Webb; interpolated into the London revue *Come Over Here* (1913).

Take Me Out to the Ball Game
Words by Jack Norworth, music by Albert von Tilzer.
York Music Corp., 1908/Jerry Vogel Music Co., Inc., 1936.
Sung by millions of Americans from March through October of every year since its premiere in Norworth and Bayes' vaudeville act, the plotted tribute to a fan is now the official 7th inning stretch song of Major League Baseball. Recordings have included major vocalists, such as Ella Logan (Columbia) and Tony Martin (Victor), and major players, among them, Phil Rizzuto, Ralph Branca and Roy Campanella (Golden Records, with Mitch Miller); featured by Gene Kelly, Frank Sinatra, Jules Munshin and Betty Garrett in the MGM musical of the same name.

Take Me 'Round in a Taxicab
Words by Edgar Selden, music by Melville J. Gideon.
Shapiro, Bernstein & Co., Inc., 1908.
Introduced by Grace Leigh with the female chorus dressed as different brands of taxis in the *Follies of 1908* and Ziegfeld's roof garden show Jardin de Paris.

Take Me to that Land of Jazz
Words by Bert Kalmar and Edgar Leslie, music by Pete Wendling.
Waterson, Berlin & Snyder, 1919/Mills Music Inc.
Marion Harris's top-selling record for the Victor label.

Take Me to That Swanee Shore
Words by L. Wolfe Gilbert, music by Lewis F. Muir.
Mills Music Inc., 1912/Alfred Music Co., Inc., 1939.
Dixieland nostalgia interpolated by George Austin Moore into *Broadway to Paris* (musical, 1912) and recorded by Arthur Collins and Byron G. Harlan (Victor, Columbia) and the Victor Military Band.

Take Me to the Cabaret
Words and music by Will Dillon.
Leo Feist Inc., 1912.
Billy Murray's recording (Victor) popularized this invitation with its references to specific night clubs and restaurants.

Take Me to the Midnight Cake-walk Ball
Words and music by Eddie Cox, Arthur Jackson, and Maurice Abrahams.
Kalmar, Puck & Abrahams Consolidated Mus, 1915.
Introduced by Daphne Pollard in the *Passing Show of 1915;* recorded by Elida Morris (Rex).

Take These Flowers, Old Lady
Words by Edward B. Marks, music by Joseph W. Stern.
Joseph W. Stern & Co., 1904.
This plotted ballad was based on an incident in the life of the veteran actress Mrs. G. H. Gilbert, while she was on tour in a mining town in Colorado.

Take Your Girlie to the Movies If You Can't Make Love at Home
Words by Edgar Leslie and Bert Kalmar, music by Pete Wendling.
Waterson, Berlin & Snyder, 1919/Mills Music Inc., 1932.
Advice from Beatrice Fairfax recorded by Billy Murray (Victor) and Irving Kaufman (Emerson) and revived by Kay Kyser (Brunswick) and Phil Harris (Victor).

The Tale of a Bumble Bee
Words by Frank Pixley, music by Gustav Luders.
M. Witmark & Sons, 1901.
Bucolic ballad of a flirtatious bee. Introduced by Gertrude Quinlan and William Norris in *King Dodo* (musical, 1901).

The Tale of a Stroll
Words by George Totten Smith, music by Byrd Dougherty.
Original copyright, 1905.
Blow-by-blow description of a flirtation interpolated by Maria Stanley during the long run of *The Wizard of Oz* (musical, 1903-).

Tammany
Words by Vincent Bryan, music by Gus Edwards.
M. Witmark & Sons, 1905.
Topical satire on New York municipal politics, which was then controlled by the Tammany Hall machine. Introduced by Jefferson de Angelis in *Fantana* (musical, 1905); additional verses in the 1910 edition refer to William Randolph Hearst.

Tango Dip
Words by Harold Atteridge, music by Harry Carroll.
Shapiro, Bernstein & Co., Inc., 1914.
Introduced by exhibition ballroom dancers Gaby Deslys and Harry Pilcer in *The Belle of Bond Street* (musical, 1914).

Teach Me That Beautiful Love
Words and music by Joe Schenck and Gus Van.
Will Rossiter, 1912.
Close-harmony romance performed by Van and Schenck; also featured by Van Court in the Cecil B. De Mille stock tour of *The Girl on the Vase.*

Teasing
Words by Cecil Mack, music by Albert von Tilzer.
York Music Corp., 1904/Jerry Vogel Music Co., Inc., 1937.
Reine Davis and Wilmer Bentley introduced this romantic duet in *The Southerners* (musical, 1904); it was also popularized by Harry and Eva Puck in their juvenile act.

The Teddy Bears' Picnic
Words and music by John W. Bratton.
M. Witmark & Sons, 1907.
Novelty song and march that achieved great popularity in England and the United States through recordings by Arthur Pryor's Band (Victor), Mantovani's Orchestra (London), and vocalists, including Rosemary Clooney (Columbia) and Bing Crosby (Decca). Often used for animation scores.

Tee-Oodle-Um-Bam-Bo
Words by B. G. De Sylva and Arthur J. Jackson, music by George Gershwin.
T. B. Harms, 1919/Francis, Day & Hunter, Inc., 1919.
Novelty song introduced by Janet Velie and J. Clarence Harvey in *La La Lucille* (musical, 1919); it was popular as a piano roll dance tune, especially with Gershwin's own roll for Universal, which was reissued in 1972 on the album *George Gershwin Plays Gershwin and Kern* (Klavier).

The Teenie Weenie Waltz
Music by Hjalmar F. Neilsson.
Original copyright, 1915.
Popular piano waltz based on William Donahey's comic strip about babies in the *Chicago Tribune.*

Tell Me
Words by J. Will Callahan, music by Max Kortlander.
Remick Music Corp., 1919.
Ballad popularized by Al Jolson (Columbia) and Ted Straeter (Decca); also recorded as a fox-trot by Red Nichols (Brunswick). Featured in *On Moonlight Bay* (Warner Brothers, 1951).

Tell Me Dusky Maiden
Words by James Weldon Johnson and Bob Cole, music by J. Rosamond Johnson.
Joseph W. Stern & Co., 1901.
Parody of the famous "Tell Me Pretty Maiden" (1899) from the satire of *Florodora* in *The Sleeping Beauty and the Beast* (musical, 1901); recorded by Arthur Collins and Joseph Natus, S. H. Dudley, and Harry MacDonough (all for Victor).

Tell That to the Marines!
Words by Harold Atteridge and Al Jolson, music by Jean Schwartz.
Waterson, Berlin & Snyder, 1918.
Al Jolson interpolated this patriotic song, based on a James Montgomery Flagg illustration and poster, into *Sinbad* (musical, 1918) and recorded it for Columbia. Gus Edwards and Bernard S. Barron wrote a song with the same title for Edwards's acts that year. A third similarly title song was popularized by the Andrews Sisters during World War II.

Tell Us Pretty Ladies
Words by Edgar Smith, music by John Stromberg.
M. Witmark & Sons, 1901.
In *Quo Vass-Iss?* (musical, 1900), Lillian Russell and David Warfield introduced this parody of Leslie Stuart's "Tell Me Pretty

Maiden," the famous double octette from *Florodora* (1899), which was still the most popular song of the season.

Ten Thousand Cattle Straying
Words and music by Owen Wister.
M. Witmark & Sons, 1904.
Incidental music from Kirk La Shelle's play *The Virginian,* starring Dustin Farnum. Introduced by Frank Campan to establish the cattle rustling plot line.

Tess of the Storm Country, also known as **My Fisher Maid**
Words by Charles Patrick, music by Bob Allan.
Original copyright, 1915.
Promotional title song for the Famous Players Film Company's silent picture starring Mary Pickford (1915).

Texas Tommy Swing
Words and music by Val Harris and Sid Brown.
Remick Music Corp., 1911.
Vera Maxwell's dance specialty in the *Follies of 1911.*

That Baboon Baby Dance
Words by Dave Oppenheim, music by Joe Cooper.
Shapiro, Bernstein & Co., Inc., 1911.
This often featured "animal" dance was interpolated by Harry Cooper into *Hanky Panky* (1912), by Grete Meyer into *A Waltz Dream* (1908), by Ward DeWolfe into *The Girl in the Taxi* (1910), and by Blanche Ring into *The Wall Street Girl* (1912).

That Carolina Rag
Words by Maurice Burkhardt and Jack Coogan, music by Violinski.
Will Rossiter, 1911.
Featured by most of the major vaudeville vocalists and dancers, among them, Belle Baker, Frank Carter, Emma Carus, Gene Greene, Abbie Mitchell, Sophie Tucker, and the team of Wellington Cross and Lois Josephine.

That Dying Rag
Words by Irving Berlin, music by Bernie Adler.
Ted Snyder Music Publishing Co., 1911.
Novelty slow drag popularized by Sophie Tucker.

That English Rag
Words by Thomas J. Gray, music by Gus Edwards.
Remick Music Corp., 1912.
Featured in the *Follies of 1912* as the introduction for William LeBrun, "The Coster Singer."

That Girl o' Mine, see **Mirandy,**.

That Hula Hula
Words and music by Irving Berlin.
Irving Berlin Music Corp., 1915.
Syncopated Hawaiian dance promoted by the chorus in *Stop, Look, Listen* (1915). Recorded by Harry MacDonough (Victor).

That Humming Tune
Words and music by Shelton Brooks.
Will Rossiter, 1911.
Brooks's variation on the "intoxicating melody" theme was introduced by the black vaudeville team of Alexander and Scott.

That Hypnotizing Man
Words by Lew Brown, music by Albert von Tilzer.
York Music Corp., 1911/Broadway Music Corp.
A patter rag featured by Belle Baker and Louise Dresser.

That Hypnotizing Rag
Words and music by Zit (pseudonym for C. Florian Zittel).
Original copyright, 1909.
One of Blanche Ring's great successes was written for her by vaudeville critic "Zit" and interpolated into her starring vehicle *The Yankee Girl* (1910).

That Hypnotizing Strain
Words by J. W. Hamer, music by Anna Chandler.
Original copyright, 1912.
Composer and rag-time contralto Chandler made this her signature tune in the 1910's; it was also performed in vaudeville by her rivals Emma Carus and Belle Baker.

That Long Lost Chord
Words by Joe McCarthy, music by Al Piantadosi.
Leo Feist Inc., 1911.
Novelty patter rag based on the nineteenth-century art song "The Lost Chord," sung by (or, as the sheet music put it "being hunted by") Gene Greene, Leo Edwards, and Harry Tierney.

That Lullaby of Long Ago, also known as **Sweet and Low**
Words by Gus Kahn and Raymond B. Egan, music by Richard Whiting and Bud De Sylva.
Remick Music Corp., 1919.
Dixie nostalgia ballad featured by Al Jolson in *Sinbad* (musical, 1918) and *Ned Wayburn's Demi-Tasse Revue* (1920).

That Magic Strain (French)
English words by Florence O'Neill, French words by Georges Sibre, music by Florence O'Neill.
Original copyright, 1918.
Patter rag featured by songwriter O'Neill, an American cabaret artist who worked in Paris music halls.

That Mellow Strain
Words by M. M. Lewis, music by George W. Meyer.
George W. Meyer, 1912/Shawnee Press, Inc.
Patter rag featured by Dorothy Meuther, the violinist Musette, and Belle Baker; recorded by Meyer and the Peerless Quartet (Victor).

That Mesmerizing Mendelssohn Tune
Words and music by Irving Berlin.
Ted Snyder Music Publishing Co., 1909/Irving Berlin Music Corp.
A syncopated version of Mendelssohn's "Spring Song" (q.v.), which was then very popular as a vaudeville and concert dance solo. Popularized by Sophie Tucker, Josie Sandler, Con Conrad, the Dolce Sisters, and many others in vaudeville; recorded by the team of Arthur Collins and Byron G. Harlan for Victor and Columbia.

That Million Dollar Melody
Words and music by Clarence L. Gaskill.
Original copyright, 1914.
Novelty rag describing the promotional gimmicks of William Hammerstein and his rival producers.

That Mysterious Rag
Words and music by Irving Berlin and Ted Snyder.
Ted Snyder Music Publishing Co., 1911.
An early popular success for Irving Berlin, this song was adapted by Eric Satie as the "Little American Girl's" theme in the ballet *Parade* (1917). Recorded by Joan Morris and William Bolcom on their Berlin album *The Girl on the Magazine Cover* (RCA, 1979).

That Old Girl of Mine
Words by Earle C. Jones, music by Egbert van Alstyne.
Remick Music Corp., 1912.
Romantic ballad featured by Hattie Burke and Ted Lorraine, Alma Youlin, Frank Morrell, and many other vaudeville stars; recorded by the American Quartet (Victor) and by Henry Burr (Columbia).

That Russian Rag
Words and music by George L. Cobb.
Original copyright, 1918.
This classic of rag-time virtuosic piano-playing was an adaption of

Rachmaninoff's Prelude inn C-sharp minor. A Mainstay of disks, cylinders, and piano rolls, its most popular recordings were by Dave Apollon and His String Orchestra, James Reese Europe's Hell Fighter Band, and the house bands of record companies Emerson, Okeh, and Pathe.

That Sneaky Snaky Rag
Words and music by Chris Smith and Elmer Bowman.
F. B. Haviland, 1912.
Descriptive dance number. Introduced by Fanny Brice, possibly used with her imitation of Ruth St. Denis's snake dance.

That Society Bear
Words and music by Irving Berlin.
Waterson, Berlin & Snyder, 1912.
This "animal" dance features topical references to millionaires Hetty Green, Cornelius Vanderbilt, J. Pierpont Morgan, and Jay Gould; it was featured by Stella Mayhew in Winter Garden revues; recorded by Walter J. Van Brunt for Victor.

That Soothing Serenade
Words and music by Harry De Costa.
M. Witmark & Sons, 1918.
Introduced by Eugene and Willie Howard with a violin obbligato in the *Passing Show of 1918* and featured by Adele Rowland.

That Spanish Rag
Words by Will A. Heelan, music by Seymour Furth.
Original copyright, 1909.
Valeska Surratt, known for her European fashions and American rag-time, introduced this song in her vaudeville tab show, *The Girl with the Whooping Cough* (1909-1910).

That Syncopated Boogie Boo
Words by Sam M. Lewis, music by George W. Meyer.
Original copyright, 1912.
Featured by Maud Raymond in *My Best Girl* (1912) and by Bobbie and Irene Smith in vaudeville.

That Tariff War
Words by J. J. Kavanaugh, music by W. A. Sullenberger.
Original copyright, 1900.
Song and recitation published in the National Democratic Committee's *Song Book of 1900,* it advocated the candidacy of William Jennings Bryan (who is not mentioned) against William McKinley, who supported the protective tariff. Published with "That Platform," a recitation against the Ohio political boss, Republican Mark Hanna.

That Teasin' Rag
Words and music by Joe Jordan.
Joseph W. Stern & Co., 1909.
Slow drag featured in Eddie Leonard's minstrel troupe's feature act *Girls from Happyland.*

That Thing Called Love
Words and music by Perry Bradford.
Perry Bradford Music Publishing Co., 1919, 1947.
Blues featured by Sophie Tucker and recorded by Mamie Smith and Her Jazz Hounds (Okeh).

That Tumble Down Shack in Athlone
Words by Richard W. Pascoe, music by Monte Carlo and Alma M. Sanders.
Waterson, Berlin & Snyder, 1918.
This Irish variation on the Dixieland "Mammy" song was an ASCAP top-seller through recordings by Prince's Orchestra (Columbia) as a fox-trot and John McCormack (Victor) as a ballad. Major revivals include those by Phil Regan (Decca). Bing Crosby (Decca), and the Buffalo Bills (Decca).

That Wonderful Kid from Madrid
Words by Ballard MacDonald, music by Nat Osbourne.
Shapiro, Bernstein & Co., Inc., 1919.
Tribute to La Carmencita, who "made improvements on all the movements," featured by Rae Samuels and Cissie Ramsden.

That Wonderful Mother of Mine
Words and music by Clyde Hager and Walter Goodwin.
M. Witmark & Sons, 1918.
Promotional song for the FBO Picture *The Spirit of the U.S.A.* (1918); sung in vaudeville by Frank Morrell and recorded by Henry Burr (Victor). Revived by Phil Regan and Jesse Crawford (Decca) and by Eddy Arnold and the Tennessee Plowboys (Victor).

That's a Plenty
Words by Henry S. Creamer, music by Bert Williams.
Will Rossiter, 1909.
Complaint song for Williams; recorded by Arthur Collins on Columbia and, as dance music, by the New Orleans Rhythm Kings (Brunswick).

That's How He Met the Girl
Words by Vincent Bryan, music by E. Ray Goetz.
Shapiro, Bernstein & Co., Inc., 1907.
Novelty flirtation song from the *Follies of 1907,* sung by the then-

adolescent team of Tempest and Sunshine; the song describes a rendezvous entirely in terms of clothing.

That's How I Need You
Words and music by Joe Goodwin, Joe McCarthy, and Al Piantadosi.
Leo Feist Inc., 1912.
Romantic ballad featured by Emma Carus and recorded by Henry Burr for Victor.

That's Love in Honolulu, see **Oh, How She Could Yacki Hacki Wicki Wacki Woo,.**

That's My Idea of Paradise
Words and music by Irving Berlin.
Waterson, Berlin & Snyder, 1914.
Gladys Clark and Harry Bergman introduced this flirtation song in Jesse Lasky's vaudeville feature act *The Society Buds* (1914-1915).

That's the Kind of Baby for Me
Words by Alfred Harriman, music by J. C. Egan.
Broadway Music Corp., 1917.
Eddie Cantor offered this description in the *Ziegfeld Midnight Frolics of 1917.*

That's the Reason Noo I Wear a Kilt (English)
Words by Harry Lauder, music by Harry Lauder and A. B. Kendal.
T. B. Harms, 1906.
Scottish-dialect comic monologue and song for Lauder.

That's What the Daisy Said
Words by Wilbur Gumm, music by Albert von Tilzer.
Original copyright, 1903, 1910.
Demure romance popularized by Adele Ritchie and revived in 1920 by female impersonator Julian Eltinge.

Theodore
Words and music by Vincent Bryan.
Shapiro, Bernstein & Co., Inc., 1907.
Homage to Theodore Roosevelt in his last year as President.

There Are Just Two I's in Dixie
Words and music by Louis Herscher.
Pickwick Music Corp., 1947/Mills Music Inc.
Title continues "...Two Blue Eyes That Mean the World to Me." This spelling novelty variation on Dixieland ballads sold over

1,000,000 copies in the 1920's; recorded by Jack Smith for Coral Records.

There Are Two Eyes in Dixie
Words and music by Irving Berlin.
Waterson, Berlin & Snyder, 1917.
Southern nostalgia song popularized by Al Jolson.

There Are Two Sides to a Story
Words and music by Will A. Heelen and J. Fred Helf.
Joseph W. Stern & Co., 1900.
Answer song to "After the Ball" (q.v.); featured by Lottie Gibson.

There'll Be a Hot Time for the Old Men While the Young Men Are Away
Words by Grant Clarke, music by George W. Meyer.
Leo Feist Inc., 1918.
World War I novelty featured by Emma Carus and Frank Mullane.

There's a Broken Heart for Every Light on Broadway
Words by Howard Johnson, music by Fred Fisher.
Leo Feist Inc., 1915.
Sentimental ballad featured by Dolly Connolly and Edna Brown (Victor); revived by Louis Prima (Atlantic), Rosemary Clooney (Harmony), and Mel Torme (Capitol) and featured in the film biography of Fred Fisher, *Oh, You Beautiful Doll* (20th Century-Fox, 1949).

There's a Light That's Burning in the Window of the Little House upon the Hill, also known as **The Little House upon the Hill**
Words and music by Ballard MacDonald, Joe Goodwin, and Harry Puck.
Shapiro, Bernstein & Co., Inc., 1915.
Kentucky nostalgia ballad sung in vaudeville by Emma Carus, Frank Mullane, Evelyn Nesbit, Bessie Wynn, and Paul Van Dyke of the Honey Boy Minstrels.

There's a Little Bit of Bad in Every Good Little Girl
Words and music by Grant Clarke and Fred Fisher.
Leo Feist Inc., 1916/Fred Fisher Music Co., 1944.
Featured by the Avon Comedy Four, Elizabeth Brice and Charles King, Emma Carus, Sophie Tucker, and Arthur Fields; recorded by Billy Murray (Victor) as a novelty and by Jaudas' Society Orchestra and the Victor Military Band as a one-step.

There's a Little Spark of Love Still Burning
Words by Joe McCarthy, music by Fred Fisher.
Leo Feist Inc., 1914.

Ballad introduced by Kitty Gordon in the playlet *Alma's Return* (1914); recorded by Henry Burr for Victor.

There's a Little Star in Heaven That They Call Broadway
Words by Jack T. Waldron, words and music by A. Baldwin Sloane.
Joseph W. Stern & Co., 1903.
Featured by Thomas Q. Seabrooke in the musicals *A Chinese Honeymoon* (1902) and *The Red Feather* (1903).

There's a Lot of Things You Never Learn at School
Words and music by Edward Gardinier and Edwin S. Brill.
Original copyright, 1902.
Juvenile comic song interpolated by Jeanette Lowrie into *The Wizard of Oz* (musical, 1903).

There's a Lump of Sugar Down in Dixie
Words by Alfred Bryan and Jack Yellin, music by Alfred Grumble.
Remick Music Corp., 1918.
Dixie nostalgia ballad given topical novelty by references to the war-time sugar shortage and rationing; interpolated by Al Jolson into *Whirl of the World* (musical, 1914) and *Sinbad* (musical, 1918) and recorded by him for Columbia; also featured by Wellington Cross and the Farber Girls (who recorded it for Pathe) and by Marion Harris, whose Victor disc remained popular into the 1920's.

There's a Parson Only 20 Miles Away, see **When It's Moonlight on the Prairie,**.

There's a Time and a Place for Everything
Words by Al Brown, music by Chris Smith.
Remick Music Corp., 1906.
Vaudeville favorite associated with Artie Hall (on the black Theater Owners Booking Association--TOBA--circuit) and with Clarice Vance.

There's Another on Board That Might Be Saved
Words and music by Charles H. Stanley.
Original copyright, 1901.
Temperance anthem of the Blue Button Army; the metaphor of saving souls as passengers in a boat on a turbulent sea was popular in Temperance and evangelical anthems by Stanley, Gabriel, and others, and in ballads by Petrie.

There's More to the Kiss than the X-X-X
Words by Irving Caesar, music by George Gershwin.
T. B. Harms, 1919/Francis, Day & Hunter, Inc., 1919.
Novelty romance with imitative kiss sounds. Introduced by Mollie

King in *Good Morning, Judge* (musical, 1919) and interpolated by Helen Clark into *La La Lucille* (musical, 1919). Revived by Barbara Cook, Elaine Stritch, Tony Perkins, and Bobby Short on the album *Ben Bagley's George Gershwin Revisited* (MGM).

There's No North or South Today
Words and music by Paul Dresser.
Howley, Haviland & Dresser, 1901.
Tribute to the soldiers who united to fight the Spanish-American War; featured by R. J. Jose.

There's No Other Girl Like My Girl
Words by E. P. Moran, music by Maude Nugent.
Shapiro, Bernstein & Co., Inc., 1901.
Romantic ballad introduced by Eugene Canfield and Nellie Lynch in David Belasco's play *The Auctioneer* (1900).

There's One in a Million Like You
Words by Grant Clarke, music by Jean Schwartz.
Original copyright, 1912/Mills Music Inc., 1940.
Introduced by Elizabeth Brice in the *Follies of 1912* and featured in vaudeville by Emma Carus, Hattie Burke and Ted Lorraine, and Brice and Charles King.

There's One Rose That Will Never Bloom Again
Words and music by Raymond A. Browne.
Sol Bloom Publishing Co/Sol Bloom Music, 1901.
Sentimental ballad tearfully performed by Lizzie B. Raymond.

There's Something Nice about the South
Words and music by Irving Berlin.
Irving Berlin Music Corp., 1917.
Nostalgic song introduced by the close-harmony team of Gus Van and Joe Schenck in the Ziegfeld Century Grove roof garden revue *Dance and Grow Thin* (1917); recorded by them for Victor.

They Call Her Frivolous Sal, see **My Gal Sal**,.

They Didn't Believe Me
Words by Herbert Reynolds, music by Jerome Kern.
T. B. Harms, 1914.
One of Kern's most popular ballads, this was interpolated by Julia Sanderson and Donald Brian into *The Girl from Utah* (musical, 1914) and by George Grossmith and Haidee de Rance into the London hit *Tonight's the Night* (musical, 1915). The duet form was discarded, however, through sixty years of recordings by such popular soloists as Harry Belafonte (Capitol), Rudy Vallee (Capitol), Vic Damone (Mercury) and Irene Dunne (Decca). It was also

often recorded by ensembles, among them, the Melachrino Strings (Gramophone), Victor Young's Decca Orchestra, and the Tommy Dorsey Orchestra (Decca).

They Don't Hesitate Any More
Words by Bert Kalmar and Edgar Leslie, music by Harry Puck.
Kalmar, Puck & Abrahams Consolidated Mus, 1914/Mills Music Inc.
Harry and Eva Puck featured this song with its triple pun on "hesitation"--the dance, the dance step, and the dancers' reluctance to hold each other tightly in public.

They Go Wild, Simply Wild Over Me
Words by Joseph McCarthy, music by Fred Fisher.
Fred Fisher Music Co., 1917, 1945, 1963.
Popular fox-trot recorded successfully by Billy Murray (Edison), Eddie Cantor (Decca), and Marion Harris (Victor); featured in the film *For Me and My Gal* (MGM, 1943). There were political satire versions of the song popularized in the 1930's by the Wobblies (International Workers of the World) and in the 1960's by SNCC (Student Non-violent Coordinating Committee), both published in the *Peoples' Song Books.*

They Start the Victrola and Go Dancing Around the Floor
Words by Grant Clarke, music by Maurice Abrahams.
Abraham Music, 1914.
Eddie Cantor first featured this description of phonograph dates; also sung by Mabel Russell and Willie Weston.

They Were All Out of Step But Jim
Words and music by Irving Berlin.
Waterson, Berlin & Snyder, 1918/Irving Berlin Music Corp., 1929.
Comic World War I song of parents' tribute to a marching soldier; popularized by Blanche Ring, Queenie Williams, and Charles Bartholomew; recorded by Billy Murray (Victor) and the team of Gus Van and Joe Schenck (Columbia).

They'll Be Mighty Proud in Dixie of Their Old Black Joe
Words and music by Harry Carroll.
Shapiro, Bernstein & Co., Inc., 1918.
Dialect tribute to Black veteran soldiers; featured by Harry Cooper.

They're All Going to the Movies
Words and music by Thomas S. Allen.
Original copyright, 1919, 1915.
"Official" song for silent film star Pearl White, with melodramatic plot precis in the verses.

They're All Sweeties
Words by Andrew B. Sterling, music by Harry von Tilzer.
Harry Von Tilzer Music Publishing Co., 1919.
Featured by Billy Glason and by Al and Harry Klein in "The Trial of the Shimmy" number in the *Gaieties of 1919* (revue).

They're On Their Way to Mexico
Words and music by Irving Berlin.
Waterson, Berlin & Snyder, 1914.
Patriotic farewell song topical to the conflict with Mexico; popularized by Belle Baker and recorded by the Heidelberg Quartet with Will Oakland (Victor) and by the Victor Military Band.

They're Wearing 'Em Higher in Hawaii
Words by Joe Goodwin, music by Halsey K. Mohr.
Shapiro, Bernstein & Co., Inc., 1916.
This lingerie buyer's report parodied the current Hawaiian dance and song craze and the shortening hemlines in New York fashion; featured by Eddie Cantor, Harry Cooper, Al Jolson, and Billy Murray.

Think of Me Little Daddy
Words and music by Bert Whitman (pseudonym for Alberta Whitman).
Handy Brothers Music Co., Inc., 1919.
Fast-paced blues for the Whitman Sisters; recorded by the Plantation Dance Orchestra (Emerson) and by Jimmie Launceford (Vocalion).

This Is the Life
Words and music by Irving Berlin.
Waterson, Berlin & Snyder, 1914.
Comic song of a "rube" visiting New York; associated with Al Jolson and Belle Baker; recorded by Billy Murray (Victor).

Those Charlie Chaplin Feet
Words by Edgar Leslie, music by Archie Gottler.
Willie Weston featured this description of the comedian. Downs and Barton's similiar "That Charlie Chaplin Walk" was also popular in 1915.

Those Draftin' Blues
Words and music by Maceo Pinkard.
Joseph W. Stern & Co., 1918/Edward B. Marks Music Corp., 1920, 1932, 1940.
War-time lament aimed at women; recorded as a fox-trot by Art Hickman's Orchestra (Columbia) and Wilbur Sweatman's Origi-

nal Jazz Band (Columbia) and, in its World War II revival, by Tony Pastor and His Orchestra.

Those Songs My Mother Used to Sing
Words and music by H. Wakefield Smith.
M. Witmark & Sons, 1904.
Ballad featured by such minstrel troupe vocalists as Frank Coombs and Morphy, who was billed as "the Man Who Sings to Beat the Band;" recorded by Edna Brown (Victor), Carmella Ponselle (Columbia), and Thomas Chalmers (Edison).

Those Things Cannot Be Explained
Words by Junie McCree, music by Ben M. Jerome.
Howley, Haviland & Dresser, 1902.
Ten verses of topical satire on fashion, railroads, politics, etc. Introduced by lyricist McCree in *The Wild Rose* (musical, 1902).

Thousands of Years Ago
Words by P. G. Wodehouse, music by Ivan Caryll.
Chappell & Co., Inc., 1918.
Romantic ballad inspired by a mummy. Introduced by Julia Sanderson in *The Canary* (musical, 1918).

Thtop Your Thtuttering Jimmy
Words and music by Hal Blake Cowles.
Leo Feist Inc., 1919.
Answer song to "K-K-K-Katy" (q.v.) who supposedly sang it; the song enjoyed a brief novelty in 1919 roof garden revues.

Tia Da Da Tia Da Da, see **My Croony Melody,**.

Tiddley-Om-Pom (English)
Words by Fred W. Leigh, music by Orlando Powell.
Francis, Day & Hunter, Ltd., London, England, 1907.
Imitative Spanish song performed by Marie Lloyd.

The Tie That Binds
Words and music by Charles K. Harris.
Charles K. Harris Music Publishing Co., 1901.
Plotted ballad based on the melodramatic playlet of the same name, about a young couple after the death of their infant; featured by song illustrators Henry and Gallot.

Tiger Rag
Words by Harry De Costa, music by Original Dixieland Jazz Band.
Leo Feist Inc., 1917, 1932.
An all-time ASCAP top seller but in no way a rag, this jazz standard has been recorded by more than seventy major artists and ensem-

bles. Arrangements based on D. J. La Rocca's Original Dixieland Jazz Band 1917 score abound for quartets, piano, two pianos, orchestras, and jazz, dance, and marching bands. The range of major recordings stretches from the Boston "Pops" (RCA) to the Wolverine Orchestra (Brunswick); multiple recordings were made by Benny Goodman (Trio on Victor, Sextet on V Disc), Art Tatum (Brunswick, Decca), Louis Armstrong (Conqueror), and the Mills Brothers (Decca).

Tiger Rose Waltz
Music by Peter DeRose and Ivan Reid.
F. B. Haviland, 1918/Jerry Vogel Music Co., Inc.
Instrumental waltz composed for Willard Mack's melodrama *Tiger Rose,* starring Lenore Ulric.

Tilda from Old Savannah
Words and music by Chris Smith and John Larkins.
Original copyright, 1904.
Author Larkins and Dora Patterson introduced this proposal duet in *A Trip to Africa* (190).

Till We Meet Again, also known as **Smile the While You Kiss Me Sad Adieu**
Words by Richard B. Egan, music by Richard A. Whiting.
Remick Music Corp., 1918/Robbins Music Corp.
An ASCAP top seller during both World Wars, this ballad was originally recorded by the duets of Albert Campbell and Henry Burr for Emerson and Gladys Rice and Vernon Dalhart for Edison. Major revivals in the 1940's include those by Kate Smith (MGM), Eddy Duchin (Columbia), the Mills Brothers (Decca), and Nelson Eddy with Jo Stafford (Columbia).

The Time and the Place and the Girl
Words by Henry Blossom, music by Victor Herbert.
M. Witmark & Sons, 1905.
Introduced by Walter Percival in *Mlle. Modiste* (1905). Excerpts from a 1910 recording by the Victor Light Opera Company including part of this song are included in the Smithsonian Institution's album *The Early Victor Herbert.*

Tippecanoo
Words by Harry Williams, music by Egbert van Alstyne.
Shapiro, Bernstein & Co., Inc., 1904.
Indian novelty song featured by Dan McAvoy, Frank Fogerty, and Clarice Vance.

Tipperary
Words by Leo Curley, music by James M. Fulton and J. Fred Helf.

Helf & Hager, 1907.
Irish love ballad featured by Clara Morton.

Tipperary Nora
Words by Ren Shields, music by Ted Snyder.
Mills Music Inc., 1907.
Introduced by Blanche Ring and Peter Dailey in *About Town* (musical, 1906).

Tishomingo Blues
Words and music by Spencer Williams.
Edward B. Marks Music Corp., 1917, 1944.
Blues recorded by Duke Ellington's Orchestra (Brunswick) and by Buck Johnson and His New Orleans Band (Decca).

Toddle Song
Words by Herbert M. Lome, music by Byrd Dougherty.
Charles K. Harris Music Publishing Co., 1901.
Novelty song about walking in a Japanese kimono introduced in the comedy *White Lilacs* (1901).

Too Much Mustard, see **Tres Moutarde,.**

Tough-Guy Levi, see **I'm a Yiddish Cowboy,.**

The Town Where I Was Born
Words and music by Paul Dresser.
Remick Music Corp., 1905.
Nostalgic ballad with an anti-urban slant featured by John P. Curran.

Toyland
Words by Glen MacDonough, music by Victor Herbert.
M. Witmark & Sons, 1903.
Production song that served as the theme for the operetta *Babes in Toyland* (1903) was introduced by Bessie Wynn and male chorus. The first known recording, by Corinne Morgan with the Haydn Quartet (Monarch, 1904), is reproduced on the Smithsonian Institution's *The Music of Victor Herbert* album.

The Trench Trot
Words by Jack Frost, music by F. Henri Klickmann.
Original copyright, 1918.
Sophie Tucker featured this dance with military allusions in its lyrics.

Tres Moutarde, also known as **Trop Moutarde,** also known as **Too Much Mustard**

Music by Cecil Macklin.
Edward Schuberth & Co., Inc., 1911.
The most popular dance band selection of the early exhibition ballroom dance era, it was a two-step turkey trot with a tango section generally credited with popularizing tango rhythms in New York. Early recordings were made by the major studios' contract bands, among them, Prince's Band (Columbia), the Victor Military Band, and James Reese Europe's Society Orchestra. The latter group performed it live with dancers Vernon and Irene Castle. See also "Tango Is the Dance for Me."

Trop Moutarde, see **Tres Moutarde,**.

The Troubadour
Words by Harry Williams, music by W. C. Powell.
Shapiro, Bernstein & Co., Inc., 1904.
Ballad with medieval-style section featured by Viola Gillette and Louise Brehany and popularized as an instrumental recording by Pryor's Orchestra on the Victor and Monarch labels.

The Troubles of Reuben and the Maid
Words by J. Cheever Goodwin, music by Maurice Levi.
Original copyright, 1902.
The third song about "Reuben" and his wife was a feature of the 1902 Rogers Brothers' musical *At Harvard;* this one dealt with mother-in-law problems. See also "When Reuben Comes to Town" and "The Wedding of Reuben and the Maid."

True Freedom
Words by J. R. Lowell, words and music by Charles Kerr, music by Vincenzo Bellini.
Original copyright, 1900.
Charles Kerr's *Socialist Songs with Music* (1900, 1901, 1906) included this anthem created posthumously from James Russell Lowell's poem and the "Druid's Hymn" from Bellini's opera *Norma.*

The Trumpeter (American-English)
Words by J. Francis Barron, music by J. Airlie Dix.
Boosey & Hawkes Inc., 1904.
Art song featured by John McCormack (Victor); also recorded by John Charles Thomas for Victrola.

Tulip Time
Words by Gene Buck, music by Dave Stamper.
Francis, Day & Hunter GmbH Musikverlag, Hamburg, Federal Republic of Germany, 1919/T. B. Harms, 1919, 1948.
Buck and Stamper's song hit from the *Ziegfeld Follies of 1919* most

of which was composed by Irving Berlin, was recorded by John Steel (Victor). Henry Burr (Pathe), Sam Ash (Vocalion), and Joseph C. Smith's Orchestra (Victor); it can also be found on the Smithsonian Institution's album *Ziegfeld Follies of 1919.* It was also performed by Winifred Roma and Eve Lynn in the London pantomime *The Sleeping Beauty* (1920).

Tumble in Love
Words by Wilkie White, music by Malvin Franklyn.
Joseph W. Stern & Co., 1915.
Flirtation song featured in the exhibition ballroom act of Evelyn Nesbit and Jack Clifford; it ended with a whirlwind spin, the most awe-inspiring movement in acrobatic ballroom dance.

Turn Back the Universe and Give Me Yesterday
Words by J. Keirn Brennan, music by Ernest R. Ball.
M. Witmark & Sons, 1916.
Ballad popularized by Rudy Vallee.

'Twas Only an Irishman's Dream
Words by John J. O'Brien and Al Dubin, music by Rennie Cormack.
M. Witmark & Sons, 1916/Jerry Vogel Music Co., Inc., 1943.
Introduced by Blanche Ring in *Broadway and Buttermilk* (musical, 1916) and recorded by Billy Murray (Bluebird) and Henry Burr (Victor).

Twelfth Street Rag
Words by James S. Sumner, music by Euday L. Bowman.
Original copyright, 1914/Shapiro, Bernstein & Co., Inc.
By 1919, this famous rag was being billed as "Featured by America's foremost orchestras," and in 1942, when a special War Bond edition was issued, it was still a top seller. Among the many jazz greats who have recorded the original version, or Andy Razaf's 1940's lyrics, are Louis Armstrong (Columbia), Count Basie (Parlophone), Duke Ellington (Brunswick), and Andy Kirk and His Clouds of Joy (Decca).

Two Congregations
Words by Jeffrey T. Branen, music by Leo Friedman.
Sol Bloom Publishing Co/Sol Bloom Music, 1901.
Plotted ballad in which a woman refuses to marry her fiance in one church when she is told that the funeral in the other is for the girl that he abandoned; popularized by the team, the Silvers.

Two Eyes
Words by James Weldon Johnson, music by J. Rosamond Johnson.
Joseph W. Stern & Co., 1903.

Romantic ballad introduced by Marie Cahill in *Nancy Brown* (musical, 1903); also featured by Julius Steger.

Two Eyes of Brown
Words by Edward Madden, music by Stephen Howard.
Sol Bloom Publishing Co/Sol Bloom Music, 1903.
Romantic ballad interpolated by Walter Percival into *The Billionaire* (musical, 1902) and by Jessie Bartlett Davis into the 1903 revival of *Erminie.*

Typical Topical Tunes
Words by Joseph McCarthy, music by Harry Carroll.
Original copyright, 1918.
This commentary on the popular songs of the era was delivered by Harry Fox in *Oh, Look!* (musical, 1918); it made specific references to "Sweethearts" (actually, "Do You Remember" q.v.) and "Sirens" (q.v.).

U

Ugly Chile, also known as **You're Some Pretty Doll**
Words and music by Clarence Williams.
Original copyright, 1917/Shapiro, Bernstein & Co., Inc., 1946.
A jazz standard associated with Johnny Mercer, who revived it for recordings on Capitol and V Disc; it was recorded earlier (under its alternative title) by Sam Ash and His Orchestra on Columbia and by Victor's All Star Trio.

The Umpire Is a Most Unhappy Man
Words by Will M. Hough and Frank R. Adams, music by Joseph E. Howard.
Charles K. Harris Music Publishing Co., 1905/Edward B. Marks Music Corp., 1933/Jerry Vogel Music Co., Inc.
Novelty song that described the plot of the Cecil Lean/Florence Holbrook musical comedy *The Umpire* (in Chicago, 1905); revived for *I Wonder Who's Kissing Her Now* (20th Century Fox, 1947), the film biography of composer Howard.

Un-requited
Words by Winfield Blake, music by G. J. Couchois.
Original copyright, 1900.
Sentimental ballad sung by Camille D'Arville.

Uncle Sammy's at Bat
Words and music by Great Howard.
Original copyright, 1918.
This novelty patriotic anthem uses baseball references, such as "When you make your bases 1, 2, 3; France and Belgium will be free..."

Under Southern Skies
Words by Al Trahern, music by Lee Orean Smith.
Original copyright, 1902.

Promotional title song for Lottie Blair Parker's ante-bellum melodrama.

Under the Anheuser Bush, also known as **Down at the Old Bull and Bush**
Words by Andrew B. Sterling, music by Harry von Tilzer.
Harry Von Tilzer Music Publishing Co., 1903/T. B. Harms.
Originally a promotional song for the Busch brewery tours, it became an enormously popular vaudeville novelty for Nora Bayes, Josephine Sabel, Elizabeth Murray, and many others; recorded by Billy Murray and by Arthur Collins and Byron G. Harlan (all for Victor). When the vaudeville stars brought the song to London, the title was changed to "Down at the Old Bull and Bush," after a popular name for pubs, with new lyrics to fit British drinking patterns. The British version was recorded on Stanley Holloway's *Join in the Chorus* album (Vanguard).

Under the Bamboo Tree
Words and music by Bob Cole.
Joseph W. Stern & Co., 1902/Edward B. Marks Music Corp., 1932.
Cake-walk interpolated by Marie Cahill into *Sally in Our Alley* (musical, 1902) and recorded by her for Victor; revived as "Tootie's Cake-walk" in performances by Judy Garland and Margaret O'Brien in the party scene of *Meet Me in St. Louis* (MGM, 1944).

Under the Linden Tree
Words by M. E. Rourke, music by Jerome Kern.
T. B. Harms, 1907.
Introduced by Hattie Williams in *The Little Cherub* (1906).

Under the Matzos Tree
Words and music by Fred Fisher.
Fred Fisher Music Co., 1907.
Hebrew-dialect version of the "Under..." songs popularized by Emma Carus, Willie Howard, and Lillian Shaw.

Under the Mistletoe Bough
Words and music by Will Heelan and J. Fred Helf.
Original copyright, 1903.
A romantic duet introduced by Harry Bulger and Aimee Angeles in Klaw and Erlanger's Christmas pantomime *Mother Goose* (1903).

Under the Rosenbloom
Words by Alfred Bryan, music by George W. Meyer.
Joseph W. Stern & Co., 1907.
Hebrew-dialect waltz song introduced by Bonnie Thornton.

The United States Field Artillery March
Words and music by John Philip Sousa, music by E. L. Gruber.
Carl Fischer, Inc., 1917, 1945.
Sousa's arrangement of E. L. Gruber's song *The Caissons Go Rolling Along* has become a band classic. It sold 400,000 cylinders for Victor in its first year and has been recorded in every format since. Currently available discs include performances by symphonic bands led by composers Morton Gould and Henry Mancini, by resident bands for Columbia and Decca, and by the United States Marine Band.

Upper Broadway After Dark
Words by Edward Gardinier, music by Maurice Levi.
A tribute to Times Square (then considered "Upper" Broadway) introduced by Lee Harrison in *The Rogers Brothers at Harvard* (musical, 1902).

U.S.A. Forever Dry
Words and music by J. G. Dailey.
Original copyright, 1918, 1928.
This Women's Christian Temperance Union anthem was written for the period between Congress' approval of the Nineteenth Amendment and its ratification by the states.

The United States Field Artillery March [illegible]
[illegible] music by [illegible] and [illegible]
[illegible] 1918.
[illegible] arrangement [illegible] E. L. [illegible] song [illegible] [illegible] [illegible] [illegible] Sousa [illegible] has been [illegible] [illegible] [illegible] composer [illegible] [illegible] for Columbia and Decca [illegible] by the United States Marine Band.

[illegible] After Dark [illegible]
Words by Edward [illegible] Maurice [illegible]
[illegible]
introduced by Lee Harrison [illegible]
[illegible]

[illegible]
Words and music by [illegible]
Original copyright [illegible]
[illegible] written [illegible]
[illegible] approval [illegible]
[illegible] states.

V

Valse de Concert, see **A Heart That's Free,.**

Valse Exquisite, see **Pierrot and Pierrette,.**

The Vamp
Words and music by Byron Gay.
Leo Feist Inc., 1919, 1947, 1954.
Oriental fox-trot introduced by the Dolly Sisters during the national tour of the musical *Oh, Look!* (1918-1919); popular as a piano roll (QRS) and on recordings by the Emerson Military Band and Joseph C. Smith's Orchestra (Victor) as dance music; revived for Pee Wee Hunt and His Orchestra (Capitol).

The Vampire
Words by Earle C. Jones and Gene Buck, music by Bert Williams.
Remick Music Corp., 1914.
The *Ziegfeld Follies of 1914* featured a parody of Porter Emerson Browne's melodrama *A Fool There Was* (based on Kipling's poem "The Vampire"). Bert Williams performed this comic song by way of introduction.

Vanity Fair
Words and music by Stella Mayhew.
Original copyright, 1907.
Authorized promotional song for the popular amusement park; written by a soon-to-be-famous comedienne.

Venetian Moon
Words by Gus Kahn, music by Phil Goldberg (pseudonym for Philip Golby) and Frank Magine.
Remick Music Corp., 1919.
Exotic close-harmony song introduced by Eugene and Willie Howard in the *Passing Show of 1918*; also popular as a fox-trot on piano rolls (QRS) and recordings by the Plantation Jazz

Orchestra (Emerson), Casino Dance Orchestra (Pathe), and the Kentucky Serenaders (Columbia).

Vilia (English)
Words by Adrian Ross, music by Franz Lehar.
Chappell & Co., Inc., 1907.
Ross's version of this soprano aria from *The Merry Widow* (1907) has been recorded separately by Jeanette MacDonald (Victor), Kitty Carlisle (Decca), and Eleanor Steber (RCA); it was recorded as a fox-trot by Paul Whiteman (Columbia) and the Waltz Kings (Bluebird).

The Villain Still Pursued Her
Words by William Jerome, music by Harry von Tilzer.
Harry Von Tilzer Music Publishing Co., 1912.
Novelty song using dance terms and song titles to retell a plot from nineteenth-century melodrama; featured by Al Jolson in Winter Garden revues.

Violette
Words by Dolly Jardon (pseudonym for Dorothy Jardon), music by J. B. Mullen.
Original copyright, 1905.
Popular march introduced by Della Fox, a male impersonator who specialized in military characterizations; also sung in vaudeville by Joe Natus, Dan W. Quinn, and W. J. Sullivan and recorded by Albert Campbell (Columbia).

A Vision of Salome (English)
Music by Archibald Joyce.
Francis, Day & Hunter, Ltd., London, England, 1908.
An instrumental favorite recorded by Victor's Bohemian Orchestra and Prince's Orchestra (Columbia).

A Vision of Salome
Words and music by Edward Madden.
Original copyright, 1908.
Ballad introducing Gertrude Hoffmann's dance solo *A Vision of Salome* in her vaudeville act, *The Borrowed Art of Gertrude Hoffmann* (1908-1912). The lyrics, which place Salome "'neath the bright Egyptian moon," were not performed during the dance.

Votes for Women
Words and music by Nellie H. Evans.
Original copyright, 1912.
Suffragist anthem published by the College Equal Suffrage League of Columbus, Ohio, and distributed widely at Ohio state fairs and other rallying places throughout the 1910's.

Votes for Women
Words by Edward M. Zimmerman, music by Marie Zimmerman.
Original copyright, 1915.
A rallying anthem associated with the campaigns of suffragist lecturer Dr. Anna Howard Shaw.

W

Wait
Words by Charles Horwitz, music by Frederick V. Bowers.
Original copyright, 1900.
Sentimental ballad introduced by Camille D'Arville and popular as a parlor song.

Wait and See, You'll Want Me Back
Words and music by Charles R. McCarron and Carey Morgan.
Joseph W. Stern & Co., 1919.
A BMI top seller, this ballad was popularized by Lola Wentworth and Marshall Montgomery and recorded by Henry Burr (Victor).

Wait at the Gate for Me
Words by Ren Shields, music by Theodore F. Morse.
Original copyright, 1902.
Ballad of soldier leaving for the Spanish-American War sung by Harry Tally, James H. Cavanaugh, and Estelle Wills; recorded by J. W. Myers (Victor).

Wait 'till the Great Day Comes (American-English)
Words by Edward Teschemacher and Sidney D. Mitchell, music by Ivor Novello.
Ascherberg, Hopwood & Crew, Ltd., London, England, 1918.
British patriotic anthem anticipating the end of World War I.

Wait 'Till the Sun Shines, Nellie
Words by Andrew B. Sterling, music by Harry von Tilzer.
Harry Von Tilzer Music Publishing Co., 1905, 1932, 1942.
Tin Pan Alley rag-time about the ideal weather for spooning that has transcended plot and vernacular to become one of America's most popular songs. First popularized by Grace Leonard, Effie Brooklin, and a variety of juvenile and adult vau deville vocalists, it has been shared by solo artists, close-harmony ensembles, and dance bands. Memorable recordings were made by Harry Tally

(Victor) and Byron G. Harlan (Columbia, Marconi, Velvet Tone, and Zon-o-phone) in its first decade and by Arthur Godfrey and by Harry James and His Orchestra in the 1940's. Featured by Bing Crosby and Mary Martin in the 1941 film *Birth of the Blues* (Paramount) and by Jean Peters and David Wayne in the 1952 Fox film that took the song's name. Additional lyrics by George Jessel were used in the Fox version and thereafter; original lyrics (with full verse) featured by Joan Morris on her album *Vaudeville.*

Waiting at the Church (English)
Words and music by Fred W. Leigh and Henry E. Pether.
Francis, Day & Hunter, Ltd., London, England, 1906.
British music hall favorite associated with Vesta Victoria (Victor) and Ada Jones (Columbia); revived by Hattie Jacques in her London club act of the 1960's.

Waiting for the Robert E. Lee
Words by L. Wolfe Gilbert, music by Lewis F. Muir.
Mills Music Inc., 1912/Alfred Music Co., Inc., 1939.
This rag-time standard of Tin Pan Alley was introduced by Al Jolson and/or Fanny Brice in *The Honeymoon Express* (1912, during its run), into which both frequently interpolated Dixie nostalgia rags. It became a million-copy seller in sheet music (as popularized by Jolson, Brice, Amy Butler, and the team of Van and Schenck), piano rolls, and 78's, with contemporary recordings by Jolson (Decca), Dolly Connolly (Columbia), and the Victor Military Band. It was possibly the first tune ever sung in sound films, since Bobbie Gordon as "Jakie" performed it in *The Jazz Singer* (Warner Brothers, 1927); later featured by Jolson in *Jolson Sings Again* (Columbia, 1949) and by Judy Garland and Mickey Rooney in *Babes on Broadway* (MGM, 1941).

Waiting for You
Words and music by Marcus C. Connelly and Gitz Rice.
Leo Feist Inc., 1918.
Romantic ballad interpolated by John Steele into *The Maid of the Mountains* (musical, 1918) and recorded by Lewis James and His Orchestra on the Empire and Operaphone labels.

Wake Up America
Words by George Graff, Jr., music by Jack Glogau.
Leo Feist Inc., 1916.
Patriotic interventionist anthem recorded by Henry Burr (Gennett, Rex), Joseph A. Phillips (Edison), and, as a one-step, by the Victor Military Band.

Walk, Walk, Walk
Words by J. Sherrie Matthews, music by Max Hoffmann.

Howley, Haviland & Dresser, 1901.
Comic novelty introduced by Harry Bulger and J. Sherrie Matthews in their musical *The Night of the Fourth* (1901).

Walkin' the Dog
Words by Shelton Brooks.
Will Rossiter, 1916.
Fox-trot associated with Sophie Tucker, who recorded it for Victor and Pathe; among the many top-selling instrumental recordings were those by Prince's Band (Columbia), the Victor Military Band, Sy Oliver (MGM), and Bunny Berigan and His Men (Victor). Other "Walking the Dogs" were by Atteridge and Motzam (1916, q.v.), Eubie Blake and Nobel Sissle (c.1916, now lost), and George Gershwin, who revived the form for *Shall We Dance.*

Walking the Dog
Words by Harold Atteridge, music by Otto Motzan.
G. Schirmer Inc., 1916.
Novelty fox-trot introduced by Elida Morris in *A World of Pleasure* (1915) and performed by the singing and exhibition dance team of Ted Doner and Mazie King.

Waltz Me Around Again, Willie
Words by Will D. Cobb, music by Ren Shields.
Mills Music Inc., 1906/Edward B. Marks Music Corp., 1933/ Shapiro, Bernstein & Co., Inc.
This perennial favorite was introduced by Mabel Barrison in the Chicago musical *The Land of Nod* (1906) and popularized by the major vaudeville vocalists of its day, among them, Emma Carus, Louise Dresser, Della Fox, Lottie Gilson, and Blanche Ring, who interpolated it into *Miss Dolly Dollars* (1905); recorded by Billy Murray and the Heidelburg Quartet for Victor.

The Waltz Must Change to a March, Marie
Words and music by Arthur J. Lamb and J. Fred Helf.
Helf & Hager, 1905.
Plotted ballad, in which a soldier marches to war but returns for the wedding march, so associated with Neil O'Brien of Dockstader's Minstrels that it was reprinted in 1906 in a Special Dockstader Edition; also sung by former minstrels J. Aldrich Libbey and Byron G. Harlan (Victor).

Waltzing with the Girl You Love
Words and music by George Evans and Ren Shields.
Original copyright, 1905.
Romance sung in minstrel shows and vaudeville by co-author George "Honey Boy" Evans, Jere Sanford, and Frances Cossar; recorded by Joseph Natus for Victor.

War Baby's Lullaby
Words and music by Adele Farrington.
G. Schirmer Inc., 1918.
World War I art song recorded by Geraldine Farrar for Victor and Victrola.

War Brides
Words and music by John C. Calhoun.
Shapiro, Bernstein & Co., Inc., 1916.
Promotional title song for the Selznick Pictures 1916 film starring Alla Nazimova; it referred to the contemporary vernacular term for the World War I Sisters of Mercy. Shapiro, Bernstein & Co. also published a similar ballad (1916) by Ballard MacDonald and James F. Hanley, which used the same title and was associated with Al Jolson.

The War in Snider's Grocery Store
Words and music by "Hank" Hancock, Ballard MacDonald, and Harry Carroll.
Shapiro, Bernstein & Co., Inc., 1914.
Novelty song describing the war in Europe through national provisions recorded by Billy Murray (Victor).

Wasn't It Yesterday?
Words and music by Irving Berlin.
Waterson, Berlin & Snyder, 1917.
This romantic anniversary ballad was introduced by Nora Bayes.

Watch Me To-night in the Torchlight Parade
Words by Arthur J. Lamb, music by Ben. M. Jerome.
Sol Bloom Publishing Co/Sol Bloom Music, 1903.
Emma Carus introduced this invitation to a campaign rally in the summer roof garden show *The Darling of the Gallery Gods* (1903).

Watch Your Step
Words and music by Irving Berlin.
Irving Berlin Music Corp., 1914, 1915.
Despite its plot and site (at a streetcar conductors' ball), this fox-trot was an exhibition ballroom promotion dance for Mrs. Vernon Castle (as she was billed) and title song of Berlin's first complete Broadway score (1914).

Way Down in Cotton Town
Words by Edgar Leslie, music by Al Piantadosi.
Leo Feist Inc., 1909.
Dixieland romance introduced by Richard Carle in *The Echo* (musical, 1910) but associated with close-harmony ensembles

such as the Empire City Quartet and the American Quartet (Victor).

Way Down in Indiana
Words and music by Paul Dresser.
Howley, Haviland & Dresser, 1901.
Nostalgic ballad popularized by R. J. Jose.

Way Down South
Words and music by George Fairman.
Bergman, Vocco & Conn Inc., 1912.
Ballad popularized by Mabel Hite and Gene Greene (Pathe) and by close-harmony ensembles, such as the Golden Gate Trio, the Heidelberg Quartet (Victor), and the Peerless Quartet (Columbia).

Way Down Yonder in the Cornfield
Words by Will D. Cobb, music by Gus Edwards.
Mills Music Inc., 1901.
Alabama nostalgia ballad associated with minstrel George Diamond and barbershop ensembles such as the Imperial Quartet (Victor) and the Columbia Stellar Quartet.

The Way That Walker Walked Away
Words by Robert B. Smith, music by Harry T. McConnell.
Edward Schuberth & Co., Inc., 1901.
Novelty song from *The Liberty Belles* (1901) that delineates a messenger boy's taste in dime novels.

The Way to Win a Woman's Heart
Words and music by Raymond A. Browne.
Sol Bloom Publishing Co/Sol Bloom Music, 1900.
Ballad introduced by contralto Jessie Bartlett Davis.

We Are Coming
Words and music by Anna A. Gordon.
Original copyright, 1904.
March for the Cold Water Army, an arm of the Women's Christian Temperance Union; this most famous of the WCTU anthems was performed as a topical parody by the Chad Mitchell Trio in the late 1950's.

We Are Coming
Words by Edith Willis Linn, music by John Philip Sousa.
G. Schirmer Inc., 1918.
Patriotic World War I march with lyrics that came from a competition arranged by *Life,* a now-extinct humor magazine; associated with Sousa's Band. Linn won first prize and $500.

We Don't Know Where We're Going But We're on Our Way
Words and music by W. R. Williams.
Will Rossiter, 1917.
This military anthem was billed as "the American Tipperary."

We Have Fed You All for a Thousand Years
Words by anonymous lyricist , music by Rudolph von Liebich.
Original copyright, 1918.
This powerful political anthem credited to "An Unknown Proletariat" was written and published by the International Workers of the World ("Wobblies") in the late 1910's and 1920's to protest the inequal distribution of food and land.

We Never Did That Before
Words and music by Edward Laska.
Remick Music Corp., 1918.
Military novelty of World War I with topical verses about K.P., women working, flying, and Prohibition.

We Stand for Peace While Others War
Words and music by W. R. Williams.
Original copyright, 1914.
This pacifist anthem from the 1914 mid-term congressional election carried the complete text of President Wilson's non-interventionist appeal printed in its inside front cover.

We Take Our Hats Off to You, Mr. Wilson
Words and music by Blanche Merrill.
Original copyright, 1914.
Non-interventionist anthem in tribute to President Woodrow Wilson.

The Wearing of the Green
Words by T. H. Glenney.
Original copyright, 1909.
This overtly political version of the traditional Irish ballad "Arrah na Pogue" includes the chorus line "... they're hanging men and women for the wearin' of the green." A less militarist version was sung by Chauncey Olcott in his *Eileen Asthorne* in 1906.

Wed the Man That You Love or Don't Wed at All
Words by Robert H. Brennan, music by Pauline B. Story.
Original copyright, 1903.
Plotted ballad of a mother's unheeded advice; sung in vaudeville by its composer and by Ollie Halford.

Wedding Bells
Words by Harold Atteridge, music by Otto Motzan.

G. Schirmer Inc., 1916.
This narrative of a romance from the first kiss introduced a chorus processional of bridal attire in *The Show of Wonders* (revue, 1916), where it was enacted by Marilynn Miller, George Baldwin, and John T. Murray.

Wedding Bells, Will You Ever Ring for Me
Words by Sam M. Lewis and Joe Young, music by Jean Schwartz.
Waterson, Berlin & Snyder, 1918.
Romantic song associated with Al Jolson (Columbia).

The Wedding Glide
Words and music by Louis A. Hirsch.
Shapiro, Bernstein & Co., Inc., 1912.
Shirley Kellogg introduced an elaborate production number in the *Passing Show of 1912* with this exhibition ballroom song and dance; recorded by Ada Jones and Billy Murray (Victor).

The Wedding of the Reuben and the Maid
Words by Harry B. Smith, music by Maurice Levi.
The Rogers Brothers in Washington (musical, 1901) included the second installment in the musical saga of this couple, originally introduced in "When Reuben Comes to Town" (q.v). Recorded by Harry MacDonough (Climax) and the American Quartet (Victor).

The Wedding of the Shimmie and Jazz
Words and music by Howard Johnson and Cliff Hess.
Leo Feist Inc., 1919.
This novelty song describes the merging of the two popular genres into an American music. Introduced by Gene Greene.

Welcome to All Is San Diego's Call
Words and music by Earl Kennedy and Dick Kennedy.
Original copyright, 1915.
Promotional song for the San Diego Panama-California Exposition of 1915-1916.

We'll Knock the Heligo into Heligo Out of Heligoland!
Words by John O'Brien, music by Theodore F. Morse.
Leo Feist Inc., 1917.
Military song of World War I, with a risque pun about the German island fortress on the Kiel Canal, which connected the Baltic Sea and the North Sea; popularized by Florence Timponi, Neil McKinley, Johnny Dooley, and Arthur Fields (Columbia).

We're Going to Hang the Kaiser under the Linden Tree
Words and music by James Kendis and James Bockman.

Original copyright, 1917.
World War I comic threat recorded by Harry Evans and His Orchestra (Emerson).

We're Going to Take the Germ Out of Germany
Words by Arthur J. Lamb, music by Frederick V. Bowers.
Original copyright, 1917.
Patriotic novelty song for World War I.

We're Going to Take the Sword Away from William
Words and music by Willie Weston.
Kalmar, Puck & Abrahams Consolidated Mus, 1917.
Novelty song popularized by Weston; refers to the post-war pacification of Kaiser Wilhelm, the German ruler who was depicted in cartoons as a child from whom civilization is removing war toys.

We're on Our Way to France
Words and music by Irving Berlin.
Waterson, Berlin & Snyder, 1918/Irving Berlin Music Corp., 1929.
Finale of *Yip Yip Yahank,* Berlin's 1918 service revue whose cast did ship off to France during its Broadway run.

We're Ready for Teddy Again
Words by Henry D. Kerr, music by Alfred Solman.
Original copyright, 1912.
Campaign song for Theodore Roosevelt's unsuccessful run for the U.S. Presidency on the Progressive, or Bull Moose, Party line in 1912.

We've Been Chums for Fifty Years
Words and music by Thurland Chattaway.
Original copyright, 1905/Jerry Vogel Music Co., Inc., 1934.
Anniversary ballad written for and recorded by R. J. Jose.

We've Got Another Washington and Wilson Is His Name
Words and music by George Fairman.
Original copyright, 1915.
Political song in praise of Woodrow Wilson, as he approached his second presidential campaign in 1916.

We've Had a Lovely Time, So Long, Good Bye
Words by Blanche Merrill, music by Leo Edwards.
Original copyright, 1912.
The team of Clark and Bergman introduced this romantic song in Jesse Lasky's precision troupe vaudeville act, *The Trained Nurses* (1912-1913).

What Are You Going to Do to Help the Boys?
Words by Gus Kahn, music by Egbert van Alstyne.
Remick Music Corp., 1918.
Promotional song for Liberty Bond sales campaigns recorded by Harry Evans (Emerson), the Peerless Quartet (Columbia), and Charles Hart with the Shannon Four (Victor).

What Do I Care?
Words by Roy Turk, music by Walter Donaldson.
M. Witmark & Sons, 1918.
Juvenile parody of Eva Tanguay's "I Don't Care." Introduced by Frances White in the *Ziegfeld Midnight Frolics of 1918;* also known as "Whad I Care?"

What Do You Want to Make Those Eyes at Me For?
Words and music by Joe McCarthy, Howard Johnson, and Jimmie V. Monaco.
Leo Feist Inc., 1916, 1944, 1960.
Title continues: "When They Don't Mean What They Say". Introduced by Henry Lewis to and about Anna Held in *Follow Me* (musical, 1916); also popularized by Emma Carus, Larry Comer, and Grace Tyson and recorded by Ada Jones and Billy Murray (Victor). Revived for film use in 1945 for Betty Hutton to sing in *Incendiary Blonde* (Paramount) and as atmospheric music in *Nob Hill* (20th Century-Fox).

What Eve Said to Adam
Words by Harry B. Smith, music by Ludwig Englander.
Edward Schuberth & Co., Inc., 1900.
Introduced by Virginia Earl in *The Belle of Bohemia* (musical, 1900).

What Good Is Alimony on a Lonesome Night
Words by Alex Gerber, music by Anselm Goetzl.
M. Witmark & Sons, 1919.
Introduced by Ina Claire in the play *The Gold Diggers.*

What Has That Man Harrigan Done?
Words by Ballard MacDonald, music by James W. Tate.
Joseph W. Stern & Co., 1909.
Italian dialect song denouncing the prevalence of Irish dialect songs; popularized by Grace Cameron.

What Makes the World Go Round
Words and music by Harry H. Williams and Egbert van Alstyne.
Remick Music Corp., 1908.
Love song introduced by Neva Aylmar in *Nearly a Hero* (musical, 1908) and recorded by Ada Jones and Billy Murray (Victor).

What the Brass Band Played
Words by Jack Drislane, music by Theodore F. Morse.
F. B. Haviland, 1904/Jerry Vogel Music Co., Inc.
This novelty song listed in rhyme the titles of such popular songs as "Bedelia" and "Way Down in My Heart" (q.v.). Introduced by Bob Roberts; recorded by Billy Murray (Monarch, Victor), J. M. Myers (Decca, Standard Disc), and Theodore F. Morse and His Orchestra (Columbia).

What Would $50,000 Make You Do?
Words by Alfred Bryan, music by Harry Tierney.
Remick Music Corp., 1917.
Louise Dresser introduced this lament of a silent film vamp in *Have a Heart* (musical, 1917).

What You Goin' to Do When the Rent Comes 'Round?, also known as **Rufus Rastus Johnson Brown**
Words by Andrew Sterling, music by Harry von Tilzer.
Harry Von Tilzer Music Publishing Co., 1905, 1932.
The title originally continued with the alternative title. Dialect novelty song associated with Emma Carus and recorded by Arthur Collins (Columbia); revived and re-popularized in a recording by Jimmy Durante and Eddie Jackson (MGM).

What You Want and What You Get
Words and music by Raymond A. Browne.
Sol Bloom Publishing Co/Sol Bloom Music, 1905.
Fay Templeton's ironic tribute to matrimony.

What'd Yo' Do Wid de Letter, Mr. Johnson?
Words and music by Monroe H. Rosenfeld.
Original copyright, 1901.
Dialect comic song interpolated by Anna Held in *The Little Duchess* (musical, 1901).

What's the Matter with the Moon Tonight?
Words by Sydney Rosenfeld, music by A. Baldwin Sloane.
Joseph W. Stern & Co., 1902.
Buccolic romance introduced by Mabel Gilman in *The Mocking Bird* (musical, 1902).

What's the Matter with Uncle Sam?
Words by Matt C. Woodward, music by Ben M. Jerome.
Original copyright, 1903.
Patriotic comic song popularized by Truly Shattuck.

What's the Use of Dreaming
Words and music by Joseph E. Howard.

Charles K. Harris Music Publishing Co., 1906/Mills Music Inc., 1934.
Mabel Barrison introduced this ballad in the Chicago premiere of *The District Leader* (musical, 1905); it was sung on Broadway in 1906, in the show's 1911 revision, *Love and Politics,* and in *The Flower of the Ranch* (musical, 1908). Recorded by songwriter Howard with the Elm City Four and the Florodora Girls (DeLuxe) and revived by Danny Kaye for Decca; featured in the Howard biographical film *I Wonder Who's Kissing Her Now* (20th Century-Fox, 1942), with June Haver.

What's the Use of Moonlight When There's No One 'Round to Love?
Words and music by Gus Kahn and Grace LeBoy.
Will Rossiter, 1909.
Lament popularized by Katherine Rooney in her family's vaudeville act.

When a Feller Needs a Friend
Words by Bernie Grossman, music by Joseph W. Stern, Jr. and Billy Frisch.
Joseph W. Stern & Co., 1919.
Novelty song based on the *New York Tribune* comic strip used as a promotional title song for the Paramount Briggs Comedies; recorded by Henry Burr (Emerson).

When a Fellow's on the Level with a Girl That's on the Square
Words and music by George M. Cohan.
Mills Music Inc., 1907/George M. Cohan Music Publishing Co.
Introduced by Victor Moore in Cohan's *The Talk of the Town* (musical, 1905) and recorded by Billy Murray for Victor and Nassau.

When a Girl Leads the Band
Words by Will A. Heelan, music by Seymour Furth.
Shapiro, Bernstein & Co., Inc., 1907.
The famous "Boy's Dream of the Fourth of July" sequence in the 1908 musical comedy *Little Nemo* featured precision choruses, on-stage firework displays, and this song from Billy B. Van.

When a Lady Leads the Band
Words by Andrew B. Sterling, music by Lee Orean Smith.
Original copyright, 1902.
Popularized by Billie Burt, this comic march claimed that a female conductor could make everyone forget Sousa.

When Alexander Takes His Rag Time Band to France
Words and music by Alfred Bryan, Cliff Hess, and Edgar Leslie.
Waterson, Berlin & Snyder, 1918/Mills Music Inc.

The World War I adventures of Berlin's band sung by Belle Baker and Marion Harris (Victor).

When Charlie Plays the Slide Trombone in the Silver Cornet Band
Words by George V. Hobart, music by Mae Auwerda Sloane.
Original copyright, 1902.
Introduced by Marie Dressler as "Lady Oblivion" in *The Hall of Fame* (musical, 1902), this novelty march was also popular with her arch-rival, Emma Carus.

When Evening Time Comes 'Round, see **Oh, Miss Malinda,**.

When Highland Mary Did the Highland Fling
Words by Jack Mahoney, music by Harry von Tilzer.
Harry Von Tilzer Music Publishing Co., 1908.
Comic song introduced by Grace LaRue in the *Follies of 1908* and recorded by Billy Murray on the Zon-o-phone label.

When Honey Sings an Old Time Song
Words and music by Joseph B. Carey.
Sherman, Clay & Co., 1919.
Barbershop quartet favorite integrating quotations and titles of popular songs from the early 1900's; recorded by George Wilton Ballard for Edison.

When I Do the Highland Fling
Words and music by Will Heelan and J. Fred Helf.
Sol Bloom Publishing Co/Sol Bloom Music, 1903.
Comic novelty introduced by W. F. McCart in *Mother Goose* (musical, 1903).

When I Dream in the Gloaming of You
Words and music by Herbert Ingraham.
Shapiro, Bernstein & Co., Inc., 1909.
Nostalgic ballad popularized by Anna Driver and Frank Morrell; recorded by Harry Tally for Columbia and by Byron G. Harlan for Zon-o-phone.

When I Get Back to Bonnie Scotland (English)
Words and music by Harry Lauder.
Francis, Day & Hunter, Ltd., London, England, 1908/T. B. Harms, 1908.
Scottish dialect song for character monologuist Harry Lauder (Victor).

When I Get Back to the U.S.A.
Words and music by Irving Berlin.
Irving Berlin Music Corp., 1915.

This theme song of a homesick American, used to link scenes in *Stop! Look! Listen!* (revue, 1915), was accompanied by "My Country 'Tis of Thee" as an obbligato; recorded with the effect by Billy Murray and the Victor mixed voice chorus.

When I Get You Alone Tonight
Words by Joe McCarthy and Joe Goodwin, music by Fred Fisher.
Leo Feist Inc., 1912/Fred Fisher Music Co., 1940.
The catch phrase "sit near the window and pull down the shade" emerged from this character song about a shy spooner; popularized by the ventriloquist Marshall Montgomery; recorded as a duet by Ada Jones and Walter J. Van Brunt for Columbia and Van Brunt for Victor.

When I Grow Up I'm Going to Be a Soldier
Words by Jean C. Havez, music by Gus Edwards.
Gus Edwards Music Publishing Co., 1917.
Novelty song performed by "Cuddles" (Lila Lee) and the chorus in the juvenile vaudeville feature act *Gus Edwards' Bandbox Revue* (1917-1918).

When I Leave the World Behind
Words and music by Irving Berlin.
Waterson, Berlin & Snyder, 1915/Irving Berlin Music Corp.
Sentimental ballad popularized by Fritzi Scheff and Al Jolson, who recorded it for Decca; also recorded by Sam Ash (Columbia) and Henry Burr (Victor) and revived by Theresa Brewer (Coral).

When I Lost You
Words and music by Irving Berlin.
Waterson, Berlin & Snyder, 1912/Irving Berlin Music Corp., 1941.
Ballad associated with the tragic death of Berlin's first wife, Dorothy Goetz, shortly after their marriage; performed by Carrie Schenck, Lillian Washburn, William J. Dooley, and many others in vaudeville; recorded by Henry Burr (Victor) and revived by, among others, Bing Crosby (Decca), Kate Smith (MGM), and Frank Sinatra (Reprise).

When I'm Away from You Dear
Words and music by Paul Dresser.
Original copyright, 1904/Shawnee Press, Inc.
Sentimental ballad associated with contralto Jessie Bartlett Davis and counter tenor R. J. Jose, who recorded it for Victor.

When I'm Thru with the Arms of the Army, I'll Come Back to the Arms of You
Words and music by Earl Carroll.
Leo Feist Inc., 1918.

World War I variation on romance interpolated into author Carroll's *The Love Mill* (musical, 1918) but best known as a fox-trot in recordings by Prince's Band on Columbia.

When Irish Eyes Are Smiling
Words by Chauncey Olcott and George Graff, Jr., music by Ernest R. Ball.
M. Witmark & Sons, 1912/Anne-Rachel Music Corp., 1986.
This standard of Irish-American popular song was introduced by Olcott and has been performed and recorded by most of the major vocalists of that enduring genre, among them, John McCormack (Gramophone, Victor), Walter Van Brunt (Edison), Dennis Day (Victor), Kate Smith (Columbia), and Bing Crosby (Decca). It was featured twice as a title song for films--by Vitagraph in 1922 and by 20th Century-Fox in 1944, and is sung by Dennis Morgan in *My Wild Irish Rose* (Warner Brothers, 1947).

When It Comes to a Lovingless Day
Words and music by Jack Frost.
Original copyright, 1918.
Romantic/comedy novelty for Eva Tanguay in vaudeville. The title and lyrics refer to war-time rationing of meat and wheat and to Prohibition limiting alcoholic "treats" recorded by Arthur Fields for Columbia.

When It Strikes Home
Words and music by Charles K. Harris.
Charles K. Harris Music Publishing Co., 1915.
Promotional title song for the classic anti-war melodrama starring Grace Washburn (World Film Corp., 1915).

When It's All Goin' Out and Nothin' Comin' In
Words and music by Bert Williams and George Walker.
Joseph W. Stern & Co., 1902.
Complaint song about money revised by James Weldon Johnson for Williams; recorded by Tom Fletcher on Decca.

When It's Apple Blossom Time in Normandy (English)
Words and music by Mellor, Gifford, and Trevor.
Francis, Day & Hunter, Ltd., London, England, 1912/Remick Music Corp., 1912.
Narrative ballad originally introduced by Nora Bayes in *The Sun Dodgers* (musical, 1912) and popularized by Belle Storey, Gene Greene, and Grace Dixon. Although the words were of general nostalgia, World War I activities in northern France gave it new relevance and popularity; recorded by Harry MacDonough and Marguerite Dunlap for Victor and by the Victor Military Band.

When It's Moonlight on the Prairie, also known as **There's a Parson Only 20 Miles Away**
Words by Robert F. Roden, music by S. R. Henry.
Joseph W. Stern & Co., 1908.
British music hall singer Rosie Lloyd performed this "great Prairie ballad" depicting a western elopement; recorded by Harry MacDonough and the Haydn Quartet for Victor.

When It's Night-time Down in Dixieland
Words and music by Irving Berlin.
Waterson, Berlin & Snyder, 1914.
Southern nostalgia popular with barbershop-style ensembles, such as the Three Shannons and the Tip-Top Four.

When Jack Comes Sailing Home Again
Words and music by Nora Bayes.
Remick Music Corp., 1918.
This variation on "When Johnny Comes Marching Home Again" was dedicated to the Atlantic Squadron and popularized by Bayes and Jack Norworth, who was then in the Navy. Recorded by Harvey Hindermeyer (Victor).

When John McCormack Sings a Song
Words by William Jerome and E. Ray Goetz, music by Jean Schwartz.
Mills Music Inc., 1915.
Nora Bayes introduced this Irish ballad as a tribute to John McCormack.

When Kate and I Were Comin' thro' the Rye
Words by Andrew B. Sterling, music by Harry von Tilzer.
Harry Von Tilzer Music Publishing Co., 1902.
Plotted ballad of proposal and anniversary in New England; popularized by song illustrators Henry and Gallot and by Lillian Washburn; recorded by Harry MacDonough (Victor).

When Love Comes Knocking at the Door (American-English)
Words by Maud Shields, music by Evelyn Baker.
Francis, Day & Hunter, Inc., 1906.
Ballad introduced by Ethel Jackson in *The Blue Moon* (musical, 1906).

When Love Is Young
Words by Rida Johnson Young, music by Melville Ellis.
M. Witmark & Sons, 1906.
Romantic ballad introduced by Harry Woodruff in *Brown of Harvard* (musical, 1906) and frequently performed by the com-

poser Ellis in his own novelty multi-piano act; recorded by Billy Murray and the Haydn Quartet for Victor.

When Love Was Young
Words by R. J. Jose, music by E. Ray Goetz.
Howley, Haviland & Dresser, 1904.
Plotted sentimental ballad popularized and recorded by R. J. Jose, the leading proponent of melodramatic love songs of his era.

When Miss Patricia Salome Did Her Funny Little Oh-la Pa-lome
Words by Vincent Bryan, music by Harry von Tilzer.
Harry Von Tilzer Music Publishing Co., 1907, 1914.
Parody of exotic dancers and their pretenses introduced by Nora Bayes in the *Follies of 1907,* wherein she confessed that "Bridget McShane ain't from Spain."

When Mr. Shakespeare Comes to Town, also known as **I Don't Like Them Minstrel Folks**
Words by William Jerome, music by Jean Schwartz.
Howley, Haviland & Dresser, 1901.
Parody of touring productions of Shakespeare popularized by Emma Carus and Harry Bulger, who interpolated it into *The King's Carnival* (musical, 1901).

When Mother Plays a Rag on the Sewing Machine
Words by Joe McCarthy and Joe Goodwin, music by Chris Smith.
Leo Feist Inc., 1912.
1912 saw the frequent publication of novelty songs about the popularity of rag-time, including this patter rag with sound effects.

When My Bridget Malone Jiggle-Wiggles Salome
Words and music by Will J. Harris and Harry I. Robinson.
Will Rossiter, 1908.
Irish-dialect answer song to Piantadosi's "Mariutch" series.

When My Johnny Boy Goes Marching By
Words by Andrew B. Sterling, music by Harry von Tilzer.
Harry Von Tilzer Music Publishing Co., 1903.
This first hit song for juvenile stars Harry and Eva Puck concerned the Salvation Army Band.

When Old Bill Bailey Plays the Ukelele
Words and music by Charles McCarron and Nat Vincent.
Broadway Music Corp., 1917.
Songwriters often used characters from past favorites to emphasize changes in musical tastes. Here, "Bill Bailey" (q.v.) of early rag-time became part of the craze for Hawaiian music and dances;

recorded by pre-eminent vocalists Nora Bayes (Victor) and Billy Murray (Edison).

When Our Mothers Rule the World
Words by Alfred Bryan, music by Jack Wells.
Remick Music Corp., 1915.
Pacifist song of the pre-World War I era.

When Patti Sang "Home Sweet Home"
Words by Ballard MacDonald, music by Robert A. Keiser.
Shapiro, Bernstein & Co., Inc., 1917.
Tribute to soprano Adelina Patti who often ended her recitals with the nostalgic song cited in the title.

When Ragtime Rosie Ragged the Rosary
Words by Edgar Leslie, music by Lewis F. Muir.
Mills Music Inc., 1911/Alfred Music Co., Inc.
Novelty song about a volunteer organist syncopating "The Rosary," a popular concert aria (q.v.); reminiscences of Jack Benny's adolescent performances of the parody on his violin (c.1913-1915) were included in his and George Burns's comic monologues.

When Ragtime Rufus Rags the Humoresque
Words and music by Harry Ruby.
Original copyright, 1911.
Dvorak's Humoresque was a frequent target for syncopation and parody, here, as performed and recorded by M. J. O'Connell (Victor).

When Reuben Comes to Town
Words by J. Cheever Goodwin, music by Maurice Levi.
Original copyright, 1900.
This was the first in a series of popular comic novelty songs about the characters in Rogers Brothers musicals. After "Reuben" met the maid in *The Rogers Brothers in Central Park* (1900), they had a "Wedding" (q.v.) and "Troubles" (q.v.); recorded by S. H. Dudley for Victor.

When Rosie Riccoola Do the Hoola Ma Boola She's the Hit of Little Italy
Words by Andrew B. Sterling, music by Arthur Lange.
Edwin H. Morris Co.
Italian-dialect dance parodies imitative of the "Mariutch" series were revised during the craze for Hawaiian music and dance on Broadway by, among others, Suzanne Rocamora and Fanny Brice; revived as a comic novelty by Jerry Colonna with Wesley Tuttle and His Texas Stars (Capitol).

When Sousa Leads the Band
Words by William Jerome, music by Charles Horwitz and Frederick V. Bowers.
Original copyright, 1900.
Tribute to John Philip Sousa for Marie Cahill to interpolate into *Star and Garter* (revue, 1900).

When Sunday Comes to Town
Words by Vincent Bryan, music by Harry von Tilzer.
Harry Von Tilzer Music Publishing Co., 1915.
Parody of Billy Sunday's revival meetings performed by Al Jolson in *Dancing Around* (revue, 1914); see also "I Love My Billy Sunday..."

When Tetrazzini Sings
Words by Addison Burkhardt, music by Seymour Furth.
Original copyright, 1908.
The musical revue *The Minic World* (1908) featured imitations of figures in theatre, dance, and opera. In this song, "Mary McKee of Kankakee" compares herself favorably to opera singers Luisa Tetrazzini, Nellie Melba, Amelia Gatti-Cazaza, and Mary Garden.

When That Midnight Choo-Choo Leaves for Alabam'
Words and music by Irving Berlin.
Waterson, Berlin & Snyder, 1912/Irving Berlin Music Corp.
Berlin's most popular Dixieland rag with railroad rhythm effects is now associated with dancers, such as Fred Astaire, who performed it with Judy Garland in the film *Easter Parade* (MGM, 1948), but it was originally a close-harmony and/or belted song, popularized by Madge Maitland, Cleo Mayfield, and rag-time violinist Ethel Mae Barker. Also popular in close-harmony arrangements, it was performed in vaudeville by the Melnotte Twins and O'Connor Sisters and in recordings by Arthur Collins and Byron G. Harlan (Victor and Columbia).

When That Vampire Rolled Her Vampy Eyes at Me
Words and music by Lee Johnson.
Original copyright, 1917.
Dedicated to Theda Bara, this ballad quotes and alludes to her film vehicle, *The Vampire,* and to "A Fool There Was," the Kipling poem on which it was based.

When the Angelus Is Ringing
Words by Joe Young, music by Bert Grant.
Waterson, Berlin & Snyder, 1914/Warock Music, Inc.
Proposal ballad popularized by Jose Collins, Violet Carleton, and

the team of Kelly and Violette; recorded by Harvey Hindermeyer for Edison.

When the Band Goes Marching By
Words and music by Charles Shackford.
Original copyright, 1902.
Sung by Kathleen Warren and Ada Russell in *The Show Girl* (musical, 1902).

When the Band Played Home Sweet Home
Words by Fred G. Raymond, music by Harry S. Marion.
Howley, Haviland & Co., 1900.
Plotted melodramatic ballad set on a battlefield; popularized during the Spanish-American War by Gertie Lewis.

When the Band Plays "Indiana," Then I'm Humming "Home Sweet Home"
Words and music by Billy Gaston.
Shapiro, Bernstein & Co., Inc., 1918.
Ballad popularized by Gaston about a nostalgic soldier. The lyrics and music refer to contemporary popular songs such as "Indiana," "By the Sycamore Tree," "On the Banks of the Wabash," and "When the Band Played Home Sweet Home" (all q.v.).

When the Bell in the Lighthouse Rings Ding, Dong
Words by Arthur J. Lamb, music by Alfred Solman.
Joseph W. Stern & Co., 1905/Edward B. Marks Music Corp., 1932.
Tremendously popular and often parodied bass solo introduced by Augustus Reed of the George Primrose Minstrels; recorded for Victor and Victrola by Wilfred Glenn and by Frank C. Stanley.

When the Birds Go North Again
Words by Robert F. Roden, music by Max S. Wilt.
Joseph W. Stern & Co., 1900.
This death-bed ballad was popularized by Lottie Gilson and the team of Kelly and Violette.

When the Black Sheep Returns to the Fold
Words and music by Irving Berlin.
Waterson, Berlin & Snyder, 1916.
Melodramatic plotted ballad introduced by Belle Baker and recorded by the Avon Comedy Four (Victor).

When the Boys Go Marching By
Words and music by Charles W. Doty.
Original copyright, 1901.
Military march for Manuel Romain, vocalist and arranger for West's Minstrels.

When the Circus Comes to Town
Words by James O'Dea, music by Robert J. Adams.
Original copyright, 1902.
March introduced by Lotta Faust in *The Wizard of Oz* (musical, 1903).

When the Fields Are White with Cotton
Words by Robert F. Roden, music by Max S. Witt.
Joseph W. Stern & Co., 1902.
Nostalgic plotted ballad introduced by Irene Franklyn as a juvenile and performed by song illustrators Henry and Gallot; revived by Witt for his vaudeville feature act *The Singing Colleens* (1913-1915).

When the Fightin' Irish Come Home
Words by J. W. Bratton, music by Joseph H. Santley.
Leo Feist Inc., 1919.
Patriotic anthem for the Irish in the Armed Forces (and in vaudeville) associated with Pat Rooney. Also dedicated to the so-called "Irish" brigade, the 69th, was Joyce Kilmer and Victor Herbert's "When the 69th Come Back" (1919).

When the Flowers Bloom on No-Man's Land, What a Wonderful Day That Will Be
Words by Howard E. Rogers, music by Archie Gottler.
Kalmar, Puck & Abrahams Consolidated Mus, 1918.
Pacifist anthem of World War I popularized by Beatrice Lambert and Harry MacDonough, who recorded it for Victor.

When the Good Lord Makes a Record of a Hero's Deed, He Draws No Color Line, also known as **He Draws No Color Line**
Words by Val Trainor, music by Harry De Costa.
M. Witmark & Sons, 1918.
Tribute to the contributions of Black soldiers in the Civil War (verse 1) and the Spanish-American War (verse 2), dedicated to Lieutenant James Reese Europe.

When the Grown-Up Ladies Act Like Babies
Words by Joe Young and Edgar Leslie, music by Maurice Abrahams.
Warock Music, Inc.
Title continues: "I've Got to Love 'Em, That's All." Al Jolson had a success with this in *Dancing Around* (1914); it was also performed by Willie Weston and Sophye Barnard and recorded by Billy Murray (Victor).

When the Harvest Days Are Over, Jessie, Dear
Words by Howard Graham, music by Harry von Tilzer.

Shapiro, Bernstein & Co., Inc., 1900/Harry Von Tilzer Music Publishing Co., 1927/Jerry Vogel Music Co., Inc., 1938.
Melodramatic ballad of death interrupting a marriage; sung by Harry A. Ellis, Emma Carus, and Maude Nugent; recorded by Harry Macdonough for Victor.

When the Last Rose of Summer Was in Bloom
Words and music by James Kendis and James Bockman.
Original copyright, 1917.
Popularized and recorded by Harry Ellis, "the Caruso of Vaudeville." Among the other ballads that referred to Flatow's classical aria from *Martha* that year was "When the Last Rose of Summer Has Whispered 'Good-Bye,' Just Remember I Love You" by Levenson and Garton.

When the Lusitania Went Down
Words and music by Charles McCarron and Nat Vincent.
Leo Feist Inc., 1915.
Tribute to the passengers who died on the Lusitania recorded by Herbert Stuart on Columbia.

When the Moon Comes Peeping Over the Hill
Words by Bob Cole, music by J. Rosamond Johnson.
Joseph W. Stern & Co., 1902.
Ballad introduced by Irene Bentley in *The Girl from Dixie* (musical, 1903).

When the Moon Plays Peek-a-Boo
Words and music by W. R. Williams.
Will Rossiter, 1907, 1921.
Spooning croon popularized by Stella Mayhew and Maud Lambert, who interpolated it into *Lonesome Town* (musical, 1908); in its 1928 re-issue, it was billed as Jessie Royce Landis's "old favorite."

When the Right Little Girl Comes Along
Words by Paul Barnes, music by E. Ray Goetz.
Paul Dresser Music Publishing Co., 1905.
Romance introduced by Templar Saxe in *The Earl and the Girl* (1905); revived for recordings by Billy Murray (Victor) and George Alexander (Columbia).

When the Right Mr. Wright Comes Along
Words by Maurice Stonehill, music by Leo Edwards.
Original copyright, 1904.
This waltz ballad became Effie Fay's signature tune.

When the Sun Goes Down in Romany, My Heart Goes Roaming Back to You, see **Romany,**.

When the Sunset Turns to Ocean's Blue to Gold
Words by Eva Fern Buckner, music by H. W. Petrie.
Joseph W. Stern & Co., 1902/Edward B. Marks Music Corp., 1932.
Descriptive ballad praising the Pacific coast popularized by Frederick V. Bowers and recorded by Frank Howard (Zon-o-phone) and Byron G. Harlan (Columbia, Marconi); revived by Kate Smith in her late 1920's radio broadcasts.

When the Troupe Gets Back to Town
Words by George Totten Smith, music by Harry von Tilzer.
Harry Von Tilzer Music Publishing Co., 1902.
Descriptions of the repertory and life style of a travelling stock company enliven this novelty song for Marie Cahill in the musical *Sally in Our Alley* (1902).

When the Whipporwill Sings Marguerite
Words by C. M. Denison, music by J. Fred Helf.
Helf & Hager, 1906.
Sentimental ballad popularized by minstrel troupe vocalists George H. Diamond and J. Aldrich Libbey, and by Louise Brehany and Lydia Barry; recorded by both of Victor's balladeers, Frank C. Stanley and Harry Macdonough, and by their rival for Columbia, Albert Campbell.

When the Winds O'er the Sea Blow a Gale
Words by Harlow Hyde, music by H. W. Petrie.
Original copyright, 1902.
Marine ballad popularized by basses Franklyn Earl Hathaway and Edward Boas.

When There's No Light at All
Words and music by John L. Golden.
T. B. Harms, 1911.
Risque parody of moonlight, starlight, twilight, etc. songs. Introduced by Edwin Foy in *Over the River* (musical, 1912).

When There's Peace on Earth Again
Words and music by Roger Lewis, Bob Crawford, and Joseph Santley.
Leo Feist Inc., 1917.
Pacifistic anthem most popular in its instrumental version as recorded by Prince's Band for the Columbia label.

When They Play "God Save the King"
Words by Vincent P. Bryan, music by Theodore F. Morse.

Joseph W. Stern & Co., 1901.
Plotted ballad of Anglo-American friendship based on the similarities between patriotic songs of two nations--"God Save the King" and "My Country 'Tis of Thee." Introduced by Lottie Gilson.

When They're Old Enough to Know Better, It's Better to Leave Them Alone
Words by Sam M. Lewis and Joe Young, music by Harry Ruby.
Waterson, Berlin & Snyder, 1919.
Eddie Cantor performed this monologue and song in the *Ziegfeld Follies of 1919* about the perils of romance; his recording for Emerson is included in the Smithsonian Institution's album *Ziegfeld Follies of 1919.*

When Those Sweet Hawaiian Babies Roll Their Eyes
Words by Edgar Leslie, music by Harry Ruby.
Kalmar, Puck & Abrahams Consolidated Mus, 1917/Mills Music Inc.
Parody of Hawaiian songs and dances that became popular elements in Broadway revues in the 1916-1917 season; featured by Rae Samuels in the *Ziegfeld Midnight Frolics of 1917* and by Irene Bordoni and Florence Moore.

When Tommy Atkins Marries Dolly Gray
Words and music by Will D. Cobb and Gus Edwards.
Gus Edwards Music Publishing Co., 1906.
Novelty patriotic anthem using the archetypal characters of "Tommy Atkins," a British soldier, and "Dolly Gray," who bade farewell to her Civil War soldier lover in Cobb and Edwards's best known ballad. Jack Norworth and Edna Wallace Hopper offered its claim that the "English speaking race against the world will stand" in *About Town* (musical, 1906); recorded during its World War I revival of popularity by Billy Murray on Victor, Columbia, and Zon-o-phone.

When Tony Goes Over the Top
Words by Billy Frisch and Archie Fletcher, music by Alex Marr.
Italian dialect World War I military tribute popularized and recorded by Gus Van and Joe Schenck (Columbia); also performed by Lillian Shaw, Clara Morton, Billy Murray (Victor), and Arthur Collins (Pathe, Emerson).

When Tony LaBoard Played the Barber-Shop Chord
Words by Joe Young, music by Bert Grant.
Original copyright, 1911.
Italian dialect answer song to the Bert Williams' novelty "Play That Barber-Shop Chord" (q.v.); popularized by Fred Watson.

When Two Hearts Are One
Words and music by Charles Shackford.
Original copyright, 1901.
Wedding ballad popularized by Camille D'Arville and by Manuel Romain of Primrose & Dockstader's Minstrels. Weber and Fields's musical *Hoity-Toity* (1901) included a parody of this ballad entitled "When Two Little Hearts Are One" by Edgar Smith and John Stromberg, sung by DeWolf Hopper and Lillian Russell.

When Uncle Joe Plays a Rag on His Old Banjo
Words and music by Theodore F. Morse.
Leo Feist Inc., 1912.
Dixieland nostalgia popularized by Arthur Collins, who recorded it with un-credited banjos for Victor and Columbia.

When Uncle Joe Steps into France
Words by Bernie Grossman, music by Billy Winkle.
"Uncle Joe" (see above) brought his rag-time band to France via Eddie Cantor and the *Ziegfeld Follies of 1918* and the team of Arthur Collins and Byron G. Harlan on Victor 78 rpm recordings.

When We Meet at the Golden Gate
Words and music by William Tobin.
Original copyright, 1915.
Promotional song by an Oakland-based composer/publisher about the Exposition of 1915 and its effect on San Francisco's suburbs.

When We Were a Couple of Kids, see **School Days,**.

When We Were Two Little Boys
Words by Edward Madden, music by Theodore F. Morse.
Howley, Haviland & Dresser, 1903.
Plotted ballad spanning from childhood friendship to battlefield rescue. Introduced by F. W. Hollis of West's Minstrels (who sang it in a Rough Riders uniform); recorded by Billy Murray (Victor).

When Yankee Doodle Learns to "Parlez-Vous Francaise?", also known as **Quand les Francaise apprennent a "Do You Speak English?"**
Words by Will Hart, music by Ed Nelson.
Stasny Music Corp., 1917.
World War I novelty popularized by Elsie Janis and Anna Chandler (in both versions) and recorded by Arthur Fields (Columbia) and George L. Thompson (Emerson).

When You and I Were Young, Maggie
Words by George W. Johnson, music by J. A. Butterfield.

Oliver Ditson Co., 1909/Mills Music Inc.
A nostalgic ballad that gained art song status through recordings by John McCormack on Victor, Victrola, and Gramophone. Contemporary recordings by Henry Burr (Perfect and Vocalion) and the Victor trio of Harry MacDonough, Elizabeth Wheeler, and the Military Band added to its popularity. Revived by such opera singers as Jan Peerce and Placido Domingo, and also in jazz performances in the Bechet/Mezzrow arrangement.

When You Come Back, and You Will Come Back, There's a Whole World...
Words and music by George M. Cohan.
M. Witmark & Sons, 1918/George M. Cohan Music Publishing Co.
Title continues: "Waiting for You." Patriotic anthem directed at World War I soldiers performed by Cohan and Nora Bayes in the *Cohan Revue of 1918* and recorded by John McCormack for Victor.

When You Come Back They'll Wonder Who the --- You Are
Words and music by Paul Dresser.
Howley, Haviland & Dresser, 1902.
Bitter response to the public's lack of attention to the Spanish-American War veterans.

When You First Kiss the Last Girl You Love
Words by Will M. Hough and Frank R. Adams, music by Joseph E. Howard.
Charles K. Harris Music Publishing Co., 1908.
Romantic ballad from the musical *A Stubborn Cinderella* (1907, in Chicago; 1908, in New York) was introduced on Broadway by Sallie Fisher to John Barrymore; recorded by Henry Burr (Columbia).

When You Hear Love's "Hello"
Words by Harold Atteridge, music by Louis A. Hirsch and E. Ray Goetz.
Gaby Deslys introduced this telephone novelty flirtation song in *Vera Violette* (musical, 1911).

When You Know You're Not Forgotten by the Girl You Can't Forget
Words by Ed Gardinier, music by J. Fred Helf.
Helf & Hager, 1906/Jerry Vogel Music Co., Inc., 1938.
Romantic song associated with Fanny Brice who, according to legend, won her first amateur contest with it; recorded by Albert Campbell (Columbia) and the Haydn Quartet (Victor).

When You Look in the Heart of a Rose
Words by Marian Gillespie, music by Florence Methuen.

Leo Feist Inc., 1918, 1946.
ASCAP top seller through recordings by John McCormack on Victor and Victrola, Henry Burr on Aeolian and Vocalion, and by Joseph C. Smith's Orchestra (Victor).

When You Wore a Tulip and I Wore a Big Red Rose
Words by Jack Mahoney, music by Percy Wenrich.
Leo Feist Inc., 1914.
Deliberately invoking the nostalgia songs of an earlier decade, vocalists quickly made this a top seller of 1914, among them, Bernard Granville and Dolly Connolly, who interpolated it widely. Always popular in its barbershop arrangements, it was first recorded by Victor's American Quartet and the Columbia Stellar Quartet and revived as a close-harmony duet for Judy Garland and Gene Kelly in the film *For Me and My Gal* (MGM, 1942). Featured by the bands of Harry James and Jimmy Dorsey (both Columbia).

When Your Lips Pressed Mine
Words by Matt C. Woodward and Albertine Dallas, music by Franz Lehar.
Joseph W. Stern & Co., 1907.
This American version of the "Merry Widow Waltz" was not associated with a specific production of the operetta.

When You're Down in Louisville, Call on Me
Words and music by Irving Berlin.
Waterson, Berlin & Snyder, 1915/Irving Berlin Music Corp.
Dixie nostalgia rag with railroad rhythm effect popularized by Belle Baker and Nora Bayes; recorded by Arthur Chandler for Columbia and by Arthur Collins and Byron G. Harlan for Victor.

When You're in Love with Someone Who Is Not in Love with You
Words by Grant Clarke, music by Al Piantadosi.
Leo Feist Inc., 1915.
This title became the ballad hit of 1915-1916 through performances by Emma Carus and Evelyn Nesbit and recordings by Charles Harrison on Victor and by Henry Burr and Miriam Clark on Columbia 78 rpm recordings.

When You're in Town in My Home Town
Words and music by Irving Berlin.
Ted Snyder Music Publishing Co., 1911/Irving Berlin Music Corp.
A travelling salesman joke popularized by Morris Abrams and the Chicago Band; a record by Henry Burr and Elise Stevenson was a top seller for Victor.

Where Do We Go from Here?
Words and music by Howard Johnson and Percy Wenrich.
Leo Feist Inc., 1917.
Comic novelty about a cab driver's misadventures in New York became an ASCAP top seller through appearances by vaudeville's major character comics, such as Emma Carus, Harry Ellis, Arthur Fields, and Willie Weston; also popular in a barbershop arrangement through performances by the Avon Comedy Four, Brice and King, the Peerless Quarter (Columbia with Fields), and the American Quartet (Victor).

Where Go the Boats? (English)
Words by Robert Louis Stevenson, music by Cissie Loftus.
M. Witmark & Sons, 1900/Shawnee Press, Inc.
This became composer Loftus's signature tune.

Where Is My Papa Tonight?
Words by Mrs. Shacklock, music by H. M. Rogers.
Original copyright, 1902.
Plotted melodramatic ballad adapted to use by the temperance campaigners, the Blue Button Army.

Where the Black-Eyed Susans Grow
Words by Dave Radford, music by Richard Whiting.
Remick Music Corp., 1917.
Jolson interpolated this ballad into his Dixie nostalgia slot in the musical *Robinson Crusoe, Jr.* (1916) and recorded it for Decca; it was also recorded as a ballad by Henry Burr (Victor) and as dance music by Bob Grant and His Orchestra (Decca) and Sam Ash and His Orchestra on Columbia.

Where the Fairest Flowers Are Blooming
Words by Henry Blossom, music by Victor Herbert.
M. Witmark & Sons, 1903.
An imitative concert aria complete with florid cadenzas. Introduced by Fritzi Scheff in *The Prima Donna* (musical, 1908).

Where the Morning Glories Twine around the Door
Words by Andrew B. Sterling, music by Harry von Tilzer.
Harry Von Tilzer Music Publishing Co., 1905/Robbins Music Corp.
Nostalgic ballad popularized by Daphne Pollard and by the adolescent team of Harry and Eva Puck; recorded by Byron G. Harlan (Columbia) and Royal Fish (an Edison tenor) and revived by Dick Powell on Decca. The same title was used for a parlor song by Dorothy Browning and Edward Stanley also in 1905, which was published by Frank K. Root.

Where the River Shannon Flows (American-English)
Words and music by James T. Russell.
M. Witmark & Sons, 1905, 1926.
"The Irish Swanee River," as it was known, was introduced by James and John Russell in their own act. It has remained a favorite of the Irish ballad repertory through major recordings by John McCormack (Victor, Victrola), Henry Burr (Columbia, Hy-Tone), and Harry MacDonough (Victor) and revivals by Bing Crosby (Decca) and Kate Smith (Columbia).

Where the Silv'ry Colorado Wends Its Way
Words by C. H. Scoggins, music by Charles Avril.
Original copyright, 1901/Will Rossiter, 1904.
Descriptive ballad that quickly became a standard of minstrelsy vocalists like Reese V. Prosser and of such ensembles as Helen May Butler's Laddie's Military Brass Band. The sheet music sold through twenty editions by 1902 when Lottie Gilson interpolated it into the musical *The Little Magnet.* Recordings by the balladeers of the major labels, including J. W. Myers for Columbia and Walter J. Van Brunt for Victor, kept it popular through the 1920's.

Where the Southern Cross' the Yellow Dog, see **Yellow Dog Blues,**.

While the British Bull-Dog's Watching the Door (English)
Words and music by Harry Lauder.
T. B. Harms, 1915.
Patriotic anthem for Lauder in which he claims that Britain will defend her empire.

While the Old Mill Wheel Is Turning, also known as **Kiss This Rose and Say "He Loves Me"**
Words by Will D. Cobb, music by Kerry Mills.
Mills Music Inc., 1906.
Melodramatic ballad introduced by song illustrator Charles Falke and performed by Emma Carus, Henry Burr, and Albert Campbell (Columbia).

Whippoorwill
Words and music by James Blyler and F. M. Fagan.
Shapiro, Bernstein & Co., Inc., 1911.
Blyler and Brown introduced this buccolic nostalgia with bird calls in Ziegfeld's *Follies of 1911.*

Whisper That You Love Me, see **Douce Fievre,**.

The Whistler and His Dog
Words by Frank Luther, music by Arthur Pryor.

Carl Fischer, Inc., 1905, 1951.
Famous whistling specialty popularized by Pryor's Band (Columbia, Victor) and by Pryor with Prince's Band (Columbia), and its rivals; featured in the film *The Emperor Waltz* (Paramount, 1948).

Whistling Rag
Words and music by Irving Berlin.
Ted Snyder Music Publishing Co., 1911/Irving Berlin Music Corp.
Sam Dody introduced this novelty rag with whistling cadenzas.

White Blossoms
Words by Charles Hanson Towne, music by D. W. Griffith.
G. Schirmer Inc., 1919.
Love theme for D. W. Griffith's film *Broken Blossoms* (United Artists, 1919).

White Ribbon Rally
Words and music by Frances B. Damon.
Original copyright, 1917, 1928.
Set to "The Battle Hymn of the Republic," this Prohibition anthem published by the Women's Christian Temperance Union memorialized the white ribbons worn by those who took the pledge of temperance.

The White Wash Man
Words by William Jerome, music by Jean Schwartz.
Shapiro, Bernstein & Co., Inc., 1909.
Schwartz's best-selling piano rag (originally published by Cohan & Harris) was given patter lyrics by Jerome for performance by William Rock and Maude Fulton in *The Candy Shop* (musical, 1909); recorded as a banjo rag by Fred Van Eps and His Banjo Orchestra (Pathe and Columbia).

Who Knows?
Words by Paul Lawrence Dunbar, music by Ernest R. Ball.
M. Witmark & Sons, 1908, 1916.
Art song based on Dunbar's poetry; known through recordings and performances by John McCormick on Victor.

Who Paid the Rent for Mrs. Rip Van Winkle?
Words by Alfred Bryan, music by Fred Fisher.
Leo Feist Inc., 1914/Fred Fisher Music Co., 1942, 1949.
Novelty song associated with Sam Bernard, who interpolated it into *The Belle of Bond Street* (musical, 1914), and Al Jolson, who introduced it in *The Honeymoon Express* (musical, 1913) and sang it in the film *Mammy* (Warner Bros., 1930); also recorded by the Victor Military Band and the Van Eps Banjo Orchestra

(Pathe) and featured in the Fred Fisher biographical film *Oh, You Beautiful Doll* (20th Century-Fox, 1949).

Who Played Poker with Pocohontas When John Smith Went Away?
Words by Sam M. Lewis and Joe Young, music by Fred Ahlert.
Waterson, Berlin & Snyder, 1919/Mills Music Inc., 1931.
Suggestive patter song of the style associated with Al Jolson's Winter Garden revues; also recorded by Pietro for Victor.

The Whole Dam Family
Words by George Totten Smith, music by Albert von Tilzer.
York Music Corp., 1905.
Promoted as "the craze of the day," this was a suggestive novelty song about a family named Dam; performed by John F. Clarke on stage and by Billy Murray on recordings for Victor and Victrola.

Why Adam Sinned
Words and music by Alex Rogers.
Gotham-Attucks Music Publishing Co., 1904/Jerry Vogel Music Co., Inc., 1938.
Introduced by Aida Overton Walker in the musical *In Dahomey* and featured in *Bandana Land* (musical, 1907); recorded by the American Singers on Edison and by Lillian Homesley on Victor.

Why Do They All Take the Night Boat to Albany?
Words by Sam M. Lewis and Joe Young, music by Jean Schwartz.
Waterson, Berlin & Snyder, 1918.
Al Jolson's great success from *Sinbad* (musical, 1918) referred to a trip that was generally considered a euphemism for illicit sexual activity; revived by Jolson for performance in the film *Mammy* (Warner Brothers, 1930); recorded as a one-step by the Hotel Biltmore Dance Orchestra.

Why Don't the Band Play?
Words by Bob Cole and James Weldon Johnson, music by J. Rosamond Johnson.
Joseph W. Stern & Co., 1900.
Novelty song with, in at least one arrangement, vocal sound effects imitating brass instruments; featured by May Irwin in *The Belle of Bridgeport* (1908) and S. H. Dudley in his Smart Set company productions; recorded by Dudley for Victor.

Why Dont You Try?
Words by Harry H. Williams, music by Egbert van Alstyne.
Remick Music Corp., 1905.
Flirtation song recommending boardwalk rolling chairs sung by

Louise Dresser, Maude Earl, and the Empire City Quartet; recorded by Harry Tally for Victor.

The Wiggle-Woggle Dance, see **Paree,**.

Wild Cherries
Words by Irving Berlin, music by Ted Snyder.
Ted Snyder Music Publishing Co., 1909/Irving Berlin Music Corp.
Considered Snyder's best piano rag, it was set with dialect lyrics for "Little" Amy Butler and Maud Raymond; it became most popular as a piano roll and in dance music recordings by the Victor Orchestra.

The Wild Wild Women Are Making a Wild Man of Me
Words and music by Henry Lewis, Al Wilson, and Al Piantadosi.
Original copyright, 1917/Goodman Music Co., Inc., 1935.
Introduced by co-author Lewis in *Doing Our Bit* (musical, 1917) and on Emerson 78 rpm recordings; also popular as a fox-trot from recordings by Prince's Band (Columbia); revived as a novelty by Freddie "Schnickelfritz" Fischer (Decca) and by Spike Jones and His City Slickers (Bluebird).

Wilhemina
Words by Edgar Smith, music by John Stromberg.
M. Witmark & Sons, 1901.
Imitative Swiss-style song yodeled by Lillian Russell in Weber and Fields's musical *Quo Vas-Iss?* (1900).

Will Taft, We're Looking to You
Words by Walter H. Cole, music by Edward Madden.
Original copyright, 1908.
Campaign anthem for Republican candidate William Howard Taft; see also "Bill? Bill Taft."

Will the Circle Be Unbroken?
Words by Ada R. Habershon, music by Charles H. Gabriel.
Original copyright, 1907.
This gospel and country-western favorite became the signature tune of Maybell Carter and the Carter Family in the 1920's and of June Carter and Johnny Cash to this day; published in *Alexander's Hymns* and originally recorded by the Metropolitan (barbershop-style) Quartet on Edison: other top-selling recordings include those by country-western stars Roy Acuff, Roy Foley, and Eddy Arnold.

Will You Forget?
Words by P. G. Wodehouse, music by Emmerich Kalman.
T. B. Harms, 1917.

Ballad introduced by Louis Cassavant in *The Riviera Girl* (musical, 1917). The title is in response to Sigmund Romberg's classic "Will You Remember?," which was introduced six weeks earlier that season.

Will You Love Me in December as You Do in May?
Words by James J. Walker, music by Ernest R. Ball.
M. Witmark & Sons, 1905/Photo Play Music Co., Inc.
This barbershop quartet standard popularized by the American, Shannon, and Haydn Quartets (all on Victor) was one of the mainstays of the Witmark catalogue for decades.

Will You Remember?
Words by Rida Johnson Young, music by Sigmund Romberg.
G. Schirmer Inc., 1917, 1955.
The love duet from the operetta *Maytime* (1917) was introduced by Peggy Wood and Charles Purcell and was revived for the 1937 MGM film by its stars Jeanette MacDonald and Nelson Eddy. Widely but incorrectly known for its first word, "Sweetheart," it remains the best loved and most often parodied romantic duet of the period and has been cited or copied for commercials for prunes, telephone service, and many other products. Memorable recordings include the film cast album (MGM), a 1944 radio recording with MacDonald and Eddy (Pelican), and individual performances by Mario Lanza and Lawrence Welk.

Wilson--That's All
Words by Ballard MacDonald, music by George Walter Brown.
Shapiro, Bernstein & Co., Inc., 1912.
Campaign song for Woodrow Wilson, candidate for President on the 1912 Democratic ticket.

With the Last Rose of Summer, I'll Come Back to You
Words by Bob Morris, music by Alfred Solman.
Original copyright, 1911.
Romantic ballad using musical references to Flatow's aria from *Martha.*

Without the Girl Inside
Words by M. E. Rourke, words and music by Jerome Kern.
T. B. Harms, 1907.
This novelty comic song for Melville Ellis's act describes the contents of a woman's trunk.

Without You
Words by Nora Bayes, music by Irving Fisher.
T. B. Harms, 1918.

Love song associated with Bayes, who introduced it in her Suffragist musical *Ladies First* and recorded it for Columbia.

The Woman Thou Gavest Me
Words and music by Al Piantadosi.
Al Piantadosi Music, 1919.
Promotional title song for the Paramount/Artcraft Photoplay silent film of 1919, also based on Caine's melodramatic novel; recorded by vocalist and bandleader Sam Ash on Emerson and Cleartone.

A Woman's No Means 'Yes'
Words by Harry B. Smith, music by Ludwig Englander.
Original copyright, 1902.
Romantic advice introduced by Blanche Ring in *The Jewel of Asia* (1903).

Woman's Right Is Woman's Duty, also known as **Day of Hope and Day of Glory**
Words and music by Charlotte Perkins Gilman.
Original copyright, 1911.
Suffragist anthem set to "The Battle Hymn of the Republic" and published in Gilman's *The Woman's Journal;* used principally by the Empire State Campaign in New York.

Women Forever!
Music by E. T. Paull.
Paull-Pioneer Music Co., 1916, 1943.
This descriptive march promotes American women as symbols of justice, liberty, victory, and equality.

Wonderland
Words and music by Thomas S. Allen.
Original copyright, 1906.
Descriptive promotional song for an amusement park; recorded by Harry Tally on Columbia.

Won't You Be My Baby Boy?
Words by Clarence Harvey, music by Gus Edwards.
Gus Edwards Music Publishing Co., 1907.
Lillian Gohn introduced the juvenile version of this comic romance in the vaudeville feature act *Gus Edwards' School Boys and Girls;* Anna Laughlin introduced the version with adult lyrics.

Won't You Be My Honey?
Words by Jack Drislane, music by Theodore F. Morse.
F. B. Haviland, 1907.
Flirtatious song popularized by Jessamine Elliot and Alys Beane;

recorded as a duet by Ada Jones and Billy Murray for Victor and as solos by each for Columbia.

Won't You Be My Valentine?
Words by Harry B. Smith, music by Victor Herbert.
Cohan & Harris, 1908/M. Witmark & Sons.
Sung by the women's chorus to introduce "The Land of Valentines," one of the most memorable and lavish scenes in the musical *Little Nemo* (1908), which translated Winsor McKay's comic strip into Broadway design.

Won't You Fondle Me
Words and music by James Kendis and James Paley.
Shapiro, Bernstein & Co., Inc., 1904.
Flirtation song popularized by Grace LaRue and recorded by Billy Murray for Zon-o-phone and by Harry Tally for the Columbia and Concert labels.

Won't You Waltz 'Home Sweet Home' with Me for Old Times Sake?
Words and music by Herbert Ingraham.
Shapiro, Bernstein & Co., Inc., 1907.
Nostalgic ballad performed by Anna Driver and Pauline Hall.

The Woodchuck Song
Words by Robert Hobart Davis, music by Theodore F. Morse.
Original copyright, 1903.
Nonsense song interpolated by Fay Templeton into *The Runaways* (musical, 1903); the chorus includes the tongue twister "How much wood would a wood chuck chuck..."

Woodman, Woodman Spare That Tree
Words and music by Irving Berlin and Vincent Bryan.
Snyder Music Corp., 1911/Irving Berlin Music Corp., 1938.
Character song for Bert Williams, who introduced it at the Ziegfeld revue at the Jardin de Paris roof garden and then sang it in the *Follies of 1911;* recorded by Williams (Columbia) and revived by Phil Harris for Okeh, Vocalion, ARA, and RCA Victor.

Work or Fight, see **Get Busy Over Here or Over There,**.

Workers of the World Awaken!, also known as **Arise Ye Prisoners of Starvation**
Words and music by Joe Hill.
Original copyright, 1916, 1970.
Recruiting and marching anthem for the International Workers of the World, the radical trade union also known as the "Wobblies."

The World Is Waiting for the Sunrise
Words by Eugene Lockhart, music by Ernest Seitz.
Chappell & Co., Inc., 1919.
This post-war ballad and ASCAP top seller is known principally through recordings by John Steel and Fritz Kreisler (Victor's virtuosi of voice and violin) and by the Victor Salon Orchestra; it was revived for memorable recordings by the Benny Goodman Sextet (Columbia and Capitol) and by Les Paul and Mary Ford (Capitol).

Would You Rather Be a Colonel with an Eagle on Your Shoulder...
Words by Sidney Mitchell, music by Archie Gottler.
Leo Feist Inc., 1918.
Title continues: "Or a Private with a Chicken on Your Knee?" Eddie Cantor performed this military comedy song in the *Ziegfeld Follies of 1918* and in vaudeville appearances. A similarly titled song was written by Fred Fisher and Leo Edwards in 1918 and performed by Ed Morton and Gene Greene.

Would You Rather Be a Tammany Tiger than a Teddy Bear?
Words by Jeff Branen, music by W. R. Williams.
Original copyright, 1908.
Presidential election campaign song in support of William Howard Taft of Cincinnati. Lyrics refer to the cartoon symbols of the Democratic Party (the Tammany Tiger), to Taft's girth (the Ohio elephant), and to retiring President Theodore Roosevelt (the New York Teddy Bear).

Y

Yaaka Hula Hickey Dula

Words and music by E. Ray Goetz, Joe Young, and Pete Wendling.

Mills Music Inc., 1916, 1944.

Al Jolson performed this contribution to the growing repertory of parodies of Hawaiian music as an interpolation into *Robinson Crusoe, Jr.* (musical, 1916); it was recorded by the Avon Comedy Four and by Arthur Collins and Byron G. Harlan for Victor. Revivals as a jazz and/or novelty song of the 1950's included recordings by Kid Ory and His Creole Dixieland Band (Decca), Red Nichols and His Five Pennies (Brunswick), and Spike Jones and the City Slickers (Victor).

Yah-De-Dah

Music by Mel B. Kaufman.

Joseph W. Stern & Co., 1917.

Piano signature tune of Earl Fuller and His Famous Jazz Band (Emerson); featured at Rector's, New York's most famous night-club.

Yama Yama Blues

Words and music by Spencer Williams and Clarence Williams.

Shapiro, Bernstein & Co., Inc., 1919.

Patter novelty blues recorded by Clarence Williams with His Orchestra (Vocalion) and His Washboard Four (Okeh), as well as by Graeme Bell and His Australian jazz Band (Jazz Classics).

The Yama Yama Man

Words by Collin Davis, music by Karl Hoschna.

M. Witmark & Sons, 1908/Jerry Vogel Music Co., Inc., 1939.

Bessie McCoy introduced this boogie-man novelty song in *The Three Twins* (musical, 1908) and, as the surprise hit of the season, it engendered a fad for "Yama-yama pajamas" (clown costumes) and a series of children's books set in Yama Yama Land. McCoy was associated with the routine for the remainder of her long career, although it was also a popular success in a fox-trot version performed by Ada Jones with Pryor's Band on the Victor label. As Irene Foote Castle, Ginger Rogers does a "Yama Yama" in *The Story of Vernon and Irene Castle* (RKO, 1939); revived by Joan Morris for her *Vaudeville* album (Nonesuch).

Yankee Doodle Boy, also known as **I'm a Yankee Doodle Dandy**
Words and music by George M. Cohan.
Sol Bloom Publishing Co/Sol Bloom Music, 1904/Emil C. Hansen Co.
Cohan's best remembered song was, in the context of his *Little Johnny Jones* (1904), a pun relating to his character, an American jockey in London, planning to ride the horse Yankee Doodle in the Derby. It has since become an American classic, deemed somewhere between a patriotic anthem and a folk song, and has been performed and recorded as both. It was the title song of Warner Brothers' film biography of Cohan, *Yankee Doodle Dandy* (1942), where it was performed by James Cagney and cast; featured by Joel Grey and company in *George M!* on Broadway (1968).

The Yankee Girl
Words by Harry B. Smith, music by Gustave Kerker.
Joseph W. Stern & Co., 1903.
Blanche Ring interpolated the song into the musical *The Blonde in Black* (1903) and adopted it as her sobriquet. Seven years later, she named her current Broadway vehicle for this song.

Yellow Dog Blues, also known as **Where the Southern Cross' the Yellow Dog**
Words and music by W. C. Handy.
Handy Brothers Music Co., Inc., 1914, 1942.
Railroad blues that introduced the "Easy" or "E.Z. Rider" character to mainstream popular music through recordings by ensembles from Joseph C. Smith's Orchestra (Victor's dance band for New York white cabarets) to Duke Ellington's bands (Brunswick); best known from recordings by Bessie Smith on Columbia and Parlophone.

Yes She Does, see **I'm Glad I'm Married,**.

Yiddisha Nightingale
Words by Irving Berlin.
Ted Snyder Music Publishing Co., 1911.
Hebrew dialect proposal song introduced by the team of Merrill and Otto.

Yiddle on Your Fiddle Play Some Rag Time
Words and music by Irving Berlin.
Ted Snyder Music Publishing Co., 1909/Irving Berlin Music Corp.
A "Sadie" novelty song popularized by Grace Leonard, Lillian Shaw, and Fanny Brice; Brice revived it for the film *The Great Ziegfeld* (MGM, 1936).

Yip-I-Addy-I-Ay
Words by Will D. Cobb, music by John H. Flynn.
Chappell & Co., Inc., 1908/Jerry Vogel Music Co., Inc.
Blanche Ring stopped the show when she replaced the lead in the burlesque musical *The Merry Widow and the Devil* (1908) and sang this patter rag; it began the craze for the 'cello as an instrument of seduction. After becoming popular in British music halls (with lyrics adapted to London locales by George Grossmith, Jr.), it returned to Broadway in *Our Miss Gibbs* (1910). Ring's recording on Victor is included on the album *They Stopped the Show!* (Audio Rarities). Buddy Clark sang it in *Mother of Men* (Columbia, 1920) with new lyrics by Roger Brown, but the original song can be heard on Joan Morris' album *Vaudeville* (Nonesuch).

Yo' Eyes Are Open, But Yo' Sound Asleep
Words by Chris Smith, music by Billy B. Johnson.
Remick Music Corp., 1907.
Dialect comic song for Clarice Vance in performance and on Victor records.

You Ain't Heard Nothing Yet
Words by Al Jolson and Gus Kahn, music by Bud De Sylva.
Remick Music Corp., 1919.
Jolson's personal catch phrase was turned into a song for his vaudeville act. After he sang it in *The Jazz Singer* (Warner Brothers, 1919), it became the keynote to the sound film era; the song itself, a follow-up to "'N' Everything" (q.v.), was recorded successfully by Jolson (Columbia) and by his comedy rivals Eddie Cantor (Emerson) and Ernest Hare (Vocalion) and found popularity as part of a fox-trot medley by the All Star Trio (Victor).

You Can Have It, I Don't Want It
Words and music by May Hill, Clarence Williams, and Armand J. Piron.
Original copyright, 1917/Jerry Vogel Music Co., Inc./MCA, Inc.
Lillian Teece introduced this standard song.

You Cannot Make Your Shimmy Shake on Tea
Words by Rennold Wolf, words and music by Irving Berlin.
Irving Berlin Music Corp., 1919.

Character complaint song referring to the restrictions on cabaret entertainments during Prohibition; Bert Williams performed it in the *Ziegfeld Follies of 1919.*

You Cannot Shake That "Shimmie" Here
Words by Gil Wells, music by Gus Van and Joseph Schenck.
Remick Music Corp., 1919.
Popularized by Van and Schenck in their *Ziegfeld Midnight Frolics* appearances in 1919, the novelty song protested the banning of the shimmie (dance) from some cabarets as indecent; see "You Can't Shake..."

You Can't Break a Broken Heart
Words and music by Shelton Brooks.
Will Rossiter, 1915.
Ballad popularized by the Dolce Sisters.

You Can't Expect Kisses from Me
Words by Roger Lewis, music by Rubey Cowan.
Will Rossiter, 1911/Jerry Vogel Music Co., Inc., 1939.
Advice to an errant lover offered by Gladys Clark and the Dolce Sisters in vaudeville and by Ada Jones and Billy Murray on Victor 78's; revived by Les Paul for Capitol.

You Can't Get Along with 'Em or Without 'Em, You've Got to Have Them, That's All
Words by Grant Clarke, music by Fred Fisher.
Leo Feist Inc., 1916/Fred Fisher Music Co., 1944.
Patter rag associated with Larry Comer and Anna Chandler, who recorded it for Columbia.

You Can't Guess What He Wrote on My Slate
Words and music by Audrey Kingsbury.
Original copyright, 1907.
Novelty song for female impersonator Julian Eltinge in his little girl character.

You Can't Shake That Shimmie Here
Words by Alex Rogers, music by Ford T. Dabney.
Remick Music Corp., 1919.
This song was performed as a vocal novelty by Bert Williams and as an instrumental shimmie by Ford T. Dabney's Orchestra in the *Ziegfeld Midnight Frolics* of 1919 and 1920. The plot relates the ejection of a shimmying couple from an aesthetic dance contest at the Paul Swan Studio in New York.

You Didn't Want Me When You Had Me So Why Do You Want Me Now?

Words by Ben Russell and Bernie Grossman, music by George J. Bennett.
Edward B. Marks Music Corp., 1919, 1932, 1944.
Frequent recordings of this one-step lament have made it a BMI top seller; its performers range from the Aeolian Dance Orchestra (Vocalion) and Henry Burr (Victor) to the Mills Brothers (Decca) and Guy Lombardo and His Royal Canadians.

You Don't Say Nothing at All, see **Holding Hands,.**

You Keep Sending 'Em Over and We'll Keep Knocking 'Em Down
Words by Sidney D. Mitchell, music by Harry Ruby.
Waterson, Berlin & Snyder, 1918/Mills Music Inc.
Military bragging by Eddie Cantor in the war-time *Ziegfeld Follies of 1918* recorded by Arthur Fields for Columbia and by Eddie Nelson for Emerson.

You Never Miss the Water 'Till the Well Runs Dry
Words by Harry Williams, music by Egbert van Alstyne.
Remick Music Corp., 1908.
Comic monologue and song introduced by Edwin Foy in *Mr. Hamlet of Broadway* (musical, 1908); revived for recordings by the Sons of the Pioneers (Victor) and the Mills Brothers (Decca).

You-oo Just You
Words by Irving Caesar, music by George Gershwin.
Remick Music Corp., 1918.
Dixie novelty interpolated by Vivienne Segal into *Miss 1917* (revue for which Gershwin served as rehearsal pianist) and by Adele Rowland into the revue *Hitchy-Koo of 1918.*

You Splash Me and I'll Splash You
Words by Arthur Lamb, music by Alfred Solman.
Joseph W. Stern & Co., 1907/Jerry Vogel Music Co., Inc.
Alice Lloyd had a summer hit with this song about flirtation at the beach; also popularized by Adele Ritchie; recorded by Lloyd (Victor) and by Ada Jones (Columbia).

You Taught Me to Love You, Now Teach Me to Forget
Words by Jack Drislane and Alfred Bryan, music by George W. Meyer.
F. B. Haviland, 1909.
Ballad popularized by May Ward; revised in the 1940's for Woody Herman and His Orchestra.

You Will Have to Sing an Irish Song
Words by Jack Norworth, music by Albert von Tilzer.
York Music Corp., 1908.

Nora Bayes's one-time signature tune, this number was introduced in the *Follies of 1908;* it functioned both as a comment on the popularity of Irish ballads and as a Hibernian love song. Recorded by Ada Jones for Victor.

You'd Be Surprised
Words and music by Irving Berlin.
Irving Berlin Music Corp., 1919.
This risque classic of the early Eddie Cantor repertory was performed in the *Ziegfeld Midnight Frolics* and his *Follies* of Spring, 1919, and quickly appropriated by rivals Lew Cooper for the musical *Oh, What a Girl* and George Jessel for the Shuberts' *Gaieties of 1919;* Cantor's recording for Emerson, available on the Smithsonian Institution's *Ziegfeld Follies of 1919* album, includes his monologue and asides; the song was featured in Berlin's films *Blue Skies* (Paramount, 1946) and *There's No Business Like Show Business* (20th Century-Fox, 1954).

You'll Always Be the Same Sweet Girl to Me
Words by E. P. Moran, music by Maude Nugent.
Shapiro, Bernstein & Co., Inc., 1902.
Anniversay song popularized by composer Nugent and by Joseph Natus, who recorded it for Victor.

You'll Do the Same Thing Over Again
Words by Alfred Bryan, music by Albert Gumble.
Remick Music Corp., 1911.
The first two verses and chorus are regretful romances but the additional verses, as performed by Valeska Surratt, include topical parodies of baseball, suffragism, and betting; the full version was recorded by Billy Murray for Victor.

You'll Find Old Dixieland in France
English words by Grant Clarke, French words by Louis Delamarre, music by George W. Meyer.
Leo Feist Inc., 1918.
Bert Williams introduced this serious tribute to the black soldiers of World War I in the military salute ending the *Ziegfeld Midnight Frolics of 1918;* it was recorded as a fox-trot (with lyrics intact) by Van and Schenck (Columbia) and Arthur Fields (Pathe).

You'll Never Know the Good Fellow I've Been, 'Till I've Gone Away
Words and music by Jack Coogan.
Will Rossiter, 1911/Jerry Vogel Music Co., Inc., 1940.
Blues for Sophie Tucker; also performed by the black vaudeville team of Alexander and Scott and by Walter J. van Brunt (Victor).

Your Dad Gave His Life for His Country
Words by Harry J. Breen, music by T. Mayo Geary.
Original copyright, 1903.
Decoration Day ballad. Recorded by Franklyn Wallace for Zon-o-phone.

Your Eyes Have Told Me So
Words by Gus Kahn and Egbert van Alstyne, music by Walter Blaufuss.
Remick Music Corp., 1919, 1936.
The first major success of the 1920's became an ASCAP top seller primarily because of recordings by John McCormack (Victor and Victrola) and Sam Ash (Pathe) and remained one through frequent performances by Kate Smith (Columbia) on radio; featured by Doris Day in *By the Light of the Silvery Moon* (Warner Brothers, 1953; Columbia recording).

Your Eyes Say No But Your Lips Say Yes!
Words by Edward Madden, music by Ben M. Jerome.
Original copyright, 1908.
This satire of Anna Held flirtation songs was performed in *The Mimic World* (revue, 1908) and featured by Irene Bentley in casino revues that year. Joseph Santley, another target of *The Mimic World,* reversed the title for his 1924 hit (with Cliff Friend) "Your Lips Tell Me No, No, But There's Yes, Yes in Your Eyes."

Your Lips Are No Man's Land But Mine
Words by Arthur Guy Empey, music by Charles R. McCarron and Carey Morgan.
Joseph W. Stern & Co., 1918/Edward B. Marks Music Corp.
Romantic ballad introduced in Empey's war drama *Over the Top* and used as a promotional song for the Vitagraph film of that name (1918); popularized by Grace LaRue and recorded by Albert Campbell and Henry Burr.

Your Mother Wants You Home Boy
Words and music by Paul Dresser.
Howley, Haviland & Dresser, 1904.
Plotted melodramatic ballad popularized by R. J. Jose (Victor), Frank Mullane, and Nellie Florede.

You're a Grand Old Flag
Words and music by George M. Cohan.
Mills Music Inc., 1906/George M. Cohan Music Publishing Co.
The first show tune to sell a million copies, this title was introduced by Cohan in *George Washington, Jr.* (musical, 1906) and has become a patriotic favorite that was once suggested as the

national anthem. Playing Cohan, whose musicals were even then described as "flag-waving," James Cagney sang this in *Yankee Doodle Dandy* (Warner Brothers, 1942) and Joel Grey performed it on Broadway in *George M!* (1968).

You're a Great Big Lonesome Baby
Words and music by Gus Kahn, Charles L. Cooke, and Richard Whiting.
Remick Music Corp., 1917.
Cooing love song associated with Marion Davies.

You're a Million Miles from Nowhere When You're One Little Mile from Home
Words by Sam M. Lewis and Joe Young, music by Walter Donaldson.
Waterson, Berlin & Snyder, 1919.
Nostalgic morality ballad in a twenty-year-old style that became an ASCAP top seller in 1919 through performances and recordings by vocalist and bandleader Sam Ash (Pathe).

You're a Perfect Jewel to Me
Words by Gene Buck, music by Dave Stamper.
T. B. Harms, 1919.
Typical Buck/Stamper production song for the A-dancers (show girls) of the *Ziegfeld Frolics of 1919.* Here eight women portrayed different jewels (Diamond, Emerald, Amethyst, Ruby, Emerald, Saphire, Topaz) spelling out the word "Dearest," which was represented by Dolores (who, like other Ziegfeld showgirls, was known by first name only) as a Wedding Ring.

You're Here and I'm Here
Words and music by Harry B. Smith and Jerome Kern.
Leo Feist Inc., 1914.
One-step written for Irene and Vernon Castle to perform in *The Laughing Husband* (musical, 1914), this included punning references to dance steps in the lyrics. It was recorded first by the Castle's own James Reese Europe's Society Orchestra (Victor) and by Prince's Band (Columbia). Also popular as a song through performances by Grace LaRue and the duet of Olive Kline and Harry MacDonough (Victor).

You're in Love
Words by Vincent Bryan, music by Leo Edwards.
Remick Music Corp., 1906.
Introduced by Emma Carus in *Too Near Home* (musical, 1907).

You're in Love
Words by Jean Lenox, music by Harry O. Sutton.

M. Witmark & Sons, 1906.
Introduced by Raymond Hitchcock in *The Galloper* (musical, 1905).

You're in Style When You're Wearing a Smile
Words and music by Al W. Brown, Gus Kahn, and Egbert van Alstyne.
Remick Music Corp., 1918.
"Smile" songs were popular in the final years of the decade; this one was performed by Bonita and by Elizabeth Brice and recorded by Arthur Fields and Prince's Band (Columbia).

You're in the Right Church But the Wrong Pew
Words and music by Cecil Mack and Chris Smith.
Gotham-Attucks Music Publishing Co., 1908/Mills Music Inc., 1936.
This complaint song was popularized by Williams and Walker in their musical *Bandana Land* (1908), by their rival S. H. Dudley's Smart Set Company productions in vaudeville and by Clarice Vance. Phil Harris revived it in his Dixie novelty repertory.

You're My Baby
Words and music by Seymour Brown and Nat D. Ayer.
Remick Music Corp., 1912.
Romance popularized by Belle Baker and Sousa vocalist Alma Youlin; recorded by the American Quartet (Victor).

You're My Heart's Desire, see **Nellie Dean,.**

You're on the Right Road Sister But You're Goin' the Wrong Way
Words by Jean C. Havez, music by Bert Williams.
Remick Music Corp., 1912.
Comic monologue and song performed by Williams in the *Follies of 1912.*

You're Some Pretty Doll, see **Ugly Chile,.**

You're the Flower of My Heart, Sweet Adeline, also known as **Sweet Adeline**
Words by Richard H. Gerard, music by Henry W. Armstrong.
M. Witmark & Sons, 1903, 1931, 1959.
This classic of the barbershop repertory was originally popularized in minstrel troupes, which featured close harmony ensembles. Major performances and recordings include those by the Quaker City Quartet (of A. G. Field's Minstrels), Harverly's Mastodon Minstrels, the Peerless Male Quartet (Victor), and the popular revival by the Buffalo Bills in the 1950's. The song is so deeply tied to the close-harmony tradition that the women's division of

the Society for the Preservation and Encouragement of Barbershop Quartet Singing in America is named "The Sweet Adelines."

You've Got to Do That Salome Dance
Words by E. Ray Goetz, music by Louis A. Hirsch.
Remick Music Corp., 1908.
Emma Carus introduced this topical novelty in the musical *The Gay White Way* (1907), lamenting the popularity of Salome as a subject for concert and vaudeville dance in the 1908-1909 season, as well as the unsuitability of many performers' figures (including her own) for the role.

You've Got to Go In or Go Under
Words by Percival Knight, music by Gitz Rice.
G. Ricordi & C., SpA, Milan, Italy, 1918.
Used in Manners and Hay's patriotic World War I play *Getting Together* (1918) and as a popular recruitment anthem for Liberty Bonds and for non-military workers.

Z

Zamona

Words by Frederic Ranken, music by William Loraine.

M. Witmark & Sons, 1901.

"Arabian Intermezzo" recorded by Sousa's Band (Victor); a song version was interpolated into the musicals *The Girl from Up There* (1901) and *King Dodo* (1902) by Elsa Ryan.

Ze Yankee Boys Have Made a Wild French Baby Out of Me

Words by Eugene West, music by Joe Gold.

Charles K. Harris Music Publishing Co., 1919.

This song offers a Paris native's version of "How You Gonna Keep 'Em Down on the Farm..." (q.v.); popularized by Juliette Dilka.

The Zoo Step

Words by Homer Tutt, music by Clarence Wilson.

G. Schirmer Inc., 1916.

This novelty song about a dancing master combined all of the "animal" dances performed by the chorus and ballroom teams of *The Show of Wonders* (revue, 1916); recorded as a one-step by Harold Veo's Orchestra for the Victor label.

Indexes and List of Publishers

Lyricists & Composers Index

Aarons, Alfred E.
Brother Bill
Devotion
A Little Girl Like Me
O Mona San
Abeles, Edward S.
In Dreamland, In Dreamland
Abrahams, Maurice
All He Does Is Follow Them Around
At That Bully Wooly Wild West Show
He'd Have to Get Under, Get Out and Get Under to Fix Up His Automobile
Oh, What a Night
Oh! You Million Dollar Doll
Rag-Time Cowboy Joe
Rufus Johnson's Harmony Band
Take Me to the Midnight Cake-walk Ball
They Start the Victrola and Go Dancing Around the Floor
When the Grown-Up Ladies Act Like Babies
Accooe, Will
I'd Like to Be a Gunner in the Navy
Love Has Claimed Its Own
My Samoan Beauty
The Phrenologist Coon
Adams, A. Emmett
The Bells of St. Mary's
Adams, Bob
The Burning of Frisco Town
Good-Bye Christina Swanson
Not Because Your Hair Is Curly
Oh, You Candy Kid
Adams, Frank R.
Be Sweet to Me, Kid
Blow the Smoke Away
Honeymoon
I Wonder Who's Kissing Her Now
The Umpire Is a Most Unhappy Man
When You First Kiss the Last Girl You Love
Adams, Robert
I Wants a Man Like Romeo
Adams, Robert J.
Daisy Donahue
When the Circus Comes to Town
Ade, George
Hike!
My Sulu Lulu Loo
R-E-M-O-R-S-E
Adler, Bernard
Dat Lovin' Rag
Adler, Bernie
That Dying Rag
Ager, Milton
Djer-Kiss

Everything Is Peaches Down in Georgia
Ahlert, Fred
Who Played Poker with Pocohontas When John Smith Went Away?
Alan, Jack
One - Two - Three - Four
Alberts, Charles S.
Down Where the Swanee River Flows
Alexander, Melville
Hello Cupid, Send Me a Fellow
Alice
An Irishman's Lilt
Allan, Bob
Tess of the Storm Country
Allen, "Mord"
In My Old Home
Kinky
Allen, Thomas S.
Any Rags?
I Wonder What Will William Tell
I'm All Dressed Up and No Where to Go
In the Heart of the City That Has No Heart
Low Bridge - Everybody Down
My Dusky Rose
Scissors to Grind
They're All Going to the Movies
Wonderland
Allison, Andrew K.
On a Good Old Time Sleigh Ride
Allwood, Lester R.
Dress Up Your Dollars in Khaki and Help Win Democracy's Fight
Alpert, S. L.
The Hurricane
Anderson, Alfred
Come Right In, Sit Right Down and Make Yourself at Home
If I Forget
Anderson, John Murray
Greenwich Village
Anderson, Will R.
Good Night Dear
I Love You All the Time
Anonymous
We Have Fed You All for a Thousand Years
Arbuckle, Roscoe
Molly Malone, My Own
Arizona, Joe
The Preacher and the Bear
Armstrong, Harry
Can't You See That I'm Lonely?
I Love My Wife But Oh, You Kid!
I Love You Just the Same, Sweet Adeline
Nellie Dean
Armstrong, Henry W.
Dreaming in the Trenches
You're the Flower of My Heart, Sweet Adeline
Armstrong, Max
Oh, Miss Malinda
Armstrong, Verne C.
I Could Learn to Love You If You Let Me Try
Arndt, Felix
Lucky in Love
My Gal's Another Gal Like Galli-Curci
Nola
Arthurs, George
I Can't Reach That Top Note
May, May, May
Asaf, George
Pack Up Your Troubles in Your Old Kit Bag and Smile, Smile, Smile
Atteridge, Harold
America's Popular Song
Angelique
By the Beautiful Sea
Come and Dance with Me
Come Back to Me
Dancing Shoes
Dat Possum Rag
Dear I Love You So
Get a Girlie!
The Golden Stairs of Love

I Just Can't Make My Feet Behave
I Won't Come Back
The Kiss Burglar
My Cleopatra Girl
My Turkey Trotting Boy
Our Ancestors
Prunella
Ragging the Nursery Rhymes
Red Pepper Rag
Sister Susie's Started Syncopation
The Stolen Melody
Syncopatia Land
Tango Dip
Tell That to the Marines!
Walking the Dog
Wedding Bells
When Gaby Did the Gaby Glide
When I Want to Settle Down
When You Hear Love's "Hello"
You'll Call the Next Love the First
Avery
Down Among the Sugar-Cane
Avery, Dan
You're Just Too Sweet to Live
Avril, Charles
Back among the Clover and the Bees
Down in Sunny Georgia Years Ago
Where the Silv'ry Colorado Wends Its Way
Ayer, Nat D.
If You Were the Only Girl in the World
Loving Time
Oh, You Beautiful Doll
When Yankee Doodle Teddy Boy Comes Marching Home Again
You're My Baby
Ayer, S. H.
see Reya, Salis
Baker, Evelyn
When Love Comes Knocking at the Door
Baldwin, Anita
The Fond Dove and His Lady Love
Ball, Ernest R.
Dear Little Boy of Mine
For Dixie and Uncle Sam
Good Bye, Good Luck, God Bless You
Goodbye, Mother Machree
I'll Change the Shadows to Sunshine
Let the Rest of the World Go By
Let Us Have Peace
A Little Bit of Heaven, Shure They Call It Ireland
Love Me and the World Is Mine
Mother Machree
My Heart Has Learned to Love You Now Do Not Say Good-Bye
She's the Daughter of Mother Machree
Sprinkle Me with Kisses If You Want My Love to Grow
To Have, To Hold, To Love
Turn Back the Universe and Give Me Yesterday
When Irish Eyes Are Smiling
Who Knows?
Will You Love Me in December as You Do in May?
Banta, Frank E.
Razzberries
Bard, Wilkie
ABCD
Barker, G. Helene
Indianola
Barnes
I've Got Rings on My Fingers
Barnes, Fannie J.
Right Is Might
Barnes, Paul
Good-Bye, Dolly Gray
Good-Bye, Maggie May
When the Right Little Girl Comes Along
Barratt, Augustus
Just a Little Word Unspoken
The Language of Lover's Smiles
Barron, J. Francis
The Trumpeter
Barron, Ted S.
Billy
I Won't Come Back

Let's Help the Red Cross Now
Baskette, Billy
Baby's Prayers Will Soon Be Answered
Everybody Wants a Key to My Cellar
The Garden of Allah
Goodbye Broadway, Hello France
Hawaiian Butterfly
In the Land Where Poppies Bloom
Jerry, You Warra a Warrior in the War
Baum, L. Frank
Scarecrow
Bayes, Nora
ABCD
Back to My Old Home Town
Blarney
Come Along My Mandy
Falling Star
I Wonder If They're True to Me
I'm Glad I'm a Boy/I'm Glad I'm a Girl
I'm Learning Something Every Day
Just Like a Gypsy
Let's Get the Umpire's Goat
Pinkerton Detective Man
Prohibition Blues
Sadie Brady Listen Good to Me
Shine On, Harvest Moon
The Stolen Melody
Turn Off Your Light, Mr. Moon Man
When Jack Comes Sailing Home Again
Without You
Bayha, Charles
Jazz Babies' Ball
Let's Be Ready, That's the Spirit of '76
Beam, Mark
The Band Played "Nearer My God to Thee" as the Ship Went Down
Beardsley, W. L.
Mexi-Tango
Beaton, Bob
I've Loved Her Ever Since She Was a Baby
Beaton, Bobry
The Saftest of the Family
Beethoven, Ludwig von
Onward Brothers
Bellezza, Vincenzo
Liberty Forever
Bellini, Vincenzo
True Freedom
Benedek, Paul
Good Bye My Home Sweet Home
Benkhardt, Gus A.
Becky Do the Bombashay
Benkhart, Gustav
A Fool There Was
Bennett, George J.
You Didn't Want Me When You Had Me So Why Do You Want Me Now?
Bennett, John
A Hundred Years from Now
Bennett, Leo
Dat Lovin' Touch
Bennett, Theron C.
The Burning of Frisco Town
Benoit, George
My Belgian Rose
Bentley, Irene
In the Cold Grey Dawn
Berlin, Irving
Alexander and His Clarinet
Alexander's Bag-Pipe Band
Alexander's Rag-Time Band
Alice in Wonderland
Along Came Ruth
Araby
At the Devil's Ball
Becky's Got a Job in a Musical Show
The Blue Devils of France
Bring Back My Lena to Me
Call Again
Call Me Up Some Rainy Afternoon
The Chicken Walk
Come Along to Toy Town
Come Back to Me My Melody
Dat Draggy Rag
Dear Mamie, I Love You
Ding Dong

Don't Take Your Beau to the Seashore
Down in Chattanooga
Ephraham Played Upon the Piano
Everybody's Doin' It Now
Eyes of Youth
Follow the Crowd
For Your Country and My Country
From Here to Shanghai
The Girl on the Magazine Cover
Good-bye France
Good-Bye Girlie and Remember Me
The Grizzly Bear
The Hand That Rocked the Cradle Rules My Heart
Happy Little Country Girl
Harem Life
He Played It on His Fid, Fid, Fiddle-dee-dee
He's a Devil in His Own Home Town
He's a Rag Picker
How Can I Forget When There's So Much to Remember?
How Do You Do It Mabel on $20 a Week?
I Can Always Find a Little Sunshine in the Y.M.C.A.
I Didn't Go Home at All
I Have Just One Heart for Just One Boy
I Lost My Heart in Dixieland
I Love a Piano
I Love to Quarrel with You
I Never Knew
I Want to Go Back to Michigan
I Wouldn't Give 'That' for the Man Who Couldn't Dance
I'd Rather See a Minstrel Show
If I Thought You Wouldn't Tell
If That's Your Idea of a Wonderful Time, Take Me Home
If You Don't Want Me
I'll Take You Back to Italy
I'm Down in Honolulu Looking Them Over
I'm Going Back to Dixie
In My Harem
Innocent Bessie Brown
I've Got My Captain Working for Me Now
Keep Away from the Fellow Who Owns an Automobile
Keep on Walking
Kiss Me, My Honey, Kiss Me
Lead Me to That Beautiful Band
Let's All Be Americans Now
Mandy
Marie from Sunny Italy
Mister Jazz Himself
Molly-O Oh Molly
My Bird of Paradise
My Sweetie
My Wife's Gone to the Country
The New Moon
Next to Your Mother Who Do You Love?
Nobody Knows and Nobody Seems to Care
Oh! How I Hate to Get Up in the Morning
Oh, How That German Could Love
The Old Maids' Ball
Piano Man
Pick, Pick, Pick, Pick on the Mandolin, Antonio
Play a Simple Melody
Poor Little Rich Girl's Dog
A Pretty Girl Is Like a Melody
Rag-Time Violin
Ragtime Jockey Man
Ragtime Mockingbird
Ragtime Soldier Man
Run Home and Tell Your Mother
Sadie Salome Go Home
San Francisco Bound
She Was a Dear Little Girl
Smile and Show Your Dimple
Snooky Ookums
Somebody's Coming to My House
Someone Else May Be There While I'm Gone
Spanish Love

Spring and Fall
Stay Down Here Where You Belong
Stop! Stop! Stop!
Stop That Rag
Sweet Italian Love
Sweet Marie Make-a Rag-a Time-a-Dance with Me
The Syncopated Walk
Take a Little Tip from Father
Take Me Back
That Beautiful Rag
That Dying Rag
That Hula Hula
That International Rag
That Mesmerizing Mendelssohn Tune
That Mysterious Rag
That Society Bear
That's My Idea of Paradise
There Are Two Eyes in Dixie
There's Something Nice about the South
They Were All Out of Step But Jim
They're On Their Way to Mexico
They've Got Me Doin' It Now
This Is the Life
Try It on Your Piano
Wasn't It Yesterday?
Watch Your Step
We Have So Much to Be Thankful For
We're on Our Way to France
When I Get Back to the U.S.A.
When I Leave the World Behind
When I Lost You
When It's Night-time Down in Dixieland
When That Midnight Choo-Choo Leaves for Alabam'
When the Black Sheep Returns to the Fold
When You're Down in Louisville, Call on Me
When You're in Town in My Home Town
Whistling Rag
Wild Cherries
Woodman, Woodman Spare That Tree
Yiddisha Eyes
Yiddisha Nightingale
Yiddle on Your Fiddle Play Some Rag Time
You Cannot Make Your Shimmy Shake on Tea
You'd Be Surprised
You've Got Your Mother's Big Blue Eyes

Bernard, Felix
Dardanella

Bernard, Mike
Mariutch, She Come Back to Me

Bernhardt, Fred
Lillies Mean You to Me

Bierman, Emil
My Honolulu Lu

Biose, Paul
My Fox Trot Girl

Bisbee, Kenneth
Lonesome Honey for You

Black, Ben
Dry Your Tears
Midnight Maid

Black, Frank
Fall in for Your Motherland

Black, Johnny S.
Dardanella

Blake, Eubie
Ain't You Coming Back, Mary Ann, to Maryland
All of No Man's Land Is Ours
Gee! I Wish I Had Someone to Rock Me in the Cradle of Love
Gee! I'm Glad That I'm from Dixie
Good Night, Angeline
It's All Your Fault
Mammy's Little Choc'late Cullud Chile
Mirandy
On Patrol in No Man's Land

Blake, Winfield
Un-requited

Blanche, Belle
I Want a Real Nice Man

Bland, James
Carry Me Back to Old Virginny
Blaufuss, Walter
My Isle of Golden Dreams
Your Eyes Have Told Me So
Blossom, Henry
Advertising
I Want What I Want When I Want It
Kiss Me Again
My Yankee Doodle Girl
The Streets of New York
The Time and the Place and the Girl
Where the Fairest Flowers Are Blooming
Blossom, Henry M., Jr.
Ain't It Funny What a Difference Just a Few Hours Make?
In Old New York
Blue, Thomas J.
Why Don't They Set Him Free?
Blyler, James
Bumble Bee
Whippoorwill
Bockman, James
I Know What It Means to Be Lonesome
We're Going to Hang the Kaiser under the Linden Tree
When the Last Rose of Summer Was in Bloom
Boden, Harry
Can't You Take My Word?
Must You?
Boman, Elmer
All In Down and Out
Bonita
Oh, Miss Malinda
Bonny, Fred
Lovie Dear
Botsford, George
The Grizzly Bear
Pride of the Prairie
Bousquet, Louis
Madelon
Bowers, Fred. V.
Moriarty
Bowers, Frederick V.
In Naples Fair
She's a Princess Just the Same
Wait
We're Going to Take the Germ Out of Germany
When Sousa Leads the Band
Bowers, Robert Hood
Chinese Lullaby
The Moon Shines on the Moonshine
Bowles, George H.
My Skylark Love
Bowman, Elmer
Beans
Bonnie Sue Sunshine
Good Morning Carrie!
That Sneaky Snaky Rag
Bowman, Euday L.
Kansas City
Twelfth Street Rag
Bowman, Eustace
Ain't Dat an Awful Feeling
Bonnie Sue Sunshine
Brachman, James
All Is Fair in Love and War
Bradford, Perry
That Thing Called Love
Bradley, J. F.
If All My Dreams Were Made of Gold, I'd Buy the World for You
Braham, Edmund
Oh! Take Me to My Mamma Dear
Poor Barney Mulligan
Brandtford, Bert
Can't You Take My Word?
Branen, Jeff
see also Nebarb, Jeff
Branen, Jeff T.
Somebody Lied
Branen, Jeffrey T.
Good Night Is But Your Last Good Bye
I Guess I'll Take the Train Back Home
Two Congregations
Branford, Bert
Must You?

Bratton, J. W.
When the Fightin' Irish Come Home
Bratton, John W.
Billet Doux
Good-By, Teddy! You Must March! March! March!
He Ought to Have a Tablet in the Hall of Fame
My Cosy Corner Girl
My Little Lady Bug
My Sunflower Sue
The Teddy Bears' Picnic
Breen, Harry
Back to the Bleachers for Mine
Pride of the Prairie
Breen, Harry J.
Your Dad Gave His Life for His Country
Brehany, Louise
Lola
Brennan, J. Keirn
America Never Took Water and America Never Will
Dear Little Boy of Mine
For Dixie and Uncle Sam
Good Bye, Good Luck, God Bless You
Goodbye, Mother Machree
Let the Rest of the World Go By
A Little Bit of Heaven, Shure They Call It Ireland
Turn Back the Universe and Give Me Yesterday
Brennan, James A.
The Rose of No Man's Land
Brennan, Robert H.
He Died on the Fighting Line
Wed the Man That You Love or Don't Wed at All
Breuer, Ernest
It's a Long Way to Dear Old Broadway
Brice, Elizabeth
Let Me Live and Stay in Dixieland
That's Everlasting Love
Brice, Monty C.
The Daughter of Rosie O'Grady
Briel, Joseph Carl
The Perfect Song
Brill, Edwin S.
There's a Lot of Things You Never Learn at School
Briquet, Jean
Alma, Where Do You Live?
Brislane, Jack
Make Believe
Broaker, Ethel
Life, Let Me Live My Life for You
Brockman, James
Down Among the Sheltering Palms
My Fluff-a de Ruff
That's Yiddisha Love
Brooks, Shelton
All Night Long
All That I Had Is Gone
The Darktown Strutters' Ball
Ev'ry Day
Give Me One More Chance
I Want to Shimmie
I Wonder Where My Easy Rider's Gone
If I Were a Bee and You Were a Red, Red Rose
Oh! You Georgia Rose
Rufus Johnson's Harmony Band
Some of These Days
Somewhere in France
That Humming Tune
Walkin' the Dog
When You Hear Cy Riddle Play His Fiddle
You Can't Break a Broken Heart
Brown, A. Seymour
Call Me in the Morning
I Don't Want To
Loving Time
Sombody Loves You
You're a Great Big Blue-Eyed Baby
Brown, A. W.
Ragging the Nursery Rhymes
Brown, Al
There's a Time and a Place for Everything

Brown, Al H.
Remember Me to My Old Girl
Brown, Al W.
You're in Style When You're Wearing a Smile
Brown, Fleta Jan
In the Candlelight
Pansies Mean Thoughts and Thoughts Mean You
Brown, George Walter
Wilson--That's All
Brown, Harry
Bye-Bye, My Eva, Bye-Bye
Gimme Hush Money or I'll Tell on You
No, No, Positively No
Brown, Lew
Give Me the Moonlight, Give Me the Girl and Leave the Rest to Me
His Majesty, the American
I May Be Gone for a Long, Long Time
I'll Come Back to You When It's All Over
Oh by Jingo! Oh by Gee! You're the Only Girl for Me
Parisienne
Please Don't Take My Lovin' Man Away
The Ragtime Dream
Sweet Kisses That Came in the Night
That Hypnotizing Man
Brown, Martin G.
Meet Me with Spangles and Bells On
Brown, Raymond
Come, Take a Skate with Me
Brown, Seymour
Oh, You Beautiful Doll
Rebecca of Sunnybrook Farm
When Yankee Doodle Teddy Boy Comes Marching Home Again
You're My Baby
Brown, Sid
Texas Tommy Swing
Brown, Walter H.
Little Mother of Mine
Browne, Raymond A.
The Army of Peace
Baby Mine
The Brotherhood of Man
Down on the Farm
Easy Street
I Need the Money
I Think It Must Be Love
It's a Waste of Time to Worry
The Meaning of U.S.A.
My Firefly
Oh, Mr. Webster
The Proper Way to Kiss
Somebody's Coming to Town from Dixie
Take Me Back to the Old Virginia Shore
There's One Rose That Will Never Bloom Again
Today's My Wedding Day
The Way to Win a Woman's Heart
What You Want and What You Get
Bryan, Al
Billy Billy, Bounce Your Baby Doll
I Was So Young, You Were So Beautiful
I'm on My Way to Manadalay
Bryan, Alfred
Always Take a Girl Named Daisy ('cause Daisies Won't Tell)
And a Little Bit More
And Then
Angel Eyes
Cheer Up Father, Cheer Up Mother
Cleopatra
Come Josephine in My Flying Machine
Cupid's I.O.U.
Dill Pickles Rag
Don't Cry Dolly Gray
Don't Try to Steal the Sweetheart of a Soldier
Freedom of the C's
Good Luck Mary

He's My Cousin If She's Your Niece
The High Cost of Loving
I Didn't Raise My Boy to Be a Soldier
I Live Up-Town
I Love the Heart of Dixie
If Yankee Doodle Hadn't Come to Town
If You Ain't Got It, Go and Get It
I'll Wed You in the Golden Summertime
I'm Going to Do What I Please
It's the Pretty Things You Say
It's Time for Every Boy to Be a Soldier
I've Made Up My Mind to Mind a Maid Made Up Like You
Just for the Sake of Society
Love Me Like I Want to Be Loved
Love Me, Make Me Love You Like I Never Loved Before
Madelon
Nothing's Good Enough for a Good Little Girl If She's Good Enough for You
Oh, I Want to Be Good But My Eyes Won't Let Me
Oh! You Gray Haired Kid
On the Road to Calais
Only a Dream of a Golden Past
Peg o' My Heart
Please Don't Take Away the Girls
Rainbow
Sasparilla, Women, and Song
She's Good Enough to Be Your Baby's Mother...
Smother Me with Kisses and Kill Me with Love
There's a Lump of Sugar Down in Dixie
Under the Rosenbloom
What Would $50,000 Make You Do?
When Alexander Takes His Rag Time Band to France
When Our Mothers Rule the World
Who Paid the Rent for Mrs. Rip Van Winkle?
You Taught Me to Love You, Now Teach Me to Forget
You'll Do the Same Thing Over Again
You're Never to Old to Love

Bryan, Arthur
Joan of Arc, They Are Calling You

Bryan, Vincent
Be My Teddy Bear
Brother Masons
Budweiser's a Friend of Mine
Bye and Bye You'll See the Sun A-Shining
The Cubanola Glide
Ephraham Played Upon the Piano
Football
Good-Bye, Maggie May
G.O.P.
He Goes to Church on Sunday
The Heaven Born Banner
He's Me Pal
How'd You Like to Float Me
Hurrah for Baffin's Baby
I Could Love You in a Steam Heat Flat
I Remember You
I Want to Be an Actor Lady
If You Knew What I Know about Men
I'm Longing for My Old Kentucky Home
I'm the Only Mother That You Ever Knew
Imagination
In My Merry Oldsmobile
In Washington
It Was the Dutch
The Man Behind
On San Francisco Bay
Over the Moonlit Sea
Over the Pilsner Foam
Percy
The Poor Old Man
Ragging the Old Vienna Roll
Since Reuben's Gone Away
Somebody's Waiting for You

Spanish Love
Tammany
That's How He Met the Girl
Theodore
When Miss Patricia Salome Did Her Funny Little Oh-la Pa-lome
When Sunday Comes to Town
Woodman, Woodman Spare That Tree
You're in Love
Bryan, Vincent P.
Down Where the Wurzburger Flows
Flora, I Am Your Adorer
Hypnotizing Lize
I Just Can't Help from Lovin' That Man
It Must Have Been Svengali in Disguise
Meet Me When the Sun Goes Down
When They Play "God Save the King"
Brymn, James T.
Good Night Lucindy
Josephine, My Jo
My Landlady
Please Go Away and Let Me Sleep
Brymn, James Tim
The Blues
Come After Breakfast, Bring 'long You' Lunch and Leave 'fore Supper Time
Buck, Gene
Chic-Chic-Chic-Chic-Chicken
Daddy Has a Sweetheart and Mother Is Her Name
Every Girl Is Fishing
Everybody Sometime Must Love Some One
Have a Heart
I Can Live without You
I Want to Learn to Jazz Dance
Nijinski
Prunella Mine
Some Boy
Tulip Time
The Vampire
You're a Perfect Jewel to Me
Buck, Richard Henry
Dear Old Girl
Buckner, Eva Fern
When the Sunset Turns to Ocean's Blue to Gold
Bulger, Harry
Eighth Avenue
No Bird Ever Flew So High He Didn't Have to Light
Burke, Joseph
My Yiddische Butterfly
Burke, Joseph A.
If I Had a Son for Each Star in Old Glory, Uncle Sam, I'd Give Them All to You
Burke, Will F.
The Curse of a Pretty Face
Burkhardt, Addison
Don't You Think It's Time to Marry?
I Knew at First Sight That I Loved You
A Kiss for Each Day of the Week
Love Me with a Tiger Love
My Little Hindoo Belle
Paint Me a Picture of Mama
Pretty Kitty-San
Pretty Maid Adelaide
Pull the Cork Out of Erin and Let the River Shannon Flow
The Queen of the Track
Spoon Time
When Tetrazzini Sings
Burkhardt, Henry S.
That La-La Melody
Burkhardt, Maurice
That Carolina Rag
Burleigh, H. T.
Bring Her Again to Me
By an' By
By the Pool at the Third Rosses
Deep River
Ethiopia Saluting the Colors
Go Down Moses
Hard Trials
I Don't Feel No Way Tired
Joshua Fit de Battl' ob Jericho

Just You
Little Mother of Mine
Burnett, Ernie
My Melancholy Baby
Burns, James F.
Nola
Burnside, R. H.
Dooley's Alibi
The Ladder of Roses
Love
Love Laughs at Locksmiths
Burris, James
Come After Breakfast, Bring 'long You' Lunch and Leave 'fore Supper Time
Burris, James H.
Rip Van Winkle Was a Lucky Man But Adam Had Him Beat a Mile
Burris, Jim
All the Little Lovin' That I Had for You Is Gone, Gone, Gone
Ballin' the Jack
Constantly
Fifty-Fifty
Burt, Benjamin Hapgood
Alexander Jones
The Deedle-Dum-Dee
Do Re Me Fa So La Si Do
I'd Rather Two-Step Than Waltz, Bill
The Indians Along Broadway
Little Girl, You'll Do
Old Reliable Jokes
Robinson Crusoe's Isle
When You're All Dressed Up and No Place to Go
Bushman, Francis X.
My Ship of Dreams
Butterfield, J. A.
When You and I Were Young, Maggie
Buzzell, Eddie
Sweet Kisses That Came in the Night
Byers, Hale N.
Molly Malone, My Own
Byrden, Neal
I Can't Help Dreaming of You
Caddigan, Jack
The Rose of No Man's Land
Caesar, Irving
I Was So Young, You Were So Beautiful
Swanee
There's More to the Kiss than the X-X-X
You-oo Just You
Cahill, William
Do Re Me Fa So La Si Do
I Want to Be a Soldier
One Called "Mother" and the Other "Home Sweet Home"
Since Father Went to Work
Take a Trip Down to Luna with Me
Caldwell, Anne
By the Light of the Honeymoon
Every Saturday Afternoon
The First Rose of Summer
Jubilo
Lola
Stars of the National Game
Calhoun, John C.
War Brides
Callahan, J. Will
The Hour of Memory
I'm Off for Mexico
Smiles
Tell Me
Campbell, C. J.
Mah Moonlight Lou
Campbell, Charles J.
A Little Girl Like Me
Campbell, Jessie H.
The Language of Flowers
Cannon, Hugh
I Hates to Get Up Early in the Morning
Cannon, Hughey
Just Because She Made Dem Goo-Goo Eyes
Cannon, Hughie
Bill Bailey, Won't You Please Come Home
He Done Me Wrong

Cantor, Eddie
Oh! The Last Rose of Summer Was the Sweetest Rose of All
Capurro, G.
O Sole Mio
Carey, Harry
Sally in Our Alley
Carey, Joseph B.
Sierra Sue
When Honey Sings an Old Time Song
Carle, Richard
All the Girls Love Me
A Lemon in the Garden of Love
Liza
Love Is Elusive
My Madagascar Maid
Carleton, Bob
Ja-Da
Carlo, Monte
That Tumble Down Shack in Athlone
Carlson, Bert H.
San Diego, California, the Gem of the U.S.A.
Carpenter, Edward Childs
Out of His Heart He Builds a Home
Carpenter, John Alden
Khaki Sammy
Carrera, Liane Held
Joan of Arc, They Are Calling You
Carroll, Earl
Beautiful Roses
Dreaming
Dreams of Long Ago
Honey, You Were Made for Me
I've Only One Idea about the Girls and That's to Love 'Em
Montezuma
Send Me a Kiss by Wireless
So Long Letty
Sprinkle Me with Kisses If You Want My Love to Grow
When I'm Thru with the Arms of the Army, I'll Come Back to the Arms of You
Carroll, Harry
At Mammy's Fireside
By the Beautiful Sea
Dancing Shoes
I Think You're Absolutely Wonderful (What Do You Think of Me?)
I'm Always Chasing Rainbows
The Little Church around the Corner
My Turkey Trotting Boy
Nix on the Glow-Worm, Lena
On the Mississippi
Prunella
Sinbad Was in Bad All the Time
Smother Me with Kisses and Kill Me with Love
Tango Dip
There's a Girl in the Heart of Maryland with a Heart That Belongs to Me
They'll Be Mighty Proud in Dixie of Their Old Black Joe
The Trail of the Lonesome Pine
Typical Topical Tunes
Underneath the Tango Moon
The War in Snider's Grocery Store
Carus, Emma
Oh! How She Can Dance
Caruso, Enrico
Dreams of Long Ago
Liberty Forever
Caryll, Ivan
By the Saskatchewan
Good Bye Girls I'm Through
Just Because It's You
Love at the Door
Oh, So Gently
Pierrot and Pierrette
The Ping Pong Song
The Pink Lady Waltz
Thousands of Years Ago
Casey, James W.
All That Glitters Is Not Gold
Cassin, S. R.
Love Has Claimed Its Own
Castle, Irene Foote
see Castle, Mrs. Vernon

Cawthorne, Joseph
I Can Dance with Everybody But My Wife
Chandler, Anna
I Love But You
That Hypnotizing Strain
Chandler, Gus
I Love But You
Chapel, Clarence M.
Deacon Jones
Hiram Green, Good-Bye
Chapman, Lylian M.
The Boys in Blue Parade Today
Chattaway, Thurland
A Flower from the Garden of Life
I've Grown So Used to You
Kerry Mills' Barn Dance
Red Wing
We've Been Chums for Fifty Years
Christie, George
Baby Rose
Lady Angeline
Christine, Henri
Come Back to Me
French Fandango
Christy, George
If All My Dreams Were Made of Gold, I'd Buy the World for You
Clare, Sidney
Ma, He's Making Eyes at Me
Clark, Billy
I Love My Wife But Oh, You Kid!
Clark, Bobby
Just a Kiss
Clark, Kenneth S.
The Glory of the Yankee Navy
Clarke, Dave
Little Nemo and His Bear
Clarke, Grant
All He Does Is Follow Them Around
America Needs You Like a Mother, Would You Turn Your Mother Down?
At That Bully Wooly Wild West Show
Back to the Carolina You Love
Beatrice Fairfax, Tell Me What to Do
Dat's Harmony
Everything Is Peaches Down in Georgia
He'd Have to Get Under, Get Out and Get Under to Fix Up His Automobile
He's a Devil in His Own Home Town
Honolulu, America Loves You
The Honolulu Blues
I Called You My Sweetheart
I Hate to Lose You
I Love My Billy Sunday But Oh, You Saturday Night
I Want to Shimmie
If He Can Fight Like He Can Love, Good Night Germany
In the Land of Beginning Again
Oh! You Million Dollar Doll
Rag-Time Cowboy Joe
Ragtime Eyes
Regretful Blues
Ring-Ting-a-Ling
Salvation Nell
There'll Be a Hot Time for the Old Men While the Young Men Are Away
There's a Little Bit of Bad in Every Good Little Girl
There's One in a Million Like You
They Start the Victrola and Go Dancing Around the Floor
When You're in Love with Someone Who Is Not in Love with You
You Can't Get Along with 'Em or Without 'Em, You've Got to Have Them, That's All
You Can't Get Away from It
You'll Find Old Dixieland in France
Clarke, Harry
O Promise Me You'll Write to Him Today
Clarke, John Lee
Bible Stories

Clayton, Thomas
A Japanese Love Song
Clesi, N. J.
I'm Sorry I Made You Cry
Coard, Henry A.
The Gypsy's Warning
Cobb, George
All Aboard for Dixie
Cobb, George L.
Bring Me Back My Lovin' Honey Boy
Just for Tonight
That Russian Rag
Cobb, Will D.
Bye Bye Dear Old Broadway
Captain Baby Bunting of the Rocking Horse Brigade
Could You Be True to Eyes of Blue If You Looked into Eyes of Brown?
Don't Take a Girlie to Coney (You May Find a Nicer One There)
Forget
The Girl Who Cares for Me
Go Easy Mabel
Good-Bye, Dolly Gray
Good-Bye, Little Girl, Good-Bye
Good Luck and God Be with You, Laddie Boy
Have You Seen My Baby?
Have You Seen My Sweetheart in His Uniform of Blue?
Hoop-la, I'm Having the Time of My Life
I Can't Tell Why I Love You But I Do
I Just Can't Make My Eyes Behave
I Miss You in a Thousand Different Ways
I Think I Could Be Awfully Good to You
I Want Something New to Play With
If a Boy Like You Loved a Girl Like Me
If a Table at Rector's Could Talk
I'll Be with You When the Roses Bloom Again
I'll Break the Fighting Line Like You Broke This Heart of Mine
I'll Get You
I'll Never Love Another Like I Love You
I'm Crazy to Go on the Stage
I'm the Man Who Makes the Money in the Mint
In Zanzibar
Kidland
Mamie, Don't You Feel Ashamie
Mary Had a Little Lamb
Meet Me Down at the Corner
Mister Monkey
The Modern Sandow Girl
"Mumms" the Word
My Charcoal Charmer
My Lonesome Little Louisiana Lady
No Bird Ever Flew So High He Didn't Have to Light
Oh! Wouldn't That Jar You?
On a Beautiful Night with a Beautiful Girl
On the Grand Old Sand
Pan, Pan, Pan
The Peach That Tastes the Sweetest Hangs the Highest on the Tree
Please Mother, Buy Me a Baby
Sally's Sunday Hat
School Days
Since My Margarette Become-a da Suffragette
Sunbonnet Sue
Waltz Me Around Again, Willie
Way Down Yonder in the Cornfield
When Tommy Atkins Marries Dolly Gray
While the Old Mill Wheel Is Turning
The Woman Thou Gavest Me
Yip-I-Addy-I-Ay
Cohan, George M.
The American Rag Time
Forty-five Minutes from Broadway
Give My Regards to Broadway

H-A-Double R-I-G-A-N
I Want to Go to Paree, Papa
I Won't Be an Actor Any More
If I Were Only Mister Morgan
I'm All O.K. with K. and E.
In a Kingdom of Our Own
Ireland, My Land of Dreams
Mary
Maudie
Musical Moon
Oh, You Wonderful Girl
Over There
Rag Babe
So Long, Mary
When a Fellow's on the Level with a Girl That's on the Square
When You Come Back, and You Will Come Back, There's a Whole World...
Yankee Doodle Boy
You're a Grand Old Flag
Colburn, Carrie W.
The Sunflower and the Sun
Cole, Bob
Big Indian Chief
The Big Red Shawl
Come Out, Dinah, on the Green
The Conjure Man
The Countess of Alagazam
Don't Butt In
Father's Got a Job
Gimme de Leavins'
He Handed Me a Lemon
I Ain't Gwin ter Work No Mo'
I Ain't Had No Lovin' in a Long Time
I Can't Think of Nothing in the Wide, Wide World But You
I Must Have Been a-Dreamin'
If Adam Hadn't Seen the Apple Tree
I've Got Troubles of My Own
I've Lost My Teddy Bear
The Katy-Did, the Cricket and the Frog
Lazy Moon
Lindy
Magdaline, My Southern Queen
The Maid of Timbucktoo
The Maiden with the Dreamy Eyes
Mexico
My Angemima Green
My Castle on the Nile
Nobody's Lookin' But de Owl and de Moon
Oh! You Georgia Rose
The Old Flag Never Touched the Ground
Sambo and Dinah
Save It for Me
Strolling Along the Beach
Sweetest Gal in Town
Tell Me Dusky Maiden
Under the Bamboo Tree
When the Moon Comes Peeping Over the Hill
Why Don't the Band Play?
Cole, E. D.
He May Get Over It But He'll Never Look the Same
Cole, Walter H.
Will Taft, We're Looking to You
Collins, Melville
Get Happy
Confare, Thomas R.
I've Been Looking for a Girl Like You
Congdon, C. H.
Roosevelt
Connelly, Marcus C.
Waiting for You
Conrad, Con
Huckleberry Pie
Ma, He's Making Eyes at Me
Oh! Frenchy
Coogan, Jack
Cleopatra Had a Jazz Band
That Carolina Rag
You'll Never Know the Good Fellow I've Been, 'Till I've Gone Away
Cook, Charles Emerson
The Friars
The Garden of Dreams
Cook, Will Marion
Allus' the Same in Dixie

As the Sunflower Turns to the Sun
Bon Bon Buddy
Daisy Deane
Darktown Barbeque
Down De Lover's Lane
In de Evenin'
Kinky
The Little Gypsy Maid
Love Me with a Tiger Love
Lovie Joe
The Pensacola Mooch
Red Red Rose
Returned
Sweetie Dear
Whoop 'er Up with a Whoop La La
Cooke, Charles I.
I Wonder Where My Lovin' Man Has Gone
Cooke, Charles L.
You're a Great Big Lonesome Baby
Cooke, Leonard
The Sunshine of Your Smile
Cooke, Leslie
Love Sends a Little Gift of Roses
Cooper, George
Sweet Genevieve
Cooper, Joe
I've Been Floating Down the Old Green River
Oh! What a Beautiful Dream You Seem
That Baboon Baby Dance
You're a Good Little Devil
Cooper, Lew
You're a Good Little Devil
Copeland, Les
I Ain't Married No More
Corin, Joel P.
Baby Lamb
My Billy Boy
Corliss, Edward W.
Katrina
Psyche
Cormack, Rennie
Melody Chimes
O'Brien Is Tryin' to Learn to Talk Hawaiian
'Twas Only an Irishman's Dream
Costa, E.
Maurice Mattchiche
Costello, Barney
I Want Someone to Flirt with Me
If You Had All the World and Its Gold
Cottler, Archie
Mammy's Chocolate Soldier
Couchois, G. J.
Un-requited
Cowan, Rubey
It Was Just a Song at Twilight That Made Me Come Back to You
Let's Be Ready, That's the Spirit of '76
You Can't Expect Kisses from Me
Cowell, Sydney
The Maid in the Moon
Cowles, Hal Blake
Thtop Your Thtuttering Jimmy
Cox, Eddie
Honolulu, America Loves You
The Honolulu Blues
My Syncopated Melody Man
Take Me to the Midnight Cake-walk Ball
Crawford, Bob
When There's Peace on Earth Again
Crawford, Clifton
De Trop
I Want to Spread a Little Sunshine
In the *Ladies' Home Journal*
Nancy Brown
Simple Little Sister Mary Green
Crawford, Stanley
I Wants to Be the Villain in the Show
I'll Wed You in the Golden Summertime
In the Village by the Sea
Only a Dream of a Golden Past
Creamer, Henry
After You've Gone

Creamer, Henry S.
Cuddle Up Honey, Let's Make Love
Good-bye Alexander, Good-bye Honey-Boy
That's a Plenty
Cross, Wellington
Lafayette
Cunha, A. R.
My Waikiki Mermaid
Cunningham, Paul
America Never Took Water and America Never Will
Baby Love
Cupero, Eddie
Sugar Mine
Curley, Leo
Tipperary
Curtis, Billy
Prohibition, You Have Lost Your Sting
Cushing, C. C. S.
Love's Own Sweet Song
Dabney, Ford T.
The Castle Combination
Castle Half and Half
Castle Valse Classique
The Castle Walk
Oh, You Devil Rag
The Pensacola Mooch
That Minor Strain
That's Why They Call Me Shine
You Can't Shake That Shimmie Here
Dailey, J. Anton
Dreaming
Dailey, J. G.
U.S.A. Forever Dry
Dalby, Alfred R.
All Right!
Dallas, Albertine
When Your Lips Pressed Mine
Daly, Joseph M.
I'm All Dressed Up and No Where to Go
In the Heart of the City That Has No Heart
Damon, Frances B.
White Ribbon Rally
Dance, George
I Want to Be a Lidy
Danideroff, Leo
Love's Lullaby
Dareweski, H. E.
Mother's Sitting Knitting Little Mittens for the Navy
David, Lee
Romance
Sipping Cider thru' a Straw
David, Worton
Come Back to Me
Davis, Benny
Goodbye Broadway, Hello France
I Know Why--Because I'm in Love with You
Davis, Collin
The Yama Yama Man
Davis, Robert Hobart
Lady Bountiful
The Woodchuck Song
Day, Frederick
De Goblin's Glide
The Manicure Girl
Day, George W.
It Was Me
de Angelis, Jefferson
All Right!
de Caillavet, Gaston
Heure exquise qui nous grise
De Costa, Harry
Hello Central, Give Me France
That Soothing Serenade
Tiger Rag
When the Good Lord Makes a Record of a Hero's Deed, He Draws No Color Line
de Fontaine, Mrs. F. G.
Ashes of Roses
De Haven, Carter
Beautiful Eyes
Darling
I've Been Looking for a Girl Like You
Ragtime Table d'Hote

De Koven, Reginald
Chloe, I'm Waiting
Flirtation Song
The Garden of Dreams
In Society
De Sylva, B. G.
The Best of Everything
From Now On
Somehow It Seldom Comes True
Tee-Oodle-Um-Bam-Bo
De Sylva, Bud
Alexander's Got a Jazz Band Now
But - After the Ball Was Over Then He Made Up for Lost Time
By the Honeysuckle Vine
Ev'ry Morning She Makes Me Late
I Gave Her That
If She Means What I Think She Means
I'll Say She Does
The Language of Love
'N' Everything
That Lullaby of Long Ago
You Ain't Heard Nothing Yet
De Voll, Cal
Alabama Lullaby
De Witt, Francis
The Moon Shines on the Moonshine
DeAngelis, Phil
Beautiful Bird of Paradise
Dee, George
I Want to Be a Lidy
Del Riego, Teresa
O Dry Those Tears
Delamarre, Louis
Love, Here Is My Heart!
You'll Find Old Dixieland in France
Dempsey, J. E.
Garden of Roses
If I Had a Son for Each Star in Old Glory, Uncle Sam, I'd Give Them All to You
Denison, C. M.
Don't Go in the Lion's Cage Tonight, Mother
'Neath the Old Acorn Tree, Sweet Estelle
When the Whipporwill Sings Marguerite
Denni, Lucien
My Skylark Love
Deppman, Ruth
The Maid of Old Madrid
DeRose, Peter
Tiger Rose Waltz
d'Hardelot, Guy
Because
di Capua, E.
O Sole Mio
Di Milo, Rita
In the Cold Grey Dawn
Diamond, George H.
There's a Mother Old and Gray Who Needs Me Now
Dillea, Herbert
Absence Makes the Heart Grow Fonder
Mah Moonlight Lou
Susan, Dear Sue
Dillon, Harry
At the Pan-I-Marry Can
Dillon, John
At the Pan-I-Marry Can
Dillon, Will
I Want a Girl Just Like the Girl That Married Dear Old Dad
Take Me to the Cabaret
Dillon, William A.
Bonnie My Highland Lassie
Dix, J. Airlie
The Trumpeter
Dixon, Will H.
Come Right In, Sit Right Down and Make Yourself at Home
Dockstader, Lew
The Old, Old Story
Dodge, Gilbert
Pollyanna
Donaldson, James
The Road for You and Me
Donaldson, Walter
The Daughter of Rosie O'Grady

How 'Ya Gonna Keep 'Em Down on the Farm After They've Seen Paris?
Just Try to Picture Me Back Home in Tennessee
What Do I Care?
You're a Million Miles from Nowhere When You're One Little Mile from Home
Donnelly, Andrew
Bumble Bee
Donovan, Walter
The Aba Daba Honeymoon
Doro, Marie
Say! Fay!
Doty, Charles W.
When the Boys Go Marching By
Dougherty, Byrd
My Palm Leaf Maid
The Tale of a Stroll
Toddle Song
Dougherty, George Byrd
I Wonder If You're Lonely
Douglas, Charles Noel
My Cosy Corner Girl
Downing, Anita Day
Get Behind the Girls Behind the Boys
Downing, Sam
All Those in Favor Say Aye
Downs, Billy
I'm Going Back to Carolina
Dreiser, Paul
see Dresser, Paul
Dresser, Paul
The Blue and the Gray: A Mother's Gift to Her Country
Calling to Her Boy Just Once Again
The Day That You Grew Colder
The Green above the Red
The Judgement Is at Hand
My Gal Sal
There's No North or South Today
The Town Where I Was Born
Way Down in Indiana
When I'm Away from You Dear
When You Come Back They'll Wonder Who the --- You Are
Your Mother Wants You Home Boy
Drewski, Hermann E.
Sister Susie's Sewing Shirts for Soldiers
Dreyer, Dave
I Love But You
I Never Knew How Much I Loved You Until There Was Somebody Else
Dreyfus, Max
He's the Whole Show Now
Drislane, Jack
After All That I've Been to You
Arrah-Wanna
Cupid's I.O.U.
The Good Old U.S.A.
Honey Love
I'm Awfully Glad I Met You
Just a Little Rocking Chair and You
Keep a Little Cozy Corner in Your Heart for Me
Keep on the Sunny Side
What the Brass Band Played
Won't You Be My Honey?
You Taught Me to Love You, Now Teach Me to Forget
Dubin, Al
My Yiddische Butterfly
O'Brien Is Tryin' to Learn to Talk Hawaiian
'Twas Only an Irishman's Dream
Dubin, Alexander
A Fool There Was
Dudley, S. H.
If I Ever Get Back to Cincinnati
Dugdale, H. Kirkus
Bill Taft for 1908
Dunbar, Paul Lawrence
Down De Lover's Lane
Joshua Fit de Battl' ob Jericho
Li'l Gal
Returned
Who Knows?

Dunham, Billy
Good-Bye Mister Caruso
Dunham, William Vaughan
Somewhere in France
Duque, L.
Maurice Mattchiche
Duval, Billy
Roaming Romeo
Dvorak, Anton
The Hour of Memory
Eardley-Wilmot, D.
Little Grey Home in the West
Earl, Mary
Beautiful Ohio
Dreamy Alabama
Enid Waltz
My Sweetheart Is Somewhere in France
Edelheit, Harry
If You Had All the World and Its Gold
Edmonds, Shepard N.
I'm Goin' to Live Anyhow 'Till I Die
Edwards, Ed
Cutey, Tell Me Who Tied Your Tie?
Edwards, Edw.
Honey, I Will Long for You
Edwards, Edward
I Am Longing for Tomorrow When I Think of Yesterday
Edwards, Gus
Alias Jimmy Valentine
All I Want in the Wide Wide World Is You
America Never Took Water and America Never Will
Betty, You're the One Best Bet
Bohemian Rag
By the Light of the Silvery Moon
Bye Bye Dear Old Broadway
Come On, Play Ball with Me
Come, Take a Skate with Me
The Comet and the Moon
Could You Be True to Eyes of Blue If You Looked into Eyes of Brown?
Don't Take a Girlie to Coney (You May Find a Nicer One There)
Don't You Think It's Time to Marry?
Farewell Killarney
Forget
The Girl Who Cares for Me
Good-Bye, Little Girl, Good-Bye
Good Luck and God Be with You, Laddie Boy
Have You Seen My Baby?
Have You Seen My Sweetheart in His Uniform of Blue?
He's Me Pal
I Can't Tell Why I Love You But I Do
I Just Can't Make My Eyes Behave
I Miss You in a Thousand Different Ways
I Want Something New to Play With
I Want to Spoon to the Tune of the Silvery Moon
If a Boy Like You Loved a Girl Like Me
If I Only Knew Just How I Stood with You
I'll Be with You When the Roses Bloom Again
I'll Get You
I'll Never Love Another Like I Love You
I'm After Madame Tettrazzini's Job
I'm Crazy to Go on the Stage
I'm the Man Who Makes the Money in the Mint
In My Merry Oldsmobile
In Zanzibar
Just 'Round the Corner from Broadway
Keep Your Golden Gate Wide Open
Kidland
Little Miss No-One from No-Where
Liza
Louisiana Louise

Lucy Anna Lou
Ma Mamselle Honee
Mamie, Don't You Feel Ashamie
Mister Monkey
Mister Pagliatch
The Modern Sandow Girl
"Mumms" the Word
My Charcoal Charmer
My Cousin Caruso
My Lonesome Little Louisiana Lady
My Yiddische Colleen
On a Beautiful Night with a Beautiful Girl
On the Grand Old Sand
On the Old See-Saw
Pan, Pan, Pan
Paree
The Peach That Tastes the Sweetest Hangs the Highest on the Tree
Please Mother, Buy Me a Baby
Rosa Rigoletto
Sally's Sunday Hat
School Days
Shadowland
Since My Margarette Become-a da Suffragette
Sunbonnet Sue
Sweet Kitty Bellairs
Tammany
That English Rag
Way Down Yonder in the Cornfield
When I Grow Up I'm Going to Be a Soldier
When the Whole World Has Gone Back on You
When Tommy Atkins Marries Dolly Gray
Won't You Be My Baby Boy?
Edwards, Julian
The Country Girl
The Dolly Varden Song
My Own United States
Sweet Thoughts of Home
Edwards, Leo
Bye and Bye
Here's to You, My Sparkling Wine
If You Want a Little Doggie, Whistle and I'll Come to You
In the Days of Girls and Boys
Mary Had a Little Lamb
The Message of the Rose
Nosie Rosie Posie
On a Spoony Moony Night
Pierrot and Pierrette
Pretty Kitty-San
We've Had a Lovely Time, So Long, Good Bye
When the Right Mr. Wright Comes Along
You're in Love
Egan, J. C.
That's the Kind of Baby for Me
Egan, Raymond
Ain't You Coming Back to Dixieland?
Mammy's Little Coal Black Rose
So Long Mother
Some Sunday Morning
Egan, Raymond B.
Just Around the Corner
That Lullaby of Long Ago
Egan, Richard
Good-bye Cabarabian Nights
Egan, Richard B.
Till We Meet Again
Eggert, Charles
Montezuma
Ehrlich, Sam
Bunker Hill
Oh! Frenchy
Elliott, Zo
There's a Long, Long Trail
Ellis, Edwin
Napoleon's Last Charge
Ellis, Harry A.
Mothers of America, You Have Done Your Share
Ellis, Havelock
Onward Brothers
Ellis, Melville
Although I Am a Soldier, I Prefer a Private Life

The Leader of the Frocks and Frills
When Love Is Young
Eltinge, Julian
Today's My Wedding Day
Emerson, Billy
Honey Will You Miss Me When I'm Gone?
Empey, Arthur Guy
Your Lips Are No Man's Land But Mine
Engelmann, H.
Melody of Love
Englander, Ludwig
Come and Take a Stroll with Me
The Gypsy's Wedding
I Want to Be Naughty Too
The Kodak Girl
A Lesson in Flirtation
The Monk of Malabar
Plain Mamie O'Hooley
Take Me Back to Herald Square
What Eve Said to Adam
A Woman's No Means 'Yes'
Erd, Daisy M. Pratt
The Ship of Uncle Sam
Erdman, Ernie
I'm Going Back to Carolina
Eschig, Mme. C.
The Rosary
Europe, James Reese
All of No Man's Land Is Ours
Blue Eyed Sue
The Castle Combination
Castle Half and Half
The Castle Walk
Good Night, Angeline
I Ain't Had No Lovin' in a Long Time
Mirandy
On Patrol in No Man's Land
Sweet Suzanne
Valse Marguerite
Evans, Everett J.
A Rose with a Broken Stem
Evans, George
Come, Take a Trip in My Air-Ship
Come to the Land of Bohemia
In the Good Old Summertime
It's Got to Be a Minstrel Show Tonight
Waltzing with the Girl You Love
Evans, Nellie H.
Votes for Women
Everard, George
It Ain't All Honey and It Ain't All Jam
It's All Right in the Summertime
The Next Horse I Ride On
Fagan, F. M.
Whippoorwill
Fairfax, Beatrice
The Merry Widow Waltz Song
Fairman, George
Bo - la - Bo
Way Down South
We've Got Another Washington and Wilson Is His Name
Fanchon
A Debutante's Engagement Book
Mack Sennett Girls
Farrell, Fred C.
Beautiful Bird of Paradise
In the Valley of Broken Hearts
It's the Man in the Sailor Suit
The Same Old Crowd
Farrell, Joseph C.
Let's All Go Up to Maud's
Farrell, William Henry
Who Will Be with You When I'm Far Away?
Farrington, Adele
War Baby's Lullaby
Fay
Kate Kearney
Fay, Frank
I Never Knew How Much I Loved You Until There Was Somebody Else
Fearis, J. S.
Beautiful Isle of Somewhere
Feist, Felix
Can't You See That I'm Lonely?
My Billy Boy
Feist, Felix F.
Baby Lamb

The Man Who Fights the Fire
On a Starry Night
Fentress, Will A.
Meet Me in Frisco and We'll Go Out to the Fair
Field, Thomas
Enid Waltz
Fields,
On the Mississippi
Fields, Arthur
The Aba Daba Honeymoon
It's a Long Way to Berlin But We'll Get There
Fields, Harry W.
Abie, the Sporty Kid
Finck, Herman
Crusader and Tommy
In the Shadows
Finden, Amy Woodforde
Kashmiri Song
Fink, Henry
The Curse of an Aching Heart
Fisher, Fred
And a Little Bit More
Any Little Girl That's a Nice Little Girl Is the Right Little Girl for Me
Billy Billy, Bounce Your Baby Doll
Come Josephine in My Flying Machine
Dancing the Blues Away
Dardanella
Happiness
I'm on My Way to Manadalay
Ireland Must Be Heaven for My Mother Came from There
Let Me See You Smile
Love Me, Make Me Love You Like I Never Loved Before
The Mountain Maid
My Brudda Sylvest'
Oh! You Chicken
Peg o' My Heart
Pull the Cork Out of Erin and Let the River Shannon Flow
There's a Broken Heart for Every Light on Broadway
There's a Little Bit of Bad in Every Good Little Girl
There's a Little Spark of Love Still Burning
They Go Wild, Simply Wild Over Me
Under the Matzos Tree
When I Get You Alone Tonight
Who Paid the Rent for Mrs. Rip Van Winkle?
You Can't Get Along with 'Em or Without 'Em, You've Got to Have Them, That's All
Fisher, Irving
Without You
Fitch, Clyde
It Rained a Mist
Fitz, Alb. H.
The Honeysuckle and the Bee
Fitzgibbon, Bert
I Get Dippy When I Do That Two-Step Dance
If They'd Only Fight the War with Wooden Soldiers
Just a Little Rocking Chair and You
Just Because He Couldn't Sing "Love Me and the World Is Mine"
Since My Mariutch Learned the Merry Widow Waltz
Fitzgibbon, Louis
I Get Dippy When I Do That Two-Step Dance
Flatow, Leon
Everybody Loves a Jazz Band
The Garden of Allah
It's a Long Way to Berlin But We'll Get There
Fleming, Carroll
People Who Live in Glass Houses Never Should Throw Any Stones
A Rose with a Broken Stem
Flemming, Carroll
Clidee-Oh
Fletcher, Archie
When Tony Goes Over the Top

Fletcher, Lucy
Sugar Blues
Flynn, Allan
Bing! Bang! Bing 'Em on the Rhine
Flynn, John H.
Come Around to Mamie's
Hoop-la, I'm Having the Time of My Life
Ida from Idaho
Yip-I-Addy-I-Ay
Fogerty, Frank
I Wonder Why Bill Bailey Don't Come Home
The Load That Father Carried
Folloy, Frank
Rob Roy McIntosh
Stop Your Tickling Jock!
Ford, Lena Guilbert
Keep the Home Fires Burning
Ford, Walter H.
Billet Doux
My Little Lady Bug
My Sunflower Sue
Francis, W. T.
Little Widow Brown
My Particular Friend
Romeo
Francis, William T.
In Dreamland, In Dreamland
The Leader of Vanity Fair
Frankel, Abe
Ragging the Chopsticks
Franklyn, Irene
I'm a Bringing Up the Family
The Pony Ballet Girl
Redhead
Franklyn, Malvin
Tumble in Love
Franklyn, Malvin M.
That La-La Melody
Fraser-Simson, H.
Dark Grows the Sky
Freeman, Harold
Beautiful Dreams of You
My Little Rambling Rose
Freeman, Harry
I'll Be with You Honey in the Springtime
French, Frank O.
Just for Tonight
Friedland, Anatol
Are You from Heaven?
Beautiful Roses
Hello Cupid, Send Me a Fellow
Lily of the Valley
My Sist' Tetrazzin'
Pig Latin Love
Friedman, Leo
Baby Mine
Good Night Is But Your Last Good Bye
I Think It Must Be Love
Let Me Call You Sweetheart
Meet Me Tonight in Dreamland
Two Congregations
Friml, Rudolf
Gianina Mia
Love Is Like a Firefly
Frisch, Billy
Let's Help the Irish Now
When a Feller Needs a Friend
When Tony Goes Over the Top
Frost, Harold G.
Sweet Hawaiian Moonlight, Tell Her of My Love
Frost, Jack
I Wonder What's the Matter wiz My Oo-la-la
My Fox Trot Girl
The Trench Trot
When It Comes to a Lovingless Day
Fulton, James M.
Tipperary
Furber, Douglas
The Bells of St. Mary's
Furst, William
It Rained a Mist
Furth, Seymour
Budweiser's a Friend of Mine
Do It the Right Way
Everything Is Rosy, Rosie

I'm Looking for the Man That Wrote "The Merry Widow Waltz"
It Was Me
Mister Sweeney, A Brainy Man
My Pocahontas
No Wedding Bells for Me
Poor Robinson Crusoe
A Singer Sang a Song
That Spanish Rag
When a Girl Leads the Band
When Tetrazzini Sings
Fysher, A. Nilson
Beautiful Eyes
Gabriel, Charles H.
Brighten the Corner Where You Are
Crusade Glory
His Eye Is on the Sparrow
Sail On!
Will the Circle Be Unbroken?
Gage, George W.
Sleepy-Headed Little Mary Green
Gale, George W.
Line Up for Bryan
Gallur, D'Amasus G.
Louie, Take Me to the Frisco Fair
Gardinier, Ed
Bashful Betsey Brown
Captain Baby Bunting of the Rocking Horse Brigade
Dreaming in the Trenches
I'll Be Your Rain-Beau
I'm a Lady
Mary Be Wary
My Fluff-a de Ruff
My Starlight Queen
No One Can Take Your Place
On a Spoony Moony Night
Queen of the Bungalow
When You Know You're Not Forgotten by the Girl You Can't Forget
Gardinier, Edward
He's the Whole Show Now
Linda, Look Out de' Windah
On the Old See-Saw
There's a Lot of Things You Never Learn at School
Upper Broadway After Dark
Gardner, William H.
Can't Yo' Hear Me Callin', Caroline
Garrett, Lloyd
Dallas Blues
Gartner, Clarence G.
Love Is Mine
Garton, Ted
My Belgian Rose
Gaskill, Clarence
I Love You Just the Same, Sweet Adeline
Gaskill, Clarence L.
That Million Dollar Melody
Gaston, Billy
Come Dance with Me
Gee! But This Is a Lonely Town
I Can't Get Enough of Your Love
My Marguerite
When the Band Plays "Indiana," Then I'm Humming "Home Sweet Home"
Gay, Byron
O
Sand Dunes
Shoot Me Back to California Land
A Soldier's Dream
The Vamp
Geary, T. Mayo
The Man with the Ladder and the Hose
Your Dad Gave His Life for His Country
Gebest, Charles J.
I Want to Look Like Lillian Russell
Geehl, Henry E.
For You Alone
Gerard, Richard H.
You're the Flower of My Heart, Sweet Adeline
Gerber, Alex
Give Me the Sultan's Harem

Keep Your Eye on the Girlie You Love
Some Girls Do and Some Girls Don't
What Good Is Alimony on a Lonesome Night
German, Edward
A Sprig of Rosemarie
Gershovitz, Jacob
see Gershwin, George
Gershwin, George
Come to the Moon
From Now On
I Was So Young, You Were So Beautiful
Somehow It Seldom Comes True
Something about Love
Swanee
Tee-Oodle-Um-Bam-Bo
There's More to the Kiss than the X-X-X
You-oo Just You
Getsey, George
My Honey's Back
Gibson, Lillian
Lillies Mean You to Me
Gideon, Melville
Alone with You
Altogether Too Fond of You
Come and Dance with Me
When My Sist' Tetrazin' Met My Cousin Carus'
Gideon, Melville J.
And Other Things
Angelique
Mammy's Shufflin' Dance
Take Me 'Round in a Taxicab
Gifford
When It's Apple Blossom Time in Normandy
Gifford, Harry
Come Along My Mandy
Gilbert, Henry F.
Pirate Song
Gilbert, Jean
All the World Loves a Lover
Gilbert, L. Wolfe
Are You from Heaven?
Let the Flag Fly!
Lily of the Valley
Little Rag Baby Doll
Mammy's Shufflin' Dance
My Hawaiian Sunrise
Oh, What a Night
Pig Latin Love
Ragging the Baby to Sleep
Ramona
She's Dancing Her Heart Away
Take Me to That Swanee Shore
Waiting for the Robert E. Lee
Gilbert, Louis W.
Beautiful Eyes
Gillespie, Arthur
Absence Makes the Heart Grow Fonder
Darling
I Want a Man Made to Order for Me
The Last Rose of Summer Is the Sweetest Song of All
Mother Has Got the Habit Now
Sumurun
Susan, Dear Sue
Gillespie, Henry A.
Hiram Green, Good-Bye
Gillespie, Marian
When You Look in the Heart of a Rose
Gilman, Charlotte Perkins
Another Star
Woman's Right Is Woman's Duty
Gilroy, John
I Sing a Little Tenor
Instrumental Man
John Would Never Do That
Mozart Lincoln
Pansy of the Dell
Glenney, T. H.
The Wearing of the Green
Glogau, Jack
At the Yiddish Wedding Jubilee
Honey, You Were Made for Me
On the Shores of Italy
Wake Up America
Godwin, J. Cheever
The Monk of Malabar

Goetz, Coleman
Everybody Loves a Jazz Band
Homeward Bound
Goetz, E. Ray
Alexander's Bag-Pipe Band
Don't Take Your Beau to the Seashore
Everything Looks Rosy and Bright
For Me and My Gal
Havana
He Goes to Church on Sunday
How'd You Like to Float Me
If You Knew What I Know about Men
I'm Simply Crazy over You
I'm the Only Mother That You Ever Knew
In the Shadows
I've Got the Blues for Home Sweet Home
Lead Me to That Beautiful Band
My Croony Melody
Oh! You Chicken
Play That Fandango Rag
The Ragtime College Girl
Take Me Back to the Garden of Love
That Dreamy Barcarole Tune
That's How He Met the Girl
When John McCormack Sings a Song
When Love Was Young
When the Right Little Girl Comes Along
When You Hear Love's "Hello"
Yaaka Hula Hickey Dula
You've Got to Do That Salome Dance
Goetz, Ray
He Played It on His Fid, Fid, Fiddle-dee-dee
My Daddy Long-Legs
Goetzl, Anselm
What Good Is Alimony on a Lonesome Night
Golby, Philip
see Goldberg, Phil
Gold, Joe
Give Me a Syncopated Tune
Ze Yankee Boys Have Made a Wild French Baby Out of Me
Goldberg, Dora
see Bayes, Nora
Goldberg, "Rube"
Life, Let Me Live My Life for You
Golden, John
Advertising
Fall in for Your Motherland
Good Bye Girls I'm Through
I Can Dance with Everybody But My Wife
My Yankee Doodle Girl
Oh, You Candy Kid
Poor Butterfly
Golden, John L.
French Fandango
When There's No Light at All
Goldstein, Nat
Get Behind the Girls Behind the Boys
Gono, Don J.
On the Exposition Zone
Goodman, Alfred
Linger Longer Letty
Goodwin, J. Cheever
The Duchess of Central Park
Kitty
Rainbows Follow After Rain
The Troubles of Reuben and the Maid
When Reuben Comes to Town
Goodwin, Joe
Baby Shoes
Billy
Breeze, Blow My Baby Back to Me
I'm Crazy 'bout the Turkey Trot
Liberty Bell, It's Time to Ring Again
Melinda's Wedding Day
My Croony Melody
Naughty! Naughty! Naughty!
One Day in June
The Ragtime Dream
That's How I Need You

There's a Light That's Burning in the Window of the Little House upon the Hill
They're Wearing 'Em Higher in Hawaii
When I Get You Alone Tonight
When Mother Plays a Rag on the Sewing Machine
When You Play in the Game of Love
Goodwin, Walter
That Wonderful Mother of Mine
Gordon, Anna A.
For God and Home and Native Land
We Are Coming
Gottler, Archie
I Hate to Lose You
I'm Gonna Make Hay While the Sun Shines in Virginia
The Letter That Never Reached Home
Lila
The More I See of Hawaii, the Better I Like New York
Ragging the Chopsticks
Rolling Stones All Come Rolling Home Again
Those Charlie Chaplin Feet
When the Flowers Bloom on No-Man's Land, What a Wonderful Day That Will Be
Would You Rather Be a Colonel with an Eagle on Your Shoulder...
Gottschalk, L. F.
A Romance of Happy Valley
Gottschalk, Louis F.
In Florida
Lady Bountiful
Gould, William
He's the Whole Show Now
Graff, George, Jr.
I'll Change the Shadows to Sunshine
Let Us Have Peace
Patria
Wake Up America
When Irish Eyes Are Smiling
Grafton, Gerald
Fou the Noo
I Love a Lassie
Graham, Harry
Dark Grows the Sky
Graham, Howard
When the Harvest Days Are Over, Jessie, Dear
Graham, Roger
I Ain't Got Nobody Much and Nobody Cares for Me
Grant, Bert
Arrah Go On, I'm Gonna Go Back to Oregon
If I Knock the 'L' Out of Kelly, It Still Would Be Kelly to Me
Let Bygones Be Bygones and Let Us Be Sweethearts Again
Love Me at Twilight
My Daddy Long-Legs
Romany
When the Angelus Is Ringing
When Tony LaBoard Played the Barber-Shop Chord
Grant, Richard
Allus' the Same in Dixie
As the Sunflower Turns to the Sun
Granville, Bernard
It Was Just a Song at Twilight That Made Me Come Back to You
Grapewin, Charley
Pots and Pans
Gray, Roger
I Thought My Troubles Were Over, But They'd Scarce Begun
Gray, Thomas J.
Any Little Girl That's a Nice Little Girl Is the Right Little Girl for Me
If I Should Die Before I Wake, How Will I Know I'm Dead?
I'm Getting Kind of Lonesome for My Old Kentucky Pal
The Little Church around the Corner
The Marquand Glide

No One Knows Where the Old Man Goes
That English Rag
Underneath the Tango Moon
Green, Bert
The Pony Ballet Girl
Redhead
Green, Bud
And That Ain't All
Green, Eddie
A Good Man Is Hard to Find
Green, J. Ed.
Kinky
Greenbank, Percy
The Language of the Flowers
The Ping Pong Song
Greenberg, Abner
He Was Always Fooling Around
Greene, Burt
I'm a Bringing Up the Family
Greville, Eden E.
The Dawn of a Tomorrow
Grey, Clifford
Crusader and Tommy
If You Were the Only Girl in the World
Griffith, D. W.
White Blossoms
Grossman, Bernard
That Dreamy Barcarole Tune
Grossman, Bernie
Let's Help the Irish Now
The Letter That Never Reached Home
Linger Longer Letty
Say a Prayer for the Boys Out There
When a Feller Needs a Friend
When Uncle Joe Steps into France
You Didn't Want Me When You Had Me So Why Do You Want Me Now?
Grossmith, George, Jr.
Oh, So Gently
Gruber, E. L.
The United States Field Artillery March
Grumble, Alfred
There's a Lump of Sugar Down in Dixie
Gumble, Al.
Somebody's Waiting for You
Gumble, Albert
Alexander's Band Is Back in Dixieland
And He Blames My Dreamy Eyes
Call Me in the Morning
The Chanticleer Rag
Irish Fluffy Ruffles
Kewpie Doll
Little Nemo and His Bear
On a Good Old Time Sleigh Ride
Rebecca of Sunnybrook Farm
Southern Gals
You'll Do the Same Thing Over Again
You're Never to Old to Love
Gumm, Wilbur
That's What the Daisy Said
Gumm, Wilbur U.
I'm Getting Sleepy
Gutman, Arthur H.
Darling
Habershon, Ada R.
Will the Circle Be Unbroken?
Haenschen, Gustav
The Maurice Glide
Hagen, J. M.
Step into Line for Taft
Hager, Clyde
That Wonderful Mother of Mine
Hain, Joseph L.
McKinley, Our Hero, Now at Rest
Hall, Gus
Johnson Rag
Hall, W. W.
Oh! Take Me to My Mamma Dear
Poor Barney Mulligan
Hamer, J. W.
I'm Looking for a Dear Old Lady
That Hypnotizing Strain
Hamill, F. J.
The Humpty-Dumpty Kid
Hamlon, Bert
Six Times Six Is Thirty-Six

Hammerstein, Arthur
It Gets Them All
Hammerstein, Oscar
Maggie McDonahue
Hammerstein, Oscar, I
Cecelia and Amelia
Hancock, "Hank"
The War in Snider's Grocery Store
Handy, W. C.
Baby Seals Blues
Beale Street Blues
The Hesitating Blues
Joe Turner Blues
Mister Crump Blues
Ole Miss
St. Louis Blues
Yellow Dog Blues
Handy, Will C.
Oh! Didn't He Ramble
Hanegan, Ernest
The Girl with the Baby Stare
Hanley, James F.
Breeze, Blow My Baby Back to Me
The Fatal Ring
Indiana
The Modern Maiden's Prayer
Oh! Papa, Oh! Papa, Won't You Be a Pretty Papa to Me?
One Day in June
The Ragtime Volunteers Are Off to War
Rose of Washington Square
Hanlon, Bert
Huckleberry Pie
M-i-s-s-i-s-s-i-p-p-i
Harbach, Otto
see Hauerbach, Otto
Harford, Harold
I Hear You Calling Me
Hargreaves, William
The Seaside Sultan
Harper, J. D.
She Is Ma Daisy
Harper, Neal
It's Good Enough for Me
Harriman, Alfred
That's the Kind of Baby for Me
Harrington, J. P.
Sadie
Harrington, John P.
Be Good! If You Can't Be Good Be Careful
I've Told His Missus All about Him
Salome
Harris, Charles K.
Always in the Way
Belle of the Ball
Do You Think You Could Learn to Love Me?
Don't You Wish You Were Back Home Again?
Girl of My Dreams
Hello Central, Give Me Heaven
I'm Wearing My Heart Away for You
In the Good Old-Fashioned Way
In the Hills of Old Carolina
I've a Longing in My Heart for You, Louise
Just Next Door
The Last Farewell
Must We Say Good Bye Forever, Nellie Dear?
My Virginian
The Tie That Binds
When It Strikes Home
Harris, Clifford
The Story of a Clothes Line
Harris, F. Clifford
Meet Me at Twilight
Harris, Val
Texas Tommy Swing
Harris, Will J.
The Shorter They Wear 'Em the Longer They Look
When My Bridget Malone Jiggle-Wiggles Salome
Harrison, Charles William
The Phonograph March
Harrison, Louis
A Love-Lorn Lily
Hart, Charles
Down Among the Sugar-Cane
You're Just Too Sweet to Live

Hart, Joseph
The Bathing Lesson
Hart, Lorenz
Any Old Place with You
Hart, Will
When Yankee Doodle Learns to "Parlez-Vous Francaise?"
Hart, Will J.
Pollyanna
Harvey, Clarence
Won't You Be My Baby Boy?
Hauerbach, Otto
Cuddle Up a Little Closer, Lovey Mine
Every Little Movement
Gianina Mia
Love Is Like a Firefly
Havez, Jean C.
Borrow from Me
Bumble Bee
The Darktown Poker Club
Everybody Works But Father
If I Only Knew Just How I Stood with You
I'll Lend You Everything I've Got Except My Wife
I'm Cured
The Land of Nicotine
My Twilight Queen
Shovelin' Coal
When I Grow Up I'm Going to Be a Soldier
You're on the Right Road Sister But You're Goin' the Wrong Way
Hawley, Annie Andros
Der Faderland for Mine
Gay Butterfly
Hawley, Antoinette A.
Crusade Glory
Hayes, Kitty
see Hoffmann, Gertrude
Heard, James
Altogether Too Fond of You
Heartz, H. L.
Love Is Elusive
Heath, Bobbie
My Pony Boy
Heath, Bobby
Becky Do the Bombashay
Just One Day
On the Old Front Porch
Heath, E. P.
Love's Own Sweet Song
Heelan, Will
Be Satisfied with What You Have, Let Well Enough Alone
A Bit o' Blarney
A Singer Sang a Song
Under the Mistletoe Bough
When I Do the Highland Fling
Heelan, Will A.
All Is Fair in Love and War
The Boys in the Gallery for Mine
Do It the Right Way
Her Boy in the Rank and File
In the House of Too Much Trouble
Irish Fluffy Ruffles
Just What the Good Book Taught
A Little Empty Nest
The Message of the Rose
Mister Sweeney, A Brainy Man
No Wedding Bells for Me
That Spanish Rag
There Are Two Sides to a Story
When a Girl Leads the Band
Hein, Silvio
The Deedle-Dum-Dee
Don't Be What You Ain't
Her Boy in the Rank and File
He's a Cousin of Mine
I Want to Be a Drummer in the Band
If Yankee Doodle Hadn't Come to Town
Little One, Good Bye
The Maurice Tango
Old Reliable Jokes
Pawnee
When You're All Dressed Up and No Place to Go
Heinzman, John
Kiss All the Girls for Me
Heiser, L. W.
Dreaming

Heisler, Harry
The Royal Will
Held, Anna
The Girl with the Eyes and the Golden Hair
It's Delightful to Be Married
Oh, I Want to Be Good But My Eyes Won't Let Me
Helf, J. Fred
Ain't You Coming Back to Old New Hampshire, Molly?
Be Satisfied with What You Have, Let Well Enough Alone
The Bee That Gets the Honey Doesn't Hang Around the Hive
A Bit o' Blarney
The Boys in the Gallery for Mine
Captain Baby Bunting of the Rocking Horse Brigade
Colleen Bawn
Don't Go in the Lion's Cage Tonight, Mother
Du Barry, the Doll of the World
Feed the Kitty
Go Easy Mabel
Here's to Our Absent Brothers
If You Can't Be a Bell-Cow, Fall in Behind
I'll Be Waiting in the Gloaming, Sweet Genevieve
I'll Be Your Rain-Beau
I'm Tying the Leaves So They Won't Come Down
In the House of Too Much Trouble
Just What the Good Book Taught
A Little Empty Nest
Lord Have Mercy on a Married Man
Make a Noise Like a Hoop and Roll Away
'Neath the Old Acorn Tree, Sweet Estelle
No One Can Take Your Place
Please Leave the Door Ajar
Teddy Da Roose
There Are Two Sides to a Story
Tipperary
Under the Mistletoe Bough
The Waltz Must Change to a March, Marie
When I Do the Highland Fling
When the Whipporwill Sings Marguerite
When You Know You're Not Forgotten by the Girl You Can't Forget
Henley, W. E.
Bring Her Again to Me
Henry, S. R.
Indianola
I've Got the Time, I've Got the Place, But It's Hard to Find the Girl
Red Domino
Take a Trip Down to Luna with Me
When It's Moonlight on the Prairie
Herbert, Joseph
The "A la Mode" Girl
Castles in the Air
Herbert, Victor
Ah, Sweet Mystery of Life
Be Kind to Poor Pierrot
Beatrice Barefacts
The Friars
I Might Be Your "Once in a While"
I Want What I Want When I Want It
I'm Falling in Love with Some One
In the Folds of the Starry Flag
It Never, Never Can Be Love
Italian Street Song
Jack O'Lantern Girl
Kiss Me Again
March of the Toys
Molly
Naughty Marietta
'Neath the Southern Moon
Out of His Heart He Builds a Home
The Streets of New York
The Time and the Place and the Girl
Toyland
Tramp, Tramp, Tramp

Where the Fairest Flowers Are Blooming
Won't You Be My Valentine?
Herscher, Louis
There Are Just Two I's in Dixie
Hess, Cliff
Blue Eyed Blond Haired Heart Breaking Baby Doll
Homesickness Blues
Huckleberry Finn
Regretful Blues
The Wedding of the Shimmie and Jazz
When Alexander Takes His Rag Time Band to France
Hickman, Art
Dry Your Tears
Rose Room
Hicks, E. C.
Hooray for a Bryan to Lead Us
Hill, J. J.
Molasses Candy
Hill, J. Leubrie
At the Ball, That's All
The Coster's Glide
I Love My Babe, My Baby Loves Me
Loving Moon
My Friend from Kentucky
Rock Me in the Cradle of Love
Hill, Joe
Workers of the World Awaken!
Hill, May
You Can Have It, I Don't Want It
Hinkley, Irving
I Love My Steady, But I'm Crazy for My Once-in-a-While
Hirsch, Louis
Come and Dance with Me
The Land of Nicotine
Hirsch, Louis A.
Angelique
The Bacchanal Rag
The Gaby Glide
I Am So Particular
My Sumurun Girl
My Twilight Queen
The Wedding Glide
When My Sist' Tetrazin' Met My Cousin Carus'
When You Hear Love's "Hello"
You've Got to Do That Salome Dance
Hirschfield, Max
I Love You Dolly
Hite, Mabel
I Wonder If You Love Me
Hobart, George V.
Alma, Where Do You Live?
Billet Doux
By the Old Oak Tree
By the Sycamore Tree
Come and Take a Stroll with Me
Don't Be What You Ain't
Hannah Dooley, Pride of Ballyhooley
Hello Honey
I Love My Shirt Waist Best
I Love You Dolly
The Irish Girl I Love
The Kodak Girl
A Love-Lorn Lily
My Irish Maid
My Pajama Beauty
O Mona San
Pretty Polly!
Sallie, Mah Hot Tamale
Take Me Back to Herald Square
When Charlie Plays the Slide Trombone in the Silver Cornet Band
Hoffman, Aaron S.
My Palm Leaf Maid
Pinky Panky Poo
Pretty Kitty-San
Hoffmann, Gertrude
Brother Masons
G.O.P.
The Heaven Born Banner
In Washington
Kiss, Kiss, Kiss, If You Want to Learn to Kiss
On San Francisco Bay
Percy
Hoffmann, Max
American Beauty

Be My Teddy Bear
By the Old Oak Tree
By the Sycamore Tree
Emalyne, My Pretty Valentine
The Gertrude Hoffmann Glide
Hannah Dooley, Pride of Ballyhooley
I Thought I Wanted Opera
The Irish Girl I Love
M-O-N-E-Y Spells Money
My Bird of Paradise
My Dixie Land Daisy
My Eulah Eulah, My Indian Maid
My Irish Maid
My Little Japaneesee
My Pretty Zulu Lu
Over the Moonlit Sea
Pajama Polly
Paree's a Branch of Broadway
A Parisian Model
Pretty Polly!
Sunrise at the Zoo
Walk, Walk, Walk

Hogan, Ernest
- He May Get Over It But He'll Never Look the Same
- I Just Can't Keep My Eyes Off You
- Is Everybody Happy?
- The Phrenologist Coon

Holbrook, Florence
- He's a Fan, Fan, Fan

Hollaender, Victor
- see also Hollander, Victor

Hollander, Joe
- I'm Getting Sleepy

Hollander, Victor
- Swing Me High, Swing Me Low

Homer, James R.
- Mother's Hymn to Me

Hood, Basil
- The Little Wooden Soldier
- A Sprig of Rosemarie

Hope, Lawrence
- Kashmiri Song

Horsman, Edward
- Bird of the Wilderness

Horwitz, Charles
- In Naples Fair
- Moriarty
- She's a Princess Just the Same
- Wait
- When Sousa Leads the Band

Hoschna, Karl
- Cuddle Up a Little Closer, Lovey Mine
- Every Little Movement
- The Yama Yama Man

Hough, Will M.
- Be Sweet to Me, Kid
- Blow the Smoke Away
- Honeymoon
- I Wonder Who's Kissing Her Now
- The Umpire Is a Most Unhappy Man
- When You First Kiss the Last Girl You Love

Howard, Great
- Uncle Sammy's at Bat

Howard, Joseph E.
- Be Sweet to Me, Kid
- Blow the Smoke Away
- Central, Give Me Back My Dime
- Good Bye, My Lady Love
- Honey Will You Miss Me When I'm Gone?
- Honeymoon
- I Wonder Who's Kissing Her Now
- Love Me All the Time
- Somewhere in France Is the Lily
- The Umpire Is a Most Unhappy Man
- What's the Use of Dreaming
- When You First Kiss the Last Girl You Love

Howard, Richard
- I've Lost You So Why Should I Care?

Howard, Stephen
- Two Eyes of Brown

Hoyt, Harry
- If Anybody Wants to Meet a Jonah, Shake Hands with Me
- Meet Me Down at the Corner

Hubbell, Raymond
Beautiful Beautiful Girl
The Girl of the Great Divide
Hello Honey
I Knew at First Sight That I Loved You
If a Table at Rector's Could Talk
A Kiss for Each Day of the Week
The Ladder of Roses
Little Mary Gardeners
My Little Hindoo Belle
Paint Me a Picture of Mama
Poor Butterfly
Pretty Maid Adelaide
The Queen of the Track
The Star and the Flower
Huffman, Dave
The Florida Blues
Huntingdon, E. S. S.
I'm Tying the Leaves So They Won't Come Down
Hutchinson, Edward
Sammy
Hyams, John
My Little Star, I'm Looking Up to You
Hyde, Harlow
After You, My Dear Alphonse
Out Where the Breakers Roar
When the Winds O'er the Sea Blow a Gale
Ince, Thomas H.
Peace Song
Ingersoll, Edwards P.
Hymn to Liberty
Ingraham, Herbert
All That I Ask of You Is Love
Amo
Because I'm Married Now
Don't Wake Me Up I Am Dreaming
I Love My Husband But Oh You Henry
Roses Bring Dreams of You
When I Dream in the Gloaming of You
Won't You Waltz 'Home Sweet Home' with Me for Old Times Sake?
You Are the Ideal of My Dreams
Irwin, May
'Taint No Use in Lovin' That Way
Jackson, Arthur
The Best of Everything
Take Me to the Midnight Cake-walk Ball
Jackson, Arthur J.
But - After the Ball Was Over Then He Made Up for Lost Time
The Fatal Ring
From Now On
If She Means What I Think She Means
It Was Just a Song at Twilight That Made Me Come Back to You
Somehow It Seldom Comes True
Tee-Oodle-Um-Bam-Bo
Jackson, Tony
Pretty Baby
Jacobi, Victor
On Miami Shore
On the Banks of the Bronx
Jacobs-Bond, Carrie
A Hundred Years from Now
I Love You Truly
Just a-Wearying for You
A Little Bit o' Honey
A Perfect Day
James, Billy
I'm Saving Up Coupons
Janis, Elsie
Anti-Rag Time Girl
I Never Knew
I'd Rather Love What I Cannot Have Than Have What I Cannot Love
The Jazz Band
A Little Love But Not for Me
A Regular Girl
Some Sort of Somebody

Jansen, Ben
He Laid Away a Suit of Gray to Wear the Union Blue
Jardon, Dolly
Build Your Nest Away Down in My Heart
Violette
Jardon, Dorothy
see also Jardon, Dolly
Arrah-Arabia
Lotus San: A Japanese Romance
Jefferson, N. H.
I Have Shed My Last Tears for You
Jentes, Harry
I Don't Want to Get Well
Some Girls Do and Some Girls Don't
Jerome, Ben
Blooming Lize
Jerome, Ben M.
Ain't It Tough to Be So Absent-Minded?
The Girl Who Loves the Races
The Hornpipe Rag
Katy Did
Love in an Orchard
Mozart Lincoln
Sister Ann
Those Things Cannot Be Explained
Watch Me To-night in the Torchlight Parade
What's the Matter with Uncle Sam?
Your Eyes Say No But Your Lips Say Yes!
Jerome, Benjamin M.
The Dusky Salome
Jerome, M. K.
Just a Baby's Prayer at Twilight to Her Daddy Over There
Poor Little Butterfly Is a Fly Girl Now
Jerome, William
Ain't You Got Nothing to Say?
And the Green Grass Grew All Around
Any Old Time at All
Back to the Woods
Bedelia
Beneath the Moon
Chinatown, My Chinatown
Don't Go in the Water, Daughter
Don't Put Me Off at Buffalo Any More
Down in the Subway
Dreamy Fandango Tune
Eighth Avenue
Every Day Will Be Sunday When the Town Goes Dry
Everybody's Ragtime Crazy
The Flower Garden Ball
For You
The Gambling Man
The Ghost That Never Walked
Good Bye Mister Ragtime
Good-Bye, Sweet Old Manhattan Isle
Hamlet Was a Melancholy Dane
Handle me with Care
He Was a Sailor
He Was Always Fooling Around
Her Eyes of Irish Blue
Honey Love Me All the Time
I Wonder Why Bill Bailey Don't Come Home
I'm a Member of the Midnight Crew
I'm a Poor Unhappy Maid
I'm on My Way to Reno
I'm Simply Crazy over You
I'm Tired
I'm Unlucky
I've Got the Blues for Home Sweet Home
Jazz Baby
Julie
Just a Tender Spot for Father Dear
Just Try to Picture Me Back Home in Tennessee
The Kellerman Girlie
Let's Make Love among the Roses
Love Days

Love Me at Twilight
The Man Who Plays the Tambourine
McGinnis
Meet Me in Rose Time Rosie
Mister Dooley
Mother Hasn't Spoken to Father Since
My Gypsy Queen
My Hula Lula Girl
My Irish Daisy
My Irish Gibson Girl
My Irish Indian
My Irish Molly O
My Irish Rose
My Lady Hottentot
My Operatic Samson
My Sweet
My Teddy Girl
None of Them's Got Anything on Me
Nursery Rhymes
On an Automobile Honeymoon
Percy
Ring-Ting-a-Ling
Rip van Winkle Was a Lucky Man
Rosie Rosinsky
Row Row Row
Since Little Dolly Dimples Made a Hit
Since Sister Nell Heard Paderewski Play
Snap Your Fingers and Away You Go
String a Ring of Roses 'Round Your Rosie
The Villain Still Pursued Her
When John McCormack Sings a Song
When Mr. Shakespeare Comes to Town
When Sousa Leads the Band
Where the Red Red Roses Grow
The White Wash Man
You Can't Get Away from It
You're Never to Old to Love

Jessel, George
And He'd Say Oo-la-la! Wee-Wee!
Oh, How I Laugh When I Think How I Cried about You

Johns, Al
Bible Stories

Johnson, Arnold
O

Johnson, Billy
Barnyard Rag
The Moon Has His Eyes on You

Johnson, Billy B.
All In Down and Out
Good-Bye, I'll See You Some More
Yo' Eyes Are Open, But Yo' Sound Asleep

Johnson, Charles E.
Dill Pickles Rag

Johnson, Charles L.
Iola

Johnson, George W.
When You and I Were Young, Maggie

Johnson, Howard
Bring Back My Daddy to Me
Dancing the Blues Away
Homeward Bound
I Called You My Sweetheart
I Don't Want to Get Well
In the Land of Wedding Bells
Ireland Must Be Heaven for My Mother Came from There
Just as Washington Crossed the Delaware, So Will Pershing Cross the Rhine
Keep Your Eye on the Girlie You Love
M-O-T-H-E-R
The Navy Took Them Over and the Navy Will Bring Them Back
Rockaway
Some Girls Do and Some Girls Don't
There's a Broken Heart for Every Light on Broadway
The Wedding of the Shimmie and Jazz
What Do You Want to Make Those Eyes at Me For?
Where Do We Go from Here?

Johnson, J. Rosamond
The Animals' Convention
As Long as the World Goes Around
The Awakening
Big Indian Chief
The Big Red Shawl
Can You Forget
Come Out, Dinah, on the Green
The Coster's Glide
De Little Pickaninny's Gone to Sleep
Don't Butt In
Down in Mulberry Bend
Fishing
Flowers of Dixieland
I Ain't Gwin ter Work No Mo'
I Can't Think of Nothing in the Wide, Wide World But You
I Love My Babe, My Baby Loves Me
I Told My Love to the Roses
I'll Keep a Warm Spot in My Heart for You
I've Got Troubles of My Own
I've Lost My Teddy Bear
Lazy Moon
Lift Every Voice and Sing
Li'l Gal
Lindy
Lovely Daughter of Allah
Loving Moon
Magdaline, My Southern Queen
The Maiden with the Dreamy Eyes
Marie Cahill's Congo Love Song
Morning, Noon, and Night
My Castle on the Nile
Nobody's Lookin' But de Owl and de Moon
O, Southland
The Old Flag Never Touched the Ground
On Lalawana's Shore
The Pussy and the Bow-Wow
Roll Dem Cotton Balls
Sambo and Dinah
Since You Went Away
Strolling Along the Beach
Sweetest Gal in Town
Take Me in Your Arms and Say You Love Me
Tell Me Dusky Maiden
Two Eyes
When the Moon Comes Peeping Over the Hill
Why Don't the Band Play?
Johnson, James Weldon
The Animals' Convention
The Awakening
Can You Forget
Come Out, Dinah, on the Green
The Conjure Man
De Little Pickaninny's Gone to Sleep
Don't Butt In
Down in Mulberry Bend
Father's Got a Job
Fishing
Gimme de Leavins'
I Ain't Gwin ter Work No Mo'
I'll Keep a Warm Spot in My Heart for You
I've Got Troubles of My Own
The Katy-Did, the Cricket and the Frog
Lift Every Voice and Sing
Lindy
Lovely Daughter of Allah
Magdaline, My Southern Queen
The Maid of Timbucktoo
The Maiden with the Dreamy Eyes
Marie Cahill's Congo Love Song
Mexico
Morning, Noon, and Night
My Angemima Green
My Castle on the Nile
Nobody's Lookin' But de Owl and de Moon
O, Southland
The Old Flag Never Touched the Ground
On Lalawana's Shore
The Pussy and the Bow-Wow
Roll Dem Cotton Balls
Sambo and Dinah
Save It for Me

Since You Went Away
Strolling Along the Beach
Tell Me Dusky Maiden
Two Eyes
Why Don't the Band Play?
Johnson, Lee
Hearts of the World
Ramona
When That Vampire Rolled Her Vampy Eyes at Me
Johnson, Philander
Somewhere in France Is the Lily
Jolson, Al
By the Honeysuckle Vine
Ev'ry Morning She Makes Me Late
I Gave Her That
I Love the Heart of Dixie
I'll Say She Does
My Sumurun Girl
'N' Everything
On the Road to Calais
Tell That to the Marines!
You Ain't Heard Nothing Yet
Jones, Bobby
Everybody Loves a Chicken
The Raffles Dance
Jones, Earle C.
The Girl with the Big Toy Bear
I Wonder Where My Lovin' Man Has Gone
The Island of Roses and Love
Love Me Like I Want to Be Loved
My Mississippi Missus Misses Me
That Old Girl of Mine
The Vampire
Jones, Harold
The Band Played "Nearer My God to Thee" as the Ship Went Down
Jones, Stephen O.
I Thought My Troubles Were Over, But They'd Scarce Begun
Jonnes, Harry
A Picture without a Frame
Jordan, Joe
Sweetie Dear
That Teasin' Rag
Jordon, Joe
Happiness
Lovie Joe
Jordon, Julian
I Love But One, I Love But You
Jose, R. J.
I Went to See Them March Away
May Sweet May
When Love Was Young
Joyce, Archibald
Aloma
Dreaming
A Vision of Salome
Kaai, Ernest K.
Across the Sea
Kahn, Gus
Everybody Rag with Me
Ev'ry Morning She Makes Me Late
For Your Boy and My Boy
Go Slow Joe
The Good Ship Mary Ann
I Wish I Had a Girl
I'll Say She Does
A Little Bit of Irish
Memories
My Baby Talking Girl
My Isle of Golden Dreams
'N' Everything
On the Road to Home Sweet Home
Pretty Baby
Sailin' Away on the Henry Clay
So Long Mother
Some Sunday Morning
That Lullaby of Long Ago
Venetian Moon
What Are You Going to Do to Help the Boys?
What's the Use of Moonlight When There's No One 'Round to Love?
You Ain't Heard Nothing Yet
Your Eyes Have Told Me So
You're a Great Big Lonesome Baby
You're in Style When You're Wearing a Smile
Kaihan, Maewa
Now Is the Hour
Kalama, S.
One - Two - Three - Four

Kalisz, Armand
Mon Amour
Kalman, Emmerich
Love's Own Sweet Song
Will You Forget?
Kalmar, Bert
All the Quakers Are Shoulder Shakers Down in Quaker Town
Eight Little Letters Make Three Little Words
Hello Wisconsin, Won't You Find My Yonnie Yonson
If You Can't Get a Girl in the Summertime, You'll Never Get a Girl at All
In the Land of Harmony
I've Been Floating Down the Old Green River
The More I See of Hawaii, the Better I Like New York
Movin' Man Don't Take My Baby Grand
Oh! What a Pal Was Mary
Over the Garden Wall
A Regular Girl
Take Me to that Land of Jazz
Take Your Girlie to the Movies If You Can't Make Love at Home
They Don't Hesitate Any More
Where Did You Get That Girl?
Kaufman, Mel B.
Yah-De-Dah
Kavanaugh, J. J.
That Tariff War
Keating, Thomas J.
I'd Lay Down My Life for You
Keiser, Robert A.
When Patti Sang "Home Sweet Home"
Keisser, S. E.
I Went to See Them March Away
Keith, Lester W.
Come Over on My Veranda
Kellette, John William
I'm Forever Blowing Bubbles
Kelley, Tom
I'm Looking for a Dear Old Lady
Kelly, Tom
Baltimore Rag
I Wonder If You Love Me
Kemble, John
Come Over on My Veranda
Kempner, David
Late Hours
Kenbrovin, Jean
I'm Forever Blowing Bubbles
Kendal, A. B.
That's the Reason Noo I Wear a Kilt
Kendall, Marguerite
He's Coming Home on the 8 O'Clock Train
Kendis, James
Angel Eyes
Billy
Havana
He Likes Their Jukelele
I Know What It Means to Be Lonesome
If I Had My Way
We're Going to Hang the Kaiser under the Linden Tree
When the Last Rose of Summer Was in Bloom
Won't You Fondle Me
Kennedy, Dick
Welcome to All Is San Diego's Call
Kennedy, Earl
Welcome to All Is San Diego's Call
Kennedy, Tom
All Those in Favor Say Aye
Kerker, Gustave
I'm the Money Burner
The Yankee Girl
Kern, Jerome
Ballooning
Come Around on Our Veranda
De Goblin's Glide
Don't Turn My Picture to the Wall
Don't You Want a Paper, Dearie?
The Edinboro Wiggle
Eight Little Girls
The First Rose of Summer
Have a Heart

How'd You Like to Spoon with Me?
I Just Couldn't Do without You
I'd Like to Meet Your Father
I'm a Crazy Daffydil
In the Valley of Mont Bijou
I've a Million Reasons Why I Love You
Jubilo
The Land of "Let's Pretend"
The Land Where the Good Songs Go
The Language of Love
Let Us Build a Little Nest
A Little Love But Not for Me
Look in Her Eyes
The Manicure Girl
Meet Me at Twilight
Mind the Paint
O Promise Me You'll Write to Him Today
Peaches
The Picture I Want to See
Same Sort of Girl
Some Sort of Somebody
They Didn't Believe Me
Under the Linden Tree
Without the Girl Inside
You're Here and I'm Here

Kern, Jerome D.
Eastern Moon
My Otaheite Lady

Kerr, Charles
The March of the Workers
Onward Brothers
True Freedom

Kerr, G. H.
After All

Kerr, Henry D.
We're Ready for Teddy Again

Kildare, Dan
The Jazz Band

King, Charles
Let Me Live and Stay in Dixieland
That's Everlasting Love

King, Stoddard
There's a Long, Long Trail

Kingsbury, Audrey
You Can't Guess What He Wrote on My Slate

Kinnear, D. M.
Get in Line for Big Bill Taft

Kinney, Ray
Across the Sea

Kipling, Rudyard
Mother o' Mine
On the Road to Mandalay

Kirby, M. B.
O'O'O'Brien

Klein, Lou
If I Had My Way

Klein, Manuel
Acting
Laugh and the World Will Laugh with You, Weep and You'll Weep All Alone
Moon Dear
Those Days of Long Ago

Kleinkauf, Henry
Johnson Rag

Klickmann, F. Henri
I Wonder What's the Matter wiz My Oo-la-la
I'm Off for Mexico
Just a Dream of You, Dear
Little Lost Sister
My Fox Trot Girl
Sabbath Chimes
The Song of the Melorose
Sweet Hawaiian Moonlight, Tell Her of My Love
The Trench Trot

Knight, Percival
You've Got to Go In or Go Under

Koevessy, Maximilian Lichenstein
Ashes of Roses

Kohlsaat, Caroline
Bread and Roses

Kondor, Erno
The Old Gypsy

Konedski-Davis, Charles
The Aeroplane Waltz

Koninsky, Sadie
Sing Me a Song of Other Days

Kortlander, Max
Tell Me
Kreisler, Fritz
A Girl, A Man, A Night, A Dance
Kummel, Clare
Egypt, My Cleopatra
Kummer, Clare
Dearie
The Garden of Dreams
In My Dreams of You
June
Listen to Me
Other Eyes
Popular Songs
The Road to Yesterday
La Rocca, D. J.
Barnyard Blues
Lachaume, Aime
Follow the Man That Leads the Band
My Filopena Pet
Lackaye, Wilton
My Particular Friend
Lamb, Arthur
And He Blames My Dreamy Eyes
Goodbye, Sweetheart, Goodbye
Jennie Lee
Like a Star That Falls from Heaven
The Mansion of Aching Hearts
Spring Song
You Splash Me and I'll Splash You
Lamb, Arthur J.
All She Gets from the Iceman Is Ice
Any Old Port in a Storm
The Banquet in Misery Hall
Beneath the Palms of Paradise
A Bird in a Gilded Cage
The Bird on Nellie's Hat
The Bird That Never Sings
In the Heart of the Mighty Deep
The Linger Longer Girl
A Picnic for Two
The Sentinel Asleep
The Waltz Must Change to a March, Marie
Watch Me To-night in the Torchlight Parade
We're Going to Take the Germ Out of Germany
When the Bell in the Lighthouse Rings Ding, Dong
Would You Take Me Back Again?
Lambert, Maud
Come Back to Playland with Me
Lange, Arthur
America, Here's My Boy
Just One Day
On the Old Front Porch
When Rosie Riccoola Do the Hoola Ma Boola She's the Hit of Little Italy
Langstaff, A. M.
Daisy Dear
Lardner, R. N.
Gee, Its a Wonderful Game
Lardner, Ring
Prohibition Blues
Larkins, John
Common Sense
Tilda from Old Savannah
Laska, Edward
The Alcoholic Blues
Do Something
Get Busy Over Here or Over There
How'd You Like to Spoon with Me?
I Would Like to Marry You
We Never Did That Before
Lasky, Jesse
My Brudda Sylvest'
Lauder, Harry
Calligan - Call Again!
Don't Let Us Sing Anymore about War, Just Let Us Sing of Love
Early in the Morning
Every Laddie Loves a Lassie
Fou the Noo
I Love a Lassie
Inverary

I've Loved Her Ever Since She Was a Baby
Killiecrankie
The Laddies Who Fought and Won
The Portobello Lassie
Roamin' in the Gloamin'
Rob Roy McIntosh
The Saftest of the Family
She Is Ma Daisy
Stop Your Tickling Jock!
That's the Reason Noo I Wear a Kilt
Trixie from Dixie
When I Get Back to Bonnie Scotland
While the British Bull-Dog's Watching the Door

Lauder, John
Trixie from Dixie

Lawrence, Jack
Johnson Rag

Layton, Turner
After You've Gone
Good-bye Alexander, Good-bye Honey-Boy

Le Baron, William
A Girl, A Man, A Night, A Dance
On Miami Shore
On the Banks of the Bronx

Lean, Cecil
He's a Fan, Fan, Fan

LeBoy, Grace
Everybody Rag with Me
Go Slow Joe
The Good Ship Mary Ann
I Wish I Had a Girl
A Little Bit of Irish
What's the Use of Moonlight When There's No One 'Round to Love?

LeBrun, Leo
Sadie

Lee, Bert
Oh! London, Where Are Your Girls Tonight?

Lee, William
Foolish Questions

Lehar, Franz
Dear I Love You So
Heure exquise qui nous grise
I Love You So
Merry Widow Waltz
The Merry Widow Waltz Song
Vilia
When Your Lips Pressed Mine

Leigh, Fred
Rum-Tiddely-Um-Tum-Tay Out for the Day Today

Leigh, Fred W.
Goo-Goo Eyes
Poor John
Tiddley-Om-Pom
Waiting at the Church

Lemonier, Thomas
Miss Hannah from Savannah

Lemonier, Tom
I'd Like to Be a Real Lady
In My Old Home
Is Everybody Happy?
Lovie Dear

Lenox, Jean
Ain't It Funny Just What Money Does for You
And the World Goes on Just the Same
I Don't Care
I'm Trying to Find a Sweetheart
Liz'
Pierrot and Pierrette
You're in Love

Leonard, Eddie
I Want to Go Back to the Land of Cotton
Ida, Sweet as Apple Cider
Molasses Candy
Roll Them Roly Boly Eyes
Sugar Mine

Leopold, Walter
Oh! How She Can Dance

Leslie, Edgar
All the Quakers Are Shoulder Shakers Down in Quaker Town
At That Bully Wooly Wild West Show
California and You

Come On Papa
The Dixie Volunteers
For Me and My Gal
Good Luck Mary
He'd Have to Get Under, Get Out and Get Under to Fix Up His Automobile
Hello Wisconsin, Won't You Find My Yonnie Yonson
I Didn't Go Home at All
I Love My Billy Sunday But Oh, You Saturday Night
I'm a Yiddish Cowboy
I'm Awfully Glad I'm Irish
Let's All Be Americans Now
The Letter That Never Reached Home
Lonesome
Lord Have Mercy on a Married Man
Oh! What a Pal Was Mary
Oh! You Million Dollar Doll
The Police Won't Let Mariutch-a Dance, Unless She Move-a-da-Feet
Ragtime Eyes
Rolling Stones All Come Rolling Home Again
Sadie Salome Go Home
Salvation Nell
Take Me to that Land of Jazz
Take Your Girlie to the Movies If You Can't Make Love at Home
They Don't Hesitate Any More
Those Charlie Chaplin Feet
Way Down in Cotton Town
When Alexander Takes His Rag Time Band to France
When Ragtime Rosie Ragged the Rosary
When the Grown-Up Ladies Act Like Babies
When Those Sweet Hawaiian Babies Roll Their Eyes
You're a Good Little Devil

Lessing, Edith Maida
Oh! You Circus Day

Letters, Will
Has Anybody Here Seen Kelly?
Put Me Upon an Island

Levenson, Robert
My Belgian Rose

Levi, Maurice
The Aero Naughty Girls
The Brinkley Bathing Girl
The Christy Girl
The Duchess of Central Park
The Game of Love
A Great Big Girl Like Me
Hat Song
I'm a Lady
In the Swim
Linda, Look Out de' Windah
Linger Longer Lingerie
Mary Be Wary
My Starlight Queen
My Syncopated Gypsy Maid
Nancy Clancy
The Nell Brinkley Girl
Rainbows Follow After Rain
Take a Tip from Venus
The Troubles of Reuben and the Maid
Upper Broadway After Dark
The Wedding of the Reuben and the Maid
When Reuben Comes to Town

Lewis, Andy
Pinky Panky Poo

Lewis, George Alfred
Star of Happiness

Lewis, Henry
The Wild Wild Women Are Making a Wild Man of Me

Lewis, M. M.
That Mellow Strain

Lewis, Roger
Floating Down the River
When There's Peace on Earth Again
You Can't Expect Kisses from Me

Lewis, Sam
Always Take a Girl Named Daisy ('cause Daisies Won't Tell)

I Wonder Why She Kept On Saying Si Si Si Si Si Senor
I'm Gonna Make Hay While the Sun Shines in Virginia
Lewis, Sam M.
Arrah Go On, I'm Gonna Go Back to Oregon
'Cross the Great Divide, I'll Wait for You
Daddy Long Legs
Dat Lovin' Touch
Hello Central, Give Me No Man's Land
How 'Ya Gonna Keep 'Em Down on the Farm After They've Seen Paris?
Huckleberry Finn
If I Knock the 'L' Out of Kelly, It Still Would Be Kelly to Me
I'm All Bound 'Round with the Mason-Dixon Line
I'm Sorry I Ain't Got It You Could Have It If I Had It Blues
Just a Baby's Prayer at Twilight to Her Daddy Over There
Meet Me at the Station
My Mother's Rosary
Oh, How I Wish I Could Sleep Until My Daddy Comes Home
Poor Little Butterfly Is a Fly Girl Now
Rock-a-bye Your Baby with a Dixie Melody
Romany
San Francisco
Shall They Plead in Vain?
That Naughty Melody
That Syncopated Boogie Boo
Wedding Bells, Will You Ever Ring for Me
When They're Old Enough to Know Better, It's Better to Leave Them Alone
Who Played Poker with Pocohontas When John Smith Went Away?
Why Do They All Take the Night Boat to Albany?
You're a Million Miles from Nowhere When You're One Little Mile from Home
Lewis, Ted
I Know Why--Because I'm in Love with You
Liliokalani, Queen
Aloha Oe
Lincke, Paul
Castles in the Air
Fireflies
The Glow Worm
Meet Me at the Masquerade
The Queen of the Night
Lincoln, Harry J.
The Midnight Fire Alarm
Lindeman, D. S.
Mexi-Tango
Linn, Edith Willis
We Are Coming
Linton, Harry
I Sing a Little Tenor
Instrumental Man
John Would Never Do That
Pansy of the Dell
Lipton, Dan
Put Me Among the Girls
Lipton, Jack M.
Louie, Take Me to the Frisco Fair
Little, George A.
The Garden of Allah
Hawaiian Butterfly
Lloyd, Evans
Next Sunday at Nine
Somebody Lied
Lloyd, Rosie
B-I-Double L Bill
Lloyd, Vans
Remember Dear
Lockhart, Eugene
The World Is Waiting for the Sunrise
Lodge, Henry
Red Pepper Rag
Loftus, Cissie
Where Go the Boats?
Logan, Frederic Knight
Moonlight Waltz

Logan, Frederick Knight
Killarney, My Home o'er the Sea
Logan, Virginia Knight
Moonlight Waltz
Logatti, C.
Maurice Irresistable
Lohr, Hermann
Little Grey Home in the West
Loll, Harry C.
Why Don't They Set Him Free?
Lome, Herbert M.
Toddle Song
Longbrake, Arthur
Brother Noah Gave Out Checks for Rain
Cutey, Tell Me Who Tied Your Tie?
Honey, I Will Long for You
I Am Longing for Tomorrow When I Think of Yesterday
Loraine, William
Zamona
Lothrop, George E.
Boys, the Old Flag Never Touched the Ground
Lowell, J. R.
True Freedom
Lowitz, J. N.
Come Around to Mamie's
Lowitz, John B.
Bandy Legs
Lucas, Clarence
The Perfect Song
Luders, Gustav
The "A la Mode" Girl
Didn't Know Exactly What to Do
Heidelberg
The Message of the Violet
The Tale of a Bumble Bee
Luther, Frank
The Whistler and His Dog
Lutter, Howard
Shadows
Lyons, George
The Road for You and Me
MacBoyle, Darl
Bring Back Those Wonderful Days
MacConnell, Harry T.
Look It Up in the Dream Book
MacDonald, Ballard
At Mammy's Fireside
Beautiful Ohio
Breeze, Blow My Baby Back to Me
Come Along Up in the Flip Flap
Fireflies
I Wish I Had My Old Girl Back Again
Indiana
I've Got the Time, I've Got the Place, But It's Hard to Find the Girl
Love's Lullaby
The Modern Maiden's Prayer
Nix on the Glow-Worm, Lena
On a Little Farm in Normandie
On the Mississippi
Play That Barbershop Chord
The Queen of the Night
The Ragtime Volunteers Are Off to War
Rose of Washington Square
Swing Me High, Swing Me Low
That Wonderful Kid from Madrid
There's a Girl in the Heart of Maryland with a Heart That Belongs to Me
There's a Light That's Burning in the Window of the Little House upon the Hill
The Trail of the Lonesome Pine
The War in Snider's Grocery Store
What Has That Man Harrigan Done?
When Patti Sang "Home Sweet Home"
Wilson--That's All
MacDonough, Glen
Beatrice Barefacts
Jack O'Lantern Girl
Little Mary Gardeners
March of the Toys
Toyland
MacDuff, Allan W. S.
I Love My Steady, But I'm Crazy for My Once-in-a-While

MacEvoy, J. Louis
I Always Wish 'Twas You
Mack, Andrew
Eyes of Blue
For Freedom and Ireland
An Irishman's Lilt
The Legend of the Maguire
Little Tommy Murphy
Mack, Cecil
see also McPherson, R. C.
Down Among the Sugar-Cane
He's a Cousin of Mine
If He Comes In, I'm Going Out
If You Don't Want Me, Send Me to My Ma
It's Hard to Love Somebody Who's Loving Somebody Else
The Last Shot Got Him
The Little Gypsy Maid
My Country Right or Wrong
Never Let the Same Bee Sting You Twice
Please Go Away and Let Me Sleep
Scaddle-de-Mooch
Teasing
That Minor Strain
That's Why They Call Me Shine
Way Down East
You're in the Right Church But the Wrong Pew
Mack, Francis
No One Knows
Macklin, Cecil
Tango Is the Dance for Me
Tres Moutarde
Madden, Edward
Alamo
Alias Jimmy Valentine
Arrah-Arabia
Blue Bell
Build Your Nest Away Down in My Heart
By the Light of the Silvery Moon
The Chanticleer Rag
Colleen Bawn
Come Down from the Big Fig Tree
Come On, Play Ball with Me
Daddy's Little Girl
The Dusky Salome
Farewell Killarney
The Hornpipe Rag
I Love to Sit and Look at You
I Want a Gibson Man
I Want to Be a Merry Merry Widow
Kewpie Doll
A Little Boy Named 'Taps'
Lotus San: A Japanese Romance
Lucy Anna Lou
Mister Pagliatch
Moonlight Bay
My Bird of Paradise
My Cousin Caruso
My Little Rang Outang
My Sist' Tetrazzin'
My Yiddische Colleen
A Quaint Old Bird
The Red Rose Rag
Rosa Rigoletto
Sunrise at the Zoo
Two Eyes of Brown
A Vision of Salome
When My Sist' Tetrazin' Met My Cousin Carus'
When the Whole World Has Gone Back on You
When We Were Two Little Boys
Will Taft, We're Looking to You
Your Eyes Say No But Your Lips Say Yes!
Magine, Frank
Venetian Moon
Mahoney, Jack
Bing! Bang! Bing 'Em on the Rhine
Every Day Will Be Sunday When the Town Goes Dry
When Highland Mary Did the Highland Fling
When You Wore a Tulip and I Wore a Big Red Rose
Malackey, James
Inverary
Malone, Edgar
Billy
I Want to Be a Prima Donna

Manley, Dave
Melody Chimes
Manley, Julia Marion
All on Account of a Dear Little Girl
Mann, Nat D.
I Want a Man Made to Order for Me
My Sulu Lulu Loo
Marco
A Debutante's Engagement Book
Mack Sennett Girls
Marion, Harry S.
When the Band Played Home Sweet Home
Marks, Edward B.
The Old Postmaster
Take These Flowers, Old Lady
Markstein, Henrietta
I Love But One, I Love But You
Marquand, Rube
The Marquand Glide
Marr, Alex
Say a Prayer for the Boys Out There
When Tony Goes Over the Top
Marshall, Charles
I Hear You Calling Me
Marshall, Henry I.
Ask Her in Tulip Time
Be My Little Baby Bumble Bee
Bless Your Ever Loving Little Heart
Dinah
Heavenly Twins
I Want to Linger
On the 5:15
You're My Boy
Marson, Cecil
Bill? Bill Taft
Martens, Frederick H.
Liberty Forever
Martin, Easthope
Bridal Dawn
Martin, John
Hooray for a Bryan to Lead Us
Martin, Mrs. C. D.
His Eye Is on the Sparrow
Mather, Henry
Boys, the Old Flag Never Touched the Ground
Matthews, J. Sherrie
Eighth Avenue
M-O-N-E-Y Spells Money
Walk, Walk, Walk
Mattullath, Alice
Tango Is the Dance for Me
Maxwell, Elsa
I Have Never Seen the Russian Ballet
My Star
Please Keep Out of My Dreams
The Singer
The Sum of Life
A Tango Dream
Maxwell, Joseph
No One Seems to Love Me Now
Mayhew, Stella
Vanity Fair
Mayne, Leslie
Little Mary
Mayo, Fred
I'm Not Jealous
McAvoy, Dan
The Beer That Made Milwaukee Famous
McBoyle, Darl
To Have, To Hold, To Love
McCarron, Charles
Down in Honky-Tonk Town
Down Where the Swanee River Flows
Poor Pauline
When Old Bill Bailey Plays the Ukelele
When the Lusitania Went Down
McCarron, Charles K.
Blues My Naughty Sweetie Gives to Me
McCarron, Charles R.
At the Levee on Revival Day
The Concert in the Sky
The Fatal Ring
I'm Crazy about My Daddy in a Uniform

I'm Glad I Can Make You Cry
Oh Helen!
Oh, How She Could Yacki Hacki Wicki Wacki Woo
Wait and See, You'll Want Me Back
Your Lips Are No Man's Land But Mine
McCarthy, Joe
At the Yiddish Wedding Jubilee
Beatrice Fairfax, Tell Me What to Do
Billy Billy, Bounce Your Baby Doll
Dancing the Blues Away
Honey Man
I Love Her Oh! Oh! Oh!
I Think You're Absolutely Wonderful (What Do You Think of Me?)
If I Could Peep through the Window Tonight
I've Only One Idea about the Girls and That's to Love 'Em
Melinda's Wedding Day
Midnight in Dreamy Spain
Sweet Cider Time When You Were Mine
That Long Lost Chord
That's How I Need You
There's a Little Spark of Love Still Burning
What Do You Want to Make Those Eyes at Me For?
When I Get You Alone Tonight
When Mother Plays a Rag on the Sewing Machine
McCarthy, Joseph
Alice Blue Gown
Castle of Dreams
If We Can't Be the Same Old Sweethearts
I'm Always Chasing Rainbows
Ireland Must Be Heaven for My Mother Came from There
My Baby's Arms
That Dreamy Italian Waltz
They Go Wild, Simply Wild Over Me
Typical Topical Tunes
McCartney, Joe
You Made Me Love You, I Didn't Want to Do It
McConnell, Harry T.
The Way That Walker Walked Away
McCoy, Bessie
I'm a Crazy Daffydil
McCrae, John
In Flanders' Fields
McCree, Junie
Could You Learn to Love Me?
Flippity-Flop
I Would Like to Be Your Pal
Let's Go to a Picture Show
Nora Malone, Call Me by Phone
Oh, That Moonlight Glide
Put Your Arms Around Me, Honey
Those Things Cannot Be Explained
McDonald, Thomas C.
The Boys in Blue Parade Today
McEvoy, J. P.
A Perfect Day
McGill, Josephine
Duna
McKenna, William J.
Any Old Place the Gang Goes I'll Be There
Mandy Lane
McKenna, Wm. J
Has Anybody Here Seen Kelly?
McLellan, C. M. S.
By the Saskatchewan
Just Because It's You
McNamara, C. F.
Just a Dream of You, Dear
McPherson, R. C.
see also Mack, Cecil
Good Night Lucindy
Josephine, My Jo
Miss Hannah from Savannah
Mead, Freddie
You'll Fall for Someone
Mellor
When It's Apple Blossom Time in Normandy

Mellor, Tom
Come Along My Mandy
Melville, James, Jr.
Deacon Jones
Melville, Rose
I'm Thinking 'bout You Honey All the While
Mendelssohn-Bartholdi, Felix
Spring Song
Merrill, Blanche
Bye and Bye
Give an Imitation of Me
Here's to You, My Sparkling Wine
I Can't Help It
I Got a Rock
If You Want a Little Doggie, Whistle and I'll Come to You
In a Little Cottage by the Railroad Track
In the Days of Girls and Boys
Jazz Baby
Just 'Round the Corner from Broadway
My Syncopated Melody Man
Nosie Rosie Posie
Oh God! Let My Dream Come True!
Shadowland
The Tanguay Rag
We Take Our Hats Off to You, Mr. Wilson
We've Had a Lovely Time, So Long, Good Bye
Merson, Billy
The Spaniard That Blighted My Life
Methuen, Florence
When You Look in the Heart of a Rose
Meyer, Fred
The Cuckoo Bird
Meyer, George W.
Always Take a Girl Named Daisy ('cause Daisies Won't Tell)
Bring Back My Daddy to Me
'Cross the Great Divide, I'll Wait for You
Cupid's I.O.U.
Everything Is Peaches Down in Georgia
For Me and My Gal
Good-Bye Girlie and Remember Me
The High Cost of Loving
Homeward Bound
Honey Love
I Live Up-Town
I Love My Billy Sunday But Oh, You Saturday Night
If He Can Fight Like He Can Love, Good Night Germany
I'm a Lonesome Melody
I'm Awfully Glad I Met You
I'm Crazy 'bout the Turkey Trot
In the Land of Beginning Again
In the Land of Wedding Bells
I've Got the Blues for Home Sweet Home
Johnny's in Town
Just as Washington Crossed the Delaware, So Will Pershing Cross the Rhine
Let's All Be Americans Now
Lonesome
Love Me Like I Want to Be Loved
Loving Eyes
My Mother's Rosary
San Francisco
That Mellow Strain
That Naughty Melody
That Syncopated Boogie Boo
There'll Be a Hot Time for the Old Men While the Young Men Are Away
Under the Rosenbloom
You Taught Me to Love You, Now Teach Me to Forget
You'll Find Old Dixieland in France
Meyer, Joe
Midnight Maid
Pack Your Duds for San Francisco
Middleton, J. A.
I Told My Love to the Roses
Mierisch, Ferd E.
At the Levee on Revival Day

Boom-Tum-Ta-Ra-Ra-Zing-Boom
The Junk Man Rag
My Landlady
Mierisch, Ferdinand E.
The Concert in the Sky
Milford, Bliss
It's Lonesome Here
Miller, Adelbert E.
The Song of the Melorose
Miller, Francis Trevelyan
Star of Happiness
Miller, Madge Marie
Just You
Mills, A. J.
Ship Ahoy
Mills, Frederick W.
Get in Line for Big Bill Taft
Mills, Kerry
Any Old Port in a Storm
I Think I Could Be Awfully Good to You
I'd Like to Be the Fellow That Girl Is Waiting For
I'll Break the Fighting Line Like You Broke This Heart of Mine
I'll Come Back to You When It's All Over
In the City of Sighs and Tears
Just for the Sake of Society
Kerry Mills' Barn Dance
Let's All Go Up to Maud's
Like a Star That Falls from Heaven
The Longest Way 'Round Is the Sweetest Way Home
Meet Me in St. Louis, Louis
The Ragtime College Girl
Red Wing
She's Dancing Her Heart Away
Take Me Around Again
While the Old Mill Wheel Is Turning
Minzey, Frank
I'm Thinking 'bout You Honey All the While
Mitchell, Sidney
Aloma
Blue Eyed Blond Haired Heart Breaking Baby Doll
Mammy's Chocolate Soldier
Would You Rather Be a Colonel with an Eagle on Your Shoulder...
Mitchell, Sidney D.
Bluin' the Blues
Razzberries
Wait 'till the Great Day Comes
You Keep Sending 'Em Over and We'll Keep Knocking 'Em Down
Mockton, Lionel
The Language of the Flowers
Mohr, Halsey K.
I'm a Yiddish Cowboy
Liberty Bell, It's Time to Ring Again
The Police Won't Let Mariutch-a Dance, Unless She Move-a-da-Feet
They're Wearing 'Em Higher in Hawaii
Monaco, James V.
I Love Her Oh! Oh! Oh!
You Made Me Love You, I Didn't Want to Do It
Monaco, Jimmie V.
Beatrice Fairfax, Tell Me What to Do
Honolulu, America Loves You
The Honolulu Blues
I Called You My Sweetheart
If We Can't Be the Same Old Sweethearts
Oh, Mr. Dream Man
Oh! You Circus Day
Row Row Row
What Do You Want to Make Those Eyes at Me For?
Monaco, Jimmy V.
Don't Take Advantage of My Good Nature
Monckton, Lionel
Little Mary
Montgomery, Billie
The Story Book Ball

Montgomery, Dave
Must You?
Moran, E. P.
I Love Her Oh! Oh! Oh!
Little One, Good Bye
No Wedding Bells for Me
There's No Other Girl Like My Girl
You'll Always Be the Same Sweet Girl to Me
Moran, Ed
Bye and Bye You'll See the Sun A-Shining
Feed the Kitty
I Sent My Wife to the 1000 Isles
Moran, Edward
Go Easy Mabel
Teddy Da Roose
Moran, Edward P.
Are You a Buffalo?
Everything Is Rosy, Rosie
Poor Robinson Crusoe
Morel, Neil
Hiawatha
Moret, Neil
The Island of Roses and Love
Mickey
Moonlight
Peggy
Morgan, Carey
Blues My Naughty Sweetie Gives to Me
I'm Crazy about My Daddy in a Uniform
I'm Glad I Can Make You Cry
Keep Your Head Down, 'Fritzie Boy'
My Hawaiian Sunrise
Oh Helen!
Sipping Cider thru' a Straw
Wait and See, You'll Want Me Back
Your Lips Are No Man's Land But Mine
Morgan, Jimmie
Frisco's Kitchen Stove Rag
Roaming Romeo
Morgan, Jimmy
Cleopatra Had a Jazz Band
I Know Why--Because I'm in Love with You
Moriarty, George
Remember Me to My Old Girl
Moriarty, George J.
Love Me Like the Ivy Loves the Old Oak Tree
Morris, Bob
With the Last Rose of Summer, I'll Come Back to You
Morris, Melville
Kewpie Doll
Morris, William
The March of the Workers
Morse, Dolly
Blue Bell
Morse, Theodore F.
The Army of Peace
Arrah-Wanna
Blue Bell
The Brotherhood of Man
Come Down from the Big Fig Tree
Daddy's Little Girl
Dear Old Girl
The Good Old U.S.A.
Happy Hooligan
Hurrah for Baffin's Baby
Hypnotizing Lize
I Want to Be a Merry Merry Widow
If They'd Only Fight the War with Wooden Soldiers
In the Valley of Broken Hearts
It's the Man in the Sailor Suit
Just a Little Rocking Chair and You
Keep a Little Cozy Corner in Your Heart for Me
Keep on the Sunny Side
A Little Boy Named 'Taps'
M-O-T-H-E-R
Make Believe
My Little Rang Outang
One Called "Mother" and the Other "Home Sweet Home"

People Who Live in Glass Houses Never Should Throw Any Stones
The Proper Way to Kiss
A Quaint Old Bird
Salvation Nell
The Same Old Crowd
Since Reuben's Gone Away
Sing Me Love's Lullaby
Wait at the Gate for Me
We'll Knock the Heligo into Heligo Out of Heligoland!
What the Brass Band Played
When They Play "God Save the King"
When Uncle Joe Plays a Rag on His Old Banjo
When We Were Two Little Boys
Won't You Be My Honey?
The Woodchuck Song
Mortimer, Robert
The Man of the Hour
Motzan, Otto
Walking the Dog
Wedding Bells
Muir, Lewis F.
Little Rag Baby Doll
Oh, What a Night
Play That Barbershop Chord
Play That Fandango Rag
Rag-Time Cowboy Joe
Ragging the Baby to Sleep
Take Me to That Swanee Shore
Waiting for the Robert E. Lee
When Ragtime Rosie Ragged the Rosary
Mullen, J. B.
I Could Love You in a Steam Heat Flat
I'm Longing for My Old Kentucky Home
Imagination
It Was the Dutch
The Load That Father Carried
The Man Behind
Over the Pilsner Foam
Pretty Little Dinah Jones
Violette
Munson, Eddie
Ida, Sweet as Apple Cider
Murphy, C. W.
Goo-Goo Eyes
Has Anybody Here Seen Kelly?
Put Me Among the Girls
The Seaside Sultan
Murphy, Stanley
The Baltimore Bombashay
Be My Little Baby Bumble Bee
Bless Your Ever Loving Little Heart
Dinah
Heavenly Twins
I Want to Linger
I'm on My Way to Dublin Bay
Johnny, Get a Girl
Love Me While the Loving Is Good
My Little Service Flag Has Seven Stars
Oh, How She Could Yacki Hacki Wicki Wacki Woo
On the 5:15
The Palm Beach Dip
Put on Your Old Grey Bonnet
Sinbad Was in Bad All the Time
Murray, Fred
It Ain't All Honey and It Ain't All Jam
It's All Right in the Summertime
The Next Horse I Ride On
Nathan, Caspar
Little Lost Sister
Nathan, J. S.
Nulife
Nathan, Joseph S.
The Man Who Fights the Fire
Neal, Henry V.
Our Boys in Overalls
Neale, Arthur
The Florida Blues
Nebarb, Jeff
She's the Daughter of Mother Machree
Neilsson, Hjalmar F.
The Teenie Weenie Waltz

Nelson, Ed
When Yankee Doodle Learns to "Parlez-Vous Francaise?"
Nelson, Eddie
It's All Your Fault
Nelson, Edward G.
I'm Not Jealous
Nesbit, Edith
The Hope of the Ages
Nevin, Arthur
Mamselle
Nevin, Ethelbert
Mighty Lak' a Rose
The Rosary
Newman, Olive Fields
I'll Be With You Honey When It's Honeysuckle Time
Newton, Eddie
Casey Jones
Newton, Harry L.
Mariutch, She Come Back to Me
Nichols, George A.
My Drowsy Babe
Nicholson, Nick
Marie from Sunny Italy
Noble, Johnny
Across the Sea
Norman,
Beckie, Stay in Your Own Backyard
Norman, Harold
Way Down East
Northrup, Theodore
My Little Star, I'm Looking Up to You
Norton, George A.
All That Glitters Is Not Gold
Mister Crump Blues
My Melancholy Baby
Round Her Neck, She Wears a Yeller Ribbon
Norworth, Jack
ABCD
Back to My Old Home Town
Blarney
Come Along My Mandy
Falling Star
Holding Hands
Honey Boy
I'm Glad I'm a Boy/I'm Glad I'm a Girl
I'm Glad I'm Married
I'm Learning Something Every Day
I'm Sorry
Let's Get the Umpire's Goat
Pinkerton Detective Man
Sadie Brady Listen Good to Me
Shine On, Harvest Moon
Smarty
Take Me Out to the Ball Game
Turn Off Your Light, Mr. Moon Man
You Will Have to Sing an Irish Song
Novello, Ivor
Keep the Home Fires Burning
The Radiance in Your Eyes
Wait 'till the Great Day Comes
Nugent, Maude
My Irish Daisy
My Irish Indian
My Little Creole Babe
My Swee' Kimona
Rosie and Josie
There's No Other Girl Like My Girl
You'll Always Be the Same Sweet Girl to Me
O'Brien, John
We'll Knock the Heligo into Heligo Out of Heligoland!
O'Brien, John J.
'Twas Only an Irishman's Dream
O'Connor, Shaumus
MacNamara's Band
O'Day, James
Pawnee
O'Dea, James
By the Light of the Honeymoon
Daisy Donahue
Every Saturday Afternoon
Hiawatha
I Wants a Man Like Romeo
Iola
Moonlight
Red Domino

Sammy
Stars of the National Game
Susan, Dear Sue
When the Circus Comes to Town
O'Donnell, Charlie
My Pony Boy
Ogden, Ina Duley
Brighten the Corner Where You Are
O'Hara, Geoffrey
K-K-K-Katy
O'Kane, T. C.
Mack and Teddy
Olcott, Chauncey
Day Dreams
Ireland! A Gra Ma Chree
Laugh and the World Will Laugh with You, Weep and You'll Weep All Alone
The Limerick Girls
Mother Machree
My Own Dear Irish Queen
When Irish Eyes Are Smiling
Oliver
Kate Kearney
Olman, Abe
Down Among the Sheltering Palms
Faugh-a Ballagh
Johnny's in Town
Oh Johnny, Oh Johnny, Oh!
O'Malley, Jack
Coster Rag
O'Neill, Dannie
Jerry, You Warra a Warrior in the War
O'Neill, Florence
That Magic Strain
Onivas, D.
Indianola
Openshaw, John
Love Sends a Little Gift of Roses
Oppenheim, Dave
Oh! What a Beautiful Dream You Seem
On the Shores of Italy
That Baboon Baby Dance
Oppenheim, James
Bread and Roses
O'Reilley, P. J.
For You Alone
Original Dixieland Jazz Band
Tiger Rag
Osbourne, Nat
On a Little Farm in Normandie
Take Me Back to the Garden of Love
That Wonderful Kid from Madrid
Overbolt, Miles
A Romance of Happy Valley
Owen, Anita
Daisies Won't Tell
Paley, Herman
And Then
Angel Eyes
Cheer Up Father, Cheer Up Mother
Don't Cry Dolly Gray
Havana
She's Good Enough to Be Your Baby's Mother...
Paley, James
Billy
Won't You Fondle Me
Paley, Lou
Come to the Moon
Something about Love
Palmer, Scott A.
San Diego, California, the Gem of the U.S.A.
Parker, Sidney
Clidee-Oh
Pascoe, Richard W.
That Tumble Down Shack in Athlone
Patrick, Charles
Tess of the Storm Country
Paull, E. T.
The Battle of Gettysburg
The Battle of the Nations
The Burning of Rome
Herald of Peace
The Roaring Volcano
Silver Sleigh Bells
Women Forever!
Pease, Harry
I Don't Want to Get Well

I'm Not Jealous
Penn, Arthur A.
Carissima
Smilin' Through
Penn, William A.
Easy Street
Penn, William H.
All on Account of a Dear Little Girl
Dolly
The Girl with the Baby Stare
Honey Boy
The Honeysuckle and the Bee
Maurice's Rag
Pansy Faces
Piking the Pike
Sadie, You'se Ma Lady-Bird
The Sunflower and the Sun
Perkins, Ray
Shall They Plead in Vain?
Perry, Edmund J.
Everybody Shimmies Now
Perry, George
The Story Book Ball
Pestalozzo, A.
Ciribiribin
Pether, Henry E.
Molly Dear, It's You I'm After
Poor John
Waiting at the Church
Petrie, H. W.
After You, My Dear Alphonse
Good Fellows
Out Where the Breakers Roar
When the Sunset Turns to Ocean's Blue to Gold
When the Winds O'er the Sea Blow a Gale
Petrova, Olga
The Road to Romany
Phillips, William King
The Florida Blues
Piantadosi, Al
At the Yiddish Wedding Jubilee
Baby Shoes
The Curse of an Aching Heart
Good-Bye Mister Caruso
Good Luck Mary
Honey Man
I Didn't Raise My Boy to Be a Soldier
If You Had All the World and Its Gold
I'll Still Believe in You
I'm a Yiddish Cowboy
I'm Awfully Glad I'm Irish
I'm Looking for a Dear Old Lady
I've Only One Idea about the Girls and That's to Love 'Em
Melinda's Wedding Day
My Mariuccia Take a Steamboat
Oh God! Let My Dream Come True!
On the Shores of Italy
Send Me Away with a Smile
That Dreamy Italian Waltz
That Long Lost Chord
That's How I Need You
Way Down in Cotton Town
When You Play in the Game of Love
When You're in Love with Someone Who Is Not in Love with You
The Wild Wild Women Are Making a Wild Man of Me
The Woman Thou Gavest Me
Pickthall, Marjorie
Duna
Pilcer, Harry
The Gaby Glide
Pinero, Arthur
Mind the Paint
Pinkard, Maceo
Don't Cry, Little Girl, Don't Cry
Easy Pickins'
He's Had No Lovin' for a Long, Long Time
Jazz Babies' Ball
Lila
Mammy o' Mine
Those Draftin' Blues
Piron, A. J.
I Wish I Could Shimmy Like My Sister Kate

Piron, Armand J.
You Can Have It, I Don't Want It
Pixley, Frank
Didn't Know Exactly What to Do
Heidelberg
The Message of the Violet
The Tale of a Bumble Bee
Pollack, Lew
Everybody Wants a Key to My Cellar
Oh! Harry! Harry!
Pollock, Channing
I Want to Look Like Lillian Russell
The Language of Lover's Smiles
Ponce, Phil
Oh! The Last Rose of Summer Was the Sweetest Rose of All
Poole, George O.
My Onliest Little Dolly
Porter, Cole
Alone with You
Altogether Too Fond of You
Hitchy's Garden of Roses
I Introduced
Porter, Lew
Mothers of America, You Have Done Your Share
Pounds, Jessie Brown
Beautiful Isle of Somewhere
Powell, Felix
Pack Up Your Troubles in Your Old Kit Bag and Smile, Smile, Smile
Powell, Orlando
May, May, May
Rum-Tiddely-Um-Tum-Tay Out for the Day Today
Salome
Tiddley-Om-Pom
Powell, W. C.
The Troubadour
Powell, William C.
The Woman Thou Gavest Me
Powers, James T.
Can't You Take My Word?
Pryor, Arthur
The Whistler and His Dog
Puck, Harry
California and You
Johnny, Get a Girl
Loving Eyes
Over the Garden Wall
There's a Light That's Burning in the Window of the Little House upon the Hill
They Don't Hesitate Any More
Where Did You Get That Girl?
Pulitzer, Walter
The Dawn of a Tomorrow
Queen, John
Ain't Dat a Shame?
I Hates to Get Up Early in the Morning
Just Because She Made Dem Goo-Goo Eyes
Quigley, C. F.
If All My Dreams Were Made of Gold, I'd Buy the World for You
Radford, Dave
Mary Pickford, the Darling of Them All
Where the Black-Eyed Susans Grow
Ragas, H. W.
Bluin' the Blues
Railey, Thomas T.
A Heart That's Free
Randall, Carl
Bolsheveki Glide
Ranken, Frederic
Zamona
Ray, Lillian
The Sunshine of Your Smile
Raymond, Fred G.
When the Band Played Home Sweet Home
Reed, Dave
Lady Angeline
My Heart Has Learned to Love You Now Do Not Say Good-Bye
Reed, Dave, Jr.
General Hardtack on Guard
Let Mary Go Round on the Merry-Go-Round
Love Me and the World Is Mine

My Princess Zulu Lulu
Reid, Ivan
Tiger Rose Waltz
Reilley, James M.
Hello Central, Give Me France
Reisner, C. Francis
Frisco's Kitchen Stove Rag
Goodbye Broadway, Hello France
Remington, Earle
Mister E. Z. Mark
Reya, Salis
The Captain of the Golf Club
Reynolds, Herbert
Auf Wiedersehn
They Didn't Believe Me
Rice, Edward E.
Googy-Oo
Rice, Gitz
Dear Old Pal of Mine
Keep Your Head Down, 'Fritzie Boy'
On the Road That Leads to Home
Waiting for You
You've Got to Go In or Go Under
Richards, Sam
On Furlough
Riley, James Whitcomb
The Messiah of Nations
Robb, A. L.
If You Can't Be a Bell-Cow, Fall in Behind
Robb, Arthur L.
He Ought to Have a Tablet in the Hall of Fame
Robe, Harold
Dear Old Pal of Mine
Robert, Camille
Madelon
Roberts, C. Luckeyth
The Junk Man Rag
Rockaway
Roberts, Lee S.
Smiles
Roberts, Robert S.
May Sweet May
Robinson, Charles
Flora, I Am Your Adorer
Robinson, Harry I.
When My Bridget Malone Jiggle-Wiggles Salome
Robinson, J. B.
Mack and Teddy
Robinson, J. Russel
He's Coming Home on the 8 O'Clock Train
Prohibition, You Have Lost Your Sting
Robinson, Lilla Cayley
The Glow Worm
Robinson, Willard
Kansas City
Robyn, Alfred G.
Ain't It Funny What a Difference Just a Few Hours Make?
A Heart That's Free
In Old New York
Roden, Robert F.
Ain't You Coming Back to Old New Hampshire, Molly?
My Heart's Tonight in Texas by the Silvery Rio Grande
Please Leave the Door Ajar
When It's Moonlight on the Prairie
When the Birds Go North Again
When the Fields Are White with Cotton
Rodgers, Richard
Any Old Place with You
Rogers, Alex
Believe Me!
Bon Bon Buddy
Fas' Fas' World
The Harbor of Lost Dreams
I May Be Crazy But I Ain't No Fool
I'd Like to Be a Real Lady
I'm a Jonah Man
In de Evenin'
The Island of By and By
Let It Alone
Nobody
Red Red Rose
Rockaway
Why Adam Sinned

You Can't Shake That Shimmie Here
Rogers, Dick
Baltimore Rag
Rogers, E. W.
Following in Father's Footsteps
Rogers, Ed
Everybody Has a Whistle Like Me
Rogers, Edward
Mrs. Carter, You're a Tartar
Rogers, Gus
Queen of the Bungalow
Rogers, H. M.
Where Is My Papa Tonight?
Rogers, Howard E.
Don't Take Advantage of My Good Nature
If He Can Fight Like He Can Love, Good Night Germany
When the Flowers Bloom on No-Man's Land, What a Wonderful Day That Will Be
Rogers, Max
Queen of the Bungalow
Rogers, Robert Cameron
The Rosary
Rohmer, Sax
Kelly Has Gone to Kingdom Come
Rolfe, Walter
The Song That I Hear in My Dreams
Roma, Caro
Can't Yo' Hear Me Callin', Caroline
Romain, Manuel
I Would If I Could But I Can't
Romberg, Sigmund
America's Popular Song
Auf Wiedersehn
Come Back to Me
Darling
I Just Can't Make My Feet Behave
I'd Be Happy Anywhere with You
The Kiss Burglar
The Kiss Waltz
My Cleopatra Girl
Our Ancestors
Sister Susie's Started Syncopation
Will You Remember?
Romilli, G.
Slowly Stealing Up and Down the River
Ronklyn, George
My Mariuccia Take a Steamboat
Rooney, Julia
If You Love Your Baby Google Google All the Time
Rooney, Pat
I Love to Sit and Look at You
Make Yourself at Home
Pansy
Take Me Back to Babyland
Rose, Ed
Baby Shoes
The Bee That Gets the Honey Doesn't Hang Around the Hive
Don't Worry
Everybody Wants a Key to My Cellar
Faugh-a Ballagh
I'd Like to Be the Fellow That Girl Is Waiting For
Oh Johnny, Oh Johnny, Oh!
Take Me Around Again
Rose, Shelton
Kentucky Rose
Rosenfeld, Monroe
B-I-Double L Bill
Rosenfeld, Monroe H.
The Bird That Never Sings
The Lily or the Rose
What'd Yo' Do Wid de Letter, Mr. Johnson?
Rosenfeld, Sydney
France, Glorious France
In Silence
A Kiss in the Dark
Sly Musette
What's the Matter with the Moon Tonight?
Rosey, George
Maybe
Rosey, Joseph
Lonesome
Ross, Adrian
I Love You So

Love at the Door
Love, Here Is My Heart!
Maud, Maud, Maud
Vilia
Rourke, M. E.
see also Reynolds, Herbert
The Edinboro Wiggle
Eight Little Girls
I'd Like to Meet Your Father
In the Valley of Mont Bijou
I've a Million Reasons Why I Love You
A Lemon in the Garden of Love
Look in Her Eyes
The Lover's A.B.C.
Under the Linden Tree
Without the Girl Inside
Rowe, James
Love Lifted Me
Royle, Edwin Milton
Don't Be What You Ain't
Rubens, Paul
The Fife and Drum
I Can't Take My Eyes off You
I Love You, Ma Cherie
If You'll Walk with Me
Rubens, Paul A.
The Argentine
Coo!
The Girl You Love
I Love the Moon
My Toreador
Ruby, Harry
And He'd Say Oo-la-la! Wee-Wee!
Come On Papa
Daddy Long Legs
The Dixie Volunteers
Hello Wisconsin, Won't You Find My Yonnie Yonson
Oh! The Last Rose of Summer Was the Sweetest Rose of All
A Regular Girl
When Ragtime Rufus Rags the Humoresque
When They're Old Enough to Know Better, It's Better to Leave Them Alone
When Those Sweet Hawaiian Babies Roll Their Eyes
You Keep Sending 'Em Over and We'll Keep Knocking 'Em Down
Rule, Bert
I Want to See My Ida Hoe in Idaho
Rumshisky, J. M.
Mamenu
Russell, Alma L.
Abie, the Sporty Kid
Russell, Ben
You Didn't Want Me When You Had Me So Why Do You Want Me Now?
Russell, James T.
Where the River Shannon Flows
Rutter, Herbert
Calligan - Call Again!
Ryan, Benny
M-i-s-s-i-s-s-i-p-p-i
Sanders, Alma M.
That Tumble Down Shack in Athlone
Sandwith, Mrs. M. T. E.
Clavelitos
Santley, Joseph
Ask Her in Tulip Time
Hawaiian Butterfly
When There's Peace on Earth Again
Santley, Joseph H.
When the Fightin' Irish Come Home
Schenck, Joe
Baby's Prayers Will Soon Be Answered
Don't Try to Steal the Sweetheart of a Soldier
If I Could Peep through the Window Tonight
In the Land Where Poppies Bloom
Midnight in Dreamy Spain
My Old Log Cabin Home
Oh! How She Can Sing
Open Up the Golden Gates to Dixieland and Let Me into Paradise

Teach Me That Beautiful Love
Schenck, Joseph
You Cannot Shake That "Shimmie" Here
Scherr, A.
Mamenu
Schertzinger, Victor
Marcheta
Schertzinger, Victor L.
Peace Song
Schindler, Paul
Oh Fudge!
Schleif, Lucy
Does This Railroad Lead to Heaven?
Schmid, Johann
Garden of Roses
Schneider, C. N.
The Sunflower and the Sun
Schonberg, Chris
Alexander's Got a Jazz Band Now
Molly Malone, My Own
Schuster, Ernest J.
Floreine
Schuster, Ira
Keep Your Eye on the Girlie You Love
The Navy Took Them Over and the Navy Will Bring Them Back
Schwartz, Jean
Ain't You Got Nothing to Say?
America Needs You Like a Mother, Would You Turn Your Mother Down?
America's Popular Song
Any Old Time at All
At the Music Hall
Back to the Carolina You Love
Back to the Woods
The Band of Reubenville
Bedelia
Beneath the Moon
Chinatown, My Chinatown
Come Back to Me
Don't Go in the Water, Daughter
Don't Put Me Off at Buffalo Any More
Down in the Subway
Dreamy Fandango Tune
Everybody's Ragtime Crazy
Everything Looks Rosy and Bright
The Flower Garden Ball
For You
Freedom of the C's
The Gambling Man
The Ghost That Never Walked
The Golden Stairs of Love
Good Bye Mister Ragtime
Good-Bye, Sweet Old Manhattan Isle
Hamlet Was a Melancholy Dane
Handle me with Care
He Was a Sailor
Hello Central, Give Me No Man's Land
Her Eyes of Irish Blue
Honey Love Me All the Time
I Just Can't Make My Feet Behave
I Love the Heart of Dixie
I'm a Member of the Midnight Crew
I'm a Poor Unhappy Maid
I'm All Bound 'Round with the Mason-Dixon Line
I'm on My Way to Reno
I'm Simply Crazy over You
I'm Tired
I'm Unlucky
I've Made Up My Mind to Mind a Maid Made Up Like You
Julie
Just a Tender Spot for Father Dear
The Kellerman Girlie
The Kiss Burglar
Let's Make Love among the Roses
Love Days
The Man Who Plays the Tambourine
McGinnis
Meet Me in Rose Time Rosie
Mister Dooley
Mother Hasn't Spoken to Father Since
My Gypsy Queen
My Hula Lula Girl
My Irish Daisy

My Irish Gibson Girl
My Irish Indian
My Irish Molly O
My Irish Rose
My Operatic Samson
My Sweet
My Teddy Girl
None of Them's Got Anything on Me
Nursery Rhymes
On an Automobile Honeymoon
On the Level, You're a Devil
O'O'O'Brien
Percy
Please Don't Take Away the Girls
Pots and Pans
Ragging the Old Vienna Roll
Ragtime Eyes
Ring-Ting-a-Ling
Rip van Winkle Was a Lucky Man
Rock-a-bye Your Baby with a Dixie Melody
Rosie Rosinsky
Sasparilla, Women, and Song
Since Little Dolly Dimples Made a Hit
Since Sister Nell Heard Paderewski Play
String a Ring of Roses 'Round Your Rosie
Syncopatia Land
Tell That to the Marines!
There's One in a Million Like You
Wedding Bells, Will You Ever Ring for Me
When Gaby Did the Gaby Glide
When I Want to Settle Down
When John McCormack Sings a Song
When Mr. Shakespeare Comes to Town
Where the Red Red Roses Grow
The White Wash Man
Why Do They All Take the Night Boat to Albany?
You Can't Get Away from It
You'll Call the Next Love the First

Schwartz, Paul
The Stolen Melody
Schwartz, Phil
Dat Possum Rag
Scoggins, C. H.
Back among the Clover and the Bees
Down in Sunny Georgia Years Ago
Where the Silv'ry Colorado Wends Its Way
Scott, Bennett
Ship Ahoy
Scott, Clement
Now Is the Hour
Scott, Maurice
I've Got Rings on My Fingers
Scotto, Vincent
It's Delightful to Be Married
Seeley, Blossom
I'm Getting Kind of Lonesome for My Old Kentucky Pal
The Marquand Glide
My Sweet Suzanna
Seibert, T. Lawrence
Casey Jones
Seitz, Ernest
The World Is Waiting for the Sunrise
Selden, Edgar
All That I Ask of You Is Love
I Get Dippy When I Do That Two-Step Dance
I Love My Husband But Oh You Henry
If You'll Walk with Me
I'm Looking for a Dear Old Lady
I'm Looking for the Man That Wrote "The Merry Widow Waltz"
Katy Did
My Marguerite
My Pocahontas
Take Me 'Round in a Taxicab
Shackford, Charles
Bygone Days in Dixie
The Face in the Firelight
Love Will Find a Way
When the Band Goes Marching By

When Two Hearts Are One
Shacklock, Mrs.
Where Is My Papa Tonight?
Shafer, Ada
Bill Taft for 1908
Shannon, J. R.
Coster Rag
Too-ra-loo-ra-loo-ra
Shapiro, Ted
Lafayette
Shaw, James W.
Maurice Hesitation
Sheridan, Frank
O Sole Mio
Sherman, Terry
Good-Bye Christina Swanson
Sherman, Tom
I Want to Be a Prima Donna
Sherwood, Ray
Shadows
Shields, Maud
When Love Comes Knocking at the Door
Shields, Ren
Bill Was There
Come, Take a Trip in My Air-Ship
Come to the Land of Bohemia
Go Easy Mabel
In the Good Old Summertime
It's Got to Be a Minstrel Show Tonight
It's Moonlight All the Time on Broadway
The Longest Way 'Round Is the Sweetest Way Home
Make a Noise Like a Hoop and Roll Away
Tipperary Nora
Wait at the Gate for Me
Waltz Me Around Again, Willie
Waltzing with the Girl You Love
Shiers, Ralph
That Dreamy Barcarole Tune
Shisler, Charles
Bring Me a Rose
Sibre, Georges
That Magic Strain
Sidney, George
Oh Fudge!
Sidney, Harry
The Last Rose of Summer Is the Sweetest Song of All
Siegel, Al
Prohibition, You Have Lost Your Sting
Silesu, Lao
Love, Here Is My Heart!
Silver, Abner
Merrily We'll Roll Along
Silver, Alex
Give Me the Sultan's Harem
Silver, Morris
I've Been Looking for a Girl Like You
Silvers, Louis
Bohemian Rag
I'm Going to Spend My Vacation with a Dear Old Relation
Silverwood, J. B.
Keep Your Golden Gate Wide Open
Simons, Seymour B.
Just Like a Gypsy
Sissle, Noble
Ain't You Coming Back, Mary Ann, to Maryland
All of No Man's Land Is Ours
Gee! I Wish I Had Someone to Rock Me in the Cradle of Love
Gee! I'm Glad That I'm from Dixie
Good Night, Angeline
It's All Your Fault
Mammy's Little Choc'late Cullud Chile
Mirandy
My Heart for You Pines Away
On Patrol in No Man's Land
Skidmore, Will E.
I'm Trying to Teach My Sweet Papa Right from Wrong
It Takes a Long Tall Brown-Skin Gal to Make a Preacher Lay His Bible Down

It's Nobody's Business But My Own
Skinner, Ralph M.
A Little Girl Like Me
Mah Moonlight Lou
Sloane, A. B.
A Love-Lorn Lily
The Pride of Newspaper Row
Sloane, A. Baldwin
Alexander's Bag-Pipe Band
Foolish Questions
France, Glorious France
Greenwich Village
Heaven Will Protect the Working Girl
In Silence
Love
Love Laughs at Locksmiths
Sly Musette
There's a Little Star in Heaven That They Call Broadway
What's the Matter with the Moon Tonight?
Sloane, Mae A.
My Pajama Beauty
Sloane, Mae Auwerda
Jack O'Lantern
My Evalyne
Nancy, Oh Miss Nancy
Sallie, Mah Hot Tamale
Spring Fashions
When Charlie Plays the Slide Trombone in the Silver Cornet Band
Smalley, Victor H.
Dat Lovin' Rag
Smith, Cecil
The Last Shot Got Him
Smith, Chris
After All That I've Been to You
Ain't Dat an Awful Feeling
All In Down and Out
All the Little Lovin' That I Had for You Is Gone, Gone, Gone
At the Levee on Revival Day
Ballin' the Jack
Barnyard Rag
Beans
The Blues
Boom-Tum-Ta-Ra-Ra-Zing-Boom
Bye-Bye, My Eva, Bye-Bye
Come After Breakfast, Bring 'long You' Lunch and Leave 'fore Supper Time
Common Sense
The Concert in the Sky
Constantly
Down Among the Sugar-Cane
Down in Honky-Tonk Town
Farmyard Blues
Fifty-Fifty
Fishing
Gee But Ain't America a Grand Old Place
Gimme Hush Money or I'll Tell on You
Good-Bye, I'll See You Some More
Good Morning Carrie!
He's a Cousin of Mine
He's My Cousin If She's Your Niece
The Honky-Tonky Monkey Rag
I Have Shed My Last Tears for You
I Want a Little Lovin' Sometimes
If He Comes In, I'm Going Out
If I Could Only Sleep Like Rip Van Winkle
If I Ever Get Back to Cincinnati
If You Ain't Got It, Go and Get It
If You Don't Want Me, Send Me to My Ma
It's Hard to Love Somebody Who's Loving Somebody Else
The Junk Man Rag
Mister Yodeling Man
My Country Right or Wrong
Never Let the Same Bee Sting You Twice
No, No, Positively No
Rip Van Winkle Was a Lucky Man But Adam Had Him Beat a Mile
Rubber Necking Moon
Scaddle-de-Mooch
She's a Patient of Mine

That Sneaky Snaky Rag
There's a Time and a Place for Everything
Tilda from Old Savannah
When Mother Plays a Rag on the Sewing Machine
Yo' Eyes Are Open, But Yo' Sound Asleep
You're in the Right Church But the Wrong Pew
You're Just Too Sweet to Live

Smith, Edgar
All I Want in the Wide Wide World Is You
The American Billionaire
As on Moonlit Waves We Ride
At the Music Hall
Beautiful Arizona
Chloe, I'm Waiting
Dream One Dream of Me
Easy Money
Flowers of Dixieland
The Game of Love
A Great Big Girl Like Me
Heaven Will Protect the Working Girl
I'm a Respectable Working Girl
Little Widow Brown
Love a la Mode
Ma Blushin' Rosie, My Posie Sweet
Ma Mamselle Honee
My Japanese Cherry Blossom
My Syncopated Gypsy Maid
Nancy Clancy
Nothing Doing
The Opera
The Queen of Society
Romeo
Tell Us Pretty Ladies
Wilhemina

Smith, George Totten
And Other Things
Brother Bill
Daisy Dear
Devotion
Down the Line with Molly
I Ain't a-Goin' to Weep No More
I Wants to Be the Leading Lady
My Drowsy Babe
My Honolulu Lu
My Little Chick
Piking the Pike
The Tale of a Stroll
When the Troupe Gets Back to Town
The Whole Dam Family

Smith, H. Wakefield
Those Songs My Mother Used to Sing

Smith, Harry B.
The Aero Naughty Girls
Be Kind to Poor Pierrot
The Brinkley Bathing Girl
The Christy Girl
The Comet and the Moon
De Cakewalk Queen
De Trop
Flirtation Song
Follow the Man That Leads the Band
The Gypsy's Wedding
Hat Song
I Want to Be Naughty Too
I'd Like to Be a Gunner in the Navy
If All the Stars Were Mine
I'm the Money Burner
In Disguise
In Florida
In Society
In the Swim
Jack O'Lantern
Kiss, Kiss, Kiss, If You Want to Learn to Kiss
The Land of "Let's Pretend"
A Lesson in Flirtation
Linger Longer Lingerie
The Little Gypsy Maid
Mamselle
Maud, Maud, Maud
Meet Me at the Masquerade
My Filopena Pet
The Nell Brinkley Girl
A Parisian Model
Plain Mamie O'Hooley

Same Sort of Girl
Spring Fashions
Take a Tip from Venus
The Wedding of the Reuben and the Maid
What Eve Said to Adam
A Woman's No Means 'Yes'
Won't You Be My Valentine?
The Yankee Girl
You're Here and I'm Here
Smith, Henry Clay
Somebody's Coming to Town from Dixie
Smith, Howard E.
Love Lifted Me
Smith, Julia
Our Boys in Overalls
Smith, Lee Orean
Under Southern Skies
When a Lady Leads the Band
Smith, Robert
Look It Up in the Dream Book
Smith, Robert B.
All the World Loves a Lover
Come Down, Ma Evening Star
Don't Turn My Picture to the Wall
The Girl of the Great Divide
I Might Be Your "Once in a While"
The Leader of Vanity Fair
Little Miss No-One from No-Where
Sweet Kitty Bellairs
The Way That Walker Walked Away
Smith, Robert H.
The Leader of the Frocks and Frills
Smith, Russell
My Heart for You Pines Away
Snyder, Ted
Alexander and His Clarinet
Beautiful Eyes
Bonnie Sue Sunshine
Bring Back My Lena to Me
Come Back to Me My Melody
Dear Mamie, I Love You
Don't Worry
Eight Little Letters Make Three Little Words
I Wonder Why She Kept On Saying Si Si Si Si Senor
If I Thought You Wouldn't Tell
I'm Going Back to Dixie
I'm Going to Do What I Please
I'm Sorry I Ain't Got It You Could Have It If I Had It Blues
In the Land of Harmony
It's the Pretty Things You Say
Kiss Me, My Honey, Kiss Me
Meet Me at the Station
Movin' Man Don't Take My Baby Grand
My Wife's Gone to the Country
Next to Your Mother Who Do You Love?
Oh, How That German Could Love
Piano Man
She Was a Dear Little Girl
Spanish Love
Stop That Rag
Sweet Italian Love
Sweet Marie Make-a Rag-a Time-a-Dance with Me
Take a Little Tip from Father
That Beautiful Rag
That Mysterious Rag
Tipperary Nora
Wild Cherries
Solman, Alfred
All She Gets from the Iceman Is Ice
The Gibson Bathing Girl
The Gibson Widow
Good Bye My Home Sweet Home
The Lily or the Rose
The Linger Longer Girl
Little Girl, You'll Do
We're Ready for Teddy Again
When the Bell in the Lighthouse Rings Ding, Dong
With the Last Rose of Summer, I'll Come Back to You
Would You Take Me Back Again?
You Splash Me and I'll Splash You

Solman, Arthur
The Bird on Nellie's Hat
Solomon, Fred
The Dandiest Boy in Town
Solomon, Frederick
Courting
Kitty
Sousa, John Philip
America First
The American Maid
Blue Ridge, I'm Coming Back to You
Boy Scouts of America
The Fairest of the Fair
The Glory of the Yankee Navy
The Golden Star
Hail to the Spirit of Liberty
The Invincible Eagle
I've Made My Plans for the Summer
The Lambs' March
The Liberty Loan March
The Messiah of Nations
The New York Hippodrome March
Sabre and Spur
The United States Field Artillery March
We Are Coming
Spaulding, George L.
Down the Line with Molly
Speaks, Oley
On the Road to Mandalay
Speaks, Olin
Sylvia
Spencer, Herbert
Lovesick
Pansies Mean Thoughts and Thoughts Mean You
Spenser, Willard
Miss Bob White
Spikes, Benjamin
Someday Sweetheart
Spikes, John C.
Someday Sweetheart
Sping, George
Come On, Let's Razoo on Our Little Kazoo
Spink, G. A.
I've Got to Dance Till the Band Gets Through
Spink, George
Personality
Stagliano, Leonard
Joan Sawyer Tango
Stamford, John J.
MacNamara's Band
Stamper, Dave
Chic-Chic-Chic-Chic-Chicken
Daddy Has a Sweetheart and Mother Is Her Name
Every Girl Is Fishing
Everybody Sometime Must Love Some One
I Can Live without You
I Want to Learn to Jazz Dance
Nijinski
Prunella Mine
Some Boy
Tulip Time
You're a Perfect Jewel to Me
Stanford, Tony
In the Valley of Kentucky
Stange, Stanislaus
The Country Girl
The Dolly Varden Song
My Own United States
Sweet Thoughts of Home
Stanley, Charles H.
The Blue Button Army
There's Another on Board That Might Be Saved
Stanton, Frank L.
Just a-Wearying for You
Mighty Lak' a Rose
Stanzione, Carmen
A Heart That's Free
Starr, Hattie
My Chilly Baby
My Onliest Little Dolly
Stauffer, Aubrey
That Loving Traumerei
Steele, W. C.
He May Get Over It But He'll Never Look the Same

Stept, Sammy
And That Ain't All
Sterling, Andrew
I Sent My Wife to the 1000 Isles
I Want Someone to Flirt with Me
Last Night Was the End of the World
What You Goin' to Do When the Rent Comes 'Round?
Sterling, Andrew B.
Alexander, Don't You Love Your Baby No More?
All Aboard for Dreamland
America, Here's My Boy
Are You Coming Out Tonight, Mary Ann?
The Baseball Glide
Bye Bye Dearie
Can You Tame Wild Wimmen?
Do You Take This Woman for Your Lawful Wife?
Down Where the Cotton Blossoms Grow
Down Where the Swanee River Flows
Good-bye, Eliza Jane
Hannah, Won't You Open the Door?
Hearts You Lose
I Ain't Got'en No Time to Have the Blues
I Just Can't Help from Lovin' That Man
I'll Be There, Mary Dear
I'm Proud to Be a Mother of a Soldier Like You
I'm the Only Star That Twinkles on Broadway
In a Hammock Built for Two
In the City of Sighs and Tears
In the Village by the Sea
In Vacation Time
Just Another Poor Man Gone Wrong
Look Who's Here
Louisiana Louise
Mamma's Little Alabama Love
Mariutch Down at Coney Island
Meet Me in St. Louis, Louis
Merrily We'll Roll Along
My Little Coney Island
My Pretty Little Kick-a-poo
Oh! Oh! Miss Phoebe
On a Sunday Afternoon
On the Banks of the Rhine with a Stein
Strike Up the Band
Take Me Back to New York Town
They're All Sweeties
Under the Anheuser Bush
Under the Yum Yum Tree
Wait 'Till the Sun Shines, Nellie
When a Lady Leads the Band
When Kate and I Were Comin' thro' the Rye
When My Johnny Boy Goes Marching By
When Rosie Riccoola Do the Hoola Ma Boola She's the Hit of Little Italy
Where the Morning Glories Twine around the Door
White Folks Call It Chanticleer But It's Still Just Plain Chicken to Me
Whoop 'er Up with a Whoop La La
Stern, Joseph W.
The Old Postmaster
Take These Flowers, Old Lady
Stern, Joseph W., Jr.
When a Feller Needs a Friend
Stevens, D. K.
Meet Me Dear, on Saturday, a Little after Two
Stevenson, Robert Louis
Pirate Song
Where Go the Boats?
Stewart, Anita
A Cheery Smile Is as Good as a Mile on the Road to Victory
In Old Kentucky
Mary Regan
A Midnight Romance
Stewart, Dorothy
Now Is the Hour

Stewart, Grant
  Acting
Stokes, Byron D.
  The Sweetheart of Sigma Chi
Stone, Mark L.
  Piking the Pike
Stonehill, Maurice
  When the Right Mr. Wright Comes Along
Story, Pauline B.
  He Died on the Fighting Line
  Wed the Man That You Love or Don't Wed at All
Stothart, Herbert
  It Gets Them All
Strasser, Fred
  Daddy, I Love You More and More Each Day
Stromberg, John
  The American Billionaire
  As on Moonlit Waves We Ride
  Beautiful Arizona
  Come Down, Ma Evening Star
  De Cakewalk Queen
  Dream One Dream of Me
  Easy Money
  If All the Stars Were Mine
  I'm a Respectable Working Girl
  Love a la Mode
  Ma Blushin' Rosie, My Posie Sweet
  Maud, Maud, Maud
  My Japanese Cherry Blossom
  Nothing Doing
  The Opera
  The Queen of Society
  Tell Us Pretty Ladies
  Wilhemina
Suck, Marie Madeleine
  Gay Butterfly
Sullenberger, W. A.
  That Tariff War
Sullivan, Alex
  I Want to See My Ida Hoe in Idaho
Sullivan, Arthur
  The Little Wooden Soldier
Sullivan, Daisy
  Mary Pickford, the Darling of Them All
Sumner, James S.
  Twelfth Street Rag
Sunshine, Marion
  You're My Boy
Suttle, Frank M.
  My Ship of Dreams
Sutton, Harry O.
  Ain't It Funny Just What Money Does for You
  And the World Goes on Just the Same
  I Don't Care
  Liz'
  You're in Love
Sutton, Henry O.
  I'm Trying to Find a Sweetheart
Swanstone, Arthur
  Blues My Naughty Sweetie Gives to Me
Sylvester, Harry
  Naughty Eyes
Symons, Arthur
  By the Pool at the Third Rosses
Taggart, George
  Du Barry, the Doll of the World
Tagore, Rabindranath
  Bird of the Wilderness
Tannehill, Frank J.
  Take Me Back to Babyland
Tannehill, Frank, Jr.
  Maybe
Tarkington, Booth
  Boy Scouts of America
Tate, James
  The Story of a Clothes Line
Tate, James W.
  Be Good! If You Can't Be Good Be Careful
  Come Along Up in the Flip Flap
  I've Told His Missus All about Him
  What Has That Man Harrigan Done?

Taylor, Billee
I Guess I'll Take the Train Back Home
Taylor, Charles H.
My Otaheite Lady
A Quaint Old Bird
Taylor, Deems
Hard Trials
Taylor, Helen
Bridal Dawn
Taylor, Herbert H.
In the Wildwood Where the Bluebells Grew
Since Nellie Went Away
Taylor, Tell
Ciribiribin
Down by the Old Mill Stream
He Sleeps beneath the Soil of France
Terris, Dorothy
Sing Me Love's Lullaby
Terry, Fred
Beautiful Dreamy Eyes
Teschemacher, Edward
Because
Love Is Mine
Wait 'till the Great Day Comes
Thaler, Rudolf
Ciribiribin
Thardo, Claude
If You Can't Say Something Good, Don't Say Nothing at All
Thompson, DeKoven
If I Forget
Thompson, Moe
My Honey's Back
Thurban, T. W.
Kelly Has Gone to Kingdom Come
Tierney, Harry
Alice Blue Gown
Bolsheveki Glide
Castle of Dreams
Cleopatra
If You Can't Get a Girl in the Summertime, You'll Never Get a Girl at All
It's Time for Every Boy to Be a Soldier
Louisiana
M-i-s-s-i-s-s-i-p-p-i
My Baby's Arms
My Little Service Flag Has Seven Stars
Nothing's Good Enough for a Good Little Girl If She's Good Enough for You
Oh, I Want to Be Good But My Eyes Won't Let Me
Oh! You Gray Haired Kid
The Palm Beach Dip
What Would $50,000 Make You Do?
Tietjens, Paul
Scarecrow
Tilbury, Walter
On Furlough
Timberg, Harold
Get a Girlie!
Tobin, William
When We Meet at the Golden Gate
Tours, Frank E.
In Flanders' Fields
Mother o' Mine
Towne, Charles Hanson
White Blossoms
Towne, T. Martin
Right Is Might
Tracey, William
Bring Back My Daddy to Me
He's Had No Lovin' for a Long, Long Time
Mammy o' Mine
Naughty! Naughty! Naughty!
Play That Barbershop Chord
Trahern, Al
Lights of Home
Under Southern Skies
Trainor, Val
When the Good Lord Makes a Record of a Hero's Deed, He Draws No Color Line
Trevelyan, Arthur
Look into Mine Eyes Dear Heart
My Jersey Lily
My Samoan Beauty

Sadie, You'se Ma Lady-Bird
Trevor
When It's Apple Blossom Time in Normandy
Troy, Henry
Farmyard Blues
Sweet Suzanne
Tucker, Henry
Sweet Genevieve
Tucker, Sophie
Daddy, I Love You More and More Each Day
Flippity-Flop
Turk, Roy
Oh, How I Laugh When I Think How I Cried about You
What Do I Care?
Turpin, Thomas M. J.
Pan-Am Rag
Tutt, Homer
The Zoo Step
Udall, Lyn
I'd Lay Down My Life for You
US
see Creamer, Henry S.
Valverde, J.
Clavelitos
van Alstyne, Egbert
Bright Eyes Good-Bye
Cheyenne
For Your Boy and My Boy
I Wonder What's the Matter with My Eyes?
I'm Afraid to Come Home in the Dark
In Dear Old Georgia
In the Shade of the Old Apple Tree
Memories
Mister Wilson, That's All
My Baby Talking Girl
My Hindoo Man
My Irish Girl
Nava Jo
'Neath the Old Cherry Tree, Sweet Marie
Oh, How I Love My Teacher
On the Road to Home Sweet Home
Pretty Baby
Sailin' Away on the Henry Clay
Semiole
So Long Mother
That Old Girl of Mine
Tippecanoo
What Are You Going to Do to Help the Boys?
What Makes the World Go Round
What's the Matter with Father?
Why Dont You Try?
You Never Miss the Water 'Till the Well Runs Dry
Your Eyes Have Told Me So
You're in Style When You're Wearing a Smile
van Alstyne, Frank
Back, Back, Back to Baltimore
Van, Gus
Baby's Prayers Will Soon Be Answered
Don't Try to Steal the Sweetheart of a Soldier
If I Could Peep through the Window Tonight
In the Land Where Poppies Bloom
Midnight in Dreamy Spain
My Old Log Cabin Home
Oh! How She Can Sing
Open Up the Golden Gates to Dixieland and Let Me into Paradise
Teach Me That Beautiful Love
You Cannot Shake That "Shimmie" Here
Vaughan, James
Bye-O Baby Bunting
Vaughan, Robert
You'll Fall for Someone
Vernon, F. Dudleigh
The Sweetheart of Sigma Chi
Villoldo, A. G.
El Choclo
Vincent, Nat
Bring Back Those Wonderful Days
I Know What It Means to Be Lonesome
Naughty! Naughty! Naughty!

Oh! Harry! Harry!
Oh! Papa, Oh! Papa, Won't You Be a Pretty Papa to Me?
The Shorter They Wear 'Em the Longer They Look
When Old Bill Bailey Plays the Ukelele
When the Lusitania Went Down
Violinski
That Carolina Rag
Vodery, Will H.
Cuddle Up Honey, Let's Make Love
The Darktown Poker Club
I Just Can't Keep My Eyes Off You
Von Breitenbach, Albert
see Bryan, Al
von Liebich, Rudolph
We Have Fed You All for a Thousand Years
von Tilzer, Albert
The Alcoholic Blues
Back to the Bleachers for Mine
Bunker Hill
Could You Learn to Love Me?
Down Where the Swanee River Flows
Give Me the Moonlight, Give Me the Girl and Leave the Rest to Me
Goodbye, Sweetheart, Goodbye
His Majesty, the American
Holding Hands
Honey Boy
I May Be Gone for a Long, Long Time
I Want Someone to Flirt with Me
I'm Glad I'm Married
I'm Sorry
Let's Go to a Picture Show
Lonesome
The Moon Has His Eyes on You
Nora Malone, Call Me by Phone
Oh by Jingo! Oh by Gee! You're the Only Girl for Me
Oh, How She Could Yacki Hacki Wicki Wacki Woo
Oh, That Moonlight Glide
Parisienne
A Picnic for Two
Please Don't Take My Lovin' Man Away
Put Your Arms Around Me, Honey
Smarty
Spoon Time
Sweet Kisses That Came in the Night
Take Me Out to the Ball Game
Teasing
That Hypnotizing Man
That's What the Daisy Said
The Whole Dam Family
You Will Have to Sing an Irish Song
von Tilzer, Harry
Alexander, Don't You Love Your Baby No More?
All Aboard for Dreamland
And the Green Grass Grew All Around
Are You a Buffalo?
Are You Coming Out Tonight, Mary Ann?
Baby Love
The Banquet in Misery Hall
The Baseball Glide
Beneath the Palms of Paradise
A Bird in a Gilded Cage
Bye and Bye You'll See the Sun A-Shining
Bye Bye Dearie
Can You Tame Wild Wimmen?
The Cubanola Glide
Do You Take This Woman for Your Lawful Wife?
Down on the Farm
Down Where the Cotton Blossoms Grow
Down Where the Swanee River Flows
Down Where the Wurzburger Flows
Good-bye, Eliza Jane
Hannah, Won't You Open the Door?

I Ain't a-Goin' to Weep No More
I Ain't Got'en No Time to Have the Blues
I Just Can't Help from Lovin' That Man
I Remember You
I Sent My Wife to the 1000 Isles
I Want a Girl Just Like the Girl That Married Dear Old Dad
I Want to Be an Actor Lady
I Wants to Be the Leading Lady
I'll Be There, Mary Dear
I'll Lend You Everything I've Got Except My Wife
I'm Proud to Be a Mother of a Soldier Like You
I'm the Only Star That Twinkles on Broadway
In a Hammock Built for Two
In the Heart of the Mighty Deep
In Vacation Time
It Must Have Been Svengali in Disguise
Jennie
Jennie Lee
Just Another Poor Man Gone Wrong
Last Night Was the End of the World
Look Who's Here
Love Me While the Loving Is Good
Mamma's Little Alabama Love
The Mansion of Aching Hearts
Mariutch Down at Coney Island
Meet Me When the Sun Goes Down
My Firefly
My Jersey Lily
My Lady Hottentot
My Little Coney Island
My Pretty Little Kick-a-poo
Oh! Oh! Miss Phoebe
On a Sunday Afternoon
On the Banks of the Rhine with a Stein
The Sentinel Asleep
Snap Your Fingers and Away You Go
Take Me Back to New York Town
They're All Sweeties
Under the Anheuser Bush
Under the Yum Yum Tree
The Villain Still Pursued Her
Wait 'Till the Sun Shines, Nellie
What You Goin' to Do When the Rent Comes 'Round?
When Highland Mary Did the Highland Fling
When Kate and I Were Comin' thro' the Rye
When Miss Patricia Salome Did Her Funny Little Oh-la Pa-lome
When My Johnny Boy Goes Marching By
When Sunday Comes to Town
When the Harvest Days Are Over, Jessie, Dear
When the Troupe Gets Back to Town
Where the Morning Glories Twine around the Door

Wade, Herman Avery
I Want to Be Loved Like a Leading Lady

Waldron, Jack T.
There's a Little Star in Heaven That They Call Broadway

Walker, E. Raymond
No One Knows Where the Old Man Goes

Walker, George
The Fortune Telling Man
She's Getting More Like the White Folks Every Day
When It's All Goin' Out and Nothin' Comin' In

Walker, Henry
Dooley's Alibi

Walker, J. J.
Kiss All the Girls for Me

Walker, James J.
Will You Love Me in December as You Do in May?

Walker, Marshall
I'm Trying to Teach My Sweet Papa Right from Wrong
It Takes a Long Tall Brown-Skin Gal to Make a Preacher Lay His Bible Down
It's Nobody's Business But My Own
Walker, Raymond
Poor Pauline
Walker, W. Ray
The Marquand Glide
Walker, Warren Ray
At the Steeplechase
Wallace, Oliver
Hindustan
Wallace, Paul
I Wish I Had My Old Girl Back Again
Wallis, W. H.
Beautiful Dreamy Eyes
Walsh, J. Brandon
Remember Me to My Old Girl
Walton, Ellis
Carmena
Walton, Lester A.
I Just Can't Keep My Eyes Off You
Wand, Hart A.
Dallas Blues
Ward, Charles B.
Strike Up the Band
Warfield, Charles
Baby, Won't You Please Come Home
Warren, Frank
Indianola
Waters, Johnnie
Oh! You Georgia Rose
Wathall, Alfred G.
Hike!
R-E-M-O-R-S-E
Watson, Maybelle E.
My Melancholy Baby
Wayburn, Ned
Come to the Moon
I Wonder If You're Lonely
My Little Chick
Wayne, Mabel
Ramona
Weatherly, Fred E.
Danny Boy
Roses of Picardy
Webster, Howard
After All
Weeks, Harold
Chong, He Come from Hong Kong
Hindustan
Weld, Arthur
In Disguise
Wells, Gil
You Cannot Shake That "Shimmie" Here
Wells, Gilbert
The Portobello Lassie
Wells, Jack
Joan of Arc, They Are Calling You
When Our Mothers Rule the World
Wendling, Pete
All the Quakers Are Shoulder Shakers Down in Quaker Town
Oh, How I Wish I Could Sleep Until My Daddy Comes Home
Oh! What a Pal Was Mary
Take Me to that Land of Jazz
Take Your Girlie to the Movies If You Can't Make Love at Home
Yaaka Hula Hickey Dula
Wenrich, Percy
The Baltimore Bombashay
The Humpty-Dumpty Kid
In Berry Pickin' Time
It's Moonlight All the Time on Broadway
Moonlight Bay
Naughty Eyes
Put on Your Old Grey Bonnet
Rainbow
The Red Rose Rag
Sweet Cider Time When You Were Mine
When You Wore a Tulip and I Wore a Big Red Rose
Where Do We Go from Here?

Weslyn, Louis
Baby Rose
The Boy Who Stuttered and the Girl Who Lisped
Douce Fievre
Lovesick
Lucky in Love
My Gal's Another Gal Like Galli-Curci
Send Me Away with a Smile
West, Clarence
It's Good Enough for Me
West, Eugene
Everybody Shimmies Now
Give Me a Syncopated Tune
Ze Yankee Boys Have Made a Wild French Baby Out of Me
West, Paul
Ballooning
Betty, You're the One Best Bet
Come Around on Our Veranda
Don't You Want a Paper, Dearie?
The Gibson Bathing Girl
The Gibson Widow
Good-By, Teddy! You Must March! March! March!
I Just Couldn't Do without You
I Want to Be Loved Like a Leading Lady
In the Folds of the Starry Flag
Weston
I've Got Rings on My Fingers
Weston, Joe
I'm Saving Up Coupons
Weston, R. P.
Mother's Sitting Knitting Little Mittens for the Navy
Oh! London, Where Are Your Girls Tonight?
Sister Susie's Sewing Shirts for Soldiers
Weston, T. C., Sr.
I Think of Thee
Weston, Willie
Joan of Arc, They Are Calling You
We're Going to Take the Sword Away from William
White, Bob
Come Right In, Sit Right Down and Make Yourself at Home
White, G. Harris (Doc)
Gee, Its a Wonderful Game
White, George
Come Dance with Me
I Can't Get Enough of Your Love
White, James
Floating Down the River
White, Wilkie
Tumble in Love
White, William
Six Times Six Is Thirty-Six
White, Willy
Everything Looks Rosy and Bright
Oh, How I Laugh When I Think How I Cried about You
Whiting, George
Baby Love
Beautiful Eyes
My Wife's Gone to the Country
Whiting, Richard
Some Sunday Morning
That Lullaby of Long Ago
Where the Black-Eyed Susans Grow
You're a Great Big Lonesome Baby
Whiting, Richard A.
Ain't You Coming Back to Dixieland?
Dress Up Your Dollars in Khaki and Help Win Democracy's Fight
Good-bye Cabarabian Nights
I Wonder Where My Lovin' Man Has Gone
Just Around the Corner
Love Me Like the Ivy Loves the Old Oak Tree
Mammy's Little Coal Black Rose
Mary Pickford, the Darling of Them All
Till We Meet Again
Whitman, Alberta
see Whitman, Bert
Whitman, Walt
Ethiopia Saluting the Colors

Whitson, Beth Slater
Don't Wake Me Up I Am Dreaming
Let Me Call You Sweetheart
Meet Me Tonight in Dreamland
Wickes, Edw. M.
He Laid Away a Suit of Gray to Wear the Union Blue
Wilbur, Al
A Picture without a Frame
Wildman, F. Collis
Pretty Desdemona
Wiley, Winthrop
Bashful Betsey Brown
Wilkens, Richard
Daisy Deane
Williams, Bert
Blackberrying Today
Borrow from Me
Constantly
The Darktown Poker Club
Dat's Harmony
Fas' Fas' World
The Fortune Telling Man
I'm Cured
The Island of By and By
Late Hours
Let It Alone
My Landlady
She's Getting More Like the White Folks Every Day
That's a Plenty
The Vampire
When It's All Goin' Out and Nothin' Comin' In
White Folks Call It Chanticleer But It's Still Just Plain Chicken to Me
You're Gwine to Get Somethin' What You Don't Expect
You're on the Right Road Sister But You're Goin' the Wrong Way
Williams, Bert A.
Believe Me!
The Harbor of Lost Dreams
If I Should Die Before I Wake, How Will I Know I'm Dead?
Nobody
Williams, Clarence
Baby, Won't You Please Come Home
I Ain't Gonna Give Nobody None o' This Jelly Roll
Royal Garden Blues
Sugar Blues
Ugly Chile
Yama Yama Blues
You Can Have It, I Don't Want It
Williams, E. J.
Martyrs of Columbia
Williams, Edna
If the Wind Had Only Blown the Other Way
Williams, Frank
Is Everybody Happy?
Williams, Harry
Back, Back, Back to Baltimore
The Band of Reubenville
Cheyenne
I Wonder What's the Matter with My Eyes?
I'm Afraid to Come Home in the Dark
Let Bygones Be Bygones and Let Us Be Sweethearts Again
Mickey
My Irish Girl
Nava Jo
'Neath the Old Cherry Tree, Sweet Marie
Peggy
Rose Room
Semiole
Tippecanoo
The Troubadour
You Never Miss the Water 'Till the Well Runs Dry
Williams, Harry H.
Bright Eyes Good-Bye
In Dear Old Georgia
In the Shade of the Old Apple Tree
Lonesome Honey for You
My Hindoo Man
Oh, How I Love My Teacher
What Makes the World Go Round

What's the Matter with Father?
Why Dont You Try?
Williams, Henry
Mister Wilson, That's All
Williams, Malcolm
Kiss Me Good Night, Dear Love
Williams, Spencer
I Ain't Gonna Give Nobody None o' This Jelly Roll
I Ain't Got Nobody Much and Nobody Cares for Me
Royal Garden Blues
Shim-me-sha-wabble
Tishomingo Blues
Yama Yama Blues
Williams, W.
Dolly
Williams, W. R.
All That I Had Is Gone
Ev'ry Day
Gee! But There's Class to a Girl Like You
The Girl You Can't Forget
I'd Like to Live in Loveland with a Girl Like You
Loveland Days
Oh! You Georgia Rose
We Don't Know Where We're Going But We're on Our Way
We Stand for Peace While Others War
When the Moon Plays Peek-a-Boo
Would You Rather Be a Tammany Tiger than a Teddy Bear?
Wills, Nat M.
BPOE
Had She Only Let Me Dream an Hour More
Wilsky, Abe
I'm Saving Up Coupons
Wilson, Al
I'm Going to Spend My Vacation with a Dear Old Relation
The Wild Wild Women Are Making a Wild Man of Me
Wilson, Clarence
The Zoo Step
Wilson, H. Lane
Carmena
Wilson, Walter
Ain't Dat a Shame?
Wilson, Woodrow
Fall in for Your Motherland
Wilt, Max S.
When the Birds Go North Again
Wimperis, Arthur
The Argentine
Winkle, Billy
When Uncle Joe Steps into France
Wise, Hen
Bye-O Baby Bunting
Wister, Owen
Ten Thousand Cattle Straying
Witt, Max S.
The Girl with the Big Toy Bear
The Lover's A.B.C.
My Heart's Tonight in Texas by the Silvery Rio Grande
My Mississippi Missus Misses Me
When the Fields Are White with Cotton
Wodehouse, P. G.
The Land Where the Good Songs Go
Peaches
The Picture I Want to See
Thousands of Years Ago
Will You Forget?
Wolf, Rennold
I Ain't Married No More
I Want to Look Like Lillian Russell
The Language of Lover's Smiles
You Cannot Make Your Shimmy Shake on Tea
Wolff, Fanny
see Fanchon
Wood, Cyrus
Darling
Wood, Frank
Molly Dear, It's You I'm After
Wood, Haydn
Roses of Picardy
Wood, Leo
Somebody Stole My Gal

Woods, F. A.
Good Fellows
Woodward, Matt
I Am So Particular
Woodward, Matt C.
Blooming Lize
The Girl Who Loves the Races
I Want to Be a Drummer in the Band
I Wonder Why Bill Bailey Don't Come Home
Love in an Orchard
Paree
Sister Ann
What's the Matter with Uncle Sam?
When Your Lips Pressed Mine
Woodward, Matthew
For Freedom and Ireland
Little Tommy Murphy
Woodward, Matthew C.
Ain't It Tough to Be So Absent-Minded?
Woolf, Edgar Allan
Let Us Build a Little Nest
Woolf, Edgar Allen
Mon Amour
Worton, David
I Can't Reach That Top Note
Wright, Ellen
The Maid in the Moon
Wynn, Bessie
If the Wind Had Only Blown the Other Way
Not for Me
Yellin, Jack
Alexander's Band Is Back in Dixieland
All Aboard for Dixie
Bring Me Back My Lovin' Honey Boy
In Berry Pickin' Time
Johnny's in Town
Oh! How She Can Sing
Open Up the Golden Gates to Dixieland and Let Me into Paradise
Southern Gals
There's a Lump of Sugar Down in Dixie
Y'Ener
Douce Fievre
Yosco, Bob
The Road for You and Me
Young,
Beckie, Stay in Your Own Backyard
Young, Joe
Arrah Go On, I'm Gonna Go Back to Oregon
Daddy Long Legs
Hello Central, Give Me No Man's Land
How 'Ya Gonna Keep 'Em Down on the Farm After They've Seen Paris?
Huckleberry Finn
I Wonder Why She Kept On Saying Si Si Si Si Si Senor
If I Knock the 'L' Out of Kelly, It Still Would Be Kelly to Me
I'm a Lonesome Melody
I'm All Bound 'Round with the Mason-Dixon Line
I'm Gonna Make Hay While the Sun Shines in Virginia
I'm Sorry I Ain't Got It You Could Have It If I Had It Blues
Let Bygones Be Bygones and Let Us Be Sweethearts Again
Love Me at Twilight
Meet Me at the Station
Oh, How I Wish I Could Sleep Until My Daddy Comes Home
On the Level, You're a Devil
Poor Little Butterfly Is a Fly Girl Now
Rock-a-bye Your Baby with a Dixie Melody
Romany
Shall They Plead in Vain?
Way Down East
Wedding Bells, Will You Ever Ring for Me
When the Angelus Is Ringing

When the Grown-Up Ladies Act Like Babies
When They're Old Enough to Know Better, It's Better to Leave Them Alone
When Tony LaBoard Played the Barber-Shop Chord
Who Played Poker with Pocohontas When John Smith Went Away?
Why Do They All Take the Night Boat to Albany?
Yaaka Hula Hickey Dula
You're a Million Miles from Nowhere When You're One Little Mile from Home
Young, Rida Johnson
Ah, Sweet Mystery of Life
The Fife and Drum
I Can't Take My Eyes off You
I'd Be Happy Anywhere with You
I'm Falling in Love with Some One
It Never, Never Can Be Love
Italian Street Song
The Kiss Waltz
Molly
Mother Machree
Naughty Marietta
'Neath the Southern Moon
Tramp, Tramp, Tramp
When Love Is Young
Will You Remember?
Zangwill, Israel
Kiss Me Good Night, Dear Love
Zarn, G. G.
Strolling on the Pike
Zelaya, Alphonse
The Maid of Old Madrid
Ziegler, Catherine
Sweetheart, Sweetheart, I Wear the Blue
Ziegler, Rachel
Sweetheart, Sweetheart, I Wear the Blue
Zierhrer, C. M.
A Kiss in the Dark
Zimmerman, Charles
Football
Zimmerman, Edward M.
Votes for Women
Zimmerman, Marie
Votes for Women
Zimmermann, Charles A.
Anchors Aweigh
Zit
Don't Walk So Fast
Gee! I'd Like to Be the Mayor
Nothing Bothers Me
That Hypnotizing Rag
Zittel, C. Florian
see Zit

Important Performances Index

Songs are listed under the works in which they were introduced or given significant renditions. The index is organized into major sections by performance medium: Album, Movie, Musical, Performer, Revue, Television Show.

Album

After the Ball
A Bird in a Gilded Cage
Come Down, Ma Evening Star
American Popular Song
Alexander's Rag-Time Band
I Ain't Got Nobody Much and Nobody Cares for Me
My Melancholy Baby
Some of These Days
Ben Bagley's George Gershwin Revisited
There's More to the Kiss than the X-X-X
The Early Victor Herbert
The Time and the Place and the Girl
The Eighty-Six Years of Eubie Blake, Record 2
It's All Your Fault
Eubie!
Gee! I Wish I Had Someone to Rock Me in the Cradle of Love
Good Night, Angeline
Eubie Blake
Good Night, Angeline
George Gershwin Plays Gershwin and Kern
Tee-Oodle-Um-Bam-Bo
The Girl on the Magazine Cover
The Girl on the Magazine Cover
That Mysterious Rag
The Heritage of John Philip Sousa
America First
Boy Scouts of America
The Fairest of the Fair
The Glory of the Yankee Navy
The Golden Star
Hail to the Spirit of Liberty
The Lambs' March
The Liberty Loan March
The New York Hippodrome March
Sabre and Spur
The United States Field Artillery March
Join in the Chorus
If You Were the Only Girl in the World
Under the Anheuser Bush
Keep the Home Fires Burning
Keep the Home Fires Burning

Maytime
  Will You Remember?
The Merry Widow
  I Love You So
The Music of Victor Herbert
  March of the Toys
  Toyland
The Sousa and Pryor Bands
  The Glory of the Yankee Navy
Stars and Stripes Forever
  The Fairest of the Fair
They All Play Ragtime
  Pan-Am Rag
They Stopped the Show!
  Alice Blue Gown
  BPOE
  I Don't Care
  I've Got Rings on My Fingers
  Redhead
  Turn Off Your Light, Mr. Moon Man
  Yip-I-Addy-I-Ay
Tintypes
  Fifty-Fifty
  I Want to Be Loved Like a Leading Lady
  I Want What I Want When I Want It
  It's Delightful to Be Married
Vaudeville
  The Bird on Nellie's Hat
  I Don't Care
  I Just Can't Make My Eyes Behave
  Let the Rest of the World Go By
  My Castle on the Nile
  Poor John
  Shine On, Harvest Moon
  Smiles
  Wait 'Till the Sun Shines, Nellie
  The Yama Yama Man
  Yip-I-Addy-I-Ay
Ziegfeld Follies of 1919
  Bring Back Those Wonderful Days
  Everybody Wants a Key to My Cellar
  I'm Sorry I Ain't Got It You Could Have It If I Had It Blues
  I've Got My Captain Working for Me Now
  Mandy
  The Moon Shines on the Moonshine
  My Baby's Arms
  Oh! How She Can Sing
  Oh! The Last Rose of Summer Was the Sweetest Rose of All
  A Pretty Girl Is Like a Melody
  Sweet Kisses That Came in the Night
  Tulip Time
  When They're Old Enough to Know Better, It's Better to Leave Them Alone
  You'd Be Surprised

Movie

Alexander's Rag-Time Band
  Alexander's Rag-Time Band
  Everybody's Doin' It Now
  In My Harem
Alias Jimmy Valentine
  Alias Jimmy Valentine
Alma, Where Do You Live?
  Alma, Where Do You Live?
Atlantic City
  On a Sunday Afternoon
Babes in Toyland
  March of the Toys
Babes on Broadway
  Waiting for the Robert E. Lee
Belle of the Yukon
  I Can't Tell Why I Love You But I Do
The Bells of St. Mary's
  The Bells of St. Mary's
  In the Land of Beginning Again
The Big Parade
  Douce Fievre
Birth of a Nation
  The Perfect Song
Birth of the Blues
  By the Light of the Silvery Moon

Cuddle Up a Little Closer, Lovey Mine
Wait 'Till the Sun Shines, Nellie
Blue Hawaii
Aloha Oe
Blue Skies
I've Got My Captain Working for Me Now
You'd Be Surprised
Boy o' Mine
Dear Little Boy of Mine
Broadway Melody of 1938
You Made Me Love You, I Didn't Want to Do It
Broken Blossoms
White Blossoms
By the Light of the Silvery Moon
By the Light of the Silvery Moon
Circus Days
Oh! You Circus Day
Civilization
Peace Song
The Cockeyed World
K-K-K-Katy
Coney Island
Cuddle Up a Little Closer, Lovey Mine
Put Your Arms Around Me, Honey
Cover Girl
Poor John
Daddy Long-Legs
Daddy Long Legs
The Daughter of Rosie O'Grady
The Daughter of Rosie O'Grady
The Dawn of a Tomorrow
The Dawn of a Tomorrow
The Dolly Sisters
I'm Always Chasing Rainbows
East Is West
Chinese Lullaby
Easter Parade
The Girl on the Magazine Cover
I Love a Piano
I Want to Go Back to Michigan
Rag-Time Violin
Snooky Ookums
When That Midnight Choo-Choo Leaves for Alabam'
The Emperor Waltz
The Whistler and His Dog
Eyes of Youth
Eyes of Youth
The Fatal Ring
The Fatal Ring
The Firefly
Gianina Mia
Love Is Like a Firefly
For Me and My Gal
For Me and My Gal
They Go Wild, Simply Wild Over Me
When You Wore a Tulip and I Wore a Big Red Rose
The Garden of Allah
The Garden of Allah
The Great Ziegfeld
A Pretty Girl Is Like a Melody
Yiddle on Your Fiddle Play Some Rag Time
Hearts of the World
Hearts of the World
Hello, Frisco, Hello
Rag-Time Cowboy Joe
His Majesty the American
His Majesty, the American
The "I Don't Care" Girl
I Don't Care
Kiss Me, My Honey, Kiss Me
I Wonder Who's Kissing Her Now
Be Sweet to Me, Kid
Honeymoon
I Wonder Who's Kissing Her Now
The Umpire Is a Most Unhappy Man
What's the Use of Dreaming
I'll See You in My Dreams
I Wish I Had a Girl
In Old Kentucky
In Old Kentucky
In Old Oklahoma
Put Your Arms Around Me, Honey
In the Good Old Summertime
I Don't Care
In the Good Old Summertime
Meet Me Tonight in Dreamland
Play That Barbershop Chord

Put Your Arms Around Me, Honey
Incendiary Blonde
Rag-Time Cowboy Joe
What Do You Want to Make Those Eyes at Me For?
Intolerance
The Mountain Maid
Irene
Alice Blue Gown
Irish Eyes Are Smiling
Dear Little Boy of Mine
Let the Rest of the World Go By
A Little Bit of Heaven, Shure They Call It Ireland
Irish Eyes Are Smiling (1944)
When Irish Eyes Are Smiling
It Started with Eve
Clavelitos
The Jazz Singer
My Gal Sal
Waiting for the Robert E. Lee
You Ain't Heard Nothing Yet
Jennie Gerhardt
Dreaming
Jolson Sings Again
For Me and My Gal
Rock-a-bye Your Baby with a Dixie Melody
Waiting for the Robert E. Lee
You Made Me Love You, I Didn't Want to Do It
The Jolson Story
I Want a Girl Just Like the Girl That Married Dear Old Dad
Ma Blushin' Rosie, My Posie Sweet
The Spaniard That Blighted My Life
Swanee
You Made Me Love You, I Didn't Want to Do It
Jubilo
Jubilo
Kid Millions
Mandy
The King of Jazz
Nola
Las Vegas Nights
On Miami Shore
Lillian Russell
Come Down, Ma Evening Star
Ma Blushin' Rosie, My Posie Sweet
Ma, He's Making Eyes at Me
Ma, He's Making Eyes at Me
Mammy
Who Paid the Rent for Mrs. Rip Van Winkle?
Mary Regan
Mary Regan
Maytime
Will You Remember?
Meet Me in St. Louis
Meet Me in St. Louis, Louis
Under the Bamboo Tree
The Merry Widow
Heure exquise qui nous grise
Metropolitan
On the Road to Mandalay
Mickey
Mickey
A Midnight Romance
A Midnight Romance
Mighty Lak' a Rose
Mighty Lak' a Rose
Miss Information
Some Sort of Somebody
Mr. Bug Goes to Town
Be My Little Baby Bumble Bee
Mother Machree
Goodbye, Mother Machree
Mother Machree
Mother of Men
Yip-I-Addy-I-Ay
My Gal Sal
My Gal Sal
My Ship o' Dreams
My Ship of Dreams
My Wild Irish Rose
When Irish Eyes Are Smiling
Naughty Marietta
Ah, Sweet Mystery of Life
I'm Falling in Love with Some One
Italian Street Song
Tramp, Tramp, Tramp

The New Moon
The New Moon
Nob Hill
What Do You Want to Make Those Eyes at Me For?
Oh, You Beautiful Doll
Come Josephine in My Flying Machine
Dardanella
Ireland Must Be Heaven for My Mother Came from There
Oh, You Beautiful Doll
There's a Broken Heart for Every Light on Broadway
Who Paid the Rent for Mrs. Rip Van Winkle?
On Moonlight Bay
Cuddle Up a Little Closer, Lovey Mine
I'm Forever Blowing Bubbles
Moonlight Bay
Tell Me
On the Riviera
Ballin' the Jack
Over the Top
Your Lips Are No Man's Land But Mine
Patria
Patria
The Perils of Pauline
Poor Pauline
Radio Days
Chinatown, My Chinatown
Ramona
Ramona
Rebecca of Sunnybrook Farm
Rebecca of Sunnybrook Farm
A Regular Girl
A Regular Girl
The Road to Romany
The Road to Romany
A Romance of Happy Valley
A Romance of Happy Valley
Rose of Washington Square
Rose of Washington Square
Shadows
Shadows
Shine On, Harvest Moon
Shine On, Harvest Moon
Show Boat
Good Bye, My Lady Love
The Singing Fool
The Spaniard That Blighted My Life
Skirts Ahoy
Oh by Jingo! Oh by Gee! You're the Only Girl for Me
Smilin' Through
Smilin' Through
So Long Letty
So Long Letty
Some Like It Hot
Down Among the Sheltering Palms
The Spirit of the U.S.A.
That Wonderful Mother of Mine
The Star Maker
Alias Jimmy Valentine
I Can't Tell Why I Love You But I Do
School Days
Sunbonnet Sue
The Story of Vernon and Irene Castle
The Yama Yama Man
The Strawberry Blonde
Good-Bye, Little Girl, Good-Bye
Sunbonnet Sue
Sunbonnet Sue
Sweetheart of Sigma Chi
The Sweetheart of Sigma Chi
Take Me Out to the Ball Game
Take Me Out to the Ball Game
Tess of the Storm Country
Tess of the Storm Country
That's Entertainment I
You Made Me Love You, I Didn't Want to Do It
That's My Boy
Ballin' the Jack
That's the Spirit
Baby, Won't You Please Come Home
There's No Business Like Show Business
Play a Simple Melody
You'd Be Surprised

This Is the Army
Oh! How I Hate to Get Up in the Morning
Three Little Girls in Blue
If You Can't Get a Girl in the Summertime, You'll Never Get a Girl at All
Three Little Words
Where Did You Get That Girl?
Thrill of a Romance
I Want What I Want When I Want It
'Till the Clouds Roll By
The Land Where the Good Songs Go
The Time, the Place, and the Girl
Honeymoon
Tin Pan Alley
K-K-K-Katy
Two Weeks with Love
The Aba Daba Honeymoon
By the Light of the Silvery Moon
A Heart That's Free
He'd Have to Get Under, Get Out and Get Under to Fix Up His Automobile
The Vagabond Lover
If You Were the Only Girl in the World
The Virginian
My Virginian
Wabash Avenue
I've Been Floating Down the Old Green River
Wait 'Till the Sun Shines, Nellie
Wait 'Till the Sun Shines, Nellie
War Brides
War Brides
Way Down East
Way Down East
When a Feller Needs a Friend
When a Feller Needs a Friend
When Irish Eyes Are Smiling (1922)
When Irish Eyes Are Smiling
When It Strikes Home
When It Strikes Home
The Woman Thou Gavest Me
The Woman Thou Gavest Me
Yankee Doodle Dandy
Forty-five Minutes from Broadway
Give My Regards to Broadway
H-A-Double R-I-G-A-N
Mary
Over There
So Long, Mary
Yankee Doodle Boy
You're a Grand Old Flag
Ziegfeld Girl
I'm Always Chasing Rainbows

Musical

About Town
Der Faderland for Mine
I'm Sorry
Tipperary Nora
When Tommy Atkins Marries Dolly Gray
Abyssinia
I Thought My Troubles Were Over, But They'd Scarce Begun
I'll Keep a Warm Spot in My Heart for You
The Island of By and By
Let It Alone
Algy
Following in Father's Footsteps
The Seaside Sultan
All Aboard
Somebody's Coming to My House
Take Me Back
Alma, Where Do You Live?
Alma, Where Do You Live?
The Amazones
My Otaheite Lady
The American Maid
The American Maid
Angel Face
I Might Be Your "Once in a While"
Atta Boy
On a Little Farm in Normandie
The Babes and the Baron
By the Light of the Honeymoon
I Would Like to Be Your Pal

Babes in the Woods
I Would Like to Marry You
Babette
Be Kind to Poor Pierrot
Bandana Land
Bon Bon Buddy
Bye-O Baby Bunting
Fas' Fas' World
The Fortune Telling Man
In My Old Home
It's Hard to Love Somebody Who's Loving Somebody Else
Kinky
Late Hours
Red Red Rose
Somebody Lied
Why Adam Sinned
You're in the Right Church But the Wrong Pew
A Barnyard Romeo
If He Comes In, I'm Going Out
The Beauty Shop
I Want to Look Like Lillian Russell
When You're All Dressed Up and No Place to Go
The Beauty Spot
Foolish Questions
The Belle of Avenue A
The Band of Reubenville
The Belle of Bohemia
What Eve Said to Adam
The Belle of Bond Street
My Turkey Trotting Boy
Prunella
Tango Dip
Who Paid the Rent for Mrs. Rip Van Winkle?
The Belle of Bridgeport
I've Got Troubles of My Own
Magdaline, My Southern Queen
Why Don't the Band Play?
The Belle of Brittany
I Can't Reach That Top Note
The Billionaire
If Yankee Doodle Hadn't Come to Town
I'm the Money Burner
Two Eyes of Brown
The Bing Boys Are Here
If You Were the Only Girl in the World
The Black Politician
If I Ever Get Back to Cincinnati
The Blonde in Black
The Yankee Girl
The Blue Moon
Don't Go in the Lion's Cage Tonight, Mother
Don't You Think It's Time to Marry?
Meet Me Down at the Corner
When Love Comes Knocking at the Door
The Blue Paradise
Here's to You, My Sparkling Wine
The Boys and Betty
She Was a Dear Little Girl
Whoop 'er Up with a Whoop La La
The Bridal Trip
Can You Forget
Broadway and Buttermilk
'Twas Only an Irishman's Dream
Broadway to Paris
Everybody Loves a Chicken
Hello Cupid, Send Me a Fellow
My Bird of Paradise
Paree's a Branch of Broadway
The Raffles Dance
Take Me to That Swanee Shore
Broadway to Tokio
A Love-Lorn Lily
Brown of Harvard
When Love Is Young
The Canary
I Have Just One Heart for Just One Boy
I Wouldn't Give 'That' for the Man Who Couldn't Dance
O Promise Me You'll Write to Him Today
Thousands of Years Ago
The Candy Shop
Googy-Oo
Oh, You Candy Kid

The White Wash Man
The Casino Girl
Down De Lover's Lane
In Disguise
Love Has Claimed Its Own
Mamselle
The Catch of the Season
Little Girl, You'll Do
A Quaint Old Bird
A Certain Party
I'm on My Way to Reno
Champagne Charlie
I Hates to Get Up Early in the Morning
The Chaperons
Blooming Lize
The Cherry Girl
Nava Jo
Chin-Chin
Good Bye Girls I'm Through
A Chinese Honeymoon
Could You Be True to Eyes of Blue If You Looked into Eyes of Brown?
I Want to Be a Lidy
The Language of Flowers
The Leader of the Frocks and Frills
Mister Dooley
There's a Little Star in Heaven That They Call Broadway
Comin' thro' the Rye
I Guess I'll Take the Train Back Home
Coming thro' the Rye
Spoon Time
A Country Girl
Coo!
The Dairymaids
I'd Like to Meet Your Father
I've a Million Reasons Why I Love You
Dancing Around
Dancing the Blues Away
Everybody Rag with Me
The Darling of the Gallery Gods
Watch Me To-night in the Torchlight Parade
Davey's Troubles
In a Little Cottage by the Railroad Track
The Deacon and the Lady
Love Me with a Tiger Love
The Defender
I'll Be Your Rain-Beau
In the Good Old Summertime
Pinky Panky Poo
Dick Wittington
When My Sist' Tetrazin' Met My Cousin Carus'
The District Leader
What's the Use of Dreaming
Dr. Beans from Boston
Cuddle Up Honey, Let's Make Love
Doing Our Bit
The Wild Wild Women Are Making a Wild Man of Me
Dolly Varden
The Country Girl
The Duke of Duluth
G.O.P.
Percy
The Earl and the Girl
How'd You Like to Spoon with Me?
I Want a Man Made to Order for Me
I Would Like to Marry You
In Zanzibar
It's Good Enough for Me
When the Right Little Girl Comes Along
Easy Dawson
And the World Goes on Just the Same
It's a Waste of Time to Worry
The Echo
French Fandango
Way Down in Cotton Town
The Emerald Isle
Dooley's Alibi
The Little Wooden Soldier
The English Daisy
At the Music Hall
Big Indian Chief

Ma Mamselle Honee
Erminie
Two Eyes of Brown
The Explorers
My Madagascar Maid
Fantana
G.O.P.
Tammany
Fascinating Flora
Ballooning
Build Your Nest Away Down in My Heart
The Girl with the Big Toy Bear
I'd Rather Two-Step Than Waltz, Bill
The Fascinating Widow
All the World Loves a Lover
Don't Go in the Water, Daughter
Don't Take Your Beau to the Seashore
The Ragtime College Girl
Fiddle-dee-dee
Ma Blushin' Rosie, My Posie Sweet
Fifty Miles from Boston
H-A-Double R-I-G-A-N
The Fisher Maiden
Beneath the Palms of Paradise
The Floor Walkers
Absence Makes the Heart Grow Fonder
The Flower of the Ranch
What's the Use of Dreaming
Fluffy Ruffles
I Love to Sit and Look at You
Follow Me
Oh, I Want to Be Good But My Eyes Won't Let Me
Oh Johnny, Oh Johnny, Oh!
What Do You Want to Make Those Eyes at Me For?
Forty-five Minutes from Broadway
Forty-five Minutes from Broadway
Mary
So Long, Mary
Foxy Grandpa
The Bathing Lesson
Fritz in Tammany Hall
My Irish Daisy
My Sweet
The Galloper
You're in Love
The Gay White Way
Irish Fluffy Ruffles
My Irish Gibson Girl
You've Got to Do That Salome Dance
George M!
Forty-five Minutes from Broadway
Give My Regards to Broadway
H-A-Double R-I-G-A-N
Mary
Oh, You Wonderful Girl
Over There
So Long, Mary
Yankee Doodle Boy
You're a Grand Old Flag
George Washington, Jr.
You're a Grand Old Flag
The Girl and the Wizard
I Wonder If You're Lonely
Oh, How That German Could Love
The Girl behind the Counter
All She Gets from the Iceman Is Ice
The Glow Worm
I Want to Be Loved Like a Leading Lady
If You'll Walk with Me
Just Because He Couldn't Sing "Love Me and the World Is Mine"
The Girl from Dixie
Love in an Orchard
The Lover's A.B.C.
Pansy Faces
When the Moon Comes Peeping Over the Hill
The Girl from Kay's
Egypt, My Cleopatra
I Love You All the Time
Love at the Door

The Girl from Montmartre
Don't Turn My Picture to the Wall
The Girl from Up There
Zamona
The Girl from Utah
Ballin' the Jack
I'm on My Way to Dublin Bay
The Land of "Let's Pretend"
Molly Dear, It's You I'm After
Same Sort of Girl
They Didn't Believe Me
The Girl in the Taxi
That Baboon Baby Dance
The Girl on the Train
In My Dreams of You
The Girl Question
Be Sweet to Me, Kid
The Girl Who Didn't
A Tango Dream
The Girls from Gottenburg
I Remember You
Good Morning, Judge
I Was So Young, You Were So Beautiful
I'm Not Jealous
There's More to the Kiss than the X-X-X
The Governor's Son
Maudie
The Hall of Fame
The Army of Peace
I'm the Man Who Makes the Money in the Mint
The Maiden with the Dreamy Eyes
Meet Me When the Sun Goes Down
My Angemima Green
My Pajama Beauty
Nancy, Oh Miss Nancy
Sallie, Mah Hot Tamale
The Sunflower and the Sun
When Charlie Plays the Slide Trombone in the Silver Cornet Band
The Ham Tree
Eighth Avenue
Good-Bye, Sweet Old Manhattan Isle
Honey Love Me All the Time
On an Automobile Honeymoon
Where the Red Red Roses Grow
Hands Up
I'm Simply Crazy over You
Hanky Panky
That Baboon Baby Dance
Have a Heart
Look in Her Eyes
What Would $50,000 Make You Do?
He Came from Milwaukee
Bring Back My Lena to Me
Head Over Heels
Let Us Build a Little Nest
The Head Waiter
Absence Makes the Heart Grow Fonder
Mah Moonlight Lou
The Hen Pecks
In the Shadows
Let Me Live and Stay in Dixieland
The Manicure Girl
Her Soldier Boy
I'd Be Happy Anywhere with You
The Kiss Waltz
Pack Up Your Troubles in Your Old Kit Bag and Smile, Smile, Smile
High Jinks
All Aboard for Dixie
Hip! Hip! Hooray!
All I Want in the Wide Wide World Is You
His Bridal Night
Heavenly Twins
His Highness the Bey
Not Because Your Hair Is Curly
His Honor the Barber
Come After Breakfast, Bring 'long You' Lunch and Leave 'fore Supper Time
That's Why They Call Me Shine
His Honor, the Mayor
Come, Take a Skate with Me
A Little Girl Like Me

My Irish Molly O
Hodge, Podge & Co.
I Love My Shirt Waist Best
My Charcoal Charmer
My Sunflower Sue
Hoity-Toity
The American Billionaire
As on Moonlit Waves We Ride
Easy Money
My Japanese Cherry Blossom
The Queen of Society
When Two Hearts Are One
The Honeymoon Express
At Mammy's Fireside
I Love Her Oh! Oh! Oh!
Ragging the Old Vienna Roll
Snap Your Fingers and Away You Go
The Spaniard That Blighted My Life
Syncopatia Land
When Gaby Did the Gaby Glide
Who Paid the Rent for Mrs. Rip Van Winkle?
You'll Call the Next Love the First
You're a Good Little Devil
Hop o' My Thumb
Those Days of Long Ago
A Hot Old Time
The Blue and the Gray: A Mother's Gift to Her Country
The Hoyden
Advertising
Put Me Among the Girls
Humpty-Dumpty
Down in Mulberry Bend
Mexico
On Lalawana's Shore
The Pussy and the Bow-Wow
Sambo and Dinah
In and Out of Society
Bless Your Ever Loving Little Heart
In Central Park
The Duchess of Central Park
In Dahomey
I'd Like to Be a Real Lady
I'm a Jonah Man
Why Adam Sinned
In Harvard
Linda, Look Out de' Windah
In Hayti
Everybody's Ragtime Crazy
Irene
Alice Blue Gown
Castle of Dreams
It Happened in Nordland
Jack O'Lantern Girl
My Hindoo Man
It Happened in Norland
Beatrice Barefacts
Jack O'Lantern
I'll Take You Back to Italy
Oh! Papa, Oh! Papa, Won't You Be a Pretty Papa to Me?
The Jersey Lily
Bedelia
The Jewel of Asia
I Love You Dolly
The Same Old Crowd
A Woman's No Means 'Yes'
The Jolly Bachelors
Come Along My Mandy
Has Anybody Here Seen Kelly?
Sweet Marie Make-a Rag-a Time-a-Dance with Me
That Beautiful Rag
Judy Forgot
I Want a Little Lovin' Sometimes
Jumping Jupiter
Dat Possum Rag
Kafoozelum
Hiram Green, Good-Bye
King Dodo
The Tale of a Bumble Bee
Zamona
The King's Carnival
My Evalyne
When Mr. Shakespeare Comes to Town
The Knickerbocker Girl
Brother Bill
Devotion
A Knight for a Day
The Garden of Dreams
The Girl of the Great Divide

I'm Afraid to Come Home in the Dark
La Belle Paree
De Goblin's Glide
The Edinboro Wiggle
La La Lucille
The Best of Everything
From Now On
Somehow It Seldom Comes True
Tee-Oodle-Um-Bam-Bo
There's More to the Kiss than the X-X-X
Ladies First
Just Like a Gypsy
Prohibition Blues
Without You
Lady Bountiful
Lady Bountiful
The Lady in Red
Something about Love
The Land of Nod
Waltz Me Around Again, Willie
The Laughing Husband
You're Here and I'm Here
The Liberty Belles
Billet Doux
De Trop
Follow the Man That Leads the Band
I'd Like to Be a Gunner in the Navy
In Florida
Instrumental Man
Jack O'Lantern
John Would Never Do That
My Filopena Pet
Spring Fashions
The Way That Walker Walked Away
Linger Longer Letty
Linger Longer Letty
Oh by Jingo! Oh by Gee! You're the Only Girl for Me
A Little Bit of Everything
Blue Eyed Sue
The Little Blue Devil
Dancing Shoes
The Little Cafe
Just Because It's You
The Little Cherub
Meet Me at Twilight
My Irish Rose
Oh, How I Love My Teacher
Pierrot and Pierrette
Popular Songs
Say! Fay!
Under the Linden Tree
Little Dolly Dimples
Good Bye My Home Sweet Home
I'm Going Back to Carolina
The Little Duchess
Bashful Betsey Brown
Chloe, I'm Waiting
Flirtation Song
In Society
The Maiden with the Dreamy Eyes
The Man Who Plays the Tambourine
Sadie
Since Sister Nell Heard Paderewski Play
Strolling Along the Beach
What'd Yo' Do Wid de Letter, Mr. Johnson?
Little Johnny Jones
Give My Regards to Broadway
Yankee Doodle Boy
The Little Magnet
Where the Silv'ry Colorado Wends Its Way
The Little Millionaire
Musical Moon
Oh, You Wonderful Girl
Little Miss Fix-It
Turn Off Your Light, Mr. Moon Man
Little Nemo
When a Girl Leads the Band
Won't You Be My Valentine?
Lola from Berlin
Beneath the Moon
A Lonely Romeo
Any Old Place with You
Lonesome Town
When the Moon Plays Peek-a-Boo

Love and Politics
What's the Use of Dreaming
The Love Mill
When I'm Thru with the Arms of the Army, I'll Come Back to the Arms of You
Love's Lottery
Sweet Thoughts of Home
A Lucky Hoodoo
The Coster's Glide
Madame Sherry
Every Little Movement
The Madcap Princess
Little Girl, You'll Do
Maid in America
If You Want a Little Doggie, Whistle and I'll Come to You
I've Been Floating Down the Old Green River
Sister Susie's Started Syncopation
The Stolen Melody
Maid Marian
If All the Stars Were Mine
The Maid of the Mountains
Dark Grows the Sky
Waiting for You
Mammy
Why Do They All Take the Night Boat to Albany?
Mam'selle Napoleon
The "A la Mode" Girl
The Man of Mexico
My Pretty Zulu Lu
The Man Who Owns Broadway
I'm All O.K. with K. and E.
Marrying Mary
He's a Cousin of Mine
Old Reliable Jokes
Mary's Lamb
Love Is Elusive
My Madagascar Maid
The Matinee Idol
Under the Yum Yum Tree
Me, Him, and I
Over the Moonlit Sea
The Medal and the Maid
In Zanzibar
The Melting of Molly
Darling
Merry-Go-Round
Have You Seen My Baby?
The Merry Widow and the Devil
Bonnie My Highland Lassie
Yip-I-Addy-I-Ay
The Merry Widower
Dat Lovin' Rag
The Messenger Boy
Can't You Take My Word?
Pansy
Poor Robinson Crusoe
The Midnight Girl
Good Night Dear
The Midnight Songs
Goo-Goo Eyes
The Midnight Sons
I'd Like to Live in Loveland with a Girl Like You
I've Got Rings on My Fingers
Kelly Has Gone to Kingdom Come
Little Mary Gardeners
My Sist' Tetrazzin'
The Queen of the Night
The Military Maid
O Mona San
Miss Bob White
Miss Bob White
Miss Caprice
Look in Her Eyes
Miss Cuba, Jr.
The Blue and the Gray: A Mother's Gift to Her Country
Miss Information
A Little Love But Not for Me
Miss Innocence
I Want to Be Naughty Too
I Wonder What's the Matter with My Eyes?
I'm Learning Something Every Day
I've Lost My Teddy Bear
My Pony Boy
Miss Simplicity
The Girl with the Baby Stare
Mr. Bluebeard
The Beer That Made Milwaukee Famous

Hamlet Was a Melancholy Dane
I'm a Poor Unhappy Maid
Julie
On a Spoony Moony Night
Sister Ann
Mr. Hamlet of Broadway
Beautiful Eyes
The Hornpipe Rag
You Never Miss the Water 'Till the Well Runs Dry
Mr. Lode of Koal
The Harbor of Lost Dreams
Mr. Pickwick
Acting
Mlle. Mischief
And Other Things
Lonesome
Mlle. Modiste
Kiss Me Again
The Time and the Place and the Girl
Mme. Sherry
Put Your Arms Around Me, Honey
The Mocking Bird
France, Glorious France
In Silence
Sly Musette
What's the Matter with the Moon Tonight?
Modest Suzanne
All the World Loves a Lover
Molly Moonshine
Don't Be What You Ain't
Robinson Crusoe's Isle
Monte Christo, Jr.
Come Back to Me
Moonshine Mary
The Conjure Man
Mother Goose
Blue Eyed Sue
Honey Boy
In the *Ladies' Home Journal*
Pansy Faces
Under the Mistletoe Bough
When I Do the Highland Fling
Mrs. Black Is Back
Bible Stories
"Mumms" the Word
'Taint No Use in Lovin' That Way
Mrs. Delaney of Newport
Her Eyes of Irish Blue
Mrs. Wilson-Andrews
Bonnie Sue Sunshine
My Best Girl
The Language of Lover's Smiles
That Syncopated Boogie Boo
My Friend from Kentucky
At the Ball, That's All
My Friend from Kentucky
Rock Me in the Cradle of Love
My Lady
Simple Little Sister Mary Green
My Lady Friends
I Want to Spread a Little Sunshine
My Toreador
My Toreador
Nancy Brown
The Katy-Did, the Cricket and the Frog
Marie Cahill's Congo Love Song
Nava Jo
Save It for Me
Two Eyes
Nearly a Hero
I Am So Particular
I Wish I Had a Girl
A Singer Sang a Song
What Makes the World Go Round
The New Yorkers
The Kodak Girl
My Honolulu Lu
Oh Fudge!
Take Me Back to Herald Square
The Newlyweds and Their Baby
Loving Time
The Night of the Fourth
M-O-N-E-Y Spells Money
Walk, Walk, Walk
The Office Boy
Plain Mamie O'Hooley
The Proper Way to Kiss
Oh, Look!
I Think You're Absolutely Wonderful (What Do You Think of Me?)

I'm Always Chasing Rainbows
My Isle of Golden Dreams
Typical Topical Tunes
The Vamp
Oh, Mamma
I Never Knew How Much I Loved You Until There Was Somebody Else
Oh, My Dear!
Sasparilla, Women, and Song
Oh, What a Girl
My Baby Talking Girl
You'd Be Surprised
The Old Town
Good-Bye Christina Swanson
The Opera Ball
I Want a Little Lovin' Sometimes
Listen to Me
The Orchid
Come Around on Our Veranda
He Goes to Church on Sunday
Little Mary
Our Miss Gibbs
Eight Little Girls
Yip-I-Addy-I-Ay
Over the River
Maurice's Rag
Montezuma
Ring-Ting-a-Ling
When There's No Light at All
The Oyster Man
I Just Can't Keep My Eyes Off You
A Parisian Model
Be My Teddy Bear
I Just Can't Make My Eyes Behave
In Washington
It's Delightful to Be Married
Kiss, Kiss, Kiss, If You Want to Learn to Kiss
Mister Monkey
On San Francisco Bay
A Parisian Model
Piff! Paff!! Pouf!!!
For You
Gee! But This Is a Lonely Town
The Ghost That Never Walked
Since Little Dolly Dimples Made a Hit
The Pink Lady
By the Saskatchewan
Oh, So Gently
The Pink Lady Waltz
The Pleasure Seekers
At That Bully Wooly Wild West Show
The Press Agent
I Think It Must Be Love
The Pretty Mrs. Smith
Dreaming
The Prima Donna
The Honeysuckle and the Bee
Where the Fairest Flowers Are Blooming
The Prince of Pilsen
Didn't Know Exactly What to Do
Heidelberg
Imagination
It Was the Dutch
The Message of the Violet
The Prince of To-Night
I Wonder Who's Kissing Her Now
A Princess of Kensington
A Sprig of Rosemarie
Punch, Judy and Co.
Maggie McDonahue
The Quaker Girl
Just a Little Word Unspoken
Queen of the Movies
Follow the Crowd
Quo Vass-Iss?
Beautiful Arizona
I'm a Respectable Working Girl
Nothing Doing
The Opera
Tell Us Pretty Ladies
Wilhemina
The Rambler Rose
Poor Little Rich Girl's Dog
The Red Feather
Carissima
The Garden of Dreams
There's a Little Star in Heaven That They Call Broadway

The Red Moon
As Long as the World Goes Around
The Big Red Shawl
I've Lost My Teddy Bear
The Red Rose
That La-La Melody
The Red Widow
Come Dance with Me
The Rich Mr. Hoggenheimer
Any Old Time at All
Don't You Want a Paper, Dearie?
Right This Way
I've Got Rings on My Fingers
The Riviera Girl
Will You Forget?
Robinson Crusoe, Jr.
Ain't You Coming Back to Dixieland?
Down Where the Swanee River Flows
I Sent My Wife to the 1000 Isles
Just Try to Picture Me Back Home in Tennessee
Sinbad Was in Bad All the Time
Where the Black-Eyed Susans Grow
Yaaka Hula Hickey Dula
The Rogers Brothers at Harvard
Ain't It Tough to Be So Absent-Minded?
I'm a Lady
Mary Be Wary
My Starlight Queen
Rainbows Follow After Rain
The Troubles of Reuben and the Maid
Upper Broadway After Dark
The Rogers Brothers in Central Park
When Reuben Comes to Town
The Rogers Brothers in Ireland
Hannah Dooley, Pride of Ballyhooley
The Irish Girl I Love
My Irish Maid
The Rogers Brothers in London
American Beauty
By the Sycamore Tree
Queen of the Bungalow
The Rogers Brothers in Panama
Sunrise at the Zoo
The Rogers Brothers in Paris
By the Old Oak Tree
Pretty Polly!
The Rogers Brothers in Washington
In the Swim
The Wedding of the Reuben and the Maid
The Rollicking Girl
The Indians Along Broadway
Little Girl, You'll Do
Roly-Boly Eyes
Roll Them Roly Boly Eyes
The Royal Vagabond
In a Kingdom of Our Own
Rufus Rastus
Is Everybody Happy?
The Runaways
Hiawatha
A Kiss for Each Day of the Week
My Little Hindoo Belle
Pretty Maid Adelaide
The Queen of the Track
The Woodchuck Song
Running for Office
I Want to Go to Paree, Papa
If I Were Only Mister Morgan
Sally in Our Alley
Come and Take a Stroll with Me
The Girl with the Baby Stare
Sally in Our Alley
Under the Bamboo Tree
When the Troupe Gets Back to Town
The School Girl
My Cosy Corner Girl
Sergeant Brue
Dearie
Every Saturday Afternoon
Meet Me Dear, on Saturday, a Little after Two
My Irish Molly O
Sergeant Kitty
Love
Love Laughs at Locksmiths

She Knows Better Now
I'm Going Back to Dixie
She's a Good Fellow
The First Rose of Summer
Jubilo
The Shoo-Fly Regiment
I Can't Think of Nothing in the Wide, Wide World But You
If Adam Hadn't Seen the Apple Tree
My Mississippi Missus Misses Me
O, Southland
The Old Flag Never Touched the Ground
Show Boat
Good Bye, My Lady Love
The Show Girl
Hiawatha
Katrina
Psyche
When the Band Goes Marching By
The Show of Wonders
Get a Girlie!
The Silver Slipper
Although I Am a Soldier, I Prefer a Private Life
The Girl You Love
The Ping Pong Song
Sinbad
Alexander's Band Is Back in Dixieland
By the Honeysuckle Vine
Cleopatra
Hello Central, Give Me No Man's Land
I Gave Her That
I Love the Heart of Dixie
I Wonder Why She Kept On Saying Si Si Si Si Si Senor
I'll Say She Does
I'm Not Jealous
'N' Everything
On the Road to Calais
Our Ancestors
Rock-a-bye Your Baby with a Dixie Melody
Swanee
Tell That to the Marines!
That Lullaby of Long Ago
There's a Lump of Sugar Down in Dixie
Why Do They All Take the Night Boat to Albany?
The Siren
In the Valley of Mont Bijou
Sis Hopkins
I'm Thinking 'bout You Honey All the While
The Sleeping Beauty
Tulip Time
The Sleeping Beauty and the Beast
Come Out, Dinah, on the Green
Flora, I Am Your Adorer
Have You Seen My Sweetheart in His Uniform of Blue?
Kitty
My Little Star, I'm Looking Up to You
My Princess Zulu Lulu
Nobody's Lookin' But de Owl and de Moon
Nursery Rhymes
Pansy of the Dell
Rip van Winkle Was a Lucky Man
Tell Me Dusky Maiden
The Slim Princess
Bless Your Ever Loving Little Heart
Let Me Live and Stay in Dixieland
My Yankee Doodle Girl
So Long Letty
So Long Letty
The Social Whirl
I've Got to Dance Till the Band Gets Through
A Society Circus
Moon Dear
Somebody's Sweetheart
It Gets Them All
A Son of Rest
General Hardtack on Guard
My Little Rang Outang
The Soul Kiss
Cutey, Tell Me Who Tied Your Tie?
Meet Me at the Masquerade

Important Performances Index

Since My Mariutch Learned the Merry Widow Waltz
A Southern Maid
Dark Grows the Sky
The Southerners
Allus' the Same in Dixie
As the Sunflower Turns to the Sun
Daisy Deane
Darktown Barbeque
Teasing
The Spring Chicken
All the Girls Love Me
A Lemon in the Garden of Love
Oh, So Gently
Star and Garter
My Little Lady Bug
Step This Way
If I Knock the 'L' Out of Kelly, It Still Would Be Kelly to Me
Love Me at Twilight
Romany
Stop! Look! Listen!
The Girl on the Magazine Cover
I Love a Piano
That Hula Hula
The Storks
Liza
The Street Singer
Billy
Lights of Home
My Billy Boy
The Strollers
Baby Mine
The Cuckoo Bird
Good-Bye, Little Girl, Good-Bye
I'm Tired
A Lesson in Flirtation
Look It Up in the Dream Book
A Stubborn Cinderella
When You First Kiss the Last Girl You Love
The Sultan of Sulu
Hike!
My Sulu Lulu Loo
R-E-M-O-R-S-E
Sumurun
Sumurun
The Sun Dodgers
Pinkerton Detective Man
When It's Apple Blossom Time in Normandy
The Sunshine Girl
The Argentine
The Supper Club
Don't Butt In
The Maiden with the Dreamy Eyes
The Sweet Girl
Honey Will You Miss Me When I'm Gone?
Sweet Maria
Cecelia and Amelia
Sybil
I Can Dance with Everybody But My Wife
The Talk of the Town
When a Fellow's on the Level with a Girl That's on the Square
The Tenderfoot
Love Is Elusive
The Three Graces
I've Got to Dance Till the Band Gets Through
Not Because Your Hair Is Curly
Three Little Maids
The Girl You Love
I Can't Take My Eyes off You
I Love the Moon
The Three Twins
Cuddle Up a Little Closer, Lovey Mine
The Yama Yama Man
Tillie's Nightmare
Heaven Will Protect the Working Girl
The Time, the Place and the Girl
Blow the Smoke Away
The Time, the Place, and the Girl
Honeymoon
Tintypes
I Want What I Want When I Want It
Tip-Top
I Want to See My Ida Hoe in Idaho

Tonight's the Night
  They Didn't Believe Me
Too Near Home
  You're in Love
The Toreador
  All Right!
  Beautiful Dreamy Eyes
  The Language of the Flowers
  Maud, Maud, Maud
A Trip to Africa
  Tilda from Old Savannah
The Troubador
  He Ought to Have a Tablet in the Hall of Fame
Twirly-Whirly
  Come Down, Ma Evening Star
  Dream One Dream of Me
  The Leader of Vanity Fair
  Little Widow Brown
  My Particular Friend
  Romeo
The Umpire
  The Umpire Is a Most Unhappy Man
Up and Down Broadway
  Chinatown, My Chinatown
  Dreamy Fandango Tune
  The Kellerman Girlie
  My Operatic Samson
  Sweet Italian Love
  That Beautiful Rag
Vera Violette
  Angelique
  Come and Dance with Me
  The Gaby Glide
  When You Hear Love's "Hello"
Very Good Eddie
  Alone with You
  Some Sort of Somebody
The Wall Street Girl
  The Deedle-Dum-Dee
  That Baboon Baby Dance
Watch Your Step
  Play a Simple Melody
  The Syncopated Walk
  Watch Your Step
What's Next
  Faugh-a Ballagh
When Claudia Smiles
  Dinah
  Everybody Sometime Must Love Some One
  The Flower Garden Ball
  I've Got Rings on My Fingers
  You're My Boy
When Johnny Comes Marching Home
  My Own United States
The Whirl of Society
  Billy Billy, Bounce Your Baby Doll
  My Sumurun Girl
Whirl of the World
  There's a Lump of Sugar Down in Dixie
The White Hen
  Because I'm Married Now
Whoop-Dee-Doo
  Flowers of Dixieland
  In Dreamland, In Dreamland
  The Maid of Timbucktoo
Widow by Proxy
  Over the Garden Wall
The Wild Rose
  The Gypsy's Wedding
  I Sing a Little Tenor
  I'm Unlucky
  It Must Have Been Svengali in Disguise
  The Little Gypsy Maid
  Nancy Brown
  Pinky Panky Poo
  Those Things Cannot Be Explained
The Winning Girl
  Deacon Jones
A Winsome Widow
  Be My Little Baby Bumble Bee
  String a Ring of Roses 'Round Your Rosie
The Wizard of Oz
  Football
  Hurrah for Baffin's Baby
  I'll Be with You Honey in the Springtime
  Little Nemo and His Bear
  Must You?
  Sammy

Scarecrow
The Tale of a Stroll
There's a Lot of Things You Never Learn at School
When the Circus Comes to Town
Woodland
Brother Masons
No Bird Ever Flew So High He Didn't Have to Light
A World of Pleasure
Pretty Baby
The Wrong Mr. President
My Heart for You Pines Away
The Yankee Consul
Ain't It Funny What a Difference Just a Few Hours Make?
In Old New York
The Yankee Girl
The Glory of the Yankee Navy
I've Got Rings on My Fingers
Let's Make Love among the Roses
Nora Malone, Call Me by Phone
That Hypnotizing Rag
The Yankee Prince
Rag Babe
A Yankee Tourist
And the World Goes on Just the Same
My Teddy Girl
The Young Turk
I Thought I Wanted Opera
Zip Goes a Million
The Language of Love

Operetta

Apple Blossoms
A Girl, A Man, A Night, A Dance
On the Banks of the Bronx
Babes in Toyland
March of the Toys
Toyland
The Blue Paradise
Auf Wiedersehn
Dolly Varden
The Dolly Varden Song
The Firefly
Gianina Mia
Love Is Like a Firefly
Maytime
Will You Remember?
Melinda and Her Sisters
I Have Never Seen the Russian Ballet
The Merry Widow
Dear I Love You So
Heure exquise qui nous grise
I Love You So
Vilia
Mlle. Mischief
A Kiss in the Dark
Mlle. Modiste
I Want What I Want When I Want It
The Monks of Malabar
The Monk of Malabar
Naughty Marietta
Ah, Sweet Mystery of Life
I'm Falling in Love with Some One
It Never, Never Can Be Love
Italian Street Song
Naughty Marietta
'Neath the Southern Moon
Tramp, Tramp, Tramp
The Red Mill
The Streets of New York
Robin Hood
If All the Stars Were Mine
Sari
Love's Own Sweet Song
Sweethearts
I Might Be Your "Once in a While"

Orchestra

Art Hickman's Band
Rose Room
Dave Apollon and His String Orchestra
That Russian Rag
Earl Fuller and His Famous Jazz Band
Yah-De-Dah
Earl Fuller's Orchestra
Hawaiian Butterfly

James Reese Europe's Hell Fighter Band
That Russian Rag
Prince's Orchestra
Moonlight Waltz

Performer

Abbott, Al
I've Only One Idea about the Girls and That's to Love 'Em
Abrams, Morris
When You're in Town in My Home Town
Ackerman, Loni
Forty-five Minutes from Broadway
Acme Male Quartet
Mammy o' Mine
Acuff, Roy
Will the Circle Be Unbroken?
Adair, Janet
I'm Going Back to Carolina
Adams, Ida
Beautiful Beautiful Girl
By the Saskatchewan
Adams, May
In the City of Sighs and Tears
Adderly, Alma
Down in Sunny Georgia Years Ago
Adelaide and Hughes
Bohemian Rag
Pierrot and Pierrette
Adler, Flo
I'll Break the Fighting Line Like You Broke This Heart of Mine
Jennie
Aeolian Dance Orchestra
Enid Waltz
Aeolian Orchestra
In a Kingdom of Our Own
Al Goodman and His Orchestra
In Old New York
Alda, Frances
The Bells of St. Mary's
Carissima
For Your Country and My Country
I Love You Truly
Just a-Wearying for You
Mighty Lak' a Rose
Please Keep Out of My Dreams
Poor Butterfly
Sing Me Love's Lullaby
The Singer
The Sum of Life
A Tango Dream
Alexander and Scott
Next Sunday at Nine
That Humming Tune
You'll Never Know the Good Fellow I've Been, 'Till I've Gone Away
Alexander, George
When the Right Little Girl Comes Along
All Star Trio
All the Quakers Are Shoulder Shakers Down in Quaker Town
Poor Little Butterfly Is a Fly Girl Now
Ugly Chile
You Ain't Heard Nothing Yet
Allen, Edward
Oh! What a Pal Was Mary
Allen, Flo
Keep a Little Cozy Corner in Your Heart for Me
Only a Dream of a Golden Past
Allen, Flossie
I Wants to Be the Leading Lady
It's Moonlight All the Time on Broadway
Josephine, My Jo
Just a Little Rocking Chair and You
Amato, Pasquale
Since You Went Away
American Comedy Four
Melinda's Wedding Day
American Quartet
Any Little Girl That's a Nice Little Girl Is the Right Little Girl for Me
Baby Rose

The Dixie Volunteers
Do You Take This Woman for Your Lawful Wife?
Everybody Rag with Me
Everything Is Peaches Down in Georgia
I Want a Girl Just Like the Girl That Married Dear Old Dad
Let's All Be Americans Now
'Neath the Old Cherry Tree, Sweet Marie
On the 5:15
The Ragtime Dream
Rebecca of Sunnybrook Farm
Sailin' Away on the Henry Clay
That Old Girl of Mine
Way Down in Cotton Town
The Wedding of the Reuben and the Maid
Will You Love Me in December as You Do in May?
You're My Baby

American Republic Band
The Maurice Glide
The Rose of No Man's Land

American Singers
Why Adam Sinned

Ames Brothers
Absence Makes the Heart Grow Fonder
If You Had All the World and Its Gold

Ames, Molly
Run Home and Tell Your Mother

Anderson, Al and T. H. Goines
My Dusky Rose

Anderson, Marian
Deep River
Hard Trials
I Don't Feel No Way Tired

Andrews, Julie
Everybody's Doin' It Now

Andrews Sisters
I Hate to Lose You
In the Good Old Summertime
Love Sends a Little Gift of Roses
My Isle of Golden Dreams
Oh Johnny, Oh Johnny, Oh!
Pack Up Your Troubles in Your Old Kit Bag and Smile, Smile, Smile

Andrews, Talleur
Little Girl, You'll Do

Andy Kirk and His Clouds of Joy
Breeze, Blow My Baby Back to Me
Twelfth Street Rag

Angeles, Aimee
Under the Mistletoe Bough

Arbuckle, Roscoe
Oh Helen!
Sipping Cider thru' a Straw

Archer, Adele
Katrina

Armin, Walter
Here's to You, My Sparkling Wine

Armstrong, Louis
After You've Gone
Baby, Won't You Please Come Home
Bill Bailey, Won't You Please Come Home
Carry Me Back to Old Virginny
Chinatown, My Chinatown
Dallas Blues
Down in Honky-Tonk Town
Ramona
Some of These Days
Tiger Rag
Twelfth Street Rag

Arndt, Felix
Nola

Arnold, Eddy
Will the Circle Be Unbroken?

Arpin, John
Pan-Am Rag

Art Hickman and His Orchestra
Dry Your Tears

Art Hickman's Orchestra
The Hesitating Blues
Those Draftin' Blues

Arthur Pryor's Band
Daisy Donahue
Dearie
Dill Pickles Rag
Oh, You Beautiful Doll
The Red Rose Rag

Swanee
The Teddy Bears' Picnic
Ash, Sam
Bring Me a Rose
Cleopatra Had a Jazz Band
'Cross the Great Divide, I'll Wait for You
Daddy Long Legs
Give Me the Moonlight, Give Me the Girl and Leave the Rest to Me
Huckleberry Finn
I'm Simply Crazy over You
The Kiss Burglar
My Hawaiian Sunrise
Smile and Show Your Dimple
Tulip Time
When I Leave the World Behind
The Woman Thou Gavest Me
Your Eyes Have Told Me So
You're a Million Miles from Nowhere When You're One Little Mile from Home
Astaire, Adele
I Just Can't Make My Feet Behave
I Love to Quarrel with You
Astaire, Fred
I Love a Piano
I Love to Quarrel with You
Rag-Time Violin
Snooky Ookums
When That Midnight Choo-Choo Leaves for Alabam'
Where Did You Get That Girl?
You'll Fall for Someone
Astaire, Fred and Adele
My Croony Melody
Athlone, Baby
I Want Someone to Flirt with Me
Atkins, Chet
Rainbow
Atwell, Roy
Sasparilla, Women, and Song
Austin, Gene
If I Had My Way
My Melancholy Baby
The Sweetheart of Sigma Chi
Austin, Gere
Alabama Lullaby
Austin, Monte
If I Had a Son for Each Star in Old Glory, Uncle Sam, I'd Give Them All to You
M-O-T-H-E-R
Autry, Gene
Sierra Sue
Avery and Hart
Down Among the Sugar-Cane
Pretty Little Dinah Jones
You're Just Too Sweet to Live
Avon Comedy Four
Be Satisfied with What You Have, Let Well Enough Alone
Blue Bell
Honolulu, America Loves You
Ireland Must Be Heaven for My Mother Came from There
It's Moonlight All the Time on Broadway
Sweet Cider Time When You Were Mine
There's a Little Bit of Bad in Every Good Little Girl
When the Black Sheep Returns to the Fold
Where Do We Go from Here?
Yaaka Hula Hickey Dula
Awker Sisters
Always Take a Girl Named Daisy ('cause Daisies Won't Tell)
Aylmar, Neva
What Makes the World Go Round
Aylmer, Neva
Queen of the Bungalow
Aymar, Neva
Blue Eyed Sue
Baby Eleanor
Mariutch Down at Coney Island
Bageard, Jeannette
The Duchess of Central Park
In the Swim
Bailey, DeFord
The Alcoholic Blues
Bailey, Mildred
All That Glitters Is Not Gold

I'm Forever Blowing Bubbles
Bailey, Pearl
Bill Bailey, Won't You Please Come Home
Johnson Rag
Ma, He's Making Eyes at Me
Row Row Row
Bailey, Ray
Mandy Lane
Baird, Stewart
I've Made Up My Mind to Mind a Maid Made Up Like You
Baker, Belle
All Night Long
America Never Took Water and America Never Will
And Then
Are You from Heaven?
Down in Chattanooga
Eli Eli
He'd Have to Get Under, Get Out and Get Under to Fix Up His Automobile
Homeward Bound
If You Don't Want Me
I'm Sorry I Made You Cry
Melinda's Wedding Day
My Old Log Cabin Home
Oh! You Million Dollar Doll
San Francisco Bound
That Carolina Rag
That Hypnotizing Man
That Hypnotizing Strain
That Mellow Strain
They're On Their Way to Mexico
This Is the Life
When Alexander Takes His Rag Time Band to France
When the Black Sheep Returns to the Fold
When You're Down in Louisville, Call on Me
You're My Baby
Baker, Bonnie
Billy
Baker, Elise
Just Because It's You
Baker, Elsie
Dear Little Boy of Mine
Dearie
A Hundred Years from Now
Baker, Kenny
The Bells of St. Mary's
Little Grey Home in the West
Baldwin, E. J.
I've Grown So Used to You
Baldwin, George
Wedding Bells
Baldwin, Winnie
Just for Tonight
Ball, Ernest
Good Bye, Good Luck, God Bless You
If All My Dreams Were Made of Gold, I'd Buy the World for You
Ballard, George Wilton
I'd Be Happy Anywhere with You
I'm a Lonesome Melody
I'm Sorry I Made You Cry
In the Land of Beginning Again
Just Try to Picture Me Back Home in Tennessee
So Long Mother
There's a Long, Long Trail
When Honey Sings an Old Time Song
Band of Her Majesty's Royal Marines
The Fairest of the Fair
Banjo Fiends
Piano Man
Bard, Wilkie
ABCD
I Can't Reach That Top Note
Put Me Upon an Island
Barker, Ethel Mae
My Croony Melody
Barnard, Elphye
On a Beautiful Night with a Beautiful Girl
Barnard, Sophye
When the Grown-Up Ladies Act Like Babies
Barnes, Fred
Rag-Time Violin

Barnes, Stuart
I'm Looking for a Dear Old Lady
Barrison, Mabel
I've Got to Dance Till the Band Gets Through
Love Me All the Time
March of the Toys
Not Because Your Hair Is Curly
Sammy
Waltz Me Around Again, Willie
What's the Use of Dreaming
Barry, Lydia
Everybody's Doin' It Now
He Laid Away a Suit of Gray to Wear the Union Blue
In Dear Old Georgia
I've a Longing in My Heart for You, Louise
When the Whipporwill Sings Marguerite
You Are the Ideal of My Dreams
Barry Sisters
I Hate to Lose You
Bartholomew, Charles
Oh, What a Night
They Were All Out of Step But Jim
Basie, Count
Ja-Da
Royal Garden Blues
Sugar Blues
Twelfth Street Rag
Bates, Louisa
After All
Batie, Franklyn
Just for Tonight
Lady Angeline
Bayes, Nora
ABCD
Are You Coming Out Tonight, Mary Ann?
Back to My Old Home Town
Blarney
By the Light of the Silvery Moon
Come Along My Mandy
Down Where the Wurzburger Flows
Falling Star
For Dixie and Uncle Sam
Good-bye France
Good Luck and God Be with You, Laddie Boy
The Good Ship Mary Ann
Handle me with Care
Has Anybody Here Seen Kelly?
Homesickness Blues
I Wonder If They're True to Me
If You Want a Little Doggie, Whistle and I'll Come to You
I'm Glad I'm a Boy/I'm Glad I'm a Girl
I'm Learning Something Every Day
Just Like a Gypsy
Khaki Sammy
Let's Get the Umpire's Goat
Look Who's Here
Meet Me in St. Louis, Louis
Meet Me with Spangles and Bells On
Mother's Sitting Knitting Little Mittens for the Navy
Oh, How I Laugh When I Think How I Cried about You
Oh Johnny, Oh Johnny, Oh!
Over There
Pawnee
Pinkerton Detective Man
Please Keep Out of My Dreams
Prohibition Blues
Pull the Cork Out of Erin and Let the River Shannon Flow
Regretful Blues
Sadie Brady Listen Good to Me
Scaddle-de-Mooch
Shine On, Harvest Moon
The Stolen Melody
Take Me Out to the Ball Game
Turn Off Your Light, Mr. Moon Man
Under the Anheuser Bush
Wasn't It Yesterday?
When It's Apple Blossom Time in Normandy
When Jack Comes Sailing Home Again
When John McCormack Sings a Song

When Miss Patricia Salome Did Her Funny Little Oh-la Pa-lome
When Old Bill Bailey Plays the Ukelele
When You Come Back, and You Will Come Back, There's a Whole World...
When You're Down in Louisville, Call on Me
Without You
You Will Have to Sing an Irish Song

Beaton, Louise
I've a Longing in My Heart for You, Louise

Beatrice, the Rag-Time Violinist
All the Little Lovin' That I Had for You Is Gone, Gone, Gone

Beatty, Ethel
Gee! I Wish I Had Someone to Rock Me in the Cradle of Love

Beaumont Sisters
The Coster's Glide

Bechet Quintet
Ole Miss

Bechet, Sidney
After You've Gone
Rose Room

Beeson, Lulu
It's the Pretty Things You Say
Smarty

Begley, Edward
Ragging the Nursery Rhymes

Behr, Carrie
I Would Like to Be Your Pal
I Would Like to Marry You

Beiderbecke, Bix
In My Merry Oldsmobile
Royal Garden Blues
Somebody Stole My Gal

Bell, May A.
A Flower from the Garden of Life
I'm Afraid to Come Home in the Dark
My Lady Hottentot

Bender, Coombs
Oh, Mr. Dream Man

Benham, Earl
Meet Me in Rose Time Rosie

Bennett Twins
In the Heart of the City That Has No Heart

Benny Goodman Sextet
The World Is Waiting for the Sunrise

Benny Goodman Trio
Someday Sweetheart

Benny, Jack
When Ragtime Rosie Ragged the Rosary

Benson, Ray
Oh! Frenchy

Bent, Marion
The Daughter of Rosie O'Grady
I Love to Sit and Look at You

Bentley, Irene
Come Around to Mamie's
The Gypsy's Wedding
In the Cold Grey Dawn
A Lesson in Flirtation
The Little Gypsy Maid
The Lover's A.B.C.
Pansy Faces
When the Moon Comes Peeping Over the Hill
Your Eyes Say No But Your Lips Say Yes!

Bentley, Wilmer
Teasing

Bergere, Bettina
I'd Be Happy Anywhere with You

Bergman, Harry
From Here to Shanghai
Honey Love
If You Don't Want Me
Nothing's Good Enough for a Good Little Girl If She's Good Enough for You
Romany
Snooky Ookums
That's My Idea of Paradise
We've Had a Lovely Time, So Long, Good Bye

Bergman, Henry
For Me and My Gal

It's a Long Way to Berlin But We'll Get There
Jerry, You Warra a Warrior in the War
Berlin, Irving
Alexander's Rag-Time Band
Marie from Sunny Italy
Oh! How I Hate to Get Up in the Morning
Oh, How That German Could Love
Sweet Italian Love
That Beautiful Rag
That International Rag
Bernard, Al
Everybody Wants a Key to My Cellar
No, No, Positively No
Bernard, Sam
Bring Back My Lena to Me
The Indians Along Broadway
Oh, How That German Could Love
A Singer Sang a Song
Who Paid the Rent for Mrs. Rip Van Winkle?
Berri, Maude Lillian
Carmena
Mexico
On Lalawana's Shore
Bigelow, Charles
Big Indian Chief
In Washington
Romeo
Bigelow, Charles E.
At the Music Hall
Bigeon, Esther
The Hesitating Blues
Bindley, Florence
Billy
I Want to Be a Prima Donna
My Billy Boy
Bingham, Kitty
All on Account of a Dear Little Girl
Bispham, David
Pirate Song
Bjorling, Jussi
Because
Blaine, Vivian
Oh by Jingo! Oh by Gee! You're the Only Girl for Me
Blake, Eubie
Ain't You Coming Back, Mary Ann, to Maryland
Gee! I Wish I Had Someone to Rock Me in the Cradle of Love
Gee! I'm Glad That I'm from Dixie
Good Night, Angeline
Mammy's Little Choc'late Cullud Chile
Mirandy
On Patrol in No Man's Land
Blanche, Belle
I Want a Real Nice Man
If You Knew What I Know about Men
I'm the Only Mother That You Ever Knew
Pick, Pick, Pick, Pick on the Mandolin, Antonio
Bloch, Ray
Honey Boy
Blondell, Libbey
All Aboard for Dreamland
Blondell, Libbie
My Hindoo Man
My Lady Hottentot
Blondells
Josephine, My Jo
Since Reuben's Gone Away
Blyler and Brown
Whippoorwill
Boardman, Lillian
Lucy Anna Lou
Mister Pagliatch
Rosa Rigoletto
Boas, Edward
When the Winds O'er the Sea Blow a Gale
Bob Eberly and the Song Spinners
Don't Cry, Little Girl, Don't Cry

Bob Grant and His Orchestra
Where the Black-Eyed Susans Grow
Bob Wills and the Texas Playboys
I'll Say She Does
Bohannon and Corey
Hearts You Lose
The Man Who Fights the Fire
Bonita
Back, Back, Back to Baltimore
Colleen Bawn
Hannah, Won't You Open the Door?
In the Land of Harmony
Lonesome Honey for You
My Irish Rose
My Lady Hottentot
Oh, Miss Malinda
Ragging the Baby to Sleep
Semiole
Somebody's Waiting for You
Stop! Stop! Stop!
Take Me Back to the Garden of Love
You're a Great Big Blue-Eyed Baby
You're in Style When You're Wearing a Smile
Bonnie Blue Eyes and Bob Atcher
Just Because She Made Dem Goo-Goo Eyes
Boone, Pat
Anchors Aweigh
Bordoni, Irene
When Those Sweet Hawaiian Babies Roll Their Eyes
Bori, Lucrezia
Ciribiribin
Clavelitos
I Hear You Calling Me
Just You
Borrah Minevitch and His Harmonica Rascals
Dardanella
Boston "Pops" Orchestra
Tiger Rag
Boswell, Connee
I Know What It Means to Be Lonesome
Boswell Sisters
Down Among the Sheltering Palms
Bouton, May
Good-Bye, Little Girl, Good-Bye
Bowers, Fred V.
Moriarty
Bowers, Frederick V.
When the Sunset Turns to Ocean's Blue to Gold
Boyle, Jack
Back to the Carolina You Love
Bradley, Charles
I Am Longing for Tomorrow When I Think of Yesterday
Bradley, Lillian
Call Again
Take a Little Tip from Father
Brady, James B.
Ain't You Coming Back to Old New Hampshire, Molly?
Brandt, Sophie
Little Girl, You'll Do
Brehany, Louise
Carissima
Hiawatha
I'm Longing for My Old Kentucky Home
In the Village by the Sea
Iola
Lola
Moonlight
The Troubadour
When the Whipporwill Sings Marguerite
Brennan, Nan
Little Mary Gardeners
Brenner, Joe
Marie from Sunny Italy
Brewer, Theresa
When I Leave the World Behind
Brian, Donald
Ballin' the Jack
I Love You So
The Land of "Let's Pretend"
Same Sort of Girl
They Didn't Believe Me
Brice and King
I Can Live without You

Brice, Elizabeth
The Aba Daba Honeymoon
Be My Little Baby Bumble Bee
For Me and My Gal
Hawaiian Butterfly
Hello Honey
Honolulu, America Loves You
I Can Live without You
If I Had a Son for Each Star in Old Glory, Uncle Sam, I'd Give Them All to You
If I Were a Bee and You Were a Red, Red Rose
I've Only One Idea about the Girls and That's to Love 'Em
Just Around the Corner
Keep Your Eye on the Girlie You Love
Let Me Live and Stay in Dixieland
Lovie Joe
Oh Johnny, Oh Johnny, Oh!
On the Shores of Italy
Row Row Row
Sombody Loves You
Some Sunday Morning
Stop! Stop! Stop!
String a Ring of Roses 'Round Your Rosie
That's Everlasting Love
There's a Little Bit of Bad in Every Good Little Girl
There's One in a Million Like You
Where Do We Go from Here?
You're a Great Big Blue-Eyed Baby
You're in Style When You're Wearing a Smile
You're Never to Old to Love
Brice, Elizabeth, and Charles King
The Palm Beach Dip
Brice, Fanny
At the Yiddish Wedding Jubilee
Ballin' the Jack
Becky Do the Bombashay
Becky's Got a Job in a Musical Show
Do It the Right Way
The Grizzly Bear
He's a Devil in His Own Home Town
I'm a Yiddish Cowboy
Lovie Joe
Nijinski
Nix on the Glow-Worm, Lena
Pots and Pans
Rose of Washington Square
Sadie Salome Go Home
Syncopatia Land
That Sneaky Snaky Rag
Waiting for the Robert E. Lee
When Rosie Riccoola Do the Hoola Ma Boola She's the Hit of Little Italy
When You Know You're Not Forgotten by the Girl You Can't Forget
Yiddle on Your Fiddle Play Some Rag Time
Broadway Quartet
Mammy's Little Coal Black Rose
My Mariuccia Take a Steamboat
Brockman, Slater
Next to Your Mother Who Do You Love?
Bronson, Edna
Beneath the Palms of Paradise
Brooke, Belle
In the Land of Wedding Bells
Brooklin, Belle
Mamie, Don't You Feel Ashamie
Brooklin, Effie
Arrah-Wanna
Blue Bell
Wait 'Till the Sun Shines, Nellie
Brooks, Joan
I've Lost You So Why Should I Care?
Brown, Bly
Sister Susie's Started Syncopation
Brown, Edna
Baby Shoes
Daddy Has a Sweetheart and Mother Is Her Name
Hello Central, Give Me No Man's Land
I Want a Little Lovin' Sometimes

In the Candlelight
Play a Simple Melody
Sprinkle Me with Kisses If You Want My Love to Grow
There's a Broken Heart for Every Light on Broadway
Those Songs My Mother Used to Sing
The Trail of the Lonesome Pine
When You Play in the Game of Love

Brown, Harry
Ain't Dat an Awful Feeling
Bye-Bye, My Eva, Bye-Bye
Gimme Hush Money or I'll Tell on You
Good-bye, Eliza Jane

Brown, Will
My Friend from Kentucky

Browne and Scott
The Song That I Hear in My Dreams

Brubeck, Dave
Indiana

Brunell, Louise
The Bacchanal Rag

Bryant, Rose
If We Can't Be the Same Old Sweethearts

Buck Johnson and His New Orleans Band
Tishomingo Blues

Buffalo Bills
You're the Flower of My Heart, Sweet Adeline

Bulger, Harry
Brother Masons
Flora, I Am Your Adorer
M-O-N-E-Y Spells Money
My Princess Zulu Lulu
No Bird Ever Flew So High He Didn't Have to Light
Rip van Winkle Was a Lucky Man
Under the Mistletoe Bough
Walk, Walk, Walk
What's the Matter with Father?
When Mr. Shakespeare Comes to Town

Bunny Berigan and His Men
Walkin' the Dog

Burke, Billie
Good Night Dear
My Otaheite Lady

Burke, Hattie
The Good Ship Mary Ann
Let Bygones Be Bygones and Let Us Be Sweethearts Again
Molly Dear, It's You I'm After
That Old Girl of Mine
There's One in a Million Like You
When the Whole World Has Gone Back on You
Where the Red Red Roses Grow

Burke, Mabel
Johnny, Get a Girl

Burkes and Lorraine
Any Little Girl That's a Nice Little Girl Is the Right Little Girl for Me

Burkhardt, Maurice
Bring Back My Lena to Me
If He Can Fight Like He Can Love, Good Night Germany

Burnham and Greenwood
Oh, That Moonlight Glide

Burns, George
I'm Tying the Leaves So They Won't Come Down
The Red Rose Rag

Burns, George, and Gracie Allen
Meet Me at the Station

Burr, Harry
I'll Change the Shadows to Sunshine

Burr, Henry
Baby Shoes
Baby's Prayers Will Soon Be Answered
Bye Bye Dearie
California and You
Come Along to Toy Town
Daddy Long Legs
Don't Cry, Little Girl, Don't Cry
Dreamy Alabama

Give Me the Moonlight, Give Me the Girl and Leave the Rest to Me
Good Bye, Good Luck, God Bless You
Good Luck and God Be with You, Laddie Boy
Goodbye, Mother Machree
The Hand That Rocked the Cradle Rules My Heart
Hindustan
I Called You My Sweetheart
I Know What It Means to Be Lonesome
I Wonder Who's Kissing Her Now
If We Can't Be the Same Old Sweethearts
I'm Glad I Can Make You Cry
I'm on My Way to Manadalay
I'm Sorry I Made You Cry
I'm Wearing My Heart Away for You
In Berry Pickin' Time
In the Heart of the City That Has No Heart
Just a Baby's Prayer at Twilight to Her Daddy Over There
Let the Rest of the World Go By
Love Me and the World Is Mine
M-O-T-H-E-R
Meet Me Tonight in Dreamland
My Belgian Rose
My Heart Has Learned to Love You Now Do Not Say Good-Bye
Oh! What a Pal Was Mary
On the Shores of Italy
One Day in June
Peg o' My Heart
Rainbow
Red Wing
Rose of Washington Square
Sing Me Love's Lullaby
Smiles
Somewhere in France Is the Lily
Stay Down Here Where You Belong
The Story Book Ball
Take Me Back
That Old Girl of Mine
That Wonderful Mother of Mine
That's How I Need You
There's a Little Spark of Love Still Burning
There's a Long, Long Trail
Till We Meet Again
To Have, To Hold, To Love
The Trail of the Lonesome Pine
Tulip Time
'Twas Only an Irishman's Dream
Wait and See, You'll Want Me Back
Wake Up America
When a Feller Needs a Friend
When I Leave the World Behind
When I Lost You
When You and I Were Young, Maggie
When You First Kiss the Last Girl You Love
When You Look in the Heart of a Rose
When You're in Love with Someone Who Is Not in Love with You
When You're in Town in My Home Town
Where the Black-Eyed Susans Grow
Where the River Shannon Flows
While the Old Mill Wheel Is Turning
Would You Take Me Back Again?
You Didn't Want Me When You Had Me So Why Do You Want Me Now?
Your Lips Are No Man's Land But Mine

Burt, Billie
When a Lady Leads the Band

Burt, Harriet
Honeymoon

Burt, Hazel
I've Grown So Used to You

Burt, Lillian
The Good Old U.S.A.

Burt, Nellie
I Wants a Man Like Romeo
Burt, Sadie
Baby Love
Butler, Amy
Colleen Bawn
It's the Pretty Things You Say
A Little Boy Named 'Taps'
San Francisco Bound
Stop! Stop! Stop!
Waiting for the Robert E. Lee
Butler, Ethel Mae
Loveland Days
Butler, "Little" Amy
Kiss Me, My Honey, Kiss Me
Wild Cherries
Cagney, James
Forty-five Minutes from Broadway
Give My Regards to Broadway
H-A-Double R-I-G-A-N
Yankee Doodle Boy
You're a Grand Old Flag
Cagwin, Jack
Darling
Cahill, Marie
Come and Take a Stroll with Me
The Conjure Man
Do Re Me Fa So La Si Do
Don't Be What You Ain't
I Want a Little Lovin' Sometimes
I've Got Troubles of My Own
June
The Katy-Did, the Cricket and the Frog
Listen to Me
Marie Cahill's Congo Love Song
My Evalyne
My Hindoo Man
Nancy Brown
Nava Jo
Old Reliable Jokes
On a Little Farm in Normandie
Robinson Crusoe's Isle
Save It for Me
She Was a Dear Little Girl
Two Eyes
Under the Bamboo Tree
When Sousa Leads the Band
When the Troupe Gets Back to Town
Whoop 'er Up with a Whoop La La
Cahill, Mary
He's a Cousin of Mine
Cahill, William
Call Me Up Some Rainy Afternoon
Since Father Went to Work
Caine, Georgia
Any Old Time at All
Don't You Want a Paper, Dearie?
Holding Hands
How'd You Like to Spoon with Me?
I Would Like to Marry You
Pansy
Callaway, Olive
Ev'ry Day
Calloway, Cab
Baby, Won't You Please Come Home
Some of These Days
Somebody Stole My Gal
Cameron, Eleanor
I Am Longing for Tomorrow When I Think of Yesterday
Cameron, Grace
I'm Getting Sleepy
A Picnic for Two
Since Little Dolly Dimples Made a Hit
What Has That Man Harrigan Done?
Campan, Frank
Ten Thousand Cattle Straying
Campbell, Albert
California and You
Dreamy Alabama
Good Luck and God Be with You, Laddie Boy
Hindustan
Let the Rest of the World Go By
Love Me and the World Is Mine
'Neath the Old Acorn Tree, Sweet Estelle
On the Shores of Italy
One Day in June

Smiles
The Story Book Ball
Till We Meet Again
The Trail of the Lonesome Pine
Violette
When the Whipporwill Sings Marguerite
When You Know You're Not Forgotten by the Girl You Can't Forget
While the Old Mill Wheel Is Turning
Your Lips Are No Man's Land But Mine

Canfield, Eugene
There's No Other Girl Like My Girl

Cantor, Eddie
Araby
But - After the Ball Was Over Then He Made Up for Lost Time
Come On Papa
The Dixie Volunteers
Don't Take Advantage of My Good Nature
Give Me the Sultan's Harem
How 'Ya Gonna Keep 'Em Down on the Farm After They've Seen Paris?
I Love Her Oh! Oh! Oh!
I Love My Billy Sunday But Oh, You Saturday Night
I Wonder What's the Matter wiz My Oo-la-la
I'd Rather See a Minstrel Show
Ida, Sweet as Apple Cider
If He Can Fight Like He Can Love, Good Night Germany
I'm a Yiddish Cowboy
I've Got My Captain Working for Me Now
Johnny's in Town
Ma, He's Making Eyes at Me
Mandy
The Modern Maiden's Prayer
Oh! How I Hate to Get Up in the Morning
Oh, How She Could Yacki Hacki Wicki Wacki Woo
Oh! The Last Rose of Summer Was the Sweetest Rose of All
Rag-Time Violin
Roaming Romeo
That's the Kind of Baby for Me
They Go Wild, Simply Wild Over Me
They Start the Victrola and Go Dancing Around the Floor
They're Wearing 'Em Higher in Hawaii
When They're Old Enough to Know Better, It's Better to Leave Them Alone
When Uncle Joe Steps into France
Would You Rather Be a Colonel with an Eagle on Your Shoulder...
You Ain't Heard Nothing Yet
You Keep Sending 'Em Over and We'll Keep Knocking 'Em Down
You'd Be Surprised

Capron, Nell
Pansies Mean Thoughts and Thoughts Mean You

Carle, Frankie
Hindustan
I Want a Girl Just Like the Girl That Married Dear Old Dad

Carle, Richard
All the Girls Love Me
Don't Turn My Picture to the Wall
A Lemon in the Garden of Love
Liza
Love Is Elusive
My Madagascar Maid
Way Down in Cotton Town

Carleton, Violet
My Croony Melody
Pride of the Prairie
When the Angelus Is Ringing

Carlisle, Kitty
Vilia

Carmichael, Hoagy
The Darktown Strutters' Ball

Carney, William H.
Boys, the Old Flag Never Touched the Ground
Carnival Four
Just One Day
Carpenter, Carleton
The Aba Daba Honeymoon
He'd Have to Get Under, Get Out and Get Under to Fix Up His Automobile
Carroll and Fields
On the Mississippi
Carroll, Harry
The Little Church around the Corner
The Trail of the Lonesome Pine
Carroll, Johnnie
The Boys in the Gallery for Mine
My Palm Leaf Maid
Carroll, Marie
The Language of Love
Carson, Mary
I'll Change the Shadows to Sunshine
Carter, Dave
Love Me and the World Is Mine
Carter Family
Will the Circle Be Unbroken?
Carter, Frank
Hello Central, Give Me No Man's Land
If She Means What I Think She Means
The Navy Took Them Over and the Navy Will Bring Them Back
That Carolina Rag
Carter's Orchestra
Marcheta
Cartnell and Harris
Make Believe
Carus, Emma
Ain't You Got Nothing to Say?
Alexander's Rag-Time Band
Beatrice Fairfax, Tell Me What to Do
Bedelia
Cleopatra Had a Jazz Band
Everybody Loves a Jazz Band
The Face in the Firelight
The Gambling Man
The Girl Who Cares for Me
Go Easy Mabel
Good-Bye, Little Girl, Good-Bye
Handle me with Care
Has Anybody Here Seen Kelly?
Hawaiian Butterfly
The High Cost of Loving
Homeward Bound
The Honolulu Blues
I Ain't a-Goin' to Weep No More
I Can't Tell Why I Love You But I Do
I Could Learn to Love You If You Let Me Try
I Could Love You in a Steam Heat Flat
I Think I Could Be Awfully Good to You
I'll Be Your Rain-Beau
I'll Still Believe in You
I'm the Only Star That Twinkles on Broadway
In the Village by the Sea
In Zanzibar
Ireland Must Be Heaven for My Mother Came from There
Love Me Like I Want to Be Loved
Make a Noise Like a Hoop and Roll Away
Meet Me When the Sun Goes Down
Melinda's Wedding Day
Molly-O Oh Molly
Mrs. Carter, You're a Tartar
My Samoan Beauty
Nancy, Oh Miss Nancy
Oh! How She Can Dance
Oh, What a Night
On the Shores of Italy
Ragtime Eyes
The Ragtime Volunteers Are Off to War
Semiole
She's Dancing Her Heart Away
Sweet Cider Time When You Were Mine

Sweet Marie Make-a Rag-a Time-a-Dance with Me
That Carolina Rag
That Hypnotizing Strain
That's How I Need You
There'll Be a Hot Time for the Old Men While the Young Men Are Away
There's a Light That's Burning in the Window of the Little House upon the Hill
There's a Little Bit of Bad in Every Good Little Girl
There's One in a Million Like You
Under the Matzos Tree
Waltz Me Around Again, Willie
Watch Me To-night in the Torchlight Parade
What Do You Want to Make Those Eyes at Me For?
What You Goin' to Do When the Rent Comes 'Round?
What's the Matter with Father?
When Charlie Plays the Slide Trombone in the Silver Cornet Band
When Mr. Shakespeare Comes to Town
When the Harvest Days Are Over, Jessie, Dear
When You're in Love with Someone Who Is Not in Love with You
Where Do We Go from Here?
While the Old Mill Wheel Is Turning
You're in Love
You've Got to Do That Salome Dance

Caruso, Enrico
Because
Dreams of Long Ago
For You Alone
Liberty Forever
Love Is Mine
O Sole Mio
Over There

Casa Loma Orchestra
Put on Your Old Grey Bonnet

Case, Anna
Carry Me Back to Old Virginny
Dear Land of Home
Dearie
Just a-Wearying for You
Love Lifted Me
A Perfect Day

Cash, Johnny
Will the Circle Be Unbroken?

Cassavant, Louis
Will You Forget?

Castle, Irene
The Syncopated Walk
Watch Your Step

Castle, Irene and Vernon
You're Here and I'm Here

Castle Square Quartette
Lola

Castle, Vernon
The Argentine
The Syncopated Walk

Castle, Vernon and Irene
The Castle Combination
Castle Half and Half
Castle Valse Classique
The Castle Walk
Tres Moutarde
Valse Marguerite

Cavanaugh, James H.
Wait at the Gate for Me

Cawthorne, Herbert
Julie

Cawthorne, Joseph
I Can Dance with Everybody But My Wife
In the *Ladies' Home Journal*
The Land of "Let's Pretend"
My Irish Daisy
My Sweet
Nursery Rhymes
Poor Little Rich Girl's Dog
Put Me Among the Girls

The Chad Mitchell Trio
We Are Coming

Chalmers, Thomas
Those Songs My Mother Used to Sing
Chalue, Flora
Cupid's I.O.U.
Champion, Marge and Gower
Good Bye, My Lady Love
Chandler, Anna
Don't Try to Steal the Sweetheart of a Soldier
Hello Wisconsin, Won't You Find My Yonnie Yonson
I Love But You
I'm Crazy 'bout the Turkey Trot
The Letter That Never Reached Home
Never Let the Same Bee Sting You Twice
Rolling Stones All Come Rolling Home Again
She's Good Enough to Be Your Baby's Mother...
That Hypnotizing Strain
When Yankee Doodle Learns to "Parlez-Vous Francaise?"
You Can't Get Along with 'Em or Without 'Em, You've Got to Have Them, That's All
Chandler, Arthur
When You're Down in Louisville, Call on Me
Chandos, Lloyd
Love Is Mine
Chantal Twins
My Wife's Gone to the Country
Chapine
Good Bye My Home Sweet Home
Chapman, Charles
Dreaming in the Trenches
Charles A. Prince's Columbia Orchestra
Kiss Me Again
Charles Twins
I Wonder What Will William Tell
Chenoweth Cornfield Symphony Orchestra
The Last Shot Got Him
Chicago Band
When You're in Town in My Home Town
Chip, Little
My Pretty Zulu Lu
Claire, Ina
Bandy Legs
What Good Is Alimony on a Lonesome Night
Clarence Williams' Jazz Band
Breeze, Blow My Baby Back to Me
Clark, Alexander
Mister Dooley
Clark and Bergman
We've Had a Lovely Time, So Long, Good Bye
Clark, Bobby
Just a Kiss
Clark, Gladys
For Me and My Gal
From Here to Shanghai
Honey Love
If You Don't Want Me
Jerry, You Warra a Warrior in the War
Nothing's Good Enough for a Good Little Girl If She's Good Enough for You
Romany
Snooky Ookums
That's My Idea of Paradise
We've Had a Lovely Time, So Long, Good Bye
You Can't Expect Kisses from Me
Clark, Gladys, and Henry Bergman
Meet Me at the Station
Clark, Helen
Daisies Won't Tell
Don't Turn My Picture to the Wall
I'll Change the Shadows to Sunshine
Let Bygones Be Bygones and Let Us Be Sweethearts Again
Next Sunday at Nine
Rebecca of Sunnybrook Farm
So Long Letty
There's More to the Kiss than the X-X-X

Clark, Madeleine
A Little Boy Named 'Taps'
Clark, Mae
All That I Ask of You Is Love
Clark, Marguerite
Pinky Panky Poo
Clark, Miriam
When You're in Love with Someone Who Is Not in Love with You
Clark, Roy
Early in the Morning
Clarke, Helen
I'll Get You
I've Made Up My Mind to Mind a Maid Made Up Like You
Just Because It's You
Where the Red Red Roses Grow
Clarke, John F.
The Whole Dam Family
Claude, Toby
Holding Hands
In a Hammock Built for Two
The Moon Has His Eyes on You
Percy
Clayton, Bessie
De Cakewalk Queen
Jack O'Lantern Girl
Clayton, Lew
Louisiana
Cleveland, James
I Don't Feel No Way Tired
Clifford, Billy
Louisiana Louise
Clifford, Billy Single
I Just Can't Help from Lovin' That Man
Please Go Away and Let Me Sleep
Clifford, Jack
Tumble in Love
Cline, Maggie
Arrah Go On, I'm Gonna Go Back to Oregon
I Want to Be a Prima Donna
A Little Bit of Irish
O'O'O'Brien
Clooney, Rosemary
The Teddy Bears' Picnic
There's a Broken Heart for Every Light on Broadway
Clough, Arthur
Daisies Won't Tell
Red Red Rose
Clyde Doerr's Club Royal Orchestra
Can You Forget
Cohan, George M.
Give My Regards to Broadway
If I Were Only Mister Morgan
Musical Moon
Oh, You Wonderful Girl
Rag Babe
When You Come Back, and You Will Come Back, There's a Whole World...
Yankee Doodle Boy
You're a Grand Old Flag
Cohan, Josephine
I Want to Go to Paree, Papa
Maudie
Rag Babe
Cohan, Josie
Don't You Think It's Time to Marry?
Cole, Bob
The Countess of Alagazam
If Adam Hadn't Seen the Apple Tree
Sweetest Gal in Town
Cole, Nat King
Angel Eyes
Baby, Won't You Please Come Home
Coleman, Dan
Any Rags?
Mother's Hymn to Me
Pretty Little Dinah Jones
Coleman, Lillian
Sambo and Dinah
Collins, Arthur
Alexander and His Clarinet
Any Rags?
Arrah-Wanna
At the Levee on Revival Day
Baby Rose
Back to the Woods
Bye-Bye, My Eva, Bye-Bye

Central, Give Me Back My Dime
The Chanticleer Rag
Cleopatra
Come After Breakfast, Bring 'long You' Lunch and Leave 'fore Supper Time
Come Down from the Big Fig Tree
Come, Take a Skate with Me
The Cubanola Glide
Dat's Harmony
Down Among the Sugar-Cane
Down in Chattanooga
Down Where the Swanee River Flows
Everybody Works But Father
The Ghost That Never Walked
Good-bye Alexander, Good-bye Honey-Boy
I Get Dippy When I Do That Two-Step Dance
If You Don't Want Me, Send Me to My Ma
I'm a Jonah Man
I'm Crazy 'bout the Turkey Trot
I'm Going Back to Carolina
I'm Going Back to Dixie
Just Because She Made Dem Goo-Goo Eyes
Lovie Joe
Lucy Anna Lou
Mammy's Shufflin' Dance
Moriarty
Mother Hasn't Spoken to Father Since
My Croony Melody
My Dusky Rose
My Sumurun Girl
My Wife's Gone to the Country
Nobody
Oh, How She Could Yacki Hacki Wicki Wacki Woo
Oh, That Moonlight Glide
The Old Maids' Ball
On the 5:15
The Preacher and the Bear
A Quaint Old Bird
Rag Babe
Ragtime Soldier Man
Round Her Neck, She Wears a Yeller Ribbon
Rufus Johnson's Harmony Band
Sailin' Away on the Henry Clay
Sipping Cider thru' a Straw
Sweetest Gal in Town
Take Me to That Swanee Shore
Tell Me Dusky Maiden
That International Rag
That Mesmerizing Mendelssohn Tune
That's a Plenty
Under the Yum Yum Tree
Underneath the Tango Moon
What You Goin' to Do When the Rent Comes 'Round?
When Tony Goes Over the Top
When Uncle Joe Plays a Rag on His Old Banjo
When Uncle Joe Steps into France
When You're Down in Louisville, Call on Me
Who Will Be with You When I'm Far Away?

Collins, Jose
Dark Grows the Sky
Rebecca of Sunnybrook Farm
When the Angelus Is Ringing

Collins, Lottie
California and You
My Turkey Trotting Boy

Colonna, Jerry
Can't Yo' Hear Me Callin', Caroline
When Rosie Riccoola Do the Hoola Ma Boola She's the Hit of Little Italy

Columbia Band
Any Rags?
I'm on My Way to Dublin Bay

Columbia Orchestra
Enid Waltz

Columbia Quartet
Everybody's Doin' It Now
My Pony Boy
Nellie Dean
Way Down East

Columbia Stellar Quartet
Carry Me Back to Old Virginny
Way Down Yonder in the Cornfield
Comer, Imogene
A Rose with a Broken Stem
Comer, Larry
If I Had a Son for Each Star in Old Glory, Uncle Sam, I'd Give Them All to You
You Can't Get Along with 'Em or Without 'Em, You've Got to Have Them, That's All
Comfort, Vaughn
Honey, I Will Long for You
Como, Perry
Because
If We Can't Be the Same Old Sweethearts
If You Had All the World and Its Gold
Marcheta
Nobody
Roses of Picardy
Condon, Eddie
Dill Pickles Rag
Ida, Sweet as Apple Cider
Coney, Joseph
The Language of the Flowers
Coniff, Ray
Cuddle Up a Little Closer, Lovey Mine
Connolly, Dolly
In Berry Pickin' Time
Naughty Eyes
Ragtime Mockingbird
The Red Rose Rag
Sweet Cider Time When You Were Mine
There's a Broken Heart for Every Light on Broadway
Waiting for the Robert E. Lee
When You Wore a Tulip and I Wore a Big Red Rose
Connor, Nadine
'Neath the Southern Moon
Conrad, Con
That Mesmerizing Mendelssohn Tune
Conroy, Nick
The Load That Father Carried
Consolidated Quartet
For Dixie and Uncle Sam
Conway's Band
The Battle of Gettysburg
The Battle of the Nations
California and You
Dreamy Alabama
Good-Bye, Dolly Gray
Have a Heart
I Love Her Oh! Oh! Oh!
Napoleon's Last Charge
Sweetie Dear
Cook, Olga
Molly Malone, My Own
Cook, Will J.
In the Hills of Old Carolina
Coombs, Frank
Those Songs My Mother Used to Sing
Cooper, Harry
That Baboon Baby Dance
They'll Be Mighty Proud in Dixie of Their Old Black Joe
They're Wearing 'Em Higher in Hawaii
Cooper, Lillian Kemble
Hitchy's Garden of Roses
Cordelia Mitchell and the Three Mitchells
Let Me See You Smile
Corinne
Lonesome
Cossar, Frances
Waltzing with the Girl You Love
Cotton, Idalene
My Mariuccia Take a Steamboat
Court, Van
Teach Me That Beautiful Love
Courtney, Birdie
Altogether Too Fond of You
Courtney, Perqueta
Please Don't Take My Lovin' Man Away

Courtney Sisters
Blue Eyed Blond Haired Heart Breaking Baby Doll
Bye and Bye
I'm Going Back to Dixie
On a Good Old Time Sleigh Ride
That Dreamy Italian Waltz
Coverdale, Minerva
Come Dance with Me
Coward, Noel
Alexander's Rag-Time Band
Cowl, Jane
Smilin' Through
Cox, Ray
It's the Pretty Things You Say
Coyne, Joseph
I Love You So
Crawford, Clifton
I Want to Spread a Little Sunshine
The Language of Lover's Smiles
Simple Little Sister Mary Green
Crawford, George
Sally's Sunday Hat
Crawford, Jesse
Auf Wiedersehn
The Bells of St. Mary's
Kate Kearney
Little Grey Home in the West
The Perfect Song
Roses of Picardy
That Wonderful Mother of Mine
Critereon Quartet
Carry Me Back to Old Virginny
My Gal Sal
Crosby, Bing
Alexander's Rag-Time Band
Alias Jimmy Valentine
The Bells of St. Mary's
Danny Boy
Dear Little Boy of Mine
Dear Old Girl
Down by the Old Mill Stream
I Can't Tell Why I Love You But I Do
I'd Like to Live in Loveland with a Girl Like You
If I Had My Way
In the Good Old Summertime
In the Land of Beginning Again
I've Got My Captain Working for Me Now
A Little Bit of Heaven, Shure They Call It Ireland
MacNamara's Band
Marcheta
Mighty Lak' a Rose
Moonlight Bay
Mother Machree
My Isle of Golden Dreams
My Melancholy Baby
Nobody
Now Is the Hour
Play a Simple Melody
Pretty Baby
Row Row Row
School Days
Sierra Sue
Some of These Days
Someday Sweetheart
The Spaniard That Blighted My Life
Sunbonnet Sue
The Sweetheart of Sigma Chi
The Teddy Bears' Picnic
Too-ra-loo-ra-loo-ra
Wait 'Till the Sun Shines, Nellie
When I Lost You
When Irish Eyes Are Smiling
Where the River Shannon Flows
Crosby, Bob
Pack Up Your Troubles in Your Old Kit Bag and Smile, Smile, Smile
Crosby, Julia
The Song That I Hear in My Dreams
Cross, Wellington
And That Ain't All
Come On Papa
The Golden Stairs of Love
Lafayette
Let's Be Ready, That's the Spirit of '76
Make Believe
Oh Helen!

There's a Lump of Sugar Down in Dixie
Crummit, Frank
Same Sort of Girl
"Cuddles"
When I Grow Up I'm Going to Be a Soldier
Cugat, Xavier
Kashmiri Song
Cullen, James H.
Eighth Avenue
Curran, John P.
Come to the Land of Bohemia
I'll Wed You in the Golden Summertime
In the City of Sighs and Tears
In the Village by the Sea
Jennie Lee
My Irish Rose
The Town Where I Was Born
Curren, Frances
I Won't Be an Actor Any More
Curtis, Vera
Baby Rose
Dailey, Dan
Play a Simple Melody
Dailey, Peter
Tipperary Nora
Dailey, Peter F.
I Hates to Get Up Early in the Morning
I Love My Shirt Waist Best
My Charcoal Charmer
My Sunflower Sue
Dale and Boyle
Next Sunday at Nine
Dale, Viola
Amo
Roses Bring Dreams of You
Dalhart, Vernon
The Alcoholic Blues
Can't Yo' Hear Me Callin', Caroline
The Curse of an Aching Heart
I'll Be with You When the Roses Bloom Again
I'm All Bound 'Round with the Mason-Dixon Line
Let Me Call You Sweetheart
Mickey
Till We Meet Again
Daly, Dan
The Kodak Girl
My Honolulu Lu
Oh Fudge!
Take Me Back to Herald Square
Daly, Lucy
Mah Moonlight Lou
Daly, Nellie
Down in Mulberry Bend
The Pussy and the Bow-Wow
Dandy, Jess
Imagination
It Was the Dutch
Daniels, Frank
The Girl with the Baby Stare
I Can't Reach That Top Note
Plain Mamie O'Hooley
The Proper Way to Kiss
Darcy, Maurice
The Irish Girl I Love
Darden, Leonie
Dolly
Darin, Bobby
I Wonder Who's Kissing Her Now
Darnel, Bill
Love Me, Make Me Love You Like I Never Loved Before
D'Arville, Camille
In Naples Fair
Sadie, You'se Ma Lady-Bird
Un-requited
Wait
When Two Hearts Are One
Davenport, Harry
Follow the Man That Leads the Band
David, Trevelyan
Dear Land of Home
Davies, Marion
You're a Great Big Lonesome Baby
Davies, Reine
Come On, Let's Razoo on Our Little Kazoo
Meet Me Tonight in Dreamland

Davis, Jessie Bartlett
Good Night Is But Your Last Good Bye
Remember Dear
Two Eyes of Brown
The Way to Win a Woman's Heart
When I'm Away from You Dear
Davis, Lillian
You've Got Your Mother's Big Blue Eyes
Davis, Reine
No One Knows Where the Old Man Goes
Oh! What a Beautiful Dream You Seem
Teasing
Davis, Sammy, Jr.
Pretty Baby
Davis, Thomas
I Wish I Had My Old Girl Back Again
Dawn, Hazel
Alice in Wonderland
Just Because It's You
Dawson, Eli
Boom-Tum-Ta-Ra-Ra-Zing-Boom
Day, Dennis
By the Light of the Silvery Moon
Danny Boy
A Little Bit of Heaven, Shure They Call It Ireland
Mother Machree
Too-ra-loo-ra-loo-ra
Day, Doris
Be My Little Baby Bumble Bee
By the Light of the Silvery Moon
Cuddle Up a Little Closer, Lovey Mine
I Wish I Had a Girl
I'm Forever Blowing Bubbles
Moonlight Bay
Pretty Baby
Your Eyes Have Told Me So
Day, Edith
Alice Blue Gown
de Angelis, Jefferson
All Right!
Beautiful Dreamy Eyes
Dooley's Alibi
Foolish Questions
G.O.P.
Tammany
De Forrest, Muriel
Swanee
de Gogorza, Emilio
Mother o' Mine
De Haven and Sidney
Mandy Lane
De Haven, Carter
Darling
Honey Man
Honey, You Were Made for Me
I'm a Member of the Midnight Crew
I've Been Looking for a Girl Like You
Pride of the Prairie
Ragtime Table d'Hote
de los Angeles, Victoria
Clavelitos
de Lussan, Zelie
I Love But One, I Love But You
De Mar, Carrie
The Bathing Lesson
Deacon, Arthur
On a Beautiful Night with a Beautiful Girl
Dean, Sidney
Honey Will You Miss Me When I'm Gone?
Delmore, Grace
It's the Pretty Things You Say
DeMar, Grace
All He Does Is Follow Them Around
Demarest, Frances
Every Little Movement
Denny, Will F.
Beautiful Dreamy Eyes
Deslys, Gaby
Angelique
Come and Dance with Me
Come Back to Me
The Gaby Glide

I'll Get You
My Turkey Trotting Boy
Tango Dip
When Gaby Did the Gaby Glide
When You Hear Love's "Hello"
You'll Call the Next Love the First
You're a Good Little Devil
Devereaux, Jack
The Longest Way 'Round Is the Sweetest Way Home
DeVoie, Bessie
Hannah Dooley, Pride of Ballyhooley
The Irish Girl I Love
My Irish Maid
DeWolfe, Ward
I'd Be Happy Anywhere with You
That Baboon Baby Dance
d'Harville, Madeleine
The Maurice Glide
The Maurice Tango
Di Dio, Mlle.
Paree
Diamond, George
Be Satisfied with What You Have, Let Well Enough Alone
Her Boy in the Rank and File
Just Next Door
Way Down Yonder in the Cornfield
Diamond, George H.
Down on the Farm
Down Where the Cotton Blossoms Grow
Down Where the Swanee River Flows
I'm Longing for My Old Kentucky Home
In the House of Too Much Trouble
In the Village by the Sea
My Drowsy Babe
There's a Mother Old and Gray Who Needs Me Now
When the Whipporwill Sings Marguerite
Dickson, Dorothy
Peggy
Dietrich and Sheridan
Please Leave the Door Ajar
Dietrich, Rene
'Cross the Great Divide, I'll Wait for You
Dilka, Juliette
Ze Yankee Boys Have Made a Wild French Baby Out of Me
Dixie Jazz Band
Lila
Dixon, Grace
When It's Apple Blossom Time in Normandy
Doane, Frank
The Sunflower and the Sun
Dockstader, Lew
Are You a Buffalo?
Back to the Woods
The Bee That Gets the Honey Doesn't Hang Around the Hive
Don't Butt In
Everybody Works But Father
Father's Got a Job
Feed the Kitty
Go Easy Mabel
G.O.P.
He Handed Me a Lemon
He Played It on His Fid, Fid, Fiddle-dee-dee
It Was the Dutch
Lord Have Mercy on a Married Man
Make a Noise Like a Hoop and Roll Away
The Man Behind
Meet Me in St. Louis, Louis
Mister Wilson, That's All
No One Can Take Your Place
No Wedding Bells for Me
Oh! Wouldn't That Jar You?
The Old, Old Story
Shovelin' Coal
Dody, Sam
My Brudda Sylvest'
That Dreamy Italian Waltz
Whistling Rag

Doherty, Jimmy
  I'd Like to Be the Fellow That Girl Is Waiting For
Doherty Sisters
  On a Starry Night
  On the Banks of the Rhine with a Stein
Dolan, Phil
  'Cross the Great Divide, I'll Wait for You
  In the Heart of the City That Has No Heart
Dolce Sisters
  Bring Me Back My Lovin' Honey Boy
  Loveland Days
  Mammy's Shufflin' Dance
  Oh! You Circus Day
  That Mesmerizing Mendelssohn Tune
  You Can't Break a Broken Heart
  You Can't Expect Kisses from Me
Dolly, Jansci
  Heavenly Twins
Dolly, Jansci and Roszika
  My Isle of Golden Dreams
Dolly, Roszika
  Heavenly Twins
Dolly Sisters
  Bumble Bee
  I'm Always Chasing Rainbows
  The Vamp
Doner, Ted
  Walking the Dog
Donlin, Mike
  My Brudda Sylvest'
  Stars of the National Game
Donner, Kitty
  Our Ancestors
Dooley, Johnny
  The Shorter They Wear 'Em the Longer They Look
  We'll Knock the Heligo into Heligo Out of Heligoland!
Dooley, William J.
  On the Old Front Porch
  When I Lost You
D'Oro, Marie
  Eastern Moon
D'Orsay, Elizabeth
  All That I Had Is Gone
Dorsey, Jimmy
  Johnson Rag
  Lily of the Valley
Dorsey, Tommy
  Love Sends a Little Gift of Roses
Downey, Morton
  Killarney, My Home o'er the Sea
Doyle and Dixon
  At Mammy's Fireside
Doyle, James T.
  Daddy's Little Girl
Dream Girls
  If He Can Fight Like He Can Love, Good Night Germany
Dresser, Louise
  Cheer Up Father, Cheer Up Mother
  Go Slow Joe
  Honey Boy
  I Remember You
  I Want to Be Loved Like a Leading Lady
  I'd Lay Down My Life for You
  I'm Sorry
  In the Shade of the Old Apple Tree
  Just Because He Couldn't Sing "Love Me and the World Is Mine"
  My Gal Sal
  Oh, You Candy Kid
  She's Good Enough to Be Your Baby's Mother...
  Take Me Back to Babyland
  That Hypnotizing Man
  Under the Yum Yum Tree
  Waltz Me Around Again, Willie
  What Would $50,000 Make You Do?
  Why Dont You Try?
Dressler, Marie
  A Great Big Girl Like Me
  Heaven Will Protect the Working Girl
  He's the Whole Show Now

I Have Never Seen the Russian Ballet
Pretty Kitty-San
She's Good Enough to Be Your Baby's Mother...
When Charlie Plays the Slide Trombone in the Silver Cornet Band
Drew, Grace
Naughty Eyes
Driscoll, Jack
Love Me Like the Ivy Loves the Old Oak Tree
Driver, Ann
In the Shade of the Old Apple Tree
Driver, Anna
Angel Eyes
Blue Bell
Come Down from the Big Fig Tree
The Gambling Man
Hoop-la, I'm Having the Time of My Life
Oh! You Chicken
Only a Dream of a Golden Past
Pawnee
The Trail of the Lonesome Pine
When I Dream in the Gloaming of You
Won't You Waltz 'Home Sweet Home' with Me for Old Times Sake?
You Are the Ideal of My Dreams
Du-For, Harry
I've Got the Blues for Home Sweet Home
Duchene, Maria
'Neath the Southern Moon
Duchin, Eddy
Alice Blue Gown
Dudley, S. H.
Come After Breakfast, Bring 'long You' Lunch and Leave 'fore Supper Time
Cuddle Up Honey, Let's Make Love
If I Ever Get Back to Cincinnati
The Man Behind
Tell Me Dusky Maiden
When Reuben Comes to Town
Why Don't the Band Play?
You're in the Right Church But the Wrong Pew
Duke Ellington's Orchestra
Beale Street Blues
Tishomingo Blues
Duncan Sisters
I Ain't Got'en No Time to Have the Blues
I Want to See My Ida Hoe in Idaho
Melody Chimes
Dunlap, Marguerite
Lindy
When It's Apple Blossom Time in Normandy
Dunmore, Eveleen
Mandy Lane
Dunn, Arthur
Courting
I Want to Be a Drummer in the Band
Just a Tender Spot for Father Dear
A Kiss for Each Day of the Week
Dunne, Thomas Potter
America Needs You Like a Mother, Would You Turn Your Mother Down?
Since My Mariutch Learned the Merry Widow Waltz
DuPre, Jeannette
I Want to Be a Merry Merry Widow
Durante, Jimmy
What You Goin' to Do When the Rent Comes 'Round?
Who Will Be with You When I'm Far Away?
Durbin, Deanna
Because
Clavelitos
Kiss Me Again
Poor Butterfly
Earl Fuller's Famous Jazz Band
I'm Sorry I Made You Cry

Earl Fuller's Orchestra
How 'Ya Gonna Keep 'Em Down on the Farm After They've Seen Paris?
Sand Dunes
Earl Fuller's Rector Novelty Orchestra
Castle Valse Classique
Earl, Mary
My Sweetheart Is Somewhere in France
Earl, Maude
Why Dont You Try?
Earl, Virginia
Down De Lover's Lane
I Could Learn to Love You If You Let Me Try
I'm Looking for the Man That Wrote "The Merry Widow Waltz"
Love
Love Laughs at Locksmiths
What Eve Said to Adam
Earle, Ermine
The Fife and Drum
Earle, Maude
On the Old See-Saw
Early, John
Absence Makes the Heart Grow Fonder
Eddie Condon and His Orchestra
Sweet Cider Time When You Were Mine
Eddy, Jenny
I'll Be There, Mary Dear
Eddy, Nelson
Ah, Sweet Mystery of Life
I'm Falling in Love with Some One
'Neath the Southern Moon
A Perfect Day
The Rosary
Sylvia
Tramp, Tramp, Tramp
Will You Remember?
Edison Band
The Maurice Glide
The Maurice Tango
Edison Military Band
Indianola
Edison's Concert Band
The Hurricane
Edison's Hungarian Orchestra
Every Little Movement
Ediss, Connie
All She Gets from the Iceman Is Ice
Edwards, Cliff
I Wonder Who's Kissing Her Now
Edwards, "Cuddles"
If I Only Knew Just How I Stood with You
Edwards, Gus
I'm Crazy to Go on the Stage
My Cousin Caruso
Rosa Rigoletto
Edwards, Leo
My Cousin Caruso
That Long Lost Chord
Eldee, Lillian
Coo!
Elinore and Williams
Just as Washington Crossed the Delaware, So Will Pershing Cross the Rhine
Elinore, Kate
Next to Your Mother Who Do You Love?
Ellington, Duke
Royal Garden Blues
Twelfth Street Rag
Yellow Dog Blues
Ellinore, May
Are You Coming Out Tonight, Mary Ann?
Ellinore Sisters
Her Eyes of Irish Blue
Ellis, Harry
Bring Me a Rose
Can't You See That I'm Lonely?
Good-Bye, Dolly Gray
I Want to Be a Soldier
Iola
'Neath the Old Cherry Tree, Sweet Marie

When the Last Rose of Summer Was in Bloom
Where Do We Go from Here?

Ellis, Harry A.
Down Where the Cotton Blossoms Grow
The Heaven Born Banner
I'll Be Waiting in the Gloaming, Sweet Genevieve
Mothers of America, You Have Done Your Share
Somebody's Waiting for You
When the Harvest Days Are Over, Jessie, Dear

Ellis, Melville
Come Around on Our Veranda
Goo-Goo Eyes
I've Got to Dance Till the Band Gets Through
When Love Is Young
Without the Girl Inside

Ellison, Glen
I Wish I Had My Old Girl Back Again
Roamin' in the Gloamin'
She Is Ma Daisy

Elsie, Lily
I Love You So

Eltinge, Julian
All the World Loves a Lover
Come Over on My Veranda
Don't Go in the Water, Daughter
Don't Take Your Beau to the Seashore
Holding Hands
In the Land of Wedding Bells
Loving Eyes
The Ragtime College Girl
That's What the Daisy Said
Today's My Wedding Day
You Can't Guess What He Wrote on My Slate

Emerson, Billy
Honey Will You Miss Me When I'm Gone?

Emerson, Ida
Be Sweet to Me, Kid
Good Bye, My Lady Love
Just Next Door

Emerson, James
Ain't You Coming Back to Old New Hampshire, Molly?

Emerson Military Band
Indianola
Madelon
Mammy o' Mine
The Midnight Fire Alarm
The Rose of No Man's Land
The Vamp

Emerson Xylo-pheinds
Bo - la - Bo

Emerson's Dance Orchestra
Oh! What a Pal Was Mary

Emery Deutch and His Royal Gypsy Orchestra
The Old Gypsy

Empire City Quartet
All That I Ask of You Is Love
Down Where the Wurzburger Flows
Way Down in Cotton Town
Why Dont You Try?

Empire City Quartette
Bright Eyes Good-Bye
Good Luck Mary
In the Village by the Sea
Mariutch Down at Coney Island
'Neath the Old Cherry Tree, Sweet Marie

Enoch Light and His Clover Leaf Four
I Love Her Oh! Oh! Oh!

Errol, Bert
Beautiful Roses

Errol, Leon
Angel Eyes

Estellita, La Belle
A Picnic for Two

Etting, Ruth
I Ain't Got Nobody Much and Nobody Cares for Me
Let Me Call You Sweetheart
Ramona
Shine On, Harvest Moon

Europe's "Hell Fighters" Band
All of No Man's Land Is Ours
Europe's Hell Fighters Band
Indianola
Europe's Society Orchestra
The Castle Combination
Castle Half and Half
The Castle Walk
I Ain't Had No Lovin' in a Long Time
Valse Marguerite
Euterpean Quartet
Beautiful Isle of Somewhere
Evan and St. John
The Boys in the Gallery for Mine
Evans, Charles
He Was Always Fooling Around
Evans, Dale
Love Lifted Me
Put Your Arms Around Me, Honey
Evans, George
Feed the Kitty
It's Got to Be a Minstrel Show Tonight
Waltzing with the Girl You Love
Evans, Harry
What Are You Going to Do to Help the Boys?
Evett, Robert
The Little Wooden Soldier
Fair, Nancy
My Baby Talking Girl
Fairbanks, Madeleine and Marion
The Chicken Walk
Falk, Eleanor
Cecelia and Amelia
He's Me Pal
Falk, Elinore
My Drowsy Babe
Pajama Polly
Falke, Charles
Always in the Way
The Banquet in Misery Hall
Be Satisfied with What You Have, Let Well Enough Alone
I'll Break the Fighting Line Like You Broke This Heart of Mine
In the City of Sighs and Tears
Just What the Good Book Taught
Keep on the Sunny Side
Like a Star That Falls from Heaven
People Who Live in Glass Houses Never Should Throw Any Stones
A Picture without a Frame
Please Leave the Door Ajar
Please Mother, Buy Me a Baby
While the Old Mill Wheel Is Turning
Fanchon and Marco
Meet Me at the Station
Farber Girls
There's a Lump of Sugar Down in Dixie
Farber Sisters
Alexander's Band Is Back in Dixieland
Everything Is Peaches Down in Georgia
If He Can Fight Like He Can Love, Good Night Germany
I'm Crazy about My Daddy in a Uniform
I'm Not Jealous
Mammy's Shufflin' Dance
Farleigh, Harry
Love Has Claimed Its Own
Farrar, Geraldine
Gay Butterfly
Mighty Lak' a Rose
Shadows
Slowly Stealing Up and Down the River
War Baby's Lullaby
Farrell, Eileen
Danny Boy
Farrell, Marguerite
If I Knock the 'L' Out of Kelly, It Still Would Be Kelly to Me
Naughty! Naughty! Naughty!
Fats Waller and His Rhythm Boys
The Darktown Strutters' Ball
Faust, Lotta
Sammy
When the Circus Comes to Town

Favor, Ed. M.
He Ought to Have a Tablet in the Hall of Fame
Hello Central, Give Me Heaven
I Want to Be a Lidy
Fay, Effie
When the Right Mr. Wright Comes Along
Fay, Elfie
The Band of Reubenville
Fay, Frank
I Never Knew How Much I Loved You Until There Was Somebody Else
My Baby Talking Girl
On the Level, You're a Devil
Faye, Alice
Come Down, Ma Evening Star
Rag-Time Cowboy Joe
Rose of Washington Square
Felmar, Rose
In the Land of Harmony
Fender, Harry
Freedom of the C's
Fenton, Marie
Movin' Man Don't Take My Baby Grand
Fields, Arthur
Along Came Ruth
And That Ain't All
Bring Back Those Wonderful Days
Can You Tame Wild Wimmen?
Do Something
Goodbye Broadway, Hello France
He's a Cousin of Mine
He's Had No Lovin' for a Long, Long Time
Honolulu, America Loves You
I Don't Want to Get Well
I Might Be Your "Once in a While"
I Never Knew
If He Can Fight Like He Can Love, Good Night Germany
I'll Come Back to You When It's All Over
Jazz Baby
Madelon
Mickey
My Baby Talking Girl
Oh! Frenchy
Oh, How I Laugh When I Think How I Cried about You
Pig Latin Love
Please Go Away and Let Me Sleep
Ragging the Chopsticks
Rock-a-bye Your Baby with a Dixie Melody
Send Me Away with a Smile
Stay Down Here Where You Belong
We'll Knock the Heligo into Heligo Out of Heligoland!
When It Comes to a Lovingless Day
When Yankee Doodle Learns to "Parlez-Vous Francaise?"
Where Do We Go from Here?
You Keep Sending 'Em Over and We'll Keep Knocking 'Em Down
You'll Find Old Dixieland in France
You're in Style When You're Wearing a Smile
Fields, Gracie
Now Is the Hour
Fields, Harry
All That I Ask of You Is Love
Fields, Harry W.
Abie, the Sporty Kid
Fields, Lew
The High Cost of Loving
Hiram Green, Good-Bye
Fields, Nat
Bless Your Ever Loving Little Heart
Fields, Sadie
Mariutch Down at Coney Island
On the Banks of the Rhine with a Stein
Fields, Shep
Dear Old Pal of Mine
Finley, Agnes
Cutey, Tell Me Who Tied Your Tie?

Fischer, Freddie "Schnickelfritz"
  The Wild Wild Women Are Making a Wild Man of Me
Fisher, Gladys
  Scissors to Grind
Fisher, Grace
  Get a Girlie!
  Naughty! Naughty! Naughty!
Fisher, Irving
  Alice in Wonderland
Fisher, Lola
  Other Eyes
Fisher, Marie
  I'd Like to Be the Fellow That Girl Is Waiting For
Fisher, Sallie
  All the World Loves a Lover
  Anti-Rag Time Girl
  Dearie
  The Garden of Dreams
  In My Dreams of You
  In the Valley of Kentucky
  Play a Simple Melody
  When You First Kiss the Last Girl You Love
Fisher, Susie
  Blue Eyed Sue
Fitzgerald, Ella
  Angel Eyes
  Baby, Won't You Please Come Home
  The Darktown Strutters' Ball
  My Melancholy Baby
  Sugar Blues
Fitzgibbon, Bert
  If They'd Only Fight the War with
  Jerry, You Warra a
    Warrior in the
    War
    Wooden Soldiers
  Since My Mariutch Learned the Merry Widow Waltz
Fitzhugh, Anna
  In My Merry Oldsmobile
Fitzin, Anna
  My Star
Fleman and Miller
  Make Believe
Fleming, James A.
  Cutey, Tell Me Who Tied Your Tie?
Fletcher, Tom
  When It's All Goin' Out and Nothin' Comin' In
Florede, Nellie
  Daisy Donahue
  Take Me Back to New York Town
  Your Mother Wants You Home Boy
Flowers, Edward
  I'll Be with You When the Roses Bloom Again
Flynn, Josie
  In My Harem
  In the City of Sighs and Tears
  In the Land of Harmony
Flynn, Kitty
  Somebody's Coming to Town from Dixie
Fogarty, Johnny
  Not Because Your Hair Is Curly
Fogerty, Frank
  I Wonder Why Bill Bailey Don't Come Home
  Tippecanoo
Foley, Roy
  Will the Circle Be Unbroken?
Foo, Lee Tong
  My Irish Rose
Ford T. Dabney's Band
  Easy Pickins'
Ford T. Dabney's Orchestra
  The Castle Combination
  Castle Half and Half
  Castle Valse Classique
  The Pensacola Mooch
  Poor Little Butterfly Is a Fly Girl Now
  Scaddle-de-Mooch
  You Can't Shake That Shimmie Here
Foreman, Charles
  Like a Star That Falls from Heaven

Forrest, Helen
I Wish I Could Shimmy Like My Sister Kate
Fougere, Mlle.
Take Me Around Again
Four Clefs
I Must Have Been a-Dreamin'
Four Musical Colbys
Bright Eyes Good-Bye
Fox, Della
Any Little Girl That's a Nice Little Girl Is the Right Little Girl for Me
Good-Bye, Maggie May
The Honeysuckle and the Bee
I'll Break the Fighting Line Like You Broke This Heart of Mine
I'm Afraid to Come Home in the Dark
In the Shade of the Old Apple Tree
Little Miss No-One from No-Where
Violette
Waltz Me Around Again, Willie
Fox, George B.
Cutey, Tell Me Who Tied Your Tie?
Fox, Harry
Alexander's Band Is Back in Dixieland
The Girl on the Magazine Cover
Honey Boy
I Lost My Heart in Dixieland
I Love a Piano
I Think You're Absolutely Wonderful (What Do You Think of Me?)
I'm All Bound 'Round with the Mason-Dixon Line
I'm Always Chasing Rainbows
The Language of Love
Meet Me at the Station
Typical Topical Tunes
Foy, Eddie, Jr.
The Streets of New York
Foy, Edwin
And the Green Grass Grew All Around
Chinatown, My Chinatown
Dreamy Fandango Tune
The Dusky Salome
Feed the Kitty
Gee! But This Is a Lonely Town
The Ghost That Never Walked
Hamlet Was a Melancholy Dane
He Goes to Church on Sunday
He Was a Sailor
The Hornpipe Rag
I'm a Poor Unhappy Maid
I'm Tired
I'm Unlucky
It Must Have Been Svengali in Disguise
It's Good Enough for Me
The Kellerman Girlie
My Operatic Samson
Oh, How I Love My Teacher
The Poor Old Man
Ring-Ting-a-Ling
Sister Ann
When There's No Light at All
You Never Miss the Water 'Till the Well Runs Dry
Foye, Edward J.
The Face in the Firelight
Francis, Connie
I'm Sorry I Made You Cry
Frank Messina and the Mavericks
Sweetest Gal in Town
Frank Novak and His Rootin' Tootin' Boys
Has Anybody Here Seen Kelly?
If I Knock the 'L' Out of Kelly, It Still Would Be Kelly to Me
I've Got Rings on My Fingers
Franklyn, Irene
Come Around on Our Veranda
I'm a Bringing Up the Family
Little One, Good Bye
The Pony Ballet Girl
Redhead
When the Fields Are White with Cotton
Frantzen's Society Orchestra
He's Had No Lovin' for a Long, Long Time

Frary, Julia
Every Saturday Afternoon
Lonesome
Fraser, Agnes
In Zanzibar
Fred Van Eps and His Banjo Orchestra
The White Wash Man
Fred Waring and His Pennsylvanians
The Bells of St. Mary's
Marcheta
Strike Up the Band
Fred Waring's Pennsylvanians
Lila
Frederick, Pauline
A Sprig of Rosemarie
Freear, Miss Louie
I Want to Be a Lidy
Freer, Margaret
I Know What It Means to Be Lonesome
French, Charles K.
The Animals' Convention
Friganza, Trixie
Everything Is Rosy, Rosie
Feed the Kitty
The Game of Love
I'm Looking for the Man That Wrote "The Merry Widow Waltz"
Nancy Clancy
No Wedding Bells for Me
Nosie Rosie Posie
Poor Barney Mulligan
Smarty
Somebody's Waiting for You
Frisco, Joe
Frisco's Kitchen Stove Rag
Fulton, Maude
The Boy Who Stuttered and the Girl Who Lisped
Oh, You Candy Kid
The White Wash Man
Gall, Yvonne
Bird of the Wilderness
Galli-Curci, Amelita
Clavelitos
Kiss Me Again
Gannon, Ila
Budweiser's a Friend of Mine
Gannon, Ula
I'm Sorry
Garland, Judy
For Me and My Gal
I Don't Care
I Love a Piano
I Want to Go Back to Michigan
Meet Me in St. Louis, Louis
Meet Me Tonight in Dreamland
Play That Barbershop Chord
Put Your Arms Around Me, Honey
Rag-Time Violin
Smilin' Through
Snooky Ookums
Under the Bamboo Tree
Waiting for the Robert E. Lee
When That Midnight Choo-Choo Leaves for Alabam'
When You Wore a Tulip and I Wore a Big Red Rose
You Made Me Love You, I Didn't Want to Do It
Garnella, May Shirk
In the Good Old-Fashioned Way
Garner, Erroll
Ja-Da
Garner, Jack
I Love to Sit and Look at You
Garrison, Mabel
Khaki Sammy
Kiss Me Again
Gassman, Josephine
My Hindoo Man
Gaston, Billy
My Marguerite
When the Band Plays "Indiana," Then I'm Humming "Home Sweet Home"
Gateson, Marjorie
I've Made Up My Mind to Mind a Maid Made Up Like You
Gaxton, William
Some Girls Do and Some Girls Don't
Gaynor, Mitzi
I Don't Care

Gene Roderich's Orchestra
Come to the Moon
Gennett Military Band
It's Time for Every Boy to Be a Soldier
George, Marie
Baby Mine
George S. Reed and the Lads of Melodie
My Marguerite
Gerard, Frances
Pansies Mean Thoughts and Thoughts Mean You
Gershwin, George
Tee-Oodle-Um-Bam-Bo
Gibson, Gertie
Everybody Has a Whistle Like Me
Gibson, Lottie
There Are Two Sides to a Story
Gillespie, Joseph
Don't You Wish You Were Back Home Again?
Gillette, Viola
I'm Glad I'm Married
The Troubadour
Gillham, Art
I Wish I Had My Old Girl Back Again
Gillot and Henry
People Who Live in Glass Houses Never Should Throw Any Stones
Gilman, Mabel
Mamselle
Sly Musette
The Sunflower and the Sun
What's the Matter with the Moon Tonight?
Gilman, Mabelle
The Army of Peace
France, Glorious France
In Silence
The Maiden with the Dreamy Eyes
Gilroy, John
Instrumental Man
John Would Never Do That
Gilroy, Mamie
Lady Bountiful
Gilson, Lottie
The Boys in Blue Parade Today
Could You Be True to Eyes of Blue If You Looked into Eyes of Brown?
Honey Love
Let's All Go Up to Maud's
Meet Me in St. Louis, Louis
Waltz Me Around Again, Willie
When the Birds Go North Again
When They Play "God Save the King"
Where the Silv'ry Colorado Wends Its Way
Gittelman, Ben
The Star and the Flower
Gladdish, Fred
Absence Makes the Heart Grow Fonder
All Is Fair in Love and War
Maybe
Glamm, Louise
My Belgian Rose
Glaser, Lulu
And Other Things
Beneath the Moon
The Country Girl
The Dolly Varden Song
The Honeysuckle and the Bee
A Kiss in the Dark
Glason, Billy
Can You Tame Wild Wimmen?
Just Another Poor Man Gone Wrong
They're All Sweeties
Glass, Bonnie
Beautiful Eyes
Gleason, Billy
On the Old Front Porch
Glen Gray and the Casa Loma Orchestra
Blow the Smoke Away
Castle of Dreams
Chinatown, My Chinatown
Dallas Blues
If I Had My Way

Sierra Sue
Glenn, Julius
My Friend from Kentucky
Glenn Miller and His Orchestra
Beautiful Ohio
Glenn, Wilfred
When the Bell in the Lighthouse Rings Ding, Dong
Glose, Augusta
Billet Doux
Gluck, Alma
Bird of the Wilderness
Carmena
Carry Me Back to Old Virginny
Little Grey Home in the West
A Perfect Day
The Rosary
Godfrey, Arthur
Dear Old Girl
Down by the Old Mill Stream
I Wish I Had a Girl
Wait 'Till the Sun Shines, Nellie
Gohn, Lillian
Won't You Be My Baby Boy?
Gold, Belle
Somebody's Coming to Town from Dixie
Golden, Beatrice
The Girl You Love
Golden, Marta
I Can't Help Dreaming of You
Goldman Band
The Fairest of the Fair
Gonne, Lillian
Ragging the Nursery Rhymes
Goodman, Benny
After You've Gone
Beale Street Blues
Ciribiribin
I Hate to Lose You
Poor Butterfly
Rose Room
Royal Garden Blues
Shim-me-sha-wabble
Somebody Stole My Gal
Tiger Rag
Gordon and Chacon
My Dusky Rose
Gordon, Kitty
Alma, Where Do You Live?
Dreaming
Love at the Door
There's a Little Spark of Love Still Burning
Gould, William
Ain't It Tough to Be So Absent-Minded?
Simple Little Sister Mary Green
Grable, Betty
Cuddle Up a Little Closer, Lovey Mine
Put Your Arms Around Me, Honey
Grady, Lottie
Dat Lovin' Rag
Graeme Bell and His Australian Jazz Band
Yama Yama Blues
Grandy, Louise
In Vacation Time
Grannon, Ila
Beautiful Eyes
A Little Bit of Irish
Grant, Bob
Goodbye Broadway, Hello France
Grant, Mamie
Oh! Oh! Miss Phoebe
Granville, Bernard
Are You from Heaven?
Beautiful Beautiful Girl
Dancing Shoes
It Was Just a Song at Twilight That Made Me Come Back to You
My Country Right or Wrong
When You Wore a Tulip and I Wore a Big Red Rose
Graveure, Louis
I Told My Love to the Roses
Sylvia
Gray, Maude
Let's Go to a Picture Show
Green, Alice
The Land Where the Good Songs Go

Green, Ethel
If I Had My Way
Innocent Bessie Brown
There's a Girl in the Heart of Maryland with a Heart That Belongs to Me
Green, George Hamilton
Castle Valse Classique
Melody of Love
Greene, Gene
Casey Jones
From Here to Shanghai
Honolulu, America Loves You
I Didn't Raise My Boy to Be a Soldier
I Wonder Where My Lovin' Man Has Gone
I'm Going Back to Dixie
Just a Dream of You, Dear
M-O-T-H-E-R
Oh, You Beautiful Doll
On the Mississippi
Piano Man
Rag-Time Cowboy Joe
Rag-Time Violin
Row Row Row
Rufus Johnson's Harmony Band
That Carolina Rag
That Long Lost Chord
Way Down South
The Wedding of the Shimmie and Jazz
When It's Apple Blossom Time in Normandy
Greenwood, Charlotte
Back to the Bleachers for Mine
Linger Longer Letty
Oh by Jingo! Oh by Gee! You're the Only Girl for Me
Greenwood, Winnifred
Over the Pilsner Foam
Grey, Joel
Forty-five Minutes from Broadway
Give My Regards to Broadway
H-A-Double R-I-G-A-N
So Long, Mary
Yankee Doodle Boy
You're a Grand Old Flag
Grossmith, George
They Didn't Believe Me
Grossmith, George Jr.
My Cosy Corner Girl
Grunning, Louise
The Proper Way to Kiss
Guerite, Laura
Beautiful Eyes
Gunning, Louise
The Road to Yesterday
Guy Lombardo and His Royal Canadians
Can't You See That I'm Lonely?
Come Back to Me
Cuddle Up a Little
Closer, Lovey
Mine
Dardanella
Huckleberry Finn
If I Had My Way
I'm Simply Crazy over You
I've Been Floating Down the Old Green River
I've Got the Time, I've Got the Place, But It's Hard to Find the Girl
Just a Baby's Prayer at Twilight to Her Daddy Over There
The Perfect Song
Smiles
You Didn't Want Me When You Had Me So Why Do You Want Me Now?
Guyer, Thomas, and Beth Stone
Daddy's Little Girl
Just a Little Rocking Chair and You
Gynt, Mirsky
It's the Pretty Things You Say
Hackett, Dolly
Pretty Baby
Hackett, Thomas
'Neath the Old Acorn Tree, Sweet Estelle
Hale, Alan
Any Old Place with You

Hale, Helen
My Teddy Girl
Halford, Ollie
Wed the Man That You Love or Don't Wed at All
Hall, Artie
The Blues
There's a Time and a Place for Everything
Hall, Jessie Mae
Lights of Home
Hall, Josephine
Brother Bill
O Mona San
Hall, Pauline
I Knew at First Sight That I Loved You
Look into Mine Eyes Dear Heart
Won't You Waltz 'Home Sweet Home' with Me for Old Times Sake?
Halley, William
All He Does Is Follow Them Around
Hamilton, Bessie
I'm Glad I Can Make You Cry
Hamlin, Frank
The Awakening
Hampton, Lionel
Nola
Handy, W. C.
Mister Crump Blues
St. Louis Blues
Handy's Band
The Florida Blues
Joe Turner Blues
Handy's Orchestra
Ole Miss
Harcourt and May
I Must Have Been a-Dreamin'
Hare, Ernest
By the Honeysuckle Vine
I Gave Her That
I'll Say She Does
You Ain't Heard Nothing Yet
Hare, Winifred
The Maid in the Moon

Harlan, Byron G.
Alexander and His Clarinet
At the Levee on Revival Day
Baby Rose
Bye-Bye, My Eva, Bye-Bye
Captain Baby Bunting of the Rocking Horse Brigade
Central, Give Me Back My Dime
The Chanticleer Rag
Come, Take a Skate with Me
The Cubanola Glide
Daddy's Little Girl
Down Among the Sugar-Cane
Down in Chattanooga
Good-bye Alexander, Good-bye Honey-Boy
The Good Old U.S.A.
Hello Central, Give Me Heaven
I'm Crazy 'bout the Turkey Trot
I'm Going Back to Dixie
Lucy Anna Lou
Mammy's Shufflin' Dance
Meet Me in Rose Time Rosie
Moriarty
Mother Hasn't Spoken to Father Since
My Cousin Caruso
My Croony Melody
My Wife's Gone to the Country
Nora Malone, Call Me by Phone
Oh, How She Could Yacki Hacki Wicki Wacki Woo
The Old Maids' Ball
On the 5:15
Ragtime Soldier Man
Round Her Neck, She Wears a Yeller Ribbon
Rufus Johnson's Harmony Band
School Days
Sipping Cider thru' a Straw
Sweetest Gal in Town
Take Me to That Swanee Shore
That International Rag
That Mesmerizing Mendelssohn Tune
Under the Yum Yum Tree
Underneath the Tango Moon
Wait 'Till the Sun Shines, Nellie

The Waltz Must Change to a March, Marie
When I Dream in the Gloaming of You
When the Sunset Turns to Ocean's Blue to Gold
When Uncle Joe Steps into France
When You're Down in Louisville, Call on Me
Where the Morning Glories Twine around the Door
Who Will Be with You When I'm Far Away?
Harlan, Otis
My Little Lady Bug
Harold Veo's Orchestra
The Zoo Step
Harris, Dixie
Loveland Days
Harris, Marion
Beale Street Blues
Good-bye Alexander, Good-bye Honey-Boy
He Done Me Wrong
Homesickness Blues
I Ain't Got Nobody Much and Nobody Cares for Me
I'm Gonna Make Hay While the Sun Shines in Virginia
Jazz Baby
Mammy's Chocolate Soldier
My Syncopated Melody Man
Take Me to that Land of Jazz
There's a Lump of Sugar Down in Dixie
They Go Wild, Simply Wild Over Me
When Alexander Takes His Rag Time Band to France
Harris, Phil
Constantly
The Darktown Poker Club
Down Among the Sugar-Cane
He's a Cousin of Mine
I Ain't Gonna Give Nobody None o' This Jelly Roll
On the Mississippi
Play a Simple Melody
The Preacher and the Bear
Row Row Row
Take Your Girlie to the Movies If You Can't Make Love at Home
Woodman, Woodman Spare That Tree
You're in the Right Church But the Wrong Pew
Harrison, Charles
In the Land of Beginning Again
The Land Where the Good Songs Go
Roses of Picardy
She's the Daughter of Mother Machree
When You're in Love with Someone Who Is Not in Love with You
Harrison, James F.
I Called You My Sweetheart
Harrison, Lee
Upper Broadway After Dark
Harrison, Louis
My Angemima Green
Harrold, Orville
Ah, Sweet Mystery of Life
I'm Falling in Love with Some One
It Never, Never Can Be Love
The Radiance in Your Eyes
Tramp, Tramp, Tramp
Harry Evans and His Orchestra
We're Going to Hang the Kaiser under the Linden Tree
Harry Salter and His "Stop the Music" Orchestra
Are You a Buffalo?
Hart, Al
I Sing a Little Tenor
Hart, Albert
Love in an Orchard
Hart, Charles
Alabama Lullaby
Beans
Lovely Daughter of Allah
My Belgian Rose
Oh! What a Pal Was Mary
So Long Mother
Somewhere in France Is the Lily

What Are You Going to Do to Help the Boys?
Hart, Charles, and Elliot Shaw
The Rose of No Man's Land
Hart, Charles H.
It's Time for Every Boy to Be a Soldier
Hart, Joseph
The Bathing Lesson
Hart, Kitty
Gimme Hush Money or I'll Tell on You
I Ain't Got Nobody Much and Nobody Cares for Me
Harvard and Cornell
I Am Longing for Tomorrow When I Think of Yesterday
Harvey, Bert
All the Quakers Are Shoulder Shakers Down in Quaker Town
Harvey, J. Clarence
Tee-Oodle-Um-Bam-Bo
Harvey, Josephine
All on Account of a Dear Little Girl
Harvey, Morton
I Didn't Raise My Boy to Be a Soldier
If You Don't Want Me, Send Me to My Ma
Hathaway, Franklyn Earl
When the Winds O'er the Sea Blow a Gale
Haverly's Mastodon Minstrels
You're the Flower of My Heart, Sweet Adeline
Hawley, Jenny
Oh! Take Me to My Mamma Dear
Hayden, Ola
Paint Me a Picture of Mama
The Star and the Flower
Haydn Quartet
Blue Bell
Heidelberg
Lazy Moon
Red Red Rose
When It's Moonlight on the Prairie
When Love Is Young
When You Know You're Not Forgotten by the Girl You Can't Forget
Will You Love Me in December as You Do in May?
Hayes, Mary
Now Is the Hour
Hayes, Roland
By an' By
Go Down Moses
Morning, Noon, and Night
Hayward Trio
Melinda's Wedding Day
Hayworth, Rita
Poor John
Hazzard, John E.
The Best of Everything
From Now On
The Head Waiter
Susan, Dear Sue
Healey, Dan
Gee! But There's Class to a Girl Like You
Hearn, Lew
In the Land of Harmony
Take Me Back to the Garden of Love
Heath, Bobby
On the Old Front Porch
Heath, Frankie
Parisienne
Please Don't Take My Lovin' Man Away
Hedges Brothers and Jacobson
On San Francisco Bay
Heidelberg Quartet
Roll Dem Cotton Balls
They're On Their Way to Mexico
Way Down South
Heidelberg Quintette
By the Beautiful Sea
Heidler, Fred
The Aba Daba Honeymoon
Held, Anna
Bashful Betsey Brown
Be My Teddy Bear
Chloe, I'm Waiting
The Comet and the Moon

Dinah
Flirtation Song
The Game of Love
The Girl with the Eyes and the Golden Hair
I Just Can't Make My Eyes Behave
I Want Something New to Play With
I Want to Be Naughty Too
I Wonder What's the Matter with My Eyes?
I'm Learning Something Every Day
In Society
In Washington
It's Delightful to Be Married
I've Lost My Teddy Bear
Kewpie Doll
Kiss, Kiss, Kiss, If You Want to Learn to Kiss
The Maiden with the Dreamy Eyes
Mister Monkey
Nancy Clancy
Oh, I Want to Be Good But My Eyes Won't Let Me
A Parisian Model
Rubber Necking Moon
Strolling Along the Beach
What'd Yo' Do Wid de Letter, Mr. Johnson?

Helf, Sadie
Ain't You Coming Back to Old New Hampshire, Molly?
I'm Tying the Leaves So They Won't Come Down

Hemus, Percy
Khaki Sammy
On the Road to Home Sweet Home

Hengler Sisters
Kitty
Pretty Maid Adelaide
Sunrise at the Zoo

Henricks, Barbara
Deep River

Henry and Gallot
In the Valley of Kentucky
The Tie That Binds
When Kate and I Were Comin' thro' the Rye
When the Fields Are White with Cotton

Henry, Eleanor
Ain't You Coming Back to Old New Hampshire, Molly?
Colleen Bawn

Herbert, Joseph
Come and Take a Stroll with Me
The Man Who Plays the Tambourine

Herman, Al
Give Me the Sultan's Harem
In the Land of Wedding Bells
Merrily We'll Roll Along

Herman, Woody
Dallas Blues

Herz, Ralph
Meet Me at the Masquerade

Hickman, Art
Dry Your Tears

Hilliard, Robert
A Fool There Was

Hilo Hawaiian Orchestra
Aloma

Hilo Orchestra
My Bird of Paradise

Hindermeyer, Harvey
Garden of Roses
Good Night Dear
When Jack Comes Sailing Home Again
When the Angelus Is Ringing

Hitchcock, Raymond
Ain't It Funny What a Difference Just a Few Hours Make?
And the World Goes on Just the Same
I Introduced
I'm All Dressed Up and No Where to Go
I'm All O.K. with K. and E.
It's a Waste of Time to Worry
When You're All Dressed Up and No Place to Go
You're in Love

Hite, Mabel
Beautiful Eyes
Because I'm Married Now
Do You Think You Could Learn to Love Me?
I Wonder If You Love Me
I'm on My Way to Reno
My Brudda Sylvest'
My Wife's Gone to the Country
Stars of the National Game
Way Down South
Ho, Don
Aloha Oe
Hobson, Florence
Barnyard Rag
Hodges Brothers
Always Take a Girl Named Daisy ('cause Daisies Won't Tell)
Hoffmann, Gertrude
I Want a Gibson Man
Lotus San: A Japanese Romance
My Bird of Paradise
My Eulah Eulah, My Indian Maid
Hogan, Ernest
He May Get Over It But He'll Never Look the Same
I Just Can't Keep My Eyes Off You
I'm Goin' to Live Anyhow 'Till I Die
Is Everybody Happy?
The Phrenologist Coon
Holbrook, Florence
He's a Fan, Fan, Fan
Hollis, F. W.
It's the Man in the Sailor Suit
When We Were Two Little Boys
Holloway, Stanley
If You Were the Only Girl in the World
Under the Anheuser Bush
Home Town Girls
I'm on My Way to Dublin Bay
Homer, Genevieve
Daddy's Little Girl
Homer, James R.
Mother's Hymn to Me
Homesley, Lillian
Why Adam Sinned
Hope, Maidie
My Toreador
Hoppe, Vera
I Want Someone to Flirt with Me
Hopper, DeWolf
Acting
The American Billionaire
Beautiful Arizona
Love a la Mode
Nothing Doing
The Opera
Those Days of Long Ago
Hopper, Edna Wallace
Come, Take a Trip in My Air-Ship
The Girl You Love
I Just Couldn't Do without You
The Ping Pong Song
When Tommy Atkins Marries Dolly Gray
Horace Heidt and His Brigadiers
Sugar Blues
Horace Wright and His Ukelele Orchestra
O'Brien Is Tryin' to Learn to Talk Hawaiian
Horitz, Jos. F.
Jennie Lee
Hotel Biltmore Dance Orchestra
Why Do They All Take the Night Boat to Albany?
Howard, Anna
Alice in Wonderland
Howard, Eugene
Beautiful Eyes
Good-Bye Girlie and Remember Me
He Was Always Fooling Around
I Have Shed My Last Tears for You
That Soothing Serenade
That's Yiddisha Love
Venetian Moon
Howard, Eugene and Willie
Bye Bye Dearie
Howard, Frank
On Lalawana's Shore

When the Sunset Turns to Ocean's Blue to Gold
Howard, Joseph E.
Be Sweet to Me, Kid
Blow the Smoke Away
Central, Give Me Back My Dime
Honey Will You Miss Me When I'm Gone?
I Wonder Who's Kissing Her Now
Howard, Olin
Linger Longer Letty
Howard, Willie
The Bacchanal Rag
Beautiful Eyes
Good-Bye Girlie and Remember Me
He Was Always Fooling Around
I Have Shed My Last Tears for You
I'm Going to Spend My Vacation with a Dear Old Relation
My Yiddische Butterfly
Ragtime Jockey Man
That Soothing Serenade
That's Yiddisha Love
Under the Matzos Tree
Venetian Moon
Howard, Willie and Eugene
Lady Angeline
Howe, Gilby
The Blue and the Gray: A Mother's Gift to Her Country
Hoy Sisters
Oh! Papa, Oh! Papa, Won't You Be a Pretty Papa to Me?
Hull, Caroline
Deacon Jones
Hunt, Pee Wee
Dill Pickles Rag
O
Hunter, Alberta
Beale Street Blues
Hunter, Edna
Spring Fashions
Hunting, Dorothy
By the Old Oak Tree
Hussey, Jimmy
America Needs You Like a Mother, Would You Turn Your Mother Down?
Hutchinson, Kathryn
Psyche
Hutton, Betty
Rag-Time Cowboy Joe
What Do You Want to Make Those Eyes at Me For?
Imperial Comedy Quartette
I'll Be With You Honey When It's Honeysuckle Time
The Imperial Four
The Load That Father Carried
Imperial Quartet
Way Down Yonder in the Cornfield
Irwin, May
Bible Stories
Bonnie Sue Sunshine
Eight Little Letters Make Three Little Words
I Ain't Gwin ter Work No Mo'
I Just Can't Help from Lovin' That Man
I'm Afraid to Come Home in the Dark
I'm Going Back to Dixie
Magdaline, My Southern Queen
"Mumms" the Word
No Wedding Bells for Me
Over the Garden Wall
The Peach That Tastes the Sweetest Hangs the Highest on the Tree
'Taint No Use in Lovin' That Way
Why Don't the Band Play?
Isham Jones' Juniors
Nola
Italian Trio
In the Shade of the Old Apple Tree
Ives, Burl
Brighten the Corner Where You Are
Early in the Morning
Ivy, Elsie
Take Me Back

Jack Fina and His Orchestra
Baltimore Rag
Jack Teagarden and the Capitol Jazzmen
I'm Sorry I Made You Cry
Jackson, Eddie
What You Goin' to Do When the Rent Comes 'Round?
Jackson, Ethel
I Love You So
Miss Bob White
When Love Comes Knocking at the Door
Jacques, Hattie
Waiting at the Church
James, Daisy
I Want to Go Back to Michigan
James, Harry
Alice Blue Gown
Ciribiribin
James, Lewis
Dreamy Alabama
Garden of Roses
James Reese Europe's "Hell Fighters"
The Darktown Strutters' Ball
James Reese Europe's Hell Fighters Band
How 'Ya Gonna Keep 'Em Down on the Farm After They've Seen Paris?
James Reese Europe's "Hell Fighters" Band
Ja-Da
James Reese Europe's Hell Fighters Band
Mirandy
James Reese Europe's Society Orchestra
Tres Moutarde
You're Here and I'm Here
James Reese Europe's 369th Infantry Band
Jazz Baby
Jan Garber and His Orchestra
I Love My Babe, My Baby Loves Me
Janis, Elsie
Advertising
Anti-Rag Time Girl
Are You from Heaven?
Ballin' the Jack
Bless Your Ever Loving Little Heart
The Chicken Walk
Crusader and Tommy
El Choclo
Give Me the Moonlight, Give Me the Girl and Leave the Rest to Me
I Never Knew
I'd Rather Love What I Cannot Have Than Have What I Cannot Love
It's a Long Way to Dear Old Broadway
The Jazz Band
Let Me Live and Stay in Dixieland
A Little Love But Not for Me
My Yankee Doodle Girl
The Picture I Want to See
A Regular Girl
Some Sort of Somebody
When Yankee Doodle Learns to "Parlez-Vous Francaise?"
Jardon, Dorothy
Alamo
Are You from Heaven?
Daisy Dear
Homeward Bound
The Language of Flowers
The Last Rose of Summer Is the Sweetest Song of All
Lotus San: A Japanese Romance
Jarman, Irene
I'm Glad I'm Married
Jarrott, John
Mexi-Tango
Jaudas' Society Orchestra
Ain't You Coming Back to Dixieland?
Beautiful Ohio
Castle Valse Classique
Djer-Kiss
Goodbye Broadway, Hello France
Have a Heart

I Didn't Raise My Boy to Be a Soldier
I'm on My Way to Dublin Bay
The Kiss Waltz
My Bird of Paradise
Jefferson Airplane
Ja-Da
Jelly Roll Morton's New Orleans Jazzmen
Oh! Didn't He Ramble
Jermon, Irene
Let's Go to a Picture Show
Jerry Murad's Harmonicats
Every Little Movement
Jessel, George
Don't Take Advantage of My Good Nature
I'll Get You
Oh, How I Laugh When I Think How I Cried about You
You'd Be Surprised
Jesters
On the 5:15
She Is Ma Daisy
Jimmy Dorsey and His Orchestra
All That Glitters Is Not Gold
Johnny Dodds and the Black Bottom Stompers
Joe Turner Blues
Johnson, Billy B.
Good-Bye, I'll See You Some More
Johnson, Carroll
Bye-Bye, My Eva, Bye-Bye
I'm Goin' to Live Anyhow 'Till I Die
Johnson, Estelle
Good-Bye, I'll See You Some More
Johnson, J. Rosamond
The Big Red Shawl
The Countess of Alagazam
O, Southland
Sweetest Gal in Town
Johnson, Lonnie
Kansas City
Jolson, Al
After You've Gone
Ain't You Coming Back to Dixieland?
Alexander's Rag-Time Band
At Mammy's Fireside
Billy Billy, Bounce Your Baby Doll
By the Honeysuckle Vine
Cleopatra
Come Back to Me
Dancing the Blues Away
Dat Lovin' Touch
Down Among the Sheltering Palms
Down Where the Swanee River Flows
Everybody Rag with Me
Ev'ry Morning She Makes Me Late
For Me and My Gal
From Here to Shanghai
He'd Have to Get Under, Get Out and Get Under to Fix Up His Automobile
Hello Central, Give Me No Man's Land
I Gave Her That
I Love Her Oh! Oh! Oh!
I Love My Billy Sunday But Oh, You Saturday Night
I Love My Steady, But I'm Crazy for My Once-in-a-While
I Love the Heart of Dixie
I Sent My Wife to the 1000 Isles
I Want a Girl Just Like the Girl That Married Dear Old Dad
I Wish I Had a Girl
I Wonder Why She Kept On Saying Si Si Si Si Si Senor
I'll Say She Does
I'm All Bound 'Round with the Mason-Dixon Line
I'm Down in Honolulu Looking Them Over
I've Got My Captain Working for Me Now
Just Try to Picture Me Back Home in Tennessee
Ma Blushin' Rosie, My Posie Sweet
Mammy's Little Coal Black Rose
Mother's Sitting Knitting Little Mittens for the Navy

Movin' Man Don't Take My Baby Grand
My Sumurun Girl
'N' Everything
Oh, How I Wish I Could Sleep Until My Daddy Comes Home
Oh, What a Night
On the Road to Calais
Pretty Baby
Ragging the Old Vienna Roll
Rock-a-bye Your Baby with a Dixie Melody
Sinbad Was in Bad All the Time
Sister Susie's Sewing Shirts for Soldiers
Snap Your Fingers and Away You Go
So Long Mother
Someone Else May Be There While I'm Gone
The Spaniard That Blighted My Life
Swanee
Tell Me
Tell That to the Marines!
That Loving Traumerei
That Lullaby of Long Ago
There Are Two Eyes in Dixie
There's a Lump of Sugar Down in Dixie
They're Wearing 'Em Higher in Hawaii
This Is the Life
The Villain Still Pursued Her
Waiting for the Robert E. Lee
Wedding Bells, Will You Ever Ring for Me
When I Leave the World Behind
When Sunday Comes to Town
When the Grown-Up Ladies Act Like Babies
Where the Black-Eyed Susans Grow
Who Paid the Rent for Mrs. Rip Van Winkle?
Who Played Poker with Pocohontas When John Smith Went Away?
Why Do They All Take the Night Boat to Albany?
Yaaka Hula Hickey Dula
You Ain't Heard Nothing Yet
You Made Me Love You, I Didn't Want to Do It
You've Got Your Mother's Big Blue Eyes

Jolson, Harry
My Hawaiian Sunrise

Jones, Ada
All Aboard for Dixie
All Night Long
Beatrice Fairfax, Tell Me What to Do
Beautiful Eyes
Billy
By the Beautiful Sea
Call Me Up Some Rainy Afternoon
Cuddle Up a Little Closer, Lovey Mine
Cupid's I.O.U.
The Deedle-Dum-Dee
Don't You Think It's Time to Marry?
Don't You Want a Paper, Dearie?
Down on the Farm
Googy-Oo
Has Anybody Here Seen Kelly?
I Just Can't Make My Eyes Behave
I Live Up-Town
I Want to Be a Merry Merry Widow
If That's Your Idea of a Wonderful Time, Take Me Home
If You Can't Get a Girl in the Summertime, You'll Never Get a Girl at All
I'll Take You Back to Italy
I'm Glad I'm a Boy/I'm Glad I'm a Girl
I'm Sorry
I've Got Rings on My Fingers
Kiss, Kiss, Kiss, If You Want to Learn to Kiss
Mandy Lane
Meet Me Down at the Corner
My Pony Boy

Nix on the Glow-Worm, Lena
Nora Malone, Call Me by Phone
O'Brien Is Tryin' to Learn to Talk Hawaiian
Oh Johnny, Oh Johnny, Oh!
Poor John
The Ragtime Dream
Row Row Row
Smarty
So Long Letty
Sombody Loves You
Some Boy
Some Sunday Morning
Sprinkle Me with Kisses If You Want My Love to Grow
Waiting at the Church
The Wedding Glide
What Makes the World Go Round
When I Get You Alone Tonight
When You Play in the Game of Love
Won't You Be My Honey?
The Yama Yama Man
You Can't Expect Kisses from Me
You Splash Me and I'll Splash You

Jones, Allan
Gianina Mia
I Love You Truly
Love Is Like a Firefly

Jones and Sutton
Good Morning Carrie!

Jones, Bobby
Everybody Loves a Chicken

Jones, Ella
Love Me Like I Want to Be Loved

Jones, Isham
Dallas Blues

Jose, R. J.
The Bird That Never Sings
The Blue and the Gray: A Mother's Gift to Her Country
Calling to Her Boy Just Once Again
The Day That You Grew Colder
Dear Old Girl
The Green above the Red
I Went to See Them March Away
In the Wildwood Where the Bluebells Grew
I've Grown So Used to You
Just for Tonight
May Sweet May
Since Nellie Went Away
There's No North or South Today
Way Down in Indiana
We've Been Chums for Fifty Years
When I'm Away from You Dear
When Love Was Young
The Woman Thou Gavest Me
Your Mother Wants You Home Boy

Joseph C. Smith's Orchestra
Come On Papa
Dear Old Pal of Mine
Dry Your Tears
Hindustan
How 'Ya Gonna Keep 'Em Down on the Farm After They've Seen Paris?
I Was So Young, You Were So Beautiful
In a Kingdom of Our Own
Mammy o' Mine
Mickey
My Sweetie
Oh! Frenchy
Oh Johnny, Oh Johnny, Oh!
Oh! What a Pal Was Mary
Sweet Hawaiian Moonlight, Tell Her of My Love
The Vamp
When You Look in the Heart of a Rose
Yellow Dog Blues

Josephine, Lois
The Golden Stairs of Love
Make Believe

Juanita Hall Choir
Lift Every Voice and Sing

Kalisz, Armand
Mon Amour
Romance

Karle, Theo
Little Mother of Mine

Karp, Sophia
Eli Eli
Kaufman, Irving
Blues My Naughty Sweetie Gives to Me
Everybody Wants a Key to My Cellar
Nobody Knows and Nobody Seems to Care
Rockaway
Take Your Girlie to the Movies If You Can't Make Love at Home
Kaufman, Jack
Nobody Knows and Nobody Seems to Care
Kay Kyser and His Orchestra
He's a Devil in His Own Home Town
I Don't Want to Get Well
Kaye, Danny
Ballin' the Jack
Oh by Jingo! Oh by Gee! You're the Only Girl for Me
What's the Use of Dreaming
Kaye, Sammy
Cuddle Up a Little Closer, Lovey Mine
Hindustan
I Want a Girl Just Like the Girl That Married Dear Old Dad
Keaton, Joe, Nora, and Buster
Down Where the Wurzburger Flows
Keefe, Baby Zena
All Aboard for Dreamland
I Want to Be an Actor Lady
I Want to Linger
In the Shade of the Old Apple Tree
In Vacation Time
Just Next Door
Smarty
Kelley, Tom
The Banquet in Misery Hall
Kellogg, Shirley
My Yiddische Colleen
The Wedding Glide
Kelly and Violette
Bright Eyes Good-Bye
Bye Bye Dearie
In Dear Old Georgia
In the Shade of the Old Apple Tree
Iola
Moonlight
My Hindoo Man
The Sunflower and the Sun
When the Angelus Is Ringing
When the Birds Go North Again
Kelly, Gene
For Me and My Gal
Ida, Sweet as Apple Cider
Moonlight Bay
Take Me Out to the Ball Game
When You Wore a Tulip and I Wore a Big Red Rose
Kelly, Georgie
I Love My Husband But Oh You Henry
Kelly, Maud Alice
Honey Will You Miss Me When I'm Gone?
Kent, Charles
Mothers of America, You Have Done Your Share
Kent, William
Please Don't Take Away the Girls
Kentucky Serenaders
Venetian Moon
Keyes, Nelson
Alone with You
Kid Ory and His Creole Dixieland Band
Yaaka Hula Hickey Dula
Kid Ory's Creole Jazz Band
Oh! Didn't He Ramble
Kimball Brothers
Come Over on My Veranda
King, Charles
The Aba Daba Honeymoon
Are You from Heaven?
Be My Little Baby Bumble Bee
For Me and My Gal
Hawaiian Butterfly
Honolulu, America Loves You
I Can Live without You
I Was So Young, You Were So Beautiful

If I Had a Son for Each Star in Old Glory, Uncle Sam, I'd Give Them All to You
If I Were a Bee and You Were a Red, Red Rose
Keep Your Eye on the Girlie You Love
Let Me Live and Stay in Dixieland
On the Shores of Italy
Play a Simple Melody
Some Sunday Morning
String a Ring of Roses 'Round Your Rosie
That's Everlasting Love
There's a Little Bit of Bad in Every Good Little Girl
There's One in a Million Like You
When I Want to Settle Down
Where Do We Go from Here?

King, Hetty
I've Got the Time, I've Got the Place, But It's Hard to Find the Girl
Ship Ahoy

King, Jack
I'm Sorry I Made You Cry

King, Mazie
Walking the Dog

King, Mollie
I Was So Young, You Were So Beautiful
I'm Not Jealous
There's More to the Kiss than the X-X-X

King Trio
Movin' Man Don't Take My Baby Grand

Kingore, Margaret
I've a Longing in My Heart for You, Louise
Must We Say Good Bye Forever, Nellie Dear?

Kingston, Mindell
The Baltimore Bombashay
Don't Take a Girlie to Coney (You May Find a Nicer One There)
Innocent Bessie Brown

Kirby, Gerald
Altogether Too Fond of You

Kirk, Ethel
My Croony Melody
On a Good Old Time Sleigh Ride

Kirstein, Dorothy
I Love You So

Kirsten, Dorothy
Kiss Me Again

Klein, Al
They're All Sweeties

Klein, Harry
They're All Sweeties

Kline, Olive
I Can Live without You
I Might Be Your "Once in a While"
A Little Bit o' Honey
The Message of the Violet
You're Here and I'm Here

Knickerbocker Quartet
Let's All Be Americans Now
Sally in Our Alley

Knight, Percival
Just a Little Word Unspoken
On the Banks of the Bronx

Koenig, Carl M.
Out Where the Breakers Roar

Kostelanetz, Andre
Auf Wiedersehn
Kiss Me Again
The Rosary
The Streets of New York

Kreisler, Fritz
Beautiful Ohio
Love Sends a Little Gift of Roses
Mighty Lak' a Rose
On Miami Shore
Poor Butterfly
The Rosary
Since You Went Away
The World Is Waiting for the Sunrise

Krupa, Gene
Blues My Naughty Sweetie Gives to Me
Down by the Old Mill Stream
Sierra Sue

Kyser, Kay
Blues My Naughty Sweetie Gives to Me
Take Your Girlie to the Movies If You Can't Make Love at Home
Laine, Frankie
On the Road to Mandalay
Lalor, Frank
Googy-Oo
I Think It Must Be Love
Lambert, Beatrice
When the Flowers Bloom on No-Man's Land, What a Wonderful Day That Will Be
Lambert, "Happy" Jack
Lead Me to That Beautiful Band
Lambert, Marie
Moonlight
Lambert, Maud
And a Little Bit More
Baby Rose
By the Light of the Honeymoon
Come Back to Playland with Me
Gee! But There's Class to a Girl Like You
The Girl You Can't Forget
He Done Me Wrong
I'd Like to Live in Loveland with a Girl Like You
If All My Dreams Were Made of Gold, I'd Buy the World for You
I'll Change the Shadows to Sunshine
Kelly Has Gone to Kingdom Come
The Linger Longer Girl
Maud, Maud, Maud
Meet Me Tonight in Dreamland
My Sist' Tetrazzin'
Oh, Miss Malinda
Oh! You Circus Day
The Queen of the Night
When the Moon Plays Peek-a-Boo
Lancaster, Tom
Brother Noah Gave Out Checks for Rain
Landis, Jessie Royce
Meet Me Tonight in Dreamland
The Story Book Ball
Lane, Lillian
My Gal's Another Gal Like Galli-Curci
Lang Thompson and His Orchestra
Billy
Langdon, Hardie
The Banquet in Misery Hall
Hearts You Lose
Langford, Frances
Carry Me Back to Old Virginny
Langley, Leland
O Dry Those Tears
Lanza, Mario
Because
Gianina Mia
I'm Falling in Love with Some One
Tramp, Tramp, Tramp
LaPomme, Irma
The Longest Way 'Round Is the Sweetest Way Home
Larkin and Larkin
I'm Awfully Glad I'm Irish
Larkins and Patterson
My Drowsy Babe
Larkins, John
Common Sense
Tilda from Old Savannah
LaRue, Grace
Budweiser's a Friend of Mine
Don't You Think It's Time to Marry?
Hiawatha
I May Be Gone for a Long, Long Time
I Wish I Had a Girl
Little One, Good Bye
Love Me at Twilight
My Firefly
My Pocahontas
Poor Butterfly
Roses of Picardy
She's Dancing Her Heart Away
The Sum of Life
A Tango Dream
When Highland Mary Did the Highland Fling
Won't You Fondle Me

Your Lips Are No Man's Land But Mine
You're Here and I'm Here
Lauder, Harry
Calligan - Call Again!
Don't Let Us Sing Anymore about War, Just Let Us Sing of Love
Early in the Morning
Every Laddie Loves a Lassie
Fou the Noo
I Love a Lassie
Inverary
I've Loved Her Ever Since She Was a Baby
Killiecrankie
The Laddies Who Fought and Won
The Portobello Lassie
Roamin' in the Gloamin'
Rob Roy McIntosh
The Saftest of the Family
She Is Ma Daisy
Stop Your Tickling Jock!
That's the Reason Noo I Wear a Kilt
Trixie from Dixie
When I Get Back to Bonnie Scotland
While the British Bull-Dog's Watching the Door
Laughlin, Anna
I'll Be with You Honey in the Springtime
In a Hammock Built for Two
Love Me All the Time
Won't You Be My Baby Boy?
Launceford, Jimmie
Put on Your Old Grey Bonnet
Think of Me Little Daddy
Laurent, Marie
All That I Ask of You Is Love
Back, Back, Back to Baltimore
In the Shade of the Old Apple Tree
Laurenti, Mario
Love Is Mine
Lavarre, Marie
Louisiana
Lawrence, Gertrude
Poor John
Lawrence, Mary
Naughty Eyes
Lean, Cecil
Here's to You, My Sparkling Wine
He's a Fan, Fan, Fan
Lee, Eula
Emalyne, My Pretty Valentine
Leigh, Grace
How'd You Like to Float Me
Take Me 'Round in a Taxicab
Leighton, Harry
Little Girl, You'll Do
Leite, June Ululani
Across the Sea
Lennox, Fred
Ma Mamselle Honee
Leon, Daisy
Cuddle Up a Little Closer, Lovey Mine
Havana
I Don't Want To
On the Old See-Saw
Sombody Loves You
Leonard, Eddie
I Want to Go Back to the Land of Cotton
Ida, Sweet as Apple Cider
If I Could Only Sleep Like Rip Van Winkle
I'm Goin' to Live Anyhow 'Till I Die
Molasses Candy
Roll Them Roly Boly Eyes
That Teasin' Rag
Leonard Feather's Hiptet
The Fortune Telling Man
Leonard, Grace
Ain't It Funny Just What Money Does for You
Hoop-la, I'm Having the Time of My Life
I Ain't a-Goin' to Weep No More
Ida from Idaho
Keep on the Sunny Side
Wait 'Till the Sun Shines, Nellie
Yiddle on Your Fiddle Play Some Rag Time

Leoni, Henri
I Love You, Ma Cherie
Kiss, Kiss, Kiss, If You Want to Learn to Kiss
Leonia Williams and Her Dixie Band
I Wish I Could Shimmy Like My Sister Kate
Les Brown and His Band of Renown
A Good Man Is Hard to Find
Leslie, Alice A.
My Hula Lula Girl
Lessing, Madge
Good-Bye, Little Girl, Good-Bye
Levey, Carlotta
The Gambling Man
Levey, Ethel
And a Little Bit More
I Am So Particular
I'd Rather Two-Step Than Waltz, Bill
Meet Me in St. Louis, Louis
Sweetie Dear
Lewis, Dave
Budweiser's a Friend of Mine
Hiram Green, Good-Bye
Lewis, Gertie
When the Band Played Home Sweet Home
Lewis, Henry
Oh Helen!
Oh Johnny, Oh Johnny, Oh!
What Do You Want to Make Those Eyes at Me For?
The Wild Wild Women Are Making a Wild Man of Me
Lewis James and His Orchestra
Waiting for You
Lewis, Jerry
Ballin' the Jack
Rock-a-bye Your Baby with a Dixie Melody
Lewis, Robert
Bring Back My Daddy to Me
How Can I Forget When There's So Much to Remember?
Lewis, Ted
Blues My Naughty Sweetie Gives to Me
I Know Why--Because I'm in Love with You
Shim-me-sha-wabble
Leybourne, Harry
If I Thought You Wouldn't Tell
Libbey and Trayer
The Sunflower and the Sun
Libbey, J. Aldrich
Ain't You Coming Back to Old New Hampshire, Molly?
He Laid Away a Suit of Gray to Wear the Union Blue
Hello Central, Give Me Heaven
The Honeysuckle and the Bee
In the Wildwood Where the Bluebells Grew
The Sentinel Asleep
The Waltz Must Change to a March, Marie
When the Whipporwill Sings Marguerite
Liberace
Johnson Rag
The Rosary
Lichter, Anna
The Message of the Violet
Light, Enoch
Under the Yum Yum Tree
Lightner, Winnie
Floating Down the River
Lilie, Carrie
I'm on My Way to Manadalay
The Ragtime Dream
Lindon, Grace
I'm All Bound 'Round with the Mason-Dixon Line
Linton, Harry
Instrumental Man
John Would Never Do That
Little Jerry
I Wonder What Will William Tell
Lloyd, Alice
Bandy Legs
Coster Rag
I Didn't Go Home at All
The Little Church around the Corner
May, May, May

The Story of a Clothes Line
You Splash Me and I'll Splash You
Lloyd, Marie
Rum-Tiddely-Um-Tum-Tay Out for the Day Today
Tiddley-Om-Pom
Lloyd, Rosie
When It's Moonlight on the Prairie
Lockett, Lou and Jack Waldron
If You Can't Get a Girl in the Summertime, You'll Never Get a Girl at All
Loftus, Cissie
Where Go the Boats?
Logan, Ella
The Curse of an Aching Heart
I'm Forever Blowing Bubbles
Take Me Out to the Ball Game
Lombardo, Guy, and His Royal Canadians
Alice Blue Gown
Long, Avon
Nobody
Loraine, Violet
If You Were the Only Girl in the World
Lorraine, Lillian
Ballin' the Jack
Beautiful Beautiful Girl
The Blue Devils of France
Bumble Bee
Come On, Play Ball with Me
Daddy Has a Sweetheart and Mother Is Her Name
Dancing Shoes
Kidland
Linger Longer Lingerie
My Cleopatra Girl
My Pony Boy
Play That Fandango Rag
Ring-Ting-a-Ling
Smother Me with Kisses and Kill Me with Love
Some Boy
Sweet Kitty Bellairs
Swing Me High, Swing Me Low
Underneath the Tango Moon
Lorraine, Ted
The Good Ship Mary Ann
Let Bygones Be Bygones and Let Us Be Sweethearts Again
That Old Girl of Mine
There's One in a Million Like You
Where the Red Red Roses Grow
Louis Jourdan and His Tympany Five
Lovie Joe
Louisiana Five Jazz Orchestra
I Ain't Got'en No Time to Have the Blues
Lowe, Isabel
On the Level, You're a Devil
Lowe, Isabelle
Darling
Lowrie, Jeanette
There's a Lot of Things You Never Learn at School
Lund, Baby
Just Next Door
On a Sunday Afternoon
Lupino, Stanley
Crusader and Tommy
Lydecker, George
Good-Bye, Little Girl, Good-Bye
Lydy, Beth
The Kiss Waltz
Lynch, Nellie
There's No Other Girl Like My Girl
Lynn, Eve
Any Old Place with You
Lyons and Yosco
The Road for You and Me
Lythgoe, David
Hiawatha
Lyton, Fritzie
Melody Chimes
MacDonald, Donald
Something about Love
MacDonald, Jeanette
Ah, Sweet Mystery of Life
I Love You Truly
Italian Street Song
Love Is Like a Firefly
A Perfect Day

- Smilin' Through
- Vilia
- Will You Remember?

MacDonough, Harry
- Absence Makes the Heart Grow Fonder
- Alice in Wonderland
- Araby
- Auf Wiedersehn
- Day Dreams
- Dear Old Girl
- Down by the Old Mill Stream
- Down Where the Cotton Blossoms Grow
- Every Little Movement
- For Freedom and Ireland
- The Garden of Dreams
- Garden of Roses
- Good-Bye, Dolly Gray
- Good Bye, My Lady Love
- Heidelberg
- I Can't Tell Why I Love You But I Do
- I Love You All the Time
- If a Boy Like You Loved a Girl Like Me
- I'll Be with You When the Roses Bloom Again
- I'm Simply Crazy over You
- I'm Wearing My Heart Away for You
- Kate Kearney
- The Last Rose of Summer Is the Sweetest Song of All
- The Letter That Never Reached Home
- Love Me and the World Is Mine
- Mandy Lane
- The Mansion of Aching Hearts
- My Cosy Corner Girl
- My Heart Has Learned to Love You Now Do Not Say Good-Bye
- Nancy Brown
- 'Neath the Old Acorn Tree, Sweet Estelle
- Queen of the Bungalow
- Red Wing
- Sunbonnet Sue
- Tell Me Dusky Maiden
- That Hula Hula
- To Have, To Hold, To Love
- The Wedding of the Reuben and the Maid
- When It's Apple Blossom Time in Normandy
- When It's Moonlight on the Prairie
- When Kate and I Were Comin' thro' the Rye
- When the Flowers Bloom on No-Man's Land, What a Wonderful Day That Will Be
- When the Harvest Days Are Over, Jessie, Dear
- When You and I Were Young, Maggie
- The Woman Thou Gavest Me
- You're Here and I'm Here

MacFarlane, George
- Can't Yo' Hear Me Callin', Caroline
- Come Down from the Big Fig Tree
- Good Night Dear
- I'm Glad I'm Married
- I'm Proud to Be a Mother of a Soldier Like You
- Look in Her Eyes
- M-O-T-H-E-R

Mack, Andrew
- Eyes of Blue
- For Freedom and Ireland
- An Irishman's Lilt
- The Legend of the Maguire
- Little Tommy Murphy
- Pull the Cork Out of Erin and Let the River Shannon Flow

Mack, Cecil
- St. Louis Blues

Mack, Joe
- Call Me Up Some Rainy Afternoon

Mack, Lillian
- He Laid Away a Suit of Gray to Wear the Union Blue

Mack, Neil
Say a Prayer for the Boys Out There
MacKenzie, Giselle
It's Delightful to Be Married
Maginn, Bonnie
On a Spoony Moony Night
Mahoney, Paul
M-i-s-s-i-s-s-i-p-p-i
Maitland, Madge
Mariutch, She Come Back to Me
My Mariuccia Take a Steamboat
We Have So Much to Be Thankful For
Mamie Smith and Her Jazz Hounds
That Thing Called Love
Manhattan Trio
I'm a Lonesome Melody
Manion, George
Since Sister Nell Heard Paderewski Play
Manion, Jack
Movin' Man Don't Take My Baby Grand
Manning, Irene
Mary
So Long, Mary
Mantelli, Mme. Eugenie
Girl of My Dreams
Mantovani
Kiss Me Again
Love, Here Is My Heart!
The Teddy Bears' Picnic
Marble, Marie
My Pretty Zulu Lu
Marble, Mary
My Little Japaneesee
Marek Weber and His Orchestra
Dreaming
Marlowe, James C.
H-A-Double R-I-G-A-N
Marquand, Rube
The Marquand Glide
Martin, Dean
Ballin' the Jack
The Sweetheart of Sigma Chi
Martin, Tony
Beautiful Ohio
Come Back to Me
Take Me Out to the Ball Game
Marx Brothers
Sailin' Away on the Henry Clay
Marx, Julius (Groucho)
Farewell Killarney
If a Boy Like You Loved a Girl Like Me
Mason, Delia
The Girl You Love
Mathews and Bulger
Eighth Avenue
Mathews, Zoa
I'm Longing for My Old Kentucky Home
Matthews, J. Sherrie
Walk, Walk, Walk
Maxwell and Simpson
No One Seems to Love Me Now
Maxwell, Vera
Texas Tommy Swing
May, Allen
In the Hills of Old Carolina
May, Edna
I Love You, Ma Cherie
Lonesome
My Cosy Corner Girl
May Stafford and Her Jazz Band
If You Don't Want Me, Send Me to My Ma
Mayfair Orchestra
Sumurun
Mayfield, Cleo
When That Midnight Choo-Choo Leaves for Alabam'
Mayhew, Stella
I Won't Come Back
If He Comes In, I'm Going Out
My Sumurun Girl
Stop That Rag
That Beautiful Rag
That Society Bear
When the Moon Plays Peek-a-Boo
Maynard, Claire
In the Land of Harmony
McAvoy & Brooks
Cutey, Tell Me Who Tied Your Tie?

McAvoy, Charles
  Alexander, Don't You Love Your Baby No More?
McAvoy, Dan
  The Beer That Made Milwaukee Famous
  The Girl with the Baby Stare
  Hypnotizing Lize
  I'm the Man Who Makes the Money in the Mint
  My Angemima Green
  Sallie, Mah Hot Tamale
  Tippecanoo
McCart, W. F.
  When I Do the Highland Fling
McCormack and Margaret Irving
  Somebody's Coming to Town from Dixie
McCormack, John
  Because
  Bridal Dawn
  Dear Old Pal of Mine
  Duna
  Goodbye, Sweetheart, Goodbye
  I Hear You Calling Me
  In Flanders' Fields
  Ireland Must Be Heaven for My Mother Came from There
  Kashmiri Song
  Keep the Home Fires Burning
  Killarney, My Home o'er the Sea
  Little Grey Home in the West
  Little Mother of Mine
  Love, Here Is My Heart!
  Love Sends a Little Gift of Roses
  Marcheta
  Mighty Lak' a Rose
  Molly
  Mother Machree
  Mother o' Mine
  The Rosary
  Roses of Picardy
  Send Me Away with a Smile
  Since You Went Away
  The Sunshine of Your Smile
  Sweet Genevieve
  There's a Long, Long Trail
  The Trumpeter
  When Irish Eyes Are Smiling
  When You and I Were Young, Maggie
  When You Come Back, and You Will Come Back, There's a Whole World...
  When You Look in the Heart of a Rose
  Where the River Shannon Flows
  Who Knows?
  Your Eyes Have Told Me So
McCormack, Owen J.
  Back to the Carolina You Love
McCoy, Baby Nellie
  I'm Tying the Leaves So They Won't Come Down
McCoy, Bessie
  French Fandango
  I'm a Crazy Daffydil
  The Yama Yama Man
McCoy, Gertrude
  Rosa Rigoletto
McCoy, Nellie
  I Miss You in a Thousand Different Ways
McCoy, Trixie
  Roll Dem Cotton Balls
McCree, Junie
  Be Sweet to Me, Kid
  Could You Learn to Love Me?
  I Would Like to Be Your Pal
  I Would Like to Marry You
  Let's Go to a Picture Show
  Those Things Cannot Be Explained
McDermott, Billy
  Cupid's I.O.U.
  I'm Awfully Glad I Met You
McDonald, Christie
  At the Music Hall
McDonald, William
  Good Fellows
McDonough, Leonora
  My Gal's Another Gal Like Galli-Curci
McIntyre and Heath
  Good-Bye, Sweet Old Manhattan Isle

McIntyre & Heath
Honey Love Me All the Time
McIntyre and Heath
Where the Red Red Roses Grow
McIntyre, Leila
Have You Seen My Sweetheart in His Uniform of Blue?
Honey Boy
My Little Star, I'm Looking Up to You
Pansy Faces
Pansy of the Dell
McIveagh, John
Sambo and Dinah
McKinley, Neil
All He Does Is Follow Them Around
How Do You Do It Mabel on $20 a Week?
I Called You My Sweetheart
We'll Knock the Heligo into Heligo Out of Heligoland!
Yiddisha Eyes
McKinley's Cotton Pickers
Shim-me-sha-wabble
McRae, Gordon
Cuddle Up a Little Closer, Lovey Mine
McVeigh, John
The Pussy and the Bow-Wow
Meader, George
I Never Knew
Mehlinger, Artie
I'm Simply Crazy over You
Melachrino Strings
The Pink Lady Waltz
Melchior, Lauritz
For You Alone
I Love You Truly
I Want What I Want When I Want It
Mellette Sisters
The Kiss Burglar
Melnotte Twins
Always Take a Girl Named Daisy ('cause Daisies Won't Tell)
Melodious Monarchs
Salvation Nell
Menuhin, Yehudi
Kashmiri Song
Mercer, Johnny
Ugly Chile
Meredith Willson and His Orchestra
Cuddle Up a Little Closer, Lovey Mine
The Sunshine of Your Smile
Merman, Ethel
Play a Simple Melody
Merrell, Helen
The Fond Dove and His Lady Love
Merrill and Otto
Yiddisha Nightingale
The Merry Macs
Ma, He's Making Eyes at Me
Methuin, Jeanette
Montezuma
Metropolitan Quartette
Honey, I Will Long for You
Meuther, Dorothy
That Mellow Strain
Meyer Davis' Hotel Astor Orchestra
If I Had My Way
Meyer, John E.
Bonnie My Highland Lassie
Meyers, Charlotte
'Cross the Great Divide, I'll Wait for You
Meyers, Louise
I Want Someone to Flirt with Me
Mighty Clouds of Joy
I Don't Feel No Way Tired
Mike Speciale and His Bamboo Gardens Orchestra
I Wish I Had My Old Girl Back Again
Miley, Kathryn
I Want to Be Loved Like a Leading Lady
I'll Be With You Honey When It's Honeysuckle Time
Just One Day
Keep on the Sunny Side
Lily of the Valley
A Little Boy Named 'Taps'
The Mansion of Aching Hearts

My Mariuccia Take a Steamboat
Next to Your Mother Who Do You Love?
You're a Great Big Blue-Eyed Baby
Millar, Gertie
Little Mary
Miller, Eddie
America's Popular Song
Miller, Glen
Alice Blue Gown
Miller, Glenn
Johnson Rag
Moonlight Bay
Oh Johnny, Oh Johnny, Oh!
Peg o' My Heart
Miller, Marilynn
Wedding Bells
Mills Brothers
Baby, Won't You Please Come Home
Carry Me Back to Old Virginny
Chinatown, My Chinatown
Down Among the Sheltering Palms
The Glow Worm
If I Had My Way
Just a Dream of You, Dear
Meet Me Tonight in Dreamland
Moonlight Bay
My Gal Sal
Put on Your Old Grey Bonnet
Sweet Genevieve
Tiger Rag
Till We Meet Again
You Didn't Want Me When You Had Me So Why Do You Want Me Now?
You Never Miss the Water 'Till the Well Runs Dry
Mills, Jerry
Dat Lovin' Rag
Minzey, Frank
I'm Thinking 'bout You Honey All the While
Mitchell, Abbie
As Long as the World Goes Around
Darktown Barbeque
I've Lost My Teddy Bear
Red Red Rose
Returned
Rubber Necking Moon
That Carolina Rag
Mitchell and Marron
Colleen Bawn
Mitzi
Let Us Build a Little Nest
Love's Own Sweet Song
Moffo, Anna
Italian Street Song
Moncrieff, Gladys
Dark Grows the Sky
Monday, Arthur
Love's Lullaby
Montgomery & Moore
Just for Tonight
Montgomery and Perry
The Story Book Ball
Montgomery and Stone
Football
Good-Bye Christina Swanson
Montgomery, Billy
When You Hear Cy Riddle Play His Fiddle
Montgomery, Billy, and Florence Moore
Oh! You Circus Day
Montgomery, Dave
Hurrah for Baffin's Baby
Must You?
Montgomery, David
The Streets of New York
Montgomery, Marshall
Wait and See, You'll Want Me Back
When I Get You Alone Tonight
Montgomery, William
At That Bully Wooly Wild West Show
He Was Always Fooling Around
Montrose, Louise
My Drowsy Babe
Moon, George
The Bacchanal Rag
Mooney, May
Love Will Find a Way

Moonlight Trio
The Rose of No Man's Land
Moore, Carrie
If All the Stars Were Mine
Moore, Florence
At That Bully Wooly Wild West Show
He Was Always Fooling Around
I've Been Floating Down the Old Green River
The More I See of Hawaii, the Better I Like New York
Southern Gals
When Those Sweet Hawaiian Babies Roll Their Eyes
When You Hear Cy Riddle Play His Fiddle
Moore, George Austin
By the Old Oak Tree
Just a Dream of You, Dear
Paree's a Branch of Broadway
Red Pepper Rag
She's a Patient of Mine
Take Me to That Swanee Shore
Moore, Grace
Ciribiribin
Moore, Victor
Forty-five Minutes from Broadway
When a Fellow's on the Level with a Girl That's on the Square
Mora, Helene
Forget
I Wants to Be the Leading Lady
Jennie Lee
The Message of the Rose
Moran, Pauline
Arrah-Wanna
Morgan, Corinne
In Dreamland, In Dreamland
The Moon Has His Eyes on You
Nobody's Lookin' But de Owl and de Moon
Toyland
Morgan, Cy
Oh, Mr. Dream Man
Morgan, Dennis
A Pretty Girl Is Like a Melody
Morgan, Edwin
Melody Chimes
Morgan, Olive
Parisienne
Moriarty, George J.
Love Me Like the Ivy Loves the Old Oak Tree
Morley, Victor
How'd You Like to Spoon with Me?
I Would Like to Marry You
Mormon Tabernacle Choir
Anchors Aweigh
Smilin' Through
Morphy
Those Songs My Mother Used to Sing
Morrell, Frank
Don't Wake Me Up I Am Dreaming
Down by the Old Mill Stream
Honey, I Will Long for You
I'd Like to Be the Fellow That Girl Is Waiting For
I'll Be With You Honey When It's Honeysuckle Time
I'm Going Back to Carolina
The Longest Way 'Round Is the Sweetest Way Home
Love Days
That Old Girl of Mine
That Wonderful Mother of Mine
When I Dream in the Gloaming of You
Would You Take Me Back Again?
You Are the Ideal of My Dreams
Morrell, Olive
Oh, So Gently
Morris, Elida
Happy Little Country Girl
The High Cost of Loving
If You Don't Want Me, Send Me to My Ma
Kiss Me, My Honey, Kiss Me
Stop! Stop! Stop!
Take Me to the Midnight Cake-walk Ball
Walking the Dog

When You Play in the Game of Love
Morris, Joan
A Bird in a Gilded Cage
The Bird on Nellie's Hat
Come Down, Ma Evening Star
The Girl on the Magazine Cover
I Just Can't Make My Eyes Behave
Let the Rest of the World Go By
My Castle on the Nile
Poor John
Shine On, Harvest Moon
Smiles
Wait 'Till the Sun Shines, Nellie
The Yama Yama Man
Yip-I-Addy-I-Ay
Morrisey Sisters
A Rose with a Broken Stem
Morton, Clara
Daisy Donahue
Down Among the Sugar-Cane
I'm Afraid to Come Home in the Dark
Tipperary
When Tony Goes Over the Top
Morton, Dorothy
I'll Be with You When the Roses Bloom Again
Morton, Ed
Brother Noah Gave Out Checks for Rain
He's a Devil in His Own Home Town
If He Comes In, I'm Going Out
I'm a Lonesome Melody
The Last Shot Got Him
Somebody Lied
Morton, Jelly Roll
Ballin' the Jack
Beale Street Blues
Moss, Alice
It Was Just a Song at Twilight That Made Me Come Back to You
Moulan, Frank
My Sulu Lulu Loo
R-E-M-O-R-S-E
Mound City Four
In Dear Old Georgia
Mouvet, Maurice
The Junk Man Rag
Just a Kiss
The Maurice Glide
Maurice Hesitation
Maurice Irresistable
Maurice Mattchiche
The Maurice Tango
Maurice's Rag
The Raffles Dance
Movey, Ethel
I'll Get You
Mozart Comedy Four
Mamie, Don't You Feel Ashamie
Mudge, Eva
It's the Man in the Sailor Suit
Mullane, Frank
All That I Ask of You Is Love
Dear Old Girl
I Want to Go Back to Michigan
I'll Come Back to You When It's All Over
In the Land of Wedding Bells
Let's Help the Irish Now
A Little Bit of Irish
The Little Church around the Corner
Oh! What a Beautiful Dream You Seem
Take Me Back to the Garden of Love
There'll Be a Hot Time for the Old Men While the Young Men Are Away
There's a Light That's Burning in the Window of the Little House upon the Hill
The Trail of the Lonesome Pine
Your Mother Wants You Home Boy
Murray, Billy
Ain't It Funny What a Difference Just a Few Hours Make?
The Alcoholic Blues
Alexander's Bag-Pipe Band
All Night Long

Allus' the Same in Dixie
And He'd Say Oo-la-la! Wee-Wee!
And That Ain't All
Any Little Girl That's a Nice Little Girl Is the Right Little Girl for Me
Arrah-Wanna
Because I'm Married Now
Billy
Blues My Naughty Sweetie Gives to Me
Bon Bon Buddy
By the Light of the Silvery Moon
Can You Tame Wild Wimmen?
Casey Jones
Cheyenne
The Cubanola Glide
Cuddle Up a Little Closer, Lovey Mine
Cupid's I.O.U.
Dardanella
Dearie
Don't Be What You Ain't
Don't You Think It's Time to Marry?
Down in the Subway
Everybody Wants a Key to My Cellar
Everybody Works But Father
Foolish Questions
The Gaby Glide
Gee! But This Is a Lonely Town
The Ghost That Never Walked
Googy-Oo
The Grizzly Bear
He'd Have to Get Under, Get Out and Get Under to Fix Up His Automobile
He's a Devil in His Own Home Town
Honey Boy
I Ain't Got'en No Time to Have the Blues
I Can Dance with Everybody But My Wife
I Love My Wife But Oh, You Kid!
I Sent My Wife to the 1000 Isles
I Wish I Had a Girl
I'd Rather Two-Step Than Waltz, Bill
I'll Take You Back to Italy
I'm Glad I'm a Boy/I'm Glad I'm a Girl
I'm Glad I'm Married
I'm Sorry
In My Merry Oldsmobile
Indianola
I've Been Floating Down the Old Green River
I've Got My Captain Working for Me Now
I've Got Rings on My Fingers
Kiss, Kiss, Kiss, If You Want to Learn to Kiss
Lazy Moon
Meet Me in Rose Time Rosie
Mother Hasn't Spoken to Father Since
My Cosy Corner Girl
My Cousin Caruso
My Irish Maid
My Irish Molly O
No Wedding Bells for Me
Not Because Your Hair Is Curly
Oh, How I Laugh When I Think How I Cried about You
Oh, You Beautiful Doll
Play a Simple Melody
Play That Barbershop Chord
Poor Little Butterfly Is a Fly Girl Now
Rainbow
The Red Rose Rag
Sister Susie's Sewing Shirts for Soldiers
Smarty
Snooky Ookums
Some Sort of Somebody
Some Sunday Morning
Somebody's Coming to Town from Dixie
The Story Book Ball
The Streets of New York
Take a Little Tip from Father
Take Me to the Cabaret

Take Your Girlie to the Movies If You Can't Make Love at Home
There's a Little Bit of Bad in Every Good Little Girl
They Go Wild, Simply Wild Over Me
They Were All Out of Step But Jim
They're Wearing 'Em Higher in Hawaii
They've Got Me Doin' It Now
This Is the Life
'Twas Only an Irishman's Dream
The War in Snider's Grocery Store
The Wedding Glide
What Makes the World Go Round
What the Brass Band Played
What's the Matter with Father?
When a Fellow's on the Level with a Girl That's on the Square
When Highland Mary Did the Highland Fling
When I Get Back to the U.S.A.
When Love Is Young
When Old Bill Bailey Plays the Ukelele
When the Grown-Up Ladies Act Like Babies
When the Right Little Girl Comes Along
When Tommy Atkins Marries Dolly Gray
When Tony Goes Over the Top
When We Were Two Little Boys
The Whole Dam Family
Won't You Be My Honey?
Won't You Fondle Me
You Can't Expect Kisses from Me
You'll Do the Same Thing Over Again
You're Gwine to Get Somethin' What You Don't Expect

Murray, Elizabeth
Alexander's Band Is Back in Dixieland
All Aboard for Dixie
Bedelia
Bring Me Back My Lovin' Honey Boy
Don't Worry
Floating Down the River
Hannah, Won't You Open the Door?
I'm Afraid to Come Home in the Dark
Mamie, Don't You Feel Ashamie
Mister Dooley
Molly Dear, It's You I'm After
Mother Has Got the Habit Now
No One Knows Where the Old Man Goes
On the 5:15
Put Your Arms Around Me, Honey
Sailin' Away on the Henry Clay
Under the Anheuser Bush

Murray, John T.
Wedding Bells

Musette
That Mellow Strain

Myers, J. M.
What the Brass Band Played

Myers, J. W.
Big Indian Chief
Bunker Hill
The Good Old U.S.A.
The Message of the Violet
Mexico
Nava Jo
Wait at the Gate for Me

Nagle, Anna
Alice Blue Gown

Nagore, Anna
My Lonesome Little Louisiana Lady

Nares, Owen
The Picture I Want to See

Nash, Madeleine
We Have So Much to Be Thankful For

Natus, Joe
Violette

Natus, Joscph
Back to the Woods
Calling to Her Boy Just Once Again
A Flower from the Garden of Life

I'll Be with You When the Roses Bloom Again
Just for the Sake of Society
My Jersey Lily
Tell Me Dusky Maiden
Waltzing with the Girl You Love
You'll Always Be the Same Sweet Girl to Me
Naudain, May
The Glow Worm
Nazarro, James
I'm All Bound 'Round with the Mason-Dixon Line
Nelson, Clara
I'd Like to Live in Loveland with a Girl Like You
Nelson, Eddie
If He Can Fight Like He Can Love, Good Night Germany
I'll Say She Does
Nelson, Ozzie
Casey Jones
The Sweetheart of Sigma Chi
Nesbit, Evelyn
Sprinkle Me with Kisses If You Want My Love to Grow
There's a Light That's Burning in the Window of the Little House upon the Hill
Tumble in Love
When You're in Love with Someone Who Is Not in Love with You
Nestor, John
The Meaning of U.S.A.
Nevada, Emma
I Always Wish 'Twas You
New Orleans Rhythm Kings
Bluin' the Blues
That's a Plenty
Nicander, Edwin
Any Old Time at All
Nichells, Rhoda
Lucky in Love
Nichols, Nellie V.
Give Me the Sultan's Harem
I Didn't Raise My Boy to Be a Soldier
Southern Gals
Nichols, Red
Alice Blue Gown
Ida, Sweet as Apple Cider
Tell Me
Nickerson, Baby Edna
Run Home and Tell Your Mother
Nolan, Peggy
Billy
Nonette
I'd Like to Live in Loveland with a Girl Like You
Kentucky Rose
Mammy's Shufflin' Dance
Norris, William
March of the Toys
The Tale of a Bumble Bee
North, Bobby
My Yiddische Colleen
North, Olive
I'm a Lonesome Melody
Norton, Clara
Hiawatha
Norton, Ed
Mariutch Down at Coney Island
Norton, Ned "Cork"
Believe Me!
Norval, James
Blow the Smoke Away
Norworth, Jack
ABCD
All He Does Is Follow Them Around
And That Ain't All
Back to My Old Home Town
Blarney
Can You Tame Wild Wimmen?
Come Along My Mandy
Falling Star
Feed the Kitty
A Good Man Is Hard to Find
Honey Boy
I Want to Spread a Little Sunshine
I'm Glad I'm a Boy/I'm Glad I'm a Girl
I'm Glad I'm Married
I'm Learning Something Every Day
I'm Sorry

Let's Get the Umpire's Goat
Pinkerton Detective Man
Sadie Brady Listen Good to Me
Shine On, Harvest Moon
Smarty
Take Me Out to the Ball Game
Turn Off Your Light, Mr. Moon Man
When Jack Comes Sailing Home Again
When Tommy Atkins Marries Dolly Gray

Nugent, Maude
Don't Put Me Off at Buffalo Any More
The Gambling Man
My Irish Indian
My Lady Hottentot
My Little Creole Babe
My Swee' Kimona
Rip van Winkle Was a Lucky Man
Rosie and Josie
When the Harvest Days Are Over, Jessie, Dear
You'll Always Be the Same Sweet Girl to Me

Oakes, Billy
Dear Mamie, I Love You
If I Thought You Wouldn't Tell
I'm Going to Do What I Please

Oakland, Will
My Twilight Queen
They're On Their Way to Mexico

O'Brien, Margaret
Under the Bamboo Tree

O'Brien, Neil
The Waltz Must Change to a March, Marie

O'Brien, Tom
The Light That Failed

O'Connell, M. J.
When Ragtime Rufus Rags the Humoresque

O'Day, Ida
I'm Sorry

Olcott, Chauncey
Day Dreams
Ireland! A Gra Ma Chree
Ireland, My Land of Dreams
Kate Kearney
Killarney, My Home o'er the Sea
Laugh and the World Will Laugh with You, Weep and You'll Weep All Alone
The Limerick Girls
A Little Bit of Heaven, Shure They Call It Ireland
Mother Machree
My Own Dear Irish Queen
Too-ra-loo-ra-loo-ra
The Wearing of the Green
When Irish Eyes Are Smiling

Oliver, Sy
Ramona
Walkin' the Dog

Olivier, Laurence
Put Me Among the Girls

O'Neil, Emma
I Don't Want To
'Neath the Old Acorn Tree, Sweet Estelle
Rufus Johnson's Harmony Band

O'Neil, Nellie
The Pride of Newspaper Row

O'Neill, Emma
In the Heart of the City That Has No Heart

O'Neill, Florence
That Magic Strain

Original Dixieland Five
Barnyard Blues

Original Dixieland Jazz Band
Barnyard Blues
Bluin' the Blues
Lindy
Royal Garden Blues
Tiger Rag

Original Jazz Hounds
All That I Had Is Gone

Orpheus Comedy Four
Katy Did

Orpheus Quartet
Ain't You Coming Back to Dixieland?
Carry Me Back to Old Virginny

If All My Dreams Were Made of Gold, I'd Buy the World for You
Mamie, Don't You Feel Ashamie
Mammy's Little Coal Black Rose
Orr, Ann
Some Sort of Somebody
O'Shea, Michael
The Streets of New York
Packwell, Maud
Let Me See You Smile
Palmer, Bee
Give Me a Syncopated Tune
I Want to Shimmie
Palmer, Clara
Love Me with a Tiger Love
Mary Be Wary
Meet Me Down at the Corner
Pankey, Anna Cook
O, Southland
Paradise Island Trio
Across the Sea
Parker, Flora
Darling
Honey Man
Honey, You Were Made for Me
I Wonder If You're Lonely
I've Been Looking for a Girl Like You
Parker, Florence
Courting
Parks, John
Spoon Time
Parr, Albert
The Message of the Violet
Partridge, Emma
If All My Dreams Were Made of Gold, I'd Buy the World for You
Pathe Dance Orchestra
Just Try to Picture Me Back Home in Tennessee
Patricola, Miss
Fifty-Fifty
Patterson, Dora
Tilda from Old Savannah
Patti, Adelina
The Last Farewell
Paul, Les
I'm Forever Blowing Bubbles
Now Is the Hour
You Can't Expect Kisses from Me
Paul, Les, and Mary Ford
Blow the Smoke Away
Paul Whiteman and His Orchestra
Ramona
Paul Whiteman's Orchestra
Nola
Pauline War and Her Plantation Quartet
Alexander, Don't You Love Your Baby No More?
Pavarotti, Luciano
O Sole Mio
Payne, Herbert
Good Bye, Good Luck, God Bless You
Pearce, Etta
Percy
Pearl, Kathryn
I Want to Be a Merry Merry Widow
Pearse, Frank
Back among the Clover and the Bees
Pee Wee Hunt and His Orchestra
The Vamp
Peerce, Jan
The Rosary
Sylvia
When You and I Were Young, Maggie
Peerless Quartet
Any Old Place the Gang Goes I'll Be There
Any Old Time at All
At the Devil's Ball
Back to the Carolina You Love
Cheer Up Father, Cheer Up Mother
Ding Dong
For Dixie and Uncle Sam
For Your Boy and My Boy
From Here to Shanghai
Goodbye Broadway, Hello France
He's a Rag Picker
I Can Always Find a Little Sunshine in the Y.M.C.A.

I Didn't Raise My Boy to Be a Soldier
I Hate to Lose You
I May Be Gone for a Long, Long Time
If I Had My Way
I'm Proud to Be a Mother of a Soldier Like You
In the Candlelight
Jazz Babies' Ball
Just a Dream of You, Dear
Liberty Bell, It's Time to Ring Again
My Bird of Paradise
My Daddy Long-Legs
The Navy Took Them Over and the Navy Will Bring Them Back
The Ragtime Dream
Salvation Nell
Sweet Genevieve
The Syncopated Walk
That Mellow Strain
Way Down South
What Are You Going to Do to Help the Boys?
You're the Flower of My Heart, Sweet Adeline

Peppino
Back to the Carolina You Love

Percival, Walter
The Time and the Place and the Girl
Two Eyes of Brown

Perfect Harmony Quartet
All That I Had Is Gone

Perry, Charles
Colleen Bawn

Perry, George
Oh! You Georgia Rose

Peters, Bernadette
Oh, You Wonderful Girl

Phil Harris and His Dixieland Syncopators
I've Been Floating Down the Old Green River

Philadelphia Orchestra
Sylvia

Philbrick, Will
Dat Possum Rag

Phillips, Joseph A.
Daisies Won't Tell
I've Made Up My Mind to Mind a Maid Made Up Like You
Wake Up America

Phillips, William
The Face in the Firelight

Pied Pipers
Cuddle Up a Little Closer, Lovey Mine

Pietro
Who Played Poker with Pocohontas When John Smith Went Away?

Pilcer, Harry
The Gaby Glide
I'll Get You
My Turkey Trotting Boy
Prunella
Tango Dip
When Gaby Did the Gaby Glide
You'll Call the Next Love the First
You're a Good Little Devil

Pinza, Ezio
For You Alone

Plantation Dance Orchestra
Think of Me Little Daddy

Plantation Jazz Orchestra
Dardanella
Venetian Moon

Pollard, Daphne
The Cubanola Glide
I Love My Wife But Oh, You Kid!
Take Me to the Midnight Cake-walk Ball
Where the Morning Glories Twine around the Door

Polla's Clover Garden Orchestra
I'll Get You

Pons, Lily
Kiss Me Again

Ponselle, Rosa
Carry Me Back to Old Virginny
Keep the Home Fires Burning
Kiss Me Again
A Perfect Day

The Rosary
Powell, Dick
Over There
Where the Morning Glories Twine around the Door
Powell, Jane
A Heart That's Free
Power, James T.
The Man Behind
Powers, James T.
Can't You Take My Word?
Love Me, Make Me Love You Like I Never Loved Before
Powers, John T.
Put Me Upon an Island
Premier Quartet
Alexander's Band Is Back in Dixieland
Bing! Bang! Bing 'Em on the Rhine
Chong, He Come from Hong Kong
The Dixie Volunteers
I Love You Just the Same, Sweet Adeline
Moonlight Bay
Preservation Hall Jazz Band
Bill Bailey, Won't You Please Come Home
Presley, Elvis
Aloha Oe
O Sole Mio
Price, Leontyne
Deep River
Prima, Louis
Alice Blue Gown
Some Sunday Morning
There's a Broken Heart for Every Light on Broadway
Primrose, George
Lazy Moon
Liz'
Oh! Didn't He Ramble
Primrose, George H.
The Honeysuckle and the Bee
Prince's Band
Back to the Carolina You Love
Beale Street Blues
Beautiful Roses
Castle Half and Half
Cleopatra Had a Jazz Band
Dreaming
Everybody Rag with Me
Everything Is Peaches Down in Georgia
Floreine
Good-bye Alexander, Good-bye Honey-Boy
Good Bye Girls I'm Through
Huckleberry Finn
I'll Come Back to You When It's All Over
In the Land of Beginning Again
Indianola
It's a Long Way to Berlin But We'll Get There
It's Time for Every Boy to Be a Soldier
Joe Turner Blues
The Ladder of Roses
Maurice Irresistable
Naughty! Naughty! Naughty!
On the Mississippi
Pretty Baby
Red Pepper Rag
Sailin' Away on the Henry Clay
Send Me Away with a Smile
Sister Susie's Sewing Shirts for Soldiers
Smiles
So Long Letty
So Long Mother
Somewhere in France Is the Lily
Sprinkle Me with Kisses If You Want My Love to Grow
Tres Moutarde
Walkin' the Dog
When I'm Thru with the Arms of the Army, I'll Come Back to the Arms of You
When There's Peace on Earth Again
The Whistler and His Dog
The Wild Wild Women Are Making a Wild Man of Me
You're Here and I'm Here
Prince's Dance Orchestra
Dear Little Boy of Mine

Prince's Military Band
Red Wing
Prince's Orchestra
Beautiful Ohio
Bring Me a Rose
Cheer Up Father, Cheer Up Mother
Chinatown, My Chinatown
Fireflies
The Florida Blues
The Glow Worm
I Sent My Wife to the 1000 Isles
I'm on My Way to Dublin Bay
I'm Sorry I Made You Cry
Just a Baby's Prayer at Twilight to Her Daddy Over There
Marcheta
Memories
Sing Me Love's Lullaby
Sweet Hawaiian Moonlight, Tell Her of My Love
A Vision of Salome
Prosser, Reese
If All My Dreams Were Made of Gold, I'd Buy the World for You
Prosser, Reese V.
Where the Silv'ry Colorado Wends Its Way
Pruette, William
I Want What I Want When I Want It
Pryor's Band
The Glow Worm
I Can't Tell Why I Love You But I Do
The Whistler and His Dog
The Yama Yama Man
You're a Great Big Blue-Eyed Baby
Pryor's Orchestra
The Troubadour
Puck, Eva
Good Bye, My Lady Love
Johnny, Get a Girl
Loving Eyes
Mamma's Little Alabama Love
My Little Coney Island
My Pretty Little Kick-a-poo
Teasing
They Don't Hesitate Any More
When My Johnny Boy Goes Marching By
Where Did You Get That Girl?
Where the Morning Glories Twine around the Door
Puck, Harry
California and You
Johnny, Get a Girl
Loving Eyes
Mamma's Little Alabama Love
My Little Coney Island
My Pretty Little Kick-a-poo
Teasing
They Don't Hesitate Any More
When My Johnny Boy Goes Marching By
Where Did You Get That Girl?
Where the Morning Glories Twine around the Door
Puck, Harry and Eva
All Aboard for Dreamland
On a Sunday Afternoon
Puckett, Riley
Everybody Works But Father
Purvis, James
The Good Old U.S.A.
Quaker City Quartet
In Dear Old Georgia
You're the Flower of My Heart, Sweet Adeline
Quigley, Thomas J.
Let Me See You Smile
Roses Bring Dreams of You
Quinlan, Gertrude
The Manicure Girl
The Tale of a Bumble Bee
Quinn, Dan W.
Blooming Lize
Brother Masons
General Hardtack on Guard
Just Because She Made Dem Goo-Goo Eyes
Mister Dooley
Oh! Didn't He Ramble
Rip Van Winkle Was a Lucky Man But Adam Had Him Beat a Mile

Violette
Ralph Flanagan and His Orchestra
Baltimore Rag
Ramsden, Cissie
That Wonderful Kid from Madrid
Ramsden, Cissy
If You Can't Get a Girl in the Summertime, You'll Never Get a Girl at All
Ramsey, Alice
Rock Me in the Cradle of Love
Randall, Carl
Bolsheveki Glide
Randegger, Mme. Alberto
A Japanese Love Song
Randolph, Amanda
Mammy's Little Choc'late Cullud Chile
Ransome, John W.
Didn't Know Exactly What to Do
It Was the Dutch
Rappold, Marie
Sing Me Love's Lullaby
Rath, Joe
I'm All Dressed Up and No Where to Go
Rawlston, Zelma
I Want a Man Made to Order for Me
Ray Benson and His Orchestra
Madelon
Ray Kinney and His Hawaiians
Across the Sea
Aloma
Sweet Hawaiian Moonlight, Tell Her of My Love
Ray Noble and His Orchestra
If I Had My Way
Raymond, Al
Pick, Pick, Pick, Pick on the Mandolin, Antonio
Raymond, Dot
Cupid's I.O.U.
Raymond, Lizzie B.
Sadie Salome Go Home
There's One Rose That Will Never Bloom Again
Raymond, Maud
Because I'm Married Now
Clidee-Oh
I Thought I Wanted Opera
I've Got to Dance Till the Band Gets Through
My Irish Girl
That Dreamy Barcarole Tune
That Syncopated Boogie Boo
Wild Cherries
Raymond, Ray
Piano Man
Raymond, Ruby
The Aba Daba Honeymoon
Everybody's Doin' It Now
I'm Going to Do What I Please
Pick, Pick, Pick, Pick on the Mandolin, Antonio
The Rays
The Blue and the Gray: A Mother's Gift to Her Country
Rays
My Jersey Lily
Reardon, George
On the Road to Home Sweet Home
Red Nichols
I'm Sorry I Made You Cry
Red Nichols and His Five Pennies
Can't Yo' Hear Me Callin', Caroline
Indiana
Rose of Washington Square
Shim-me-sha-wabble
Yaaka Hula Hickey Dula
Redmond, Rita
My Jersey Lily
Stop! Stop! Stop!
Reed, Augustus
When the Bell in the Lighthouse Rings Ding, Dong
Reed Orchestra
Fireflies
Regan, Phil
The Daughter of Rosie O'Grady
Has Anybody Here Seen Kelly?
A Little Bit of Heaven, Shure They Call It Ireland

Peg o' My Heart
Sunbonnet Sue
That Wonderful Mother of Mine
Reilley, William J. "Sailor"
Any Old Place the Gang Goes I'll Be There
Reliance Quartette
Be Satisfied with What You Have, Let Well Enough Alone
Remus, Percy
The Radiance in Your Eyes
Rey, Alvino
I Wish I Had a Girl
Reynolds, Debbie
The Aba Daba Honeymoon
Alice Blue Gown
He'd Have to Get Under, Get Out and Get Under to Fix Up His Automobile
Rice, Gilda
Ain't You Coming Back to Old New Hampshire, Molly?
Rice, Gladys
Good Bye, Good Luck, God Bless You
Naughty! Naughty! Naughty!
Till We Meet Again
Rice, John C.
Ma Mamselle Honee
Rosie Rosinsky
Richards, Tom
The Kiss Waltz
Richmond, McKee
I'm a Member of the Midnight Crew
Riley's Cabaret Orchestra
I'm Glad I Can Make You Cry
Ring, Blanche
Absence Makes the Heart Grow Fonder
All That Glitters Is Not Gold
Bedelia
Bing! Bang! Bing 'Em on the Rhine
Bonnie My Highland Lassie
Bye and Bye You'll See the Sun A-Shining
Come Josephine in My Flying Machine
Come, Take a Skate with Me
The Deedle-Dum-Dee
Der Faderland for Mine
Everybody Sometime Must Love Some One
Faugh-a Ballagh
The Flower Garden Ball
Good Bye, My Lady Love
I Love You Dolly
In the Good Old Summertime
Irish Fluffy Ruffles
I've Got Rings on My Fingers
Kate Kearney
Killarney, My Home o'er the Sea
Let's Make Love among the Roses
A Little Girl Like Me
The Meaning of U.S.A.
Meet Me Dear, on Saturday, a Little after Two
Molly Dear, It's You I'm After
My Irish Gibson Girl
My Irish Molly O
Nora Malone, Call Me by Phone
Pinky Panky Poo
The Same Old Crowd
Semiole
That Baboon Baby Dance
That Hypnotizing Rag
They Were All Out of Step But Jim
Tipperary Nora
'Twas Only an Irishman's Dream
Waltz Me Around Again, Willie
A Woman's No Means 'Yes'
The Yankee Girl
Yip-I-Addy-I-Ay
Ritchie, Adele
Ballooning
Build Your Nest Away Down in My Heart
The Girl with the Big Toy Bear
I'd Rather Two-Step Than Waltz, Bill
I'm Trying to Find a Sweetheart
The Leader of the Frocks and Frills
The Moon Has His Eyes on You
A Picnic for Two
Rebecca of Sunnybrook Farm

That's What the Daisy Said
When the Whole World Has Gone Back on You
You Splash Me and I'll Splash You
Robert Shaw Chorale
Every Little Movement
Roberts, Bob
Back, Back, Back to Baltimore
Good-bye, Eliza Jane
I Ain't Had No Lovin' in a Long Time
No Wedding Bells for Me
The Poor Old Man
Sadie Salome Go Home
What the Brass Band Played
Roberts, "Lucky"
The Junk Man Rag
Robeson, Paul
After the Battle
By an' By
De Little Pickaninny's Gone to Sleep
Deep River
Down De Lover's Lane
Go Down Moses
Just a-Wearying for You
Li'l Gal
Mighty Lak' a Rose
Sylvia
Robey, George
If You Were the Only Girl in the World
Robinson, Ethel
Come, Take a Trip in My Air-Ship
Robson, Eleanor
The Dawn of a Tomorrow
Kiss Me Good Night, Dear Love
Rocamora, Suzanne
Amo
I'll Be With You Honey When It's Honeysuckle Time
On the Old See-Saw
When Rosie Riccoola Do the Hoola Ma Boola She's the Hit of Little Italy
Rochester, Claire
Along Came Ruth
I'm a Lonesome Melody
Rochester, Clare
Last Night Was the End of the World
Rock, William
The Boy Who Stuttered and the Girl Who Lisped
If You'll Walk with Me
Oh! You Gray Haired Kid
The White Wash Man
Rodeheaver, Homer A.
Brighten the Corner Where You Are
His Eye Is on the Sparrow
Love Lifted Me
Rogers Brothers
My Starlight Queen
Linda, Look Out de' Windah
Rogers, Ginger
The Yama Yama Man
Rogers, Lara
The Lily or the Rose
Rogers, Roy
Love Lifted Me
Rogers, Walter B.
Absence Makes the Heart Grow Fonder
Roland, Ruth
I'll Come Back to You When It's All Over
Romain, Manuel
The Curse of an Aching Heart
Daddy Has a Sweetheart and Mother Is Her Name
I Wish I Had My Old Girl Back Again
I Would If I Could But I Can't
Mammy's Little Coal Black Rose
She's Dancing Her Heart Away
She's the Daughter of Mother Machree
When the Boys Go Marching By
When Two Hearts Are One
Romaine, Claire
Maud, Maud, Maud
Romaine, Margaret
My Skylark Love

Rooney, Katherine
What's the Use of Moonlight When There's No One 'Round to Love?
Rooney, Mickey
Waiting for the Robert E. Lee
Rooney, Pat
The Daughter of Rosie O'Grady
I Love to Sit and Look at You
Linda, Look Out de' Windah
Make Yourself at Home
When the Fightin' Irish Come Home
Rooney, Pat, Jr.
The Daughter of Rosie O'Grady
Rooney Sisters
If You Love Your Baby Google Google All the Time
I'm Getting Sleepy
Rosenblatt, Cantor Joseph
Duna
Eli Eli
Ross, Charles J.
Budweiser's a Friend of Mine
Ross, Lillian
Molly Dear, It's You I'm After
Rounseville, Robert
I Love You So
Rowland, Adele
The Hesitating Blues
Lily of the Valley
Mammy o' Mine
Mammy's Little Coal Black Rose
Pack Up Your Troubles in Your Old Kit Bag and Smile, Smile, Smile
Something about Love
That Soothing Serenade
You-oo Just You
Rubell, Leah
Marie from Sunny Italy
Rucker, John
Gimme de Leavins'
Ruggles, Charles
My Baby Talking Girl
Russell, Ada
When the Band Goes Marching By
Russell, Annie
It Rained a Mist
Russell, Bobbie
I Want to Go Back to Michigan
Russell Brothers
Where the River Shannon Flows
Russell, Dorothy
In Vacation Time
Russell, Leah
Mary Had a Little Lamb
Russell, Lillian
As on Moonlit Waves We Ride
Come Down, Ma Evening Star
Flowers of Dixieland
If a Boy Like You Loved a Girl Like Me
In Dreamland, In Dreamland
In the Days of Girls and Boys
The Island of Roses and Love
The Leader of Vanity Fair
Little Widow Brown
Love a la Mode
The Maid of Timbucktoo
The Opera
The Queen of Society
Tell Us Pretty Ladies
Wilhemina
Russell, Mabel
The Dandiest Boy in Town
Just a Little Rocking Chair and You
They Start the Victrola and Go Dancing Around the Floor
Russell, Marie
My Hawaiian Sunrise
On the Shores of Italy
Russell, Zella
I Wonder What Will William Tell
Rutan's Song Birds
Run Home and Tell Your Mother
Ruth, Babe
And That Ain't All
Rutland, Belle
I'm on My Way to Manadalay
Ryan, Elsa
Zamona

Ryan, Kathryn
I Love My Husband But Oh You Henry
Sabel, Josephine
A Bit o' Blarney
Easy Street
Let Mary Go Round on the Merry-Go-Round
My Palm Leaf Maid
Take Me Back to the Garden of Love
Under the Anheuser Bush
Sadler, Josie
On the Banks of the Rhine with a Stein
A Picnic for Two
Sam Ash and His Orchestra
Ugly Chile
Where the Black-Eyed Susans Grow
Sam Lanin's Orchestra
Roamin' in the Gloamin'
Samuels, Rae
America Needs You Like a Mother, Would You Turn Your Mother Down?
Back to the Carolina You Love
Don't Take Advantage of My Good Nature
Fishing
The Good Ship Mary Ann
Harem Life
He's a Rag Picker
If He Can Fight Like He Can Love, Good Night Germany
It Takes a Long Tall Brown-Skin Gal to Make a Preacher Lay His Bible Down
Southern Gals
That Wonderful Kid from Madrid
When Those Sweet Hawaiian Babies Roll Their Eyes
Sanderson, Julia
The Argentine
I Have Just One Heart for Just One Boy
I Wouldn't Give 'That' for the Man Who Couldn't Dance
I'd Like to Meet Your Father
I'm on My Way to Dublin Bay
In the Valley of Mont Bijou
I've a Million Reasons Why I Love You
The Land of "Let's Pretend"
O Promise Me You'll Write to Him Today
Same Sort of Girl
They Didn't Believe Me
Thousands of Years Ago
Sandler, Josie
That Mesmerizing Mendelssohn Tune
Sanford, Jere
Always in the Way
I'm Wearing My Heart Away for You
Waltzing with the Girl You Love
Santley, Joseph
Ask Her in Tulip Time
Do Something
The First Rose of Summer
Homeward Bound
The Honolulu Blues
Some Girls Do and Some Girls Don't
Sarkozi, Feri
The Old Gypsy
Sarto, Andrea
By the Saskatchewan
Rainbow
Spanish Love
Sawyer, Ivy
Ask Her in Tulip Time
The First Rose of Summer
Sawyer, Joan
The Aeroplane Waltz
Joan Sawyer Tango
Mexi-Tango
Saxe, Templar
Don't Go in the Lion's Cage Tonight, Mother
When the Right Little Girl Comes Along

Sayao, Bido
Carry Me Back to Old Virginny
Scanlan, Walter
The Sunshine of Your Smile
Scanlon, Walter
I'll Be with You When the Roses Bloom Again
Schaffer, Bela Piroska
The Old Gypsy
Scheff, Fritzi
Be Kind to Poor Pierrot
Kiss Me Again
When I Leave the World Behind
Where the Fairest Flowers Are Blooming
Schenck, Carrie
When I Lost You
Schenck, Joe
Baby's Prayers Will Soon Be Answered
Don't Try to Steal the Sweetheart of a Soldier
He Likes Their Jukelele
Huckleberry Finn
I Ain't Got'en No Time to Have the Blues
I Don't Want to Get Well
In the Land Where Poppies Bloom
My Baby's Arms
My Little Rambling Rose
Open Up the Golden Gates to Dixieland and Let Me into Paradise
Send Me Away with a Smile
Southern Gals
Sweet Kisses That Came in the Night
Teach Me That Beautiful Love
There's Something Nice about the South
They Were All Out of Step But Jim
When Tony Goes Over the Top
You'll Find Old Dixieland in France
Schumann-Heink, Ernestine
Ashes of Roses
Danny Boy
Every Little Movement
If I Forget
The Rosary
A Soldier's Dream
Sweet Thoughts of Home
Scott, Cyril
Although I Am a Soldier, I Prefer a Private Life
The Ping Pong Song
Scott, Henri
On the Road to Mandalay
Seabrooke, Thomas Q.
The Bird on Nellie's Hat
The Maiden with the Dreamy Eyes
There's a Little Star in Heaven That They Call Broadway
Seals, B. F.
Baby Seals Blues
Seeley, Blossom
The Darktown Strutters' Ball
The Good Ship Mary Ann
I Love a Piano
I'm Getting Kind of Lonesome for My Old Kentucky Pal
Mammy's Little Coal Black Rose
The Marquand Glide
My Bird of Paradise
My Sweet Suzanna
Sister Susie's Started Syncopation
Seeley, Sallie
Just 'Round the Corner from Broadway
Seeley, Sally
Shadowland
Segal, Vivienne
Auf Wiedersehn
You-oo Just You
Selbini, Lalla
My Fluff-a de Ruff
Selvin's Novelty Orchestra
I Know Why--Because I'm in Love with You
Seymour, Katie
In Disguise
Shackford, Charles
Bygone Days in Dixie
Shackleford, Malcolm
Come Down from the Big Fig Tree

Shannon Four
Any Old Time at All
What Are You Going to Do to Help the Boys?
Shannon Quartet
I May Be Gone for a Long, Long Time
Nellie Dean
Will You Love Me in December as You Do in May?
Shattuck, Truly
Alma, Where Do You Live?
And a Little Bit More
I Can't Help Dreaming of You
What's the Matter with Uncle Sam?
Shaw, Artie
Hindustan
Shaw, Lillian
I Got a Rock
Under the Matzos Tree
When Tony Goes Over the Top
Yiddle on Your Fiddle Play Some Rag Time
Shaw, Oscar
Some Girls Do and Some Girls Don't
Shearer, Norma
Smilin' Through
Shepperly Sisters
Melody Chimes
Sherbo's Novelty Orchestra
Alabama Lullaby
Sherwood, Walter
No One Knows
Shirley, Florence
A Girl, A Man, A Night, A Dance
Shore, Dinah
All That Glitters Is Not Gold
I Can't Tell Why I Love You But I Do
My Isle of Golden Dreams
Play a Simple Melody
Sidney Bechet and His New Orleans Feet Warmers
I Ain't Gonna Give Nobody None o' This Jelly Roll
Sweetie Dear
Siegrist, Topsy
If You'll Walk with Me
Sills, Beverly
It Never, Never Can Be Love
Italian Street Song
'Neath the Southern Moon
The Silvers
Two Congregations
Simon Paskal and His Orchestra
Mamenu
Simpson, Cheridah
Carissima
Havana
Pride of the Prairie
Sinatra, Frank
I'm Sorry I Made You Cry
Kiss Me Again
Oh! What a Pal Was Mary
The Sunshine of Your Smile
Take Me Out to the Ball Game
When I Lost You
Sissle, Noble
Ain't You Coming Back, Mary Ann, to Maryland
All of No Man's Land Is Ours
Can't Yo' Hear Me Callin', Caroline
Gee! I Wish I Had Someone to Rock Me in the Cradle of Love
Gee! I'm Glad That I'm from Dixie
Good Night, Angeline
How 'Ya Gonna Keep 'Em Down on the Farm After They've Seen Paris?
Mammy's Little Choc'late Cullud Chile
Mirandy
On Patrol in No Man's Land
Royal Garden Blues
Sisters Howard
Over the Pilsner Foam
Slavin, John
The Girl of the Great Divide
Slavin, John E.
Mister Dooley

Slavin, John H.
Courting
Slavin, John P.
I've Got to Dance Till the Band Gets Through
Smith, Bessie
After You've Gone
Alexander's Rag-Time Band
Baby, Won't You Please Come Home
I Ain't Got Nobody Much and Nobody Cares for Me
Yellow Dog Blues
Smith, Bobbie
That Syncopated Boogie Boo
Smith, Chris
The Concert in the Sky
Farmyard Blues
Good-Bye, I'll See You Some More
Smith, Irene
That Syncopated Boogie Boo
Smith, Irene and Bobbie
I'm on My Way to Dublin Bay
Smith, Jack
There Are Just Two I's in Dixie
Smith, Kate
If I Had My Way
Mother Machree
My Melancholy Baby
Now Is the Hour
Peg o' My Heart
Some Sunday Morning
Till We Meet Again
Too-ra-loo-ra-loo-ra
When I Lost You
When Irish Eyes Are Smiling
When the Sunset Turns to Ocean's Blue to Gold
Where the River Shannon Flows
Your Eyes Have Told Me So
Smith, Sue
In a Hammock Built for Two
Snyder, Ted
Sweet Italian Love
That Beautiful Rag
Sodero's Band
Ciribiribin
Solar, Willie
Huckleberry Pie
I Miss You in a Thousand Different Ways
Sons of the Pioneers
There's a Long, Long Trail
You Never Miss the Water 'Till the Well Runs Dry
Sousa's Band
America First
Blue Ridge, I'm Coming Back to You
The Fairest of the Fair
Hail to the Spirit of Liberty
In the Good Old Summertime
The Invincible Eagle
Iola
The Liberty Loan March
Moonlight
The New York Hippodrome March
On the Mississippi
The Preacher and the Bear
We Are Coming
Zamona
Southern Sons
Lift Every Voice and Sing
Spencer, Attie
I Need the Money
She's a Princess Just the Same
Spencer, Elizabeth
Baby Shoes
I Hear You Calling Me
I'm on My Way to Manadalay
Just Because It's You
Let the Rest of the World Go By
My Sweetheart Is Somewhere in France
Spike Jones and His City Slickers
By the Beautiful Sea
Come Josephine in My Flying Machine
The Glow Worm
MacNamara's Band
Oh by Jingo! Oh by Gee! You're the Only Girl for Me
Pack Up Your Troubles in Your Old Kit Bag and Smile, Smile, Smile

Red Wing
The Wild Wild Women Are Making a Wild Man of Me
Yaaka Hula Hickey Dula
Spiro, Sidonie
I'd Be Happy Anywhere with You
Spooner, Allie
Good-bye, Eliza Jane
Spooner, Edna May
A Little Empty Nest
Stacy, Jess
Breeze, Blow My Baby Back to Me
Stafford, Jo
Rag-Time Cowboy Joe
Smiles
Stanley, Frank
Rainbow
Stanley, Frank C.
Belle of the Ball
By the Light of the Honeymoon
Bye Bye Dearie
Come, Take a Trip in My Air-Ship
Falling Star
The Girl Who Cares for Me
Goodbye, Sweetheart, Goodbye
Honey Boy
In Dear Old Georgia
Meet Me in Rose Time Rosie
The Moon Has His Eyes on You
Nobody's Lookin' But de Owl and de Moon
Sambo and Dinah
When the Bell in the Lighthouse Rings Ding, Dong
When the Whipporwill Sings Marguerite
Stanley, Gertrude
On a Starry Night
Stanley, Maria
The Tale of a Stroll
Stanley, Marion
My Irish Maid
Starr, Carrie
I Love My Steady, But I'm Crazy for My Once-in-a-While
Starr, Hattie
My Chilly Baby
Sweetheart, Sweetheart, I Wear the Blue
Starr, Kay
Honeymoon
Steber, Eleanor
Danny Boy
I Love You So
Vilia
Steel, John
The Hand That Rocked the Cradle Rules My Heart
My Baby's Arms
A Pretty Girl Is Like a Melody
Tulip Time
The World Is Waiting for the Sunrise
Steele, John
Waiting for You
Steger, Julius
Castles in the Air
Two Eyes
Stellar Quartet
Nellie Dean
Sterling Trio
Don't Try to Steal the Sweetheart of a Soldier
Stevenson, Alice
I've Lost My Teddy Bear
Stevenson, Douglas
Good Bye Girls I'm Through
Stevenson, Elise
The Garden of Dreams
When You're in Town in My Home Town
Stewart, Anita
A Cheery Smile Is as Good as a Mile on the Road to Victory
Mary Regan
Stewart, William G.
My Own United States
Stone, Amelia
All I Want in the Wide Wide World Is You
Mon Amour
Romance
Spoon Time
Stone, Fred
Hurrah for Baffin's Baby

I'll Take You Back to Italy
Scarecrow
The Streets of New York
Stone, Marmion
Always Take a Girl Named Daisy ('cause Daisies Won't Tell)
Stone, Paul Russell
At Mammy's Fireside
Storey, Belle
When It's Apple Blossom Time in Normandy
Storm, Gale
Sunbonnet Sue
Story, Belle
The Flower Garden Ball
On a Good Old Time Sleigh Ride
Rebecca of Sunnybrook Farm
Take Me Back to the Garden of Love
Story, Pauline B.
He Died on the Fighting Line
Wed the Man That You Love or Don't Wed at All
Straeter, Ted
Tell Me
Streisand, Barbra
My Melancholy Baby
Stuart, Herbert
When the Lusitania Went Down
Sullivan, W. J.
Violette
Sunday, Sylvia
Love's Lullaby
Sunshine and Tempest
Melody Chimes
Sunshine, Marion
Dinah
I Live Up-Town
That's How He Met the Girl
You're My Boy
Surratt, Valeska
Parisienne
Please Don't Take My Lovin' Man Away
That Dreamy Italian Waltz
That La-La Melody
That Spanish Rag
You'll Do the Same Thing Over Again
Sydell, Rose
I'm Awfully Glad I'm Irish
Sykes, Jerome
If Yankee Doodle Hadn't Come to Town
I'm the Money Burner
Sylva, Marguerite
Miss Bob White
Sylvester, Nellie
My Jersey Lily
Symonds, Lottie West
My Irish Indian
Talbot, Walter
I've Grown So Used to You
Talliaferro, Mabel
I Think of Thee
Tally, Harry
Ballooning
Bye Bye Dearie
Can't You See That I'm Lonely?
Good-Bye, Sweet Old Manhattan Isle
In Dear Old Georgia
My Dusky Rose
My Irish Molly O
My Little Creole Babe
Wait at the Gate for Me
Wait 'Till the Sun Shines, Nellie
When I Dream in the Gloaming of You
Wonderland
Won't You Fondle Me
Tanguay, Eva
Come On, Play Ball with Me
Gee! I'd Like to Be the Mayor
Get Happy
Give an Imitation of Me
I Can't Help It
I Don't Care
If You Had All the World and Its Gold
M-O-T-H-E-R
Mothers of America, You Have Done Your Share
Nothing Bothers Me

Personality
The Tanguay Rag
When It Comes to a Lovingless Day
Tascott
Ain't Dat a Shame?
Any Rags?
The Gambling Man
Hannah, Won't You Open the Door?
If You Can't Be a Bell-Cow, Fall in Behind
Mother's Hymn to Me
The Sentinel Asleep
Tate, Harry
Fishing
Tatum, Art
Indiana
Ja-Da
St. Louis Blues
Tiger Rag
Tauber, Richard
For You Alone
I Love the Moon
Kiss Me Again
Love, Here Is My Heart!
Marcheta
The Rosary
Roses of Picardy
Taylor, Billee
I Guess I'll Take the Train Back Home
I Won't Come Back
Taylor, Charlotte
Always Take a Girl Named Daisy ('cause Daisies Won't Tell)
'Cross the Great Divide, I'll Wait for You
Taylor, Eva
I Wish I Could Shimmy Like My Sister Kate
Taylor, Sally
My Gal's Another Gal Like Galli-Curci
Teal, Raymond
Bunker Hill
The Mansion of Aching Hearts
Oh, Mr. Webster
Please Go Away and Let Me Sleep
Ted Lewis and His Band
Barnyard Blues
Ted Lewis and His Jazz Band
Bo - la - Bo
Teece, Lillian
You Can Have It, I Don't Want It
Tempest and Sunshine
Oh, That Moonlight Glide
Tempest, Florenz
I Live Up-Town
Oh! What a Beautiful Dream You Seem
On the Grand Old Sand
That's How He Met the Girl
Templeton, Fay
Dream One Dream of Me
Easy Money
Fishing
I'm a Respectable Working Girl
Lindy
A Love-Lorn Lily
Ma Blushin' Rosie, My Posie Sweet
Mary
My Japanese Cherry Blossom
My Little Hindoo Belle
My Particular Friend
Sleepy-Headed Little Mary Green
What You Want and What You Get
The Woodchuck Song
Tenney, Harry
I'm Glad I Can Make You Cry
Terriss, Ellaline
Nava Jo
Teyte, Maggie
Just You
Kashmiri Song
Little Grey Home in the West
Thardo, Claude
I Wants to Be the Villain in the Show
If You Can't Say Something Good, Don't Say Nothing at All
In Dear Old Georgia
In the Shade of the Old Apple Tree
Little One, Good Bye

That Quartette
Come to the Land of Bohemia
Cutey, Tell Me Who Tied Your Tie?
Theis' Detroit Ritz Orchestra
Can You Forget
Theodore F. Morse and His Orchestra
What the Brass Band Played
Thigpen, Lynn
Fifty-Fifty
Thomas, John Charles
Little Mother of Mine
Mother o' Mine
On the Road to Mandalay
The Trumpeter
Thomashefsky, Boris
Eli Eli
Thompson, George L.
When Yankee Doodle Learns to "Parlez-Vous Francaise?"
Thornton, Bonnie
Under the Rosenbloom
Three Jesters
MacNamara's Band
Three Shannons
When It's Night-time Down in Dixieland
Thropp, Clara
I Get Dippy When I Do That Two-Step Dance
Tibbett, Lawrence
Killarney, My Home o'er the Sea
On the Road to Mandalay
Tierney, Harry
If You Can't Get a Girl in the Summertime, You'll Never Get a Girl at All
That Long Lost Chord
Tiffany, Maud
Everybody's Doin' It Now
Take a Little Tip from Father
Tighe, Harry
All I Want in the Wide Wide World Is You
Tilford
Come Back to Me My Melody
Keep Away from the Fellow Who Owns an Automobile
Tilley, Vesta
Following in Father's Footsteps
Oh! London, Where Are Your Girls Tonight?
On Furlough
The Seaside Sultan
Tillotson, Merle
Sweet Genevieve
Timberg, Hattie
Oh! You Million Dollar Doll
Timberg, Herman
In a Little Cottage by the Railroad Track
School Days
Timponi, Florence
I Don't Want To
We'll Knock the Heligo into Heligo Out of Heligoland!
Tinney, Frank
On a Little Farm in Normandie
Tip-Top Four
When It's Night-time Down in Dixieland
Tommy Dorsey and His Band
Marcheta
Tony Pastor and His Orchestra
Those Draftin' Blues
Torme, Mel
Oh, You Beautiful Doll
There's a Broken Heart for Every Light on Broadway
Tracy, Arthur
Just a-Wearying for You
Traubel, Helen
Carry Me Back to Old Virginny
I Love You Truly
Someday Sweetheart
Tree, Charles
Dear Land of Home
Trentini, Emma
Ah, Sweet Mystery of Life
Gianina Mia
It Never, Never Can Be Love
Italian Street Song
Love Is Like a Firefly
Naughty Marietta

Trimbell, Fannie
In the Valley of Broken Hearts
Trix, Helen
The Bird on Nellie's Hat
Blue Bell
The Next Horse I Ride On
Snooky Ookums
The Story of a Clothes Line
The Troubadour Four
In the House of Too Much Trouble
Troy, Henry
Bye-O Baby Bunting
Farmyard Blues
Sweet Suzanne
Tucker, Orin
Billy
Tucker, Sophie
After You've Gone
Alexander's Got a Jazz Band Now
All Those in Favor Say Aye
And That Ain't All
At the Yiddish Wedding Jubilee
Baby Lamb
Beatrice Fairfax, Tell Me What to Do
Cleopatra Had a Jazz Band
Daddy, I Love You More and More Each Day
The Darktown Strutters' Ball
Don't Take Advantage of My Good Nature
Don't Walk So Fast
Down in Honky-Tonk Town
Everybody Shimmies Now
Ev'ry Day
Flippity-Flop
Floating Down the River
A Good Man Is Hard to Find
The Grizzly Bear
Hawaiian Butterfly
Hello Wisconsin, Won't You Find My Yonnie Yonson
He's a Rag Picker
He's Coming Home on the 8 O'Clock Train
The Honky-Tonky Monkey Rag
I Ain't Got Nobody Much and Nobody Cares for Me
I Can't Get Enough of Your Love
I Wonder Where My Easy Rider's Gone
I'm Crazy about My Daddy in a Uniform
I'm Going Back to Carolina
I'm Going to Do What I Please
I'm Gonna Make Hay While the Sun Shines in Virginia
I'm Trying to Teach My Sweet Papa Right from Wrong
It's All Your Fault
It's Lonesome Here
Jazz Babies' Ball
Just for Tonight
Keep on Walking
Keep Your Eye on the Girlie You Love
Lily of the Valley
Little Rag Baby Doll
Mammy's Chocolate Soldier
My Honey's Back
My Old Log Cabin Home
Oh! Harry! Harry!
Oh Helen!
Oh Johnny, Oh Johnny, Oh!
Oh! Papa, Oh! Papa, Won't You Be a Pretty Papa to Me?
Prohibition, You Have Lost Your Sting
Rockaway
Rolling Stones All Come Rolling Home Again
Some Girls Do and Some Girls Don't
Some of These Days
Someday Sweetheart
Sweet Cider Time When You Were Mine
That Carolina Rag
That Dying Rag
That Mesmerizing Mendelssohn Tune
That Naughty Melody
That Thing Called Love
There's a Little Bit of Bad in Every Good Little Girl
The Trench Trot

Walkin' the Dog
You'll Never Know the Good Fellow I've Been, 'Till I've Gone Away
You're a Great Big Blue-Eyed Baby
Turner, Alan
Goodbye, Sweetheart, Goodbye
How Can I Forget When There's So Much to Remember?
Turner, Florence
Lonesome
Tyson, Grace
Mister Sweeney, A Brainy Man
United States Marine Band
America First
Boy Scouts of America
The Fairest of the Fair
The Golden Star
The Invincible Eagle
The Lambs' March
The Liberty Loan March
The New York Hippodrome March
University Six
Lila
Valentino, Rudolph
Kashmiri Song
Vallee, Rudy
After All That I've Been to You
Casey Jones
I Love the Moon
If You Were the Only Girl in the World
They Didn't Believe Me
Turn Back the Universe and Give Me Yesterday
Van and Schenck
Honey Man
If I Could Peep through the Window Tonight
Mandy
Midnight in Dreamy Spain
My Hawaiian Sunrise
My Old Log Cabin Home
Oh! How She Can Sing
You Cannot Shake That "Shimmie" Here
Van, Billy
Poor Robinson Crusoe
Van, Billy B.
The Coster's Glide
When a Girl Leads the Band
Van Brunt, Walter
Don't Wake Me Up I Am Dreaming
I Live Up-Town
The Trail of the Lonesome Pine
Van Brunt, Walter J.
Bless Your Ever Loving Little Heart
Don't Turn My Picture to the Wall
Good Bye, Good Luck, God Bless You
He Played It on His Fid, Fid, Fiddle-dee-dee
In My Harem
My Sumurun Girl
Next Sunday at Nine
Somebody's Coming to My House
That Society Bear
When I Get You Alone Tonight
Where the Red Red Roses Grow
You'll Never Know the Good Fellow I've Been, 'Till I've Gone Away
Van Dyke, Paul
There's a Light That's Burning in the Window of the Little House upon the Hill
Van Eps Banjo Quartet
Chong, He Come from Hong Kong
Van Eps, Fred
The Maurice Tango
Van Eps Trio
I Wonder What Will William Tell
Razzberries
Van, Gus
Baby's Prayers Will Soon Be Answered
Beans
Don't Try to Steal the Sweetheart of a Soldier
He Likes Their Jukelele
Huckleberry Finn
I Ain't Got'en No Time to Have the Blues

I Don't Want to Get Well
In the Land Where Poppies Bloom
My Baby's Arms
My Little Rambling Rose
Open Up the Golden Gates to Dixieland and Let Me into Paradise
Piano Man
Send Me Away with a Smile
Southern Gals
Sweet Kisses That Came in the Night
Teach Me That Beautiful Love
There's Something Nice about the South
They Were All Out of Step But Jim
When Tony Goes Over the Top
You'll Find Old Dixieland in France

van Studdiford, Grace
The Garden of Dreams

Vance, Clarice
Alexander Jones
All In Down and Out
Back, Back, Back to Baltimore
Bedelia
Common Sense
He's a Cousin of Mine
He's My Cousin If She's Your Niece
I Can't Tell Why I Love You But I Do
I'd Rather Two-Step Than Waltz, Bill
If Anybody Wants to Meet a Jonah, Shake Hands with Me
If You Can't Be a Bell-Cow, Fall in Behind
I'm Afraid to Come Home in the Dark
I'm Goin' to Live Anyhow 'Till I Die
I'm Longing for My Old Kentucky Home
Salome
She's Good Enough to Be Your Baby's Mother...
There's a Time and a Place for Everything
Tippecanoo
Yo' Eyes Are Open, But Yo' Sound Asleep
You're in the Right Church But the Wrong Pew

Vaughan, Sarah
Bill Bailey, Won't You Please Come Home

Velie, Janet
From Now On
Somehow It Seldom Comes True
Tee-Oodle-Um-Bam-Bo

Vera Ellen
Where Did You Get That Girl?

Vesta, Netta
The Moon Has His Eyes on You

Victor Dance Orchestra
The Pink Lady Waltz

Victor Herbert and His Orchestra
The Streets of New York

Victor Herbert's Orchestra
Kiss Me Again
March of the Toys
The Rosary

Victor Light Opera company
Love's Own Sweet Song

Victor Lombardo and His Orchestra
I'm Gonna Make Hay While the Sun Shines in Virginia

Victor Military Band
All He Does Is Follow Them Around
At the Ball, That's All
Castle Half and Half
Chinatown, My Chinatown
Down Among the Sheltering Palms
Floreine
The Flower Garden Ball
The Gertrude Hoffmann Glide
Honolulu, America Loves You
I Can Dance with Everybody But My Wife
If I Knock the 'L' Out of Kelly, It Still Would Be Kelly to Me
I'm on My Way to Dublin Bay
I'm Simply Crazy over You

Joe Turner Blues
Kansas City
Liberty Forever
Madelon
Maurice Hesitation
Maurice Mattchiche
The Maurice Tango
Naughty! Naughty! Naughty!
On San Francisco Bay
On the Mississippi
Over the Moonlit Sea
Same Sort of Girl
Silver Sleigh Bells
Sister Susie's Sewing Shirts for Soldiers
The Syncopated Walk
Take Me to That Swanee Shore
They're On Their Way to Mexico
Tres Moutarde
Waiting for the Robert E. Lee
Wake Up America
Walkin' the Dog
When It's Apple Blossom Time in Normandy
When You and I Were Young, Maggie
Where Did You Get That Girl?

Victor Orchestra
Melody of Love
Wild Cherries

Victor Salon Orchestra
Chinese Lullaby
Marcheta
The Perfect Song

Victoria, Vesta
All She Gets from the Iceman Is Ice
And He Blames My Dreamy Eyes
Come Along Up in the Flip Flap
It Ain't All Honey and It Ain't All Jam
It's All Right in the Summertime
I've Told His Missus All about Him
Mother Hasn't Spoken to Father Since
The Next Horse I Ride On
Poor John
Waiting at the Church

Vincent, Helen
In the Days of Girls and Boys
I've Only One Idea about the Girls and That's to Love 'Em
You've Got Your Mother's Big Blue Eyes

Vincent Lopez and His Orchestra
Nola

Vincent, Querita
Just Because She Made Dem Goo-Goo Eyes

Vogel, Jerry
Jerry, You Warra a Warrior in the War

Vokes, May
I'm Afraid to Come Home in the Dark

von Studdiford, Grace
Can You Forget
If All the Stars Were Mine

Wadsworth's Novelty Orchestra
Ole Miss

Waikiki Hawaiian Orchestra
Aloma

Wakefield, Willa Holt
He's Me Pal

Waldorf-Astoria Dance Orchestra
Chinese Lullaby
On Miami Shore

Walker, Aida Overton
Good Morning Carrie!
I'd Like to Be a Real Lady
I'll Keep a Warm Spot in My Heart for You
The Island of By and By
It's Hard to Love Somebody Who's Loving Somebody Else
Kinky
Lovie Dear
Miss Hannah from Savannah
Oh, You Devil Rag
That's Why They Call Me Shine
Why Adam Sinned

Walker, George
Bon Bon Buddy
Pretty Desdemona

She's Getting More Like the White Folks Every Day
You're in the Right Church But the Wrong Pew
Walker, Margaret
Spring Fashions
Wallace, Franklyn
Your Dad Gave His Life for His Country
Wallace, Grace
If He Can Fight Like He Can Love, Good Night Germany
Waller, Fats
After You've Gone
The Curse of an Aching Heart
I'm Sorry I Made You Cry
Oh! Frenchy
Somebody Stole My Gal
Sugar Blues
Waller, Thomas "Fats"
Beale Street Blues
Walsh, Billy
Be Satisfied with What You Have, Let Well Enough Alone
Walsh, Marie
Make Yourself at Home
Walton, Florence
The Junk Man Rag
Just a Kiss
Maurice Mattchiche
The Raffles Dance
Waltz Kings
Vilia
Ward, Fannie
Meet Me in Rose Time Rosie
Ward, May
Alexander, Don't You Love Your Baby No More?
Any Little Girl That's a Nice Little Girl Is the Right Little Girl for Me
The Bird on Nellie's Hat
I'm Awfully Glad I Met You
I'm Looking for the Man That Wrote "The Merry Widow Waltz"
You Taught Me to Love You, Now Teach Me to Forget
Ward, Will J.
I Didn't Raise My Boy to Be a Soldier
When the Whole World Has Gone Back on You
Warfield, David
Tell Us Pretty Ladies
Waring, Fred
Over There
The Rosary
Warren, Kathleen
When the Band Goes Marching By
Warren, Leonard
On the Road to Mandalay
Washboard Sam and His Band
Save It for Me
Washburn, Blanche
One Called "Mother" and the Other "Home Sweet Home"
Washburn, Lillian
When I Lost You
When Kate and I Were Comin' thro' the Rye
Waters, Ethel
His Eye Is on the Sparrow
St. Louis Blues
Someday Sweetheart
Waters, Hattie
Pansy
Watkins, Billy
Baby Love
Watson, Fred
When Tony LaBoard Played the Barber-Shop Chord
Watson, Harry
The Comet and the Moon
Watson, Harry, Jr.
Handle me with Care
Watson, Nora
In the Candlelight
Watson Sisters
Mister Jazz Himself
Webb, Dorothy
Take Me in Your Arms and Say You Love Me
Webb, Teddy
Here's to You, My Sparkling Wine

Weeks, Marion
Beautiful Roses
Wehle, Charlotte
My Palm Leaf Maid
Welch, Ben
My Mariuccia Take a Steamboat
Welk, Lawrence
Aloha Oe
Every Little Movement
O
Wentworth, Lola
Wait and See, You'll Want Me Back
Werrenrath, Reinald
By the Saskatchewan
Let Us Have Peace
Love Sends a Little Gift of Roses
Pirate Song
The Radiance in Your Eyes
Weslyn, Louis
Lovesick
Lucky in Love
West, DeForest
Sing Me a Song of Other Days
West, Mae
And Then
Everybody Shimmies Now
West, Will
Crusader and Tommy
Oh, How I Love My Teacher
Weston, Cecilia
Take Me Back to New York Town
Weston, Eddie and Cecilia
Keep on the Sunny Side
Weston, Fields, and Carroll
Lady Angeline
Weston, Joe
Melody Chimes
Weston, Lucy
Be Good! If You Can't Be Good Be Careful
Weston, Willie
For Your Country and My Country
Hello Wisconsin, Won't You Find My Yonnie Yonson
Homeward Bound
I Called You My Sweetheart
In the Land of Wedding Bells
I've Got the Blues for Home Sweet Home
Rufus Johnson's Harmony Band
They Start the Victrola and Go Dancing Around the Floor
Those Charlie Chaplin Feet
We're Going to Take the Sword Away from William
When the Grown-Up Ladies Act Like Babies
Where Do We Go from Here?
Wheaton, Anna
The Bacchanal Rag
Wheeler, Bert and Betty
The Honolulu Blues
I'm a Lonesome Melody
Wheeler, Earl
Baby Rose
Wheeler, Elizabeth
Good Night Dear
When You and I Were Young, Maggie
Wheeler, Frederick
Brighten the Corner Where You Are
On the Road to Mandalay
Wheeler, Van Rensselar
Could You Be True to Eyes of Blue If You Looked into Eyes of Brown?
Whitbeck, Jane
My Heart's Tonight in Texas by the Silvery Rio Grande
White City Quartette
'Neath the Old Cherry Tree, Sweet Marie
White, Elsie
I'll Come Back to You When It's All Over
In the Land of Wedding Bells
White, Frances
M-i-s-s-i-s-s-i-p-p-i
Oh! You Gray Haired Kid
Six Times Six Is Thirty-Six
What Do I Care?
White, George
Come Dance with Me

White, Lee
Give Me One More Chance
Oh! You Georgia Rose
White, Pearl
They're All Going to the Movies
White, Sam
Louisiana
Whiteman, Paul
Chinese Lullaby
The Darktown Strutters' Ball
M-i-s-s-i-s-s-i-p-p-i
Poor Butterfly
Rag-Time Cowboy Joe
Rose Room
Vilia
Whitfield, Frederick
Absence Makes the Heart Grow Fonder
Whitford, Annabelle
The Christy Girl
The Gibson Bathing Girl
Take a Tip from Venus
Whiting and Burt
Love Me While the Loving Is Good
Whiting, George
Do You Take This Woman for Your Lawful Wife?
Whiting, Margaret
Now Is the Hour
Whitman Sisters
Think of Me Little Daddy
Whitney, Salem Tutt
My Heart for You Pines Away
Wilbur, Clarence
After You, My Dear Alphonse
Wilbur Sweatman and His Orchestra
The Florida Blues
Wilbur Sweatman's Original Jazz Band
Bluin' the Blues
Indianola
Those Draftin' Blues
Wiley, Lee
Memories
Wiley, Stella
Any Rags?
Williams and Walker
The Fortune Telling Man
Good Morning Carrie!
Williams, Andy
Aloha Oe
Williams, Bert
All In Down and Out
Believe Me!
Blackberrying Today
Borrow from Me
Bring Back Those Wonderful Days
Come Right In, Sit Right Down and Make Yourself at Home
Constantly
The Darktown Poker Club
Dat's Harmony
Ephraham Played Upon the Piano
Everybody Wants a Key to My Cellar
Fas' Fas' World
The Harbor of Lost Dreams
He's a Cousin of Mine
I Ain't Married No More
I May Be Crazy But I Ain't No Fool
I Thought My Troubles Were Over, But They'd Scarce Begun
I'd Rather See a Minstrel Show
If I Should Die Before I Wake, How Will I Know I'm Dead?
If You Ain't Got It, Go and Get It
I'll Lend You Everything I've Got Except My Wife
I'm a Jonah Man
I'm Cured
I'm Sorry I Ain't Got It You Could Have It If I Had It Blues
In de Evenin'
It Was Me
It's Nobody's Business But My Own
Late Hours
Let It Alone
My Castle on the Nile
My Landlady
Nobody
The Phrenologist Coon
Play That Barbershop Chord

Pretty Desdemona
Rip Van Winkle Was a Lucky Man But Adam Had Him Beat a Mile
She's Getting More Like the White Folks Every Day
Somebody Lied
That Minor Strain
That's a Plenty
The Vampire
When It's All Goin' Out and Nothin' Comin' In
White Folks Call It Chanticleer But It's Still Just Plain Chicken to Me
Woodman, Woodman Spare That Tree
You Cannot Make Your Shimmy Shake on Tea
You Can't Get Away from It
You Can't Shake That Shimmie Here
You'll Find Old Dixieland in France
You're Gwine to Get Somethin' What You Don't Expect
You're in the Right Church But the Wrong Pew
You're on the Right Road Sister But You're Goin' the Wrong Way

Williams, Clarence
Baby, Won't You Please Come Home
I Wish I Could Shimmy Like My Sister Kate
Yama Yama Blues

Williams, Evan
A Little Bit o' Honey

Williams, Frank
Brother Masons

Williams, Harry
In Berry Pickin' Time

Williams, Hattie
Don't Turn My Picture to the Wall
I Love You All the Time
I'm a Lady
The Indians Along Broadway
My Irish Rose
My Starlight Queen
Pierrot and Pierrette
Popular Songs
Say! Fay!
Under the Linden Tree

Williams, Irene
The Message of the Violet

Williams, Lottie
Good Morning Carrie!

Williams, Maud
Carissima

Williams, Queenie
They Were All Out of Step But Jim

Wills, Estelle
Wait at the Gate for Me

Wills, Nat C.
The Poor Old Man

Wills, Nat M.
Alexander Jones
Bill Was There
BPOE
General Hardtack on Guard
G.O.P.
Had She Only Let Me Dream an Hour More
If a Table at Rector's Could Talk
The Man Behind

Wilson Family
Good Morning Carrie!

Wilson, Francis
The Cuckoo Bird
He Ought to Have a Tablet in the Hall of Fame
Look It Up in the Dream Book
The Monk of Malabar

Wilson, Grace
The Last Rose of Summer Is the Sweetest Song of All
Mammy's Shufflin' Dance
Mariutch, She Come Back to Me

Windom, Constance
I Can't Take My Eyes off You

Winter, Winnona
Meet Me at Twilight

Winterhalter, Hugo
All That I Ask of You Is Love

Wisdom, Eleanor
'Neath the Old Acorn Tree, Sweet Estelle
Withee, Mabel
Our Ancestors
Witherspoon, Herbert
Mother o' Mine
Pirate Song
"The Woman in White"
In the House of Too Much Trouble
Wood, James
The Song That I Hear in My Dreams
Woodruff, Harry
When Love Is Young
Woody Herman and His Orchestra
You Taught Me to Love You, Now Teach Me to Forget
Wright, Ruth
I'm Tying the Leaves So They Won't Come Down
Wynn, Bessie
All That I Ask of You Is Love
And Then
Beautiful Dreams of You
By the Beautiful Sea
Call Me in the Morning
Chic-Chic-Chic-Chic-Chicken
Don't Wake Me Up I Am Dreaming
Honey Man
If the Wind Had Only Blown the Other Way
I'll Never Love Another Like I Love You
I'm After Madame Tettrazzini's Job
I'm Looking for a Dear Old Lady
In the Candlelight
Not for Me
Roses Bring Dreams of You
Somebody's Waiting for You
There's a Light That's Burning in the Window of the Little House upon the Hill
Toyland
You Are the Ideal of My Dreams
You're a Great Big Blue-Eyed Baby
Wynn, Ed
Put Me Upon an Island
Wynne, Mona
My Little Rang Outang
Xavier Cugat's Waldorf Astoria Orchestra
Let Me Call You Sweetheart
Yerkes' Jazarimba Band
I'll Say She Does
Yerkes' Jazarimba Orchestra
And He'd Say Oo-la-la! Wee-Wee!
Mammy o' Mine
Yerkes' Novelty Five
Easy Pickins'
Yohn, May
Down in the Subway
Yolo, Alta
Always in the Way
Yorke, Alice
Cuddle Up a Little Closer, Lovey Mine
Youlin, Alma
Mammy's Shufflin' Dance
That Old Girl of Mine
You're My Baby
Young, John
On the Road to Home Sweet Home
Young, John E.
By the Saskatchewan
Just Because It's You
Young, Lester
Indiana
Young, Margaret
Jerry, You Warra a Warrior in the War
Young, Myrtle
I've Got the Blues for Home Sweet Home
Yvette
My Belgian Rose
Zelaya, Alphonse
The Maid of Old Madrid
Zon-o-phone Concert Band
The Gaby Glide

Play

Acushla Machree
  Say a Prayer for the Boys Out There
Alma's Return
  There's a Little Spark of Love Still Burning
Along Came Ruth
  Along Came Ruth
The American Way
  A Lemon in the Garden of Love
Arrah-na-Pogue
  An Irishman's Lilt
Asthorne, Eileen
  The Wearing of the Green
The Auctioneer
  There's No Other Girl Like My Girl
Barry of Barrymore
  Laugh and the World Will Laugh with You, Weep and You'll Weep All Alone
  Mother Machree
The Bird of Paradise
  Aloha Oe
  Beautiful Bird of Paradise
  One - Two - Three - Four
The Blue Mouse
  Love Me All the Time
The Bold Soger Boy
  Little Tommy Murphy
The Cinderella Man
  Out of His Heart He Builds a Home
Daddy Long-Legs
  My Daddy Long-Legs
The Dawn of a Tomorrow
  The Dawn of a Tomorrow
Du Barry
  Du Barry, the Doll of the World
East Is West
  Chinese Lullaby
Eileen Asthorne
  Day Dreams
The Entertainer
  Put Me Among the Girls
The Fifth Commandment
  Castles in the Air
Garrett O'Magh
  Ireland! A Gra Ma Chree
Getting Together
  Dear Old Pal of Mine
  On the Road That Leads to Home
  You've Got to Go In or Go Under
The Girl and the Judge
  It Rained a Mist
The Girl and the Taxi
  Ragtime Table d'Hote
The Gold Diggers
  What Good Is Alimony on a Lonesome Night
Good Gracious Annabelle
  Other Eyes
Happiness
  Happiness
The Heart of Paddy Whack
  A Little Bit of Heaven, Shure They Call It Ireland
Huckleberry Finn
  The Animals' Convention
  Courting
  Good Night Lucindy
  I Want to Be a Drummer in the Band
  Just a Tender Spot for Father Dear
Killarney, My Home o'er the Sea
  Killarney, My Home o'er the Sea
Lights of Home
  Lights of Home
Little Lost Sister
  Little Lost Sister
The Little Princess
  Dolly
Love Watches
  Good Night Dear
The Member of the Wedding
  His Eye Is on the Sparrow
Merely Mary Ann
  Kiss Me Good Night, Dear Love
The Mind the Paint Girl
  Mind the Paint
The Morals of Marcus
  Eastern Moon
The New Lady Bantock
  Meet Me in Rose Time Rosie

Old Limerick Town
The Limerick Girls
Over Night
O Sole Mio
Over the Top
Your Lips Are No Man's Land But Mine
Peg o' My Heart
Peg o' My Heart
Pollyanna
Pollyanna
Ragged Robin
Laugh and the World Will Laugh with You, Weep and You'll Weep All Alone
Rebecca of Sunnybrook Farm
Rebecca of Sunnybrook Farm
The Rebel
Eyes of Blue
For Freedom and Ireland
A Romance of Athlone
Kate Kearney
Romeo and Juliet
To Have, To Hold, To Love
Shameen Dhu
Too-ra-loo-ra-loo-ra
Smilin' Through
Smilin' Through
Terrance
My Own Dear Irish Queen
Tiger Rose
Tiger Rose Waltz
Tom Jones
The Road to Yesterday
Uncle Tom's Cabin
Clidee-Oh
Under Southern Skies
Under Southern Skies
The Virginian
Ten Thousand Cattle Straying
The Voice of McConnell
Ireland, My Land of Dreams
The Way to Kenmare
The Legend of the Maguire
The White Chrysanthemum
I Just Couldn't Do without You
White Lilacs
Toddle Song

Radio Show

The Pepsodent Hour Featuring Amos and Andy
The Perfect Song
Stop the Music
Are You a Buffalo?

Revue

All-Star Varieties Jubilee
Dinah
Army Play-by-Play
Fall in for Your Motherland
The Big Show
Poor Butterfly
Broadway to Paris
The Gertrude Hoffmann Glide
Just a Kiss
Bubbling Brown Sugar
Nobody
The Century Girl
Alice in Wonderland
The Chicken Walk
He Likes Their Jukelele
Century Grove Revue
Bolsheveki Glide
Century Midnight Whirl
Peggy
The Chocolate Dandies
Mammy's Little Choc'late Cullud Chile
Cohan Revue of 1918
Regretful Blues
Come Over Here
Take Me in Your Arms and Say You Love Me
Dance and Grow Thin
There's Something Nice about the South
Dancing Around
When Sunday Comes to Town
When the Grown-Up Ladies Act Like Babies
The Darling of the Gallery Gods
Mozart Lincoln
Demi-Tasse Revue
Come to the Moon

Eubie!
Gee! I Wish I Had Someone to Rock Me in the Cradle of Love
Good Night, Angeline
Everything
Come Along to Toy Town
Follies of 1908
The Brinkley Bathing Girl
Hat Song
The Nell Brinkley Girl
Shine On, Harvest Moon
Take Me 'Round in a Taxicab
When Highland Mary Did the Highland Fling
You Will Have to Sing an Irish Song
Follies of 1911
Bumble Bee
Dat's Harmony
Do It the Right Way
Ephraham Played Upon the Piano
I'm a Crazy Daffydil
It Was Me
My Landlady
My Yiddische Colleen
Pots and Pans
Texas Tommy Swing
Whippoorwill
Woodman, Woodman Spare That Tree
Follies of 1909
The Aero Naughty Girls
The Baltimore Bombashay
Believe Me!
Blarney
By the Light of the Silvery Moon
The Christy Girl
Come On, Play Ball with Me
Falling Star
I'm After Madame Tettrazzini's Job
I'm Glad I'm a Boy/I'm Glad I'm a Girl
Linger Longer Lingerie
Take a Tip from Venus
Follies of 1907
Be Good! If You Can't Be Good Be Careful
Budweiser's a Friend of Mine
Bye Bye Dear Old Broadway
The Gibson Bathing Girl
Handle me with Care
How'd You Like to Float Me
Meet Me with Spangles and Bells On
The Modern Sandow Girl
My Pocahontas
On the Grand Old Sand
That's How He Met the Girl
When Miss Patricia Salome Did Her Funny Little Oh-la Pa-lome
Follies of 1910
The Comet and the Moon
Constantly
Don't Take a Girlie to Coney (You May Find a Nicer One There)
The Grizzly Bear
I'll Lend You Everything I've Got Except My Wife
In de Evenin'
Kidland
Lovie Joe
Mister Sweeney, A Brainy Man
Nix on the Glow-Worm, Lena
The Pensacola Mooch
Play That Fandango Rag
Sweet Kitty Bellairs
Swing Me High, Swing Me Low
That Minor Strain
White Folks Call It Chanticleer But It's Still Just Plain Chicken to Me
You're Gwine to Get Somethin' What You Don't Expect
Follies of 1912
Beautiful Beautiful Girl
Blackberrying Today
Borrow from Me
Bumble Bee
Daddy Has a Sweetheart and Mother Is Her Name
Row Row Row
Some Boy
That English Rag
There's One in a Million Like You

You're on the Right Road Sister But You're Goin' the Wrong Way
Gaby
Spanish Love
Gaieties of 1919
Freedom of the C's
I've Made Up My Mind to Mind a Maid Made Up Like You
Jazz Babies' Ball
Please Don't Take Away the Girls
They're All Sweeties
You'd Be Surprised
Greenwich Village Follies
Give Me the Sultan's Harem
Greenwich Village Follies of 1919
Bo - la - Bo
I Know Why--Because I'm in Love with You
Gus Edwards' Merry-Go-Round
Betty, You're the One Best Bet
Gus Edwards' 1914 Song Revue
Just 'Round the Corner from Broadway
Gus Edwards' Song Revue of 1911
I Want to Spoon to the Tune of the Silvery Moon
Gus Edwards' Song Revue of 1909
My Cousin Caruso
Gus Edwards' Song Revue of 1910
Lucy Anna Lou
My Cousin Caruso
Rosa Rigoletto
Gus Edwards' Song Revue of 1912
Mister Pagliatch
Higgeldy-Piggeldy
The Game of Love
A Great Big Girl Like Me
Nancy Clancy
Hip Hip Hooray
The Ladder of Roses
Hitchy-Koo of 1918
You-oo Just You
Hitchy-Koo of 1919
Hitchy's Garden of Roses
I Introduced
Hitchy-Koo of 1917
I May Be Gone for a Long, Long Time
Six Times Six Is Thirty-Six
Hoity-Toity
Love a la Mode
Hullo America
Crusader and Tommy
Give Me the Moonlight, Give Me the Girl and Leave the Rest to Me
The Jazz Band
The Picture I Want to See
The Jolly Bachelors
Stop That Rag
Jubilee
The Island of Roses and Love
Lambs' Gambol of 1914
He Was Always Fooling Around
The Lambs' March
Let's Go
A Debutante's Engagement Book
Mack Sennett Girls
The Mimic World
When Tetrazzini Sings
Your Eyes Say No But Your Lips Say Yes!
Miss 1917
The Land Where the Good Songs Go
Midnight in Dreamy Spain
The Palm Beach Dip
Peaches
You-oo Just You
Ned Wayburn's Demi-Tasse Revue
That Lullaby of Long Ago
Ned Wayburn's Demi-Tasse Revue of 1919
Swanee
Passing Show of 1918
I Just Can't Make My Feet Behave
I'm Going to Spend My Vacation with a Dear Old Relation
My Baby Talking Girl
On the Level, You're a Devil
Smiles
That Soothing Serenade
Venetian Moon

Passing Show of 1915
Take Me to the Midnight Cake-walk Ball
Passing Show of 1914
Bohemian Rag
Passing Show of 1919
America's Popular Song
I'm Forever Blowing Bubbles
The Kiss Burglar
Molly Malone, My Own
Passing Show of 1917
Goodbye Broadway, Hello France
It's a Long Way to Berlin But We'll Get There
Meet Me at the Station
Passing Show of 1916
Nothing's Good Enough for a Good Little Girl If She's Good Enough for You
Pretty Baby
Passing Show of 1913
Do You Take This Woman for Your Lawful Wife?
The Golden Stairs of Love
Love Me While the Loving Is Good
Ragging the Nursery Rhymes
When I Want to Settle Down
Passing Show of 1912
The Bacchanal Rag
Ragtime Jockey Man
Red Pepper Rag
The Wedding Glide
The School Girl
Lonesome
The Show of Wonders
Louisiana
My Yiddische Butterfly
Naughty! Naughty! Naughty!
Wedding Bells
The Zoo Step
Shuffle Along
Ain't You Coming Back, Mary Ann, to Maryland
Good Night, Angeline
On Patrol in No Man's Land
Star and Garter
When Sousa Leads the Band
Stop! Look! Listen!
When I Get Back to the U.S.A.
Telling the Tale
Altogether Too Fond of You
Temptations
Spanish Love
That's It
Midnight Maid
This Is the Army
For Your Country and My Country
Oh! How I Hate to Get Up in the Morning
Tintypes
Fifty-Fifty
I Want to Be Loved Like a Leading Lady
It's Delightful to Be Married
Tout Suite Elizabet
Just Around the Corner
Twiddle Twaddle
My Syncopated Gypsy Maid
Venus of Broadway
Greenwich Village
The Whirl of the World
My Cleopatra Girl
Smother Me with Kisses and Kill Me with Love
Words and Music
Everything Looks Rosy and Bright
A World of Pleasure
Walking the Dog
Yip Yip Yahank
Ding Dong
For Your Country and My Country
I Can Always Find a Little Sunshine in the Y.M.C.A.
Mandy
Oh! How I Hate to Get Up in the Morning
We're on Our Way to France
Ziegfeld Follies of 1918
The Blue Devils of France
But - After the Ball Was Over Then He Made Up for Lost Time
Come On Papa

Frisco's Kitchen Stove Rag
I Want to Learn to Jazz Dance
If She Means What I Think She Means
The Navy Took Them Over and the Navy Will Bring Them Back
Oh! How I Hate to Get Up in the Morning
Roaming Romeo
When Uncle Joe Steps into France
Would You Rather Be a Colonel with an Eagle on Your Shoulder...
You Keep Sending 'Em Over and We'll Keep Knocking 'Em Down

Ziegfeld Follies of 1915
My Country Right or Wrong

Ziegfeld Follies of 1914
Baby Love
The Darktown Poker Club
I'm Cured
Prunella Mine
Rock Me in the Cradle of Love
The Vampire

Ziegfeld Follies of 1919
Bring Back Those Wonderful Days
Everybody Wants a Key to My Cellar
Harem Life
I'd Rather See a Minstrel Show
It's Nobody's Business But My Own
I've Got My Captain Working for Me Now
Johnny's in Town
Mandy
The Moon Shines on the Moonshine
My Baby's Arms
Oh! How She Can Sing
Oh! The Last Rose of Summer Was the Sweetest Rose of All
A Pretty Girl Is Like a Melody
Sweet Kisses That Came in the Night
Tulip Time
When They're Old Enough to Know Better, It's Better to Leave Them Alone
You Cannot Make Your Shimmy Shake on Tea
You'd Be Surprised

Ziegfeld Follies of 1917
The Dixie Volunteers
I Ain't Married No More
The Modern Maiden's Prayer

Ziegfeld Follies of 1916
Have a Heart
Nijinski

Ziegfeld Follies of 1913
At the Ball, That's All
Be My Little Baby Bumble Bee
Hello Honey
I Can Live without You
If a Table at Rector's Could Talk
You Can't Get Away from It
You're Never to Old to Love

Ziegfeld Follies of 1931
Shine On, Harvest Moon

Ziegfeld Follies of 1927
Daddy Has a Sweetheart and Mother Is Her Name

Ziegfeld Follies of 1923
Daddy Has a Sweetheart and Mother Is Her Name

Ziegfeld Midnight Frolics of 1918
What Do I Care?
You'll Find Old Dixieland in France

Ziegfeld Midnight Frolics of 1915
M-i-s-s-i-s-s-i-p-p-i
Oh, How She Could Yacki Hacki Wicki Wacki Woo
Scaddle-de-Mooch

Ziegfeld Midnight Frolics of 1919
The Moon Shines on the Moonshine
Oh! The Last Rose of Summer Was the Sweetest Rose of All
You Cannot Shake That "Shimmie" Here
You Can't Shake That Shimmie Here
You're a Perfect Jewel to Me

Ziegfeld Midnight Frolics of 1917
That's the Kind of Baby for Me
When Those Sweet Hawaiian Babies Roll Their Eyes
Ziegfeld Midnight Frolics of 1916
Every Girl Is Fishing
Oh! You Gray Haired Kid
Ziegfeld Midnight Frolics of 1920
You Can't Shake That Shimmie Here
Ziegfeld Moulin Rouge
Borrow from Me

Television Show

Celebrating Gershwin
Come to the Moon
I Know Why the Caged Bird Sings
Lift Every Voice and Sing
Roots: The Next Generation
Lift Every Voice and Sing

Vaudeville Act

The Borrowed Art of Gertrude Hoffmann
A Vision of Salome
Buster Brown's Holiday
My Mississippi Missus Misses Me
Charles D. Lawlor and Daughters
Since Father Went to Work
Christy's Minstrels
If All My Dreams Were Made of Gold, I'd Buy the World for You
Cohan and Harris' Minstrel Show
The American Rag Time
Any Old Port in a Storm
Cohan & Harris' Minstrels
Good Bye Mister Ragtime
Lead Me to That Beautiful Band
Love Days
McGinnis
Meet Me in Rose Time Rosie
None of Them's Got Anything on Me
Cupid's Ladder
Lucky in Love
Darktown Follies
At the Ball, That's All
Exceeding the Speed Limit
Darling
The Gibson Girl Review
The Gibson Widow
The Girl with the Whooping Cough
That Spanish Rag
Girlies
My Irish Girl
Girls from Happyland
That Teasin' Rag
Gorman's Minstrels
My Mississippi Missus Misses Me
Gus Edwards' Bandbox Revue
If I Only Knew Just How I Stood with You
When I Grow Up I'm Going to Be a Soldier
Gus Edwards' Blonde Typewriters
Liza
Gus Edwards' Newsboys
Farewell Killarney
If a Boy Like You Loved a Girl Like Me
Gus Edwards' 1914 Revue
Shadowland
Gus Edwards' Rube Kids
On the Old See-Saw
Gus Edwards' School Boys and Girls
He's Me Pal
School Days
Sunbonnet Sue
Won't You Be My Baby Boy?
Gus Edwards' School Days
Have You Seen My Baby?
On the Old See-Saw
Gus Edwards' Song Revue
Liza
Gus Edwards' Song Revue of 1910
Alias Jimmy Valentine
Gus Edwards' Song Revue of 1913
Alias Jimmy Valentine
Since My Margarette Become-a da Suffragette
Gus Edwards' Song Revue of 1912
On a Beautiful Night with a Beautiful Girl

Gus Hill's Minstrels
I'm Glad I Can Make You Cry
Hanky-Panky
When You Hear Cy Riddle Play His Fiddle
A Hot Old Time
My Jersey Lily
Johnson and Dean Review
Royal Garden Blues
La Domino Rouge
Red Domino
The Lady Bountiful Minstrels
Somebody Stole My Gal
Lew Dockstader and His Big Minstrels
My Twilight Queen
Lew Dockstader's Minstrels
I Want to Be a Soldier
The Land of Nicotine
Moriarty
Sugar Mine
Max Witt's Singing Colleens
The Last Rose of Summer Is the Sweetest Song of All
When the Fields Are White with Cotton
Max Witt's Six Sophomores and a Freshman
Kiss All the Girls for Me
Napanese Honeymoon
Abie, the Sporty Kid
Ned Wayburn's Daisy Dancers
Daisy Dear
My Little Japaneesee
Ned Wayburn's Girls
My Little Chick
Ned Wayburn's Hello, Paris
Loving Moon
Ned Wayburn's Minstrel Misses
My Dixie Land Daisy
A Night in the Jardin de Danse
The Little Church around the Corner
Original English Pony Ballet
My Gypsy Queen
Primrose and Dockstader's Minstrels
Absence Makes the Heart Grow Fonder
A Real Girl
Take Me Back to the Garden of Love
S. H. Dudley's Smart Set Company
Don't Walk So Fast
Seven Hoboes
My Brudda Sylvest'
The Society Buds
That's My Idea of Paradise
A Song Romance
Romance
30 Minutes at Sheepshead
Betty, You're the One Best Bet
The Trained Nurses
If You Don't Want Me
We've Had a Lovely Time, So Long, Good Bye
Vogel's Minstrels
The Curse of a Pretty Face
The Wireless Belles
Send Me a Kiss by Wireless

Chronological Index

1900

Absence Makes the Heart Grow Fonder
After All
All on Account of a Dear Little Girl
Beautiful Arizona
Billet Doux
A Bird in a Gilded Cage
The Blue and the Gray: A Mother's Gift to Her Country
By the Silvery Rio Grande, *see* My Heart's Tonight in Texas by the Silvery Rio Grande
Calligan - Call Again!
Calling to Her Boy Just Once Again
Castles in the Air
Crusade Glory
The Dandiest Boy in Town
De Cakewalk Queen
Do You Think You Could Learn to Love Me?
Down De Lover's Lane
The Duchess of Central Park
Early in the Morning
Eyes of Blue
A Flower from the Garden of Life
The Fond Dove and His Lady Love
For Freedom and Ireland
Good-Bye, Dolly Gray
The Green above the Red
Hail to the Spirit of Liberty
I Ain't a-Goin' to Weep No More
I Ain't Gwin ter Work No Mo'
I Can't Tell Why I Love You But I Do
I Love But One, I Love But You
I Love My Shirt Waist Best
I Love You, Ma Cherie
I Must Have Been a-Dreamin'
I Need the Money
I Won't Be an Actor Any More
If All the Stars Were Mine
In Naples Fair
In the House of Too Much Trouble
Ireland! A Gra Ma Chree
I've a Longing in My Heart for You, Louise
I've Got Troubles of My Own
A Japanese Love Song
Just Because She Made Dem Goo-Goo Eyes
Just What the Good Book Taught
Killiecrankie
Lift Every Voice and Sing
Little Tommy Murphy
Longing to Be by Your Side, *see* Absence Makes the Heart Grow Fonder
Look into Mine Eyes Dear Heart
A Love-Lorn Lily

Love Will Find a Way
Ma Blushin' Rosie, My Posie Sweet
Mack and Teddy
Magdaline, My Southern Queen
Mamselle
The Midnight Fire Alarm
The Monk of Malabar
My Charcoal Charmer
My Chilly Baby
My Drowsy Babe
My Heart's Tonight in Texas by the Silvery Rio Grande
My Jersey Lily
My Little Lady Bug
My Sunflower Sue
Nothing Doing
O Mona San
Oh! Oh! Miss Phoebe
Oh! Wouldn't That Jar You?
The Old Postmaster
On Furlough
The Opera
A Picture without a Frame
The Pride of Newspaper Row
The Rosary
Rosie and Josie
The Sentinel Asleep
She's a Princess Just the Same
Sing Me a Song of Other Days
Sleepy-Headed Little Mary Green
The Star and the Flower
Strike Up the Band
That Tariff War
There Are Two Sides to a Story
True Freedom
Un-requited
Wait
The Way to Win a Woman's Heart
What Eve Said to Adam
When Reuben Comes to Town
When Sousa Leads the Band
When the Band Played Home Sweet Home
When the Birds Go North Again
When the Harvest Days Are Over, Jessie, Dear
Where Go the Boats?
Why Don't the Band Play?

1901

Ain't Dat a Shame?
All That Glitters Is Not Gold
The American Billionaire
An Ante-bellum Sermon, *see* Joshua Fit de Battl' ob Jericho
Are You a Buffalo?
As on Moonlit Waves We Ride
Ashes of Roses
At the Pan-I-Marry Can
Baby Mine
Bashful Betsey Brown
Beautiful Isle of Somewhere
The Belle of Washington, D.C., *see* In the Swim
The Brotherhood of Man
Can't You Take My Word?
Cecelia and Amelia
Chloe, I'm Waiting
Clidee-Oh
Come Out, Dinah, on the Green
The Country Girl
The Cuckoo Bird
The Curse of a Pretty Face
De Trop
The Dolly Varden Song
Don't Butt In
Don't Put Me Off at Buffalo Any More
Down Where the Cotton Blossoms Grow
Dreaming in the Trenches
Easy Money
Eighth Avenue
Everybody Has a Whistle Like Me
Flirtation Song
Flora, I Am Your Adorer
Forget
The Fortune Telling Man
The Girl You Love
Good Morning Carrie!
Good Night Is But Your Last Good Bye
He Died on the Fighting Line
He Laid Away a Suit of Gray to Wear the Union Blue
He Ought to Have a Tablet in the Hall of Fame

Hello Central, Give Me Heaven
The Honeysuckle and the Bee
The Hope of the Ages
Hypnotizing Lize
I Don't Like Them Minstrel Folks, *see* When Mr. Shakespeare Comes to Town
I Hates to Get Up Early in the Morning
I Love You Truly
I Want to Be a Lidy
I Wants to Be the Leading Lady
I'd Lay Down My Life for You
I'd Like to Be a Gunner in the Navy
Ida from Idaho
I'll Be with You When the Roses Bloom Again
I'm a Respectable Working Girl
I'm Goin' to Live Anyhow 'Till I Die
I'm Tired
In Disguise
In Florida
In Society
In the Good Old-Fashioned Way
In the Heart of the Mighty Deep
In the Swim
In the Valley of Kentucky
The Invincible Eagle
Iola
I've Grown So Used to You
Jack O'Lantern
Josephine, My Jo
Joshua Fit de Battl' ob Jericho
Just a Message from the Camp Fire, *see* He Died on the Fighting Line
Just a-Wearying for You
Kitty
The Kodak Girl
The Language of the Flowers
A Lesson in Flirtation
Let Mary Go Round on the Merry-Go-Round
The Light That Failed
Li'l Gal
A Little Empty Nest
The Little Wooden Soldier
Look It Up in the Dream Book
Love Has Claimed Its Own
M-O-N-E-Y Spells Money
Ma Poppy Belle, *see* Easy Money
Mah Moonlight Lou
The Maid in the Moon
The Maiden with the Dreamy Eyes
Mamie, Don't You Feel Ashamie
The Man Who Plays the Tambourine
The March of the Workers
Maud, Maud, Maud
Maudie
Maybe
McKinley, Our Hero, Now at Rest
Mighty Lak' a Rose
Miss Bob White
Miss Hannah from Savannah
Mother's Hymn to Me
Mrs. Carter, You're a Tartar
Must We Say Good Bye Forever, Nellie Dear?
My Castle on the Nile
My Evalyne
My Filopena Pet
My Honolulu Lu
My Japanese Cherry Blossom
My Lady Hottentot
My Lonesome Little Louisiana Lady
My Onliest Little Dolly
My Samoan Beauty
My Swee' Kimona
My Toreador
The Mysterious Melody, *see* Are You a Buffalo?
Nancy Brown
Nobody's Lookin' But de Owl and de Moon
O Dry Those Tears
Oh Fudge!
The Old Flag Never Touched the Ground
Onward Brothers
Our Boys in Overalls
Pan, Pan, Pan
Pansy
The Pawn Shop Man, *see* My Onliest Little Dolly
The Phrenologist Coon
The Ping Pong Song
The Queen of Society

Rip van Winkle Was a Lucky Man
A Rose with a Broken Stem
The Royal Will
Sadie
Sadie, You'se Ma Lady-Bird
Sallie, Mah Hot Tamale
Sally's Sunday Hat
She's Getting More Like the White Folks Every Day
Simple Little Sister Mary Green
Spring Fashions
The Sunflower and the Sun
Susan, Dear Sue
Sweetheart, Sweetheart, I Wear the Blue
Take Me Back to Herald Square
The Tale of a Bumble Bee
Tell Me Dusky Maiden
Tell Us Pretty Ladies
There's Another on Board That Might Be Saved
There's No North or South Today
There's No Other Girl Like My Girl
There's One Rose That Will Never Bloom Again
The Tie That Binds
Toddle Song
Two Congregations
Walk, Walk, Walk
Way Down in Indiana
Way Down Yonder in the Cornfield
The Way That Walker Walked Away
The Wedding of the Reuben and the Maid
What'd Yo' Do Wid de Letter, Mr. Johnson?
When Mr. Shakespeare Comes to Town
When the Boys Go Marching By
When They Play "God Save the King"
When Two Hearts Are One
Where the Silv'ry Colorado Wends Its Way
Wilhemina
Zamona

1902

Acting
After You, My Dear Alphonse
Ain't It Tough to Be So Absent-Minded?
All Is Fair in Love and War
The Animals' Convention
Any Rags?
The Army of Peace
At the Steeplechase
Back among the Clover and the Bees
Back to the Woods
The Banquet in Misery Hall
The Bathing Lesson
Because
Bill Bailey, Won't You Please Come Home
The Bird That Never Sings
Blooming Lize
The Blue Button Army
Bygone Days in Dixie
The Captain of the Golf Club
Carmena
Come and Take a Stroll with Me
Come Down, Ma Evening Star
Coo!
Could You Be True to Eyes of Blue If You Looked into Eyes of Brown?
Courting
Der Faderland for Mine
Didn't Know Exactly What to Do
Does This Railroad Lead to Heaven?
Dooley's Alibi
Down in Dear Old Sunny Georgia Years Ago, *see* Down in Sunny Georgia Years Ago
Down in Sunny Georgia Years Ago
Down on the Farm
Down the Line with Molly
Down Where the Wurzburger Flows
Dream One Dream of Me
Du Barry, the Doll of the World
Emalyne, My Pretty Valentine
The Face in the Firelight
Follow the Man That Leads the Band
Following in Father's Footsteps
France, Glorious France

The Gambling Man
The Girl Who Loves the Races
The Girl with the Baby Stare
The Glow Worm
Good Night Lucindy
The Gypsy's Wedding
Hamlet Was a Melancholy Dane
Happy Hooligan
Have You Seen My Sweetheart in His Uniform of Blue?
Heidelberg
Hike!
Honey Will You Miss Me When I'm Gone?
I Always Wish 'Twas You
I Just Can't Help from Lovin' That Man
I Love the Moon
I Sing a Little Tenor
I Want to Be a Drummer in the Band
I Want to Be an Actor Lady
I Wants a Man Like Romeo
I Wants to Be the Villain in the Show
I Went to See Them March Away
I Wonder Why Bill Bailey Don't Come Home
I'd Like to Be a Real Lady
If Yankee Doodle Hadn't Come to Town
If You Can't Be a Bell-Cow, Fall in Behind
I'll Be There, Mary Dear
I'll Be with You Honey in the Springtime
I'll Be Your Rain-Beau
I'll Wed You in the Golden Summertime
I'm a Lady
I'm the Man Who Makes the Money in the Mint
I'm the Money Burner
I'm Unlucky
I'm Wearing My Heart Away for You
In Silence
In the City of Sighs and Tears
In the Good Old Summertime
In the Hills of Old Carolina
Instrumental Man
It Must Have Been Svengali in Disguise
It Rained a Mist
It's Got to Be a Minstrel Show Tonight
It's the Man in the Sailor Suit
Jennie
Jennie Lee
John Would Never Do That
Just a Tender Spot for Father Dear
Just for Tonight
Just Next Door
Katrina
Katy Did
Lady Bountiful
The Leader of the Frocks and Frills
The Lily or the Rose
The Limerick Girls
Linda, Look Out de' Windah
The Little Gypsy Maid
Liza
Louisiana Louise
Love a la Mode
The Mansion of Aching Hearts
Mary Be Wary
May Sweet May
The Meaning of U.S.A.
Meet Me When the Sun Goes Down
The Message of the Rose
The Message of the Violet
The Messiah of Nations
Microbes on the Brain, *see* Poor Barney Mulligan
Mister Dooley
My Angemima Green
My Eulah Eulah, My Indian Maid
My Firefly
My Gypsy Queen
My Madagascar Maid
My Otaheite Lady
My Own United States
My Pajama Beauty
My Particular Friend
My Pretty Zulu Lu
My Princess Zulu Lulu
My Starlight Queen
My Sulu Lulu Loo
Nancy, Oh Miss Nancy

Nursery Rhymes
Oh! Didn't He Ramble
Oh, Mr. Webster
On a Sunday Afternoon
O'O'O'Brien
Paint Me a Picture of Mama
Pajama Polly
Pansy of the Dell
The Phonograph March
Pinky Panky Poo
Pirate Song
Please Go Away and Let Me Sleep
Please Leave the Door Ajar
Poor Barney Mulligan
Pretty Little Dinah Jones
Pretty Maid Adelaide
The Proper Way to Kiss
Psyche
The Queen of the Track
R-E-M-O-R-S-E
Rainbows Follow After Rain
Returned
Romeo
Sally in Our Alley
Sammy
Scarecrow
Since Reuben's Gone Away
Since Sister Nell Heard Paderewski Play
Sly Musette
The Song That I Hear in My Dreams
The Stein Song, *see* Heidelberg
Strolling Along the Beach
Take Me Back to the Old Virginia Shore
There's a Lot of Things You Never Learn at School
Those Things Cannot Be Explained
The Troubles of Reuben and the Maid
Under Southern Skies
Under the Bamboo Tree
Upper Broadway After Dark
Wait at the Gate for Me
What's the Matter with the Moon Tonight?
When a Lady Leads the Band
When Charlie Plays the Slide Trombone in the Silver Cornet Band
When It's All Goin' Out and Nothin' Comin' In
When Kate and I Were Comin' thro' the Rye
When the Band Goes Marching By
When the Circus Comes to Town
When the Fields Are White with Cotton
When the Moon Comes Peeping Over the Hill
When the Sunset Turns to Ocean's Blue to Gold
When the Troupe Gets Back to Town
When the Winds O'er the Sea Blow a Gale
When You Come Back They'll Wonder Who the --- You Are
Where Is My Papa Tonight?
A Woman's No Means 'Yes'
You'll Always Be the Same Sweet Girl to Me

1903

The "A la Mode" Girl
Ain't Dat an Awful Feeling
Ain't It Funny What a Difference Just a Few Hours Make?
All Right!
Allessandro's Love Song, *see* Ramona
Although I Am a Soldier, I Prefer a Private Life
Always in the Way
American Beauty
The Apple, Apple, Apple of My Eye, *see* Love in an Orchard
Be Kind to Poor Pierrot
Beautiful Dreamy Eyes
Bedelia
The Beer That Made Milwaukee Famous
Beneath the Palms of Paradise
Bill Was There
The Boys in Blue Parade Today
The Boys in the Gallery for Mine

Brother Bill
The Burning of Rome
By the Sycamore Tree
Congo Love Song, *see* Marie Cahill's Congo Love Song
Daisy Donahue
Dear Old Girl
Devotion
Down at the Old Bull and Bush, *see* Under the Anheuser Bush
Down Where the Swanee River Flows
Egypt, My Cleopatra
The Fife and Drum
Flowers of Dixieland
The Garden of Dreams
General Hardtack on Guard
Girl of My Dreams
Good-bye, Eliza Jane
Good Fellows
Had She Only Let Me Dream an Hour More
He May Get Over It But He'll Never Look the Same
He Was a Sailor
Hearts You Lose
Her Boy in the Rank and File
Her Eyes of Irish Blue
Here's to Our Absent Brothers
He's the Whole Show Now
Hiawatha
The Humpty-Dumpty Kid
Hurrah for Baffin's Baby
I Could Love You in a Steam Heat Flat
I Knew at First Sight That I Loved You
I Love You Dolly
I Think of Thee
I Want to Go to Paree, Papa
I Would If I Could But I Can't
Ida, Sweet as Apple Cider
If I Were Only Mister Morgan
I'm a Jonah Man
I'm a Poor Unhappy Maid
In Old New York
In the Valley of Broken Hearts
In the Village by the Sea
An Irishman's Lilt
It Was the Dutch
Julie
June
Kashmiri Song
The Katy-Did, the Cricket and the Frog
A Kiss for Each Day of the Week
The Language of Flowers
The Last Farewell
Lazy Moon
The Leader of Vanity Fair
Like a Star That Falls from Heaven
Lindy
Little Mary
Little Widow Brown
Love
Love at the Door
Love in an Orchard
Love Is Elusive
Love Laughs at Locksmiths
The Lover's A.B.C.
Ma Mamselle Honee
Maggie McDonahue
The Maid of Timbucktoo
Mamma's Little Alabama Love
March of the Toys
Marie Cahill's Congo Love Song
Mary Had a Little Lamb
Meet Me Dear, on Saturday, a Little after Two
Melody of Love
Mister E. Z. Mark
Moriarty
Mother o' Mine
Mozart Lincoln
Must You?
My Cosy Corner Girl
My Dixie Land Daisy
My Hula Lula Girl
My Little Coney Island
My Little Creole Babe
My Little Hindoo Belle
My Little Japaneesee
My Little Rang Outang
My Little Star, I'm Looking Up to You
My Own Dear Irish Queen

My Palm Leaf Maid
My Waikiki Mermaid
Nava Jo
Oh! Take Me to My Mamma Dear
On a Spoony Moony Night
On a Starry Night
Only a Dream of a Golden Past
Out Where the Breakers Roar
Over the Pilsner Foam
Pansy Faces
People Who Live in Glass Houses Never Should Throw Any Stones
Plain Mamie O'Hooley
Please Mother, Buy Me a Baby
Queen of the Bungalow
Ramona
The Same Old Crowd
Save It for Me
The Seaside Sultan
Sister Ann
Sound of the Times, *see* Lindy
A Sprig of Rosemarie
Sweet Adeline, *see* You're the Flower of My Heart, Sweet Adeline
That's What the Daisy Said
There's a Little Star in Heaven That They Call Broadway
Toyland
Two Eyes
Two Eyes of Brown
Under the Anheuser Bush
Under the Mistletoe Bough
Watch Me To-night in the Torchlight Parade
Wed the Man That You Love or Don't Wed at All
What's the Matter with Uncle Sam?
When I Do the Highland Fling
When My Johnny Boy Goes Marching By
When We Were Two Little Boys
Where the Fairest Flowers Are Blooming
The Woodchuck Song
The Yankee Girl
Your Dad Gave His Life for His Country
You're the Flower of My Heart, Sweet Adeline

1904

Alexander, Don't You Love Your Baby No More?
All Aboard for Dreamland
Allus' the Same in Dixie
As the Sunflower Turns to the Sun
At the Music Hall
Back, Back, Back to Baltimore
The Bal Tabarin, *see* Meet Me at the Masquerade
Be Satisfied with What You Have, Let Well Enough Alone
Beatrice Barefacts
Bible Stories
Big Indian Chief
Billy
A Bit o' Blarney
Blue Bell
Blue Eyed Sue
Bunker Hill
By the Old Oak Tree
Cheyenne
Come Down from the Big Fig Tree
Come, Take a Trip in My Air-Ship
The Countess of Alagazam
Daisy Deane
Darktown Barbeque
Dolly
Down in Mulberry Bend
Down in the Subway
Fishing
For God and Home and Native Land
For You
The Game of Love
The Ghost That Never Walked
Gimme de Leavins'
The Girl Who Cares for Me
The Girl with the Eyes and the Golden Hair
Give My Regards to Broadway
Good-By, Teddy! You Must March! March! March!
Good-Bye, Little Girl, Good-Bye
Good Bye, My Lady Love

A Great Big Girl Like Me
Hannah, Won't You Open the Door?
He Done Me Wrong
Honey Boy
I Can't Take My Eyes off You
I Love You All the Time
I May Be Crazy But I Ain't No Fool
I Want to Be a Soldier
I'll Never Love Another Like I Love You
I'm a Yankee Doodle Dandy, *see* Yankee Doodle Boy
I'm Crazy to Go on the Stage
I'm Longing for My Old Kentucky Home
I'm Thinking 'bout You Honey All the While
Imagination
In Dreamland, In Dreamland
In the Folds of the Starry Flag
In the *Ladies' Home Journal*
In Zanzibar
It's All Right in the Summertime
Jack O'Lantern Girl
Just for the Sake of Society
Kate Kearney
Kiss Me Good Night, Dear Love
The Legend of the Maguire
Let's All Go Up to Maud's
Lights of Home
A Little Boy Named 'Taps'
Little Miss No-One from No-Where
Lola
Lonesome
Make Yourself at Home
The Man Behind
The Man with the Ladder and the Hose
Meet Me at the Masquerade
Meet Me in St. Louis, Louis
Mexico
Mister Wilson, That's All
"Mumms" the Word
My Little Chick
My Pretty Little Kick-a-poo
Nancy Clancy
No Bird Ever Flew So High He Didn't Have to Light
No One Can Take Your Place
No One Seems to Love Me Now
The Old, Old Story
On Lalawana's Shore
Over the Moonlit Sea
Piking the Pike
Poor Robinson Crusoe
The Preacher and the Bear
Pretty Kitty-San
Pretty Polly!
The Pussy and the Bow-Wow
A Quaint Old Bird
Right Is Might
Rosie Rosinsky
The Saftest of the Family
Sambo and Dinah
Scissors to Grind
Semiole
Since Little Dolly Dimples Made a Hit
Stop Your Tickling Jock!
The Story of a Clothes Line
Strolling on the Pike
Sweet Thoughts of Home
'Taint No Use in Lovin' That Way
Take a Pike at the Pike with Me, *see* Piking the Pike
Take These Flowers, Old Lady
Teasing
Ten Thousand Cattle Straying
Those Songs My Mother Used to Sing
Tilda from Old Savannah
Tippecanoo
The Troubadour
The Trumpeter
We Are Coming
What the Brass Band Played
When I'm Away from You Dear
When Love Was Young
When the Right Mr. Wright Comes Along
Why Adam Sinned
Won't You Fondle Me
Yankee Doodle Boy
Your Mother Wants You Home Boy

1905

ABCD
After the Battle
And the World Goes on Just the Same
The Band of Reubenville
Bright Eyes Good-Bye
Brother Masons
Bye-Bye, My Eva, Bye-Bye
Can't You See That I'm Lonely?
Carissima
Central, Give Me Back My Dime
Come Around to Mamie's
Come Over on My Veranda
The Conjure Man
Daddy's Little Girl
The Day That You Grew Colder
Deacon Jones
Dearie
Don't Be What You Ain't
Easy Street
Everybody Works But Father
Football
Fou the Noo
Gee! But This Is a Lonely Town
Gimme Hush Money or I'll Tell on You
Good-Bye, I'll See You Some More
Good-Bye, Maggie May
Good-Bye, Sweet Old Manhattan Isle
Goodbye, Sweetheart, Goodbye
G.O.P.
Hannah Dooley, Pride of Ballyhooley
The Heaven Born Banner
He's Me Pal
Hiram Green, Good-Bye
Honey Love Me All the Time
How'd You Like to Spoon with Me?
I Could Learn to Love You If You Let Me Try
I Don't Care
I Love a Lassie
I Think I Could Be Awfully Good to You
I Want a Man Made to Order for Me
I Want What I Want When I Want It
I Would Like to Be Your Pal
I Would Like to Marry You
If a Boy Like You Loved a Girl Like Me
If I Were on the Stage, *see* Kiss Me Again
I'll Be Waiting in the Gloaming, Sweet Genevieve
I'll Break the Fighting Line Like You Broke This Heart of Mine
I'm Getting Sleepy
I'm on My Way to Dublin Bay
I'm the Only Star That Twinkles on Broadway
I'm Trying to Find a Sweetheart
In a Hammock Built for Two
In Dear Old Georgia
In My Merry Oldsmobile
In the Cold Grey Dawn
In the Shade of the Old Apple Tree
In Vacation Time
The Indians Along Broadway
Inverary
The Irish Girl I Love
Is Everybody Happy?
It's a Waste of Time to Worry
It's Good Enough for Me
Just a Little Rocking Chair and You
Keep a Little Cozy Corner in Your Heart for Me
Kiss Me Again
Let Me See You Smile
A Little Girl Like Me
Little Girl, You'll Do
Liz'
The Load That Father Carried
Ma Scotch Bluebell, *see* I Love a Lassie
Moon Dear
The Moon Has His Eyes on You
Moonlight
My Dusky Rose
My Gal Sal
My Hindoo Man
My Irish Daisy
My Irish Indian
My Irish Maid
My Irish Molly O
My Sweet
My Syncopated Gypsy Maid

Nellie Dean
Nobody
Oh, So Gently
On an Automobile Honeymoon
On the Banks of the Rhine with a Stein
One Called "Mother" and the Other "Home Sweet Home"
A Picnic for Two
Pretty Desdemona
Remember Dear
Robinson Crusoe's Isle
Rufus Rastus Johnson Brown, *see* What You Goin' to Do When the Rent Comes 'Round?
She Is Ma Daisy
Spoon Time
Swing Me High, Swing Me Low
The Tale of a Stroll
Tammany
They Call Her Frivolous Sal, *see* My Gal Sal
The Time and the Place and the Girl
The Town Where I Was Born
The Umpire Is a Most Unhappy Man
Violette
Wait 'Till the Sun Shines, Nellie
The Waltz Must Change to a March, Marie
Waltzing with the Girl You Love
We've Been Chums for Fifty Years
What You Goin' to Do When the Rent Comes 'Round?
What You Want and What You Get
When the Bell in the Lighthouse Rings Ding, Dong
When the Right Little Girl Comes Along
Where the Morning Glories Twine around the Door
Where the River Shannon Flows
The Whistler and His Dog
The Whole Dam Family
Why Dont You Try?
Will You Love Mc in December as You Do in May?
You're My Heart's Desire, *see* Nellie Dean

1906

Ain't You Coming Back to Old New Hampshire, Molly?
Ain't You Got Nothing to Say?
Alamo
All In Down and Out
All the Girls Love Me
Anchors Aweigh
Any Old Time at All
Are You Coming Out Tonight, Mary Ann?
Arrah-Wanna
The Bee That Gets the Honey Doesn't Hang Around the Hive
The Bird on Nellie's Hat
Blow the Smoke Away
The Burning of Frisco Town
By the Light of the Honeymoon
Captain Baby Bunting of the Rocking Horse Brigade
Carry Me Back to Old Virginny
Colleen Bawn
Come, Take a Skate with Me
Daisy Dear
Day Dreams
Do Re Me Fa So La Si Do
Don't Go in the Lion's Cage Tonight, Mother
Don't You Think It's Time to Marry?
Don't You Want a Paper, Dearie?
Dreaming
Every Saturday Afternoon
Everything Is Rosy, Rosie
Farewell Killarney
Father's Got a Job
Forty-five Minutes from Broadway
The Good Old U.S.A.
He Handed Me a Lemon
He's a Cousin of Mine
His Eye Is on the Sparrow
Holding Hands
Honeymoon
The Hurricane
I Guess I'll Take the Train Back Home
I Just Can't Make My Eyes Behave
I Miss You in a Thousand Different Ways

I Thought My Troubles Were Over, But They'd Scarce Begun
If Adam Hadn't Seen the Apple Tree
If Anybody Wants to Meet a Jonah, Shake Hands with Me
If I Ever Get Back to Cincinnati
If You Can't Say Something Good, Don't Say Nothing at All
I'll Keep a Warm Spot in My Heart for You
I'm Sorry
In Old New York, *see* The Streets of New York
In Washington
The Island of By and By
It Ain't All Honey and It Ain't All Jam
It's Delightful to Be Married
I've Got to Dance Till the Band Gets Through
The Judgement Is at Hand
Keep on the Sunny Side
Kiss All the Girls for Me
Kiss, Kiss, Kiss, If You Want to Learn to Kiss
Kiss This Rose and Say "He Loves Me", *see* While the Old Mill Wheel Is Turning
A Lemon in the Garden of Love
Let It Alone
The Linger Longer Girl
Little One, Good Bye
Look Who's Here
Love Me and the World Is Mine
Mariutch, She Come Back to Me
Mary
Mary Is a Grand Old Name, *see* Mary
Meet Me at Twilight
Meet Me Down at the Corner
Mister Monkey
Mother Has Got the Habit Now
My Billy Boy
My Irish Girl
My Irish Rose
My Little Rambling Rose
My Mariuccia Take a Steamboat
My Mississippi Missus Misses Me
The Next Horse I Ride On
No Wedding Bells for Me
Not Because Your Hair Is Curly
Oh, How I Love My Teacher
Old Reliable Jokes
On San Francisco Bay
A Parisian Model
Pawnee
Percy
Percy
Pierrot and Pierrette
Poor John
The Poor Old Man
Popular Songs
Red Domino
Say! Fay!
School Days
Shovelin' Coal
Silver Sleigh Bells
Since Father Went to Work
Since Nellie Went Away
So Long, Mary
Somebody's Waiting for You
Sorry, I Ain't Got It, You Could Have It If I Had It Blues, *see* All In Down and Out
Spring Song
The Streets of New York
Sugar Mine
Sweetie Dear
That's the Reason Noo I Wear a Kilt
There's a Time and a Place for Everything
Waiting at the Church
Waltz Me Around Again, Willie
What's the Use of Dreaming
When Love Comes Knocking at the Door
When Love Is Young
When the Whipporwill Sings Marguerite
When Tommy Atkins Marries Dolly Gray
When We Were a Couple of Kids, *see* School Days
When You Know You're Not Forgotten by the Girl You Can't Forget

While the Old Mill Wheel Is Turning
Wonderland
You Don't Say Nothing at All, *see* Holding Hands
You're a Grand Old Flag
You're in Love
You're in Love

1907

Advertising
Ain't It Funny Just What Money Does for You
All I Want in the Wide Wide World Is You
All She Gets from the Iceman Is Ice
And a Little Bit More
And He Blames My Dreamy Eyes
Ballooning
Be Good! If You Can't Be Good Be Careful
Be My Teddy Bear
Be Sweet to Me, Kid
Because I'm Married Now
Beneath the Moon
Bon Bon Buddy
Bonnie Sue Sunshine
The Boy Who Stuttered and the Girl Who Lisped
BPOE
Brother Noah Gave Out Checks for Rain
Budweiser's a Friend of Mine
Build Your Nest Away Down in My Heart
Bye Bye Dear Old Broadway
Bye Bye Dearie
The Chocolate Drop, *see* Bon Bon Buddy
Come Along My Mandy
Come Around on Our Veranda
Come to the Land of Bohemia
Common Sense
Dat Lovin' Rag
Don't Worry
Eastern Moon
The Elks Song, *see* BPOE
Fas' Fas' World
The Friars
Get Happy
The Gibson Bathing Girl
The Girl of the Great Divide
The Girl with the Big Toy Bear
The Gypsy's Warning
Handle me with Care
He Goes to Church on Sunday
Honey Boy
How'd You Like to Float Me
I Can't Think of Nothing in the Wide, Wide World But You
I Get Dippy When I Do That Two-Step Dance
I Just Can't Keep My Eyes Off You
I Just Couldn't Do without You
I Love You So
I Want a Gibson Man
I Want a Girl Just Like the Girl That Married Dear Old Dad
I Want to Be a Merry Merry Widow
I Wish I Had a Girl
I'd Like to Meet Your Father
I'd Rather Two-Step Than Waltz, Bill
If You'll Walk with Me
I'm Afraid to Come Home in the Dark
I'm Looking for the Man That Wrote "The Merry Widow Waltz"
I'm Tying the Leaves So They Won't Come Down
In the Wildwood Where the Bluebells Grew
Irish Fluffy Ruffles
It May Not All Be True, *see* Don't Worry
It's Hard to Love Somebody Who's Loving Somebody Else
I've a Million Reasons Why I Love You
I've Been Looking for a Girl Like You
I've Made My Plans for the Summer
I've Told His Missus All about Him
Just Because He Couldn't Sing "Love Me and the World Is Mine"
A Kiss in the Dark
The Land of Nicotine

The Last Rose of Summer Is the Sweetest Song of All
Late Hours
Lila
Little Nemo and His Bear
Loving Eyes
Make Believe
Marie from Sunny Italy
Mariutch Down at Coney Island
Mariutch Make a the Hootch a Ma Kootch, *see* Mariutch Down at Coney Island
May, May, May
Meet Me with Spangles and Bells On
Merry Widow Waltz
The Modern Sandow Girl
My Cigarette Maid, *see* The Land of Nicotine
My Fox Trot Girl
My Irish Gibson Girl
My Pocahontas
My Teddy Girl
My Twilight Queen
'Neath the Old Acorn Tree, Sweet Estelle
'Neath the Old Cherry Tree, Sweet Marie
No, No, Positively No
No One Knows
Not for Me
Nothing Bothers Me
On the Grand Old Sand
On the Old See-Saw
On the Road to Mandalay
Paree
The Peach That Tastes the Sweetest Hangs the Highest on the Tree
The Police Won't Let Mariutch-a Dance, Unless She Move-a-da-Feet
Pride of the Prairie
Put Me Among the Girls
The Queen of the Night
Rob Roy McIntosh
Rum-Tiddely-Um-Tum-Tay Out for the Day Today
Somebody Lied
Sunrise at the Zoo
Take Me Around Again
Take Me Back to New York Town
The Teddy Bears' Picnic
That's How He Met the Girl
Theodore
Tiddley-Om-Pom
Tipperary
Tipperary Nora
Under the Linden Tree
Under the Matzos Tree
Under the Rosenbloom
Vanity Fair
Vilia
When a Fellow's on the Level with a Girl That's on the Square
When a Girl Leads the Band
When Miss Patricia Salome Did Her Funny Little Oh-la Pa-lome
When the Moon Plays Peek-a-Boo
When Your Lips Pressed Mine
The Wiggle-Woggle Dance, *see* Paree
Will the Circle Be Unbroken?
Without the Girl Inside
Won't You Be My Baby Boy?
Won't You Be My Honey?
Won't You Waltz 'Home Sweet Home' with Me for Old Times Sake?
Yo' Eyes Are Open, But Yo' Sound Asleep
You Can't Guess What He Wrote on My Slate
You Splash Me and I'll Splash You

1908

Aloha Oe
The American Rag Time
And Other Things
Any Old Port in a Storm
Arrah-Arabia
B-I-Double L Bill
Betty, You're the One Best Bet
The Big Red Shawl
Bill? Bill Taft
Bill Taft for 1908
Bonnie My Highland Lassie
Come Along Up in the Flip Flap

Cuddle Up a Little Closer, Lovey Mine
Daisies Won't Tell
Dear I Love You So
Don't Go in the Water, Daughter
Down Among the Sugar-Cane
The Dusky Salome
The Fairest of the Fair
Farewell to Thee, *see* Aloha Oe
The Farrar Waltz, *see* Gay Butterfly
Feed the Kitty
Fireflies
The Garden of Dreams
Gay Butterfly
Gee! But There's Class to a Girl Like You
Get in Line for Big Bill Taft
The Gibson Widow
Goo-Goo Eyes
Good Bye Mister Ragtime
Good Night Dear
Googy-Oo
H-A-Double R-I-G-A-N
Harrigan, *see* H-A-Double R-I-G-A-N
Hat Song
Have You Seen My Baby?
A Heart That's Free
Hooray for a Bryan to Lead Us
The Hornpipe Rag
I Ain't Had No Lovin' in a Long Time
I Am So Particular
I Hear You Calling Me
I Love to Sit and Look at You
I Remember You
I Want to Be Loved Like a Leading Lady
I Want to Be Naughty Too
I Want to Go Back to the Land of Cotton
I Wonder If They're True to Me
I Wonder What's the Matter with My Eyes?
If You Love Your Baby Google Google All the Time
I'm a Yiddish Cowboy
I'm Glad I'm Married
In My Old Home
It's Moonlight All the Time on Broadway
It's the Pretty Things You Say
I've Lost My Teddy Bear
Kerry Mills' Barn Dance
Kinky
Laugh and the World Will Laugh with You, Weep and You'll Weep All Alone
Line Up for Bryan
The Longest Way 'Round Is the Sweetest Way Home
Lotus San: A Japanese Romance
Love Days
Love Me Like I Want to Be Loved
Lovesick
Loving Time
Make a Noise Like a Hoop and Roll Away
The Man Who Fights the Fire
Mandy Lane
McGinnis
Meet Me in Rose Time Rosie
The Merry Widow Waltz Song
Mother Hasn't Spoken to Father Since
My Brudda Sylvest'
My Fluff-a de Ruff
Naughty Eyes
The Nell Brinkley Girl
None of Them's Got Anything on Me
Nulife
O, Southland
Oh, Miss Malinda
The Old Maids' Ball
Pansies Mean Thoughts and Thoughts Mean You
Put Me Upon an Island
Rag Babe
Rainbow
Red Red Rose
Redhead
The Road to Yesterday
Roses Bring Dreams of You
Shine On, Harvest Moon
Since My Mariutch Learned the Merry Widow Waltz
A Singer Sang a Song

Smarty
Stars of the National Game
Step into Line for Taft
Sunbonnet Sue
Sweetest Gal in Town
Take a Trip Down to Luna with Me
Take Me Out to the Ball Game
Take Me 'Round in a Taxicab
There's a Parson Only 20 Miles Away, *see* When It's Moonlight on the Prairie
Tough-Guy Levi, *see* I'm a Yiddish Cowboy
Valse de Concert, *see* A Heart That's Free
A Vision of Salome
A Vision of Salome
What Makes the World Go Round
When Evening Time Comes 'Round, *see* Oh, Miss Malinda
When Highland Mary Did the Highland Fling
When I Get Back to Bonnie Scotland
When It's Moonlight on the Prairie
When My Bridget Malone Jiggle-Wiggles Salome
When Tetrazzini Sings
When You First Kiss the Last Girl You Love
The White Wash Man
Who Knows?
Will Taft, We're Looking to You
Won't You Be My Valentine?
Would You Rather Be a Tammany Tiger than a Teddy Bear?
The Yama Yama Man
Yes She Does, *see* I'm Glad I'm Married
Yip-I-Addy-I-Ay
You Never Miss the Water 'Till the Well Runs Dry
You Will Have to Sing an Irish Song
Your Eyes Say No But Your Lips Say Yes!
You're in the Right Church But the Wrong Pew
You've Got to Do That Salome Dance

1909

Abie, the Sporty Kid
The Aero Naughty Girls
Alexander Jones
All the Nice Girls Love a Sailor, *see* Ship Ahoy
Alma, Where Do You Live?
Amo
Angel Eyes
As Long as the World Goes Around
Baby Lamb
The Baltimore Bombashay
Bandy Legs
Beautiful Eyes
Believe Me!
The Belle of Brittany, *see* I Can't Reach That Top Note
Blarney
Boys, the Old Flag Never Touched the Ground
The Brinkley Bathing Girl
By the Light of the Silvery Moon
Bye-O Baby Bunting
Carnations, *see* Clavelitos
Casey Jones
The Christy Girl
Ciribiribin
Clavelitos
Come After Breakfast, Bring 'long You' Lunch and Leave 'fore Supper Time
Come On, Play Ball with Me
Come Right In, Sit Right Down and Make Yourself at Home
Could You Learn to Love Me?
The Cubanola Glide
The Dawn of a Tomorrow
Everybody's Ragtime Crazy
Falling Star
Foolish Questions
For You Alone
Garden of Roses
Gee But Ain't America a Grand Old Place
Gee! I'd Like to Be the Mayor
Glad, *see* The Dawn of a Tomorrow
The Glory of the Yankee Navy
Go Easy Mabel

Good-Bye Christina Swanson
Good-Bye Girlie and Remember Me
Good-Bye Mister Caruso
Good Luck Mary
Hail the Waistmakers!
The Harbor of Lost Dreams
Has Anybody Here Seen Kelly?
Heaven Will Protect the Working Girl
He's a Fan, Fan, Fan
Heure exquise qui nous grise
I Am Longing for Tomorrow When I Think of Yesterday
I Can't Reach That Top Note
I Didn't Go Home at All
I Love My Husband But Oh You Henry
I Love My Wife But Oh, You Kid!
I Thought I Wanted Opera
I Want to Be a Prima Donna
I Wish I Had My Old Girl Back Again
I Wonder If You're Lonely
I Wonder Who's Kissing Her Now
I'd Like to Be the Fellow That Girl Is Waiting For
If I Could Only Sleep Like Rip Van Winkle
If I Thought You Wouldn't Tell
If the Wind Had Only Blown the Other Way
If You Ain't Got It, Go and Get It
I'm a Bringing Up the Family
I'm a Member of the Midnight Crew
I'm After Madame Tettrazzini's Job
I'm All O.K. with K. and E.
I'm Awfully Glad I Met You
I'm Glad I'm a Boy/I'm Glad I'm a Girl
I'm Going to Do What I Please
I'm Learning Something Every Day
I've Got Rings on My Fingers
I've Loved Her Ever Since She Was a Baby
Let's Get the Umpire's Goat
Let's Go to a Picture Show
Linger Longer Lingerie
Little Mary Gardeners
Lonesome
Love Me All the Time
Madame Venus, *see* Take a Tip from Venus
Mamenu
Meet Me Tonight in Dreamland
My Cousin Caruso
My Pony Boy
My Sist' Tetrazzin'
My Wife's Gone to the Country
Next to Your Mother Who Do You Love?
Nora Malone, Call Me by Phone
Oh, You Candy Kid
Oh, You Devil Rag
Ood-kay Oo-yay Earn-lay Oo-tay Ove-Lay Ee-may?, *see* Could You Learn to Love Me?
Personality
Play That Fandango Rag
The Pony Ballet Girl
Put on Your Old Grey Bonnet
Rip Van Winkle Was a Lucky Man But Adam Had Him Beat a Mile
Sadie Salome Go Home
Sail On!
Salome
She Was a Dear Little Girl
Ship Ahoy
Stop That Rag
The Sum of Life
Sweet Italian Love
Sweet Marie Make-a Rag-a Time-a-Dance with Me
Take a Tip from Venus
Take Me Back to Babyland
That Hypnotizing Rag
That Mesmerizing Mendelssohn Tune
That Spanish Rag
That Teasin' Rag
That's a Plenty
Way Down in Cotton Town
The Wearing of the Green
What Has That Man Harrigan Done?
What's the Use of Moonlight When There's No One 'Round to Love?

When I Dream in the Gloaming of You
When You and I Were Young, Maggie
Wild Cherries
Yiddle on Your Fiddle Play Some Rag Time
You Taught Me to Love You, Now Teach Me to Forget

1910

Ah, Sweet Mystery of Life
Alexander and His Clarinet
Alias Jimmy Valentine
All That I Ask of You Is Love
Any Little Girl That's a Nice Little Girl Is the Right Little Girl for Me
Back to My Old Home Town
Back to the Bleachers for Mine
Baltimore Rag
Beckie, Stay in Your Own Backyard
Becky Do the Bombashay
Bring Back My Lena to Me
By the Saskatchewan
Call 00-00-00-00-0, *see* I Want a Real Nice Man
Call Me Up Some Rainy Afternoon
Can You Forget
The Chanticleer Rag
Chinatown, My Chinatown
Come Back to Me
Come Josephine in My Flying Machine
Come Over and Love Me Some More, *see* Stop! Stop! Stop!
The Comet and the Moon
Constantly
Coster Rag
Cupid's I.O.U.
Cutey, Tell Me Who Tied Your Tie?
Dat Draggy Rag
Dat Possum Rag
De Little Pickaninny's Gone to Sleep
Dill Pickles Rag
Doing That Grizzly Bear, *see* The Grizzly Bear
Don't Take a Girlie to Coney (You May Find a Nicer One There)
Don't Wake Me Up I Am Dreaming
Don't Walk So Fast
Down by the Old Mill Stream
Dream Melody, *see* Ah, Sweet Mystery of Life
Dreamy Fandango Tune
Eight Little Girls
The End of a Perfect Day, *see* A Perfect Day
Every Laddie Loves a Lassie
Every Little Movement
Flippity-Flop
French Fandango
Give an Imitation of Me
The Grizzly Bear
Havana
Honey, I Will Long for You
Hoop-la, I'm Having the Time of My Life
I Can't Help It
I Love My Steady, But I'm Crazy for My Once-in-a-While
I Want a Real Nice Man
I Want Someone to Flirt with Me
I Wonder If You Love Me
I'd Like to Live in Loveland with a Girl Like You
If He Comes In, I'm Going Out
If I Should Die Before I Wake, How Will I Know I'm Dead?
I'll Be With You Honey When It's Honeysuckle Time
I'll Lend You Everything I've Got Except My Wife
I'm Awfully Glad I'm Irish
I'm Falling in Love with Some One
I'm Looking for a Dear Old Lady
I'm Looking for a Dear Old Lady
I'm on My Way to Reno
In de Evenin'
In My Dreams of You
Innocent Bessie Brown
It Never, Never Can Be Love
Italian Street Song

I've Got the Time, I've Got the Place, But It's Hard to Find the Girl
Just a Dream of You, Dear
The Kellerman Girlie
Kelly Has Gone to Kingdom Come
Kidland
Kiss Me, My Honey, Kiss Me
Let Me Call You Sweetheart
Let Me Live and Stay in Dixieland
Let's Make Love among the Roses
Look Out for Jimmy Valentine, *see* Alias Jimmy Valentine
Love Me with a Tiger Love
Lovie Joe
Lucy Anna Lou
The Manicure Girl
Mr. Moon Man, Turn Off Your Light, *see* Turn Off Your Light, Mr. Moon Man
Mister Sweeney, A Brainy Man
Molasses Candy
Mother Machree
My Heart Has Learned to Love You Now Do Not Say Good-Bye
My Heart Is Thine, *see* O Sole Mio
My Operatic Samson
My Yankee Doodle Girl
Napoleon's Last Charge
Naughty Marietta
'Neath the Southern Moon
Nix on the Glow-Worm, Lena
O Sole Mio
Oh, How That German Could Love
Oh, That Moonlight Glide
Oh! You Chicken
The Pensacola Mooch
A Perfect Day
Philomene, *see* French Fandango
Piano Man
Play That Barbershop Chord
Put Your Arms Around Me, Honey
Ragtime Table d'Hote
Rosa Rigoletto
Rubber Necking Moon
Sadie Brady Listen Good to Me
She's a Patient of Mine
Some of These Days
Stop! Stop! Stop!
Sweet Kitty Bellairs
Sweet Suzanne
The Tanguay Rag
Teddy Da Roose
That Beautiful Rag
That Dreamy Barcarole Tune
That Dreamy Italian Waltz
That La-La Melody
That Loving Traumerei
That Minor Strain
That's Everlasting Love
That's Why They Call Me Shine
That's Yiddisha Love
There's a Mother Old and Gray Who Needs Me Now
Today's My Wedding Day
Tramp, Tramp, Tramp
Try It on Your Piano
Turn Off Your Light, Mr. Moon Man
Under the Yum Yum Tree
Way Down East
What's the Matter with Father?
When My Sist' Tetrazin' Met My Cousin Carus'
When Yankee Doodle Teddy Boy Comes Marching Home Again
White Folks Call It Chanticleer But It's Still Just Plain Chicken to Me
Whoop 'er Up with a Whoop La La
Yiddisha Eyes
You Are the Ideal of My Dreams
You're Gwine to Get Somethin' What You Don't Expect
You're Just Too Sweet to Live

1911

Alexander's Rag-Time Band
All the World Loves a Lover
Angelique
Another Star
The Argentine
Baby Rose
Barnyard Rag
The Baseball Glide
Belle of the Ball
Billy

Bless Your Ever Loving Little Heart
Bumble Bee
Come and Dance with Me
The Coster's Glide
Cuddle Up Honey, Let's Make Love
Dat Lovin' Touch
Dat's Harmony
Day of Hope and Day of Glory, *see* Woman's Right Is Woman's Duty
De Goblin's Glide
Dear Land of Home
Dear Mamie, I Love You
The Deedle-Dum-Dee
Do It the Right Way
Don't Take Your Beau to the Seashore
The Edinboro Wiggle
Eight Little Letters Make Three Little Words
Ephraham Played Upon the Piano
Everybody's Doin' It Now
Farmyard Blues
Fishing
The Gaby Glide
Gee, Its a Wonderful Game
Go Slow Joe
Honey Love
Honey Man
The Honky-Tonky Monkey Rag
How Do You Do It Mabel on $20 a Week?
I Always Dream of Bill, *see* Billy
I Got a Rock
I Live Up-Town
I Love My Babe, My Baby Loves Me
I Think It Must Be Love
I Want a Little Lovin' Sometimes
I Want Something New to Play With
I Want to Be in Dixie, *see* I'm Going Back to Dixie
I Want to Spoon to the Tune of the Silvery Moon
I Won't Come Back
I'd Rather Love What I Cannot Have Than Have What I Cannot Love
If All My Dreams Were Made of Gold, I'd Buy the World for You
If I Forget
If You Knew What I Know about Men
I'm a Crazy Daffydil
I'm Crazy 'bout the Turkey Trot
I'm Getting Kind of Lonesome for My Old Kentucky Pal
I'm Going Back to Dixie
I'm the Only Mother That You Ever Knew
In the Days of Girls and Boys
In the Land of Harmony
In the Shadows
In the Valley of Mont Bijou
The Island of Roses and Love
It Was Me
Killarney, My Home o'er the Sea
Let Us Have Peace
Lillies Mean You to Me
A Little Bit of Irish
Little Grey Home in the West
Little Lovin' Honey Man, *see* Honey Man
Lord Have Mercy on a Married Man
Love Is Mine
Love Me, Make Me Love You Like I Never Loved Before
Lovie Dear
Loving Moon
The Maid of Old Madrid
Mammy's Shufflin' Dance
Mister Yodeling Man
Molly-O Oh Molly
Mon Amour
Movin' Man Don't Take My Baby Grand
Musical Moon
My Melancholy Baby
My Sweet Suzanna
My Sweetheart, *see* Mon Amour
My Yiddische Colleen
Oh, Mr. Dream Man
Oh, You Beautiful Doll
Oh, You Wonderful Girl
The Pink Lady Waltz
Pots and Pans
Rag-Time Violin
Ragging the Old Vienna Roll
The Ragtime College Girl

Red Pepper Rag
The Red Rose Rag
Roamin' in the Gloamin'
Run Home and Tell Your Mother
Same Sort of Girl
Send Me a Kiss by Wireless
The Spaniard That Blighted My Life
Spanish Love
Take Me Back to the Garden of Love
Texas Tommy Swing
That Baboon Baby Dance
That Carolina Rag
That Dying Rag
That Humming Tune
That Hypnotizing Man
That Long Lost Chord
That Mysterious Rag
Too Much Mustard, *see* Tres Moutarde
Tres Moutarde
Trop Moutarde, *see* Tres Moutarde
When Ragtime Rosie Ragged the Rosary
When Ragtime Rufus Rags the Humoresque
When There's No Light at All
When Tony LaBoard Played the Barber-Shop Chord
When You Hear Love's "Hello"
When You're in Town in My Home Town
Whippoorwill
Whistling Rag
With the Last Rose of Summer, I'll Come Back to You
Woman's Right Is Woman's Duty
Woodman, Woodman Spare That Tree
Yiddisha Nightingale
You Can't Expect Kisses from Me
You'll Do the Same Thing Over Again
You'll Never Know the Good Fellow I've Been, 'Till I've Gone Away

1912

After All That I've Been to You
Alexander's Bag-Pipe Band
And the Green Grass Grew All Around
At the Devil's Ball
At the Levee on Revival Day
Baby Seals Blues
The Bacchanal Rag
The Band Played "Nearer My God to Thee" as the Ship Went Down
Be My Little Baby Bumble Bee
Beans
Beautiful Beautiful Girl
Beautiful Bird of Paradise
Beautiful Dreams of You
Becky's Got a Job in a Musical Show
Berceuse Tendre, *see* Love's Lullaby
Billy Billy, Bounce Your Baby Doll
Blackberrying Today
The Blues
Borrow from Me
Bread and Roses
Bye and Bye
Call Again
Call Me in the Morning
Come Back to Me My Melody
Come Back to Playland with Me
Daddy Has a Sweetheart and Mother Is Her Name
Dallas Blues
Dearie, Won't You Call Me Dearie, *see* Next Sunday at Nine
Don't Turn My Picture to the Wall
Dreams of Long Ago
Everybody Loves a Chicken
The Gertrude Hoffmann Glide
Gianina Mia
The Golden Stairs of Love
He Played It on His Fid, Fid, Fiddle-dee-dee
Hello Cupid, Send Me a Fellow
He's Coming Home on the 8 O'Clock Train
I've Got the Blues But I'm Too Blamed Mean to Cry, *see* The Blues
Just a Little Word Unspoken
Keep Away from the Fellow Who Owns an Automobile

Lady Angeline
The Language of Lover's Smiles
Last Night Was the End of the World
The Last Shot Got Him
Lead Me to That Beautiful Band
Let Us Be Sweethearts Again, *see* Just a Little Word Unspoken
Let Us Build a Little Nest
Listen to Me
Lonesome Honey for You
Louie, Take Me to the Frisco Fair
Love Is Like a Firefly
Love Lifted Me
Lovely Daughter of Allah
Love's Lullaby
Love's Own Sweet Song
The Marquand Glide
The Maurice Glide
The Maurice Tango
Maurice's Rag
Melody Chimes
Mind the Paint
Mister Pagliatch
Montezuma
Moonlight Bay
My Bird of Paradise
My Landlady
My Marguerite
My Sumurun Girl
Next Sunday at Nine
No One Knows Where the Old Man Goes
Nosie Rosie Posie
Oh! What a Beautiful Dream You Seem
Oh, What a Night
Oh! You Circus Day
Oh! You Georgia Rose
On a Beautiful Night with a Beautiful Girl
On Moonlight Bay, *see* Moonlight Bay
On the Mississippi
Paree's a Branch of Broadway
Parisienne
Pick, Pick, Pick, Pick on the Mandolin, Antonio
Pinkerton Detective Man
Please Don't Take My Lovin' Man Away
Rag-Time Cowboy Joe
Ragging the Baby to Sleep
Ragtime Eyes
Ragtime Jockey Man
Ragtime Mockingbird
Ragtime Soldier Man
Remember Me to My Old Girl
Ring-Ting-a-Ling
The Roaring Volcano
Roll Them Roly Boly Eyes
Roosevelt
Row Row Row
Snap Your Fingers and Away You Go
Some Boy
Somebody's Coming to Town from Dixie
Spring and Fall
String a Ring of Roses 'Round Your Rosie
Sumurun
The Sweetheart of Sigma Chi
Take a Little Tip from Father
Take Me in Your Arms and Say You Love Me
Take Me to That Swanee Shore
Take Me to the Cabaret
Teach Me That Beautiful Love
That English Rag
That Hypnotizing Strain
That Mellow Strain
That Old Girl of Mine
That Sneaky Snaky Rag
That Society Bear
That Syncopated Boogie Boo
That's How I Need You
There's One in a Million Like You
The Villain Still Pursued Her
Votes for Women
Waiting for the Robert E. Lee
Way Down South
The Wedding Glide
We're Ready for Teddy Again
We've Had a Lovely Time, So Long, Good Bye
When I Get You Alone Tonight

When I Lost You
When Irish Eyes Are Smiling
When It's Apple Blossom Time in Normandy
When Mother Plays a Rag on the Sewing Machine
When That Midnight Choo-Choo Leaves for Alabam'
When Uncle Joe Plays a Rag on His Old Banjo
Wilson--That's All
You're My Baby
You're on the Right Road Sister But You're Goin' the Wrong Way

1913

All Aboard for Dixie
All Aboard for Dixieland, *see* All Aboard for Dixie
All the Little Lovin' That I Had for You Is Gone, Gone, Gone
Always Take a Girl Named Daisy ('cause Daisies Won't Tell)
The American Maid
And Then
Anti-Rag Time Girl
At Mammy's Fireside
At That Bully Wooly Wild West Show
At the Ball, That's All
The Awakening
Boom-Tum-Ta-Ra-Ra-Zing-Boom
Brighten the Corner Where You Are
Bring Me Back My Lovin' Honey Boy
Chic-Chic-Chic-Chic-Chicken
Come Dance with Me
Come On, Let's Razoo on Our Little Kazoo
The Concert in the Sky
'Cross the Great Divide, I'll Wait for You
The Curse of an Aching Heart
Danny Boy
Darling
Deep River
Dinah
Do You Take This Woman for Your Lawful Wife?
Don't You Wish You Were Back Home Again?
Down in Chattanooga
Dreaming
El Choclo
Everybody Sometime Must Love Some One
Floating Down the River
Floreine
The Flower Garden Ball
A Fool There Was
Good Bye My Home Sweet Home
Happy Little Country Girl
He'd Have to Get Under, Get Out and Get Under to Fix Up His Automobile
Hello Honey
Honey, You Were Made for Me
I Can Live without You
I Can't Get Enough of Your Love
I Don't Want To
I Love Her Oh! Oh! Oh!
I Want to Look Like Lillian Russell
I Wonder Where My Easy Rider's Gone
If a Table at Rector's Could Talk
If I Had My Way
If You Don't Want Me
I'll Change the Shadows to Sunshine
I'll Get You
I'll Still Believe in You
I'm All Dressed Up and No Where to Go
I'm Going Back to Carolina
I'm on My Way to Manadalay
In a Little Cottage by the Railroad Track
In My Harem
In the Candlelight
In the Heart of the City That Has No Heart
The Junk Man Rag
Just a Kiss, *see* The Raffles Dance
Just a Kiss
Just Because It's You
Just for Tonight

Keep on Walking
Keep Your Golden Gate Wide Open
The Little Church around the Corner
Little Rag Baby Doll
Look in Her Eyes
Love Me While the Loving Is Good
Lucky in Love
Maori Farewell Song, *see* Now Is the Hour
Marcheta
Martyrs of Columbia
Maurice Hesitation
Maurice Irresistable
Maurice Mattchiche
Melinda's Wedding Day
Memphis Blues, *see* Mister Crump Blues
Mister Crump Blues
My Friend from Kentucky
My Heart for You Pines Away
My Old Log Cabin Home
My Skylark Love
Now Is the Hour
Oh! You Million Dollar Doll
The Old Gypsy
On a Good Old Time Sleigh Ride
On the Old Front Porch
Over the Garden Wall
Peg o' My Heart
The Raffles Dance
The Raffles Dance, *see* Just a Kiss
Ragging the Nursery Rhymes
The Ragtime Dream
Rebecca of Sunnybrook Farm
Sabbath Chimes
Salvation Nell
San Francisco Bound
Since My Margarette Become-a da Suffragette
Since You Went Away
Snooky Ookums
Sombody Loves You
Somebody's Coming to My House
The Song of the Melorose
Syncopatia Land
Take Me Back
A Tango Dream
Tango Is the Dance for Me
That International Rag
That Naughty Melody
That's an Irish Lullaby, *see* Too-ra-loo-ra-loo-ra
There's a Girl in the Heart of Maryland with a Heart That Belongs to Me
There's a Long, Long Trail
They've Got Me Doin' It Now
Those Days of Long Ago
To Have, To Hold, To Love
Too-ra-loo-ra-loo-ra
The Trail of the Lonesome Pine
Trixie from Dixie
Underneath the Tango Moon
Valse Marguerite
A Ven Cigany, *see* The Old Gypsy
We Have So Much to Be Thankful For
When Gaby Did the Gaby Glide
When I Want to Settle Down
When the Whole World Has Gone Back on You
When You Hear Cy Riddle Play His Fiddle
When You Play in the Game of Love
When You're All Dressed Up and No Place to Go
Where Did You Get That Girl?
Where the Red Red Roses Grow
Who Will Be with You When I'm Far Away?
Why Don't They Set Him Free?
The Woman Thou Gavest Me
Would You Take Me Back Again?
You Can't Get Away from It
You Made Me Love You, I Didn't Want to Do It
You'll Call the Next Love the First
You'll Fall for Someone
You're a Good Little Devil
You're a Great Big Blue-Eyed Baby
You're My Boy
You're Never to Old to Love
You've Got Your Mother's Big Blue Eyes

1914

The Aba Daba Honeymoon
The Aeroplane Waltz
All He Does Is Follow Them Around
All That I Had Is Gone
Along Came Ruth
At the Yiddish Wedding Jubilee
Baby Love
Back to the Carolina You Love
Ballin' the Jack
Beautiful Roses
Bird of the Wilderness
Bohemian Rag
Bring Her Again to Me
By the Beautiful Sea
California and You
Can't Yo' Hear Me Callin', Caroline
The Castle Combination
Castle Half and Half
Castle Valse Classique
The Castle Walk
Cleopatra
Daddy, I Love You More and More Each Day
Dancing the Blues Away
The Darktown Poker Club
Douce Fievre
Down Among the Sheltering Palms
Everybody Rag with Me
Fifty-Fifty
The Florida Blues
Follow the Crowd
Give Me One More Chance
Good Bye Girls I'm Through
The Good Ship Mary Ann
He Was Always Fooling Around
Herald of Peace
He's a Devil in His Own Home Town
He's a Rag Picker
He's My Cousin If She's Your Niece
The High Cost of Loving
A Hundred Years from Now
Hymn to Liberty
I Have Shed My Last Tears for You
I Love to Quarrel with You
I Want to Go Back to Michigan
I Want to Linger
I Wonder What Will William Tell
I Wonder Where My Lovin' Man Has Gone
If That's Your Idea of a Wonderful Time, Take Me Home
I'm Cured
I'm Off for Mexico
I'm Saving Up Coupons
I've Only One Idea about the Girls and That's to Love 'Em
Joan Sawyer Tango
Just 'Round the Corner from Broadway
Kansas City
Kewpie Doll
The Lambs' March
The Land of "Let's Pretend"
Let Bygones Be Bygones and Let Us Be Sweethearts Again
A Little Bit of Heaven, Shure They Call It Ireland
Little Lost Sister
Love Me Like the Ivy Loves the Old Oak Tree
MacNamara's Band
Mary Pickford, the Darling of Them All
Mexi-Tango
My Cleopatra Girl
My Croony Melody
My Daddy Long-Legs
My Turkey Trotting Boy
My Virginian
On the 5:15
On the Shores of Italy
Pan-Am Rag
Play a Simple Melody
Poor Pauline
The Portobello Lassie
Prunella
Prunella Mine
Rock Me in the Cradle of Love
Roll Dem Cotton Balls
Rufus Johnson's Harmony Band
St. Louis Blues
San Francisco
Shadowland
She's Dancing Her Heart Away

Sister Susie's Sewing Shirts for Soldiers
Smother Me with Kisses and Kill Me with Love
Stay Down Here Where You Belong
Sylvia
The Syncopated Walk
Tango Dip
That Million Dollar Melody
That's My Idea of Paradise
There's a Little Spark of Love Still Burning
They Didn't Believe Me
They Don't Hesitate Any More
They Start the Victrola and Go Dancing Around the Floor
They're On Their Way to Mexico
This Is the Life
Tia Da Da Tia Da Da, *see* My Croony Melody
Twelfth Street Rag
The Vampire
The War in Snider's Grocery Store
Watch Your Step
We Stand for Peace While Others War
We Take Our Hats Off to You, Mr. Wilson
When It's Night-time Down in Dixieland
When the Angelus Is Ringing
When the Grown-Up Ladies Act Like Babies
When You Wore a Tulip and I Wore a Big Red Rose
Where the Southern Cross' the Yellow Dog, *see* Yellow Dog Blues
Whisper That You Love Me, *see* Douce Fievre
Who Paid the Rent for Mrs. Rip Van Winkle?
Yellow Dog Blues
You're Here and I'm Here

1915

Araby
Auf Wiedersehn
The Battle of the Nations
Beatrice Fairfax, Tell Me What to Do
Beautiful Eyes
Chere, a toi mon coeur, *see* Love, Here Is My Heart!
Duna
Ethiopia Saluting the Colors
The Girl on the Magazine Cover
Here's to You, My Sparkling Wine
The Hesitating Blues
I Didn't Raise My Boy to Be a Soldier
I Love a Piano
I Love the U.S.A.
If I Only Knew Just How I Stood with You
If I Were a Bee and You Were a Red, Red Rose
If They'd Only Fight the War with Wooden Soldiers
If We Can't Be the Same Old Sweethearts
If You Can't Get a Girl in the Summertime, You'll Never Get a Girl at All
If You Want a Little Doggie, Whistle and I'll Come to You
I'm a Lonesome Melody
I'm Proud to Be a Mother of a Soldier Like You
I'm Simply Crazy over You
It Was Just a Song at Twilight That Made Me Come Back to You
It's All Your Fault
I've Been Floating Down the Old Green River
Joe Turner Blues
Just Try to Picture Me Back Home in Tennessee
Just You
Keep the Home Fires Burning
Kentucky Rose
The Ladder of Roses
Les Beaux Yeux, *see* Beautiful Eyes
The Little House upon the Hill, *see* There's a Light That's Burning in the Window of the Little House upon the Hill

A Little Love But Not for Me
Love, Here Is My Heart!
Loveland Days
M-O-T-H-E-R
Meet Me in Frisco and We'll Go Out to the Fair
Memories
Molly Dear, It's You I'm After
Mother's Sitting Knitting Little Mittens for the Navy
My Bird of Paradise
My Country Right or Wrong
My Fisher Maid, *see* Tess of the Storm Country
My Mother's Rosary
My Ship of Dreams
The New York Hippodrome March
Nola
On the Exposition Zone
Pack Up Your Troubles in Your Old Kit Bag and Smile, Smile, Smile
Pack Your Duds for San Francisco
The Perfect Song
Please Keep Out of My Dreams
The Radiance in Your Eyes
Scaddle-de-Mooch
She's the Daughter of Mother Machree
Shoot Me Back to California Land
The Singer
Sister Susie's Started Syncopation
Smile, Smile, Smile, *see* Pack Up Your Troubles in Your Old Kit Bag and Smile, Smile, Smile
So Long Letty
Some Sort of Somebody
Sprinkle Me with Kisses If You Want My Love to Grow
The Stolen Melody
The Sunshine of Your Smile
Take Me to the Midnight Cake-walk Ball
The Teenie Weenie Waltz
Tess of the Storm Country
That Hula Hula
There's a Broken Heart for Every Light on Broadway
There's a Light That's Burning in the Window of the Little House upon the Hill
They're All Going to the Movies
Those Charlie Chaplin Feet
Tumble in Love
Votes for Women
Welcome to All Is San Diego's Call
We've Got Another Washington and Wilson Is His Name
When I Get Back to the U.S.A.
When I Leave the World Behind
When It Strikes Home
When John McCormack Sings a Song
When Our Mothers Rule the World
When Sunday Comes to Town
When the Lusitania Went Down
When We Meet at the Golden Gate
When You're Down in Louisville, Call on Me
When You're in Love with Someone Who Is Not in Love with You
While the British Bull-Dog's Watching the Door
You Can't Break a Broken Heart

1916

Alice in Wonderland
America First
Arise Ye Prisoners of Starvation, *see* Workers of the World Awaken!
Arrah Go On, I'm Gonna Go Back to Oregon
Baby Shoes
Beale Street Blues
Boy Scouts of America
By the Pool at the Third Rosses
The Chicken Walk
Don't Cry Dolly Gray
Down in Honky-Tonk Town
Down Where the Swanee River Flows
Every Girl Is Fishing
Fall in for Your Motherland
For Dixie and Uncle Sam
Get a Girlie!
The Girl You Can't Forget

Good Bye, Good Luck, God Bless You
Have a Heart
Heavenly Twins
Homesickness Blues
Honolulu, America Loves You
The Honolulu Blues
The Hour of Memory
I Ain't Got Nobody Much and Nobody Cares for Me
I Can Dance with Everybody But My Wife
I Have Never Seen the Russian Ballet
I Sent My Wife to the 1000 Isles
I Told My Love to the Roses
I'd Be Happy Anywhere with You
If I Knock the 'L' Out of Kelly, It Still Would Be Kelly to Me
If You Don't Want Me, Send Me to My Ma
If You Had All the World and Its Gold
If You Were the Only Girl in the World
I'm Down in Honolulu Looking Them Over
I'm Gonna Make Hay While the Sun Shines in Virginia
I'm Sorry I Made You Cry
Ireland Must Be Heaven for My Mother Came from There
It's Lonesome Here
I've Got the Blues for Home Sweet Home
I've Lost You So Why Should I Care?
Johnny, Get a Girl
Just One Day
Keep Your Eye on the Girlie You Love
The Kiss Waltz
The Laddies Who Fought and Won
Let's Be Ready, That's the Spirit of '76
The Letter That Never Reached Home
Louisiana
Love Me at Twilight
M-i-s-s-i-s-s-i-p-p-i
Mammy's Little Coal Black Rose
The Man of the Hour
Moonlight Waltz
Morning, Noon, and Night
My Hawaiian Sunrise
Naughty! Naughty! Naughty!
Never Let the Same Bee Sting You Twice
Nijinski
O'Brien Is Tryin' to Learn to Talk Hawaiian
Oh God! Let My Dream Come True!
Oh, I Want to Be Good But My Eyes Won't Let Me
Oh! You Gray Haired Kid
Ole Miss
Other Eyes
Out of His Heart He Builds a Home
Peace Song
Pierrot and Pierrette
Poor Butterfly
Pretty Baby
Rolling Stones All Come Rolling Home Again
Romany
Roses of Picardy
San Diego, California, the Gem of the U.S.A.
She's Good Enough to Be Your Baby's Mother...
Shim-me-sha-wabble
Sierra Sue
Some Girls Do and Some Girls Don't
Sweet Cider Time When You Were Mine
Sweet Genevieve
There's a Little Bit of Bad in Every Good Little Girl
They're Wearing 'Em Higher in Hawaii
Turn Back the Universe and Give Me Yesterday
'Twas Only an Irishman's Dream
Valse Exquisite, *see* Pierrot and Pierrette
Wake Up America
Walkin' the Dog
Walking the Dog

War Brides
Wedding Bells
What Do You Want to Make Those Eyes at Me For?
When the Black Sheep Returns to the Fold
When the Sun Goes Down in Romany, My Heart Goes Roaming Back to You, *see* Romany
Women Forever!
Workers of the World Awaken!
Yaaka Hula Hickey Dula
You Can't Get Along with 'Em or Without 'Em, You've Got to Have Them, That's All
The Zoo Step

1917

Ain't You Coming Back to Dixieland?
Alexander's Got a Jazz Band Now
All Night Long
America, Here's My Boy
America Needs You Like a Mother, Would You Turn Your Mother Down?
Any Old Place the Gang Goes I'll Be There
Are You from Heaven?
Ask Her in Tulip Time
Barnyard Blues
The Battle of Gettysburg
The Bells of St. Mary's
Blue Ridge, I'm Coming Back to You
The Boys in Navy Blue, *see* Blue Ridge, I'm Coming Back to You
Bring Back My Daddy to Me
By an' By
Cleopatra Had a Jazz Band
The Darktown Strutters' Ball
The Dixie Volunteers
Do Something
Don't Try to Steal the Sweetheart of a Soldier
Everybody Loves a Jazz Band
Everything Looks Rosy and Bright
The Fatal Ring
Faugh-a Ballagh
For Me and My Gal
For Your Country and My Country
From Here to Shanghai
The Garden of Allah
Give Me the Moonlight, Give Me the Girl and Leave the Rest to Me
The Glad Song, *see* Pollyanna
Go Down Moses
Good Luck and God Be with You, Laddie Boy
Good Night, Angeline
Goodbye Broadway, Hello France
Greenwich Village
Hawaiian Butterfly
He Likes Their Jukelele
He Sleeps beneath the Soil of France
Hello Central, Give Me France
Hello Wisconsin, Won't You Find My Yonnie Yonson
Homeward Bound
How Can I Forget When There's So Much to Remember?
Huckleberry Finn
I Ain't Married No More
I Called You My Sweetheart
I Can't Help Dreaming of You
I Don't Feel No Way Tired
I Don't Want to Get Well
I Love But You
I Love My Billy Sunday But Oh, You Saturday Night
I May Be Gone for a Long, Long Time
If I Had a Son for Each Star in Old Glory, Uncle Sam, I'd Give Them All to You
I'll Come Back to You When It's All Over
I'll Take You Back to Italy
I'm All Bound 'Round with the Mason-Dixon Line
In Berry Pickin' Time
In the Land of Wedding Bells
Indiana
It Takes a Long Tall Brown-Skin Gal to Make a Preacher Lay His Bible Down

It's a Long Way to Berlin But We'll Get There
It's Time for Every Boy to Be a Soldier
Joan of Arc, They Are Calling You
Johnson Rag
Just as Washington Crossed the Delaware, So Will Pershing Cross the Rhine
Khaki Sammy
Laddie Boy, *see* Good Luck and God Be with You, Laddie Boy
The Land Where the Good Songs Go
Let My People Go, *see* Go Down Moses
Let the Flag Fly!
Let's All Be Americans Now
Let's Help the Red Cross Now
Liberty Bell, It's Time to Ring Again
The Liberty Loan March
Lily of the Valley
A Little Bit o' Honey
Little Mother of Mine
Love's Lullaby of Dreams, *see* Sing Me Love's Lullaby
Mammy's Little Choc'late Cullud Chile
Meet Me at the Station
Mister Jazz Himself
The Modern Maiden's Prayer
The More I See of Hawaii, the Better I Like New York
My Sweetheart Is Somewhere in France
My Sweetie
My Yiddische Butterfly
Nothing's Good Enough for a Good Little Girl If She's Good Enough for You
Oh, How She Could Yacki Hacki Wicki Wacki Woo
Oh Johnny, Oh Johnny, Oh!
Oh! Papa, Oh! Papa, Won't You Be a Pretty Papa to Me?
On the Road to Home Sweet Home
One Day in June
One - Two - Three - Four
Over There
The Palm Beach Dip
Patria
Peaches
The Picture I Want to See
Pollyanna
Poor Little Rich Girl's Dog
Pull the Cork Out of Erin and Let the River Shannon Flow
Quand les Francaise apprennent a "Do You Speak English?", *see* When Yankee Doodle Learns to "Parlez-Vous Francaise?"
The Ragtime Volunteers Are Off to War
Ramona
Red Wing
Regretful Blues
The Road for You and Me
Rockaway
Rose Room
Round Her Neck, She Wears a Yeller Ribbon
Sailin' Away on the Henry Clay
Say a Prayer for the Boys Out There
Send Me Away with a Smile
The Ship of Uncle Sam
The Shorter They Wear 'Em the Longer They Look
Sinbad Was in Bad All the Time
Sing Me Love's Lullaby
Six Times Six Is Thirty-Six
Slowly Stealing Up and Down the River
Smile and Show Your Dimple
Smiles
So Long Mother
Some Sunday Morning
Someone Else May Be There While I'm Gone
Somewhere in France
Somewhere in France Is the Lily
Southern Gals
The Story Book Ball
That's Love in Honolulu, *see* Oh, How She Could Yacki Hacki Wicki Wacki Woo
That's the Kind of Baby for Me
There Are Two Eyes in Dixie

There's Something Nice about the South
They Go Wild, Simply Wild Over Me
Tiger Rag
Tishomingo Blues
Ugly Chile
The United States Field Artillery March
Wasn't It Yesterday?
We Don't Know Where We're Going But We're on Our Way
We'll Knock the Heligo into Heligo Out of Heligoland!
We're Going to Hang the Kaiser under the Linden Tree
We're Going to Take the Germ Out of Germany
We're Going to Take the Sword Away from William
What Would $50,000 Make You Do?
When I Grow Up I'm Going to Be a Soldier
When Old Bill Bailey Plays the Ukelele
When Patti Sang "Home Sweet Home"
When Rosie Riccoola Do the Hoola Ma Boola She's the Hit of Little Italy
When That Vampire Rolled Her Vampy Eyes at Me
When the Last Rose of Summer Was in Bloom
When There's Peace on Earth Again
When Those Sweet Hawaiian Babies Roll Their Eyes
When Yankee Doodle Learns to "Parlez-Vous Francaise?"
Where Do We Go from Here?
Where the Black-Eyed Susans Grow
White Ribbon Rally
The Wild Wild Women Are Making a Wild Man of Me
Will You Forget?
Will You Remember?
Yah-De-Dah
You Can Have It, I Don't Want It
You're a Great Big Lonesome Baby
You're Some Pretty Doll, *see* Ugly Chile

1918

After You've Gone
Alone with You
Altogether Too Fond of You
Baby's Prayers Will Soon Be Answered
Beautiful Ohio
Bing! Bang! Bing 'Em on the Rhine
The Blue Devils of France
Bolsheveki Glide
Bridal Dawn
Bring Me a Rose
But - After the Ball Was Over Then He Made Up for Lost Time
Bye and Bye You'll See the Sun A-Shining
Can You Tame Wild Wimmen?
Cheer Up Father, Cheer Up Mother
A Cheery Smile Is as Good as a Mile on the Road to Victory
Come On Papa
Crusader and Tommy
Dark Grows the Sky
Darling
The Daughter of Rosie O'Grady
Dear Little Boy of Mine
Dear Old Pal of Mine
Ding Dong
Djer-Kiss
Don't Cry, Little Girl, Don't Cry
Don't Let Us Sing Anymore about War, Just Let Us Sing of Love
Dress Up Your Dollars in Khaki and Help Win Democracy's Fight
Dry Your Tears
Every Day Will Be Sunday When the Town Goes Dry
Everybody Shimmies Now
Everything Is Peaches Down in Georgia
Ev'ry Day
Ev'ry Morning She Makes Me Late
For Your Boy and My Boy
Frisco's Kitchen Stove Rag

Get Behind the Girls Behind the Boys
Get Busy Over Here or Over There
Good-bye Alexander, Good-bye Honey-Boy
Good-bye Cabarabian Nights
Good-bye France
A Good Man Is Hard to Find
Goodbye, Mother Machree
Happiness
He Draws No Color Line, *see* When the Good Lord Makes a Record of a Hero's Deed, He Draws No Color Line
Hearts of the World
Hello Central, Give Me No Man's Land
Hindustan
Huckleberry Pie
I Can Always Find a Little Sunshine in the Y.M.C.A.
I Hate to Lose You
I Have Just One Heart for Just One Boy
I Just Can't Make My Feet Behave
I Love the Heart of Dixie
I Think You're Absolutely Wonderful (What Do You Think of Me?)
I Want to Learn to Jazz Dance
I Want to See My Ida Hoe in Idaho
I Wonder Why She Kept On Saying Si Si Si Si Senor
If He Can Fight Like He Can Love, Good Night Germany
If I Could Peep through the Window Tonight
If She Means What I Think She Means
I'll Be True to the Whole Regiment, *see* Madelon
I'll Say She Does
I'm Always Chasing Rainbows
I'm Crazy about My Daddy in a Uniform
I'm Glad I Can Make You Cry
I'm Going to Spend My Vacation with a Dear Old Relation
I'm So Used to You Now, *see* I Hate to Lose You
I'm Trying to Teach My Sweet Papa Right from Wrong
In Flanders' Fields
In the Land of Beginning Again
In the Land Where Poppies Bloom
Indianola
Ireland, My Land of Dreams
It Gets Them All
It's a Long Way to Dear Old Broadway
Ja-Da
The Jazz Band
Just a Baby's Prayer at Twilight to Her Daddy Over There
K-K-K-Katy
Keep Your Head Down, 'Fritzie Boy'
Liberty Forever
Ma, He's Making Eyes at Me
Madelon
Mammy's Chocolate Soldier
Merrily We'll Roll Along
Mickey
Midnight in Dreamy Spain
Mirandy
Mothers of America, You Have Done Your Share
My Baby Talking Girl
My Belgian Rose
My Honey's Back
My Little Service Flag Has Seven Stars
My Star
My Syncopated Melody Man
'N' Everything
The Navy Took Them Over and the Navy Will Bring Them Back
O Promise Me You'll Write to Him Today
Oh! Frenchy
Oh! Harry! Harry!
Oh Helen!
Oh! How I Hate to Get Up in the Morning
Oh, How I Wish I Could Sleep Until My Daddy Comes Home

Oh! London, Where Are Your Girls Tonight?
On the Level, You're a Devil
On the Road That Leads to Home
Our Ancestors
Per Sempre Liberta!, *see* Liberty Forever
Roaming Romeo
Rock-a-bye Your Baby with a Dixie Melody
The Rose of No Man's Land
Sabre and Spur
Smile the While You Kiss Me Sad Adieu, *see* Till We Meet Again
A Soldier's Dream
Somebody Stole My Gal
Sweet Hawaiian Moonlight, Tell Her of My Love
Tell That to the Marines!
That Girl o' Mine, *see* Mirandy
That Magic Strain
That Russian Rag
That Soothing Serenade
That Tumble Down Shack in Athlone
That Wonderful Mother of Mine
There'll Be a Hot Time for the Old Men While the Young Men Are Away
There's a Lump of Sugar Down in Dixie
They Were All Out of Step But Jim
They'll Be Mighty Proud in Dixie of Their Old Black Joe
Those Draftin' Blues
Thousands of Years Ago
Tiger Rose Waltz
Till We Meet Again
The Trench Trot
Typical Topical Tunes
Uncle Sammy's at Bat
U.S.A. Forever Dry
Wait 'till the Great Day Comes
Waiting for You
War Baby's Lullaby
We Are Coming
We Have Fed You All for a Thousand Years
We Never Did That Before
Wedding Bells, Will You Ever Ring for Me
We're on Our Way to France
What Are You Going to Do to Help the Boys?
What Do I Care?
When Alexander Takes His Rag Time Band to France
When I'm Thru with the Arms of the Army, I'll Come Back to the Arms of You
When It Comes to a Lovingless Day
When Jack Comes Sailing Home Again
When the Band Plays "Indiana," Then I'm Humming "Home Sweet Home"
When the Flowers Bloom on No-Man's Land, What a Wonderful Day That Will Be
When the Good Lord Makes a Record of a Hero's Deed, He Draws No Color Line
When Tony Goes Over the Top
When Uncle Joe Steps into France
When You Come Back, and You Will Come Back, There's a Whole World...
When You Look in the Heart of a Rose
Why Do They All Take the Night Boat to Albany?
Without You
Work or Fight, *see* Get Busy Over Here or Over There
Would You Rather Be a Colonel with an Eagle on Your Shoulder...
You Keep Sending 'Em Over and We'll Keep Knocking 'Em Down
You-oo Just You
You'll Find Old Dixieland in France
Your Lips Are No Man's Land But Mine
You're in Style When You're Wearing a Smile
You've Got to Go In or Go Under

1919

Across the Sea
Ain't You Coming Back, Mary Ann, to Maryland
Alabama Lullaby
The Alcoholic Blues
Alexander's Band Is Back in Dixieland
Alice Blue Gown
All of No Man's Land Is Ours
All the Quakers Are Shoulder Shakers Down in Quaker Town
All Those in Favor Say Aye
Aloma
America Never Took Water and America Never Will
America's Popular Song
And He'd Say Oo-la-la! Wee-Wee!
And That Ain't All
Any Old Place with You
At the Fall of Babylon, *see* The Mountain Maid
Baby, Won't You Please Come Home
The Best of Everything
Blue Eyed Blond Haired Heart Breaking Baby Doll
Blues My Naughty Sweetie Gives to Me
Bluin' the Blues
Bo - la - Bo
Breeze, Blow My Baby Back to Me
Bring Back Those Wonderful Days
By the Honeysuckle Vine
Castle of Dreams
Chinese Lullaby
Chong, He Come from Hong Kong
Come Along to Toy Town
Come Back to Me
Come to the Moon
Daddy Long Legs
Dancing Shoes
Dardanella
A Debutante's Engagement Book
Don't Take Advantage of My Good Nature
Dreamy Alabama
Easy Pickins'
Eli Eli
Enid Waltz
Everybody Wants a Key to My Cellar
Eyes of Youth
Fifteen Years on the Erie Canal, *see* Low Bridge - Everybody Down
The First Rose of Summer
Freedom of the C's
From Now On
Gee! I Wish I Had Someone to Rock Me in the Cradle of Love
Gee! I'm Glad That I'm from Dixie
A Girl, A Man, A Night, A Dance
Give Me a Syncopated Tune
Give Me the Sultan's Harem
Golden Shores of Miami, *see* On Miami Shore
The Golden Star
The Hand That Rocked the Cradle Rules My Heart
Hard Trials
Harem Life
He's Had No Lovin' for a Long, Long Time
His Majesty, the American
Hitchy's Garden of Roses
How 'Ya Gonna Keep 'Em Down on the Farm After They've Seen Paris?
I Ain't Gonna Give Nobody None o' This Jelly Roll
I Ain't Got'en No Time to Have the Blues
I Gave Her That
I Introduced
I Know What It Means to Be Lonesome
I Know Why--Because I'm in Love with You
I Lost My Heart in Dixieland
I Love You Just the Same, Sweet Adeline
I Might Be Your "Once in a While"
I Never Knew
I Never Knew How Much I Loved You Until There Was Somebody Else
I Want to Shimmie
I Want to Spread a Little Sunshine

I Was So Young, You Were So Beautiful
I Wish I Could Shimmy Like My Sister Kate
I Wonder What's the Matter wiz My Oo-la-la
I Wouldn't Give 'That' for the Man Who Couldn't Dance
I-yay Ove-lay Oo-yay Earie-day, *see* Pig Latin Love
I'd Rather See a Minstrel Show
I'm Forever Blowing Bubbles
I'm Not Jealous
I'm Sorry I Ain't Got It You Could Have It If I Had It Blues
In a Kingdom of Our Own
In Hitchy's Garden, *see* Hitchy's Garden of Roses
In Old Kentucky
It's Nobody's Business But My Own
I've Got My Captain Working for Me Now
I've Made Up My Mind to Mind a Maid Made Up Like You
Jazz Babies' Ball
Jazz Baby
Jerry, You Warra a Warrior in the War
Johnny's in Town
Joyous Springtime Bring Me Love, *see* Enid Waltz
Jubilo
Just Another Poor Man Gone Wrong
Just Around the Corner
Just Like a Gypsy
The Kiss Burglar
Lafayette
The Language of Love
Let the Rest of the World Go By
Let's Help the Irish Now
Life, Let Me Live My Life for You
Linger Longer Letty
Love Sends a Little Gift of Roses
Low Bridge - Everybody Down
Mack Sennett Girls
Mammy o' Mine
Mandy
Mary Regan
Midnight Maid
A Midnight Romance
Molly
Molly Malone, My Own
The Moon Shines on the Moonshine
The Mountain Maid
My Baby's Arms
My Desert Rose, *see* Sand Dunes
My Gal's Another Gal Like Galli-Curci
My Isle of Golden Dreams
The New Moon
Nobody Knows and Nobody Seems to Care
O
Oh by Jingo! Oh by Gee! You're the Only Girl for Me
Oh, How I Laugh When I Think How I Cried about You
Oh! How She Can Dance
Oh! How She Can Sing
Oh! The Last Rose of Summer Was the Sweetest Rose of All
Oh! What a Pal Was Mary
On a Little Farm in Normandie
On Miami Shore
On Patrol in No Man's Land
On the Banks of the Bronx
On the Road to Calais
Open Up the Golden Gates to Dixieland and Let Me into Paradise
Outside of That Every Little Thing's All Right, *see* Harem Life
Peggy
Pig Latin Love
Please Don't Take Away the Girls
Poor Little Butterfly Is a Fly Girl Now
A Pretty Girl Is Like a Melody
Prohibition Blues
Prohibition, You Have Lost Your Sting
Ragging the Chopsticks
Razzberries
A Regular Girl
The Road to Romany
Romance

A Romance of Happy Valley
Rose of Washington Square
Royal Garden Blues
Sand Dunes
Sasparilla, Women, and Song
Shadows
Shall They Plead in Vain?
Sipping Cider thru' a Straw
Smilin' Through
Someday Sweetheart
Somehow It Seldom Comes True
Something about Love
Star of Happiness
Sugar Blues
Swanee
Sweet and Low, *see* That Lullaby of Long Ago
Sweet Kisses That Came in the Night
Take Me to that Land of Jazz
Take Your Girlie to the Movies If You Can't Make Love at Home
Tee-Oodle-Um-Bam-Bo
Tell Me
That Lullaby of Long Ago
That Thing Called Love
That Wonderful Kid from Madrid
There Are Just Two I's in Dixie
There's More to the Kiss than the X-X-X
They're All Sweeties
Think of Me Little Daddy
Thtop Your Thtuttering Jimmy
Tulip Time
The Vamp
Venetian Moon
Wait and See, You'll Want Me Back
The Wedding of the Shimmie and Jazz
What Good Is Alimony on a Lonesome Night
When a Feller Needs a Friend
When Honey Sings an Old Time Song
When the Fightin' Irish Come Home
When They're Old Enough to Know Better, It's Better to Leave Them Alone
White Blossoms
Who Played Poker with Pocohontas When John Smith Went Away?
The Woman Thou Gavest Me
The World Is Waiting for the Sunrise
Yama Yama Blues
You Ain't Heard Nothing Yet
You Cannot Make Your Shimmy Shake on Tea
You Cannot Shake That "Shimmie" Here
You Can't Shake That Shimmie Here
You Didn't Want Me When You Had Me So Why Do You Want Me Now?
You'd Be Surprised
Your Eyes Have Told Me So
You're a Million Miles from Nowhere When You're One Little Mile from Home
You're a Perfect Jewel to Me
Ze Yankee Boys Have Made a Wild French Baby Out of Me

List of Publishers

A directory of publishers of the songs included in *Popular Music,* 1900-1919. Publishers that are members of the American Society of Composers, Authors, and Publishers or whose catalogs are available under ASCAP license are indicated by the designation (ASCAP). Publishers that have granted performing rights to Broadcast Music, Inc., are designated by the notation (BMI). Publishers whose catalogs are represented by SESAC, Inc., are indicated by the designation (SESAC).

The addresses were gleaned from a variety of sources, including ASCAP, BMI, SESAC, *Billboard* magazine, and the National Music Publishers' Association. As in any volatile industry, many of the addresses may become outdated quickly. In the interim between the book's completion and its subsequent publication, some publishers may have been consolidated into others or changed hands. This is a fact of life long endured by the music business and its constituents. The data collected here, and throughout the book, are as accurate as such circumstances allow.

A

A. R. White
Address unknown

Alfred Music Co., Inc.
Address unknown

American Music, Inc. (BMI)
9109 Sunset Blvd.
Hollywood, California 90069

Anne-Rachel Music Corp. (ASCAP)
c/o Chappell & Co., Inc.
810 Seventh Avenue
New York, New York 10019

Arnett Delonais
Address unknown

B

Bell & Cee Music Co. (ASCAP)
Address unknown

List of Publishers

Belwin-Mills Publishing Corp. (ASCAP)
1776 Broadway, 11th Fl.
New York, New York 10019

Irving Berlin Music Corp. (ASCAP)
1290 Avenue of the Americas
New York, New York 10019

Sol Bloom Publishing Co/Sol Bloom Music
Defunct

Blossom Music Corp. (ASCAP)
322 W. 48th Street
New York, New York 10036

Boosey & Hawkes Inc. (ASCAP)
24 W. 57th Street
New York, New York 10019

Boston Music Co. (ASCAP)
116 Boylston Street
Boston, Massachusetts 02116

Leonard Gould Bottler (ASCAP)
Address unknown

Bourne Co. (ASCAP)
437 Fifth Avenue
New York, New York 10016

Perry Bradford Music Publishing Co.
104-49 165th Street
Jamaica, New York 11433

Broadway Music Corp. (ASCAP)
135 W. 50th Street, Suite 1920
New York, New York 10020

Fred Burch Music (BMI)
2805 Shauna Court
Nashville, Tennessee 37214

C

Calumnet
Address unknown

Chappell & Co., Inc. (ASCAP)
810 Seventh Avenue
New York, New York 10019

John Church Co. (ASCAP)
Bryn Mawr, Pennsylvania 19010

Clef Music Publishers (ASCAP)
Address unknown

Cohan & Harris Music Publishers
Defunct

George M. Cohan Music Publishing Co. (ASCAP)
c/o Freddy Bienstock Enterprises
1619 Broadway
New York, New York 10019

M. M. Cole
Address unknown

D

Dajon (ASCAP)
Address unknown

Oliver Ditson Co. (ASCAP)
1712 Chestnut Street
Philadelphia, Pennsylvania 19103

Paul Dresser Music Publishing Co.
Defunct

E

Gus Edwards Music Publishing Co.
see Belwin-Mills Publishing Corp.

F

Famous Music Corp. (ASCAP)
Gulf & Western Industries, Inc.
1 Gulf & Western Plaza
New York, New York 10023

Leo Feist Inc. (ASCAP)
see MCA Music

B. Feldman & Co., Ltd. (ASCAP)
c/o Abels, Clark & Osterberg
224 E. 50th Street
New York, New York 10022

Carl Fischer, Inc. (ASCAP)
62 Cooper Square
New York, New York 10003

Fred Fisher Music Co. (ASCAP)
c/o Fisher Music Corp.
1619 Broadway
New York, New York 10019

Fisher Music Corp. (ASCAP)
1619 Broadway
New York, New York 10019

Forster Music Publishers, Inc. (ASCAP)
216 S. Wabash Avenue
Chicago, Illinois 60604

Sam Fox Publishing Co., Inc. (ASCAP)
73-941 Highway 111, Suite 11
Palm Desert, California 92260

Francis, Day & Hunter, Inc. (ASCAP)
c/o The Big 3
7165 Sunset Blvd.
Hollywood, California 90046

G

Goodman Music Co., Inc. (ASCAP)
825 West End Avenue, Apt. 9A
New York, New York 10025

Gotham-Attucks Music Publishing Co.
see Belwin-Mills Publishing Corp.

H

Handy Brothers Music Co., Inc. (ASCAP)
200 W. 72nd Street
New York, New York 10023

Emil C. Hansen Co. (ASCAP)
Address unknown

Harms, Inc. (ASCAP)
488 Madison Avenue
New York, New York 10022

T. B. Harms (ASCAP)
see Welk Music Group

Charles K. Harris Music Publishing Co. (ASCAP)
1740 Broadway
New York, New York 10019

F. B. Haviland
see Jerry Vogel Music Co., Inc.

Helf & Hager Music Co/Helf Music Pub. Co
see Lark Music, Inc.

Howley, Haviland & Co.
see Jerry Vogel Music Co., Inc.

Howley, Haviland & Dresser
see Jerry Vogel Music Co., Inc.

J

Joseph Morris Co.
Address unknown

K

Kalmar, Puck & Abrahams Consolidated Music
see Belwin-Mills Publishing Corp.

L

La Salle Music Publishers, Inc. (ASCAP)
1740 Broadway
New York, New York 10019

Lark Music, Inc. (BMI)
Music Administration Service Co.
c/o SAS, Inc.
1414 Avenue of the Americas
New York, New York 10019

Laurel Music Corp. (ASCAP)
22 W. 48th Street
New York, New York 10036

Leeds Music Corp. (ASCAP)
c/o Mr. John McKellen
445 Park Avenue
New York, New York 10022

Lewis Music Publishing Co., Inc. (ASCAP)
Ashley Dealer's Inc.
263 Veteran's Blvd.
Carlstadt, New Jersey 07072

M

Edward B. Marks Music Corp. (BMI)
1790 Broadway
New York, New York 10019

Mayfair Music Corp. (ASCAP)
31 W. 54th Street
New York, New York 10019

MCA, Inc. (ASCAP)
c/o Mr. John McKellen
445 Park Avenue
New York, New York 10022

MCA Music (ASCAP)
Division of MCA Inc.
445 Park Avenue
New York, New York 10022

Melrose Music Corp. (ASCAP)
31 W. 54th Street
New York, New York 10019

George W. Meyer
Address unknown

Miller Music Corp. (ASCAP)
see United Artists Music Co., Inc.

Mills Music Inc. (ASCAP)
see Belwin-Mills Publishing Corp.

Morley Music Co., Inc. (ASCAP)
c/o Eastman & Eastman
39 W. 54th Street
New York, New York 10019

Edwin H. Morris Co. (ASCAP)
see MPL Communications Inc.

MPL Communications Inc. (ASCAP)
c/o Lee Eastman
39 W. 54th Street
New York, New York 10019

N

New World Music Corp. (NY) (ASCAP)
75 Rockefeller Plaza
New York, New York 10020

Norworth Music Co.
Defunct

O

Original copyright

P

E. T. Paull

Paull-Pioneer Music Co.
see Shawnee Press, Inc.

Penn Music Co. (ASCAP)
c/o George Mysels
1315 N. Orange Drive
Hollywood, California 90028

Photo Play Music Co., Inc. (ASCAP)
143-66 Beech Avenue
Flushing, New York 11355

Al Piantadosi Music
see Alfred Music Co., Inc.

Pickwick Music Corp. (ASCAP)
445 Park Avenue
New York, New York 10022

Theodore Presser Co. (ASCAP)
Presser Place
Bryn Mawr, Pennsylvania 19010

R

Remick Music Corp. (ASCAP)
488 Madison Avenue
New York, New York 10022

Robbins Music Corp. (ASCAP)
see United Artists Music Co., Inc.

Homer A. Rodeheaver
Defunct

Will Rossiter (ASCAP)
173 W. Madison Street
Chicago, Illinois 60602

S

G. Schirmer Inc. (ASCAP)
866 Third Avenue
New York, New York 10022

Edward Schuberth & Co., Inc. (SESAC)
263 Veterans Blvd.
Carlstadt, New Jersey 07072

Shapiro, Bernstein & Co., Inc. (ASCAP)
Att: Leon Brettler
10 E. 53rd Street
New York, New York 10022

Shawnee Press, Inc. (ASCAP)
Division of Waring Enterprises, Inc.
Delaware Water Gap, Pennsylvania 18327

George Simon, Inc. (ASCAP)
c/o George Simon, Inc.
2147 Sunshine Circle
Palm Springs, California 92262

Snyder & Berlin Co.
Defunct

Snyder Music Corp. (ASCAP)
6255 W. Sunset Blvd.
Hollywood, California 90028

Ted Snyder Music Publishing Co. (ASCAP)
P.O. Box 2327
Palm Desert, California 92260

Larry Spier, Inc. (ASCAP)
401 Fifth Avenue
New York, New York 10016

Spike's Music (BMI)
c/o Jeffrey Berger
2131 Capitol Avenue, Suite 300
Sacramento, California 95816

Stasny Music Corp. (ASCAP)
1619 Broadway
New York, New York 10019

Jos. W. Stern & Co.
Defunct

T

Tempo Music (ASCAP)
c/o Alexandria House
P.O. Box 300
Alexandria, Indiana 46001

U

United Artists Music Co., Inc.
6753 Hollywood Blvd.
Los Angeles, California 90028

V

Venus Music Corp. (ASCAP)
1841 Broadway
New York, New York 10023

Jerry Vogel Music Co., Inc. (ASCAP)
501 Fifth Avenue, 15th Fl.
New York, New York 10017

Harry Von Tilzer Music Publishing Co.
see Welk Music Group

W

Warner Brothers, Inc. (ASCAP)
9000 Sunset Blvd.
Los Angeles, California 90069

Warock Music, Inc. (ASCAP)
400 Madison Avenue
New York, New York 10017

Waterson, Berlin & Snyder
see Belwin-Mills Publishing Corp.

Welk Music Group
1299 Ocean Avenue, Suite 800
Santa Monica, California 90401

Clarence Williams Music (ASCAP)
c/o John McKellen
MCA Inc.
445 Park Avenue
New York, New York 10022

M. Witmark & Sons (ASCAP)
488 Madison Avenue
New York, New York 10022

Y

York Music Corp.
Defunct